MEGAMALL ON THE HUDSON

Planning, Wal-Mart and Grassroots Resistance

David Porter and Chester L. Mirsky

Trafford

2003

National Library of Canada Cataloguing in Publication

Porter, David, 1939-
      Megamall on the Hudson : planning, Wal-Mart and grassroots resistance /
David Porter and Chester L. Mirsky.
      Includes bibliographical references and index.
      ISBN 1-55369-855-X
          I.Mirsky , Chester L., 1943- II. Title.

HF5430.4.N48P67 2002   307.3Õ33Õ097473   C2002-904634-3

TRAFFORD

This book was published *on-demand* in cooperation with Trafford Publishing.
On-demand publishing is a unique process and service of making a book available for retail
sale to the public taking advantage of on-demand manufacturing and Internet marketing.
On-demand publishing includes promotions, retail sales, manufacturing, order fulfilment,
accounting and collecting royalties on behalf of the author.

Suite 6E, 2333 Government St., Victoria, B.C. V8T 4P4, CANADA
Phone   250-383-6864   Toll-free   1-888-232-4444 (Canada & US)
Fax   250-383-6804   E-mail   sales@trafford.com
Web site   www.trafford.com   TRAFFORD PUBLISHING IS A DIVISION OF TRAFFORD HOLDINGS LTD.
Trafford Catalogue #02-0668   www.trafford.com/robots/02-0668.html

10   9   8   7   6   5   4   3   2   1

CONTENTS

PART THREE - PROJECT REVIEW

PART FOUR - PROJECT DECISION

PART FIVE - CONCLUSION

APPENDIXES

Acknowledgements

For several decades now, we have participated in various land-use struggles and encouraged thoughtful and democratic planning in the Hudson Valley of New York, hoping through our efforts with many others to save the beautiful rural landscape and small-town lifestyle for its present and future human and non-human inhabitants. Each of us brought to this realm of active local politics extensive backgrounds of earlier community organizing, commitment to genuine grassroots empowerment and research and writing on similar historical and contemporary political issues. This background and our own personal immersion in the rich ecology of this region led us to intense commitments in many local and regional land-use battles.

As our experience deepened, our learnings in this arena broadened, culminating especially in the intense megamall land-use struggle described in this book.

Along with the gained deeper insights we have chosen to share here, we have enriched our own lives in each struggle with new friendships and new inspiring confirmations of vital grassroots resistance to authoritarian decision-making and elitist local regimes. Many of our "Ashbury" friends and hard-working associates in the particular megamall struggle described here were especially in our minds as we spent six long years preparing this book. We would like to acknowledge many of them here. But our decision discretely to fictionalize names and places which could identify actual actors and locales of this drama prevents us from stating these names. In any case, you know who you are and we thank you abundantly for your own commitment, support and friendship during the particular megamall struggle and in the years since as we prepared the present book.

We also could never say enough for the sustaining encouragement and love from our wives Nancy Schniedewind and Gloria Kapilow and endless patience and support from our children David Porter, Noelle Parker, Jesse and Daniel Schniedewind and Jon, Rebecca and Daniel Mirsky during the nearly ten years of project opposition and manuscript preparation.

Finally, we wish to thank Open Space Institute for its early interest in the project and its grant in 1996 which allowed us to prepare the first, much longer, draft of the manuscript. The book has changed considerably since then but, of course, OSI as well as any of the actual community groups referred to by substitute names in this account are not responsible for any of the contents or analyses in any versions of this project.

ONE

INTRODUCTION: PURPOSE, NATURE AND CONTEXT OF THE STUDY

The co-authors of this book have worked side-by-side for over a decade as leaders of a grassroots community group closely monitoring, critiquing, and sometimes struggling against land-use decisions made by local officials in Ashbury, New York, a small town in the upstate Hudson Valley. One of the authors teaches at the State University of New York/Empire State College, the other at New York University School of Law. Over four decades, the first has investigated and written on a variety of grassroots contexts of community participatory empowerment, historically and in the present, in the U.S. and abroad. For a similar period, the second has researched and written extensively about historical socio-legal contexts of the U.S. criminal justice system, focusing on the role of courtroom actors and the impact they have on the form of law and the method by which law is understood and employed on a day-to-day basis.

Eight years ago, each of us became involved in an on-going struggle to prevent construction of a Wal-Mart megamall on the outskirts of Ashbury. To a large extent, the formal framework for this struggle was the official New York state regulations for evaluating environmental impacts of development projects, the State Environmental Quality Review Act (SEQRA) process. Several months after the conclusion of that process in 1996, we recognized that we had an intense story to tell, were uniquely in an insider's position to do so, and had a responsibility to share it with others. From this realization came our plan for the present project.

As participant-observers, our principal goals in this book are twofold. First, we provide a uniquely detailed panorama of the landscape of struggle, a case-study in "insurgent planning,"[1] with the hope that accounts of so-called "rational-legal" assertions by developers and their allies and lay efforts to overcome them will prove useful for grassroots activists facing similarly contested terrain in New York state and elsewhere.[2]

Second, we step back from the immediacy of conflict and analyze the nature of the regulatory politics arena more generally. In doing so, our experience sheds light on important questions concerning environmental policymaking, the relation between corporate power, the law and scientific expertise, and the limits and possibilities of popular initiative from below in presentday American politics. The authors consider the extent to which statist law, however formally "participatory," can empower citizens to reacquire control over material forces which shape their everyday existence.

Participatory research inevitably produces a somewhat different set of knowledge than research by outside analysts. We believe that the detailed "insider" roles of each of us as central actors in the context under study provide great strength to our account of the ongoing process. At the same time, we continually infuse the study with the same sort of data--objective official and unofficial record--available to any meticulous outside researcher (i.e., minutes and transcriptions of board meetings, the documentary file in the planning board office, newspaper accounts, etc.) to elucidate the wider socio-legal context.

As with many community studies, our choice to substitute different names for people, places and companies (except for Wal-Mart) involved in the immediate struggle or which might identify its location helps to assure that readers will focus on the broader principles, issues and dynamics at stake, rather than on specific behaviors of particular persons and companies. Since we are explicit about our own biases, readers also will understand that the lens through which this account is presented is not the typical lens of traditional public administration, planning or organizational theory. The book not only questions the legitimacy of formal structures and processes, but analyzes critically the dynamics of ideology, power, knowledge, control and resistance.[3] As central partisan participants in the community struggle, we were in no position to interview those whom we opposed, during or after the described events. Thus, we have avoided ascribing motives or strategies to the latter except when reasonably supported by the public record. We are equally cautious in referring to the elusive topic of "prevailing community sentiment."

At the same time, we found that the central conclusions derived from our own participation and subsequent more "distanced" analysis well complement themes and principles articulated by non-participant researchers examining similar policy-making contexts and issues elsewhere. We have cited such references throughout our account, but especially in Chapters Two, Sixteen, Seventeen and Eighteen, to encourage readers to understand that our analysis goes quite beyond the particular personalities and forces involved in this specific local struggle. While the two-year Ashbury experience was not unique, we believe that the narrative details and extensive directly-quoted dialogue from our specific context provide convincing power for our analysis[4] and engage and contribute to existing literature in a range of scholarly fields.

As with any book, some readers will differ from the authors in their interpretations of events and their overall analysis, just as differences in perspective existed within the community under discussion itself. We have tried to present enough material from all major actors to allow such differences to become clear. We trust that our combination of participatory and traditional research and analysis will therefore be received as providing unique access to the dynamics and meaning of the local land-use planning process and "participatory" opportunities within liberal democracy more generally.

We assume that the account has a certain dramatic appeal of its own which may entrance some readers as the actual experience of struggle did for those locally in the middle of it. We intend that the book will be valuable for scholars, activists and interested lay readers alike. With this in mind, we use language which is hopefully accessible and meaningful to all.

We also begin Parts Two, Three and Four with brief introductions to the major tasks, issues and dynamics of the particular stage of the environmental impact review process involved. For community activists immediately involved in local struggles who wish to use this book as a quick guide to the potentials and pitfalls of the SEQRA process (and comparable environmental impact assessment processes in other states and countries), the second chapter and part of the third (on SEQRA) as well as the introductions to Parts Two, Three and Four will orient them as to the direct pragmatic issues at stake in each section of the book. In Part Five, our concluding section, Chapter Sixteen creates a detailed overall theoretical framework within and also against which the final two chapters provide analysis for understanding the broader political significance of the case-study, environmental impact assessment and local land-use planning more generally.

Background and Purpose

Our book explores the system of land-use management employed by people within a small community in the Hudson Valley of New York to sustain and foster their daily lives. Land-use management has always been central in the definition of small towns, particularly in areas such as this Valley where beautiful and delicate topography are defining characteristics, and the use of the land itself has a substantial impact on the lives of the inhabitants and their social and economic identity. We believe, as cultural anthropologist Constance Perin stated, that "[w]hatever governs relationships among land uses . . . [are] as well organizing principles for relationships among land users."[5] Even more explicitly, as Nicholas Blomley suggests, "socially produced space is saturated with power relations."[6]

In the long evolution of local land use planning in modern society, we have passed from more communal forms to an emphatically laissez-faire model based on governmental support and individual and corporate decision-makers, to increasing use of political regulation mainly through planning and zoning and, eventually, such tools as mandated environmental impact review. Only in the last phase of this evolution has the opportunity arisen for a return to more communitarian, participatory modes of decision-making.

Much of the more radical strife within the English Civil War and the aftermath of the American Revolution was in fact caused by the accurate perception of subsistence farmers that communal land rights and communal decision-making were increasingly replaced by individualistic speculative and commercial land-use essentially unaccountable to people at the grassroots level--a privatization of power relations which, over several generations, became increasingly invisible as the social artifact it was. At the same time that land-use and decision-making became more individualized, government maintained a framework of consistent intervention through expropriation, land grants, corporate charters, development of local infrastructure, and protection of the dominant economic interests through the army, police and the courts.[7]

By the late 19th and early 20th centuries, the accumulation of grievances of social exploitation, especially in urban areas, became so great that social movements sought and eventually obtained a variety of reforms through formal political legislation. Among these was urban zoning. However, as with earlier forms of government intervention, zoning also had major benefits for those already with an economic advantage, primarily through providing a more orderly and predictable framework in which to make land-investment decisions, and the likelihood of increased property value for land already possessed. Without stating so directly, zoning also provided, for some neighborhoods or communities, a convenient regulatory device to exclude outsiders on the basis of class, race or ethnicity.[8]

At the same time, political decision-making was retained in the hands of existing urban governing regimes, now assisted by a coterie of professional planners to provide "rational" guidance and thus a "scientific" imprimatur to the planning and code administrative decisions to be made. Implicit in the new zoning enterprise was creation of what would eventually appear as a detailed a priori framework of urban spatial order, concealing the power relations and contestations involved within and between each designated locale.[9]

While zoning and compliance administration provided some degree of coherence in a previously laissez-faire context, the advantages of zoning were commonly eroded through individualist entrepreneur demands for use variances, special permits, frequent re-zoning and other devices, all of which, in the hands of existing political regimes, became highly politicized rather than decided primarily on the basis of professional planning criteria.[10] For this reason, a new wave of land-use policy reform urged the development of local comprehensive or "master" plans which could articulate a meaningful set of broad community goals to which zoning codes, government projects and other legal protective measures would be accountable.

Public participation in these various processes was typically limited, at best, to "informational meetings," advisory referenda and public meetings of the local decision-making boards, as well as periodic electoral opportunity to influence the personnel of the governing regime itself. However, formal power was relegated to elected or appointed officials, assisted by professional experts, and heavily influenced by those private development interests which supported maintaining the rich lode of investment opportunity in local land development. In combination, largely-unaccountable government officials, developers, and others in the business community who gained from expansion of the local community constituted what urban sociologist Harvey Molotch referred to as "the growth machine."[11]

While environmental protection became an area of governmental regulation from the late 19th century on from motivations of basic health and safety and from a desire to "conserve" natural resources for longer-range economic exploitation, more serious concerns with overall environmental degradation due to the ravenous appetite of local "growth machines" and the overall "growth economy" did not gain substantial recognition in public consciousness or legislation until the 1960s. Riding the crest of environmental consciousness more generally, specific legally-mandated "environmental impact assessment" processes for government and private development projects were first enacted in the late 1960s and throughout the 1970s. NEPA at the national level and "little NEPAs" at the state level, including New York's SEQRA (State Environmental Quality Review Act), identified specific realms of potential adverse environmental impact and created specific environmental review processes to be incorporated in the broader scheme of governmental regulatory approval.

Because of the large scope of potential environmental impact, the particularly intense direct effect on citizens of development decisions and the popular grassroots demand for participatory deliberative decision-making in many policy realms at the time,[12] NEPA and the little NEPAs typically included, as part of the review and decision-making process for every project, a substantial space for grassroots citizens' participation. While still within the broader framework and dynamics of the capitalist political economy, these new "participatory enclaves" were the closest approximations to date of the old communitarian tradition of grassroots "moral economy" approaches to land-use decision-making from the 18th century and earlier. (By 1995, as two close observers of participatory decision-making noted, at the federal level, NEPA [along with the Freedom of Information Act] is currently still the "most profoundly" driving and shaping force in officially authorized public participation.[13])

Each of the above transitions in the evolution of local land-use decision-making came about over time, sometimes only after major clashes and as part of broader changes in the political culture of the country more generally. Yet predominance of certain approaches in cultures of public policy decision-making at a particular phase of the society's evolution, at both local and national levels, did not eliminate adherents of older approaches from earlier political cultures. Thus, in presentday America are believers, spokespeople and political actors for various rival ideologies. Many, if not most, current local land-use debates include some participants across this political spectrum.

This book seeks to clarify the nature of these alternative ideologies, their particular orientation toward land-use policy and how it is made, and the power-based interactions between them within the local decision-making political culture and process of contemporary America. It attempts to do so through a micro-scale case study of the workings of SEQRA, New York's "little NEPA," as they became known in a small community's intense experience with considering a proposed retail megamall within its midst.

In the concluding three chapters, the authors analyze the broader meaning of this experience and the spectrum of land-use ideologies by placing the local struggle and issues within the theoretical contexts of both urban political economy and participatory democracy more generally. Our analysis of SEQRA and participatory land-use planning, as it applies to local communities, is at the intersection of these two large bodies of theoretical work. The first, from the interdisciplinary field of urban studies, concerns the political economy of municipal regimes. The second, from especially political science and political philosophy, concerns the theory of participatory democracy.

Urban political economy theory concentrates especially on the dynamics of power within specific urban regimes as well as overall constraints imposed by state and national government prerogatives and by overall regional, national and international economies. From this literature, we set forth leading hypotheses concerning reformist potentials for expanding the external and internal boundaries of power, to be tested for analytic usefulness by our own case study.

Participatory democracy theory views contemporary mainstream democratic theory as contemptuous of the potential value of grassroots citizens' contribution to deliberative policy-making and complacently satisfied with an elitist assumption that democracy should be basically an arena for the more privileged and sophisticated few, however broadly defined that elite may be. Participatory democracy theorists reject these assumptions and the diminished quality of life which elite democracy implies for the vast majority of individuals. They advocate the value of fuller political experience for everyone in a society as well as various models for achieving it. From such theories, we derive critical criteria with which to judge the actual participatory democratic content of local applications of SEQRA.

This particular case-study analysis of Ashbury experience with the SEQRA process provides an especially useful vantage point for examining the explicatory power of current theories in these two realms. From an analytical standpoint, the single project focus has clear starting and ending points, with the entire procedural range of environmental impact analysis stages in between. The context was small enough to easily identify principal actors and principal structural factors. A full transcript of public meetings as well as personal observation and other documentation permit a precise delineation of competing ideologies as they vied with each other through the various detailed phases of impact review.

From a theoretical perspective, the small community scale of the conflict, more conducive to face-to-face interaction, to expectations of community accountability, and to relative simplicity of issues, allows for much easier testing of the potentials of progressive local reform and participatory democratic forms than do similar experiments in more dense complex metropolitan settings with far more problematic claims to "community." The very size of the setting also made more credible activists' claim that this was a fundamental local crisis, with the basic, long-range well-being of the community at risk. Because stakes were so large, each side invested far more effort and rhetoric than would have typified decision-making processes for smaller development proposals.

There were also important factors objectively favoring significant grassroots influence. The particular issue involved. a project commencement, not an attempt to reverse a development already vested with official approvals, let alone with on-site construction and thus a much larger potential private loss at stake. Grassroots groups were largely privileged in race and class terms and thus were more likely to gain attention in the formal process. As articulated by activists, the issue itself was not a radical challenge to the nature of the local political regime nor an attack on the legitimacy of capitalism more generally. It was well within the bounds of mainstream "legitimate" political discourse. For these various reasons, one reasonably would expect maximum potential influence by grassroots voices through the participatory opportunities available, since otherwise the very credibility of "rationalist" scientism and legal liberalism would be at risk.

Local politics are the realm most accessible to grassroots citizens. Within this realm, local land-use planning is one of the core policy decisionmaking areas and generally the one most available for democratic community intervention. In turn, the SEQRA process (and similar environmental impact assessment processes elsewhere) is the single most open arena for such participation. In other words, **if participatory democracy would work**

anywhere within the larger framework of the liberal capitalist political economy, it should work here. If it does not work convincingly at this scale and within this type of context, its overall function is not definable in these terms, and the political exercise is something other than what it claims to be.

Rather than fatalistically accept "structural" assumptions that "you can't fight City Hall" or that "Wal-Mart is too powerful to be stopped"--both of which were articulated within the upstate New York local community under study, grassroots activists decided to test the limits of the land-use planning "participatory enclave" provided by the SEQRA law, to see if "horizontal planning" was indeed possible within the present political economic system. The narrative and analysis to follow, by two leading participant-observers in this local struggle, provide a uniquely detailed and grassroots-level account, through each step of a development proposal review, of the potentials and limits experienced in this apparently democratic enclave.

Specifically, while acknowledging the present variety of urban regimes in the United States generally, the present case study will examine the flexibility for change of a particular political regime and will compare this with theoretical findings in the field concerning the extent to which a local political economy within the larger framework of American liberal capitalism is capable of opening its land-use policy-making process to full public participation. We will explore the boundaries of participatory planning procedurally promised by legal liberalism and the limits actually experienced, and the substantive development policy meaning of the participation allowed. On the basis of this experience, we will speculate in Chapter Seventeen on the broader import of these lessons for the potential of participatory influence in opening up urban regimes and in influencing local urban development and planning more specifically.

The case study thus becomes a normative test not only of the limits of the specialized law and practice of environmental impact review, but also of the limited democracy of local small-town regimes and the obstacles to meaningful participatory civic roles within the confines of capitalist economy generally. Competing constructions of reality--professional-legal and communitarian-experiential--become a central focus of the study as we consider the extent to which statist law can empower citizens to reacquire control over material forces which shape their everyday existence.[14] The particular local process described in this book was one moment in the ongoing dynamic resolution of this contradiction. Though, as Manuel Castells suggests, we are still merely at "the prehistory of the social sciences,"[15] we believe that the current case study helps to elucidate the important questions to address.

TWO INTRODUCTION: COMPETING LAND-USE PLANNING IDEOLOGIES; ORGANIZATION OF THE BOOK

In the first chapter, we described successive stages of dominant land-use ideology in this society from the 18th century to the present. The political dynamics behind the nature and functioning of environmental impact reviews generally, New York's SEQRA law in particular and the specific case study of this book must be understood in these ideological dimensions.

Who Should Decide and How?

We have chosen four typologies, commonly reflected in the literature on local political economy and local planning, to represent the wide spectrum of perspectives about human relationship with "natural resources" generally and the role of the community in determining specific types of land use. These four perspectives have appeared with different strengths historically and at present. While each can exist abstractly, their actual ability to be translated into public policy depends on receptive political cultures and structural contexts at the level of concern, from local urban regimes to those at national and international scales.

Each perspective derives from (and reenforces) broad assumptions about the primacy of business vs. non-business values in public policy, the role of market capitalism in organizing a society's economic activity, the proper relationship between governing structures and economic organization, the importance of equity claims for social allocation and redistribution, the centrality of ecological consciousness in determination of economic and non-material social objectives, and the primacy of rationalist scientism as the arbiter of social policy. In general terms, following the spectrum from "minimalist" to "pragmatic capitalist" to "regulator" and to "ecologist" perspectives, there is ever-greater attention to communitarian and inter-generational equity over individualist current rights--and the procedural and substantive redistribution which follows, more inclusion of non-"rationalist" or non-"scientistic" forms of reasoning, more balance of other social realms with the economic rather than the latter's primacy, and more ecocentric instead of solely anthropocentric worldviews.

We explain in this account how representatives of the four ideologies were influential in the contexts of the original and continuing political debate about the state environmental impact review law and in the particular struggle concerning the megamall in Ashbury. While any typology is artificial when applied to complex human attitudes and behavior, we believe that as generalized positions on a continuous spectrum, each has a particular internal logic significantly distinguishable from the others. Each has its own consistent psychological, economic, social and political appeal. Defining here major traits of the four perspectives will clarify the larger ideological meaning and intent of particular actions in succeeding chapters--often beyond the conscious understanding of the actors themselves at the time. While initially created on the basis of our own empirical observations, the chosen typology, we discovered, is commonly represented in theoretical literature on urban political economy and urban planning and well reflects current discussion of urban regimes and participatory democracy.[1]

Focusing on free, autonomous individuals as the basic social units, the **"minimalist" perspective** on land-use planning is committed to the predominance of property rights and market values. It maintains that laissez-faire individualist entrepreneurial motivation is the proper driving force behind the economic and general flourishing of a society. By this perspective, property rights derived from a natural process of Darwinian struggle for survival, not from explicit governmental action.

> .... [T]hey evolved from the bedrock of communities of people who survived . . . . When property rights are secure, the owner has an incentive to improve his assets, to maximize their value. . . . Property rights cause people to conserve natural resources and guard scarce environmental assets.[2]

Alternatively, if private appropriation of scarce natural resources deprives others of their use, this loss of freedom will be generally compensated for by the overall material well-being of society resulting from a free market system.[3] By this logic, privately-initiated growth equals progress, with few questions asked. "Land-use planning" is reserved essentially for private sector investors and developers, and their own privately-retained planners, as well as the unsparing logic of the free market ("market rationality"). Thus, historically, as James Howard Kunstler expressed it:

> Speculation became the primary basis for land distribution--indeed, the commercial transfer of property would become the basis of American land-use planning, which is to say hardly any planning at all. Somebody would buy a large tract of land and subdivide it into smaller parcels at a profit--a process that continues in our time.[4]

If mutually-beneficial coordination is needed, it can occur among entrepreneurs themselves, without interference by the government. At the most, governmental intervention in land-use should be minimal and reserved for emergency situations only.

Despite apparent hostility to the state, in the contemporary U.S. political context, obviously even "minimalist" developers must interact with it to some degree in order to carry on economic activity. The "minimalist" model itself is dependent upon prior:

> government stipulations regarding rights and privileges among market participants (for example, deeds, leases, and sales contracts). Without such government "regulation" there could be no exchange of place [a real estate market] at all. The State actively sustains the commodity status of land.

Similar necessary government intervention in developing urban infrastructure is crucial in determining market outcomes.[5] This dependence on the state, however, tends to be unacknowledged, since "[m]ost people generalize from the microeconomic meeting of buyer and seller making a deal to the larger market system. They divorce the microexchange from the social organization that permeates each economic act."[6] Furthermore, government has always reserved some rights, as with hunting and fishing controls, exercise of police power, taxation and eminent domain.[7] However, whatever the benefit gained by private property owners through acceptance of essential government support and thus collaboration with the state, "minimalists" also resist government by opposing any new legislation restricting free market dynamics and by seeking deregulation through non-enforcement or revocation.[8]

The **"pragmatic capitalist" perspective** is equally committed to the preeminance of market values over others, but recognizes that laissez-faire capitalism produces internal contradictions among capitalists themselves and between the various segments of society generally, through respective rewards and damage from the system. Both types of contradiction can be dysfunctional to efficient, stable economic activity and both threaten periodically even the viability of the system as a whole. For this reason, mediating statist intervention in the market is acceptable, but only to the degree necessary to preserve the viability and "legitimacy" of the free market system itself. As well, "pragmatic capitalists" often are ready to mobilize government planning tools and public intervention for purely social exclusionary, rather than environmental, objectives.

"Pragmatic capitalist" land-use planners thus accept the concepts of local traffic and parking regulations, municipal zoning and municipal water and sewer treatment facilities to encourage the proximity of similar uses and maximization of market values of land.

> In the new-property market [of undeveloped land], land-use regulations reduce investment uncertainty: effective ahead of development, they are designed wholly to protect and recapture monetary and social values. Municipal adoption of a zoning map. . . [is] transferring some of the risk from the individual investor to the

collectivity . . . .

Zoning also reduces uncertainty for owners of already-used property, concerned that nearby, new property development might lessen their own property values. [9] As perceived by "common-sense," only those environmental impacts which pose immediate egregious threats to the continued viability and growth of the community deserve government regulation, and then only on a case-by-case basis with the burden of proof falling on the regulators. The need for environmental "planning" may be convincingly articulated, but is preferably a matter of designing suggestive guidelines rather than imposing "command and control" restrictions. As such, governmental intervention (with the "social exclusionist" exception) should be only the midwife of private sector planning. Professional planners may be called upon, on a case-by-case basis, but only as instrumentalist technicians subservient to those in political power.

As with the growth of the law and legalism under capitalism more generally, for "pragmatic capitalists," the prime purpose of land-use regulation and planning is to establish a sense of orderly process, rather than leaving growth completely to the whims of the market and naked power itself. Not only does this guarantee some space for entrepreneurial activity for the somewhat-less powerful, it also gives a cloak of "objective bureaucratized" legitimacy, among the broader population, for insider and outsider elites involved in the process of real estate development generally. [10] Aside from these economic and legitimacy motivations, such land-use regulatory tools also assist those interested in social exclusion, on the basis of class, race, or ethnicity. Concerning manipulative uses of planning practice generally, Charles Hoch points out, "The danger of technocratic rationality comes not from the commitment to reason but from the use of particular technical findings to discredit the legitimate purposes of other individuals as irrelevant, self-interested, or even stupid." [11]

To guarantee that mediative governmental intervention does not go beyond the bounds of maintaining minimally orderly process to assure continued economic growth, or to accomplish social exclusion, "pragmatic capitalists" trust only themselves, not those committed to redistributive values, to position the various regulatory bodies involved. Significant participation by the public in such processes is anathema, unless effectively controlled and channeled by "pragmatic capitalist" leaders to assure support for pre-existing "developer-friendly" or social exclusionary agendas. "Planning" and land-use regulation generally are best carried out by trusted local elites and professionals of the same ideological orientation, beyond the scrutiny and control of the public and "special interest groups" who would use regulation to effectively redistribute private wealth to their own ends. [12]

In turn, despite the "rational" and "regulatory" implications of the planning profession, many planning experts (primarily the "traditional technicians" and "passive hybrids" identified by Elizabeth Howe[13]) have internalized their functionally and politically circumscribed role, viewing the "public interest" as essentially whatever elected public officials declare it to be. They define their limited influence as derived from technical expertise and abstain from advocacy, willing to acknowledge and maintain existing arrangements of power. As John Friedmann portrays in discussing the orientation of the "policy analysis" school generally, technocrats of this type practice "[i]ncremental analysis [which] is parsimonious in its demands for information, concentrates on the consequences of limited change, and can be modeled to yield determinate solutions."[14]

Variations of this perspective are bureaucratic development entrepreneurs at state and national levels of government. As Serge Taylor analyzed, project and agency managers in federal agencies typically "are not rewarded for either thinking about or pointing out the potentially adverse 'side effects' of their policies." They "tend not to want errors or dubious decision premises to be exposed to critical scrutiny by outsiders."[15]

"Pragmatic capitalist" planning thus hopes to avoid direct confrontation with applicants through excessive project delays, denials or lawsuits so as to preserve the image of developer self-restraint, responsibility and even "environmentalism," and to minimize broader grassroots critiques of market justice more generally. This cautious non-confrontational approach is also promoted as a way to assure "community," since it aims to discourage polarization between proponents and opponents of any particular projects and the public's explicit awareness of interest polarization more generally.[16]

"Regulator" land-use planners have more rigorous and consistent environmental concerns, recognizing that threats to individual investments, economic growth and community viability occur from gradual longer-range and systemic accretion of environmental damage as well as from immediate, highly-visible dangers. As well, allocative equity in land-use policy (including universal enjoyment of scarce natural resources and quality of life) requires social redistribution for those presently less favored and less empowered and for future generations alike. In their view, regulatory intervention addresses higher "public interest" values than those produced by individual or corporate capitalist intervention and the market alone. As Bruce Williams and Albert Matheny state, environmental and other realms of "social regulation" (such as workplace and consumer safety) concerning non-market products of economic activity are designed "to remedy the failure of the private market to price adequately the negative externalities of many productive practices" which impose "economically unjustifiable costs on certain groups in the population

. . . ." Social regulation thus attempts to redistribute costs back to those responsible for their appearance--corporations and, indirectly, consumers themselves.[17]

"Regulator" land-use planners thus attempt to promote and conscientiously administer legislation, from local to national levels, which will provide enforceable protective guidelines and mitigation by which to assure only future development which is appropriate.[18] At the same time, they understand that, to remain legitimate, bureaucratic regulation demands procedural equity (fairness) in criteria, application of rules, review process and outcomes, without favoritism for politically-favored elites.

Confrontation is expected and accepted since planning, by its nature, is understood by "regulators" to be political. To be effective (or "socially rational") in this context, planners must be assertive in pressing their claims. As acknowledged generally throughout current literature on planning theory, such activism typically takes one or several of three forms: in-house political lobbying to resist "pragmatic capitalist" officials, diligent and forceful technical research and presentation of findings, or open advocacy for and potential mobilization of greater grassroots participation supportive of planners' positions.[19]

"In-house lobbyists" (Howe's "active planners" or Throgmorton's "policy analysts") blend science and politics in trying "to persuade elected and appointed officials to use the planner's advice."[20] For them, planning is "a tool for accomplishing particular goals to which they [are] committed." They "developed political support and mobilized it on particular issues, accumulated and called in political debts, and generally lobbied actively. In addition, they used information strategically."[21]

"Forceful researchers" (Howe's "technician activists" or Throgmorton's "advocacy planners")

> use rigorous scientific techniques in support of a chosen set of values or interests. . . . [They] help clarify and express their client's ideas, help inform the public about the range of available alternatives, point out biases in other plans, and ground the evaluation of plans in a clearly articulated (and passionately held) set of values.[22]

To take advantage of "the 'straight' and 'competent' associations with the technical image to build a more activist role," they emphasize "the importance of good technical analysis" and providing "objective information to decision-makers" to get results.[23]

"Participatory advocates" (Howe's "process planners" or Throgmorton's "political entrepreneurs") "bring diverse constituencies (or advocacy groups) into new coalitions, which, in turn, . . . provide organizational and political support for the political entrepreneurs who established them."[24] They have "an overriding concern with the legitimacy of the planning process and a concern with keeping it open and responsive to input from a wide variety of groups."[25]

Whatever their concerns with substantive or allocative equity, doubts of some as to the overall "sustainability" of constant growth, and occasional questions about the instrumentalist, anthropocentric view of nature, "regulators" do not challenge the overall legitimacy of capitalist political economy. They also share the technocratic assumption that expert rational discourse, as embodied in the conscientious performance of modern science, can fairly and reasonably evaluate existing and potential environmental conditions relevant to the merits of any proposed development project. Nevertheless, in contrast with "minimalists" and "pragmatic capitalists," most "regulators" reject the position that policy alternatives can be solely or primarily commodified--determined, that is, by a balancing test which relies solely on estimates of dollars or dollar-equivalents gained or lost. In part, this stems from "regulators'" recognition that protection and enhancement of non-materialistic goals, such as aesthetic landscapes, community bonds and civic participation, are valuable in themselves.

The **"ecologist" perspective** on land-use planning is concerned that endless "development" itself is the problem[26] and that effective long-range and cumulative "mitigation" in most cases is meaningless and impossible. From a "lesser-of-evils" calculation, despite sharing with "minimalists" a deep distrust of the state and bureaucratic control and deep recognition of the potential value of non-governmental "civil society," "ecologists" believe that reliance on autonomous capitalist market dynamics, imbued as they are with the logic and ethics of individualism, endless growth, and private power centers, offers even less acceptable alternatives to their own goal of communitarian society within ecological balance. Turning full circle to the traditional position of North America's original inhabitants, "ecologists" agree that a community should always carry out its activities with the equal welfare of the seventh future generation in mind. It asks that we critically distance ourselves from contemporary "civilization," as does poet Gary Snyder when he observes:

> Our skills and works are but tiny reflections of the wild world that is innately and loosely orderly. There is nothing like stepping away from the road and heading into a new part of the watershed. Not for the sake of newness, but for the sense of coming home to our whole terrain.[27]

For "ecologists," typically with bioregionalist, social ecology, deep ecology or ecofeminist orientations,[28] there is no separation between people and their environment. Ecologists contend that, consciously or not, people live in complete interdependence with all that exists. While supporting individuals' opportunities to flourish, "ecologists" believe that materialist advancement at the expense of the natural environment is an illusory gain. A clear statement of this position half a century ago was Aldo Leopold's forward to his *A Sand County Almanac*: "We abuse land because we regard it as a commodity belonging to us. When we see land as a community to which we belong, we may begin to use it with love and respect."[29] By contrast, "ecologists" see much of what was built in America in the last fifty years as "depressing, brutal, ugly, unhealthy, and spiritually degrading . . . the whole destructive, wasteful, toxic, agoraphobia-inducing spectacle that politicians proudly call 'growth.'"[30]

In the context of the wider capitalist political economy, this perspective doubts that government allied with capitalism has the will and ability to consistently prioritize long-range ecological concerns over short-range economic profits. As Raymond Rogers states, "The history of environmental policy is a history of <u>responses</u> to the appearance of environmental problems which are, in turn, generated by the priorities of industrial exploitation." Typical of the "ecologist" perspective is his view that "to accept a limited environmental agenda which operates as a kind of 'add-on' to the forces of development . . . is to doom conservation of the natural world to a rapidly accelerating failure."[31] In the context of local-level land use, undesirable "development" by those outside the community is perceived as a form of involuntary servitude, only made possible by the alliance of governmental and capitalist interests. Ecologists contend that while government may acknowledge "social justice" (procedural and distributive equity) and "sustainable economy" as legitimate concerns, its program is fundamentally overtaken by capitalism's constant need to expand and its insatiable desire for private gain, rather than to coordinate community resources as a "commons" for the benefit of all of its members, let alone to conceive of "community" and "benefit" in ecocentric instead of anthropocentric terms.[32]

While "ecologists" respect the informative potentials of scientific inquiry, they reject rationalist scientism's claim to privileged status in determination of social policy--understanding "natural science," "economic science" and "legal science" to be subservient social institutions within the overall framework and logic of capitalism and industrial society generally.[33] "Scientific" assurances about the safety of nuclear reactors and of stored nuclear waste for thousands of years are only among the most dramatic empirical sources for this distrust in the environmental realm generally. By contrast, for ecologists, to abrogate feelings

> play[s] willingly and directly into the hands of instrumental rationality, the same rationality that sees nature not as an experience of our very selves but as a human utility, a commodity, an externality. We sacrifice ourselves--and thus nature--to the very ideology that is wild

nature's most intractable enemy.[34]

Implied in this perspective as well is a critique of overly-rationalist self-justifications and behavior even among "ecologists" themselves.[35]

"Ecologists" are committed to effective community governance through empowerment of citizens to make their own decisions from below, instead of seeking reforms (as do "regulators") from what they view as the fundamentally-flawed alliance of hierarchical politics, technocratic expertise and capitalism.[36] Opposed to governance through corporations and bureaucrats both, "ecologists" endorse the concept of decentralized "home rule." But for them, the logic of "home rule" is participatory democracy, not domination by local elites. Inclusive deep democracy, they believe, will produce better community policy as a product of both seriously-considered multiple perspectives and greater ecological sensitivity. Thus, "ecologists" challenge existing governance structures at the same time that they problematize environmental issues.[37]

"Ecologist" professional planners within the state, in the words of Michael Brooks, can only "function as a watchdog, as a 'guerrilla in the bureaucracy,' as an agent of radical social change or as one who monitors communication flows and guards against the dissemination of false information." However, as he modestly observes, it would be naive to expect such roles "to be played by the vast majority of governmentally employed planners who function in systems that do not generally reward such activities."[38] Despite their structural determinism, if crisis at any level (including local land-use disputes) compels "ecologists" (activists and community-based professional planners alike) to move beyond mere critique and utopian theory, they usually find themselves (aside from possible involvement in extralegal forms of direct action[39]) in a "serious planner" alliance with those of "regulator" perspective. An observer such as Friedmann stresses, "One of the most difficult requirements for radical planners is the ability to live with contradictions."[40] Howe agrees, pointing out that, however compelling the theoretical approach that leads critical planners "essentially to reject the legitimacy of the political systems in which they work[,] . . . the tension and contradiction this implies for any practicing planner makes its adoption difficult."[41] Thus, "ecologists" recognize that:

> [r]adical planning, always based on people's self-organized actions, stands in necessary opposition to the established powers and, more particularly, the state. . . . Still, it would be wrong to ignore the state's existence or to treat it as an adversary only.[42]

Across the overall ideological spectrum, in any particular political context, the forcefulness and clarity with which any political actor presents her/his particular planning perspective may differ significantly, depending on personality dynamics, ideological self-consciousness and articulateness.[43]

Nevertheless, strengths or weaknesses of these personal factors do not affect the basic logic and implications of any of the four ideological positions. In any case, specific words and actions of individuals throughout the local drama described in this book were sufficiently consistent, in our view, to justify the label we chose for each political actor.

In the dynamics of polarization typical of contemporary American politics, it is common for "minimalists" and "pragmatic capitalists" to ally together in policy battles in what could be called a **"light planning"** growth coalition, while "regulators" and "ecologists" join together to pursue an agenda of **"serious planning."** The fact of coalition by no means precludes internal disputes within each alliance, but at the time of fierce struggle between the two poles it is pragmatic bonding rather than the differences which tends to prevail. Nevertheless, for any outside observer, the reality of actors operating within these two pragmatic coalitions sometimes obscures the actual core values of particular individuals.[44] One must at least act like a "pragmatic capitalist" or "regulator" player in order to be appointed to and participate on a local planning board, adopting at least some degree of that "normal discourse" shared by one of these two perspectives, even though one has "minimalist" or "ecologist" core values. (Though one's desire to serve on such a board is also a value statement itself.)[45]

In the current state of American politics, with strong gravitation toward the center generally, it is "pragmatic capitalists" and "regulators," together a kind of "governing consensus," which tend to dominate their respective coalitions since neither "minimalists" nor "ecologists" fundamentally believe in the discourse, appropriateness, or even legitimacy of governmental "regulatory planning."[46]

Organization of Book

Following the theoretical groundwork of this chapter, Part One of our account provides the background readers need to comprehend the specific political arena in which these dynamics of larger theoretical import occur. Chapter Three thus introduces the specific local Ashbury context of recent decades in order to clarify its own urban regime transitions, land-use planning practice, and the presence of alternative community voices. The chapter also presents the main forces behind the Wal-Mart project as well as their commercial development predecessors at the same site. It addresses the overall origin, purpose and statutory framework of the New York State Environmental Quality Review Act (SEQRA), its relationship to the similar federal NEPA and other states' "little NEPAs," and general trends in its impact on land-use planning within New York state.

Part Two is concerned with agenda-making, the first stage of environmental impact assessment and the first stage in any public policy review. Chapter Four establishes the implicit and explicit political nature of this process, including basic ideological contestations, as the developer, town planning officials, the latter's consultants and the mobilized public all articulate and pressure for initial definitions of a proper environmental impact review and the role of the public within it. Chapter Five describes the specific agenda-setting arena of the scoping process, the first formal stage for assessment definitions once the decision is made for an environmental impact statement (EIS). Within this stage, the political stance of each actor becomes more explicit. Chapter Six examines the appropriation of scientific and technical discourse by the developer in advancing the merits of its project in a draft EIS. Chapter Seven explains how confrontation on the specific land-use policy at hand escalates to the point where the community movement must challenge the very legitimacy, by democratic and ethical criteria, of the existing local regime. Chapter Eight demonstrates how the voice of the grassroots public comes to be clearly articulated through both expert and lay discourse within the officially-legitimized context of the EIS public hearing.

Part Three explains the equally politicized stage in which specific environmental and economic impacts of the megamall proposal were researched and analyzed, following the official conclusion of the agenda-setting stage. Chapter Nine discusses the procedural standards followed by the planning board and continually contested by the activist public in order to establish a level playing field for fair consideration of substantive evidence presented. Chapter Ten describes critical substantive issues themselves in the realms of stormwater, water quality, traffic and economic impact, as well as the basis for alternative analytical methodologies and interpretations of actual impact significance. Chapter Eleven presents external non-impact review challenges to the project through tax-abatement policy, litigation, street demonstrations and the electoral arena, all employed by community activists to enhance their influence in the face of the flawed "participatory democratic" and biased EIS review.

Part Four sets forth the final stage of environmental impact review, in which the planning board came to determine the fate of the Wal-Mart megamall. Chapter Twelve describes how the planning board arrived at a summary of its own research of substantive impact issues in a "comments-responses" document. Chapter Thirteen articulates the politicized struggle within the planning board as demonstrated in alternative impact "findings" statements, as well as new efforts by activists to influence the process even at this late stage. Chapter Fourteen presents the final phase of procedural maneuvers and dramatic decisions to conclude the environmental impact review process, alongside the larger context of an electoral challenge to the existing local governing regime.

Part Five provides a more extensive theoretical framework within which to analyze the deeper political dynamics and significance of the case-study experience as well as their ultimate implications for American politics more generally. Chapter Fifteen follows major actors of the local struggle during ensuing months and years in order to help evaluate the deeper local impact of the overall environmental impact review process and ultimate decision. Chapter Sixteen identifies essential traits of progressive urban regimes and moderate participatory democracy and the implications of both for local participatory political culture. Chapter Seventeen employs this analytical framework to develop a deeper understanding of the dynamics and more basic political meanings of the case-study and larger SEQRA experience. On the basis of the two previous chapters, Chapter Eighteen critiques the limitations of the theoretical models of progressive urban regimes and moderate participatory democracy and suggests broader implications for the future of American politics.

PART ONE   BACKGROUND

THREE

THE EVOLVING LOCAL
POLITICAL ECONOMY, THE
PROJECT AND SEQRA

Ashbury Evolution

By 1930, the bucolic, tree-lined town of Ashbury in Forest County, a few miles west of the Hudson River and below Albany, had nearly 1500 residents and a reasonable agriculturally-oriented economic base, significantly strengthened by the state Normal School, to protect against the worst ravages of the Great Depression.[1] Though Ashbury first accepted modern municipal regulatory powers for traffic and parking problems in the previous decade, this community, just as most rural small towns of the era, remained unaffected by the first wave of "pragmatic capitalist" urban zoning land-use controls reaching the larger urban centers in that same interwar decade.

Nevertheless, when a local newspaper, supported by the Normal School and "a group of our leading business and professional men," launched in 1930 a "Campaign for the Greater Development of Ashbury" and a 52-week series of articles about various phases of community development, the optimistic promise of rationalist science, expertise and planning was already in the air. At the same time, the newspaper editorialized that "the best index to the prosperity of any community is its growth--a steady increase in the number of its inhabitants."[2] A new urban regime was readying itself in the wings.

Consistent with this growing "pragmatic capitalist" ideology, in 1937, the Village government[3] set up a zoning committee, responding to urgings from the "establishment" women's Ashbury Study Club. Its goals, among others, were "to protect our village for the future from unsanitary conditions, building and factories." The committee, in turn, recommended zoning in order "to protect [a citizen] from unreasonable injuries by his neighbors who would seek private gain at his expense." But transition to a new local regime was stillborn. Zoning was rejected by "minimalist" voters in the following year by a 106 to 63 margin.[4]

Foreshadowing this 1938 vote, by nearly a two-to-one majority, Ashbury voters in 1932 endorsed the more conservative Republican Herbert Hoover for a second presidential term over Gov. Franklin Roosevelt, the Hudson Valley's own regional candidate.[5] Even in Roosevelt's 1936 sweep, Ashbury and Forest County overall supported Republican Landon. Clearly, the surfaced interest among some local citizens for more coordinated "civic improvement" did not imply the community's endorsement of New Deal politics or any form of major governmental regulatory intervention.

However, important new factors soon appeared which made further regime challenges and transitions inevitable. Throughout much of the country, the first two decades after World War II saw a tremendous upsurge of population, consumer spending, demographic mobility, use of automobiles and expansion of housing. Slogans of "growth" and "development" became popularized among large numbers to describe enthusiastically the energetic spree of long-delayed materialistic consumption, expansion of the business sector and government investment in domestic infrastructure. Ashbury participated in all of these trends.

The most significant new elements in the local job market were the coming of IBM to the area in the 1950s, the incorporation of the State Teachers College into the new State University of New York (SUNY) system and the College's subsequent rapid expansion in the 1960s and 70s. Stimulated by the presence of the College, regional proximity to New York City as well as other artist colonies in the area and an emerging countercultural back-to-the-land movement, by the late 60s the Ashbury area also experienced a major influx of artists and crafts people as well.

Announced in 1938, begun in the Thomas Dewey administration and completed in 1955 under Governor Harriman, the New York State Thruway, running parallel to and on the west side of the Hudson from just north of New York City to Albany, impacted Ashbury enormously. In physical terms, it divided the town north to south for eight miles, with about 80% of town land to the west and 20% (largely farmland) to the east.[6] More importantly, the Thruway exit for Ashbury now permitted daily commuting to the city for a hearty few and exposed the town for the first time to large numbers of metropolitan and Long Island day or weekend visitors, many of whom increasingly became interested in escaping the stress of city life or the rapid malling and suburbanization of their own communities.[7] Easy road access, the striking scenic beauty and famous rockclimbing challenge of a nearby mountain range, expanding student numbers at the college and job opportunities at area IBM plants attracted many persons specifically to Ashbury who would normally never have considered it.

Between the wide variety of groups migrating to the area over the past few decades, Ashbury emerged as an unusually diverse and stimulating community--a bit of urban sophistication in the country[8] with a median age 9 years younger than that of Forest County generally.[9]

In the consciousness of its residents and others, "Ashbury" was not a single "place," but a multiplicity of place-images. It was simultaneously a rural farming center, primarily focused on apple crops; an empty or transitory land-space for developmental expansion of all sorts, thus a potential opportunity for self-profit or supposed reduction in taxes through an enlarged assessment base; a time-space of Dutch legacy; a place of safe suburban or exurban living, and perhaps upscale gentrification; an environmental and recreational mecca, focused on the nearby mountain range, with its famed 200-foot climbing cliffs, and the lower slopes and plains between that ridge and a tree-lined local river; a small-town rural setting where fresh air, open spaces and tree-lined streets combined with friendliness and volunteer networking to preserve a sense of genuine community; a nexus of creative arts, crafts and music; a unique tourism destination based on the arts, environment and history; a college town revolving around the intellectual and cultural needs and interests of faculty, administration and students; and a legacy of 60s street spontaneity and diversity associated primarily with students, youth generally and other survivors of the politics and counter culture of that era.[10] As Blomley suggested generally, "landscape is continually in a state of contestatory becoming"[11] and as Massey states, places are better thought of not "as areas with boundaries around" but as "articulated moments in networks of social relations and understandings. . . . [E]ach place is the focus of a distinct <u>mixture</u> of wider and more local social relations."[12]

Within each individual's consciousness and between individuals, such aesthetic, economic, environmental, social and historical images competed for influence, though by nature some images of Ashbury were logically more complementary or more antithetical than others. These amalgams and contrasts of images, in turn, roughly overlapped with, influenced and were influenced by the competing ideologies of land-use planning described in Chapter Two. Planning "minimalists" tended almost exclusively to be those who saw Ashbury primarily in farming or development terms and who saw little reason to abandon the native Dutch descendant and WASP leadership which had characterized Ashbury for nearly three centuries. "Pragmatic capitalists" likewise saw Ashbury as a place for development potential. But they also recognized that certain minimal regulatory guidelines and governmental intervention were needed to provoke interest by outside investors and tourists as well as to prevent internal breakdowns of land-use, investments and infrastructure systems already in place. "Regulators" commonly were found among those attracted to Ashbury by the college, IBM or recreation and among those who sought to escape city stress or the Paramus-type commercialization, congestion and degradation of their previous suburban communities. Finally, "ecologists" were most frequently drawn from those who admired the town's counter-cultural, youthful, artistic, environmental and communitarian dimensions.

Between 1940 and 1950, the population of the Ashbury community rose 33.2% from its base of 2815, five times faster than Forest County as a whole.

During the next decade, local population rose 55.8%, about twice the rate of the county. From 1960 to 1970, especially because of the SUNY campus expansion, Ashbury grew another 78.3%, from 5800 to 10,415, again about five times faster than the overall county. Thus, in the three decades from 1940 to 1970, its period of massive growth, the population of Ashbury almost quadrupled, an enormous strain on the land base and politics of the community.[13]

By 1992, commercial farms (primarily producing apples and sweet corn) accounted for 79% of overall farm cropland acreage in Forest County, but overall farm acreage had declined by nearly 2/3 since 1950. Rising taxes, the cost of farming and ever-greater dominance of the market by larger farms put great strains on the ability of smaller farms to survive. From a land speculator perspective, on the other hand, as an Ashbury farmer (and president of the County Farm Bureau) expressed it, the steady increase of land values "provided [the farmer] with some security."[14]

This combination of declining sustainability of small farms and expanding residential need, in turn, led to a sharp increase in local housing on old farmland, primarily through proliferation of suburban-type subdivisions and apartment complexes. By 1980, 61% of the community's housing structures had been constructed in the 25-year span of 1950 to 1974. With expanding population and consumption patterns came investment in new retail facilities. In the single decade between 1967 and 1977, retail sales in Ashbury rose 82% (adjusted for inflation). In 1956, one of the classic large inns catering for years to the summer resort trade, as well as magnificent maples around it, were cut down to make way for the first "uptown" strip plaza. The decades-long march of ugly retail sprawl up the main thoroughfare to the outskirts of town was well underway, destroying beautiful old trees lining the road as it proceeded. From 1968 to 1979 came a wave of two major shopping centers, two smaller strip centers and four fast-food chain outlets.

This rapid commercial expansion eastward created havoc with the historic downtown business district for well over a decade, while the leapfrogging of grocery store chains resulted in the first major mall casualty, an eyesore empty or underused grocery facility left behind by Grand Union, reoccupied finally by a chain drug store outlet in 1986.[15] By 1988, there were approximately 300,000 sq. ft. of retail space along the Main Street-Rte. 354 corridor in the Town of Ashbury east of the village line, added to about 1/3 of that amount in the Village.[16]

Nevertheless, just four years later, the Ashbury Development Corporation pitched to outside investors the claim that roughly half of the Ashbury population's $109 million in retail purchases went to regional malls at least fifteen miles away and could therefore be totally recouped if new retail space was built in Ashbury. It specifically encouraged commercial sprawl even further east, on land near the intersection of the Thruway exit and Rte. 354.[17]

Community Land-Use Planning

In the early 1950s, after state statutory legislation authorizing establishment of planning boards and zoning for local towns,[18] the state Planning Department began prodding individual towns to set up such mechanisms along with creation of local master plans. Community land-use planning and zoning in Ashbury, however, were too late and ultimately too weak to prevent urban sprawl and the helter-skelter transformation of the community. Such goals were not top priorities of the new postwar local urban regime, despite its new emphases in other realms.[19]

The transition was slow in coming. In 1948, responding to the request of the local League of Women Voters chapter, the Ashbury Study Club and the male "establishment" Ashbury Club, the Village Mayor appointed a new committee to study village zoning. In a series of articles in the local press, the League emphasized the growth pressures already occuring and the fact that a community could not rely alone on the good intentions of every single owner to assure its well-being. One year later, however, the Village Trustees' proposed ordinance was publicly opposed by the new "minimalist"-leaning Ashbury Business Men's Association and rejected by voters by almost a 3-to-1 majority, 337 to 118.[20]

It took another seven years before a newly-ascended "pragmatic capitalist" coalition legitimated its perspective through adoption, finally, of a Village zoning code--much due to community shock and anguish at replacement of a beautiful old inn with a strip mall.[21] In favor of the ordinance in 1956 were the League of Women Voters, the Garden Club, the Chamber of Commerce and the School Board. An extensive survey of town residents by the League of Women Voters in 1954-55 had discovered that, next to "parking facilities," "zoning" was the most frequent response to the question, "What do you think Ashbury needs?" The vast majority of such responses came from village residents.[22] Authoring the ordinance was the Village Board attorney, who was also a longtime leader in Republican politics, a member of the 1948 Village zoning committee, and eventually Forest County District Attorney in the early 1960s. Clearly, the "pragmatic capitalist" position had been accepted.

Shortly thereafter, in turn, zoning was proposed for the whole town as a way to preserve community character and residential property values by prohibiting inappropriate business or industrial activities in residential areas. After much raucous and inflammatory debate,[23] in March 1958, town citizens voted 379 to 278 in a non-binding referendum to approve the concept of zoning generally, though this vote still left the town without a specific zoning code in place.[24]

In 1960, the Town adopted its first zoning ordinance, thus legalizing the victory of the "pragmatic capitalist" perspective and urban regime in the three-decade ideological struggle over Ashbury land-use policy. The new code created residential, commercial and industrial zones and permitted-use tables covering the entire community. Overall, the zoning scheme primarily acknowledged, legitimized and further encouraged the already-existing "order" of land-use patterns determined to date by private developers, rather than establishing new restrictive long-range planning.[25] In effect, the door remained open to unaccountable outside forces and a few local elites to determine the community's fate.[26] As in other communities, the "growth machine" was now entrenched with the imprimatur of official land-use planning. By late 1968, the machine was so effective that even planning board members admitted that they lacked adequate background to deal with the various development issues before them and thus moved to hire their first outside planning consultant.[27]

In actuality, these initial steps toward land-use planning, like the local traffic and parking regulations of the 1920s, were minimal in intent and effect, eliminating only the most egregious violations of common-sense community standards.[28] Additionally, however, the intricacies of zoning and subdivision regulations and their amendment now offered a further manipulable arena (not accessible to the average citizen) for lawyers representing special business interests. Lawyers sought zoning and accompanying site-plan regulations to assure a reduced-risk environment which actually facilitated development. Thus, developers "have not lost in the bargain the freedom to develop with the fewest restrictions on their project as possible, which as poor losers they [kept] trying to regain."[29] To be sure that their intent was carried out, the "pragmatic capitalist" Town Board re-enforced the limited impact of Ashbury zoning by assuring a pro-developer orientation of most members appointed to the newly-established planning board. In 1966, for example, the seven-person planning board[30] included the president of the Ashbury Savings Bank, two owners of major commercial apple orchards and an employee of the regional electric utility company.[31]

The shift in land-use policy from "minimalist" to "pragmatic capitalist" orientation accompanied the broadening of predominant political-economic power in Ashbury by the 1960s. The old regime alliance of Dutch descendant families and other businessmen and professionals of northern European descent[32] extended itself to include a more active and now well-established coalition of large commercial farmers (with speculative land interests of their own) and younger local businessmen, a number of whom were second-generation Italian-Americans also linked by bonds of ethnic loyalty and intermarriage of their own.[33] The coming of age of this broader power alliance, energizing especially the local Republican Party, was symbolized also in the widened ethnic membership of local "establishment" social clubs--the Ashbury Club for men and the Ashbury Study Club for women.[34] The importance of this shift in coalition regime definition was symbolized by the ascension of an ambitious central figure within it, Joe Enrico. An Ashbury insurance agency owner, 26-year old Enrico became Town Clerk in 1956, then served as its youngest Town Supervisor from 1960 through 1968, Chair of the County Board of Supervisors in 1967, and first Chair of the Republican-dominated new Forest County Legislature in 1968.[35] Enrico prided himself as a pragmatic leader who got things done, contrasting, in his words, with "the highly sophisticated theories of many political scientists [which] have been found wanting."[36]

Following the two-year preparation of a community master plan, never officially adopted by Enrico's Town Board,[37] the 1950s "pragmatic capitalist" ideological approach to town land-use planning and the "free market" power base behind it remained the determining forces in Ashbury's urban regime and this policy arena for another three decades.[38] However, community voices criticizing the ineffectiveness of this "light planning" approach appeared at various times from the 1960s on.[39] Some of these voices appeared from within the dominant regime itself.

For example, despite a revised zoning ordinance in 1969 explicitly based on Master Plan objectives,[40] even Supervisor Bob Tapani, a large apple-grower and himself part of this political regime, in 1971 foresaw that heavy new population growth would make it difficult to retain open space, "against great pressure to see the area altered into a concrete or asphalt jungle." Nevertheless, Tapani, the Town Board and Town planning board all favored widening Main Street from two to four lanes a mile westward into the village.[41] Similarly, by 1986, the executive director of the Ashbury Chamber of Commerce admitted the obvious--the deterioration of environmental quality in Ashbury--and called for good planning to reverse the trend. But she also saw existing local regulation--through municipal planning boards--as merely anti-business red tape. For her, the apparent solution was business-led "planning," in actuality a contradictory effort, to prevent the "choking" of Ashbury.[42] Under the local "pragmatic capitalist" regime, planning boards would only be "bargaining" boards, not enforcers of serious environmental planning which might significantly restrict developers' freedom.[43]

After years of talk, Village and Town governments eventually decided in 1985 to renew an attempt at comprehensive planning through creation of a new master plan.[44] But because of Town-Village rivalries, two years passed before appointing a full joint committee and beginning to meet. Another three years were then consumed for the committee to complete studies and a report, a further four years for the Town planning board to re-shape that recommendation into the weakened version it preferred and another year for a substantial (though still incomplete) official comprehensive plan to be adopted by the Town Board in 1995.

Despite evidence over two decades of substantial and growing community support for serious land-use planning to protect what remained of the valuable rural small-town character and beautiful scenery of the area, official positions of the Town Board and planning board during this entire period showed little evolution. While periodically challenged, the "pragmatic capitalist" urban regime remained in place.

Evolution of Local Environmental Movement

Not until the early 1970s did Ashbury experience public critiques of town land-use planning from more rigorous "serious planning" environmentalist positions. By 1973, for example, Village planning board member and Democratic candidate for Town Board Paul Hurley explicitly and emphatically made land-use planning the primary issue of his campaign. From his apparent "regulator" perspective, the choice was:

> whether or not [voters] want to continue to live in a semi-rural community or one that is being urbanized by the onslaught of a greedy realtor, with the assistance of our elected officials, who want to sell our community to the highest bidder in land speculation or a national developer. . . . We can no longer afford to tolerate public officials who make their decisions in rooms away from public scrutiny. We can no longer afford to tolerate public officials who seem only to respond to and protect their own selfish interests and those of their friends without regard for the welfare of the community.[45]

In turn, Hurley's running mate for Town Board was apparently the first ever to raise the impropriety of a business-dominated Town Board which had "difficulty reflecting a non-business viewpoint or holding concepts which might not be beneficial to business while helping the community."[46]

Complementing these campaign statements were local critics, such as those with "Community United for Proper Development" (of which Hurley was a member), who denounced provisions for planned unit developments (PUDs) or for apartments outside the village as needlessly moving Ashbury in the "bedroom community" direction. Some of these active critics, as in CUPD, emerged from New Left and counter-cultural contexts of the 1960s which emphasized grassroots empowerment, nature over artificiality and disdain for state and corporate hierarchy. This new "ecologist" voice was concerned that endless "development" itself was the problem and that effective mitigation in most cases was meaningless and impossible.

From the mid-60s on, Hudson Valley residents were embroiled in a series of highly-publicized, hotly-contested regional environmental struggles against a massive power plant on a prominent mountain overlooking the Hudson, conversion of a large military airport to potentially large-scale civilian use, construction of nuclear plants in Acton (just east of Ashbury) and across the Hudson and development of a major corporation's hotel and condominium complex on the ridge overlooking Ashbury on the west. While regional in nature (and of national interest in two of the cases), each of these battles recruited new voices from the Ashbury area to land-use issues, developed greater sophistication about organizing, the environment and politics, and left an experiential activist legacy which infused the local political climate for years to come.

The ten-year difficult but victorious struggle to stall and eventually defeat the hotel-condominium complex (and its supporters in the local business community, the county legislature and the state government) and to bring the whole of the nearby mountain site into the state fold of public parks provided a tremendous wealth of confidence, organizing experience and conscious ecological self-identity to large numbers of Ashbury residents. The seeds were thus sown for sustained critical local grassroots activity in the realm of land-use policy generally.[47] Such a victory was timely since, as one regional writer dramatically expressed shortly thereafter:

> There is a war going on in the Hudson valley, a conflict that is causing more impact on the land than did the Revolutionary War. Battles are taking place sporadically but with predictable regularity in town halls and city council meetings up and down the river, where real estate developers and neighborhood defenders square off over the fate of a particular parcel of land.[48]

In January 1985, several individuals--including Kevin Scully, a leader of the Mountain Protection League campaign, and a veteran of Ashbury Homeowners Association and CUPD[49] campaigns, and Alex McBride, an eight-year resident of Ashbury at the time--invited over twenty residents of Ashbury and its neighboring town to the south to participate in forming a new organization, Citizens Linked for Environmental Action and Responsibility (CLEAR).[50] Most were veterans of the Mountain Protection League struggle, actively concerned about other local planning issues or living in some proximity to the site of another newly-announced major proposed development. Task groups formed to gather information concerning existing zoning, potential land trusts, scenic roads, education, long-range development planning, preservation of farmlands, and fiscal implications of development. Significant numbers in the community were obviously concerned about such issues and new CLEAR members were ready to put time and energy into developing effective changes in Ashbury policy. In general orientation, the group ranged mainly from "regulator" to "ecology" land-use policy perspectives. An immediate aim of CLEAR was to oppose a new proposal to build a 700-unit "planned unit development" (PUD) in a 200-acre plot located toward the western edge of town between the Van Wyck River and the mountain ridge, an area zoned for a maximum density of one house per 1.5 acres. This massively oversized residential and conference center would dramatically alter the appearance, traffic density and character of the town's most scenic "west-of-the-river" area. It thus represented a dramatic assault on the character of the community at a time when "light planning" dominance of the planning board left Ashbury in a very vulnerable position.[51]

During town consideration of the Amsterdam Square megamall in 1989-91, at the later site of the Moselle Plaza proposal discussed in this book, CLEAR was its leading community critic, though by no means was alone. At that time, McBride filed numerous letters and spoke out frequently to the planning board against the board's inadequate environmental review process and the developer's failure to address adverse environmental impacts. CLEAR hired professional experts in the areas of hydrogeology and economic impact and demonstrated how the project planning firm failed to use the same soil analysis standards for pesticide-laden soils which it employed for a residential subdivision one year earlier. This forced the developer, as part of the SEQRA process, to engage in extensive additional soil sampling, testing and planning for extensive mitigation. While critiques of this sort delayed the project[52] and gained support in the community, ultimately the board decided that the developer's mitigation plans would satisfy environmental standards.

Along with its willingness to engage in litigation generally, two specific activities of CLEAR were most controversial. First was its organization in 1986 of large-scale community demands for more sensitive re-zoning, including an official town moratorium against all but the smallest development projects while the master plan and subsequent rezoning were finalized.[53] Second was its litigation specifically against a residential subdivision on part of the apple orchard owned by Bob Tapani, the Republican ex-Town Supervisor, and his father.[54] In the eyes of the local "light planning" regime and its network of supporters, the latter suit symbolized a frontal attack.

Letters to local newspapers and comments at public hearings virulently denounced Scully, McBride and CLEAR. Some attacked CLEAR as simply a collection of newcomers who wished unfairly to close the door behind them now that they were inside.[55] For some CLEAR members, in terms of years of residency in Ashbury, the "outsiders" claim was correct. But of course the term was relative since all but Mohican Indians actually qualified for that label.[56] Even in relative terms, however, CLEAR had the support of many long-standing Ashbury families, while those who opposed it were frequently as fresh to the scene as those they denounced.

Some figures in the local real estate business were among the loudest in their attacks. Non-native Linda Parsons, for example, the strongest voice and influence in the local trade, president of the Ashbury Chamber of Commerce in 1984 and representative for mega-project developers east of the Thruway in 1973 and 1984, was a common hovering presence at planning board meetings, often adding her thoughts on particular proposals before the board and frequently criticizing the comments of CLEAR.[57] As a "minimalist" admirer of Ayn Rand, her view was that Ashbury planning should be left in the hands of people like herself, since they had the expertise, cared for the local beauty and wished to plan for "orderly growth." Said a critic in 1973, however, "she badgers her Republican pals to get her way, particularly in zoning for her out-of-town developers. She'd sell Ashbury to the highest bidder for a buck."[58]

Several SLAPP suits were filed or threatened in an effort to intimidate CLEAR and its leaders.[59] Additionally, at a "candidates night" public meeting in 1987 and on other public occasions thereafter, those running for town office were subjected to a McCarthyite challenge, "Are you or are you not a member of CLEAR?," as the supposed ultimate clarification of their position. Nevertheless, there was substantial community support for CLEAR's critical perspectives and actions, as indicated in other letters to the editor, comments at public meetings and consistent membership renewals.[60]

Evolving Local Political Context

Like many small rural towns across the country over the past thirty years, Ashbury during this period experienced an infusion of political concern and dedication quite different from traditional community politics up to that date.[61] The diversification of cultures and ideologies across American society generally could not help but affect the local context as well, especially concerning as sensitive and central a realm as land-use policy.[62] The influx of new residents by 1985 brought total voter enrollment in Ashbury to 6229, with 2209 Democrats, 1964 Republicans and 1901 independents.[63] One result of new consciousness and new constituents was election of the first Democrat in four decades as Town Supervisor in 1975.[64] From a long-time Ashbury family, formerly a school guidance counselor and owner of an Army-Navy store, Tom Kessler was only modestly innovative. He nevertheless symbolized a shift toward questioning the prevailing urban regime and its "pragmatic capitalist" ideology. After backing several environmental initiatives pursued by elements within his coalition, including a model recycling center, however, Kessler soon settled into the same "pragmatic capitalist" mode and laconic equilibrium of his predecessors, eventually joining the vocal public critics of CLEAR as well.

He thereby gained the endorsement of the local Conservative party in several re-election campaigns.[65]

Seeking in 1989 to reclaim the Town Supervisor post, Republicans nominated Grant Schmidt, grandson of an apple farmer and attorney (and state assemblyman), son of an attorney, ex-high school basketball teammate of Joe Enrico, charter member of the Ashbury Jaycees, member of the Ashbury Club since 1966 (and its president in 1982-83), brother of a previous Town Attorney and Supervisor, retiring IBM manager and descendant of at least 11 of the 12 original Dutch settler families. Despite his own campaign emphasis on managerial skills and fiscal stringency, Schmidt's apparent concern with environmental safeguards (he had served on the local Environmental Conservation Commission) seemed relatively appealing to those who had seen little progress in this realm for years.[66]

Regardless of Schmidt's victories in 1989 and 1991, the relative local strength of alternative land-use ideologies was by the early 90s still unclear.[67] Just one month before Magellan Construction's megamall application to the planning board in December 1993, local elections returned Schmidt to office again against a token candidate of the Democrats. At the same time, long-time moderate Democrat incumbent Edna Devilla and conservative Republican Gertrude Kraft were chosen for the two contested seats on the Town Board. The two other Board seats were occupied by liberal Mark Lyon (Citizens Party) and liberal Democrat Jerry Ritter. For those with environmental concerns, this board seemed, in relative terms, potentially the most encouraging ever.

Lyon, a past chair of the town's Environmental Conservation Commission and past member of CLEAR, had consistently sought local environmental measures from a "regulator" perspective (especially concerning recycling and rail-trail conversion) since his first election to the board in 1987. He had also suggested re-zoning the commercial district east of the Thruway to prevent megamall applications in the future. Musician-carpenter Ritter's position seemed similar to Lyon's but, after only two years on the Board, he resigned in December 1993, moving to a neighboring town. (The Board replaced him in February with Republican realtor Jay Mosher.) Devilla lived in Ashbury since 1964 and taught English at a nearby community college. She was a former president of the League of Women Voters, a regular Democratic candidate since 1971, and an eight-year veteran (from January 1975 to March 1983) and past chair (1978-81, 1983) of the Town planning board.[68] Her ease with local "old boy" conservative Republicans and her obvious political ambition apparently cautioned her against controversial stands. She, her husband (on the SUNY/Ashbury faculty) and a handful of other Democratic veterans traditionally controlled the local party organization.[69] Gertrude Kraft was a conservative past member of the Village Board and ex-member and past chair of the Ashbury Town planning board in the 1970s.[70]

In late 1993, the seven-member town planning board was chaired by Rocky Ryker, a 43-year old "minimalist" free market ideologue, a graduate of SUNY/Ashbury from White Plains, ex-county jail guard, ex-radio station employee, salesman for an industrial cleaning products company, and a sometime road manager for a nationally-known local rock band.[71] Despite his defeat as a candidate for the Village Board in early 1985, several months later, the Town Board chose Ryker over CLEAR's Scully to fill a planning board opening, a clear indication of prevailing Town Board perspectives at that time. Since that date, Ryker had moved in 1992 from vice-chair to full chair of the board (with Town Board approval), replacing Abe Kinsella, a retired IBM programmer and manager and Ashbury restaurant owner.[72]

Where Kinsella's leadership style was like a steamroller, with a domineering personal demeanor and detailed knowledge of the planning code, Ryker's was a second-rate imitation. Younger, of shorter stature, less knowledgeable, and frequently gruff and acerbic, he had a belligerent personality reminiscent of his political mentor, Joe Enrico.[73] Assured of the latter's powerful backing, he often seemed like and apparently self-consciously enjoyed the role of a schoolyard tough with those he couldn't charm with praise or control. For years at board meetings and in the press, he had denounced CLEAR and environmentalists generally as a small handful of special interests. He also viewed many of the Master Plan Committee's 1990 recommendations as a "knee-jerk response," with zoning and environmental restraints on developers that "go above and beyond what's necessary."[74] Ryker continually asserted that he and he alone would choose when and if any public testimony would be "appropriate" for environmental review of projects considered in the SEQRA process.

As Enrico's protege, Ryker also was the chair of the local Republican party. In this role, he draped himself with the cloak of a simple populist, "in tune with the long-time residents, the farmers, the blue-collar workers,"[75] while also, in open partisan manner, jealously protecting the interests of "free enterprise." He was commonly perceived as a crude opportunist, a useful local agent to carry out the decisions of Enrico, the county and Ashbury Republican boss. As such, Ryker represented the old urban regime and its "light planning" positions on land-use policy which had dominated the Ashbury planning board since the 1950s and 60s.

By late 1993, however, for the first time in the years of the Kinsella-Ryker regime, the planning board included at least three members (still a minority of the seven-person board) with apparently a more critical "regulator" planning perspective, the result of both nudging from Lyon on the Town Board and the qualifications of available candidates when replacements were needed. Jane Pelletier, a dancer, educator, travel agent and member of the Nature Conservancy and League of Women Voters, vocally identified herself as an environmentalist and often gave passionate statements of position. Ben Hillman was employed by the state Department of Transportation (not locally) and in the past had worked in a different upstate county's planning department. His more serious demeanor and stubborn attentiveness to contradictions and detail complemented an apparent strong "regulator" commitment. Ray Dalrymple was a reserved official of an area real estate developer not directly involved in the Ashbury market. He seemed reasonably knowledgeable about current "regulator" planning standards and occasionally was outspoken in their defense.

Supporting Ryker's position on almost every occasion was vice-chair Rich Maglie, an official with EnergyMax, the regional electric utility. While sometimes ideologically straddling "pragmatic capitalist" and "regulator" perspectives and with a more reasoned tone and personality, he rarely asserted himself to dispute with the chair. He had, however, ultimately voted against environmental approval of the earlier Amsterdam Square megamall proposal, apparently based on concerns over traffic and economic impacts. A similar general outlook and tone typified Lynn Whipple, a local attorney who joined the board shortly after its 1990 Amsterdam Square decision.

Rounding out the board was developer Red Davis, business partner since 1959 of his father Ernie who had sold a 57-acre tract, the land focus of this book, to developer Joe Heller in 1986. Though living by 1993 in another part of town, Red still owned a lot immediately adjacent to the Heller tract. A somewhat reserved and often seemingly-angry man on the board, he prided himself as being one of the "old Ashbury boys" who made good, graduating in the same small 1954 high school class as commercial apple farmers and former planning board members Bob Tapani and Kip Graves. He was a member of the establishment Ashbury Club from at least 1970 and its president in 1988-89. He had also served as an appointed Republican Town Board replacement for a few months in 1975 until his electoral defeat later in the same year.

With an engineering background and his own excavating and paving business, Davis was a throwback to the old "minimalist" perspective, only occasionally and begrudgingly acknowledging the validity of planning generally.[76] At one CLEAR-sponsored public forum on the environmental dangers of pesticides several years earlier, sitting with his old high school peers, he gleefully pointed out how he had inhaled huge amounts of pesticide as a farmboy growing up and still was in fine health. On the planning board, Davis enjoyed occasionally pointing out inconsistencies by an applicant or apparent serious questions that needed to be asked. But it appeared that he could always be counted upon to come around in favor of the developer as he had done with Amsterdam Square. For the most part, Davis saw the community in dichotimized terms: those individuals, like himself, whom he described as "REAL NATIVES" and those "late-comers" to the community whom he contended had not "dedicated and donated their social and economic lives and livelihood in every way possible to make Ashbury what it is so we can enjoy it." Davis, reflecting his compromised "minimalist" perspective, maintained that "God made this valley and the ridge to the west of it. We respect that gift and have obviously done a fair job of preserving it since new arrivals still find it attractive."[77]

The planning board majority thus still held to the same "light planning" coalition perspective characterizing most of its shifting membership from 1957. As with the Town Board, the actual quality of planning board accomplishments over the years had usually fallen far short of even its modest capabilities. Members often reviewed application documents for the first time at the meetings themselves, apparently rarely spoke with each other between meetings, allowed themselves to be manipulated through chair initiatives, were inhibited by the psychological need to maintain "friendly" peer relations and were often quite defensive against suggestions from the public.

For years, Abe Kinsella and others had asserted that the task of the board was to administer the zoning code, not to engage in planning.[78] From the perspective of CLEAR and others of "regulator" and "ecologist" perspectives, this ideological claim was a purposeful abrogation of responsibility, a "light planning" restraint on the significant discretionary planning role defined for that board by state law, not reflective of the environmental concerns of substantial numbers in the community.

When forced in 1990 to be responsible for processing the new master plan once recommendations were handed over by the Master Plan Committee, the board deliberated at a snail's pace on most planning policy issues involved, clearly discomforted with its role. After Kinsella stepped down, board members stated that the latter never favored the comprehensive plan and that that factor was responsible for the board's lack of progress. However, dynamics among board members themselves also left those potentially interested in long-range planning easily manipulated into acquiescence to the chair's position. Whatever the personal orientation of each member (by late 1993 those of a "regulator" perspective were never a majority), as a group the board had basically followed the will of the chair and the chair followed, in most cases, the intent of the developer.

Legislative Origins and History of SEQRA

Local land-use planning policy was also significantly affected by wider politics at the state level. Prior to enactment of the New York State Environmental Quality Review Act (hereinafter "SEQRA"), those concerned about degradation of the natural environment undertook several efforts at state-level legislation which proved unsuccessful. These efforts were spurred by the implementation of the National Environmental Policy Act (NEPA) of 1970 and legislation in other states, notably California and Minnesota, which maintained that government had a responsibility to protect the environment and to consider and mitigate the adverse environmental impacts of development.[79] These early bills were defeated in part because of general concern for the economic impact of environmental legislation during a period in which the economy was undergoing protracted difficulties.[80] The policy debate in the legislature also broke down because there was no consensus regarding the applicability of environmental law to private development, which to date required only limited governmental activity in relation to the granting of permits or approvals.

Legislators also disagreed regarding the proper role of the state in the enforcement of environmental law. While NEPA required only that the federal government consider adverse environmental impacts through appropriate study, early proposed legislation in New York sought to authorize the New York State Department of Environmental Conservation (hereinafter "DEC") to review state and local government enforcement of such laws.[81] The policy debate spurred by "minimalist" and "pragmatic capitalist" concerns over governmental restriction of free enterprise and home rule, voiced by both Governor Rockefeller and relevant leaders of the state legislature, served to scuttle ten successive bills proposed between 1970 and 1975.[82]

In 1975, newly-elected Governor Carey re-energized those concerned with the environment by stating in his first annual message to the legislature that while the state was still undergoing severe financial difficulties, "we will do what we must to preserve the natural environment for tomorrow and take our responsibilities to future generations with the same high consideration we give our own."[83] A report to Governor Carey within months by his Task Force on the Environment proposed a Critical Resources Management Act after finding first that certain elements of the natural resource base of the state, i.e., water supply, food production, flood protection, and wildlife habitat, have been "significantly diminished by uncontrolled or incompatible development, and the quality of remaining resources has been seriously impaired."[84]

The Task Force found that "[t]he quality of life, and ultimately perhaps even the existence, of future generations depends in large measure upon steps now taken to resolve through wise management and long-range conservation the otherwise insoluble dilemma posed by increasing demands upon a decreasing supply of finite resources."[85] As with the landmark state law eight decades earlier which established the Adirondack State Preserve, such a regulatory rationale was clearly "conservationist" rather than "preservationist" in orientation, justifying governmental intervention to assure that capitalism's use of natural resources might continue in the foreseeable future, as opposed to protecting nature from human use. With regard to growth, the Task Force found that "[d]evelopment needed for residential, industrial, transportation and other important purposes should have its location and nature planned so as to permit present and future resource requirements of a critical nature to be fulfilled and to allow serious hazards to be avoided."[86] The Task Force, in effect, sought to integrate the applicability of regulatory environmental law to both public and private spheres by requiring the preparation of an environmental impact statement for any action either proposed or to be approved by state or local government.[87]

The first SEQRA legislation, modeled largely on California precedents, was approved by the New York State Assembly and Senate in June 1975.[88] Its "regulator" purpose was to make environmental protection the mandate of state and local government in both the public and private sectors. Acknowledging that zoning and site-plan design regulations only minimally, at best, protected against a community's environmental degradation, the SEQRA statute, as originally enacted, presented a stark challenge to development. It raised the real possibility, for example, that a local planning board, as an agency delegated to implement the SEQRA statute, must deny approval of a shopping center whose significant adverse environmental impacts cannot be effectively mitigated, despite the fact that the planning board has no original permit jurisdiction over those natural resources which may be adversely affected and regardless of whether the plan satisfied local zoning and site-plan regulations.[89]

Opposition and Amendment to SEQRA

The SEQRA statute was signed into law by Governor Carey in August 1975, apparently in part due to his still relatively fresh presence on the Albany scene compared to veteran assertive legislative leaders committed to producing the legislation.[90] Between legislative approval and adoption, leaders of local government, developers and suppliers of construction materials, the state's major electric utilities, organized labor and state agencies themselves voiced "pragmatic capitalist" opposition (re-enforced by "localist" sentiments) to the legislation, contending that it represented a fundamental intrusion upon local government's power of home rule in the exercise of the discretion granted to town boards, planning boards and zoning boards relating to land use and development. The New York State Association of Towns, the County Officers Association and the New York Conference of Mayors and Municipal Officials were among its most vocal opponents. For example, the last of these declared an emphatically "growth machine" perspective:

> The experience of local governments with federally-required impact statements has meant delay of up to two years, increased costs, the withdrawal of developers because of these costs, mandated inflationary incentives in municipal budgets. All this comes at a time of severe economic difficulty when by general consensus all city and village officials are concerned with human needs and employment opportunities for many.[91]

In a subsequent submission, the Conference of Mayors (membership representing 98.6% of the total population living in the incorporated bodies of the state (excluding towns) asked the following rhetorical question:

> When a person applies for a license to fish or to hunt, must the protection of water, land, fish, wildlife and air resources be considered? [92]

Typical of the views of local officials was the opposition voiced by the mayor of Patchogue:

> In my 24 years of public service, the past 16 years of which I have spent as the Mayor of the Village of Patchogue--and a Democrat at that--this is the worst piece of legislation that I have ever seen the Legislature try to shove down the throats of local government. It would mean the filing of an impact statement for practically every move a Village, Town or County wishes to make.[93]

Business voiced its opposition through the Empire State Chamber of Commerce and the New York Chamber of Commerce and Industry, while organizations such as the General Contractors Association of New York, the New York State Association of Architects and the New York State AFL-CIO joined the anti-SEQRA coalition. In voicing its opposition, the General Contractors Association contended that the legislation would cause serious delays and "[d]elays will increase construction costs. Construction is the best pump primer for the economy and should not be fettered by the dampening effect of this legislation." It further insisted that this type of law "subjects every decision and review to the scrutiny of every citizen at each and every stage of the process. A fanatical fringe that is outraged by anything and compelled to protest in loud voices at the drop of a picket sign, will have a field day."[94]

The ideological panic created after SEQRA's enactment and prior to Governor Carey's signing of the bill was instructive for several reasons. First, it was apparent from the face of the debate that the combination of local government and development interests had little tolerance for restrictive acts of the central state government. Second, if a central state government sought to prevent environmentally-unfettered free market growth and development, it would have to do so not only over the objection of entrenched interests at the ground level but at a substantial cost to the state in terms of monitoring and enforcement. The legislature in Albany might pass what it thought was in the best interests of the state, but to ask those at a local level who opposed the legislation to enforce it would lead to an irreconcilable tension created by contradictory perspectives. Although the reader might conclude that the judicial system could arbitrate and mediate among the different perspectives to ensure compliance, that would presuppose an available body of citizen groups willing to act as ombudspeople and a disinterested--non-politicized--judiciary who could resolve whatever dispute arose.

In signing the SEQRA law in August 1975, Governor Carey sought to ameliorate the political threat created by the alliance of governmental and business interests which opposed the bill as contrary to the basic tenets of state-supported capitalism. In deference to the power of local government, the Governor indicated that the legislation he was signing required the Commissioner of the DEC to consult with involved state and local officials and agencies before adopting implementing regulations for SEQRA. Similar assurances were given to the construction industry. In pursuit of this non-disruptive role, the Governor signed new legislation in 1976, only gradually phasing implementation of SEQRA and also containing a schedule for the adoption of regulations and practices to implement SEQRA by state and local agencies.[95]

By 1977, the "light planning" alliance of local government and capital attempted again to exert influence on the Governor to drastically weaken or repeal the SEQRA statute. These efforts ultimately succeeded in persuading the Governor to make SEQRA less of an environmental watchdog and more a set of instructive guidelines to encourage local government and industry to become more environmentally sensitive. The language of the statute was amended to make SEQRA "more compatible with the state's economic concerns and agency resources."[96] Thus, the word "due" was substituted for the word "major" when characterizing the "consideration" that regulatory agencies must give in preventing environmental damage.[97] Similar statutory language amendments related to the findings that an agency made in deciding whether to approve a public or private action subject to SEQRA. As originally drafted in 1975, the statute required agencies to determine that "all practicable means will be taken to avoid adverse environmental effects."[98] The 1977 amendments, however, required an analytical "balancing test" whereby, "consistent with social, economic and other essential considerations, to the maximum extent practicable, adverse environmental effects revealed in the environmental impact process will be minimalized or avoided."[99] Specific requirements included within the original statute regarding the contents of an environmental impact statement (hereinafter "EIS") were also weakened.[100]

The Governor's final amendment invited the development and contracting industry to prepare the EIS itself. While such a delegation to capital had been construed as anathema under NEPA, the Governor in effect authorized the entity who proposed to damage the environment to draft the impact statement which would inform local government of the extent of that damage. Not surprisingly, these amendments received overwhelming approval in a legislature unwilling to engage in fundamental ideological conflict on the issue. It passed the amendments with little or no debate. In June 1977, the ideological panic was avoided when the new developer-friendly SEQRA legislation went into effect.

Application of SEQRA

Preparation of the EIS was the principal method which SEQRA legislation envisaged to achieve its broad policy goals. An EIS requires an environmental analysis, circulation of that analysis for public and other concerned agencies' comment, and consideration of the analysis and comments in the decision of whether to approve or disapprove of the project. The statement must include a description of (1) the proposed action and its environmental setting; (2) mitigation measures; (3) growth-inducing aspects of the proposed action; and (4) environmental effects of the proposed action and its alternatives, including its effect on the use and conservation of energy resources.[101]

Unlike NEPA, SEQRA applies to administrative bodies and, for the most part, to legislative bodies. A local agency is defined as "any local agency, board, district, commission, or governing body . . . ."[102] Thus, the environmental analysis applies to both the legislative activities of local government (passage of zoning ordinances, etc.) and local agency decision-making (such as planning board site plan approval for a developer's proposed megamall or subdivision). An EIS is required for every action that "may have a significant effect on the environment."[103]

The timing of the EIS is "to relate environmental considerations to the inception of the planning process, to inform the public and other public agencies as early as possible about proposed actions . . . , and to solicit comments which will assist the agency in the decision making process . . . ."[104] Thus, the statute directs that at the outset or upon the submission of a proposal, "[a]s early as possible . . . , the responsible agency shall make an initial determination whether an environmental impact statement need be prepared for the action."[105] (See SEQRA flow chart in the appendix.)

Once a draft EIS is adopted, SEQRA requires "peer review" circulation to assure the adequacy of the scientific data as well as distribution to interested members of the public for comment. By circulating the EIS to the public,

SEQRA directly empowers and encourages individuals and environmental organizations who oppose the project to engage in project review.[106] To the point, as leading experts on SEQRA state, "SEQRA is built around the concept of full public participation in agency decision-making."[107] SEQRA thus is a mandate, perhaps the strongest in New York state, for active citizenship as a principal means of assuring public agency performance. Not only does it elicit grassroots impact data potentially overlooked by experts, it is also a tool for local communities to protect community character and to tailor the market paradigm to culturally-derived ways of life. In effect, SEQRA provides an opportunity for non-materialistic values to guide economic policymaking.[108]

For all actions that have been the subject of an EIS, SEQRA requires the preparation of an "explicit finding" whether to approve or disapprove of the action on the basis that the requirements of the statute have been met and, "to the maximum extent practicable," adverse environmental effects revealed in the impact statement process will be minimized or avoided.[109]

Compliance with SEQRA can ultimately be obtained through judicial review.[110] While courts are not envisaged as decision-makers on adverse environmental impacts, they are available to assure literal compliance with the statute. Of course, while on the surface refusing to touch "substantive environmental issues," courts might in fact render substantive judgments in the guise of procedural rulings.[111] (This same dynamic of substantive decisions in the guise of procedural "rulings" at the level of the planning board itself is at the heart of the discussion in this book.) In addition, a court may intervene and reverse a decision contained in a finding statement when that decision is either the result of a biased process or a process which so denigrates the facts as to become "arbitrary and capricious."[112] Courts therefore are available to assure that the agency undertaking the SEQRA analysis gives a "hard look" to the adverse environmental impacts, the alternatives, and whatever mitigation is proposed before deciding whether to approve or disapprove any action.[113] Citizen groups whose members are directly impacted by a proposed project have standing to challenge a SEQRA determination in court. However, since SEQRA is a "look before you leap" statute, judicial review is to occur before a project has acquired irreversible momentum. Those seeking to challenge a final SEQRA determination in court, therefore, must proceed within the small window of time provided for by state and local law authorizing an agency's approval of the project.[114] Thus, challenges to actions of village and town planning boards pursuant to Village Law and Town Law must occur within thirty days "to either keep the project moving or stop it before too much time and money have been expended."[115]

SEQRA Implementation

Though state law requires planning boards to hold public hearings before approving site plans, essentially by that late stage both developers and boards have invested so much in the process that they are rarely diverted from the plans before them. In Ashbury, from CLEAR's earliest days, as was true for grassroots groups elsewhere, the only significant opportunity for public intervention in project review was through the promise of the apparent "regulator" SEQRA framework.

Because the statute parcels the duty of administration to virtually any state or local entity termed the lead agency, no governing body bears the ultimate responsibility to oversee compliance with the statute. Most of New York's overall Environmental Conservation Law is administered directly by the Department of Environmental Conservation (DEC).[116] However, the DEC plays a limited role in administering that part of the code concerning SEQRA. The DEC's primary responsibilities under the statute are to promulgate regulatory criteria for implementation to be followed by the lead agencies,[117] to assume an informal advisory role,[118] and to resolve disputes in determining the lead agency.[119]

Beyond the publication of manuals such as the *SEQR Handbook*, the DEC has slipped into a role of little more than monitoring the waning application of the statute throughout the state. A small staff of DEC employees assembles statistics on SEQRA compliance but nothing is done with the figures to promote adherence to the spirit of the law.

Figures assembled by the DEC tell a tale of growing disregard of SEQRA throughout New York State and portray a statute being subverted by neglect. Specifically in Forest County, the number of projects subjected to detailed environmental review dwindled radically since peaking in the late 1980s.

The first step in SEQRA compliance is to determine whether an environmental impact statement need even be filed. SEQRA requires that an environmental impact statement must be filed when a project "may have a significant effect on the environment."[120] These so-called positive declarations, like most indicators of SEQRA compliance, have been on the decline throughout the state since the mid-1980s.[121] Figure 1 shows that the number of positive declarations, statewide, peaked at 552 in 1988 and had fallen to a mere 138 in 1996, a 75% decrease in less than a decade. Importantly, from 1984 to 1994, the ratio of "pos decs" overall to "neg decs" for Type I actions showed a steady precipitous decline. In 1984, the "pos dec" total was 62% of the total for Type I action "neg decs." By 1992-94, the figure had dropped to about 21%.

Once decided that an EIS is required, a draft environmental impact statement (DEIS) is prepared.[122] In Figure 2, trends for DEISs received for five different regions--the state, the DEC's Region B,[123] Region B less its largest county,[124] the four counties contiguous to Forest west of the Hudson River,[125] and Forest County itself--show a precipitous DEIS decline. Forest County exhibited a 94% drop between its peak year (1989) and 1996. The other defined regions feature more moderate declines of between 63% and 73%.

These sharp declines are put into context when contrasted with other indices of development and economic health below. By 1996, DEISs received had fallen to 141. Figures 3 and 4 show that the pattern in Forest County followed that of the state, save for an even sharper drop off in DEISs. In Forest County, DEISs reached their apogee of 18 in 1989 before declining steadily to only one in 1996.

Such a slide in SEQRA compliance activity would not be shocking had an economic collapse brought all development in the state and Forest County to a crashing halt. Factors such as employment, population, number of businesses, housing permits, and site plans do indicate that Forest County suffered an economic contraction since the late 1980s. However, the drop in SEQRA compliance was significantly more severe than the decrease in other economic and developmental indicators and serious environmental review in Forest County wavers on the brink of extinction.

The true fate of environmental review in Forest County comes into sharp focus in a side-by-side comparison of the trends discussed above. Figure 5 examines the decline in the several factors from their peak year to the most recent year for which figures are available. DEISs fell off a staggering 94% in less than a decade (1989-1996). Employment and retail businesses showed modest declines of 3% and 1%, respectively, between the years 1987 and 1992. While residential housing permits fell off 75% between 1987 and 1994, they were the only developmental factor that even approached the attenuation in DEISs received. Moreover, site plans, the better indicator of developments likely to have an adverse environmental impact, declined only 15% over approximately the same time period that DEISs received fell off 94%.[126]

Non-SEQRA figures cannot explain the sudden evaporation of environmental review in Forest County and decline throughout the state.[127] Perhaps the decline in environmental impact assessment, "the most visible influence of environmentalism on procedures in public policy,"[128] reflected the inevitable exhaustion of an effort that was never even half-hearted. The recession of the early 90s may well have left the boards of financially strapped communities more willing to remove impediments to developers promising jobs, more open to "growth machine" logic than ever before. Growing populations can also create demands for more jobs and more amenities. So too, perhaps, it was the effect of judicial decision-making, which continues to authorize planning boards and other lead agencies to engage in informal SEQRA decisions despite

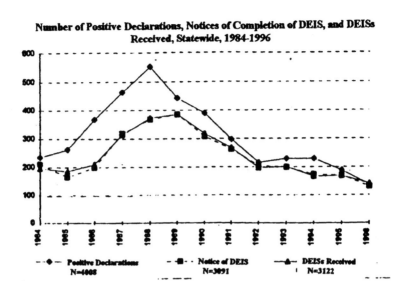

Number of Positive Declarations, Notices of Completion of DEIS, and DEISs Received, Statewide, 1984-1996

FIGURE 1

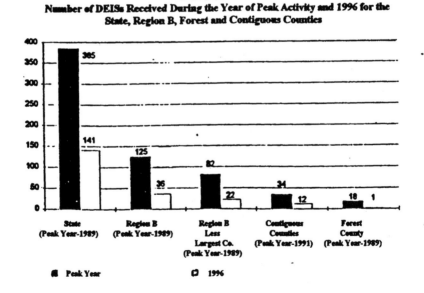

Number of DEISs Received During the Year of Peak Activity and 1996 for the State, Region B, Forest and Contiguous Counties

FIGURE 2

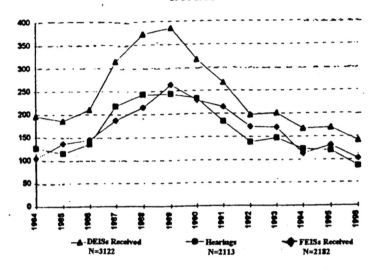

Number DEISs Received, Notices of Public Hearings and FEISs Received by DEC, Statewide 1984-1996

FIGURE 3

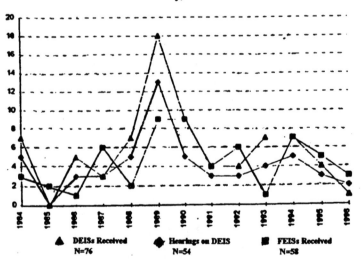

Number DEISs Received, Notices of Public Hearings and FEISs Received for Forest County, 1984-1996

FIGURE 4

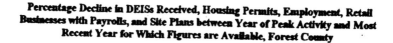

Percentage Decline in DEISs Received, Housing Permits, Employment, Retail Businesses with Payrolls, and Site Plans between Year of Peak Activity and Most Recent Year for Which Figures are Available, Forest County

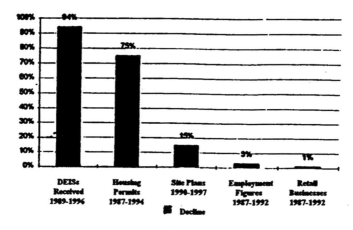

FIGURE 5

the rigor of the statute and its predisposition to an EIS as the appropriate way of addressing environmental impacts.[129] This book's account describes and analyzes the effects of these trends as they became manifest in one prolonged SEQRA case study of the mid-1990s.

The Megamall Site

The site for the controversial project focused on by this book is a 57.4 acre plot of largely open field near the eastern edge of the town (see site map in the appendix). An on-site wetland of 1.7 acres in the northeast corner of the site helped to cleanse water proceeding to the water table and to the nearby aquifer. Most stormwater from the site drains easterly, eventually flowing through a culvert under adjacent South Creighton Road into a large wet area, then ultimately into a New York State-designated wetland. The large wet area to the east of the road was identified as a significant aquifer because of the presence of a sand and gravel layer of up to 28 feet under the silt and muck just west of the Roodekill stream.

On the long western boundary of the roughly rectangular site is the multi-lane entrance and exit ramp of the New York State Thruway. On the north side is a dead-end road, Davis Lane, which angles down, in a southwesterly direction, off of New York State Route 354, the east-west extension of Main Street. In the 1930s, the plot was purchased by Ernie Davis from a descendant of one of the original Dutch settlers as part of a 134-acre tract.[130] A farmer since 1934,[131] Davis moved into the on-site late 18th-century stone house along the old Ashbury-Acton road, establishing an apple orchard on about ten acres, with dairy farming on the rest. By 1950, the dairy ceased and the orchards were leased to a tenant farmer. Ernie had started a construction firm in 1945 and apparently became increasingly interested in selling the farm.

Like many farmers of his generation, Ernie sought financial advantage from the new market for land development. In fact, the state government greatly increased his speculative land value with its March 1952 announcement of a planned Ashbury exit for the major north-south Thruway artery between New York City and Albany.[132] The Town's original zoning code, eight years later, helped to assure this land value by its designation as part of a large zone for industrial and commercial facilities. According to son Red, "the property's business/industrial designation made the tax assessment extremely high compared to its actual limited use" and gave his father extra incentive to sell out.[133]

In 1966, Davis made his first public developmental move by allowing the BigBurg hamburger chain to propose for his site an 80-seat fast-food restaurant.[134] When that project failed to proceed,[135] five years later, in 1971, Davis escalated development stakes by selling an option for the largest remaining portion of his huge tract (64 acres) to a Long Island firm. The latter planned a mammoth 200,000 sq. foot enclosed 20-store mall, the Ashbury Center (including a 54,000 sq. ft. department store and a 22,000 sq. ft. supermarket). This was phase one of a larger development (the largest commercial development in Ashbury history) to include a three-story 100,000 sq. ft. office building and a 200-unit motel. Ardently assisting in presenting the project to the planning board in 1973, local realtor Linda Parsons asked that Village water lines be extended from the west to east of the Thruway and foresaw either a similar extension of municipal sewer lines or creation of an on-site wastewater treatment plant. She also sought rezoning of 27 acres on Davis Lane and South Creighton Road from industrial to exclusively commercial use. Both the Town Board and the Town planning board acceded to her request, though the director of the county planning board then rebuked the Town for this action since it had not informed the county board beforehand as it was legally required to do and since the project "raises a spectre of chaos which to us is too high a price for both Ashbury and the other communities of Forest County dependent upon this interchange."

Though Parsons insisted that "everyone in town is in favor of this shopping center," very critical of the proposal were members of a new group of "serious planning" orientation, Community United for Proper Development--including three local attorneys (Manny Dreyfus among them), a college art professor and a Village Trustee. The group threatened to seek a legal injunction against further development of Ashbury (and FoodFeast) shopping centers because of "irreparable harm to the community." Specifically, they argued (though SEQRA was not yet available) that the local market for the proposed facilities was already met, that building the megamall would induce further undesirable Paramus-type strip malls, that extending municipal utilities would force eventual taxpayer subsidizing of sewage plant expansion and that both Ashbury and FoodFeast centers would exacerbate the already-intolerable traffic congestion on Rte. 354. Dreyfus described the mall as meeting "the needs of speculators" only and its added traffic as a step which "would strangle this town, strangle it at its neck."[136] While town decisionmakers accommodated the Long Island developer despite citizen and County Planning Board opposition, apparently the OPEC oil crisis in 1974 and the resulting economic recession caused the developer to eventually drop its plans.[137]

In early 1984, new developers announced plans for a $21 million industrial park on the same parcel and were accompanied to the planning board by realtor Linda Parsons and Ernie Davis. Planning a complex of small office units in the front (100,000 sq. ft. total) and a series of 25-50,000 sq. ft. units for "light industry" in the rear (200,000 sq. ft. total), these developers assured the board that "the project will be residential in nature" and "kept to a country setting."[138] After considerable discussion of water and sewer issues, planning board members anticipated a startup in the Spring.[139]

To the surprise of many, this latest project failed to move forward[140] and in October 1985 Davis sold the same 57-acre plot to Albany real estate investor, Joe Heller, for $258,000. Said Heller later, it was "one of the most beautiful pieces of property" he had ever seen. "I thought it was a nice piece of land at a decent price with a real winner location"[141]--in other words, "beautiful" in terms of its speculative investment value. Heller immediately submitted a plan of his own for a 300,000 sq. ft., 8-lot light industrial/commercial park at this site. Withdrawing the proposal a few months later, for the next decade he nevertheless recouped on his investment by selling development options for a succession of four separate development proposals, beginning in 1987.

New York-based developer National Development Enterprises (NDE), an international firm with an estimated $1 billion in assets, first presented an Amsterdam Plaza megamall project for the Heller site to the Ashbury Town Board in March 1988, after itself buying option rights from the most recent developer option-holders from New Windsor and White Plains, N.Y. The latter developers had recently withdrawn their own plaza plan, the fourth mega-project for the site (following the major shopping center-industrial park proposal from Heller himself in 1986, the 1984 project and the 1973 proposal by the Long Island developer).

NDE originally proposed a 225,000 square foot facility for a supermarket, department store, small stores, a bank, restaurant and a four-story hotel, along with later additional office and industrial development further south on site. The company told the Town Board that it envisioned upscale rather than discount stores and that "this is the last chance for the [Thruway] exit to have something that makes sense." While "regulator" Town Board members Lyon and Reitman[142] opposed Town Board consideration of the project until eventual new master plan recommendations could be reviewed (which they recognized could be a significant delay), Supervisor Kessler and Town Board members Devilla and Taglione, all of "pragmatic capitalist" orientation, were quite willing to proceed with project review.[143] After discovering significant community opposition and thus potential political problems in securing Town Board approval (including a zoning change for part of Heller's property), NDE withdrew its original application and resubmitted a new one in early 1989, this time to the more amenable Town planning board.[144]

NDE's 200,000 sq. ft. project (now called "Amsterdam Square"), the sixth shopping center or industrial park proposal for the site,[145] called for a major "department store" anchor of 80,000 sq. ft., an expanded FoodFeast grocery store of 65,000 sq. ft. (a 20-year lease was already signed in 1988), a bank, and a number of smaller retail stores, but without a three-story hotel as before. Despite significant community opposition, NDE eventually secured planning board SEQRA approval in August 1990. But in the context of the downward economic turn one year later, delays in obtaining other agency permits apparently led Wal-Mart, the department store anchor, to pull out.[146] Without a major department store anchor, despite spending over $100,000 on project studies and much more on options for the site,[147] NDE in turn withdrew its site plan application from the planning board in October 1991 and Medford Corporation, the owners of FoodFeast, signed a new option agreement with landowner Heller on January 8, 1992.

Specific Proposal

In early 1992, Heller applied to the planning board and received permission to divide his 57-acre parcel into two lots. The first, with 21 acres, lay entirely within the town's B-2 (Highway Business) zone. The adjacent second lot to the south was divided from the first by the same boundary line which placed it in the light industrial zone. Though Heller was the formal applicant for this change, it was designed to serve the Medford FoodFeast grocery chain which intended to pursue a new megamall proposal on the order of Amsterdam Square--a seventh giant project plan for the site. The option also anticipated a potential further shopping center in Heller's rear lot to the south.

Though Medford apparently did not relinquish its formal option for the property to Magellan Construction until late 1994,[148] the latter Albany-based company appeared before the planning board in late 1993 with an authorization from Joe Heller to represent him before that body. The Moselle Plaza project was first presented by Magellan to the full town planning board on December 20, 1993. It proposed to construct a 178,000 sq. foot shopping center consisting of a "department store" (100,000 sq. ft.), a grocery store (65,000 sq. ft.) and a small assortment of miscellaneous retail stores in two other buildings. The plan included an 18-acre paved area for 960 cars and 11 loading areas. It involved all 21.6 acres of Joe Heller's B-2 (Business-Highway) zone property, plus at least several acres in his immediately-adjacent Light Industrial zone plot to the south. Water and sewer hookups to the Village system west of the Thruway were essential.

The Magellan Construction Group, Inc. was a wholly-owned branch of the Albany construction and real estate developer firm of Crotty & Forte. The latter was incorporated in 1973 and by the mid-1990s had assets of $500 million, with annual sales in excess of $200 million. It claimed the 122nd position in a 1994 "Top 400 Contractors" U.S. list and 64th in a list of "Top 100 Construction Managers." By 1996, the firm described itself as "one of New York State's leading contractors with a growing presence and activity in the national construction market . . . [performing] work in east coast states from Maine to Florida, and [completing] projects as far west as Kansas, Texas and California." The 1996 edition of Ward's Business Directory listed the company as the number one constructor (by sales) of industrial buildings and warehouses in New York state.[149]

Its principal officers in 1994, Harold Crotty and LeRoy Forte, were well-accepted members of the Albany business elite and were well-known in the Albany area as major campaign contributors to both parties. The parent company, Crotty & Forte, had also been cited in the Albany press and in a 1992 State Legislature official report on Industrial Development Agencies as engaging in questionable activities in the IDA-financing of several projects in the Albany area.[150]

As of 1994, Magellan Construction employed 20 people under the direction of branch manager Deke Reynolds. The particular project manager for the Ashbury project was young David Jankoff. Magellan's attorney was Morris Schwab, a specialist in environmental, zoning and land use law for a Glens Falls, N.Y. firm.

From the beginning, most local observers assumed that the major "department store" anchor was Wal-Mart, though Magellan Construction never publicly acknowledged that fact throughout the many months of its struggle to gain project approval. Already by 1993, the Wal-Mart corporation was the largest retail chain in the world, the number four U.S. corporation in worth (behind General Electric, Exxon and AT&T), and the 10th most profitable U.S. company in sales (about $65 billion in 1994). It had 434,000 employees in 1993 and a market value of shares at $57.5 billion at the end of 1994. The Walton family which owned the bulk of shares in this company was listed by *Forbes* magazine as having assets worth nearly $21.7 billion collectively, while a decade earlier, it stated that Wal-Mart founder Sam Walton was the richest man in the United States.[151]

No longer the "little store that could," as *Hoover's Handbook of American Business* stated in 1994, Wal-Mart became "sometimes perceived by towns it seeks to enter as a 'model of savage capitalism.'"[152] Typical was the pattern announced by *Business Week* in 1992 when it predicted that Wal-Mart sales would gain by 25% when the retail sector generally would at best grow by 4%.[153] Clearly, the success of the former was largely at the expense of smaller retailers. In 1996, Wal-Mart CEO David Glass told stockholders, "We're going to dominate North America."[154] In the previous several years, Wal-Mart had turned toward the Northeast, its final untouched region in this country, and had begun aggressively expanding its presence. In 1992-93, Wal-Mart opened 25 stores in New York state, 8 in New Jersey and 1 in Connecticut. It planned to open another 17 in these three states in 1994.[155] Wal-Mart apparently defined Ashbury according to typical marketing profiles, with a consumer base ripe for the plucking, although, more frequently than not, it was Wal-Mart policy to avoid announcing itself as a coming anchor tenant to avoid any adverse reactions.[156]

Medford Corporation, owners of the FoodFeast grocery store chain,[157] pursued the project in Ashbury to obtain a facility double the size of its existing store. For many years, with over two dozen supermarkets, Medford had dominated the retail grocery store market in the Hudson Valley, in many cases driving out earlier stores such as Grand Union. Headquartered in Reading County to the south, fifty-year old Medford had overall assets of $275 million, annual sales of $750 million, a net worth of $10 million and some 4500 employees as of the 1992 fiscal year. By 1994, it had 27 stores in Pennsylvania, New York, New Jersey and Connecticut. Nevertheless, by the late 80s, Medford felt growing competitive pressure from other chains, superstores and discount shopping centers. Specifically, by 1986, Medford looked to expand its 12-year old Ashbury operation and to prevent a rival from moving into the attractive Heller site at the same time.[158]

As part of its regional drive to maintain and enhance its market position, by the early 90s, Medford began a major store-expansion and new store construction program for two dozen FoodFeasts in the area. To support part of this construction package (including the Ashbury megamall), Medford obtained preliminary approval by March 1993 from an Industrial Development

Agency (IDA) in adjacent Reading County to gain major tax breaks and low-cost financing--nine months before the Moselle Plaza application came before the Ashbury planning board. Though never clear to outsiders which, if any, of the three corporations--Magellan Construction, Wal-Mart or Medford--was the prime mover behind Moselle Plaza, each had strong reasons for seeking approval. No doubt each wholeheartedly supported the many months of campaign for town acceptance.[159] Each for years had accepted the larger developmental ethos of "bigger means better"--an ethos well-accepted also by the "light planning" generation of the Ashbury power structure still dominating decision-making in this town.

PART TWO   AGENDA-MAKING

INTRODUCTION

In environmental impact reviews, as with scientific research or "discovery" processes generally,[1] the first task is to identify relevant subject-matter and the method of inquiry to be used. The developer's "hypothesis," whether stated in good conscience or not, is that the project proposed will be beneficial to the community and that any adverse environmental impacts will be minimal by comparison or sufficiently mitigated. Essentially, the review body (or "lead agency") is charged with employing successively-stronger lenses, as with a microscope, to perceive the "reality" of the project's intrusion on local ecology in ever-more refined environmental and other relevant dimensions, as well as to examine potential impacts of other reasonable alternatives. At each stage of the agenda-making phase, the agency must decide if what it sees may have further hidden implications which might be significant and reasonably understood. Before reasonable impact judgments can be made, evidence must be laid out in adequate detail and accessible form to those reviewing, critiquing and making the decision. This phase thus identifies relevant issues and appropriate methodology for their exploration. Importantly, by implicit and sometimes explicit language, the SEQRA statute, regulations and official handbook also encourage grassroots citizen participation in setting the research agenda.

Based primarily or entirely on motivations of profit rather than "non-business values," a private developer obviously wishes to expedite project approval. Since the environmental review process is one of the major regulatory "permit hurdles," every developer seeks from the start to maximize the impression of project benefits for the community while minimizing images of adverse impacts. While a developer's project advocacy is a predictable opening phase, its equally predictable profit motivation means that one major participant in the local land-use planning context has every reason not to participate in an open-ended honest communication process, one of the essential prerequisites for successful participatory planning. Despite the official intent of presenting all sides of controversial issues,[2] the environmental review process from beginning to end is in great part, therefore, the drama of a developer's public relations campaign seeking hegemony over a supposed open-ended rational-legal search for the truth.

This dynamic assures that while slick graphics and rhetoric strive for the agency's attention, developers will also seek to dissuade those with official authority from asking serious research questions which might cause added delay, greater expense or even ultimate disapproval. Initially, agency decision-makers (the local town planning board in this case study) are approached, usually before an application is officially presented at an open public meeting. Nevertheless, while developers nurture "partnership" with formal decision-makers, public participation in the review process more frequently poses the greatest threat. As potential greatest recipients of the project's adverse effects and the least likely in the community to gain, ordinary citizens predictably bring the greatest skepticism and critique. While developers frequently attempt at an early stage to sell themselves to project site neighbors or to the public generally, distrusting the potential outcome of open-ended participatory inquiry, their most immediate priority is to reduce public access to and impact upon the decision-making process.[3] In addition to promoting itself with the review board, attempting to dissuade it from critical research, developers thus also seek agency complicity in denying a significant public role. If the predominant land-use ideology of board members also favors effective public exclusion, SEQRA's environmental research agenda can be greatly reduced and ultimate approval more quickly gained.

Under SEQRA, the formal starting place is the developer's project application itself and the short- or long-form environmental assessment form ("EAF") which accompanies it. These documents lay out the overall nature and purpose of the project, the basic environmental traits of the project site and surrounding area and any negative environmental impacts which the developer promises to mitigate. As Chapter Four indicates, from the discussion immediately following formal application to the SEQRA decision for a positive or negative determination (requiring or not a more detailed environmental impact statement), the basic pattern of developer-agency-public interplay becomes clear. Types of questions asked by board members, procedural and/or substantive advice from board consultants (or professional staff) and involved agencies, and degree of openness to public participation in exploring the initial research phase all reflect the ideological orientation of the official land-use decision-making regime.

Power politics are thus part and parcel of the SEQRA process from the beginning. To assure a meaningful role and adequate depth of the research process generally, grassroots citizens must become attentive and involved from the moment the project application is presented. Individual interventions may begin this process, but only organized groups are likely to mobilize oppositional power threats and thus gain sufficient board attention for any hope of real influence. Contrary to models of participatory democracy, there is rarely a neutral facilitator immediately available to assure a fair and open process. The power of anti-environmental politics to render the SEQRA statute a paper tiger through the law's gaps and interpretive subjectivity is well-illustrated in this chapter by the critical importance of ideology in defining initial board relations with the developer, in selecting and being influenced by professional consultants, and in responding to demands for a significant public role. For the case study at hand, the struggle to assure the SEQRA relevance of economic analysis and for an initial public hearing best exemplify these issues.

The chapter also portrays the developer's attempt to evade significant impact research through informal "frontloading" issue discussion to avoid an EIS, through "backloading" resolution of important issues to the post-SEQRA stage when the public would have a negligible role, and through use of a political culture among involved agencies which typically defers to these same strategies. Finally, the chapter describes typical first steps in organizing a grassroots community group oriented toward SEQRA intervention and toward unmasking, if needed, the larger political-ethical decision-making context.

A SEQRA "positive declaration" is the lead agency's official decision that an EIS will be required. While on the surface apparently authorizing a sharper analytical lens and thus a more honest inquiry with which to assess project impacts, in fact this decision simply opens the door to a new arena of potential contestation as equally affected by the larger ideological and political context as the first. Chapter Five describes how the wording of the "pos dec" resolution and official scoping document, both designed to identify the relevant topics and issues to be explored in the draft EIS, profoundly affect the seriousness of the ongoing research inquiry. It demonstrates how the importance of various adverse impacts are negotiated and how the developer lobbies to restrict the substantive ambit of the resolutions. Ultimately, through manipulation of the process by board leadership and through intervention of the board's "light planning" attorney, the potential range and depth of the scope and the public's role in its determination were, in this case, subverted.

The chapter also indicates the ongoing significance of the broader extra-SEQRA political struggle in Ashbury as it affected water and sewer availability for the project and the composition of the planning board itself. In both cases, the outcome of these non-SEQRA political battles, in turn, had direct repercussions on the nature of the ongoing SEQRA process.

The SEQRA sequel to the scoping document is a draft of the EIS itself, to be reviewed for consistency with the scoping agenda and for sufficient accuracy, clarity and detail to permit intelligent critiques concerning potential needed additional research. Chapter Six explores the SEQRA implications of a developer-prepared draft EIS and the degree to which it becomes legitimated by a scientific discourse and technical presentation of data unfamiliar to lay people, inside and outside of the board, who may seek to review the document. The typically impenetrable presentation and lack of a mechanism to assure translation for lay readers limit accessibility to critical review and prevent accountability itself. Such a document, while in facial compliance with SEQRA's statutory mandates, can easily mask inaccurate data and superficial and misleading analyses while still being accepted as "complete" by ideologically-friendly board members, with the encouragement of "light planning" board attorneys and consultants.

Environmental discourse thereby becomes appropriated by developers for their own purposes rather than a form of empowerment for genuine community inquiry into alternative futures. At the same time, to the degree that the local board can prevent the public from gaining access to SEQRA data and establishing a record at this stage, the board's threshhold for "completeness" determination becomes significantly lower and SEQRA's research purpose further subverted. Nevertheless, "freedom of information" law provides the public with at least a tool for combating such exclusion.

At a certain point in the SEQRA process, it may become necessary for community groups, as described in the present case study, to directly confront obvious prejudgment and apparent conflicts of interest which distort SEQRA's premise of fair process and open-minded inquiry. Ultimately, this entails a challenge to the political legitimacy of board decision-makers and their consultants by the terms of legal liberalism itself. As portrayed in Chapter Seven, in addition to establishing a record for eventual legal recourse by invoking legal and professional standards of proper ethical conduct, such an approach has the further advantage of calling forth the moral authority of more easily-understandable community concepts of fairness and participatory democracy as well, which in turn translate to further political pressure on decision-makers. At a certain point, however, such an attack may be perceived by some who are not direct targets, within and outside of the decision-making elite, as too personalistic and divisive, contrary to the ideal of participatory democracy, and thus provoke a backlash reluctance to consider rational SEQRA analysis or to further engage in the community struggle itself.

In the final stage of EIS agenda-making, described in Chapter Eight, the public is at last guaranteed by SEQRA a formal opportunity to critique the statement of issues and research approaches to date assembled by the developer. While not assured of a public hearing instead of written comment alone, for most projects of potential major impact, it would be difficult politically for a planning board to deny citizens the opportunity to finally register their views in person, though a struggle over the public hearing format may well ensue. Effective public participation at this stage requires a good spectrum of lay critiques. Impassioned statements "from the heart," while no doubt dismissed as not "substantive" by SEQRA criteria, help to empower the grassroots opposition and inform decision-makers that communitarian decision-making based on "moral economy" criteria may be just as important as a narrowly-interpreted legalistic definition of SEQRA relevance. The synergistic effect of public presentation in mobilizing the community can be profound. It is the moment of greatest sense of empowerment--at least on a symbolic level.

At the same time, grassroots testimony about specific environmental and economic effects by at least some citizens versed in traditional SEQRA discourse cannot be summarily dismissed. Of far greater weight for later court review and therefore of concern for the board itself, however, is testimony from professional experts retained (if resources are available) by the activist community groups. With credibility assured through familiarity with the technical language and methodology of the developer and board experts, community experts finally level the playing field and force at least the semblance of a "hard look" at the critiques presented, whatever the failings of the overall process by participatory criteria. Additional input on the draft EIS from experts in involved agencies at this same stage provides further leverage by which a deeper, more complete research agenda can be established.

FOUR   MEGAMALL APPLICATION AND INITIAL SEQRA DETERMINATION

<u>Immediate Background</u>

While the local political stalemate prevented rezoning to block a revival of Amsterdam Square, community residents were unaware of how soon Ashbury would have to face the battle over a megamall in the Heller area once again. From 1991 to late 1993, Medford planned its strategy behind closed doors. In late 1991, it gained an option from Heller to develop his property as a shopping center. Said Nelson Silveira, Medford's senior vice-president for corporate development three years later, "We had a provision in the original contract that if the developer [NDE] pulled out, we had a right to the plans and could look for somebody else."[1] Going public, Medford first obtained a two-lot subdivision approval from the Ashbury planning board in early 1992--separating the northerly 21 acres of "commercial" zoned land from the southerly "light industrial" acres—without revealing its actual plans for another mall. It then gained preliminary approval in March and June 1993 from its local Reading County IDA ("RCIDA") to receive low interest financing and major tax exemptions for constructing a shopping center at the Heller site (shortly before state statutory authority for taxpayer-assisted financing of retail shopping centers would terminate[2]). Though nominally a public action, this Medford-RCIDA process was carried out apparently with no notification to Ashbury officials, let alone to the Ashbury public.[3]

Again unbeknownst to CLEAR or others who had opposed Amsterdam Square, the Ashbury Development Corporation, a local government-funded body mandated to attract outside investors, was sending out flyers claiming that Ashbury consumers were spending $53 million on retail purchases in regional malls which in fact could be re-captured by appropriate retail development locally.[4] Medford and Wal-Mart could not have received a clearer message.

By 1993, Medford also lined up the Albany firm of Magellan Construction, its collaborator in two similar Hudson Valley projects, to formally manage and process the new Ashbury application, "to stay the course," in Silveira's words.

Financially, Medford was hurting in its overall operations. It claimed, for example, a 1994 first quarter loss of about $1.5 million. But in Ashbury, its only immediate competition was an older minor chain grocery store, only half its size, in Ashbury Plaza just across Main Street. Because of its advantage, the Ashbury FoodFeast store showed a profit by charging significantly more for a wide spectrum of items than in its other branches in the area. Nevertheless, Medford wanted even more of the local retail market. According to Silveira, there was no shelf room in the Ashbury store for one-third of the goods available from Medford's warehouse and little room for non-food items generally. FoodFeast wished to add a fresh fish section, significantly expand its produce department, expand its deli and add more prepared foods.[5] It also seemed that one major Medford motivation for seeking the new development was simply to pre-empt any major competitor from arriving on the scene with a new superstore, presumably at the Heller site, and its belief that it could not afford to build it own new facility at that site without a surrounding mall anchored by a mega-retail store.

Aside from announcing plans initially (with Magellan Construction) to the local Chamber of Commerce on October 20, 1993,[6] Medford, however, was to remain quiet throughout the official Moselle Plaza process, absent from all public aspects of the planning board's activity except for the EIS public hearing itself. However, as discussed below, Medford did engage in various public relations efforts to promote the development. Wal-Mart, in turn, followed its common policy of total silence about the project publicly, even denying to an organization in another New York community that it had any plans for an Ashbury site.[7]   In turn, preparing for the chips to fall in his favor, site owner Heller in November 1993 discretely obtained from a neighbor an option on dozens of acres adjacent to the southern boundary of his 57-acre property for potential further commercial development of his own.

Along with these other three parties, Magellan Construction also made preparations out of public view. After initial discussions with Medford and Heller (and presumably the major discount chain) and after reviewing the old Amsterdam Square plans, Magellan formulated modifications of its own and presented its plans (with Medford) to local business people two months before appearing publicly before the planning board. Meanwhile, the Albany developer's manager Deke Reynolds, who soon appeared publicly on a first-name basis with planning board chairman Ryker, on October 28, 1993 contributed $245 to the Ashbury Republican Club (also chaired by Ryker) for purchase of "Halloween candy" to be handed out to kids following the annual evening march down Main Street. However small the payment, discovered by critics a few months later, it would eventually symbolize for project opponents the cozy relationship between the developer and the planning board chair.[8]

Initial Agenda-Setting: SEQRA and Beyond

Suspicions of this arrangement began from the first moment of Magellan's public presentation of the Moselle Plaza proposal to the planning board at the meeting of December 20, 1993.[9] At that point of the agenda, Ryker informed fellow board members for the first time that he and Supervisor Schmidt had arranged the hiring of a new board attorney, Frank Rattle of Regent Park, to become its official legal consultant for this project.[10] The board's regular attorney, Don Torelli of Harvey & Plonsker, had recused himself because of his firm's involvement with FoodFeast and Magellan Construction in a joint development further south.

The retention of Frank Rattle exposed a fundamental flaw in the design of SEQRA. Board compliance with that statute would now rely on advice from one whose professional career as a "developer's lawyer" of "minimalist" ideology[11] had shown little apparent interest in environmental law issues other than to secure permits and approvals for developers who sought to avoid the force of the SEQRA statute. This pattern of pro-developer selection would be replayed by "light planners" on the board in future arrangements with professional consultants and in the political jockeying for new planning board members.

The same pro-developer bias was epitomized as well by Gene Busch, the planning board's "planning consultant" since 1974.[12] Busch was present at nearly every planning board meeting, paid at the hourly rate of $125. For the most part, he was nearly mute when decisions of significance were required of the board. Typically, Busch would listen to sentiments voiced by either the majority of the board or its most vocal members and would at some time contribute supportive reasons for their decision, thus tending to legitimate the process from an overall professional planning perspective. Thus, while Busch's voice would not be heard initially on whether an EIS should be required, should the board proceed with a negative declaration, thereby eliminating the need for an EIS, Busch would assist the board with any technical language in the declaration of non-significance of any potential adverse environmental effects.

In serving to legitimate the pro-development and anti-SEQRA bias of local planning board members, Busch assured his continued employment and built a reputation such that other similarly-minded local planning boards and developers would feel comfortable in retaining him to facilitate their efforts. In the spectrum of professional planners, Busch was a "traditional technician," a type Elizabeth Howe describes as deferential and loyal to decision-makers, apparently rarely concerned with openness of the planning process to the public, advisory rather than proactive, and apparently least influenced by "substantive values, such as a commitment to social justice, to environmental protection, or even to good land use."[13]

Magellan's Moselle Plaza in many ways replicated NDE's earlier proposal. Indeed, Magellan argued from the beginning that the planning board should keep its role focused to a narrow instrumental task. It needed simply to acknowledge the continued validity of its original 1990 SEQRA findings since "the design, layout and components of the Moselle Plaza Project are virtually identical to those of the previously approved Amsterdam project." Because the environmental setting is "substantially identical" and potential environmental impacts and mitigative measures are "essentially the same," "a supplemental environmental impact statement is not required."[14] In overall size, it was slightly smaller, about 178,000 sq. ft. of retail space versus about 200,000 for Amsterdam Square, contained fewer small retail stores and had no free-standing bank. Nevertheless, its two planned anchor stores were considerably larger--from 45,000 originally to 65,000 sq. ft. for the FoodFeast and from 80,000 earlier to 100,000 sq. ft. for the unnamed discount department store. Magellan wished merely to amend the previous SEQRA findings statement for Amsterdam Square with the submission of a supplemental Environmental Assessment Form (EAF) containing a series of generic questions and including basic details and a description of Moselle Plaza.[15]

At Ryker's encouragement, attorney Rattle actively sought to shape the direction of the board's process from this original Magellan assumption. Rattle argued at the December meeting that the project was basically an amendment to "an existing pending application" for which official findings had already been issued and that only limited consideration under SEQRA was now appropriate. He suggested that the board seek permission from all involved agencies (those that must act on eventual project permits) to again become "lead agency."

As with any application going through the SEQRA process, he said, the board could then decide whether any project factors (in this case, only new factors) might potentially cause a significant adverse impact, in which case a Supplemental Environmental Impact Statement ("SEIS") would be required. (If a positive determination is made, statutory procedures for preparing and reviewing an SEIS are no different from those for an ordinary EIS.) Using his authoritative voice as planning board attorney, he advised, however, that according to the applicant, the project was smaller than before and would have less impact than Amsterdam Square. His comments thus suggested the appropriateness of Magellan's "frontloading" attempt to gain a "negative declaration," avoiding new detailed review with significant public accountability.

As in the prior application, certain aspects of the project, including some of the parking lot and stormwater detention area, would extend beyond the commercial into the light industrial zone. Because the 1992 subdivision had now split the Heller property into two lots, with the border the same as the zone district boundary, gaining permission to use some of the southerly lot for the non-permitted retail shopping center would be more involved than earlier.[16]

Nevertheless, Rattle foresaw no major difficulty and Busch endorsed this agenda.[17]

Beyond the statutory mandate requiring the planning board to immediately proceed into the SEQRA framework, the dynamics of this first meeting demonstrated how prior collaboration between the developer, planning board chair and board professional consultants easily led the disorganized, uninformed other members of the board to accept the former's interpretation of that mandate. How to interpret SEQRA was eventually to become the dominant theme of contention in the months to follow.

Anticipating an area of major potential concern with Moselle Plaza and to further restrict the bounds of "legitimate" SEQRA inquiry, Rattle on November 15th had contacted the staff of the Division of Regulatory Affairs of the state Department of Environmental Conservation (DEC) to gain its informal opinion as to whether the discussion of business competition and the attendant possible loss of jobs fell within the purview of the SEQRA statute. As no doubt he expected, in a December 24th letter,[18] a staff member responded with the advice, augmented by a 1986 appellate court case, that SEQRA "does not protect people against economic competition and persons alleging competitive interests have no standing to sue."[19] On a related issue, the DEC official cited a 1986 Court of Appeals case to add that if an action "has the potential to change a community in such a way as to cause a major modification (emphasis added) in the existing mix of land uses then it may be reasonable to consider this issue in an environmental review."[20] No mention was made in the DEC letter of the economic balancing test required by SEQRA once an adverse environmental impact was identified.[21]

This limited response was apparently what Rattle wished to hear, to arm himself as he moved further to narrow the agenda of planning board review by eliminating any economic analysis--whether with regard to character of the community or the balancing test. However, this particular interpretative issue would reverberate in board meetings for months to come.

While events at the planning board level seemed to proceed as the chairman wished, Ryker launched a public relations campaign as well, anticipating correctly that at least some in the community would oppose the Moselle Plaza proposal. Always the politician, Ryker eagerly responded to a local weekly's inquiry by stating that Moselle Plaza would have "much, much, much reduced impact on the downtown area, if any" by comparison with Amsterdam Square, since acreage and the number of stores were scaled down.[22] He thought the plaza "could be a real asset to the community," among other things, by providing a new on-site sewage treatment plant available to others as well and by freeing up the old FoodFeast space for other uses.[23]

Ryker, however, was angry to discover that his comments were included in an article headlined as "Huge Shopping Plaza Proposed" and his own position summarized as apparently "already favorably disposed toward the huge project."[24] In his typical caustic style, he thus wrote letters to the local press, denouncing the *Tribune*'s publisher as a case of "absolute power corrupts absolutely" and his biased account as the result of the latter's personal and political differences with Ryker and "the bile this paper has spewed in the past."[25] This strongly reactive antagonism toward project critics through the press would typify Ryker's political practice and would consistently intensify emotions and commitment on the part of those actively opposed to the project.

Though some in the business community had advance warning of Moselle Plaza, activists who earlier had battled against Amsterdam Square were shocked and numbed by the December 20th announcement. They dreaded the daunting prospect of another long struggle within the context of SEQRA and with a planning board majority apparently stacked in the developer's favor from the start. The *Tribune*'s article offered slight consolation at best.

Because this project necessitated review of a previous megamall approval, CLEAR leaders and others hoped that enough time would be available to regroup for a difficult campaign. At the same moment, the planning board's own Town master plan draft was at long last being finalized, with a public hearing scheduled for February 28th. At its meeting of February 5th, CLEAR made plans to circulate among its members a detailed critique of the master plan draft and to assure a sizeable public presence. However, CLEAR also had its first internal discussion of Moselle Plaza and sought also to encourage those members of the South Creighton Association most active earlier about Amsterdam Square now to resume their participation in the public critique. The latter organization, however, was preoccupied with final appeals to the planning board to require an EIS for a wetland-infringing trailer park project which they had fought for years.

In the meantime, on January 10th planning board member Lynn Whipple, a member of the "light planning" majority, suddenly resigned because of her move to a neighboring town. Within a few days, six persons applied for the post and the informal word was that Julia Bellows, a one-year resident unknown to past community struggles, was among the most environmentally-concerned of the group. Bellows was a rising vice president and regional manager of the private banking division for a major bank chain. She was also an enthusiastic member of the Town Environmental Conservation Commission where she became known as an articulate and strong advocate of a "regulatory" position. As candidate interviews began in early February, however, CLEAR was skeptical of the Town Board's willingness to endorse a candidate of that reputation.

As January and February went by, the nature of the Moselle Plaza process and its overall political context took fuller shape. At the meeting of January 10th, for example, there was an extraordinarily revealing exchange on the planning board's role. "Regulator" Jane Pelletier suggested that the board should seek information on how the new project would affect existing shopping centers. "Light planner" Rich Maglie replied that this was addressed in the previous FEIS findings. In turn, Ryker admitted that community reaction to Amsterdam Square at that time was mixed, but claimed that the current project would have less impact with fewer small stores to compete with the downtown. When Pelletier pointed out that Moselle Plaza tenants were not identified, Ryker replied, "It's irrelevant what it is." Pelletier disagreed and asked, "How can we make an intelligent decision on approving something if we don't know what exactly we are approving?" To know at least the type of store would make a difference. Davis tried to deflect the issue by pointing out that a particular store might close in one year and be replaced by another and claimed, "it's not our call." Ryker, in turn, moved the discussion to an explicit ideological level: "Nowhere in the zoning ordinances does it say that you have any jurisdiction [concerning the type of retail store] . . . it's called capitalism." When Pelletier urged "some kind of cooperative effort," Ryker reiterated: "You can't tell these people by law what they can or cannot do in the free market." In turn, Pelletier's response articulated her "regulator" definition of planning board responsibility: "We are a planning board, so we have to plan what comes into this community . . . ." To this, Davis asserted: "We are not a planning board, we are a compliance board. The nearest we have come to planning is the master plan. What we do month after month after month is to make sure that the developer complies to the zoning ordinance." Davis later added his "light planner" reliance on legalism by accepting Rattle's interpretation that the board could only supplement its earlier findings on Amsterdam Square, not begin a SEQRA review afresh: "Legally, [Rattle] spelled out in very precise terms why we had to do what we had to do . . . He's got a lot of case law . . . and we'd be fools not to accept what he's telling us."[26]

Soon afterwards, Ryker further revealed his ideological orientation by asserting, in the *Tribune*, that those in the community who wished to have design standards for buildings such as McDonald's were proposing something that smacked of "Big Brother or architectural fascism."[27] He also was sharply critical of the public's role in the master plan public hearing on February 28th. Among the nearly 100 people who attended, an overwhelming majority of those who spoke criticized the weakening of the plan from the more restrictive version drafted by the Master Plan Committee. As that Committee's chair Amy Rossiter stated, "[The planning board] made magic here. They made all the really strong policies evaporate--disappear--and still made it longer than the [original] document." Ryker's response in the next *Tribune* was to try to denigrate and de-legitimate public hearings by isolating critics with an appeal to "the silent majority":

> I think the majority of the community really has faith in the people appointed or elected to protect their overall interests. The special interest groups like CLEAR and the Van Wyck Valley Land Trust brought out all their troops as expected because they think the louder you scream, the more relevant your message is. But we know that the majority of the community understands the beauty of the area can only be saved with a thriving, balanced economy supported by proper growth and sound businesses.[28]

Only four days earlier Julia Bellows finally was chosen for the planning board by an unusual majority of Lyon, Devilla and Schmidt. It was difficult to deny the superiority of her credentials over most, given her service for the past year on the town's own environmental conservation commission and her career in the world of business. Schmidt was also impressed with the fact that Bellows had actually read the proposed master plan and knew the difference between the commission's role of recommending and the planning board's role of enforcing.[29]

Bellows described her own position as "probably right down the middle," between those "very pro-environment" and others "not very pro-environment."[30] She thought that both perspectives had a legitimate role. Despite the cautious nature of Bellows' remarks, CLEAR and others of its perspective were hopeful that her appointment might signal (with members Pelletier, Hillman and Dalrymple) the first "regulator" majority in memory.

"Frontloading" and "Backloading" vs. Necessary Caution

In early January, the planning board sent a "lead agency request" to ten state, federal and local agencies.[31] However, only two of these agencies, the Forest County Planning Board (FCPB) and the state Department of Environmental Conservation (DEC), responded by March with more detailed statements of significant potential concern. Given the need for heightened scrutiny, the absence of any meaningful input from the DOT regarding traffic and the Army Corps regarding the effect of the project on federally-impacted wetlands underscored SEQRA's limitations as a planning tool for lead agencies. While the statute requires a proposed lead agency to give notice of its intention to proceed with a project's review to all concerned and involved agencies with future permitting authority,[32] SEQRA does not require these agencies to provide the planning board, as lead agency, with any comment on potential adverse environmental impact. Thus, notifications can be ignored and interpreted by the local planning board as either a sign of approval or lack of concern.

In his letter of February 10th, FCPB planner Henry Fowler pointed out that the developer's traffic counts were done in October 1993 during a period of massive IBM downsizing.[33] Magellan thus distorted and minimized likely longer-range traffic volumes in the area. Fowler also suggested that the developer explore a potential extension of and hookup with municipal water supplies west of the Thruway. As well, he pointed out that stormwater design must be consistent with new DEC standards and that the storage capacity of detention ponds was suspect when bottom elevations were below the known water table.[34] These critiques presented new information regarding significant adverse effects which now had to be addressed in view of post-Amsterdam Square changed circumstances before an initial SEQRA decision could be reached.[35]

Four days later, William Tholen of the DEC's regional office presented a letter containing a similar analysis. He requested that the planning board address alternatives to Magellan's planned discharge of sewage effluent into the wetlands, as well as compliance with 1993 DEC stormwater standards adopted after the previous Amsterdam Square review, fresh delineations of state wetland boundaries throughout the project area, the handling and management of pesticide-contaminated soil, additional information on potential historical resources in the area and a revised Army Corps determination concerning the extent of on-site federally-regulated wetlands to be disturbed.[36] Thus, FCPB and DEC responses served as a counterpoint to earlier Rattle and Busch positions that further environmental review was not needed.

On the same day as Tholen's reply, the board had a discussion with Magellan Construction in which the developer acknowledged its "frontloading" desire to avoid an SEIS altogether. Articulating an approach common to developers and typically accepted by the "light planning" majority in the past, Magellan argued that all conceptual environmental issues could be addressed and answered informally and satisfactorily over the next several weeks without further environmental review. All concerns would be resolved and the planning board could then issue a negative declaration, declining to engage in any further SEQRA review. Magellan maintained that "frontloading" could be effectively combined with "backloading" whereby specific design details and needed mitigations could be deferred to the site-plan review process with the board and with the various outside permitting agencies. Such a process, to follow SEQRA approval, would eliminate the opportunity for full-blown review and comment by the public on adverse environmental effects, since this is only assured when the "lead agency" makes a "positive SEQRA declaration" requiring the developer to prepare an EIS.[37]

This common attempt at "frontloading"/"backloading" a project's SEQRA review through offering initially only broad design information avoids the fact that later specific design details and mitigations can have profound negative environmental implications which are not considered at the time of the issuance of the negative determination. It also allows a developer to use all the advantages of months of advance work and public relations to impress a technically-unsophisticated board with a smooth overall plan. It defers specific technical and analytical issues to bureaucratic permitting agencies disconnected from a local community, thus enabling board members to approve a project without taking responsibility for harm to the local environment. These bureaucratic agencies, such as the DEC and the DOT, in turn, are themselves the subject of political pressure and frequently view their responsibility as facilitating construction of a project, once a local planning board has given SEQRA approval. Such agencies rarely become involved in any substantial project review, even if informal, before such determination by the lead agency.[38] Even individuals of a "regulator" perspective in such agencies are typically constrained by budget and time constraints, as well as the absence of lead agency analytical guidance, from issuing more than generalized bland critiques "usually more concerned with the 'stream' of projects improving than with any one project being changed." As well, since outside agency officials expect to be dealing with the various local lead agencies on other issues in the future, "there are strong incentives to be cooperative."[39]

In a letter to board chair Ryker of February 23rd, attorney Rattle supported Magellan's "frontloading"/"backloading" strategy of avoiding an SEIS. As in December, he contended that most of Tholen's DEC concerns were considered by the previous board's SEQRA approval findings about Amsterdam Square. A lead agency, he said, referring to the SEQRA regulations, could require an SEIS only if "there is the potential for at least one significant adverse environmental effect arising from project changes or newly discovered information or a change in circumstances." If an SEIS is required, he said, only those specific issues qualifying by these criteria could be addressed. On this basis, he suggested that since DEC's concerns with stormwater discharge and the rest were all addressed in the Amsterdam Square SEQRA findings, they would not now justify an SEIS. Only the fact of new stormwater regulations might qualify as "a change in circumstances." But he urged that the applicant and board should now simply address these and other lingering DEC concerns. Magellan could demonstrate its ability to successfully conceptualize any potential mitigation alternatives and thus eliminate the need for an SEIS. This would permit the board to issue a negative declaration, ending the SEQRA process, and to move on to site-plan review.[40]

Representatives of Magellan Construction came to the meeting of February 28th, after the board's master plan public hearing, with the expressed intent to gain board agreement that no SEIS was needed. As its attorney Morris Schwab defined it, the only potential hurdles before a negative declaration were to resolve how their project expansion into the differently-zoned southerly lot would be resolved and to address the several points made by the DEC. Each of these, he argued, could be resolved at a later date through permit application processes.[41]

Suddenly, project approval seemed imminent. If a negative declaration were issued at this meeting, neither the public nor the planning board would be able seriously to affect the ability of Moselle Plaza to go forward. It would be Amsterdam Square reborn, a fait accompli! For McBride of CLEAR and Ina Turbell, leader of the South Creighton Road neighborhood group, it was an agonizing moment to experience. Though both had gathered information demonstrating how changed circumstances since 1991 would cause significant adverse environmental project impacts, neither had yet had the time to begin a public campaign. Since Bellows had not yet taken her place on the board and both Hillman and Davis were absent, there was a potential 2-2 split between "light planners" and those from the "regulator" perspective (Ryker and Maglie vs. Pelletier and Dalrymple). But Dalrymple's concerns regarding Moselle Plaza were not yet clear and the issues at hand seemed too nebulous to force him to take a strong stand.

Anticipating legal objections which community groups might raise, Rattle now expressed concern that the board protect itself by meeting with Tholen of the DEC to satisfy SEQRA's "hard look" standard, before deferring all issues to the permit approval process.[42] Explicit points mentioned in the DEC letter, such as implications from new stormwater standards and the issue of wastewater discharge into the wetlands, would have to be clarified directly to avoid any interpretation that these comments signified major potential changes in circumstances requiring an SEIS. Since a different DEC official had reviewed the earlier Amsterdam Square and since it wasn't clear, according to Rattle, that Tholen was "up to speed" about the scope and sufficiency of the previous findings, he stated, "I think that it would behoove us to talk to him. If he comes up with something that's a change in circumstance or new information, I think you should address it. If this can be done quickly, it would make me feel a lot more comfortable."

Now upset by Rattle's delay on the verge of apparent SEQRA approval, Magellan's attorney Schwab objected, claiming that meeting with Tholen would produce no new information and that everything he had mentioned was already addressed in the Amsterdam Square findings. To call a meeting would be almost to beg DEC to give the board a reason for an SEIS. "It's not that we don't want to come meet. It's that we want to keep the project proceeding." However, in his first indication of concern for a thorough SEQRA process, Dalrymple now suggested that the meeting should occur even without

Magellan's attendance. Reading the power balance and predicting a deadlock on an issue which he wished ultimately to avoid, Ryker conceded the point. He stated that "it seems to be the feeling of the board that they would like to get at least a feeling for what Mr. Tholen was getting at. . . . Let's go to the DEC, get it cleared up and then come back."

As quickly as that, the door opened at least slightly to a more careful review. Both Dalrymple and Pelletier said they had not yet had time to compare the two shopping center projects to determine if an SEIS was needed. Pelletier said she thought the business context had changed in three years and Dalrymple said he had concerns even beyond those brought up by the DEC. Schwab, Rattle and then Ryker backed off to a position of merely setting up a format and time frame to complete the SEQRA determination. Though ready to approve the present project now, Ryker stated his intention to have the board finish its comparison at the meeting of March 14th at which time a definite decision regarding the need or not for an SEIS could occur. The rush to judgment was delayed.[43]

The disputed meeting with the DEC was anti-climactic, with Tholen simply restating concerns voiced in his earlier letter and Rattle informing him of the nature of the original Amsterdam Square findings. The more important result of the delay, however, became apparent at the March 14th meeting. Pelletier now elaborated upon her economic and wastewater concerns. Ben Hillman, with some detailed questioning, demanded more information on stormwater plans, traffic and economic impacts. To demonstrate "light planners'" adherence to SEQRA, in turn, Maglie and Davis requested more details on traffic and economics, while Davis voiced concern that the board determine whether Magellan's project was identical to Amsterdam Square. New board member Julia Bellows provided a neutral, but thorough, level of inquiry and participated in discussion of every realm. She sought information about new DEC standards on wastewater, updated economic and fiscal impact data, and accurate traffic figures.

Magellan now confronted a strategic political choice. Breaking down before their eyes were their own and Ryker's piggybacking upon Amsterdam Square findings and reliance on Rattle's and Busch's advice to avoid further SEQRA review because allegedly the projects were substantially the same. Magellan had to decide whether it could afford politically to continue pressing for fast-track "frontloading"/"backloading" or, alternatively, whether to accept a potential full-blown SEIS, with full public participation, substantive comments by independent consultants and a formal final determination based on the record after significant expense of more time and money. To continue the strategy of fast-track "frontloading"/"backloading" and to obtain conceptual approval without an SEIS from at least one of the "regulator" majority comprised of Pelletier, Dalrymple, Bellows and Hillman, Magellan would have to provide significantly more information than already submitted. Rattle's approach, similar to Busch's, was to agree to permit additional information-gathering without an SEIS, after which the board would issue a negative declaration. The latter would contend that the board had taken a "hard look" at all changes in circumstances and adverse environmental impacts and that it was satisfied that all issues were adequately addressed by the developer and would be satisfactorily resolved. Although a somewhat more complex approach than Busch's (in that it required some data gathering and analysis), Rattle continued to maintain that economic impact had no legitimate role in SEQRA review and that no further information in this realm was needed. After prompting by Busch, however, Rattle acknowledged that economics might have some relevance if a development caused blight in the community. When Davis also indicated that he wouldn't approve the project unless questions about economic impact were answered (whether a legitimate SEQRA issue or not), the die was cast. By the end of the meeting, Magellan came to accept the political reality that it would have to provide more information about stormwater, wastewater, traffic and economics impacts if it had any hope of avoiding a full-blown SEIS.[44]

Summarizing, though incompletely, these informational demands after the mid-March meeting while at the same time distancing himself from them, Ryker submitted by memo to project manager David Jankoff what he called the "'laundry list' of background studies required by planning board members." This included exploration of all alternatives to an on-site sewage treatment plant, analysis of the plaza's likely economic impact on the Ashbury business community--specifically including Ashbury Plaza and the village downtown, and specific background data used to arrive at Magellan's conclusions about existing and project-generated traffic.[45] Missing from this list was any reference to the change in DEC stormwater management standards and the effect of this on the method of stormwater removal and treatment proposed by Magellan.

Public Involvement

Local *Tribune* editor George Worthy immediately celebrated a perceived political victory. In his lead editorial, he commended the board for choosing to think "long and hard about what is best for the community" and urged the Town Board "to eliminate shopping plazas right out of the code book." Quoting Supervisor Schmidt who said, "I think it is the intention of some people to kill the Moselle Plaza project--legally, illegally, or any way they can," Worthy confessed that he was one of those people. "Ashbury needs another plaza like it needs another pizza joint or bar. . . . If anyone knows of places where plazas have actually decreased the property tax rate, I would be thrilled to learn about them."[46] Worthy's discourse, and that of the first critical letter-writers to the press, raised the temperature of the debate over Moselle Plaza and signified that project construction would become a wider political issue than merely the competing perspectives of planning board members.

By the time of the April 25th meeting, Magellan Construction had turned in its engineer's more detailed report on stormwater management alternatives; a 20-page economic impact report from a hired New York City planner;[47] and an additional traffic survey to provide alternative figures from those in October. Magellan also had begun negotiations to hook up with village water and sewer systems. Through the submission of these new data, the developer hoped to avoid an SEIS and the need to design on-site water and sewer treatment facilities.

In response to the challenge posed by critics in the press, Ryker renewed his public relations campaign by stating that Ashbury Plaza and Moselle Plaza stores would well complement each other in the future and that additional cars attracted to Moselle Plaza would not clog the streets of Ashbury.[48] He was joined in welcoming the plaza by Town Board members Kraft and Mosher. However, the views of Ryker and his political allies, in turn, were countered in the press by other political figures critical of the proposed megamall and its effect on the environment and culture of the town. Town Board member Lyon, several Village trustees and Village Mayor Gary Patton all expressed serious critiques.[49]

In Ryker's absence, vice-chair Rich Maglie presided on April 25th. Before the board could proceed, Alex McBride appealed from the audience for the public to have the opportunity to verbally comment before the board made any SEQRA determination. Maglie, however, implied his intent to decide at this meeting whether an SEIS was needed. Attempting to assure that "light planning" would prevail and that an SEIS was unnecessary, Maglie quoted long passages to the board from the entire 40+-page earlier Amsterdam Square SEQRA findings statement. Through these quotations, he sought to reassure the board that all relevant issues of stormwater, traffic and economics had already been adequately considered and that no significant change in circumstances existed.

Eventually member Julia Bellows raised the need for public involvement in the process: "I don't see this as just a Planning Board Town/Village project. It's very much a public project. One that is going to impact everybody to the extent that their comment is important." Rattle, however, now invoked the authority of law to control the discretion of planning board members. Said Rattle: "You can't do it. If you do a 'pos dec', [a positive declaration that an EIS was required] then you can." Unimpressed, Bellows replied: "I just think that we have a responsibility to give the public an opportunity to provide input. Otherwise, we're not doing our job." Rattle tried again: "The law is quite clear that if you should determine this to be a negative declaration, there is no requirement, no mandate for a public hearing. It's only optional if you make a positive [declaration] and then it is optional even then." Bellows refused to be intimidated: "If it's important to me then I would go for a 'pos dec' on this . . . I'd vote for a 'pos dec' on this."[50]

A public hearing was the event that "light planners" sought most to avoid. Such a hearing would allow the public to review Magellan's proposed plan and, with assistance from outside consultants, to indicate the degree to which significant change had occurred since Amsterdam Square's final approval which might result in significant adverse environmental effects. Thus, the case for an SEIS could be persuasively made and would not rely solely on untutored views of the "regulator" majority on the planning board. Furthermore, inviting the public in, at this stage, would clearly politicize the planning board's decision even more and raise the ideological stakes surrounding the building of the proposed megamall. While CLEAR and other community groups might be counted upon to add the testimony of independent consultants to the mix, other members of the public with strong "regulator" and "ecologist" views on the environment would certainly echo the words of editorialist George Worthy and thereby increase the temperature of the debate. With such a prospect in sight, Magellan's project manager David Jankoff sought desperately to intervene in the planning board's discussion in order to shore up the "backloading" dimension of his fast-track strategy:

> A finding statement was done on this project before. Just because a finding statement has been issued, obviously it doesn't mean the project is going to be built. We realize that we have a long way to go even after the issuance of a finding statement . . . as far as coming back . . . going through all of our permits . . . doing more and decisive detailed site plan approval at that time. Public hearing, yes, but I really think it's going to be kind of confusing to bring in a public hearing now because there are a lot of questions now that I can't answer for you and you can't direct me. There's a lot of things that we have to go through with various agencies and try to scope out what we are going to do here. As the developer I will do whatever you guys recommend.

While Jankoff's plea sought to present Magellan as a non-obstructive facilitative actor which would answer all questions eventually through the site-plan and permitting process, his suggestion that Magellan was unable to answer pertinent questions at this time and that these questions should be deferred to a later date was a tactical mistake. Such acknowledgment simply whet the appetite of the new "regulator" planning board majority who correctly thought that the absence of relevant information already justified an SEIS at this juncture of the SEQRA process. The meeting ended when Maglie refused to offer more than a vague promise that at some point there would be public comment. At the same time, he said, he expected the board to be ready with a decision in one month.[51]

At a joint Town Board-planning board meeting on May 2nd, the topic of Moselle Plaza was on everyone's mind. Supervisor Schmidt attempted a positive spin by revealing that Magellan Construction had agreed to a water-sewer hook-up requiring it to pay over $300,000 to the Town and Village for various fees and infrastructure expansion. But Mark Lyon clarified that the Village Mayor had just indicated that Village approval for the hook-up would depend on a favorable economic impact analysis.[52] This was a critically important message for developer and planning board both because the Village, which controlled the water and sewage treatment plant, had absolute control over a hook-up decision. Not bound to decide the question within the environmental framework of SEQRA, the Village could deny permission based solely on the adverse economic impact the megamall would have on village businesses. If the Village denied Magellan's request, the environmental impacts of alternative on-site water supply and wastewater treatment for the megamall would become important issues when the town planning board, under SEQRA, would have to decide whether or not to require an SEIS.

Ashbury Community Together

From early in 1994, Ina Turbell and Alex McBride had scrutinized every project-related document in the files and had closely monitored board discussion at every meeting where Moselle Plaza was raised. They also began sifting through piles of documents each had collected in the previous struggle against Amsterdam Square and began making contacts with other communities where similar battles were underway.

Following the May 2nd joint meeting, Turbell and McBride decided that the best approach to coordinate "regulator" and "ecologist" political influence was to create a new grassroots organization totally focused on the issue of Moselle Plaza. Between Turbell's contacts in the community and McBride's knowledge of more active and interested members of CLEAR, on April 27th, the two leaders personally invited nearly two dozen Ashbury residents to an organizing meeting at the home of an environmentally-concerned local builder on May 5th.

That gathering was McBride's and Turbell's first attempt to demystify the SEQRA statute and planning board legal processes so as to make Moselle Plaza decision-making accessible to community members concerned with local environmental, social and economic well-being. They explained the nature of the project and specifically alerted those present to major adverse environmental impacts of Moselle Plaza in the realms already earmarked by the planning board--stormwater, wastewater, water quality, and traffic. They also explained that with the likelihood of Wal-Mart as the major anchor store, economic concerns, in the SEQRA "balancing test," would be at the forefront. In this realm especially, they cited lessons from other local communities on destructive impacts of Wal-Mart, gathered from various materials McBride and Turbell had already researched.[53]

Quick brainstorming produced the group's "Ashbury Community Together" label, chosen in part because of the combative "ACT" acronym. All present at the meeting believed in the fact of a threatened "Ashbury community." But it remained to be seen if ACT activists could successfully re-frame the struggle among the general public from a techno-legalistic battle of experts to a popular cross-ideology grassroots effort within and outside of the SEQRA framework to defend a "home community" against outside predators.[54]

Ina Turbell, a proven fine organizer and activist since the 60s, was chosen as president. ACT's method, however, was to encourage other members also to accept leadership roles, enhancing their ability to articulate issues among the wider public. The idea was to counter the top-down organizational method, typified by Magellan, with a model maximizing the political voice and creativity of the wider public. The challenge to ACT was to translate into "regulator" and "ecologist" discourse the concerns of non-elites who liked to live in the town because of its rural exurban identity, proximity to the mountains, and the natural beauty and historical resources of the Hudson Valley. While McBride would remain active in ACT, he felt it was important to retain his separate identity as CLEAR co-chair because of the long-standing presence and reputation of that organization's "regulator" and "ecologist" community planning perspectives generally, perspectives not necessarily shared by all those whom ACT sought to attract. Nevertheless, for the next two years, McBride's personal focus and that of CLEAR were directed almost exclusively to Moselle Plaza.

ACT committees were set up for fundraising, publicity, research, letter-writing and petition-gathering and initial proposals for each were quickly developed. A top priority was to petition the planning board at its next meeting, three days from then, to hold a public hearing on the plaza before determining whether or not to require an SEIS. This would immediately engage the public in the decision-making process and provide political support for those on the planning board with the "regulator" perspective. More importantly, it would provide a counterweight to Magellan's voice and make the dialogue more inclusive.

Using SEQRA as an organizing tool was resisted by some who questioned law's utility in bringing about social and political change. For them, law was captive to the professional and business elite and inaccessible as a means of empowerment. They were thus doubtful that SEQRA could actually slow down or stop the project. But the public's right to have a voice in such a monumental decision was perceived by most as a matter of simple justice, not a formal legalistic issue for the planning board to decide. Without pretending to understand intricate details of economic or traffic impacts, let alone effects on the wetlands, most knew from personal observation elsewhere the major effects of new malls on existing retail businesses and everyone had experienced frequent traffic congestion along the town's Main Street and its continuation east of the Thruway. Moreover, the group recognized that Ashbury had grown increasingly ugly as developers, in alliance with local government, had enlarged the presence of a mass retail culture through construction of the four uptown existing shopping centers.

Despite this grassroots knowledge and doubts about official process, everyone agreed, after Turbell's and McBride's presentation, that the group should focus much of its efforts during the next several weeks on the planning board's decision whether to require an SEIS. At the same time, the group recognized that the context of the planning board's decision would be multi-dimensional and political, and that therefore strong appeals, beyond SEQRA's discourse, would be needed to the Town Board, the Village Board, the local merchant community and the public at large.

A simple petition was drawn up, demanding a public hearing and stating the key economic and environmental issues presented by Moselle Plaza. Because of the short time frame, it was circulated primarily among friends and neighbors of the original ACT group. By the time the petition was presented to the board just three days later at its meeting of May 9th, about one hundred signatures had been obtained. For the new organization, this was an important first effort and public appearance.

Shortly thereafter, Turbell contacted Harry Morris, the owner of Ashbury Plaza, the town's largest shopping center. Morris had already called the Village Board and written to Mark Lyon, the Town Board's representative on the Ashbury Development Corporation, opposing the new project for failing to meet even the criteria of orderly fair competition. While Morris' opposition was rooted in self-interest--the potential loss of rent-roll at Ashbury Plaza, his support for ACT would legitimate the organization in the eyes of his tenants and those of other local businesses with similar economic concerns.

Turbell set up an informal informational meeting of herself and McBride with Morris and a number of store tenants from Ashbury Plaza for May 13th. This was the beginning, along with contacts around the petition, of a broad political coalition opposed to Moselle Plaza, including environmental activists, concerned citizens and many from the local business community.[55] Perhaps this new anti-mall alliance, newly sensitive to elements of "community" previously taken for granted, could achieve together what concerned individuals from "pragmatic capitalist," "regulator" and "ecologist" perspectives could not achieve on their own.

At the planning board meeting of May 10th, ACT members anxiously awaited the outcome of their appeal for a hearing. With Ryker still out of town, the board's strongest voice for the "minimalist" perspective" and against a public role for the opposition would not be heard. As board members appeared in the public meeting room, vice-chair Maglie distributed to them a memorandum summarizing the planning board's April 25th discussion comparing Moselle Plaza with Amsterdam Square. His explicit purpose was to organize for the next board meeting on the 23rd a topic-by-topic discussion of whatever issues remained. However, it appeared that his actual intent was to enable the board to issue a negative declaration, without an SEIS, based on Amsterdam Square's earlier SEQRA approval. Maglie admonished the Board to "stay focused" on areas of traffic, water resources and economic impact. He also turned to the legal standard for justifying an SEIS by stating emphatically, but without legal authority, "Remember, the key is not is it a significant change to the existing area but is it a significant change from the previously approved project [emphasis added]. Board members should be prepared with factual objective conclusions."[56]

Maglie's instructions sought to legitimate a narrow decision limited solely to changes in the project rather than, as anticipated by the SEQRA statute and regulations, changes in the economic climate and deterioration of existing traffic, wetlands and aquifer contexts since the previous project's approval. By capturing law's language and narrowing its definition, Maglie sought to empower those members of the board with "minimalist" and "pragmatic capitalist" perspectives to argue, amidst a "regulator" majority perspective, for issuance of a negative declaration. However, Maglie's efforts were already contradicted because Rattle had conceded at earlier meetings that any "change in circumstances" subsequent to the Amsterdam Square approval findings statement which produced a potential significant adverse environmental effect was grounds for an SEIS. For ACT and CLEAR, who later obtained Maglie's memorandum from the planning board files, his hand seemed revealed.

Only after eight more agenda items and dissolution of most of the audience over the next two hours did Maglie finally announce that "public comments" would also be heard at the May 23rd meeting. This strategy of considering issues unrelated to Moselle Plaza for the first part of a meeting would be repeated throughout the two-year process, delaying megamall discussion until near the end when most members of the public had left for home and bed. This strategy also demonstrated the power of a board minority to hold hostage "regulator" members who were not sufficiently organized to challenge the agenda procedures of the chair. Nevertheless, Maglie's final statement--that "public comments" would be considered at the next meeting--was a concession to views of the "regulator" majority which opened the door to the public to become part of formal SEQRA deliberations.

Energized by success in attaining the right to participate through a public hearing, ACT immediately sought further to explain and demystify SEQRA to make it accessible to widening numbers of the public opposed to urban sprawl and concerned about the viability of local businesses. ACT's first task was to acquaint people with the meaning of an SEIS and the SEQRA process. While the planning board might announce that public comment would be taken at a meeting, no effort would be made by the board or its secretary to educate the public regarding the relevance of that comment. Meanwhile, the reaction of most people interested in participating in the process would be to attend and voice their opposition to the proposed megamall based upon substantive reasons (dislike of urban sprawl and the demise of a small town atmosphere) which "light planning" members, upon advice of the planning board's lawyer, would find to be irrelevant to SEQRA criteria.

ACT immediately moved to prepare a new petition requesting an SEIS itself, while alerting the community about the scheduled public hearing. The language of the petition drafted by McBride and Turbell informed the public of appropriate legal reasons for an SEIS, thus assuring that the signatures would conform to SEQRA's standard. Circulated widely throughout the community, filled sheets were collected and fresh sheets distributed every few days. Within the next weeks, ACT succeeded in gathering many hundreds of signatures. With additional press publicity and through a mailing to petition signers and others, ACT hoped to obtain a large informed turnout at the late May planning board meeting.

On the morning of the May 23rd meeting, the press again quoted Ryker as praising the economic benefits of Moselle Plaza and labeling its opposition as merely those who fear competition. He claimed that taxpayers, government officials and business people favored the project. But Ryker's error was to assume that the town's governmental and property elite, which over the last 35 years had invited and encouraged large-scale commercial development, somehow represented the views of the wider public. Of course, this assumption was not without some support, given that this elite had controlled all key appointed positions at the planning and zoning board levels and had, with only the partial exception of Supervisor Kessler, an unbroken chain of Town Supervisors who had embraced this form of free market ideology and home rule.

However Ryker's attempt to manipulate the SEQRA process by discouraging public participation through remarks in the press and by marginalizing ACT in the eyes of planning board members backfired and demonstrated Ryker's flawed sense of appropriate message, tone and timing. By the time the so-called "public comment" meeting was well underway, hundreds of people had packed the meeting room at Town Hall, with many unable to get in. It was easily the largest crowd to attend a planning board function in the past decade. Of the 26 who spoke, all but 3 or 4 opposed the project.

While few were versed in the subtleties of the SEQRA statute's language, virtually everyone provided good rationales, if the board chose to use them, for requiring an SEIS. With a kind of "lay epidemiology," many spoke of the devastation to community character and tax base caused by Wal-Marts and similar megamalls in communities they had moved from or visited[57] or which existed in the Hudson Valley itself--on both sides of the river. The question of community character was very real, since the economic downswing following the 1991 acceptance of Amsterdam Square's EIS already raised the specter of blight in the town's existing shopping centers. Mayor Patton, whose statement foreshadowed Village Board opposition to the water-sewer hook-up for Moselle Plaza, spoke to applause about his fears for a future community with empty stores and abandoned businesses. Turbell presented a clear statement of critical issues concerning project damage to the wetlands and aquifer and how Magellan's proposed mitigation did not satisfy the heightened scrutiny criteria voiced by DEC's new standards. McBride offered evidence to weigh potential damage in economic and fiscal realms along with negative environmental effects and asserted the need to assume, at least for analytical purposes, that the anchor store would be Wal-Mart, a national chain with a history of devouring Main Street, USA.

At the hearing, ACT presented its petitions and a detailed 25-page letter with another 25 pages of careful documentation.[58] The letter explicitly defined, in appropriate SEQRA terms, the need for an SEIS to address issues of stormwater, wastewater, water supply, traffic, fiscal and economic impacts. For the first time before the planning board, it was argued that the need to address economic impacts was justified not only because of potential urban blight, a community character issue, but also because SEQRA mandated the need to assess the balance between adverse environmental impacts and potential economic gain, once environmental impacts were identified.[59] Detailed economic analysis was obviously required to make such an evaluation.

The public comment session quickly became a full-blown hearing providing Moselle Plaza opponents their first opportunity to voice concerns. Many attending were not versed in the legal standard appropriate to an SEIS and often spoke from the heart about local environmental degradation that town government had already permitted to occur. For these people, to turn this property into a megamall was the final stage toward what James Kunstler has termed "the geography of nowhere."

As each opponent spoke, Ryker, who chaired the meeting, did what he could to marginalize their words. Ryker was a master of body language and was not beyond snickering, raising his eyebrows, rolling his eyes, or actually belittling people with whose views he disagreed. His behavior, along with statements by a four-year resident and past head of the now-defunct Ashbury Taxpayers Association and by Supervisor Grant Schmidt, provided the only significant counterweight to what could only be described as community outrage over the project. Schmidt sought to demonstrate that the public's objections were futile, that the project was inevitable and that people ought to return to their homes with the knowledge that the elected and appointed officials of the town would adequately address everyone's concerns. Additionally, both speakers appealed to purse-strings by contending that Moselle Plaza and its anchor stores would be a tax benefit to the town in the present context where, given the downsizing of the economy, the town had to continually increase homeowner tax rates. Ominously, Schmidt contended that if the planning board were to disapprove Moselle Plaza, Magellan would only go eastward right down the highway to the neighboring town of Acton, and Ashbury would be stuck without new tax revenues, but with all the environmental liabilities.[60]

Manny Dreyfus, an active opponent of the 1973 megamall at the same location, had obtained a copy of ACT's flyer and decided to attend the meeting. Dreyfus had not been involved in CLEAR's struggle against Amsterdam Square, although he had collaborated with McBride earlier in challenging the Tapani subdivision located no more than a quarter of a mile from his home.

However, this was Dreyfus' first opportunity to observe the planning board in action and Ryker's behavior in particular. It was problematic to him that Ryker and Schmidt appeared so committed to the project in the face of what would appear to be widespread community opposition. Ryker's intransigence and apparent insider hostility to the views of the community led Dreyfus to ask whether perhaps Ryker's insistence that the project go forward without an SEIS was because of possible financial benefit for himself and others.[61] The stakes were high, with polarization increasing and growing futility increasingly apparent among speakers who opposed the project. Dreyfus decided to directly confront Ryker about his demeaning behavior which, because mostly in body language, would not appear in any written minutes of the meeting. In addition, he sought to unmask Ryker as someone who sought to hide behind a narrow SEQRA interpretation to avoid the objectives and principles upon which the statute was enacted. He blamed Ryker and the board for not caring about public sentiments while trying to force a narrow legalistic discussion devoid of socio-economic content. He accused Ryker of not respecting the seriousness of comments already made, having seen him "smirk a good deal of the time, say, when Mr. Patton spoke." He then suggested that it might be appropriate for citizens outraged by the planning board's conduct to consider requesting convening of a grand jury to investigate corruption in local government and to subpoena records of board members to determine if they were likely to benefit or to have benefitted from development of the project. As to the SEQRA issue, Dreyfus attempted to rally the audience against Ryker's attitude that public comments were a mere formality since Ryker appeared to view a negative declaration as a foregone conclusion. Given demonstrated changes of circumstances following acceptance of the Amsterdam Square project, Dreyfus stated: "We should know that it is not really our burden to prove that a SEQRA review is needed. It's Rocky Ryker's burden to show us that it isn't needed."

Dreyfus' statements immediately resonated among those who opposed the project, who were offended by Ryker's behavior and who had begun to express openly that local corruption might have been one reason why the face of Ashbury had been transformed. Ryker, in turn, accused Dreyfus of coming "dangerously close to slander," after which he quickly moved on to the next speaker and threatened to immediately close the hearing. However, this conflict-of-interest issue and Dreyfus' challenge to the chair's interpretation of legality quickly resulted in expanding the network of individuals interested in exposing the Moselle Plaza development.

Immediately following the meeting, people opposing the mall asked Dreyfus to utilize his legal skills in the effort. Additionally, Joshua Wright, a professional engineer for 27 years and a town resident for seven, introduced himself to Dreyfus and volunteered his services to those who opposed the project. Wright was an expert consultant to several planning boards in Dutchess County and a new member of the Town Environmental Conservation Commission, and had been a candidate in December to fill the one-year Town Board opening. Dreyfus immediately introduced Wright to McBride and Turbell who were familiar with the specific environmental issues raised by the project. Wright had already read Magellan's application and followed the issues in the press. On the day following the hearing, he submitted a detailed letter to the planning board explaining, from an engineering and planning perspective, how the DEC's new standards on stormwater discharge were themselves a change in circumstances which demonstrated that Magellan's existing plans, however similar to Amsterdam Square's, would now have an adverse environmental effect not previously recognized by the board and thus a clear SEQRA cause for an SEIS.

Wright's willingness to join with Dreyfus, McBride, Turbell and the ACT alliance meant that for the first time in the history of the struggle over implementation and enforcement of SEQRA at the local town level, a major development proposal would now be continuously confronted with professionals and individuals whose issue sophistication equaled that of planning board and developer consultants. Of even greater importance, Dreyfus and Wright were each willing to provide legal and engineering skills on a "pro bono" basis for the good of the community and without compensation.

Ryker, wounded by the confrontation with Dreyfus unmasking him as predisposed to Moselle Plaza for possibly extralegal reasons, immediately attempted to reestablish his authority as the sole legitimate interpreter of the law. In one interview with the press, he stated that "99% of the comments made at the hearing were not relevant" and that most of the speakers were concerned about community character rather than SEQRA matters.[62] But settled SEQRA case law contradicted Ryker's statement on community character since project-caused blight or significant change in usage which would damage or significantly alter the community's existing character was defined as a relevant environmental issue.[63]

Ethics and Organizing

Following the May 23rd meeting, ACT sought to expand its perspective and to include issues of ethics and government within its critique. Through a Freedom of Information ("FOIL") request[64] to the Forest County Board of Elections, Turbell had obtained proof that Magellan Construction's manager Deke Reynolds had contributed $245 to the Ashbury Republican Club-- just several weeks before Magellan's proposal was presented to the board. While the amount involved was small, the issue raised was consistent with Dreyfus' critique of Ryker at the May 23rd meeting and demonstrated Magellan's preference for the politics of the local Republican Party. The question of bias and apparent conflict of interest had been an issue in one of the early cases litigated under the SEQRA statute.[65] The courts concluded that the appearance of a conflict of interest would undermine public confidence and the board's decision-making process under SEQRA. The decision, which itself was not remarkable under legal liberalism's promise of a fair decision-making process, envisioned local planning boards as quasi-judicial agencies rather than political bodies with pre-existing agendas.[66]

This precedent placed into question the propriety of the planning board permitting the chairman of a political party to sit at its head when the same local party received contributions from the developer and when the same individual conspicuously favored the Moselle Plaza project, despite the merits of the claims of potential adverse environmental impact presented to the board by McBride, Turbell and others. Magellan's campaign contribution became a symbol and rallying point for those opposed to the project who ultimately believed that a fair and impartial decision on Moselle Plaza could not occur as long as Ryker was a member of the planning board.

Beyond the issue's symbolic importance politically, ACT and CLEAR decided to raise the conflict-of-interest issue immediately so that the planning board would have adequate opportunity to recuse Ryker before its decision would be tainted by his participation. Dreyfus advised the groups that legality required formal placement on the record, through written submission, any allegations and evidence which could provide grounds for judicial review and reversal of a negative declaration.

ACT was equally concerned with the status of board member Red Davis who also appeared to have a conflict of interest because of commercial property he owned adjacent to the proposed Moselle Plaza site, property which would potentially increase in value with construction of the megamall. The same issue affected Red's father, Ernie, who held considerable property adjacent to the Heller site and who had sold to Heller directly the land upon which the plaza was to be built.[67] Since Heller had clearly intended to develop the property into a massive commercial project (Moselle Plaza was the fifth such scheme under his ownership), Dreyfus and members of ACT and CLEAR believed that neither Red, on the planning board, nor Ernie, the chair of the zoning board of appeals, should be permitted to deliberate and vote on any issue related to the matter since the commercial value of their adjacent property might be enhanced and since, in any event, they would reasonably appear to favor Heller (and Magellan, his agent) who had paid a quarter of a million dollars to Ernie Davis to acquire the land. Ethics opinions issued by the State Attorney General indicated that adjacent property owners presumptively appear to have a conflict of interest.[68] Dreyfus therefore encouraged the group to preserve the record by filing a document detailing the Davises' situation and asking that the planning board recuse Red Davis from deciding whether an SEIS was required and from further participation regarding the process for Moselle Plaza.

ACT also considered Supervisor Grant Schmidt's advocacy of the development to present its own apparent conflict of interest. The Schmidt family held a 78-acre tract of property on the north side of Main Street, just west of the Thruway, which would potentially benefit, when developed, by any water-sewer infrastructure improvements resulting from Magellan's project. As a Town Board official, Grant Schmidt would have to vote on potential issues of water-sewer hook-up, improvement of Davis Lane, a town road immediately adjacent to the project site, and any adjustment of zoning boundaries dividing the Heller property.

A detailed letter was drafted to the planning board urging that Ryker and Davis recuse themselves from Moselle Plaza deliberations and that the board submit the issues to the Town Ethics Committee for its opinion. A similar letter was prepared for Schmidt. At the same time, the group prepared a press release aimed to inform the public of the government ethics issues presented for Ryker, Davis and Schmidt. Engaging the public in this debate was a strategic choice to underscore the importance of this issue to the community's process. Ethics in local government had heretofore been largely neglected in the environmental debate in Ashbury. Raising the temperature of the debate helped focus on the very viability of state law enforcement at the level of local government and, in turn, on the legitimacy of local government itself. The patterns and practices of local officials in Ashbury very much represented an old boys' network in which large property owners and their agents sought to ensure that those in power would be either themselves or those favorably disposed to their positions.

In Schmidt's June 18th reply to Turbell and McBride, also sent to the local press, he denied allegations that his family's ownership of property potentially benefiting from water and sewer line extension created a conflict of interest and stated that he had recused himself in any potential conflict-of-interest situations. To the reporter of the Regent Park Star, he stated: "This has nothing to do with me or my family's property. This is about finding a way to stop a project that a small fraction of the community does not want."[69]

As to the contribution from Deke Reynolds to local Republicans, Schmidt had earlier stated that "anyone can contribute to any party they want. There is nothing illegal in a contribution."[70] In turn, Ryker stated that the charges of conflict of interest because of Reynolds' donation were "hogwash." He contended that "There are forces in this community who are just not placing the welfare and continued economic base of the Ashbury community at the center of their interests." He claimed that Turbell and McBride "have their own agendas" and that he never had personal knowledge of any contributions to the party from Reynolds nor did he solicit them. "Frankly, I'm insulted by the accusation. I never have and never give preferential treatment before the Planning Board."[71]

Ryker's and Schmidt's denials carefully avoided the issue of "an appearance of a conflict of interest" and the effect that such appearances might have on the democratic process in the town. Their defense, continued through the months to come, was that in the absence of actual proof of personal gain or solicitation, there was nothing unethical in their behavior. Appearances, for the old boys' network, were subjective and represented only the paranoia of a marginalized ideological group.[72]

The strategy of firefighting adopted by Ryker and Schmidt was later pursued as well by Red Davis. The latter claimed that a 1990 investigation of this issue by Town Attorney Lou Tapani and planning board attorney Vince Schiffler at the time of the Amsterdam Square project had cleared him of any wrongdoing and demonstrated that there was no basis for a claim of conflict of interest.[73] However, he and the 1990 letter failed to address the issue of an <u>appearance</u> of impropriety created by the Davises' ownership of adjacent property. Nor was there any analysis of whether the public could reasonably construe that the Davises were predisposed and biased in favor of the project, because they had sold the project land to someone who had intended to develop it as a megamall and who had assigned his interests to Magellan for this purpose.

Resolution: A SEQRA Declaration

The long-awaited meeting of June 27th opened with three members present apparently favoring a negative declaration, thus SEQRA approval of the project, and three potentially on the other side. "Regulator" member Pelletier was absent on a long-planned trip. With the likely scenario that a 3-3 deadlock at this meeting would simply postpone the vote until Pelletier returned, Maglie in effect conceded the need for an SEIS to his opponents. In contrast to Ryker's authoritarian style, Maglie traditionally preferred using a "consensus" strategy to win the board to his positions. In this case, realizing that the majority was on the other side, he sought to minimize the damage to Magellan by agreeing to an SEIS, while also seeking to limit narrowly the scope of any SEQRA inquiry.

With board members taking turns revealing their positions, Maglie led off with what appeared to be a decisive call for an SEIS. However, his language was carefully worded. He said that the new stormwater regulations required developers to show the impact of a 100-year storm event, that Magellan had not done so and that planning for such an event might require larger detention and retention ponds and further expansion into the southern lot. He also reminded the board that water and sewer arrangements were still unsettled. He pointed out that the DOT's response contained no reference to the developer's April traffic figures. Thus, Magellan still had to justify its plan for traffic mitigation.

As to economics, however, Maglie sought to close the door on any further analysis other than to ask that Magellan provide additional information on tax revenues and whatever tax abatements it sought, thereby enabling the board to determine whether Moselle Plaza would pay a fair proportion of tax revenues to the town. As to further analysis of implications of the downward change in the economic climate following approval of Amsterdam Square, Maglie hoped that the majority would vote against such an inquiry. He referred to economic modeling and contentions that a downswing in the economy would exacerbate the viability of existing businesses and limit the commercial retail market: "In essence, I think I've received sufficient material--both pros and cons and those in between--on the economic impact of such a site development. I don't think I need any more material on that."[74] Maglie's view on economic analysis was to become a constant theme in his effort to preclude economic predictors, insofar as they diverted from a "common sense" view that more commercial development would improve the tax base and economy of the town.[75]

Following Maglie's response, Red Davis passed. Julia Bellows was concerned that an important aquifer had been identified previously in the area and might be adversely affected by Magellan's proposed method of stormwater control. Contrary to Maglie, she also believed that an independent economic impact analysis was important since "[Magellan's] economic impact statement wasn't as thorough or thoughtful as I'd like."[76] While a new member of the board, Bellows' comments showed "light planners" that she could not easily be overpowered. Her knowledge of institutional decision-making and her ability to articulate and analyze a complicated fact pattern gave her an authoritative voice.

Ben Hillman agreed with the need to examine stormwater, water, sewer and fiscal impacts. He pointed out that Magellan's traffic analyses had changed over time and that nothing definitive had been received from the DOT or Thruway Authority.[77] Hillman's analysis of traffic was informed by his background as a DOT employee, giving his remarks in this realm the imprimatur of legitimacy. He also was emphatic that more economic analysis was required.

Ray Dalrymple saw stormwater, water, sewer and economic issues as all justifying an SEIS. For the latter realm, the developer's report had too many subjective assumptions. Dalrymple contended that an SEIS would allow all information to be gathered in one place instead of the piecemeal submission of data and scattered reviews to date. Dalrymple's voice had its own ring of legitimacy because he was employed by a developer and was familiar with the discourse of contracting. In addition, he was not easily pigeonholed as being an environmentalist who sought to impede development and to act in disregard for the economic well-being of the community.

Planning consultant Gene Busch continued to support "light planning" members rather than the views of the new-found majority. While admitting that more information could be useful, he reiterated his earlier "frontloading" position that Moselle Plaza was not much different from its predecessor. He also endorsed the "backloading" claim that DEC's new stormwater regulations would assure ("at least in theory") that the project would have less of a negative impact than before, leaving nothing more for the planning board to do at the SEQRA stage. Without addressing traffic, economics or community character, Busch said that he didn't regard any of the project impacts as significant or ultimately adverse. Thus, by his view, none of the official

SEQRA threshholds to require an SEIS had been satisfied.

Questioning the legitimacy of issues pursued by "regulator" members, Rattle made one last intervention to insulate Magellan from an SEIS and to push the project to the post-SEQRA, site-plan review stage. Rattle was less concerned with consensus than Maglie and saw the stormwater and traffic concerns, which Maglie acknowledged, as "site-plan details" to be considered only after the approval of a negative SEQRA declaration. Although his role as attorney for the board was to give advice, Rattle presented his views authoritatively, imbued by his knowledge of legality which was privileged and understandable only by a few. "The [SEQRA] regulations are quite clear that you're not supposed to conduct site plan review while you're conducting SEQRA." He said, "You can go ahead and look at those as far as they relate to the environmental impact, but you're not supposed to go ahead and do that until you've resolved the SEQRA issue. So they shouldn't proceed together."[78] While his wording was jumbled, his apparent intent was clear. Environmental impacts could be considered by permitting agencies, he asserted, but only after the planning board's issuance of a negative declaration (i.e., during the site-plan review stage).

To someone versed in the principles and objectives of SEQRA, such language would seem to have turned the meaning of the statute on its head. Rattle apprently was hoping to narrow legitimate SEQRA inquiry through authoritative representation of what the law actually said and by delegation of authority to the administrative permitting agencies. While the regulations clearly authorized and encouraged the planning board to obtain the views of interested permitting agencies, such as the DEC and DOT, it was anticipated that the views of these agencies would be received during, not after, the SEQRA process because the planning board had its own responsibility under SEQRA, separate and apart from these agencies with permitting responsibilities.[79]

Now, however, with Busch's and Rattle's lead, Red Davis spoke of the "gray area" between SEQRA and site-plan review and argued that site-plan review should be the focus of the planning board's concerns. Site-plan review--to ensure that the project was constructed according to specifications of local law--was the proper concern of the planning board. In Davis' view, new DEC stormwater regulations meant simply that a later DEC permit would assure that the project was self-mitigating in this realm. As for fiscal impacts, he echoed Maglie's earlier position, preferring to rely on his own "common sense" rather than the analysis of independent consultants. He said, "They're so subjective. . . . You get two people doing it and you're apt to get two different decisions and you still won't know, two different reports, and you still won't know necessarily which one is correct, because it is so subjective."

Ryker concluded the round of opening statements by shrouding himself in legality and asserting that the "light planning" perspective had the only claim to legitimacy. He contrasted himself to those with the "regulator" perspective-- "I don't have the luxury of being emotionally involved in the project. I'm certainly constrained by the law."[80] Like Davis, he opposed an SEIS.

As the evening grew later, Maglie again sought to use his "conciliatory" position to forge a consensus between the different planning perspectives to narrow the range of what he viewed as an inevitable SEIS. In reviewing what he saw as the relevant issues, he again questioned whether DEC standards imposed alternative detention pond arrangements that could be managed within the 21-acre lot of the commercial zone or whether the light industrial zone was implicated as well.[81] Reynolds, who was sitting before the board, along with Morris Schwab, Magellan's lawyer, and David Jankoff, the project manager, assured Maglie that the detention ponds would be wholly contained within the 21-acre lot of the commercial zone and their construction would therefore not constitute a change in circumstances necessitating an SEIS. Thereafter, Rattle, attempting again to establish his authority as law's provider, emphasized that the board could not simply go fishing for all kinds of new information, they had to show a "significant" change to demand new data through an SEIS. "Beyond that, you are tromping around in red tape."[82.]

While Ryker, Davis and Maglie all agreed that more economic information would be useless, the latter two thought that Magellan's picture was overly optimistic. Nevertheless, Davis and Maglie contended that an inflated economic scenario was at the developer's risk, not the community's. Their common sense told them only that the project wouldn't harm the economic base of the community. Attempting to avoid SEIS inquiry about the project's traffic impacts, Reynolds revealingly asserted that traffic studies, like economic studies, were all subjective and open to interpretation and that the board should leave the decision to DOT to apply permitting standards. Later, realizing that he had gone too far and may have affronted the rational-legal pretenses of those present, he apologized for this remark.

Increasingly, however, Reynolds took on a frustrated, angry and combative stance toward the board's inability to resolve its differences over the SEIS. He began pacing the room, sometimes approaching the board's table to voice his disapproval. He indicated that he was dismayed at the endless rounds of questions and insisted on the "backloading" assertion that other agencies could answer board concerns in their detailed post-SEQRA reviews. At the same time, he reverted to Magellan's original fast-track "frontloading" position, asserting that he was willing to provide more information now, without an SEIS, and claimed that requiring the formality of the latter would not get the board significantly different data later. He urged the board to realize that

Magellan was under great pressure because of the option agreement with Heller and the legal time frame involved. Finally, with patience expended, he contended angrily, "If you're looking to vote no, please don't waste my time and money. My fear is people have made up their minds on the board that they don't want the project."[83]

Abruptly, in the face of the majority's unchanged position, Reynolds then conceded that "to move the process forward," Magellan would prepare an SEIS and satisfy its critics. No doubt he had prepared himself for such a necessity, but had hoped that those with the "light planning" perspective would be able to persuade one of the "regulator" members not to pursue an SEIS. Rattle met this concession with the admonition that an SEIS meant that the board "would have to go the whole nine yards" and he cautioned against the necessity of such an approach which would involve the public in a critique and analysis and thereby require the board to respond to all substantive comments. However, with his ire raised, Reynolds dismissed Rattle's last-gasp intervention and caustically proceeded through a tentative list of issues with the board to limit the damage created by a decision to require an SEIS. As for traffic concerns, he said, if the DOT gave no comments to the board (which he expected they wouldn't until site-review stage), "your independent traffic consultant looking at it doesn't mean a damn." When they came to economic issues, attorney Schwab took over for Reynolds and stated flatly that such analysis was "beyond the letter of the law."[84] After Schwab's several bitter exchanges on this issue with "regulator" board members, Ben Hillman stated his objection to continuing the board's process with the adversarial interventions of the developer. The four-hour meeting came to a close and the 50 attending local residents broke into applause.

Headlines about the meeting proclaimed: "New Mall Caught in Red Tape" and "Long Session Short on Results for Developers."[85] The battle for the SEIS had been won and signaled a potentially protracted struggle over the adverse environmental impacts of the proposed megamall and the nature of their review. While the "frontloading" dimension of Magellan's SEIS avoidance had failed, it was yet to be seen if its "backloading" effort would render the SEIS itself a mere pro forma exercise.

FIVE

Village Intervenes

ACT learned that the next meeting of the Village Board, on June 29th, would discuss the issue of Moselle Plaza's hookup to Village water and sewer systems. Under Ina Turbell's leadership, a number of ACT activists attended the meeting and were prepared to speak in opposition. ACT's position was that forcing Magellan to design water and sewage treatment facilities of its own on site could present a formidable roadblock to the project. Not only would Magellan have to obtain a special DEC permit approving a wastewater plant,[1] it would have to persuade the new "regulator" majority of the town planning board that these site-specific facilities would not further degrade the adjacent wetlands, streams and aquifer. ACT knew that the Town's only sewage treatment plant in the area, to the north of the Heller property, was already malfunctioning and contributing to eutrophication of the wetlands. ACT was confident that it could demonstrate to "light planners" that further deterioration had occurred since approval of Amsterdam Square and that the flow of additional effluent from the Heller site into the wetlands would further complicate the problem, leading to irreversible damage. In this context, politicizing the water and sewage hook-up issue was essential if ACT was to be successful in confronting the planning board with a "change in circumstances" which would have to be carefully examined in the SEIS. Therefore, while the law defined the relevant area of inquiry, politics would define the legal issues to be resolved.

At the late June meeting, Mayor Patton[2] immediately presented reasons against the hook-up:

> If we [approved the hookup] it would strengthen their position, so I am opposed to Magellan Construction hooking onto Village water and sewer under any circumstance. . . . [The project] would dramatically affect our three existing shopping centers . . . . It would leave this side of the Thruway without a grocery store. I have a vision of people coming off the Thruway, turning left and finding three vacant plazas. That would make a poor impression on tourists, which are a large part of our local economy.[3]

He noted that for the first time in many years, there was no vacancy in downtown stores. After additional critical comments by Turbell, Dreyfus and several other activists and Village Trustees, the Board voted unanimously to deny the hook-ups for Magellan and was roundly applauded by all activists present.

Strategically, it was the first decisive anti-mall decision by any official Ashbury body and ACT hoped that press coverage of the issue would strengthen the resolve of those members of the public and planning board with a "serious planner" perspective. With the imprimatur of local elected officials, ACT could more credibly claim its role as "community defender." It might also now resist those previously reluctant to become associated with a grassroots activist movement denigrated by Ryker and other Town officials as a radical minority without the best interests of the community at heart. Importantly also, ACT was able to expand its political base through alliance with the Downtown Merchants Group, a volunteer organization of over forty separate businesses in the village. For the first time in the struggle, the DMG had undertaken its own lobbying efforts to persuade Village Trustees that the hook-ups were not in their interest because Moselle Plaza's application was an ongoing threat to the viability of village businesses.

Preparing for the Scope

On the heels of the important planning board decision requiring an SEIS, ACT's immediate concern and that of the board was the next stage of the SEQRA process. Specifically, the planning board needed to finalize formally its positive declaration and proceed to define or "scope" out the particular agenda of issues to be researched and addressed in the SEIS.[4] How both processes were carried out would have important implications for the potential depth and breadth of substantive investigation and analysis which the planning board would be willing to undertake. This level of board commitment, in turn, would signal the potential for meaningful public input in critiquing Magellan's plans, as well as the likely duration of overall SEQRA deliberations. As evident from the fate of the previous Amsterdam Square proposal, a lengthy EIS review process might also in the end discourage the developer financially from proceeding.[5]

For these various reasons, the politics which would imbue the language of the positive declaration and define the scope of the SEQRA inquiry were likely to create new flashpoints requiring ACT's intervention, public education, and public participation. For opposite reasons, that is, to prevent significant substantive review, public participation and a lengthy process, the developer and its "light planning" allies on the board wished to obtain the shallowest positive declaration and the narrowest scoping agenda.

On July 1st, just four days after the planning board required (and Reynolds agreed to) preparation of an SEIS, Magellan's attorney Morris Schwab wrote to Rattle (instead of directly to the planning board) to narrow the issues and reduce the impact of the SEIS decision-making process. Attempting to use

Reynolds' concession as the basis for the SEIS agenda, Schwab contended that the limited inquiry for which Reynolds said Magellan Construction would submit data was "agreed to by the Board," thus eliminating the need for any further deliberative process and, in effect, tightening the boundaries of legitimate board review.

Schwab was clearly attempting to ward off, through Rattle's interpretation, the meaning and purpose SEQRA attaches to the scoping process. The *SEQR Handbook* identifies the main objectives of the scoping process and the planning board's responsibility under this process: "[i]dentify the relevant environmental issues and provide the preparers with the specific issues to be addressed; [e]liminate irrelevant issues and de-emphasize nonsignificant issues; [i]dentify the extent and quality of information needed; [i]dentify the range of reasonable alternatives to be discussed; . . . [i]dentify potential areas of mitigation; [and] [i]dentify available sources of information."[6]

Through bypassing the planning board and corresponding directly with its lawyer, Schwab apparently hoped to be able to invoke law's "waiver" and "default" principles[7] to preclude an adequate inquiry to address potential adverse environmental impacts resulting from changed circumstances following Amsterdam Square's approval. His argument was that since the planning board accepted Reynolds's concession for an SEIS, it was also bound by the limited inquiry Reynolds had proposed, and the board could not be now heard to object, having waived or defaulted on its right for a more thorough and searching scope.

In addition, Schwab hoped to persuade the board that public input was unnecessary. Public participation in identifying the extent and quality of information needed in the SEIS could result in a document which not only substantially widened the board's legitimate area of inquiry, but which addressed issues that Reynolds hoped to foreclose in his concession. Thus, Schwab stated that if hook-ups to the Village infrastructure were not available, Magellan would return to the on-site sewage disposal and water supply facilities previously approved for Amsterdam Square, thus eliminating the need for any further inquiry regarding deterioration of the wetlands.

Concerning traffic issues, Schwab contended to Rattle that Magellan would "compile the traffic data and information which has already been presented into one comprehensive report" and seek "review/conceptual approval correspondence" from the DOT. If the latter could not be obtained by Magellan, the board could obtain it itself or could waive this requirement. Magellan had already obtained and passed on to the board in June a one-page internal DOT memo implying conceptual and methodological approval, so this did not seem a formidable task.[8]

With regard to stormwater management, Schwab assured Rattle that

Magellan would demonstrate its ability to comply with the new DEC requirements and guidelines in this realm. Thus, for all three areas of SEIS review, Schwab posed a rapid, pro forma scenario.

As at the previous meeting, Schwab attempted to ally himself with Rattle's interpretation that economics was irrelevant to the SEQRA process and he reiterated Magellan's opposition to "the validity of requiring any further economic analysis" under SEQRA. However, since he acknowledged that the board was ready to commission such a study "whether we feel it is appropriate or not," he stated that Magellan would agree to allow part of its previously-established escrow fund (pursuant to SEQRA for experts retained by the board) to be used for this purpose as well. While his offer conveyed that Magellan was prepared to play a facilitative role and not be obstructionist, the SEQRA statute authorized the planning board to require the applicant to escrow enough funds to cover such expenditures, whether the applicant favored the expenditures or not.[9]

Finally, Schwab attempted to set as quick a timetable for the scoping process as possible. Magellan understood, he said, that the board would review the scoping outline of this letter no later than their next meeting on the 11th and would meet with Magellan on the 18th for finalization. Schwab's timetable obviously would preclude any public participation in the process, because by the time the public had the proposed scoping document in hand, it would not have enough time to consult with independent experts to critique Magellan's agenda.

A letter from Jankoff to Ryker on July 6th attempted to re-establish Magellan's control over the economic analysis now apparently out of its hands, since it was to be prepared by an independent consultant retained by the board. Jankoff first repeated that Magellan Construction "feels it is not warranted under SEQRA to further analyze the economics of this project." He then attempted to use what he hopefully conveyed as Magellan's power over the purse-strings to limit the expenditure made for such an analysis and thereby limit the scope of that inquiry. Jankoff stated that while the Town could use part of Magellan's escrow fund "to review, compare and contrast the economic and fiscal impacts of Moselle Plaza[,] [a]ll we ask is that we receive a copy of the proposal (price) for this report and are given the opportunity to approve the amount spent." In other words, Magellan wanted veto power over the seriousness of a study which the company itself refused to carry out. Such veto power was never intended to be granted developers under the SEQRA regulations, which permit a planning board to assess a commercial developer for up to .5% of project costs for any outside consultant reasonably required to prepare or review an EIS.[10] With an estimated cost of $10 million for Moselle Plaza (indicated in Medford's IDA application), DEC guidelines thus permitted the board to spend and bill Magellan for as much as $50,000 for outside consultants if they so wished.[11] Nevertheless, to the board on July 11th, Rattle added his legal imprimatur to Magellan's veto request.[12]

Scoping Begins

The July 11th meeting of the planning board had to address several immediate items: to finalize the positive declaration requiring an SEIS, to discuss the scoping process and to determine how to proceed with obtaining an outside analysis of economic/fiscal impacts. Each of these concerns was a new arena for conflict.

A positive declaration under SEQRA states the areas of potential significant adverse environmental impact which require EIS investigation[13] and should summarize the issues and rationales identified by the planning board in its prior discussions.[14] By implication, no realm excluded from the positive declaration could later emerge in the scoping agenda as required for discussion in the EIS. Scoping following a positive declaration amplifies the issues contained in the positive declaration and suggests a methodological approach which would provide the board with a satisfactory basis for analysis.

Ryker invited Rattle to set the basic agenda by presenting a draft positive declaration. This initiative sought to control the scope of the positive declaration by delegating it to a professional whose knowledge of law would require deference from "regulator" members who might wish to write their own document. By SEQRA guidelines, the document was to be written by the board and not by the lawyer who served as the board's consultant.[15] While it would be appropriate for the lawyer, in consultation with the board, to craft the board's language to satisfy any legal standard of relevance, SEQRA did not anticipate that the lawyer would define what was relevant, in the first instance.

Of course, the drafting of a positive declaration and the preparation of a scoping agenda require some technical familiarity with the possible adverse environmental impacts raised by an application. Lay members of the board would not normally be expected to articulate their concerns in scientific and engineering discourse. Nor would they be familiar with the meta-language of law which would legitimate the declaration through compliance with SEQRA's statutory wording and whatever gloss the courts attached to the statute through law's interpretive process. Hence, the political will of any majority of planning board members could easily become subordinated by and dependent on professional advice. Statutes such as SEQRA, containing terms subject to interpretation and discretionary application, create further dependency.

Rattle's draft positive declaration identified only three of the realms previously identified by planning board members as relevant to the SEIS-- traffic, stormwater and economics. Missing were any references to water and sewage and the impact that this project might have on the changed conditions of the adjacent wetlands and aquifer. By this time, the planning board and the community were well aware of the Village's rejection of water and sewer hook-ups for Moselle Plaza. Thus, for Rattle to be faithful to the board's earlier discussions, he would have to refer to the need to construct an effluent treatment facility and wells which did not further damage the environment. Instead, like Schwab, Rattle treated this as a non-issue, presuming that the Moselle Plaza project would simply revert to already SEQRA-approved plans for water and wastewater identified in the Amsterdam Square proposal. No mention was made of the deterioration of the wetlands following the acceptance of the earlier proposal and resulting from effluent discharge emitted by the malfunctioning North Creighton sewage treatment plant.

Ina Turbell attempted to raise water and sewage issues at the planning board meeting of the 11th in order to emphasize their importance for the positive declaration. Turbell's problem was gaining public access to the board through registering remarks at the tape-recorded meetings. As concerning earlier issues of conflict of interest, Dreyfus had alerted Turbell and other ACT members that whatever issues were raised would only be preserved for judicial review if they were made part of the record. The record, in turn, consisted of verbal remarks made at the meeting which the planning board was called upon to consider and those issues raised by correspondence and included within the planning board's file on Moselle Plaza.[16]

In this setting, the power of the chair enabled Ryker to control the flow of information. The planning board had no rules regarding public comment and normally the board had met in public but precluded any interaction with the public through comment and discussion. Since some of the members sitting around the table had their backs to the public and others spoke quietly, the public was discouraged from attending. The absence of guaranteed public involvement was a deficiency in the regulatory rules adopted by the DEC because the intent of the statute was to maximize public input so that adverse environmental impacts would not be overlooked or given short shrift.[17] However, the power vacuum created by the regulatory defect could easily be remedied by discretionary planning board rules guaranteeing access through structured public input either at the outset of a meeting or prior to any significant decision-making. By contrast, in the absence of any rules regularizing public involvement and without opposition voiced by members themselves, the chair of the planning board was free to control any agenda by precluding public involvement and delegating the planning voice to "authoritative" professionals with whom he agreed.

Ryker denied Turbell's attempt to present issues of water and sewage to the board by telling her that she was out of order and that the public had no standing at these meetings. For Ryker, while the public could be seen, they were not to be heard. However, knowing of Ryker's predisposition, Turbell succeeded in alerting some board members before the meeting, thereby instigating a board discussion concerning Rattle's narrowing of the positive declaration. The result was rewarding. At the meeting, Julia Bellows specifically raised her concern about additional mall effluent being potentially added to a wetland presently contaminated by illegal effluent from the North Creighton plant. She pointed out that this existing wetland contamination was a change in circumstances from 1990 when Amsterdam Square received SEQRA approval. It thus merited the board's fresh review of potential adverse impacts from an on-site sewage treatment plant. The issue was thereby joined but, typical of Ryker's strategy, was not resolved and would have to be reconsidered again at a subsequent meeting or once again become subordinated to the scoping agenda articulated by Ryker and Rattle.

A discussion of scoping details was also postponed. Before this was done, however, the board briefly discussed the fact that because siting of water and sewage facilities would mean an increase in infrastructure, stormwater management facilities would have a harder time fitting within the increasingly-crowded 21-acre northerly lot zoned for commercial use.

The meeting of July 11th ended with no agreement on final language to be used in the positive declaration.[18] During the one-week interlude between planning board meetings, both Magellan and the community groups actively attempted to affect the content of the positive declaration and subsequent scope. On July 13th, Rattle received a letter from Schwab urging, as Rattle had already recommended to the board, that water and sewer issues be excluded from SEQRA consideration because of the previous approval the board had given to these arrangements for the Amsterdam Square megamall.[19] In the meantime, Turbell and McBride sent to Ryker, with copies to the rest of the board, a draft positive declaration of their own to provide a point-by-point alternative to Rattle's earlier draft, utilizing the meta-languages of law and science to contest the legitimacy of Rattle's points. In the July 14th letter introducing their draft, Turbell and McBride also complained about Ryker's denial of the opportunity for public comment at the meeting of the 11th and what appeared to be Ryker's plan to continue to deny public access at any of the board meetings.[20] In the same letter, they complained that the planning board secretary had refused to provide them with a copy of Rattle's draft positive declaration and that this violated the state Freedom of Information Law. The struggle for access became an ongoing issue for the community groups. Access affected the control of information and thus the method of legitimating one planning perspective or the other.

Concerning stormwater management, the ACT-CLEAR draft positive declaration emphasized that the new DEC requirements on quantity and quality of stormwater release would necessitate larger detention basins than those designed for Amsterdam Square. Additionally, Moselle Plaza's parking area, 20% larger than that for Amsterdam Square, would significantly add to the quantity of salt and vehicle oil-products in stormwater runoff before reaching the basins. Without adequate treatment facilities, polluted stormwater would be released into the groundwater, downstream surface waters and an aquifer underlying the site. The need for extensive detention ponds, in turn, would also risk disturbing and transferring toxic pesticide-laden soils--already abundant in this former orchard site--into groundwater, surface waters and the aquifer. Furthermore, the need for larger ponds would force construction in the southerly light industrial-zoned lot which was prohibited by zoning and which also had on-site wetlands and flooding constraints of its own.

Concerning sewage issues, Turbell and McBride pointed out that a March 25, 1994 letter from a DEC engineer to Supervisor Schmidt documented that the Town's North Creighton sewage plant produced poor effluent quality and was in a state of continuing permit violations. Since the Amsterdam Square EIS assumed that this facility met water quality standards, a new study would now be needed to measure the cumulative impact on the adjacent Roodekill wetlands of the proposed Moselle Plaza plant and the defective one on North Creighton Road.

With regard to water, the ACT/CLEAR document contrasted Moselle Plaza's location of wells in the northerly commercial lot with Amsterdam Square's well sites far to the south. Water drawn from the former source was not yet demonstrated to be uncontaminated, testing might show the need for substantial treatment to remove salt, and the construction of wells could potentially cause pesticide residues to be sucked into the groundwater and aquifer through the process of pumping, thus perhaps adversely affecting the quantity and quality of water for neighbors.

Potential significant new traffic impacts, said Turbell and McBride, could be expected due to more parking spaces and expected site-generated traffic compared with Amsterdam Square; additional cumulative background traffic because of approved and currently-considered major development projects in the towns of Ashbury and Acton; and expected new levels of congestion to be caused by bridge and road expansion over the Thruway in 1995.

As for economic and fiscal effects, they said, primary new major potential impacts (since Amsterdam Square's SEQRA approval) would derive from the planned department anchor store's identification as a <u>discount</u> department store, significant new information and analysis concerning economic and fiscal impacts of such stores on rural small-town communities, the 20% increase in store size compared to Amsterdam Square and the significant downturn of the

Hudson Valley economy since 1990. Turbell and McBride contended that the large discount department store in Moselle Plaza was likely to cause significant deterioration of existing retail businesses, especially in several uptown plazas and in the downtown of Ashbury. They also pointed to likely major secondary negative impacts on the tourist trade, local banks and insurance companies.

The fiscal balance of Ashbury would be adversely affected by potential reduction of the local tax base caused from lower assessments for commercial and residential properties negatively impacted by the new mall. They also contended that there would be significant new spending for fire and police services at the new mall and ghettoized older malls. Costly new public programs to revitalize deteriorated commercial areas of the village and town would be required. At the same time, potential tax revenues from the new mall would be reduced through various tax incentive programs available to owners of the new plaza. McBride and Turbell argued that the negative economic impact would also adversely affect community character, itself a cognizable environmental issue under SEQRA.[21] The new mall, they contended, would create urban blight and damage the rural small-town atmosphere of Ashbury.

McBride and Turbell were concerned that on July 18th the board would adopt a positive declaration and then move immediately to determine the more detailed scope of the SEIS. They feared that the "regulator" majority would be unable to engage Busch or Rattle in a discourse dominated by scientism and legalism. To level the playing field and to empower the new majority, they submitted detailed documentation regarding the effluent and water issues which their draft positive declaration identified, but which they knew would be contested.

On July 18th, Ryker instructed the planning board first to consider a draft scoping document prepared by Gene Busch and handed out on this occasion for the first time. While Busch's action confirmed McBride's and Turbell's fears regarding the board's finalizing the scope before adequate discussion and information, it also demonstrated how the minority, through the chair, could control the discourse and ultimately tailor whatever decision the board reached to satisfy the "light planning" perspective. Although Rattle's draft positive declaration had been contested by the majority on the meeting of the 11th, thus implying the need for a new draft, Rattle failed to provide a revision before the board considered how to scope the issues raised by that document. Instead, following the lead of Rattle's positive declaration draft of the week before, Busch excluded any discussion of water and sewer issues. As before, Julia Bellows recommended that cumulative impact be studied for the combined Moselle Plaza sewage plant effluent and the substandard wastewater from the North Creighton plant. While Maglie attempted to minimize the significance of this issue, Pelletier and Dalrymple agreed with Bellows. Conciliatory in the face of these stubborn assertions, Busch now reaffirmed Bellows' concerns. In turn, Maglie conceded that the current validity or not of Amsterdam Square's four-year projections are "what we need to find out."

After briefly outlining potential traffic issues, Busch continued with his draft section on economic impacts. In this realm, he suggested that the board should use current data, consider changes in the local economy (such as the impact of IBM layoffs), and look at the effect of the proposed project--especially of stores like Wal-Mart or Kmart--on existing local businesses.

In Rattle's view, Busch conceded too much:

> I think one thing that this board is losing sight of is before you can require the SEIS and something to be reviewed, you have to identify the possibility or the probability that there is an adverse impact. This document is not to go on a fishing expedition to look for one. And if you can't find one . . . then it shouldn't be addressed. The potential for a significant adverse impact due to a project change or a change of circumstances must be identified first and then you look into it to see how significant it is and what can be done about it.

Taking Rattle's warning as his own cue, Magellan's attorney Schwab repeated once again his objection to a required economic analysis generally.

Without further discussion, the board minority moved to accept the positive declaration, and, despite the majority's position verbalized at the meeting of July 11th, the board voted unanimously to accept Rattle's draft of that resolution without reviewing the document to determine whether it had been amended to consider the impact of further sewage effluent and the siting of wells on the northerly portion of the Heller parcel. While Rattle had altered some language of the earlier draft, the new positive declaration was carefully worded to omit any reference to water and sewage issues to be addressed. The alliance of Ryker and Rattle, combined with the majority's inability to closely scrutinize the process, allowed "light planners" to significantly narrow the SEIS agenda.

One section of the resolution and positive declaration was devoted to "stormwater management and erosion control/water quality," but there was no section explicitly outlining well water and sewage treatment issues. Within the positive declaration itself, was the short phrase: "The existing quality of the receiving [wetlands] waters [for treated stormwater] as well as any changes in such quality since 1989/1990 needs to be determined and evaluated." Rattle's artfully ambiguous wording could be construed as having incorporated the concerns of the majority for the deteriorating condition of the wetlands, without conceding that the issue was effluent-related or that the wetlands could be adversely impacted by another sewage treatment plant. Nevertheless, despite the narrowing of the SEIS agenda, this single sentence, in the eyes of the community groups, offered now the only potential basis, however slim, for legally requiring through the scoping process that the SEIS examine the current effluent output of the North Creighton sewage plant--a significant substantive and potentially costly study.

The method of obtaining traffic and economic data, while not surprising, significantly departed from the intent and letter of the SEQRA statute and regulations permitting and encouraging that the public be provided the opportunity to submit relevant data for each scoping realm. Regarding traffic, the resolution authorizing the positive declaration implied that new data would be sought only from DOT, the Thruway Authority and the County Department of Public Works. Solicitation of this official input, rather than further data and analysis from the developer, was the scenario Magellan had requested in its July 1st letter to Rattle.

Also at this meeting, Julia Bellows informed the board that she had contacted potential economic consultants and had requested that they be prepared to complete a study by the end of August.[22] Thereafter Ryker again predicted that the SEIS process would be completed in short order--revising his end date now to the end of September.[23] Community groups, however, were guardedly more optimistic that a thorough process would occur. If it did, such a process would require many months for review and analysis of the issues.

ACT and CLEAR activists were especially frustrated to view this flawed process in forced silence from the audience when they had tried formally and informally to inform the "regulator" majority about crucial issues. This epistemological disparity between ACT/ CLEAR and unfocused "regulator" board members was unfortunately to occur repeatedly as the SEQRA process unfolded. Despite Ryker's confrontational, provocative method, bullied by Rattle's narrow but apparently authoritative citations of "the law" and without having informed themselves of relevant facts and their relationship to the SEQRA process, "regulators" were constantly defending against implicit accusations from "light planners" of disrupting genial consensus. Less experienced with and motivated about methodical details of SEQRA process and uncoordinated among themselves, by comparison with those members who favored the project and their lawyer and planner allies, the "regulator" majority was able to be manipulated into accepting formal statements that contradicted its own views. For all of the issues, attention now shifted to the next draft of the scoping document and whether "regulator" members would be prepared to take a strong stand when that document was reviewed at the next meeting.

Further Manipulations

At the August 8th meeting in a crowded office at the back of Town Hall, all seven members of the board were present but Rattle was not. Busch presented a new draft scoping document responding to members' comments of July 18th and, once again, the controversy about the North Creighton sewage plant reappeared. Eventually Busch agreed to make most changes requested by Bellows and Hillman, including reference to the planned waste management system and its relationship to the Town's North Creighton plant and further degradation of the wetlands. He agreed to send this next scoping draft back down to the board the next day by fax. Ryker asked that the board secretary, Judy Laporte, then send copies to each board member. A copy also would be given to Rattle who would in turn, following SEQRA guidelines, distribute the draft to all involved agencies for potential comments and to Magellan. Rattle's previous efforts to solicit comments from involved agencies on the scoping agenda had yielded nothing of value. Because of this, the "regulator" majority insisted that special appeals for comments be made--even by phone to more important agencies such as the DEC, DOT, Thruway Agency and Army Corps of Engineers, since their expertise might help to refine the scope and add to specific issues mentioned by the board. "Direct call," confirmed Ryker. To secretary Laporte he added, "You and I can work that out. Just remind me with a big note, as opposed to all the small notes." This new agency comment period would be left open for a month until several days before the next workshop meeting on September 12th.

On August 9th, Busch faxed the new scoping draft to the planning board office, including explicit reference to the need to study effluent quality from the North Creighton sewage plant. Laporte was then supposed to send the document to Rattle who, in turn, was to transmit it to all of the involved agencies with a covering letter asking for additional comments. Ryker would subsequently call each agency to assure solicitation of each agency's views. Whatever the plan, once Busch's new scoping draft arrived at the planning board, it simply was not distributed, thus undermining the possibility, hoped for by the "regulator" majority, that at least some comments would be received by the meeting of September 12th when the board would finalize the SEIS scoping agenda.

Changing Board Membership

In early August, ACT and CLEAR activists were stunned by news that Julia Bellows, the newest board member, was about to resign because of a job reassignment to Connecticut. While sometimes disappointed in her seemingly too cautious efforts to develop "consensus," community activists viewed her as an articulate and well-organized critical presence--in effect the additional weight and glue which allowed the "regulator" majority's first challenge to "light planner" domination of the board. Her leadership in gaining the SEQRA positive declaration and her occasional stubborn assertiveness gave hope that ultimately the mall project might be disapproved.[24] At the news of her impending resignation, activists' sense of momentum was lost. Once again, the Town Board would have to appoint a new member of the planning board. With the high stakes raised by Moselle Plaza, further politicization of the review process was likely.

This became evident when the board discussed Bellows' replacement on August 8th. Over the years, the "light planners'" perspective was able to dominate the board by appointment of like-minded individuals oftentimes politically associated with the chair. The interview process had devolved to the planning board which would then make its recommendation known to the Town Board. The Town Board, in turn, would interview applicants and normally act to confirm the planning board's recommendation. While the Town Board's rubber-stamp role began to break down in the recent past, leading to the appointment of Bellows, Pelletier and Hillman, those of the "light planning" perspective, concerned that their power was beginning to wane, hoped to reassert control through the alliance of Ryker and Schmidt and the Town Board's liaison to the planning board, Gertrude Kraft, a Republican hostile to "regulator" views.

Ryker had opposed Bellows in the Spring when he sought to secure board appointment for Sam Myers, a former social studies schoolteacher now employed by a real estate management firm. Myers was known to Ryker personally to have a "light planner" orientation compatible with his own. Moreover, Myers, like Bellows, was articulate and able to use rhetorical flourishes to marginalize his opponents. This, then, was Ryker's opportunity to redress the wrong and to re-secure "light planner" majority control over the board. When Pelletier pointed out that current Town policy for planning board vacancies was to announce them publicly and seek applications, Ryker replied, "We did that 6 months ago." Pelletier, fully aware of Ryker's intent to regain control of the board, responded, "I think we should do that again." Hillman, Dalrymple and Bellows backed her position. Replied Ryker, "If the Town Board says to do it, then we'll do it . . . . My personal feeling was that we interviewed a bunch of candidates . . . they showed interest . . . all of a sudden we have some other people that are interested? . . . It's up to the Town Board." Pelletier added, "I like a democratic process." Supposedly in jest but with bad portent, conservative Gertrude Kraft replied, "I like a Republican process too."[25]

A few days later, Kraft told the Town Board that the planning board wanted Myers to be appointed. While this assertion directly contradicted the views of the planning board majority (Kraft claimed later it was simply a "half-truth" since Ryker, the planning board chair, favored Myers), it was a necessary manipulation to secure a "light planner" majority. With a three-person Town

Board Republican majority (Schmidt, Kraft and Mosher) already committed to a closed process which would ratify Sam Myers's appointment and with Citizen Party board member Lyon absent from the meeting, only Democrat Edna Devilla could potentially have insisted on an open application process. Devilla, however, was more often than not the political ally of Schmidt and Kraft and a supporter of Ryker. When Schmidt moved to appoint Myers, Devilla voted "yes," rendering the Town Board's decision unanimous.

This vote was particularly galling to ACT and CLEAR. Whatever arguments could now be mustered in response to Magellan's SEIS would be viewed through the lens of a majority apparently predisposed in favor of the mall, thus stacking the decision-making process against a critical analysis of adverse environmental impacts and proposed mitigation.

The Final Scoping Decision

At the September 12th meeting, Ryker appeared once again in thorough command. Myers' presence confirmed the newly-constituted "light planning" majority. No one from the previous "regulator" majority inquired about involved agency responses to Busch's final scoping draft which stated understandings reached at the August 8th planning board meeting.[26] Remaining "regulator" members were not nearly as articulate as Julia Bellows and had shown, to that date, little inclination to organize themselves enough to assure that the process would reflect their views. This was the perfect context for Ryker to act as intimidator and, with Rattle's assistance, to legitimate every decision as "merely following the letter of the law."

On September 16th, Morris Schwab wrote Rattle to remind him of his written promise of August 2nd that Magellan would receive the board's final scoping document for review no later than August 15th. Having received nothing, because Busch's final draft was not transmitted, Schwab proceeded under a theory of legal estoppel[27] to assert that the board had defaulted in its obligation to Magellan and involved agencies and that it was now bound by the first scoping draft of July 18th, which omitted any reference to study wetland degradation by the Town's North Creighton treatment plant. Citing SEQRA regulations which gave the planning board only 30 days to prepare a final scope following adoption of the positive declaration, Schwab declared Busch's draft scope of July 18th as "the official, final scoping outline" which Magellan would rely upon in preparing the SEIS. Thus, Magellan would submit its Draft SEIS (DSEIS) concerning stormwater and traffic issues on the basis of a narrower environmental agenda instead of that in the board's revised scope. Since Rattle never responded to Schwab's contentions, Magellan asserted that the board was now precluded from inquiring into the condition of the wetlands subsequent to the approval of Amsterdam Square's FEIS. In turn, this omission would foreclose discussion of the further adverse environmental impact which effluent from Magellan's sewage treatment plant would have on existing deteriorated conditions.

It was clear that the planning board had failed to transmit the final scoping draft of August 8th to either Magellan or any of the involved agencies. As well, whether or not secretary Laporte had given Ryker a "big note" as a reminder, the chair had not sought fit to speak with any of the involved agencies. The entire process in which the "regulator" majority had revised Busch's original draft scope of July 18th was wasted. There now seemed no legal basis to study wetland eutrophication and effluent from the North Creighton sewage plant, important elements for assessing Moselle Plaza's potential negative effect. Though county planner Henry Fowler had earlier told the board of his interest in responding to their draft scope, neither he nor any of the agency experts who could have helped focus and refine the scoping agenda in any realm, as SEQRA regulations and the *Handbook* urged,[28] contributed to the process.

Surprised that no agency had responded to their mid-August request, at the September 26th board meeting, Pelletier and Hillman questioned whether a scoping letter had even been sent to outside agencies as intended and pointed out that the planning board's secretary had no copy of such a document. Throughout a lengthy and confusing exchange with Hillman, Rattle claimed innocence and asserted that he did invite scoping comments.[29] The disempowerment of the board's August "regulator" majority in this matter was now complete.

SIX   COMPLETENESS

DSEIS

Magellan Construction presented the Draft SEIS (DSEIS) to the board at its September 26, 1994 meeting. The document was consistent with Schwab's pre-scoping letter of July 1st indicating that little if any additional information would be needed beyond that provided for the Amsterdam Square project in 1990. Moreover, the DSEIS omitted any analysis of the condition of the wetlands to be impacted by Magellan's proposed sewage treatment plant, and it disregarded the planning board's August 9th scoping instructions. The DSEIS did not include the required study of effluent produced by the North Creighton sewage treatment plant, its effect on the wetlands, and the effect of additional effluent produced by Moselle Plaza. The two sections in the DSEIS--on traffic and stormwater--added little to existing data already on file with the board.

The materials comprising the DSEIS were little more than pro forma compliance with SEQRA's requirement for greater information. In actuality, the quality and quantity of the data represented Magellan's desire to speed the process along as quickly as possible.[1] It directly challenged the board. Prove to us, it said, that you are informed enough to demand more than symbolic gestures of compliance with SEQRA. Except for Ben Hillman, employed by the Department of Transportation (DOT) in New York City and with some background in professional planning, lay members of the board were in no position to critique Magellan's "expert" conclusions. Thus, Magellan might justifiably expect relatively quick formal acceptance of the DSEIS as "complete" for public comment.

With regard to traffic, 40 pages of prose and 132 pages of charts and tables in the DSEIS reassembled the data and analysis already transmitted to the board through various documents earlier. In that Spring 1994 phase, Magellan had attempted to ward off an SEIS through assurance that any traffic increase generated would be minimal and mitigated. All the DSEIS added was a one-paragraph introduction and a table of contents. The developer's traffic consultant[2] certified, as it had earlier, with "considered professional opinion . . . that with the completion of the improvements identified above, that safe and efficient operating conditions will exist on area roadways after the construction of the proposed Moselle Plaza shopping center."

While the technical format and language of Magellan's traffic submission had the veneer of authoritative scientific rationality, it was not easilyaccessible to board review. Basic data consisted of raw traffic counts conducted by the developer's engineer at intersections near the project site at supposed "worst case" or "peak hour" conditions,[3] funneled through a computer program utilizing standard formulas based mainly on numbers and directions of lanes, lane widths, posted speed limit and, when applicable, traffic signals. Basic data outcomes were defined in terms of expected "levels of service" of traffic flow for each lane, from A to F, based on standard professional traffic engineer methodology. "Before build" or background levels of service were then compared with "after build" levels to assess expected traffic impacts of the project at each location analyzed. Even with best intentions, lay members lacking independent traffic counts and access to computerized formulas for verification were in no position to challenge the actual outcome numbers stated by the developer's engineer and then translated into levels-of-service grades.

Magellan's traffic data could be compared independently, however, with DOT's periodic traffic counts on state roads. The board could also commission independent traffic studies to obtain their own raw data and to determine whether contradictions existed within the developer's analyses which undermined the conclusions. But a lay board unschooled in the scientism of traffic and legal discourse is hardly in a position to determine whether such an allocation of resources is necessary or whether Magellan's data could be relied upon in good faith. While thus potentially subject to scientific standards of cross-checking and replicability, when confronted by developer resources, it was improbable that the planning board could begin to penetrate Magellan's thicket of technological data and formulas, let alone have the initiative to pay for an independent traffic engineer to do the same.

In most cases, only the DOT might be capable of or likely to challenge a traffic analysis from a stance of self-confident professional equality. However, the DOT's June 1994 internal memo obtained by Magellan showed that this agency, like most state bureaucracies, was reluctant to involve itself in critical analysis during early stages of lead agency SEQRA review. Probably because of some traditional anti-SEQRA bias, a pro-development self-mission, bureaucratic compartmentalization, and limited resources, by September 1994 the DOT had only briefly and superficially reviewed Magellan's traffic studies, and then apparently mainly in terms of the quantity, rather than the quality, of data submitted. At best, the DOT would eventually examine traffic impacts more thoroughly in site plan review when Magellan applied for a DOT permit. But at the permitting stage, DOT, like most involved agencies, would be unlikely on its own to halt such a project if a community had found that environmental harm had been mitigated sufficiently to warrant SEQRA approval.

Magellan counted on the same absence of scientific peer review concerning the major impact area of stormwater management. In his July 1st letter to

Rattle, Schwab stated that the DSEIS would:

> thoroughly discuss our ability to comply with the new Department of Environmental Conservation (DEC) stormwater regulations including demonstration of ability to manage stormwater runoff on-site in a manner permitted by the new regulations and/or guidelines.

In addition, the board's original late July scoping draft, the only scoping agenda Magellan felt legally bound to follow, asked for analysis of the project-specific and cumulative effects of stormwater on on-site and off-site state and federal wetlands. However, while providing new details on its on-site stormwater management plans, Magellan Construction's engineers[4] offered no analysis of stormwater impacts of the project individually or cumulatively on the wetlands. As with the traffic analysis, the DSEIS also offered no alternative (potentially mitigating) development scenario, such as a downsized project, as required under SEQRA.[5]

The DSEIS did not even mention the existence of potentially-impacted state-designated wetlands to the east of the project.[6] It only acknowledged an "unclassified wet area east of South Creighton Road." For an "analysis" of the status of this "wet area," the document merely offered the assessment that "the receiving streams and waters of New York State are in eutrophic or nutrient rich conditions in the vicinity," without examining the extent of those negative conditions and the cumulative adverse impact of additional stormwater. As for the small on-site wetland of about one acre, seemingly protected under federal law[7], the DSEIS assured that the project will utilize its stormwater cleansing capacities "in the same manner as it functions currently."[8] In addition, the document concluded, the project "will further enhance this wetland area by replacing upland areas surrounding a portion of the wetland and allowing them to re-establish with wetland vegetation." Beyond these brief conclusions, the DSEIS assured the board that state and federal standards would have to be met for any DEC or Army Corps of Engineers permits. By implication, therefore, Magellan concluded that no further SEQRA review of wetland impacts would be appropriate and, as with traffic, all would be dealt with at the "permitting stage."

Similar to Magellan's traffic analysis, scientific and reassuring prose provided a benign interpretive gloss for the lengthy pages of engineer's raw data on drainage conditions. For the lay reader, the latter was totally inaccessible and unchallengeable. But even the prose interpretation was so immersed in specialized conceptual and technical engineering language that all but the most dedicated lay member readers would be discouraged from even attempting to understand it. Between the impenetrability of Magellan's data and the report's assurance that permitting agencies would review everything, board members could easily rationalize distancing themselves from responsibility for any real scrutiny of environmental impact. Furthermore, while the planning board would be able to consult about stormwater drainage with its own engineer, Tony Napoleon, there was no likelihood that the board would have a consultant specializing in stormwater and wetland impact.

The third area of DSEIS discussion required by the formal scope concerned economic and fiscal impacts of Moselle Plaza. Magellan Construction had objected from the beginning to including this realm as a legitimate SEQRA concern. However, so as not to delay the overall process further nor needlessly antagonize members of the board, the company had agreed to use the escrow fund to cover costs for an independent consultant to be hired by the board itself. By the September 26th meeting, the board had received five bids for this service, all from firms outside Forest County, though all but one from the lower Hudson Valley.

Busch was apparently unfamiliar with any of the firms or their previous consulting projects. In actuality, the backgrounds of the two firms favored by board members seemed quite comparable. Stuart Turner and Renwick Brothers had each conducted environmental and economic/fiscal studies for many major commercial, industrial and residential projects in the Hudson Valley, on behalf of municipalities and developers alike.[9] At the same time, none of their listed studies were on behalf of community groups who sought to challenge development based on adverse environmental and economic impacts. Renwick Brothers proposed to subcontract the economic impact analysis to Brian Marvell & Associates, Inc. Marvell at the time was chief economist for a SUNY center for policy analysis and had carried out a wide range of project analyses and economic/fiscal policy studies for government agencies, municipalities and private developers, especially in the western part of the state. His specific resume, as well, mentioned no studies on behalf of community groups opposing megamall development.

At the meeting of September 26th, the board voted for Renwick Brothers-Marvell three votes to one. A meeting with these consultants was arranged for October 13th to review their proposal and to communicate the board's scoping agenda for economic issues. Attorney Rattle once again sought to exclude analysis of any potential economic harm to local businesses and thus, indirectly, to the town through the loss of tax revenue. While such data are relevant under SEQRA in balancing environmental harm against social and economic concerns, Rattle sought to deflect the inquiry by restricting analysis to matters solely environmental, i.e., impact on community character and population. Rattle contended that the study should include only:

> [an] economic review of community character and population character, not to go off into never-never land, as some of them might tend to do. . . . There are only two legitimate things that can be

reviewed under SEQRA as economic: one is what is the development going to do to the character of the neighborhood and what's it going to do regarding the population of the area . . . . Things about general trends, I don't know. Unless they affect one of these two things, these people should not be [doing it].[10]

On October 13th, board members met with the Renwick Brothers executive vice-president, another firm associate and Marvell, as well as Reynolds and Jankoff from Magellan Construction. The presence of the latter two implied that Ryker was acting on Rattle's earlier suggestion that Magellan should have veto power over any independent consultant hired by the board. Indeed, Reynolds, hovering over the others in the tight confines of the planning board office, was an integral part of the dialogue and made a point of impressing Renwick Brothers officials and Marvell with the importance of his company as a potential employer. He contended that Magellan was the largest developer in New York state outside of New York City and that it was currently constructing six other shopping centers at that moment. By not too subtle implication, Magellan was informing Marvell that their paths might well cross again in the future.

When the issue was raised as to the analytical relevance of identifying the department store anchor, Reynolds claimed that Magellan still didn't know the future tenant. "If I knew, I would tell you," he said.[11] He also stated that their main motivation was to allow FoodFeast to move to an expanded facility as soon as possible. The other anchor would not be a "mega-store" and in any case a Wal-Mart was not necessarily worse than a Caldor in impact. He repeated Rattle's warning that the analysis must stay within the confines of SEQRA.

Later in the discussion, the Renwick Brothers vice-president and Marvell agreed to conduct the fiscal impact part of this analysis on the basis of the project's full property assessment value. In doing so, they failed to acknowledge that projected property-tax revenue figures would thus be misleading, since Magellan would seek abatements through IDA (Industrial Development Agency) financing or the 485-B program.[12] Also unmentioned was the IDA sales tax exemption for construction costs for such projects, government-financed with low-interest bonds. The consultants agreed to submit a draft report by early December and, with no objection from Reynolds, the board agreed to their employment. Ryker signed an agreement four days later.

Process Critiques

On October 14th, Alex McBride of CLEAR and Jerry Killington, vice-president of ACT, wrote to the planning board criticizing a statement by Ryker two weeks earlier to the press that the planning board (i.e., public funds) would pick up any tab for an economic analyst beyond the $10,000 maximum which Magellan said it would pay.[13] McBride and Killington stated that this was totally inappropriate since taxpayers would thereby subsidize a developer and a $10,000 cap would potentially restrict the board from gaining important and appropriate in-depth followup studies in response to comments on the DSEIS.

Moreover, the letter criticized the apparent conflict of interest and resulting bias on the part of Frank Rattle, the board's reviewing attorney for this project. They cited the scoping document fiasco as underlining "the importance for the Board of receiving sufficient and timely legal advice to assure a level playing field for all parties concerned." They pointed out that Rattle recently had represented the Cairo Corporation, developers of a new Kmart megastore in nearby Regent Park. Given that Magellan had not publically excluded Kmart as the potential anchor discount department store tenant for Moselle Plaza, Rattle should recuse himself until such information could be provided.

Again, such a letter was sent to establish a clear record of SEQRA and non-SEQRA procedural violations since a "light planning" majority was apparently back in control and the matter was likely to end up in the courts. While they had little hope that the letter itself would change views of the "light planning" majority and while they knew that courts deferred to the substantive expertise of a lead agency, an attack based on a claim of unfair process, stemming from bias and conflict of interest, might well prevail.

FoodFeast on the Defense

Beyond confronting the legal process of the board to assure proper SEQRA review, beginning in the summer of 1994, Ashbury Community Together moved more vigorously toward consolidating its base of support and reaching further outward to non-members who opposed Moselle Plaza on substantive grounds. The goal was to mobilize greater explicit public opposition and thereby move the Moselle Plaza decision from the formal procedural realm to that of explicit politics and substance. Under the reign of legal liberalism whatever substantive conclusions the planning board agreed upon would likely withstand the judicial "hard look" standard of a fair and reasoned decision-making process, given the cover supplied by Magellan's paperwork, provided the board complied with SEQRA's minimal procedural requirements. But substantive conclusions might still depend upon a voting majority of lay people who were not immune from the politics of the community.

Letter-writing to the local press thus remained a high priority both to introduce ACT and to effectively explain and politicize the issues. For example, Fran Killington's letter to FoodFeast, printed in the *Tribune* of July 21st, repeated critiques of the mall and criticized FoodFeast's in-store shopper petition campaign which favored the project and offered only two over-simplified choices: no upgrade of the existing store or Moselle Plaza. "The citizens of Ashbury are smarter than that," she said. FoodFeast should instead consider expanding at its present site or another location west of the Thruway and without Wal-Mart. Killington's theme of possible alternatives, coupled with the characterization of Ashbury as a "small town of stubborn individualists," sought to encourage the new emerging anti-mall "populist alliance" between small business people and those with "regulator" or "ecologist" views from professional, counter-cultural and other non-business backgrounds.

At the end of the summer, ACT urged members and others to send pre-printed postcards to Medford's management, emphasizing the alternatives mentioned by Killington and calling for a mutually satisfactory resolution between the town and FoodFeast, without Moselle Plaza. Paul Halpern, president and chief operating officer of Medford, responded defiantly to the press. He said, "We're committed to the new mall. . . . We've already signed the contracts." He questioned the "community" nature of ACT since "We've been told this effort was initiated by a group of shopowners who made these cards available to their customers."[14] But Medford executives were apparently confused about whether their "enemy" was economic, cultural, or political since, at about this same time, one of them privately told a local journalist, "You people in Ashbury are just a bunch of old hippies who would oppose anything like this."[15]

To stop the public relations erosion, Halpern sent separate letters to each postcard writer[16] claiming that no alternatives existed[17] and that customers would only benefit from expanded grocery offerings. Halpern also presented a seemingly more reasonable rationalization. He specifically claimed that local authorities had told FoodFeast in 1985 that worsening traffic on Main Street would require expansion east of the Thruway instead.

For numerous reasons, Halpern's letter was hardly a public relations coup. Its reference to a "thoughtfully-designed, neighborhood-style shopping center" sought to de-politicize the image of standard big-box Wal-Mart centers, but only insulted its readers. FoodFeast's claimed sensitivity to concerns about traffic congestion omitted reference to the major additional traffic impact to be caused by Wal-Mart alone. Reference to many additional categories of potential retail products re-enforced fears that FoodFeast and the plaza generally would eat up existing retail facilities. Finally, the claim that "local authorities" discouraged earlier efforts to expand on site backfired, with Town Board denials, and resulted in further politicizing the issue of who was responsible for "malling" Ashbury.

The Local Media

During the Fall months of 1994, ACT continued to speak with local newspaper reporters to educate them regarding the reasons for opposing Moselle Plaza. This began to bear fruit through an increase in coverage and more favorable tone of articles. For months the *Tribune* had run basically uncritical reports about Moselle Plaza and the planning board process.

In the October 20th issue of the *Tribune*, however, editor George Worthy committed the paper to opposing Moselle Plaza.[18] The editorial entitled "Developmentally Disabled" stated:

> To set the record straight, most of us here at the *Tribune* think the whole project stinks. In fact, if the Ashbury planning board approves this commercial atrocity, we all might as well pack our bags and leave town. Who wants to stick around and watch visionless cretins destroy our community parcel by parcel.

After deflating the developer's promise of major tax relief, Worthy concluded, "let's not be wooed by sleazy developers promising us the moon when we know that we are going to be the ones left with the bill." Not only was Worthy's support a welcome boost to ACT and CLEAR, the language of the editorial further politicized the struggle and focused the community on the planning board's SEQRA decision as the key to whether Moselle Plaza would be built. This was a portent of continuing *Tribune* support for the duration of the struggle and an assurance that ACT's and CLEAR's efforts would be publicized as much as the actions of the "light planning" majority.

Potentially as significant as the *Tribune*'s position was the fact that the owner-publisher of the rival weekly *Ashbury Chronicle*, Burt Tompkins, a small-government populist who frequently voiced anti-regulatory themes, had already published one editorial and would write two more in the Fall of 1994 against Moselle Plaza. With a more traditional readership of longtime area residents receptive to conservative Republican ideology, compared to the somewhat more liberal and "counter-cultural" interests of the newer *Tribune*, the *Ashbury Chronicle* in the past had sometimes strongly editorialized against CLEAR. On the other hand, Tompkins had once listed CLEAR's co-chair Alex McBride as one of his local "people of the decade" and had praised him and others for "awakening Ashbury residents to the dangers that growth can cause."[19] Despite his unpredictability, Tompkins was a staunch advocate of anything to reduce the burden on local taxpayers. It was this concern, more than anything else, which turned him against the new project. Moreover, Tompkins' support demonstrated the growing community alliance against Moselle Plaza, ranging from "pragmatic capitalist" to "ecologist" residents. It was only such an alliance which could begin to isolate the Ryker-Rattle consensus from the body of the community and have an impact on the planning board's decision-making process.

Another media episode in this period well dramatized the issues and public dynamics of the struggle. On an October 4th hour-long call-in radio talk show from the SUNY/Ashbury campus FM station, Rocky Ryker and Ina Turbell were interviewed side-by-side. Responding to Turbell's explanation of environmental and economic issues from ACT's perspective, Ryker initially moved from his original stance as a neutral planning board administrator to an outright advocate of the mall.

In his usual pugnacious style, Ryker early on repeated Magellan's incredulous assertion about the identity of the anchor department store: "Who that is, what store that will be, is anybody's guess at this time. The developer has said that they are negotiating with many stores, and it is very early in the process at this time."[20] Furthermore, though Ryker had flatly asserted months earlier that no economic impact review was needed, he now sought to deflate critiques of Wal-Mart by appealing, in almost post-modern rhetoric, to the ideology of progress:

> We have no idea what the impact will be, and nobody does. Anybody who says that they do is trying to read their future. . . . [I]f you look at a sunset, you might see a beautiful sunset. If I look at a sunset, I might see something really ugly, really horrible looking. It is possible. If it is one of the super stores, there are many possible impacts, some of them good, some of them bad. You might look at something and say it is good; I might say it is bad, or vice versa. It is up to the community to make a success of the community. It is not one store; it is not one person; it is not one organization.

To marginalize ACT and CLEAR and those who opposed the project, Ryker addressed the specific reputation of Wal-Mart which he attributed to critics of the free market:

> . . . [O]pponents of growth and development are using the fear tactic of the name Wal-Mart or the super store in much the same way that people are using a button-pushing name like a super-dump or a mega-dump to scare people. And Wal-Mart has come into other communities with positive and negative results, and they are using--some people and some organizations are using that same type of scare tactic to underline the end result of what they want, which is no growth. That's just one person's opinion. . . .[W]hether or not it is Wal-Mart, Kmart or SUNY Mart doesn't really matter. If you are a bad business person, you're not going to survive, and if you are a good business person, you will.

Turbell responded that this laissez-faire philosophy, relying totally on market self-regulation, strongly contradicted the expressed intent of the Town's Comprehensive Plan to protect, through governmental intervention, the future character of the community and the economic vitality of the business sector. Ryker's philosophy, she contended, also contradicted the specific role of the planning board to uphold its legal responsibilities. Ryker then proceeded to characterize himself again as a humble public servant and upholder of law and order without the partisan perspective of a pro-development ideologue:

> I give hundreds of hours of my time, and the planning board members do. We don't all agree on anything, but we do it because we believe in the community of Ashbury, and we work very hard, and we do the best we can. And if certain people and certain groups don't like it, I am still going to do it the way I see it. I follow the law, I follow the oath I took to serve the best interest of health of the community and welfare of the community of Ashbury, and I will continue to do so until I am either replaced or removed.

He later added a touch of Darwinist inevitability in which he identified himself with the "guiding hand" of progress:

> . . . [I]f it wasn't progress for a community to grow, if a community is not allowed to breathe and find its own identity and change its identity as time goes on, then that community will really wither up and die.[21]

Ryker's responses to Turbell, couched as they were in homilies, were strikingly devoid of specific data to substantiate Magellan's contention that whatever adverse environmental impacts might occur from building Moselle Plaza would be outweighed by specific social and economic benefits. In the absence of data, Ryker turned to ideology. For him, this meant politicizing the megamall in apocalyptic "minimalist" terms as a struggle between what's good in America--growth and development in a free market economy--and what's bad--a regulatory state inhabited by visionless NIMBYs who seek to control the enterprising human spirit.

Unable to hide what appeared to be his antagonism for environmental laws, which, it seemed, he believed were anti-development, Ryker denied SEQRA's role in either modifying or disapproving a project, while also dropping his mask of objectivity. When referring to whether the Heller site was appropriate for a megamall, he stated:

> It is a [Rte.] 354 corridor. It is properly used for business and commercial development; as long as [Moselle Plaza] is planned properly and screened so it does not become a visual blight to the community, that's fine. It is exactly what this community needs and wants.

It was not surprising when the final caller, apparently unaware of Ryker's official role, referred to him as "the person who is representing the development."[22]

Freedom of Information

While seeking to create broad community discussion of the proposal, activists also could not neglect the official decision-making arena. In the face of pro forma compliance and obfuscation from Magellan and its allies on the planning board and the inability of "regulatory" members effectively to critique data submitted by Magellan's experts, ACT and CLEAR themselves would have to review Magellan's submissions, Rattle's advice and whatever data involved agencies provided to assure a meaningful critique.

SEQRA anticipated and encouraged public participation in the process, even envisioning the public as monitors or ombudspersons. However, the statute provided no means by which community groups could apply for and obtain government funds to serve this vital role. Nor did SEQRA explicitly require public access to the planning board's ongoing process of gathering information. In order to counter a developer's "expert" assertions on traffic, stormwater or economics issues with what was relevant, persuasive and required by law, the public would first need timely access to whatever information was provided the planning board, long before the board declared it as a "complete" draft EIS for public review. Thereafter, those with equivalent expert knowledge could begin the process of detailed comparison and cross-checking to determine whether Magellan's conclusions were sustainable.

Negotiating access to planning board files could occur informally, through established relationships with the planning board secretary and members of the board who were in possession of relevant data or it could occur formally through a legal request pursuant to New York's Freedom of Information Law (FOIL). However, reliance on FOIL could prove time-consuming and awkward, involving ultimately an exchange of legal letters and consultation by the planning board with its attorneys, followed either by compliance, limited access, or denial of access and judicial review. For ACT and CLEAR to have timely impact on the process, responses to data submitted to the planning board would have to be in the hands of board members prior to the next meeting in order to empower "regulators" among them to raise critical issues. This could prove a formidable stumbling block to any community group, even those like CLEAR and ACT which had professional expertise available to critique the process. As one SEQRA legal expert sees it, this access obstacle is a major flaw for the integrity of SEQRA since "in reality this [FOIL] process often takes months. It is not uncommon for a requester to wait a year or two to receive documents."[23] Penalties for FOIL non-compliance in New York state are non-existent. As stated by Robert Freeman, director of New York State's

Committee on Open Government which monitors FOIL, "If you think FOIL is the remedy, it's not a particularly good remedy. When push comes to shove, the last resort is a lawsuit."[24] But few grassroots groups can afford this additional expense and even an ultimately favorable court ruling may produce documents which have long since lost their usefulness for a review process already completed.

Magellan submitted its DSEIS on traffic and stormwater impacts to the planning board on September 26th. When McBride went to the board office in early October to obtain a copy, the secretary informed him, on Ryker's instruction, that it was not and would not be made available until after the board had officially accepted it as "complete."[25] Ryker's response complied with the board's discretionary responsibility under SEQRA, which required public distribution of a draft EIS only when accepted by the board as "complete." Given that it was precisely the board's determination of "completeness" which ACT and CLEAR wished to influence, Ryker's procedural decision was specifically intended to exclude the public from meaningful participation in this stage of the SEQRA process.

On October 17th, following the procedure recommended by New York State's Committee on Open Government, McBride wrote an official FOIL request for a copy of the DSEIS. Four days later, Ryker denied his request, claiming that his denial was only consistent with past board policy.[26] When McBride then spoke by phone with state FOIL monitor Robert Freeman, the latter assured him that the DSEIS should be fully accessible to the public under rules of the FOIL statute. But McBride realized that it might be as late as November 25th, three days before Ryker's likely request for a "completeness" vote, before an appeals process to the Town Board might produce a copy of the DSEIS.[27] A rejected appeal would necessitate judicial action and further delay. Thus, despite FOIL, Ryker's manipulations could effectively block public access to a document essential for influencing the SEQRA process at this stage. Nevertheless, on October 31st, apparently after consulting Rattle, Ryker retracted his earlier position, now approving public access to the DSEIS. The immediate issue was resolved. Ryker had overplayed his hand.[28]

RCIDA Disclosure

This process of establishing the right of access to public documents replicated a process that McBride had initiated earlier with the Reading County Industrial Development Agency (RCIDA). In June 1994, ACT began to consider alternative opportunities for public intervention in the overall approval process beyond SEQRA. When shortly thereafter, Rattle mentioned at a board meeting that RCIDA was apparently financing Moselle Plaza, McBride realized that with a likely upcoming economic/fiscal impact analysis, it was essential that the public learn more about the IDA role and about government participation in Magellan's project financing generally.

McBride thus sent a FOIL letter to the Reading County IDA on July 15, asking for any documents relating to the Moselle Plaza project. However, it took two follow-up calls and a formally-worded letter referring to the agency's legal obligation to reply within five days before McBride received a letter from IDA administrator, attorney Abe Sanford, listing a long series of relevant documents. After McBride forwarded the copying fee for 119 pages of material, the IDA package arrived in mid-November.

Included were Medford's March 9, 1993 application for IDA funding for Moselle Plaza and other projects, as well as March 11 and June 9, 1993 preliminary approvals by RCIDA.[29] The documents revealed much about the nature and process of IDA activity previously unknown to the Ashbury public. More significantly, they revealed the degree of potential financial benefit the local county agency was willing to provide to Medford, at public expense, and the degree to which Medford had massaged its intentions in its application for IDA-backed bond funding and major tax abatements.

RCIDA operated under the New York State Industrial Development Act which authorized county governments to establish agencies with the power to issue low-interest rate mortgages backed by government bonds for local economic development and to approve abatements for sales tax for construction costs, mortgage recording and ongoing local property taxes. The statute was not designed to encourage expansion of megamalls which would displace or eliminate existing local economies. However, a loophole in the law enabled large commercial retailers with home offices in one county to apply for low interest rate financing of supermarkets and megastores in another county as long as the application did not involve the closing of any existing store owned by the same company or the movement of that store from one town to another.[30]

Medford's expansion plans beyond its home Reading County did not, in the first instance, have to be shared with the residents of those counties. Medford only needed to persuade its local county IDA that its overall plans were worthy of support. Without apparently notifying officials or the community of Ashbury of Medford's application, RCIDA had on its own thus granted Medford a first major stage of approval for a megamall successor to Amsterdam Square--nine months before Moselle Plaza plans were presented to the Ashbury planning board. However, though Medford planned to relocate the existing Ashbury FoodFeast to Moselle Plaza, its IDA application stated "not applicable" when asked if the project would result in an existing plant being closed. When asked if the project would meet local zoning requirements, Medford responded "yes." But this reply, like the first, was misleading since

Magellan later admitted that Moselle Plaza could not be wholly contained within Heller's commercial lot alone, a fact that should have been obvious from the outset. Yet both Medford statements were material to application approval.[31] After a subsequent request from McBride and a reminder letter in legal language from Dreyfus, Sanford sent on a second packet of material giving detailed insight into RCIDA procedures as well as the nature and timing of Medford's 1991 option with Heller. Activists thus gained new informational leverage for later ACT and CLEAR advantage.[32]

Planning Board and Town Board

On November 8th, 1994, "regulator" planning board member Jane Pelletier won a seat on the Town Board by a decisive voter majority. This was a short-range change since it merely filled for one more year the seat of an unexpired term. Since Pelletier ran on a "regulator" platform and her opponent, incumbent appointee Jay Mosher, with "minimalist" themes, the former's victory was a good omen. Nevertheless, while opponents of Moselle Plaza could now be assured of increased influence on the Town Board, three planning board seats--a majority--suddenly were up for appointment by that same body. These included the seat of Pelletier herself once she took Town Board office in January, the seat of Ray Dalrymple who had to resign after December for personal reasons, and the seat of Red Davis, a "minimalist" planner whose seven-year term ended at the close of 1994, but who sought and was likely to obtain re-appointment for another term. With Pelletier's election and Dalrymple's resignation, planning board composition appeared to favor Moselle Plaza all the more. Ryker's "light planning" majority now outnumbered "serious planners" 4 to 1.

Opponents of Magellan Construction recognized that the new appointments by the Town Board were critical for maintaining a "serious planning" perspective on the planning board and ultimately to defeat Moselle Plaza. Should two individuals with "regulator" views join Ben Hillman, "light planners'" advantage would be reduced to one, with both Ryker and Davis subject to possible disqualification on judicial review. On the other hand, should the new appointees share the same views as the current "light planning" majority, the fact that two members should have been disqualified might not be enough to persuade a court to reverse a planning board SEQRA decision favorable for Magellan.[33]

The Anti-Sprawl Network

To better inform the community of the nature of Magellan's threat, ACT and CLEAR meanwhile sought to place in national context the social, environmental and economic issues posed by a Wal-Mart-dominated megamall.

Activists understood that the experience of other towns throughout the country would be persuasive in reaching that wider public yet undecided about Moselle Plaza. McBride had earlier contacted the National Trust for Historic Preservation and Al Norman, author of an article on Wal-Mart and leader of a successful local referendum campaign against it in Greenfield, Massachusetts. These contacts, in turn, connected McBride with a growing network of individuals and groups around the country who were struggling with the same issues ACT and CLEAR faced in Ashbury.[34] Norman's monthly *Sprawl-Busters Newsletter*, begun in mid-1994, was a valuable resource of arguments, evidence and tactics used by community groups in a similar position. Readers discovered that their own battles were not unique and that there were increasing numbers around the United States with a shared anti-sprawl perspective. Research by Norman and others had amassed data which established likely patterns of economic blight faced by local communities when confronted with a Wal-Mart megamall. A December 1st ACT forum on the issues distributed such materials to the wider Ashbury public.[35]

Moving Toward Completion

At the planning board meeting of November 28th, Ryker, Rattle and Reynolds pressured members to make a tentative "completeness" decision about the developer's traffic and stormwater sections of the DSEIS. As Reynolds constantly reminded the board, "time is money." It was obviously to Magellan's advantage to avoid too close a scrutiny of its own DSEIS claims. Ryker also argued that the "completeness" decision should have nothing to do with whether board members liked or disliked the substantive content, framing it as merely a minor technical vote on whether the developer had addressed all scoping issues. In effect, Ryker was instructing the board that any questions members might have on methodology, factual presentation, sources or logic were not relevant at this stage, despite the fact that such issues were critically important to determining the completeness of the DSEIS. Apparently, for Ryker, completeness was limited to the mere presence of developer responses to issues raised in the scope, without concern for the adequacy of the responses themselves. Nonetheless, sufficiently clear, direct and analytically-serious responses from Magellan were crucial for meaningful public and outside agencies input at the time of the public hearing. Likewise, for the board itself to make the most reliable assessments later about severity of impacts and possibilities of mitigations, it needed more than conclusory statements from the developer, appended to computerized printouts of raw data. Thus, Ryker's effort to marginalize "completeness" as a technical concern only contradicted the proclaimed purpose of SEQRA which required that a lead agency "should ensure that all relevant information has been presented and analyzed . . . ."[36]

To assure that a decision on "completeness" was made without further delay, Ryker asked Gene Busch to comment upon whether Magellan had adequately addressed the issues raised by the board's scope. Busch proceeded to list several issues from the scoping agenda, in stormwater and traffic realms, that Magellan had failed to specifically address. While seemingly challenging the completeness of Magellan's response, in fact Busch's objection was one of form, not substance. He gave no judgment as to whether Magellan's responses were analytically complete. He thereby effectually complemented Ryker's and the "light planning" majority's stance.

Planning Board engineering consultant Tony Napoleon's two-page critique of the stormwater portion of the DSEIS was received at the board office on November 15th, but was not distributed to board members until the November 28th meeting itself. Napoleon's comments were few, but he raised several issues which could be seen as significant if the board had familiarized itself with his response and was inclined to follow its logic.

Ben Hillman and Jane Pelletier objected to the pressures from Ryker and Rattle and insisted that the completeness discussion be deferred until December 19th as agreed to by the board two weeks earlier. But Reynolds argued against further delay and Magellan's attorney, Morris Schwab, threatened the board with a lawsuit since it had already exceeded the 60-day limit provided by SEQRA regulations.[37] He insisted that if Magellan responded to the critiques of Busch and Napoleon by December 19th, the board would be legally and morally wrong to prolong the completeness process beyond that date. With the "light planning" majority fully in control, a 4-2 vote (Dalrymple was absent) overrode Hillman and Pelletier.[38]

The Independent Economic Study

At least 50 observers attended the planning board meeting of December 5th. Alerted especially through ACT's public meeting of December 1st, community people (including many from Ashbury businesses) recognized that Marvell's preliminary economic impact report would potentially be decisive in affecting the megamall outcome and the well-being of Ashbury generally. By the time Marvell presented his first few statements, the tone and ultimate conclusion of the report became clear. Marvell saw the mall in positive economic terms as an advantage to the town and compatible with existing businesses. The report anticipated a modest growth of the local economy, saw the project construction phase and new jobs as welcome additional stimuli, stated that there was ample consumer demand presently unfulfilled by local retailers and promised that the project would have minimal impact on local retailers. In any case, "the heightened competition among the [local] retailers will make the consumers of Ashbury the clear winner from the project." He further assured the board and audience that Wal-Marts in places like Huntington, Long Island, Detroit and Atlanta had not hurt local business. As to potential impact on the downtown area, he dismissed downtown merchants as catering mainly to the transient population of students, their parents and tourists--including a lot of "headshops" and restaurants. "Our assessment is that the Wal-Mart type of a store will bring business into the downtown area. . . . So we don't think it will have a negative impact. . . . [I]t will not have a devastating impact on the downtown area . . . ."[39]

The audience was stunned and outraged and broke into laughter at this one-sided presentation which sounded more pro-Moselle Plaza than the report by Magellan Construction itself. While Marvell's brief discussion was vulnerable to critics in its gaps of research topics as well as for what it asserted, it was especially discouraging to activists that the "independent" perspective so strongly fought for had ultimately accepted so fully the framework Magellan had presented months before. While analytical sections within the brief report were of questionable scientific validity, the overall aura of "objectivity" was especially alarming. Many activists left the meeting assuming that Marvell and Renwick Brothers had simply assessed their future prospects and decided that, as Reynolds had emphasized, since Magellan was "the largest developer outside of New York City" within the state, it was no trifle to risk angering.

Fortunately for ACT and CLEAR, press coverage of the report was attentive and to the point. An editorial in the *Tribune* expressed the common reaction of skepticism about scientism and economic projections generally:

> If Brian Marvell says a Wal-Mart will be good for us, it must be true. He is the pro, and he has the projected sales per capita to prove it. Marvell's vision of Ashbury is a good example of what happens when you start looking at the world through numbers. If you spend enough time translating the world into numbers and charts, sooner or later you start getting the two confused. Inevitably, you start thinking that you can translate numbers into reality.[40]

While certainly an understandable popular response to scientism, to follow this logic completely would leave critics almost entirely outside of the SEQRA process. Moreover, on judicial review, great deference is given to an administrative process which is assumed to have been informed by the cultural prestige of natural science. Thus, to show the fallacy of Marvell's conclusions and that they were determined contrary to scientific rationality demanded that critics also become as immersed and articulate in scientific methodology as either Marvell or the developers themselves.

Ryker, of course, was delighted. He later told the press that the Marvell report was eminently fair and that the analyst had done a good job.[41] At the meeting itself, following Marvell's report, Ryker pressured board members to immediately review this last DSEIS document for "completeness" status as well. Said Ryker:

> [The economic consultants] said they will allow us to submit written comments to them to incorporate in their final document. Hopefully, I'd like to see if there is written comment by the Board by Thursday so they can get it addressed by Monday.

While it was appropriate for the board to instruct Marvell about the completeness of his report, it was not for the latter to "allow" the board to submit written comments. By adopting Marvell's deferential phrasing and tone, Ryker's remarks disempowered the two remaining and present "regulator" members of the board who were now granted only three days to scrutinize and critique a document which took two months for the expert himself to prepare. Since these members lacked both the time and expertise to analyze and critique the report, Ryker foreclosed any debate about completeness and assured that the Marvell final draft to be voted on at the meeting of the 19th would be nearly identical to the preliminary report presented on the 5[th.]

Final Consideration

Adding to the momentum created by Ryker's response, at the same December 5th meeting, Red Davis sought to define the term "completeness" to preclude any critical inquiry into the adequacy of Marvell's data or interpretation. He contended that disagreements that board members might have with the report would likely concern merely its conclusions, a substantive area which, under SEQRA, would be addressed only once the report was accepted by the board.

As interpreted by Davis and Ryker, the completeness stage of the SEQRA process concerned only a literal judgment about whether the document "addressed" the scoping items laid out earlier by the board. Yet the board was urged by critics to judge whether Marvell's economic study, as well as Magellan's presentation on stormwater and traffic, contained adequate and sufficient data, employed appropriate methodology and gave analytical consideration to the concerns raised in the board's scope. Although "light planners'" thus sought to diminish the importance of the "completeness" stage, it was the only opportunity for the board to determine whether the breadth and scope of the DSEIS would enable the public and involved agencies to adequately address Magellan's conclusions about the underlying environmental and economic issues. Once the DSEIS was presented for mandated public review, the responses and substantive comments would be framed by the manner in which issues were addressed in a document which the board had determined to be "complete" for SEQRA purposes.

Any board member who dared ask for significant revisions or greater analysis at this stage risked being accused of hypertechnical or nitpicking behavior, of bias against the project as a whole, or of ignorance about the limited inquiry the board was authorized to underake pursuant to the SEQRA statute. Such an atmosphere of social discipline, in which dissent was unwelcome and marginalized, clearly was meant to control and disempower "regulator" members of the board. Time constraints, the lack of significant assistance from the board's planner and engineer, and the difficulty of understanding each analytical realm well enough to pass critical judgment on DSEIS compliance combined to make independent in-depth critiques nearly impossible. The initial stage of the SEQRA process thus became virtually meaningless as a phase of clarification and focus toward objective debate, while the stamp of lead agency approval as a "complete" document would convey legitimacy upon the DSEIS which it by no means possessed when it first emerged from Magellan's and Marvell's offices.

In December, Turbell encouraged town resident and professional engineer Joshua Wright to submit his own independent critique of Magellan's DSEIS stormwater discussion prior to the board's determination of "completeness" on December 19th. Wright's experienced perspective and his willingness to directly challenge the developer's engineer in writing were a major asset for the anti-mall struggle, as already demonstrated in his detailed May and June submissions on the need for an SEIS.

The audience at the December 19th meeting was packed with about 50 opponents to the project. Ryker again arranged for the Moselle Plaza topic to be placed at the bottom of the agenda, thereby assuring attrition among those in the crowd who could not remain for over an hour or more until the topic was reached. As before, there was no period for public comment. Ryker called first on Rattle to instruct the board on its legal options. Rattle opened with a reminder that the board "can either reject [the DSEIS] as incomplete or accept it as complete." However, most of his subsequent legal advice referred to the technical process the board would have to follow to approve the DSEIS as "complete" and to proceed from there. Rattle's approach, therefore, was to treat "completeness" as a fait accompli, without articulating any procedures needed should the board reject the document and require further submission by the developer. This lack of balance, added to pressures from the previous meetings, clearly set the stage for a decision by the "light planning" majority to accept the DSEIS as submitted.

Rattle stated that once the board accepted the document as "complete," it must then determine whether or not to restrict public comments to writing alone or to include also a public hearing, emphasizing that a public hearing was not mandatory under SEQRA. Ryker and Rattle were obviously speaking to those in the audience as well to remind them and "regulator" board members that the amount and nature of process which the majority had to tolerate would be determined by themselves, not by project opponents. To those assembled, the announcement that even a public hearing was uncertain seemed an insult and provocation, given the intensity of community concern about the project. If public critique of the DSEIS were confined to the more distant, impersonal, and more easily dismissed mode of written comments, there would surely be an intense community outcry. No doubt Ryker and Rattle were both aware of this, but each chose to state publicly this potential option, as if to purposefully remind those present whose turf the SEQRA process was on and whose discourse would dominate the proceedings.[42]

Gene Busch was then invited to further set the tone. But again, as in November, he offered little on the "completeness" of DSEIS issues from a position of professional planning expertise. His non-advice was an open door to the board's "light planning" majority. Said Busch:

> I think where all that leaves us is the board needs to make a decision of completeness. I've tried to look at this with the perspective that has all the information been provided . . . that we are really comfortable with to access the project. . . . There are a lot of issues that have been raised that have been addressed in the document.

He added that the board should rely on DOT, DEC and other outside agencies for technical analysis of project impacts. When Busch mentioned the thinness of the final Marvell report, Ryker apologetically interjected, "They were only working on a dime." Essentially, Busch's "summary" avoided issues of substance while addressing only matters of form from which a finding of "completeness" could be made.

Ryker's "minimalist" intent was further revealed in the ensuing quick exchange:

Ryker:	Board comment?
Pelletier:	I didn't see anything from Renwick Brothers about a 50% tax abatement. I know they said that they were not going to address that issue but I don't feel that it is complete unless it is.
Ryker:	Comment noted.

No engagement with the issue raised. No invitation to other board members to engage themselves.

When Pelletier then proceeded to question the absence of data on the effect of the new culvert and larger size stormwater drainage pipes on the adjacent wetlands, Busch replied that Magellan's plan was probably acceptable. Ryker attacked more directly, demanding the source of her critique. When she identified it as professional engineer Joshua Wright, a member of the Town's Environmental Conservation Commission, Ryker dismissed his "outsider" remarks as irrelevant for the present stage of the SEQRA process. Said he, they should be presented in the public comment period instead. Magellan's attorney Schwab voiced his agreement. Despite this stone wall of defense, Pelletier continued to attempt at least to put issues on the floor. But to those in the audience, it was obvious that Pelletier, who was not very familiar with Magellan's analytical method, was being browbeaten into silence. Ryker's bullying approach as chair was never more explicit.

While Pelletier's attempted critique and analysis were attacked, the written remarks of Ben Hillman were totally ignored. Hillman was absent at this meeting but had left for the board a detailed, six-page identification of DSEIS areas concerning stormwater and water quality, traffic and economic impact still incomplete and inadequate for public review by the terms of the board's August 9th scope. All of Hillman's suggested items were significant enough to warrant rejecting the existing revised DSEIS as inadequate, thus requiring Magellan Construction and Marvell to revise and re-submit once again. However, Hillman's critique and request were not even acknowledged at the meeting.

After the overall brief discussion, Ryker asked board members to register their views. Davis said, "I think it's time to get into a public forum." Maglie and Dalrymple echoed this apparently populist theme, with Maglie opportunistically adding that the public wants to see the document and the board needs the public input and the only way to get it would be to declare the document complete. Ryker added: "We could look at this ad infinitum, but now it's the public's turn." All but Pelletier then voted the DSEIS "complete." A public hearing was scheduled for January 30th. Myers congratulated the planning board for its fine efforts. Pelletier dryly observed to a reporter, "Completeness does not mean much."[43]

While the board's "light planner" majority was currently clearly in control, political pressure from the anti-mall groups could potentially affect the new board appointments and thus reduce the "light planning" majority to a one-vote advantage. Because of the bias and conflict-of-interest arguments against Ryker and Davis, a one-vote "light planner" advantage was not necessarily reliable given a reasonable standard of judicial review which mandated that the process be conducted fairly and impartially.

Magellan sought to limit this potential vulnerability and to neutralize the advocacy of the community groups. In early December, Ina Turbell was invited by Deke Reynolds to meet for lunch. Turbell agreed, hoping to persuade Reynolds to either withdraw the application or substantially downsize and eliminate plans for a Wal-Mart-anchored megamall. She thought that persuasive environmental issues raised about stormwater management and traffic might be accepted by Magellan as irrefutable. She reviewed for Reynolds the range of ACT objections to Moselle Plaza, including the potential economic damage to the town. Rather than addressing such issues, however, Reynolds' response was to try to persuade Turbell that it was in ACT's and CLEAR's best interest to withdraw their objections. Reynolds asked Turbell what it would take for the group to drop its opposition. Did ACT want a new park, a new wetland, a sewage plant east of the Thruway or what? He claimed that Magellan was willing to spend whatever money it took to make it appear that community groups had achieved a substantial compromise from Magellan. This, he contended, would enable the groups to withdraw their objections with dignity while also enhancing the image of Magellan as a community-minded developer. Rejected out of hand by Turbell, Reynolds' unsuccessful ploy was a sobering reminder of the formidable stakes involved for Magellan. It also starkly revealed Reynolds' willingness and capacity, through "sweetening" the pie for major participants, to diminish the integrity of the SEQRA review process, dependent upon public scrutiny but ultimately on the number of approval votes Magellan could obtain from the planning board.[44]

SEVEN CHALLENGING PLANNING BOARD IDEOLOGY AND POLITICS

Strategizing Beyond SEQRA

Though frustrated with "light planner" manipulations resulting in a shallow "completeness" review, ACT and CLEAR activists were ready psychologically to move on to a new, more intense phase of the SEQRA struggle--the official public comment period. At the same time, the specific ideological context of the planning board promised to continue preventing a serious environmental impact review, no matter how significant, detailed and rational were the analytical critiques of Magellan's DSEIS. More than ever, it seemed likely that the Moselle Plaza battle would end up in the courts because the "light planning" majority would prevail and approve the project.

Fortunately, by the end of December, ACT and CLEAR were able to obtain full-time legal advice without fee. A six-month research leave from teaching enabled Dreyfus to devote significant time to political and legal strategizing and to preparing needed documentation for a proper legal record. Conceptualizing and strategizing about issues to be presented for judicial review would also assist in further politicizing issues in the community, potentially at best resulting in the removal of Ryker and Davis from the board and replacing Rattle as counsel. Addition of new planning board members from a "regulator" perspective, not only to fill vacancies created by the resignations of Pelletier and Dalrymple, but also to replace Ryker and Davis, could dramatically shift the balance of power on the board and its attitude toward Moselle Plaza. To use leverage outside of the SEQRA realm was important precisely because the SEQRA context for considering Moselle Plaza seemed already corrupted by pro-developer legal and political bias.

All parties recognized that apparent procedural compliance with SEQRA would satisfy the "hard look" standard of judicial review if the planning board went through the motions of requiring a positive declaration, engaging in scoping and a completeness determination, and ultimately approving an SEIS after responding to public review and comment. If a decision approving Moselle Plaza were to be overturned in the courts, ACT and CLEAR would have to demonstrate that the integrity of the process was tainted by a combination of bias, prejudice, interest and corruption. While raw ingredients for such a case existed, Dreyfus argued that it would be up to those challenging the process to present to the planning board and the Town Board a record of their objections with documented reasons elaborating the basis for their conclusions. Dreyfus emphasized that administrative law complainants would be best advised to place grievances on the public record as early as possible to demonstrate to a later judge that due process violations could have been corrected, but were not, by the agency involved. Such an attack, in turn, would have to demonstrate that the adverse environmental impacts of Moselle Plaza were substantial and that any fair-minded person would have considered those issues differently but for the reasons that tainted the decision-making of Ryker and Davis and the advice of Rattle.

Thus, while the community groups' attack would have to personalize the dispute, the rationality underlying the merits of the environmental critique would have to be preserved. Moreover, the success of any arguments from community groups for judicial reversal could depend on the ability to assure that at least three votes on the planning board were for disapproval. Only with the board closely deadlocked could a bias-disqualifying ruling concerning Ryker, Davis and/or Rattle be confidently argued as material enough (potentially affecting the SEQRA decision) to persuade a reviewing court that the error in permitting these people to participate substantially prejudiced the rights of the community groups. With this strategy in mind, ACT and CLEAR began to challenge the "light planning" majority's narrow channeling of the SEQRA process, as well as the legitimacy of the decisionmakers themselves.

By the time Rattle filed a notice of DSEIS "completeness" with the DEC and other agencies on December 27th, activist plans were already underway for a twofold attack. First, the biased, manipulative context in which the SEQRA process was conducted had to become a matter of public debate. Second, preparations were needed for strong, detailed critiques on the merits of the DSEIS. The board had agreed, when it accepted the DSEIS as "complete," to legitimate its decision by holding a public hearing in which testimony and exhibits could be offered. The hearing was scheduled for January 30th, though written public comments could be received until February 13th.

The New Year's Attack

In the final week of December, Dreyfus, McBride and Turbell assembled documents and a list of issues to submit to the Town Board in order to neutralize if not undermine "light planners'" dominance of the planning board. The bold plan was to call for replacing Ryker as chair, recusing Ryker and Red Davis from deliberations on Moselle Plaza, and replacing Rattle as planning board attorney.[1] With no illusions that any of these goals would be easily attained, the three activist leaders agreed that placing evidence and these requests on record might inhibit more flagrant procedural violations and at least educate the public. It might also later prove flaws in the legal procedural record through which an eventual pro-developer SEQRA decision by the planning board could be challenged in court. The Town Board was selected as the forum to hear these issues because, under state law, that board had absolute discretion to appoint and remove the planning board chair.[2] In addition, that board had legal authority to remove members for "good cause" based upon conflicts of interest and ethical improprieties. While the planning board had sole statutory authority to appoint its attorney, the Town Board could recommend to the planning board that it not retain the services of a lawyer whose professional biases appeared to preclude the rendering of impartial advice.[3] Since the Town Board had the power of the purse, such a recommendation would carry considerable weight and it would also place the planning board in an awkward legal position should a court be asked to review its determination.[4]

This strategy, however, was also risky. Its confrontational nature would be abrasive compared to the relative placid nature of bureaucratic board discussions and agendas. In sharp contrast with the superficially benign Town Board politics of "civility," the activists' strategy would be perceived quickly for what it was, a direct attack on the larger structure of "light planning" domination in Ashbury. Despite the fact that "regulator" Jane Pelletier was now joining the five-person Town Board, her only obvious direct ally would be Citizen Party member Mark Lyon. Even then, it was unclear if Pelletier and Lyon themselves would be supportive of a direct confrontation over individual officials. Beyond these two, the only hope for positive resolution was a favorable vote from Democrat Edna Devilla. But Devilla's own long-time entrenchment in the local power structure and her unwillingness to stand out as a dissenter made such support quite doubtful. It was rumored, in fact, that Devilla planned to run in November 1995 as an unopposed candidate for Town Supervisor if Grant Schmidt chose not to run. In such a context, she was highly unlikely, even if she believed the critique about Ryker, Davis and Rattle, to risk public perception as a confrontational politician.

Beyond the difficulty of winning Town Board votes for replacement and recusal, activists also feared that with at least two seats to fill on the planning board, a hostile polarized majority on the Town Board might feel so provoked that it would choose additional "light planners" to consolidate Ryker's control. That would be a major disaster because it would eliminate the likelihood of any favorable scenario. Likewise, activists also foresaw that a direct attack on Ryker and Davis might be so offensive to the only potential planning board swing votes, Maglie and Myers, that the whole effort might backfire by further solidifying their loyalty to Ryker and Davis and the hard-line "light planning" position. Though both Maglie and Myers had shown by the time of the "completeness" vote that they would support Magellan Construction, it seemed to activists still premature to completely write them off as unreachable by later argument and community appeals.

Finally, there was also the danger of alienating some within the anti-mall struggle, within and outside of ACT and CLEAR. For many opposed to Moselle Plaza from "regulator" or "ecologist" perspectives, confrontational politics seemed contrary to their communitarian ideal. They believed in the power of friendly persuasion or, at the least, that extra-SEQRA challenges were emotional and political diversions from the appropriate central focus. Dreyfus, by personality and profession, felt comfortable with confrontation when a situation seemed to require it. McBride and Turbell had for years, patiently but with increasing frustration, observed the biased performance of the planning board, while attempting unsuccessfully to engage it in rational dialogue through the official discourse of the SEQRA process. Abused by the pretenses of legalist "civility," they also now concluded that the time was ripe for this bolder strategy. There was too much at stake to allow entrenched decision-makers to persist without a fundamental public challenge of the integrity of the planning board's decision-making process itself.

The takeoff point for this new approach was the Town Board's organizational meeting of January 2nd. Traditionally, this was the occasion when new Town Board members were sworn in and the year's committee assignments parcelled out--a brief and uninteresting meeting concluded by light refreshments for the Board, other town officials and whichever few local citizens might attend. Scrambling through piles of documents and drafts of letters down to the final minutes before the meeting began, Turbell, McBride and Dreyfus presented the board and a packed audience of supporters with totally new dynamics.

When Supervisor Schmidt, toward the beginning of the meeting, ritually offered the public the chance to make comments, the activist tornado swept through. On behalf of CLEAR, McBride arose, distributed a 7-page statement (with 16 exhibits) and read the main text aloud. He formally requested that the Town Board not reappoint Ryker as planning board chair for 1995 since he had "acted (or failed to act) in a manner which is at substantial variance from his official role as impartial community servant." As chair of the planning board, he "should not pre-judge the merits of any application pending before him" and "should conduct himself when dealing with the public with the appearance of propriety."[5]

Challenging Ryker by the criteria of bureaucratic impartiality, McBride stated that Ryker's relationship with the public was arbitrary and denigrating. Throughout his tenure, he normally prevented public input and intentionally insulted its worth when the public was allowed to speak. Most recently, on December 19th, he had failed even to acknowledge receipt of Joshua Wright's critique of the DSEIS stormwater treatment discussion and precluded any direct verbal remarks by Wright at the same meeting. His arbitrary action thus had eliminated the possibility of informed board discussion relevant to the issue of "completeness."

McBride then recited examples when Ryker's favorable bias toward Moselle Plaza was explicitly stated to the press even before the board had reviewed the data in any depth. As explained privately to McBride by Bellows, Pelletier and Hillman, Ryker also had attempted to intimidate board members opposed to his own positions on projects with angry tirades in the planning board office at the back of Town Hall.[6]

McBride stated that Ryker "had diminished the impartial reputation" of the planning board chair position by continuing to chair the local Republican party at the same time, thus raising issues of "patronage and partisanship." This appearance of impropriety was most evident when Magellan Construction's manager had contributed to the local party just prior to its own formal application to the board.

McBride's next argument was that Ryker had failed to comply with accepted regulatory processes for SEQRA and FOIL, as well as the Town Board's guidelines for appointment of planning board members. Concerning SEQRA violations, McBride specifically cited Ryker's failure to process the August 8th draft scope as requested by the board, thus precluding examination of crucial relevant environmental issues in the DSEIS; his promise to use taxpayer funds to subsidize Marvell's economic impact study; his failure in October to extend the time period for board review of the developer's DSEIS; and his ruling on December 19th that the Marvell report would be deemed as "complete" even though an addendum was already promised for later on. McBride also referred to Ryker's denial of public access to the DSEIS, in contradiction of FOIL, and his manipulation of the board vacancy issue by securing the appointment of Sam Myers when Julia Bellows had resigned. Said McBride, it was time for the Town Board to accept responsibility for proper governance. A new board chair should be immediately designated and Ryker should be recused from any further deliberations on Moselle Plaza.

Following this presentation which the Board received in stunned silence, McBride immediately proceeded to a second CLEAR letter requesting the Town Board not to reappoint Red Davis to a new term on the planning board and to direct Red's father, Ernie Davis, to recuse himself from any deliberations the zoning board of appeals might have concerning a variance request for Magellan's project. The basis for these requests was an appearance of impropriety, on grounds already made public by ACT and CLEAR the previous June.

Supervisor Schmidt, however, responded that Red Davis had already been reappointed to the planning board at the Town Board's last meeting in December, several days earlier. This was surprising and extralegal since Davis' term did not expire until the end of the calendar year,[7] but McBride immediately requested that in that case the Town Board should request his recusal from Moselle Plaza deliberations.

McBride also challenged the credibility of regular planning board attorney Don Torelli's 1991 investigation of the Davis land-holdings since at that time Torelli's own firm, Harvey & Plonsker, represented applicants for a FoodFeast plaza in a town in neighboring Reading County. This actual conflict of interest should have precluded Torelli from participating in the 1991 investigation and indeed from participating in any legal capacity for the board concerning Amsterdam Square at all.

Ina Turbell then proceeded into a detailed, well-documented analysis of the specific conflict of interest of the same law firm, based mainly on documentary discoveries several years earlier by CLEAR activist Ellen Scott as well as Spring 1994 research by Turbell and McBride both. Through news clippings, records from Reading County and two towns, Turbell suggested that the firm of Harvey & Plonsker represented the FoodFeast development in Reading County at the same time as acting as counsel for the Ashbury planning board while it considered FoodFeast-anchored Amsterdam Square. She also established that the law firm might also have been a direct partner in that same Reading County development at the same time and until 1994.[8]

Finally, Turbell showed how Don Torelli continued as Ashbury planning board attorney throughout the Spring of 1992 at a time when Medford applied to the same board for subdivision of the Heller property. "It's good that they finally told the Planning Board [in 1993] about the conflict of interest, but it was three or four years too late."[9] Turbell asked the Town Board to refer these matters to a newly-constituted Town Ethics Committee and to remove the firm from its legal representation of the planning board.[10]

Dreyfus, in turn, alleged that Frank Rattle had not provided neutral counsel to the planning board but acted instead as an advocate for the developer. He promised that CLEAR would provide detailed documentation regarding Rattle's employment by the Cairo group, the developer of the Super Kmart in nearby Regent Park, and the misleading and one-sided nature of advice Rattle provided the planning board. He stressed that a lawyer's professional behavior had to be constrained when there was an appearance of a conflict of interest.

These challenges clarified that community activists would not wait and react to planning board business as usual and that the contested terrain would involve not only SEQRA but the local political economy in which SEQRA decisions were made. After heated discussion among its members, the Town Board agreed to review the various charges and requests at its January 12th meeting.

The day after the organizational meeting, McBride presented to the Town Board on behalf of CLEAR a closely-argued 6-page letter detailing reasons why Rattle should be relieved by the board from "all responsibilities as attorney representing the Ashbury Planning Board in the Moselle Plaza matter." He also requested appointment of a replacement who should not attempt "to influence the decision of the Board on the merits of the application . . . [and who] should not have any clients who are likely to benefit by the construction of Moselle Plaza."

McBride's letter enumerated the issues behind his request. He began with the fact that Rattle was appointed in Ashbury at a time when he legally represented a Kmart developer in Regent Park, without any apparent inquiry by Ryker or self-admission by Rattle about ethical problems involved when there was a reasonable possibility that Kmart would be the anchor for Moselle Plaza. McBride then discussed how, at the decisive June 27, 1994 meeting, Rattle used his position as counsel to try several times to discourage the board from issuing a SEQRA positive declaration. He then provided a detailed description of the fiasco created by Rattle's failure to disseminate the board's August 8th scoping document with which he disagreed, how the various outside agencies never received the opportunity to comment upon that draft and how the DSEIS approved by the board as "complete" on December 19th was thus fundamentally weakened by this omission.

To assure that the record was as direct and complete as possible, McBride then submitted on January 4th a separate letter to the planning board itself. Here he asked Ryker, Davis and Rattle to recuse themselves for the various reasons cited already to the Town Board.

Ryker Reacts

The strategy ACT and CLEAR adopted sought as well to provoke those from the "light planning" perspective to respond publicly to the charges raised at the Town Board meeting. The expectation was that Rocky Ryker, whose short fuse was notorious,[11] would respond in language which would add further weight to charges of bias. As to Davis and Rattle, conflict-of-interest issues might provoke either a response or withdrawal from the process. This strategy of public revelation sought to empower outsiders by eliminating the monopoly of "expert" procedural knowledge and the advantage this provided to "light planners" in control of local government. Whistle-blowing gave ACT and CLEAR an opportunity to exercise power from without by defining the discourse of accountability and legitimacy in terms which contradicted insiders' traditional understanding of acceptable practices and political relationships.

Ryker responded the day after the January 2nd public meeting. To the Regent

Park *Star*, he said that he never allowed personal feelings about a project or anything else to affect his objectivity. He said that people like McBride and "the 40 or so others" opposing the plaza make up "a small minority of the Ashbury population." Concerning the conflict of interest and bias charges, "Obviously, they're grasping at straws. This is not the first time they have twisted the facts to try and prove a point."[12]

A few days later, he told the same reporter that the Harvey & Plonsker conflict-of-interest issue didn't exist, since by as early as November 1990 the Amsterdam Square project had died. But this assertion was contradicted by correspondence in the planning board file. Specifically, it showed that the developer of that project, in which Medford was a major anchor, still actively pursued permits with outside agencies at least as late as May 1991, when Harvey & Plonsker, at the time representing (and partners investing in) a shopping center project in Reading County (to be anchored by Medford), acted as the Ashbury planning board's lawyers reviewing Amsterdam Square. Concerning the law firm's conflict of interest at the time of Heller's property subdivision on behalf of Medford, in the Spring of 1992, Ryker claimed that "it was a basic, simple procedure, by the books. No advice from counsel was needed."[13] He did not mention that Torelli was present at planning board meetings where the subdivision was considered and gave the planning board advice regarding the propriety of severing Heller's commercial property from that designated for light industrial use.

In the same week, to the reporter for the *Tribune*, Ryker stated that the issues raised about Harvey & Plonsker were "non-issues at this point. They were designed to create a smoke screen to cloud the real issue." He claimed that there was ample opportunity for public input at planning board meetings and that "no one's been denied the opportunity to speak at a public hearing." Overall, he said, the issues brought up by CLEAR and Ashbury Community Together were invalid, simply an effort to obstruct Moselle Plaza. "I'd like to see them shut up and go away because they are not dealing with facts. I think we're doing good work, and they seem to be the only one with this conflict or this agenda."[14]

For the Londonville *Post*, the day after the Town Board meeting, Ryker repeated his denunciation of McBride's charges as products of "a very vocal and rude minority. I have served and will continue to serve this community's other 10,000 members to the best of my abilities." Concerning the Magellan Construction manager's October 1993 contribution to local Republicans, several weeks before presenting its project application to the board, amazingly Ryker now acknowledged knowing about it at the time. Just seven months earlier he had totally denied awareness of the contribution. The *Post*'s reporter stated that Ryker "laughed off the question of impropriety." Said Ryker: "If

Mr. Dreyfus thinks the decisions of a seven-member board can be swayed by a $200 donation, he should think again. I'm only one vote, and I'm a person of high moral character."[15]

At the first planning board meeting of January after CLEAR and ACT allegations and demands to the Town Board, the "light planning" majority felt the need to publicly reaffirm Ryker's role as chair in an effort to persuade the Town Board to re-appoint him. Their public justification for support revealed shamelessly the reality of "light planning" ideology. As Rich Maglie, the vice-chair, stated:

> The chairman job is a very demanding one. And in Rocky we've found a person who has been more than willing to put the extra time in . . . a person who has been always willing to go the extra mile for applicants and help them through what can be a very confusing process.

In response to the critique that the board was controlled by entrenched relationships which monopolized the decision-making process, Maglie also recommended that the Town Board now make the chair position a rotating two-year appointment. After all, Maglie said, the position demanded enormous time and every board member ought to learn the details of the planning approval process through such responsibility. However, to assure that Ryker would remain as chair throughout the Moselle Plaza process and to dispel the notion that reform was at all connected to activist critiques, he suggested that the proposed rotation begin after another twelve months, so everyone could adjust to the new schedule. Red Davis and Sam Myers readily agreed. Only Ben Hillman, now the lone member from the summer's "regulator" majority, insisted that rotation of office should begin right away.[16]

To Their Own Defense

Since the Town Board had promised to review ACT's and CLEAR's allegations and requests at their meeting on the 12th, Ryker was not alone in mounting a defense. Responding for himself and his son Red, Ernie Davis asserted to the *Tribune* that no conflict of interest existed since Red never owned the property sold to Heller and since so much time had passed since its sale. "I don't think there's any conflict of interest when it's been sold for that period of time."[17] He omitted to explain that original SEQRA approval for the Amsterdam Square project (including the vote of Red Davis) was given in 1990, just five years after the sale. Nor did he comment on the fact that both he and his son continued to own adjacent properties whose commercial value would be enhanced with project approval by the planning board and zoning board of appeals (of which Ernie was chair).

Speaking to the *Tribune*, attorney Rattle, in turn, claimed no conflict of interest existed since he represented the Cairo Group, the developer of the Kmart shopping mall, not Kmart itself. "I have never represented Kmart in any capacity. I have nothing to do with them. They didn't pay my bills."[18] Rattle thus framed the propriety of attorney conduct into a narrow concern with actual conflict of interest (who paid his bills) without addressing the wider and more appropriate issue of the apparent conflict of interest for a lawyer representing a public agency. He stated that his advice to the planning board on Magellan Construction's project had been responsible. "You have to be objective. My job is to make sure the board obeys the regulations and follows the regulations and make sure the applicant follows the regulations." As for the scope of the SEIS, "I just didn't think it had to be very broad." Concerning the failure of the board's August 8th draft scope to be sent out to other agencies, he claimed that he thought it had been, but that wasn't his job. "I didn't participate in that part." He didn't comment on his failure to correct the error by informing Magellan that the draft scope to which the DSEIS referred had been superceded by the planning board's new version. Rattle's final remarks attempted to counterattack CLEAR's claims by marginalizing the source: "The whole thing is just ridiculous. They apparently oppose the project and they obviously don't like the way things are going."[19] In more formal terms, Rattle repeated the same arguments in a 5-page letter to Ashbury Town Attorney Lou Tapani (whose brother and father were Rattle's clients when CLEAR sued the planning board over SEQRA issues concerning their development in 1987[20]).

Not surprisingly, Rattle, like Ryker, described his actions as simply protecting the board by following, not creating, the law. This ideological characterization contrasted with an activist view of the law which "light planners" attributed to ACT and CLEAR and those who opposed the project. Allegedly, the latter were defilers of the law, having little respect for its mandates and for the democratic process leading to its enactment. As a servant of the law, Rattle portrayed his job as guiding the board through the otherwise undecipherable thicket of regulations and case law so that it would emerge unscathed from potential attacks by the developer alleging non-compliance. However, he exhibited no concern with a potential reversal of the board's decision because of a lawsuit from the public.

Finally, the law firm of Harvey & Plonsker presented its own defense as well. In statements to the press, Vince Schiffler (predecessor to Torelli as board attorney from the same firm) admitted that Torelli had represented FoodFeast in the Reading County project and that members of the firm were financially involved. But he claimed that all of this happened after Amsterdam Square's consideration in Ashbury. Concerning Don Torelli's failure to recuse himself when Medford sought to subdivide Heller's lot in 1992, Torelli himself claimed, "I only knew the applicant as being Mr. Heller. It was a straight forward subdivision along the zoning line." He failed to mention that Heller's agent before the board stated that the subdivision was sought because FoodFeast wished to build at the location. Furthermore, Medford paid the bill for the subdivision application. Apparently oblivious to these actual circumstances and to the significance of conflict-of-interest concerns generally, Torelli then added, "I don't tell the board how to vote. As an attorney, I am not the policy maker or the planner or the engineer."[21]

In his 7-page letter of January 9th to the Town Board, Don Torelli acknowledged that Turbell, "for the most part, has submitted accurate data and documentation to your Board." However, her assumptions and conclusions, he said, were not supported by the data since she relied on factually incorrect news articles and used other facts out of context. He claimed that his firm had not represented FoodFeast until November 1992 and had never represented Heller, the developer of Amsterdam Square, Magellan Construction or any other entity with an interest in the Amsterdam Square project or the Heller subdivision. Clearly Torelli's admission that his firm represented FoodFeast contradicted his final assertion. Beyond that, as with Rattle's letter, however, this defense technically argued that before November 1992, when Harvey & Plonsker represented the planning board on the Amsterdam Square or Heller subdivision, there was no <u>actual</u> conflict of interest, but failed to disclose substantial evidence of the firm's <u>apparent</u> conflict of interest.

Torelli admitted, as Ryker's defense of the firm had not, that he had done research for and provided advice to Ashbury town officials as late as March 1991 concerning the site plan stage of the Amsterdam Square proposal. He also admitted that Heller's agent in early 1992 told the planning board that Medford had asked her to submit the application for subdivision of the Heller lot, a matter also upon which Torelli advised the planning board. The <u>apparent</u> conflict of interest became clear upon Torelli's detailed description of his firm's relationship with FoodFeast prior to November 1992, before the firm was formally retained by Medford.[22] The apparent if not actual conflict of interest of this closely-connected business relationship was plain to see, though the firm did not disclose this fact at the time to the planning board as it was professionally obligated to do and continued to refuse to acknowledge its significance, once Turbell disclosed the facts to the town.[23] What ACT and CLEAR confronted, at its core, was the question of legitimacy of local small-town government and law's capacity to be responsive to the needs of those other than business interests and the governing elite.

Preparing for the Hearing

By the time of the January 12th meeting, five other critical documents had been submitted to the Town Board. Newly-elected Board member Jane Pelletier verified by memorandum various allegations of Ryker's bias and irresponsibility on the planning board. Among these, she pointed out that it was the chair's responsibility to assure that all board members have "equal access to all information concerning the planning board and its functions in a timely manner." Nevertheless, she said:

> A number of times while on the planning board, I have received important material just minutes before the meeting or have been given material during the meeting, or have found out at the end of a meeting that an addition has been made to the agenda and have been expected to act immediately on the matter and/or material.

She also strongly disapproved of Ryker asserting his own opinions to the media as if he was speaking on behalf of the board. "Mr. Ryker has taken license to speak on behalf of the planning board on many occasions and I, as a planning board member at that time and not always holding the same opinion as Mr. Ryker, take issue with this liberty."

Pelletier's critique was complemented by a handwritten letter from ex-planning board member Julia Bellows. She opened with a call for change in planning board leadership, then presented a list of grievances of her own. Agendas were prepared at the last minute and were incomplete; applicants were not adequately guided through the SEQRA process; Ryker's attendance was irregular; he failed to promote communication and cooperation with other Town bodies; and he failed to help orient new members to SEQRA and overall Board goals, let alone find speakers and other sources of new planning ideas.

More importantly, concerning accusations of prejudice, Bellows stated:

> There is the appearance of favoritism by how the meetings are conducted. There is the appearance of bias, via facial and body expressions, and whisperings with other board members, during public comment meetings.[24] . . . The Chairman has inappropriately discussed Board issues with the press. He has left the impression that his views are the consensus of the Planning Board. The Chairman reduces the effectiveness of member participation by expressing impatience with points of view and/or presentation style. . . . Many decisions are made arbitrarily by the Chairman that should be voted upon by the full Board.

Stated by one as tactful and temperate as Julia Bellows, this was a damning insider list of grievances and corroborated the public perspective already placed on the record by ACT and CLEAR.

In turn, at the invitation of Town Attorney Lou Tapani, Dreyfus wrote the latter a 9-page letter-brief on January 10th (forwarded also to the Town Board and planning board) analyzing in detail the Town Board's legal authority to remove Ryker as chair and to recommend to Ryker and Davis that should they vote on Moselle Plaza, they would subject themselves to removal for cause.[25] As to the attorneys, he explained the legal authority which precluded them from representing a public body without informed consent when an apparent conflict of interest existed.[26]

Tapani, a Republican and brother of ex-Supervisor Bob, was part of the political clique which dominated town politics since the early 1960s. While Tapani's manner was gracious and in style even-handed, his advice to town officials was enabling and consistently avoided any threat to their position. He followed Dreyfus with a 10-page letter to the Town Board on the same issues on January 11th and with a supplementary letter on the next day.

Concerning the potential reappointment of Ryker as planning board chair, Tapani was certainly aware of that board's vote several days earlier to keep Ryker as chair for another year. Nevertheless, Tapani suggested simply that materials received by the Town Board be passed on to the planning board for its review before the latter body made its recommendation for the chair position to the Town Board. As for the rest, Tapani claimed to find no legal grounds for decisive Town Board or Town Ethics Board action, as activists requested, in part because he failed to acknowledge a distinction between actual and apparent conflict of interest, a critical distinction in Dreyfus' argument concerning Red and Ernie Davis, Rattle and the firm of Harvey & Plonsker.

The Showdown: First Phase

The stage was thus set for the January 12th Town Board meeting by ample documentation from each side. Following Tapani's verbal explanation of the points in his letters, there ensued two and a half hours of heated exchanges between board members, attorneys and members of the audience, many of whom were supporters of ACT and CLEAR. Supervisor Schmidt said that he didn't see "any statement from any meeting that would indicate Mr. Ryker has pre-judged this project." ACT members and others who had seen Ryker in action confronted Schmidt's characterizations and demanded that Ryker be held to a standard of accountability. Said one ACT activist:

> I've been to the town planning meetings and see the applicants hanging out with the board. The public is told to shut up and can't hear what's going on. . . . In watching the process I have lost faith. . . . Why can't we clean this operation up, so it can function in a way we can have confidence?

Throughout the give-and-take, Ryker stood alone at the back of the room with what appeared at first to be an air of disinterest and contempt for the process initiated by his critics. When he finally did speak, he described himself as a man dedicated solely to the interests of the community and, while personalizing all issues, attacked the motives of McBride, Turbell, and

Dreyfus,[27] as well as his longtime Town Board critic, Mark Lyon. Ryker claimed that since the time of his appointment to the planning board:

> I have tried . . . to keep all of my personal and political feelings separate. I have succeeded. Whether or not you believe me or not, that is up to you. Everybody seems to know what is in my mind. . . . I have not played games with [public access to] documents. I have not attempted to do anything other than what I am pledged to do for this community. You may not like what I do, you may not agree with what I do, but nobody in this room or in any other room is going to imply that there is any personal gain, political agenda, or anything else. That is blatantly untrue.
>
> . . . To accuse the Davis family of a conflict of interest or illegal gain is just absurd. These people are people who built the community, 50 years or more. I defy anybody making accusations to make these kinds of claims. We have sat week after week, month after month, at, in my case, financial loss. Why? Because we came here 26, 7, 8, whatever, 10 years ago, we love this community. We will continue to serve this community the way we see it until such time as we are either removed or not reappointed. And if that's the will, that's fine. But if this Town Board serves the will of three people with a grudge and agenda . . . . I am not the easiest person to get along with. However, I do have a lot of friends. Some people like me, some people don't. I do not go out of my way to cultivate people. I go out of my way to serve the community. I will continue to do so proudly and, I think, extremely capably.

Also defending themselves, at length and vociferously, were attorneys Vince Schiffler and Don Torelli of the Harvey & Plonsker firm. At one point waving a copy of the lawyer's Code of Professional Responsibility, Schiffler claimed that his firm had been unfairly criticized. "I've heard just about enough. . . . In fact, there is no conflict of interest. . . . In fact, it's absurd to even suggest that [there is some kind of conspiracy]. What's clear here is that there is some kind of agenda. . . . It's absolutely crazy." He challenged Dreyfus about the relevance of the Professional Code for such instances of apparent conflict of interest and contended that all that was required was his firm's claim that it had no actual conflict because of its involvement in Reading County until November 1992, when the firm was first retained to represent Medford. Ultimately, the impact of the law firm's defense distinguishing between actual and apparent conflicts was lost on most of the audience who supported ACT's and CLEAR's position. As summarized by an Ashbury resident:

> I'm confused. I'd like to see an attorney that has no connection to any of this. I feel you have a little too much experience--maybe we need

someone a little more naive! The Forest County phone book is full of lawyers. Can't we find one who has not represented FoodFeast, Kmarts or anyone else involved here?

Though Lyon, Pelletier and Schmidt were ready to vote on the various issues at the meeting's conclusion, both Devilla and Kraft stated that they were not. The Board chose to defer all issues to its next meeting on January 19th.[28]

Two days before that meeting, Dreyfus sent a new 13-page letter to the Town Board, summarizing the position of CLEAR and ACT but with reference now also to the letters of Tapani and Torelli as well as data presented at the January 12th meeting. Dreyfus contested Tapani's interpretations in several respects. Challenging Tapani's assertion that planning board members are "not performing judicial functions" and are thus not held to the high standards of impartiality of a quasi-judicial agency, Dreyfus enumerated the various adjudicatory functions required by SEQRA which thus required recusal when lack of impartiality and prejudgment have occurred. He also disputed Tapani's suggestion that Ryker's opinions were mere philosophical differences as opposed to prejudgment of the facts, the latter being sufficient ground for disqualification. Among other matters, he also recommended specific ways in which the Town Board should amend the Ethics Code, broaden the powers of the Town Ethics Board and intervene concerning various planning board procedural issues.

However, such reforms designed to provide meaningful, substantive and unbiased SEQRA reviews were far from the agenda of "light planning" insiders who controlled the Town's political and economic agenda. Acting as a lightning rod for the "light planners," on January 19th, the very day of the Town Board meeting, the *Tribune* quoted Ryker as asserting, "I'm a person of opinion. And I have a right to voice that opinion in the back room with other board members." He claimed that Julia Bellows and Jane Pelletier were criticizing him because of their own personal agendas.

> If they cannot force feed their agendas down the throats of the community, desperate people take desperate measures. It seems like there's a witch hunt out there. The opponents of this project and growth in general cannot fight fairly. And when it seems like they're going to lose, they fight nasty. I hope the community at large takes it from where it comes.

More unsettling, however, was the reaction of Magellan Construction. During this same period, Ina Turbell called Deke Reynolds in order to better gauge Magellan's response to these events. She also expected another Magellan invitation to a direct meeting and a new attempt to buy off ACT's and CLEAR's opposition. If such an opportunity developed, she was prepared to expose such an offer to the public. This time on the phone, however, Reynolds was immediately vicious. From the nature of his remarks, it appeared to Turbell that Ryker had already provided Reynolds with details from the Town Board meeting. Furthermore, Reynolds accused herself, McBride and Dreyfus of "gangster" tactics and assured her that they would destroy the jobs of each of them. For Turbell, the threat soon appeared actualized when she lost, without notice, her accountant position for a private estate, legally represented by Frank Rattle. It was a badly unsettling blow to Turbell. Though temporarily free to devote even more time to the struggle against Moselle Plaza, with two young children, her contribution to family income was much needed.

The Showdown: Second Phase

The Town Board meeting of January 19th promised to be a critical showdown and Town Hall was packed with a highly attentive audience. It was obvious to all that with Schmidt and Kraft opposing Lyon and Pelletier on all issues, Edna Devilla had the swing vote for the one decision the Town Board could not avoid--appointment of a planning board chair for the coming year. Devilla remained uncommitted and much was personally at stake. It was assumed that Devilla wished to run for Supervisor in November should Schmidt not seek re-election and it was obvious that Ryker was highly unpopular with Democrats, whether activist or not. On the other hand, Devilla's instincts were always self-protective. She recoiled almost viscerally to any emotional statements by others before the Board and seemed to despise the idea that popular agitation might be a legitimate reason to act. Two days before the meeting, she told the press merely that she liked the idea of a rotating two-year term for planning board chairs, but then claimed not to know if the planning board's recommendation implied just one more year for Ryker or as many as three.[29]

During the public input at this meeting, only one voice was offered for Ryker's support--that of recently-appointed planning board member Sam Myers who indeed owed his office to Ryker's and Kraft's manipulations. Said Myers, "In my personal opinion, I've never seen Rocky attack anybody. . . . Some of these charges don't seem to have much credibility."

The Board then proceeded to CLEAR's and ACT's requests, as presented by Dreyfus, that it become a fact-finding hearing body to consider whether it should recommend to Ryker, Red Davis and Ernie Davis that they recuse themselves from any deliberations on Moselle Plaza. The Board also had to deal with the two groups' requests that the Board recommend to the planning board that it consider removing attorneys Rattle, Torelli and the latter's firm from their positions as planning board counsel.

Schmidt claimed, "I have reviewed documentation from both sides . . . 2 1/2 inches of it. And after discussing it all with our attorney, I just don't feel that this is an issue that should be decided by the Town Board." He then read through a full-page statement, intended as a resolution, in which Schmidt alleged that potential conflicts of interest or the appearance of such were impossible to avoid in a a small town. The inevitable "moral panic" would assure theoretically that virtually no qualified long-time residents would serve on local boards since anyone who ever had any kind of relationship with other townspeople would always have to recuse themselves.

Rather than focusing on potential appearances of conflicts of interest, said Schmidt, the Town Board should try simply to find people of undisputed integrity to serve on boards and then trust them to act by their conscience on a case-by-case basis. It would be impossible for town officials to judge others' behavior since they themselves "have the same relationships." Therefore, he said, the Town Board should leave to the planning board and ZBA members the question of whether there was a conflict of interest. "We have faith in their judgment." The same was true, he said, concerning the limited number of local attorneys or law firms with expertise on land-use law. By necessity, these would be firms that regularly represented developers. Hence, an "appearance of conflict of interests" would have to be distinguished from "actual conflicts of interest."

Lyon and Pelletier strongly disagreed with Schmidt's proposed resolution. Lyon asked, "If we have an opinion as to a certain matter, then we should not make that opinion known?" Schmidt replied that he had "personal confidence in the personal integrity of every member of every board that we appoint." Lyon responded:

> You can't just say absolve yourself of considering any allegations that are made . . . . I think we have an obligation to look into those matters. . . . You can't just shy away from facts that might be unpleasant or difficult to deal with.

After additional discussion, Schmidt's resolution was tabled by votes of Lyon, Pelletier and Devilla. Lyon then moved for fact-finding reviews of conflict-of-interest charges against Ryker, Red Davis and the firm of Harvey & Plonsker. After Schmidt accused Lyon of a conflict of interest because of his pre-Town Board membership in CLEAR, that motion also failed, with Devilla now joining the two Republicans, Schmidt and Kraft. Pelletier complained:

> What you're saying is we're going to recuse ourselves from any obligation. We have to have checks and balances. Right now what we have before us is a lot of potentially explosive issues. I'll sweat on this. We shouldn't just wash our hands. Everybody's potentially good and everybody's potentially bad.

Devilla, unsettled by Pelletier's remarks, then moved to untable Schmidt's original resolution. With her support, it again came to the floor and this time it passed by a 3-2 vote.

Following the board majority's failure to address conflict-of-interest charges and its acceptance of Schmidt's resolution, prospects appeared dim for a negative vote on the critical issue of reappointing Ryker as planning board chair. Lyon took the lead by instead nominating Maglie to be planning board chair for 1995 and by assuring the Board that he had said he would serve if elected. After a small discussion among Board members, Devilla offered a portent of her likely vote with an ironically supportive defense of Ryker:

> I just think that, as a very active Democrat, I disagree . . . that his being chairman of the Republican Party is a conflict. I may have other disagreements with Rocky, but I don't think that's an issue. I sat and watched that [Planning] Board for eight years, up until last year ago in January, and I never saw--and I couldn't tell Republicans from Democrats in the audience--and I never saw. He was equally authoritarian to everyone. . . . As a Democrat and knowing how broke we always are, I don't know what we'd do, probably collapsed in sheer surprise if anybody had given us a donation. . . . I think it was dumb, but I don't think that that's going to make or break Moselle Plaza. . . . People do dumb . . . . I'm not going to crucify Rocky because Magellan Construction gave him $245 for the Republican Party. I sat there for eight years and saw him be equally rude to everybody. . . . I don't know why they did [give the money to the Republicans and not the Democrats]. But I don't think he's going to vote for Moselle Plaza because they gave $245 to the Republicans . . . . His price is higher than that.

After bursts of laughter throughout the room at the last remark, the vote proceeded around the table. As expected, Pelletier and Lyon voted yes to replace Ryker with Maglie. Kraft voted no, emphasizing that "Mr. Ryker has done an excellent job." Everyone knew that the final vote, Schmidt's, would also be in Ryker's camp. The critical moment had arrived. With dead silence in the room and much hesitation, Devilla voted yes, in support of Maglie. Barely believing what they heard, the large audience let out a collective sigh of relief and elation and a strong round of applause. As if suddenly appalled at what she had done, Devilla immediately asked for the floor. Speaking out directly to Ryker who stood dejectedly at the back of the meeting room, she came as close as possible to verbally reversing her vote.

> I would like to say, Rocky, don't go yet. I would like to say that I think the things that have been said against Rocky are, in many cases, are highly out of order. I sat there for eight years and watched him and, joking aside, he was both polite and rude to everybody. I had no indication that he treated people unfairly. He knows his stuff. I think

it's probably time for a change.

. . . The point is that I think Rocky has taken a lot of bad P.R., a lot of bad flak the last few weeks. He is not as bad as you all want to make him out and I think that it's been unfortunate for him. I think it's made his tenure very difficult. I think none of us is perfect and a lot of the things that have been said against him were much more a case of style than they were of substance and you may not like people who are rude or who may talk with other people on the board or who smile at the audience. And maybe in the best of all possible worlds, the Planning Board chairman is sweet and nice. . . . But each of us has our own styles and Rocky had a right to have his own style. The Town Board has supported him, Republicans and Democrats alike, for a number of years, as its Planning Board member and as the chairman of the Planning Board. And I apologize to Rocky for the way he's been treated in the last few weeks. And even though I voted for Rich and I think Rich will be super, and I've seen Rich in action too over the years, I don't like to see Rocky maligned the way he's been maligned the last several weeks.[30]

After Devilla's ringing endorsement of insider politics, the audience realized why Ryker and those of the "light planning" perspective had been entrenched for so many years and how very narrow the activists' victory had been. Devilla reduced all grievances about Ryker to personality differences, as he had himself, without acknowledging that his ideological position may have corrupted the objective role Ryker was supposed to play under SEQRA and other bureaucratic rules in place. In the eyes of community groups, these rules implied that meaningful and seriously-considered public input was at the heart of SEQRA integrity. Personality was a factor insomuch as it biased Ryker against allowing the public or dissenting board members to be heard and against considering the potential validity of their positions. But personality, in Ryker's case, simply intensified an already-proclaimed ideological predisposition toward "light planning" policy which facilitated development at every turn.

Moreover, Devilla herself over the years had shown much of the same rudeness and disdain for public critiques of development as Ryker, so no doubt she was especially willing to discount its relevance for fair process. Likewise, Devilla failed to acknowledge ideology as a factor since she herself identified with the "light planning" perspective and had therefore backed Ryker for many years. She also could not admit that Ryker's manipulations of the board and of SEQRA were very political--not in terms of the Republican-Democrat dichotomy to which she wished to reduce the term "politics," but in terms of "light planners'" dominance over "regulator" board members and the public.

Devilla's brief concession that it was now "time to change" was apparently only a matter of public relations. In her eyes, Rocky unfortunately had to be sacrificed since wrongly distrustful people had made his "tenure very difficult." A certain level of credibility of government with the public had to be maintained even when accusations of improper behavior were false. After hearing this speech, some in the audience assumed that Devilla had now made her opening bid for a bipartisan nomination for Town Supervisor in case Schmidt chose later to retire.

While ACT and CLEAR were elated to witness the "beheading" of Ryker, as the *Tribune* described it, the statements of Devilla, Schmidt's summary dismissal of conflict-of-interest issues and the explicit rationale behind their dismissal indicated how deeply entrenched "insider politics" were in Ashbury generally and thus how heavily protected was the "light planning" approach to land-use policy.

Ryker's reaction to his dismissal was predictably vicious. To the *Star* reporter, he labeled the attacks as a "witchhunt, plain and simple. It's obvious who's pulling the strings." A few days later he told the same journalist that he was considering suing Turbell and McBride if the attacks continued. To the *Post* reporter, he said, "Unfortunately, those who scream the loudest and with the least information got their way." Worst were his statements to the *Tribune*: "I got onto the planning board to give something back to the community I love. I'm not going to let these people run me out." Those who caused his unseating, he said, were "environmental fascists." Then, taking the term even further, he demagogically identified himself with the victims of fascist oppression, arguing that the Town Board's move had frightening overtones:

> Like the Nazis. First they killed the Catholics, and nobody said anything. Then they killed the gays, and nobody said anything. Then they killed the Jews and nobody said anything. Pretty soon there was nobody left to say anything.

Contending that a silent majority of "light planning" residents had not been heard, he claimed that there was widespread support for his reappointment despite the fact that it was never publicly expressed to the Town Board: "Maybe these people were home with their families. Maybe they had two jobs." Claiming never to be a quitter, he asked, "You think I had a big mouth before? You ain't seen nothing yet."[31]

Emotions at A Peak

The final Town Board drama concerning conflict-of-interest and bias charges came at its next meeting on the 26th. Even before this time, a number of activists, including Turbell herself, had become increasingly nervous that so much focus on negative issues, however important the principles, was causing public attention to be unwisely diverted from Moselle Plaza. The SEQRA process was approaching its greatest climax to date, the official public hearing where large numbers could finally register their sentiments about Magellan's DSEIS. The fear was that people potentially or already opposed to the mall would become disillusioned with the struggle because they perceived only shrill and caustic personal attacks.

An *Ashbury Chronicle* editorial by conservative Burt Tompkins, they said, was a case in point. Tompkins' support was important for building a broad community coalition. Already, for months, Tompkins had editorialized against Moselle Plaza. Now, it seemed, he was on the verge of standing on the sidelines. His new editorial, entitled, "Paranoia in Ashbury," urged "opponents [to] get away from this embarrassing sideshow and zero in on the important issues: traffic and taxes."[32]

From the middle of January, therefore, Turbell and others urged that no more verbal presentations on bias and conflicts of interest be made at Town Board meetings which might further divert attention or support from the SEQRA struggle itself. Dreyfus, on the other hand, from his legal background, felt that it was a top priority to establish a complete official record of the various charges and the local government's failure to dispose of them properly, since it was likely that the plaza issue would ultimately be decided in court. Thus he insisted that the planning board also be directly confronted with the accusations and given the opportunity to remedy the situation through recusal of those who were biased in favor.

Dreyfus argued that megamall opponents should demonstrate that they had tried every official recourse potentially available to disqualify those votes and that the Town Board, planning board and individuals concerned had refused to respond positively to these official requests. This especially concerned Rattle who was the planning board's and not the Town Board's appointment. Furthermore, not only was a record of written requests essential, such requests needed to be verbally presented or summarized directly to the boards involved-- and at the beginnings of the meetings concerned--since judges frequently read no further than the first few pages of a transcript. By contrast, Turbell and others challenged not only the continued public focus on such issues, but the insistence on effectively dominating the public input period and overall tone of Town Board meetings with this agenda. They argued that such tactics would alienate much-needed community support among those who believed that once the project's adverse impacts were known, the planning board, as a reasonable group of neighbors, would certainly disapprove. The larger background debate about the legitimacy of local government and its dependence on an agenda of an entrenched group of insiders was not an issue that many activists could claim as their own.[33]

However, substantive and procedural issues came to a head once again at the January 26th Town Board meeting. On that occasion, McBride read from Dreyfus' letter to the Town Board of the previous day. Dreyfus had pointed out that it was standard procedure for jury trials to be based on a cross-section of local residents and that dismissal of potential jurors because of questions of their potential fairness or impartiality did not undermine the system. Additionally, Dreyfus had described the responses of Ryker and Davis to ACT's and CLEAR's professional expert witnesses as having already demonstrated bias. At the planning board meeting of January 23rd, Davis had contended that placing the community groups' experts first at the public hearing would prevent the public from speaking until midnight or 1 AM, despite the fact that ACT and CLEAR had requested only the first fifty minutes. Ryker, in turn, had stated disdain for hearing from the public's "paid experts" generally (though two of the three would be unpaid volunteers). Furthermore, Ryker's continuing bias was illustrated by his statement at the same meeting that "until such time as the full list of the members of CLEAR and the financial contributors to ACT are divulged, I don't even recognize you people as having a right to ask us to do anything."[34] Dreyfus also cited Ryker's description of the community groups as Nazis and fascists as not only indicating bias but in itself so outrageous as to provide "cause" for his removal.

Despite the relevance of these arguments and new evidence, at the Town Board meeting itself Schmidt refused to budge. "You're not going to direct what this board does," he said to Dreyfus. When Lyon, in turn, moved for a revived Ethics Committee to offer opinions on hypothetical conflict-of-interest scenarios, the same majority as the week before defeated his proposal. Devilla said she opposed the strategy of considering ethics issues as they arose, one-by-one, preferring an across-the-board review instead. The matters were dropped. Responding, however, to Dreyfus' additional public evidence and his stated sense of insult when activists, some of whom were Jewish, were called Nazis and fascists, Ryker added his final word in speaking to the *Tribune*'s reporter:

> I took offense at their comments. I'm a fighter. I'll fight back. I want them to feel the hurt, the pain, they tried to inflict on me. If it hurt them, I'm glad. They're sore losers. Like cry babies, they go running to the Town Board, "Mommy, Daddy, please help me." [Nevertheless,] I will treat [their information] equally with every other piece of information I receive. Just because I find the leaders of the organizations personally obnoxious, offensive and repugnant doesn't mean I can't look at the facts objectively.[35]

EIGHT

THE PUBLIC'S OFFICIAL OPPORTUNITY TO BE HEARD

Professional Experts

Christmas 1994 brought the welcome news story that the Vermont Environmental Board had just denied Wal-Mart's application for a megamall in St. Albans, Vermont, involving the same types of adverse environmental and economic impacts as in Ashbury. To underline the significance of economic issues, ACT had submitted to the planning board at the May hearing an economic impact critique of the Vermont project by economists Thomas Muller and Elizabeth Humstone. Ashbury activists were encouraged that the logic of this analysis had now been accepted by an official government body, even though in a different state.

Meanwhile, SEQRA required that the written comment period, from Dec. 19th to Feb. 13th, be open to the public and that anyone could speak at the public hearing on Moselle Plaza slated for January 30th.[1] However, only data that satisfied SEQRA's definition of relevance was required to be considered by the planning board as "substantive comments." This meant that data of a "rational," "scientific" nature were a necessary prerequisite to comment upon the adequacy of similar data submitted by the developer as part of the DSEIS.[2] Lay opinions that the traffic condition of the town would deteriorate, that the wetlands would be degraded, and that the character of the community would be debased, while seemingly within the realm of everyday common sense, would not likely satisfy such criteria and could be disregarded. Thus, while the well-intentioned public might conscientiously respond in writing or in oral remarks at the public hearing, without adequate "rational" basis, critical comments could be met with lawful condescension. Epistemological issues thus became paramount.[3]

ACT and CLEAR concluded that to persuade planning board members of the "substantive" nature of their comments on adverse environmental impacts, their best chance would come through the use of professional experts skilled and credentialed in the use of legitimized discourse. Likewise, in case the struggle ended in court, an anti-mall case built on a record of testimony from expert witnesses would be essential. Magellan Construction had its own professional engineer and traffic engineer, professional economist Marvell had prepared the economic analysis and Busch and Napoleon were in the wings to potentially endorse the developer's scheme as the planning board's own professionals.

However, SEQRA provided no similar resources to the public and community groups.[4] While the statute assumed that the public would monitor the process and serve as ombudspeople, without specific provisions allocating fees for experts hired by the public, the potential for this role was undermined by statutory design.

ACT and CLEAR required resources to create a level playing field in which "legitimized" critical comment could be made part of the official SEQRA discourse. Bake sales would not be enough. And while Dreyfus was able to balance the scales by countering legal interpretations and opinions of Rattle and Schwab, without cost to the groups ("pro bono"), similar professional expertise in other realms would also be needed at little or no expense. Ashbury was not a wealthy community and national environmental organizations, such as the Environmental Defense Fund, the Natural Resources Defense Council and the Sierra Club, traditionally demonstrate little interest in a local struggle of this sort.

Fortunately, local professional engineer Joshua Wright had already voluntarily reviewed Magellan's preliminary materials on stormwater issues and commented upon them at scoping and "completeness" stages. He was also committed to further pro bono critiques. Professionally, Wright was increasingly frustrated by the analytical shallowness and compromises of working for established engineering firms dependent on cultivating long-range financial arrangements with municipalities and developers. He was ready to launch out on his own as an independent engineer whose "regulator" planning concerns would be represented in his work.

Inhibiting professional pressures made it difficult to find anyone in the local area sufficiently uncompromised to submit detailed critical analyses in the areas of traffic and economics. To cover both sets of issues, ACT and CLEAR thus sought experts outside of the region who were not concerned with future local employment nor with maintaining friendly peer relations with Magellan and experts hired by the developer or Town.[5] Ideally, activists wished to find persons with experience analyzing similar megamall projects elsewhere and who had shown the will to take critical positions. For this reason, McBride called Constance Beaumont at the National Trust for Historic Preservation, the organizer of an anti-sprawl conference in Boston he attended in early December.[6] Her suggested contact, in turn, encouraged McBride to call Maynard Smith, a professor of land-use planning at the University of Massachusetts-Amherst, who had also helped prepare the community group's economic impact analysis for St. Albans. Besides teaching, Smith had published extensively in professional journals. In private consulting firms, he had specialized in industrial and master planning and had critiqued numerous shopping mall proposals in the northeast. He was also on National Guard assignment as a Colonel in the Office of the Chief of Staff of the U.S. Army. From a scientific and political perspective, his credentials seemed impeccable.

Beaumont's contact also recommended Stanley Case, a Bethesda, Maryland traffic engineer, who had also analyzed adverse impact in the St. Albans struggle. He was a longtime specialist in transportation planning and traffic engineering who was also a lawyer. He had qualified as an expert witness in 17 states, including New York, and had previously held major transportation planning positions in the Baltimore-D.C. areas. He had carried out traffic and transportation studies for governments and developers throughout the United States and around the world for over 40 years and had published extensively in a wide array of professional journals. His credentials and methodology would satisfy any test for substantive reliability adopted by the planning board. Moreover, like Wright and Smith, Case's comments after reviewing the DSEIS could not be ignored without jeopardizing "light planners'" confidence that their Moselle Plaza approval decision would be upheld in the courts.

When McBride spoke with the two experts by phone on January 4th, each was interested and available. Smith offered to prepare a written critique of Marvell's economic analysis and to appear at the public hearing for $2000. Case was willing to do the same concerning Magellan's traffic data for the cost of travel and lodging alone. In his words, he had worked so many years on the other side, he was now trying to balance the scale by providing expertise for community groups.

McBride immediately sent off to each of them detailed documentation about Amsterdam Square and Moselle Plaza projects, including relevant DSEIS sections, planning board resolutions, articles from the local press and lengthy lists of significant impact issues in each area which McBride himself had assembled. Smith and Case agreed to have a draft statement written within two weeks.

The Community Prepares

ACT and CLEAR activists were also intensely engaged in researching evidence and preparing their own statements for the January 30th public hearing. While delegation to professionals might satisfy the techno-legal dimension of SEQRA planning, a local voice which contextualized these data in terms of the community's moral authority was essential to make the dialogue meaningful to the wider public and to continue to politicize the issues. For traffic and economics realms, McBride regularly communicated with Case and Smith, not only to provide further details, but to integrate their respective analyses into the presentation that CLEAR itself intended to make. As part of the earlier SEQRA process, Ashbury engineer Joshua Wright had already prepared several lengthy analyses for stormwater and wetlands issues. Now he and Turbell built upon these to further refine the case and integrate it into communitarian concern for the wetlands and aquifer dimensions of the local ecology. This process enabled Turbell as well to prepare her own extensive critique on behalf of ACT. While Magellan, an out-of-town developer, would depend upon highly-paid outside experts with little or no connection to the town, the two community groups would speak in a local voice informed and corroborated by expert data but which originated from within the town itself.

On January 9th, ACT sent a mailing to hundreds in the community, largely those who had already actively supported ACT's position or signed petitions. The letter brought readers up to date on the SEQRA process and sought donations to cover additional publicity, while urging further circulation of the anti-mall petition and a large turnout at the public hearing. In addition, CLEAR sent a letter to its members on the 22nd, announcing the significance of the change in planning board chair for a more open process, while encouraging attendance and testimony on the 30th. A list of 22 potential substantive issues was enclosed.

The IDA issue was especially attractive to several leaders of the Ashbury Downtown Merchants Group (DMG) who had linked with ACT and CLEAR in devising a strategy to oppose the mall. Using McBride's draft analysis of IDA-derived fiscal benefits for Moselle Plaza as well as megamall fiscal impact analyses for other communities, the DMG began circulating an anti-tax abatement petition among its members and customers in downtown stores. It also submitted a letter to the Town Board on January 5th asking the Town to oppose tax relief for the project. At the Town Board meeting of the 19th, at the peak of confrontation on the conflict-of-interest charges, the DMG president presented its petition with 400 signatures--including 45 of the 65 DMG members.

The DMG statement described the economic and fiscal damage expected from Magellan's megamall. It also informed the Town Board that New York state had passed IDA reforms in 1993 (just after RCIDA's Medford approvals) which intentionally banned malls of this sort from IDA benefits because of unfair economic advantages these gave to retail store chains over local competitors--without compensating gains for the community. The DMG cited documents from the press and state legislature providing additional critiques of IDA abuses and helping to intensify the reaction of Ashbury residents against IDA benefits for Moselle Plaza.[7] At the January 23rd planning board meeting, the DMG also asked that board's support in its request to the Town Board for IDA status denial.

Ground Rules
After replacing Ryker, Maglie insisted to the press that the planning board

wouldn't change much under his leadership, "it will probably just be a little less flamboyant."[8] He also stated that "Rocky and I have a great working relationship. I hope to continue it." Ryker, in turn, predicted that Maglie "will be a very good chairman. He's got my full support."[9] Community activists were well aware of their friendship and remained wary of Maglie's potential for independence, given that Ryker continued to participate in the process as a regular planning board member. Nevertheless, Maglie's ideological perspective toward planning over the years seemed less rigidly "free market" than Ryker's and his mild personality seemed both less hostile to the public and less able to impose a personal agenda on the board. After the January 19th meeting, both McBride and Turbell personally congratulated Maglie on his new position. While not the decisive break from Ryker they would have liked, both were hopeful that Maglie would help make the SEQRA process more open and fair.

At the planning board meeting of the 23rd, Maglie assured CLEAR and ACT, against objections from Ryker and Davis, that the community groups' professional experts would be allotted the first 50 minutes at the public hearing and that necessary microphones and audio-visual equipment would be provided. Maglie's compromise gave greater latitude to the public than could ever have been hoped for under Ryker's reign and seemed to assure the public that legitimate environmental issues would receive a just hearing. Finally, Maglie agreed that the meeting would be scheduled for the high school auditorium to assure that everyone who wished to could attend.

On January 30th, the date of the hearing, McBride, Dreyfus and several others met Maynard Smith and Stanley Case for the first time and accompanied them through different parts of the town they would refer to in their reports. The experts' confident critiques of the inadequate and shoddy data submitted by Magellan and by Marvell were reassuring. It would be difficult for the planning board to adopt conclusions, without comment, which professional expertise on record would now show were flawed from both methodological and substantive perspectives.

The Public Hearing

Though ACT and CLEAR had both publicized the event, they had no sense of how many would attend. By the beginning of the hearing, however, over 500 turned out. While many were familiar faces, many others were unknown personally to any of the three leaders and some of these individuals immediately signed their names to speak. It was still unclear how the evening would proceed.

As the minutes and hours unfolded, activists realized that no script could have been better prepared. Maglie first invited the Ashbury FoodFeast manager to present the views of Medford on its desire to relocate to Moselle Plaza. With the assistance of an architect's rendering, the manager briefly explained the benefits the town would obtain from a new facility, arguing that FoodFeast could not provide its customers with a desirable quality and range of items at its current location. In addition, he contended that if the project was rejected, FoodFeast would have to consider relocating to another town, leaving Ashbury without a large supermarket. As the only public officials ready to speak, Mayor Gary Patton and Carl Dunning, members of the Village Board, then described the damage the megamall would cause to the downtown and pointed to similar dynamics already experienced elsewhere in the region.

On behalf of the community groups, Joshua Wright then outlined major negative impacts likely from the project's stormwater management plan and discussed the failure of the DSEIS to adequately address such issues. Concerning stormwater quality, Wright stated that in the 1970s, the federal Environmental Protection Agency had discovered that "the concentration of pollutants in stormwater discharge were greater at the first part of a storm than the concentrations contained in raw sewage." For this reason, DEC had eventually issued its stormwater regulations in 1993.

Wright then described the critical location of the project itself:

> . . . it's pretty much at the top of the watershed of the Roodekill [stream]. Whatever impacts happen from the Moselle discharge of the stormwater [are] going to affect the Roodekill all the way down to Perch Pond--it's quite a reach--and then on down to Yellow Creek to the Hudson. The area around the Roodekill is a very sensitive environment. We need to really make sure that whatever is going to be developed on this parcel is adaptable, to be able to make sure that that sensitive environment isn't compromised.

Wright pointed out how the proposed system would fail to remove soluble phosphate, nutrient and salt contaminants and thus do significant damage to the delicate balance of the wetlands. While the DSEIS minimized the impact of de-icing salt, Wright stated that the amount used for 14 acres of mall pavement would be the equivalent of salt used for 5 1/4 miles of highway, but concentrated all together. Finally, he spoke of the great increase in volume of project area stormwater compared to present conditions and, with overlay maps, demonstrated how the project's stormwater retention ponds would intrude illegally upon existing on-site federally-designated wetlands. While Wright's written submission developed each point in considerably more detail, his verbal statement was simple and clear enough to dramatize the significance of this stormwater/wetlands realm to the planning board and audience alike. It was an auspicious beginning which could not be dismissed, out of hand, by those with a "light planning" perspective.

Stanley Case then summarized his analysis and conclusions from reviewing

Magellan's traffic study.

> The project would have a significant impact on traffic conditions on the Route 354 corridor from Creighton Road through Green Corners Road. Taking the Traffic Impact study that was prepared for this project at face value, there would be large increases in delay of travel through the principal intersections. . . . This is not good news for motorists.

Case stressed that the situation would be much worse than admitted by Magellan because of serious shortcomings in its methodology. These included failure to consider other nearby substantial developments, incomplete traffic growth projections, exaggerated lane widths at intersections,[10] combining very different lane delays at specific intersections in order to imply more acceptable "average" traffic flows and "arbitrary and unwarranted reductions in trip generation." Concerning the final distortion, he said, "I've been doing this work for 40 years, and I have never seen the kind of discounting of traffic that took place in this analysis." Most dramatically, he asserted that "even if the recommended road improvements are made--and there's no assurance of that-- that both Green Corners and Creighton Road" intersections would experience peak hour conditions deteriorating from today's B or C to an E level. "Levels of service E and F are not acceptable in New York State and just about everywhere else." While Ben Hillman could no doubt understand Case's analysis, the glazed look on the faces of other planning board members seemed to suggest that scientific discourse, while the asserted basis for legal action, could only legitimate members' pre-existing ideology. When ideology conflicted with scientific rationality, board members might simply pick and choose that which supported their views and discard that which did not.

Land-use planner Maynard Smith was the community groups' final professional consultant. He led off quickly with a shocking expose of the Marvell report's failure to address basic questions in the official scoping agenda. The report, he said, described no impact on the town's overall fiscal position, only data on revenues, and no impact on town and school taxes. "In this case, we have no knowledge of whether there will be a net tax increase or a net tax decrease to a specific homeowner in the town." Similarly, while there was data on the projected number of jobs to be created, "there is nothing in the report about the jobs lost and . . . about the characteristics of the jobs that are to be gained." While the report claims that the project will have no impact on downtown merchants, Marvell "offers little backing for that statement beyond raw data." The report therefore failed to comply with the scoping agenda concerning impacts on town fiscal position, school taxes, jobs created, household income, and existing businesses.

Smith then reviewed Marvell's flawed assumptions and evidence concerning likely future regional growth rates, geographical extent of the likely retail consumer base, local market leakage, the effect of other proposed megamalls in the same Hudson Valley region, typical effects of Wal-Marts on traditional downtowns, secondary and tertiary negative impacts beyond those affecting Wal-Mart's direct local competition, typical patterns of Wal-Mart sales expansion over time, Wal-Mart's slower pattern of job expansion proportional to increased sales, and declines in tax values for empty commercial space resulting from construction of the megamall.

He then summarized the likely impact of Moselle Plaza on community character which, under SEQRA, was the original link to make economics relevant to a finding of adverse environmental impact:

> Your town evolved steadily and slowly over time. There isn't a big bang that occurred to cause any major transformation of that community. For the first time, you are going to have a major development on the other side of the [Thruway] that's equal to 90 shops in the village . . . . That's five times the size of your Agway, and it is going to be on the other side of the highway. This is a big bang. Rules of thumb are that as long as commerce is growing in concert with growth, it is okay. When you get something that is a substantial grower, indeed you're getting a disruptive agent, such as the case with this project.

Turbell then proceeded, with a series of maps, to present the board and audience with visual images of the wetlands and project impacts on water quality. She explained Amsterdam Square's earlier, more extensive and preferable plans for stormwater treatment ponds; delineated on-site federally-declared wetlands endangered by Magellan's groundwater and stormwater plans; discussed potential contamination of on-site groundwater, a major aquifer and nearby state-designated wetlands through salt piles, pesticide residues from past orchard use and stormwater residues; and addressed the impact of effluent discharge from Moselle Plaza's on-site sewage treatment plant on the Roodekill stream and adjacent wetlands. Turbell's effort helped to open access for "regulator" board members and the general public to technical issues previously unfamiliar and too complex.

A representative of the Town's official Environmental Conservation Committee then described their intent to pursue a detailed study of the large aquifer in the Creighton Road-Rte. 354 area and requested that the mall project not be given SEQRA approval without extensive analysis of that aquifer and its potential degradation. Artist Fran Killington then spoke on the "visual blight" the concrete block megamall would create at "the gateway to Ashbury and the mountain range, not only for residents but for the tourist trade we want to encourage." She suggested instead that the site combine a mini-park with a tourist welcome and information center.

A highlight of the hearing was Sara Miller's set of on-screen overlays dramatically illustrating, with concentric circles, precisely the retail market zones already or about to be claimed by Wal-Mart and other big-box megastores in surrounding towns and cities of the region. In actuality, she said, the uncontested Ashbury retail market would have only about 13,000 people. She posed the relevant question of how many Wal-Marts could survive in such a saturated region. "If one of them should close--and maybe it is the one that's built in Ashbury--if that comes to be, what effect will that have on our community?"

Shortly thereafter came what one paper called "the evening's peak disclosure." Andrew Kirk, the owner of a one-hour photo store in Ashbury Plaza, several weeks earlier had informed McBride that he had direct personal knowledge that the planned big-box department store for Moselle Plaza would be a Wal-Mart. This was the first confirmation anyone in ACT/CLEAR ranks had received that their assumption was correct.[11] Magellan Construction had consistently refused to identify that anchor and always insisted that it wasn't yet known. Beyond offering to contribute funds to ACT, Kirk then agreed to testify at the public hearing. Facing the large crowd on that occasion, Kirk stated that in April 1994 he had called a Magellan Construction official he knew earlier from a different context. Potentially interested in locating his store at Moselle Plaza, he told the official that he would have no motivation to do so if the megamall anchor was a Kmart or Wal-Mart since each chain had its own quick-photo division. His Magellan contact told him the deal was not yet finalized, but he would let him know. Several weeks later, still in April 1994, he informed Kirk that the anchor would be a Wal-Mart. Kirk's account not only confirmed community suspicions, it also publicly exposed Magellan as a duplicitous applicant. For Magellan and for Wal-Mart (which itself had denied any plans for Ashbury), it was a public relations disaster.

In his own statement a few minutes later, McBride chose to emphasize the "preciousness" of the present day Ashbury community by integrating the earlier statements of the experts with his own "common sense" analysis of various impacts Moselle Plaza would have on community character. To exemplify differences between scales of retail activity, he spoke of current cooperation between the several drug stores in town. If one of them ran low on a product, it could call up the others to temporarily replenish its stock. In contrast, an unaccountable mega-store would simply devour existing small stores such as these. "Competition of this second sort," he said, "is like placing an NFL team on the same football field with the high school team and then approving the results as the survival of the fittest." He concluded by suggesting that:

> a project sponsored and promoted by one of the state's largest
> contractors, by a major 32-store supermarket chain and by the world's
> largest retailer controlled in turn by one of the world's richest families
> . . . [was] unlikely by definition to be much concerned with the
> interests of a community the size of Ashbury.

He cited the bad faith of all three companies in publicly hiding the name of the
main anchor as precisely the sort of relationship with outside interests which
the community did not want.

At least two dozen more spoke out against the project. By contrast, only a
local realtor-developer friend of Ryker--who reminded people that "landowners
have a right to develop their property"--and two more FoodFeast employees
spoke in favor. All speakers against the mall received loud applause, reflecting
sentiments of the vast majority attending the hearing.

Some speakers, such as professional horticulturalist Bob Martin, gave further
expert testimony concerning technical aspects to be considered. Others, such
as Ashbury resident Gail Garvey, made clear to the developers the strength of
community opposition: "Let me assure Magellan Construction and Medford
that they will fight an uphill battle. We will have no dead stores and no dead
streams in Ashbury." Most simply spoke with common sense intuition and
from the heart. Against the backdrop of scientific rationality, initially relied
upon at the hearing by the community groups, such sentiments took on added
significance. One area resident, for example, challenged FoodFeast's claimed
need to expand with a series of questions and answers, loudly cheered by the
audience after each one: "I shop in your FoodFeast and I find what I need. You
need fish? We've got Rizzo's. You need a pharmacy? We've got Almond and
McCleary's. You need a deli? We've got The Deli." Toward the end of the
hearing, ACT vice-president Jerry Killington dramatically presented to the
board the anti-plaza petition with about 1600 signatures.

The *Tribune* later reported the response of Medford and Magellan
Construction officials throughout the several hours of testimony. Huddled
together in a corner of the auditorium, they reacted

> . . . impatiently when speakers went beyond loose time-limits, tried to
> catch Mr. Ryker's or the Chair's eye while tapping a timepiece,
> seemed contemptuous of many points of view, laughed or shrugged at
> serious objections to the project, [and] offered no defense of the plan
> other than [the store manager's] pale statement . . . . It was as if [the
> officials] had decided to be present only to gauge the strength of the
> opposition, to plan the next move, and to proceed with a "public be
> damned" attitude.[12]

Ryker, in turn, displayed the same non-verbal antipathy for public comment
which Julia Bellows had accused him of in her memo two weeks earlier to the

Town Board and which he demonstrated at the first public hearing in May. This time, however, Ryker chose to wear a tee shirt with Hebrew inscriptions rather than his usual sweatsuit attire garnished with the American flag or some other patriotic message. The Hebrew, it appeared, was related to his "brownshirt" accusation previously voiced in the press against ACT and CLEAR.

ACT and CLEAR activists were elated with the nature and dynamics of the public hearing.[13] The anti-mall testimony was broad in scope and substantial in every area of the official SEQRA agenda. For the most part, it appeared to satisfy SEQRA's "substantive comment" standard which would require a response by the developer and the planning board before a final determination could be reached. Moreover, because of the turnout and crowd reaction at the auditorium, it was now increasingly difficult for Ryker, Davis and those who supported the "light planning" perspective to marginalize the opposition as a small group of malcontents. From all appearances, a significant number of the community was opposed to Moselle Plaza. Most speakers also submitted written copies of their speeches and, in some cases, much more detailed comments as well. On behalf of CLEAR, McBride's written remarks amounted to 53 separate issues in 33 pages; Turbell submitted 24 issues in 32 pages for ACT. Each of the professional experts handed in expanded statements as well, all assembled and submitted together with an introductory memorandum from Dreyfus. The latter included, as well, all of the maps and overlays with sequential exhibit numbers. An impressive substantive record was now created.

Media Coverage

ACT and CLEAR realized from the beginning that the planning board's decision whether to approve Moselle Plaza was inherently a political choice normatively couched in an environmental cost-benefit analysis. SEQRA established no precise formula to determine whether the social and economic side of the equation outweighed the environmental damage, but instead left determination to the discretion of the planning board. That decision, in turn, would depend on which voting group within the planning board could muster a majority. At the public hearing, only one "regulator" board member remained, with two positions vacant, awaiting appointments by the elected Town Board. It was therefore essential for the community groups to create political pressure on elected officials to assure that new appointees to the planning board reflected what was rapidly becoming a more environmentally-conscious community on this specific issue. If new members of the planning board would join with Ben Hillman in disapproving the megamall, community groups would be one vote away from a majority. Along the way, activists would have formidable insider allies on the board who could demand that

Magellan respond to each of the substantive comments on the DSEIS. Failure on Magellan's part to comply, coupled with a whitewash from the "light planning" majority would create a credible court record for reversal, given the majority's vulnerability to attack based upon the procedural record of bias and conflicts of interest.

In this context, the local media became an important contested terrain. Fortunately, the *Tribune* had a large portion of each paper devoted to letters submitted from the public. ACT and CLEAR members had sent letters from March 1994 on to publicize each stage of concerns, thus effectively educating a significant part of the local community and politicizing the overall struggle. Moreover, editorial writers for the two local weeklies had begun in the Fall to assume an advocacy posture by explicitly opposing the mall. In January, regular news stories in both papers and the three regional dailies covered the attacks against Ryker and his "light planning" allies which led to the former's removal as chair. Solid investigative journalism to pursue data and leads suggested by the community groups could offer additional important leverage in gaining ever more public support in the weeks and months ahead.

The public hearing provided an opportunity for the media to fully understand the debate and to familiarize itself with the legal and scientific discourse which framed SEQRA analysis. Articles in the local weeklies--the *Ashbury Chronicle* and the *Tribune*--were especially detailed. The latter publication complemented its intense favorable coverage on the public hearing with a series of related articles: an account of the decades-long demise of one reporter's Hudson Valley hometown due to precisely the same development dynamics at issue in Ashbury; an article on the Town Board's evasion of conflict-of-interest issues at its January 26th meeting; coverage about the DMG's mounting campaign against IDA tax abatements; and an editorial by the publisher against large projects that adversely affect taxpayers and "violate our sense of scale." The *Tribune*'s next issue maintained this momentum with a strong investigative report challenging the accuracy and depth of the Marvell report on economic impact and with a powerful editorial entitled, "Just say no."

> After last week's public hearing on Moselle Plaza, it's pretty obvious that a very large majority of the people in Ashbury are passionately opposed to the proposed mega-plaza. In fact, if the developers had any sense or compassion, they would pack up their bags and catch the next bus out of town. . . . [Whichever SEQRA decision is made,] there will be trouble. If the project is passed on to the final level of review, the community will rebel and start chaining their children to bulldozers and trees. If the project is turned down, the developers will take their case to court. The planning board is in the hot seat no matter what it does. But the choice before them is clear and simple. They get to

decide if Ashbury has a government for and of the people or if it has a government despite the people.

The combination of investigative journalism, editorials, and letters buoyed ACT's and CLEAR's hopes that the "light planning" majority would ultimately be isolated as pariahs acting from self-interest, either ideological or aggrandizing, with whom elected officials would be reluctant to identify.

Involved Agencies

Beyond critiques from the public and outside professional experts, the official public comment period until February 13th also was open to responses from the broad list of "involved" agencies at local, county, state and federal levels.[14] The potential depth and breadth of these critiques were critically important in influencing the planning board and, if need be, the courts, since such agencies were automatically under SEQRA considered as offering "expert testimony."[15]

Of the six "involved agency" letters received during this official period of public comment, none were decisively opposed to the project, though serious questions were raised.[16] On traffic impacts, some Forest County Planning Board (FCPB) comments were comparable to those of Stanley Case, including the need to include better projections of expected traffic growth in the future and the unacceptability of "E" level traffic conditions.[17] The Forest County Department of Public Works (FCDPW), in turn, unexpectedly demanded that its own consultant independently analyze the impact of traffic on local roads-- with the cost of the study to be paid by the developer.[18] By contrast, the Department of Transportation (DOT), an agency which originally had opposed the SEQRA statute's adoption and viewed it as hostile to its principal road-building mission, provided a brief superficial review of the DSEIS, assuring the planning board that "the methodology used for [traffic] analysis seems to be reasonable," judged by DOT permitting standards.[19]

On stormwater issues, the FCPB questioned the accuracy of Magellan's stormwater and detention pond figures and the adequacy of its stormwater management system to prevent higher runoff than already existed. The FCDPW rejected, as it had for the Amsterdam Square project, Magellan Construction's plan to add a second culvert pipe for the flow of additional stormwater under South Creighton Road to wetlands on the east, therefore requiring the developer to "provide a solution for the [stormwater] drainage on site." Meanwhile, the DEC stressed concern with protecting state-designated wetlands, thus recommending, as with Amsterdam Square, stormwater and wastewater treatment alternatives whenever possible to avoid intruding upon those areas.[20] Most importantly, it asked that the types of detailed information usually required for DEC permits at the site-plan stage of review also now be included as part of the SEIS. Likewise, the NYS Thruway Authority was critical of the quality of the DSEIS,

> due to the overall lack of written material to guide the reviewer through the work. The technical appendix that presents the work must have a narrative that specifically shows how the design storms and runoff were completed. . . . This narrative must include a discussion of pre and post-development flows entering Authority lands and exactly how these post-development flows will be held to pre-development levels.

The Thruway Authority was also concerned to discover on February 7th that Magellan intended to reconfigure the Rte. 354-Thruway ramp intersection and that additional site stormwater flows would be discharged into the Thruway's drainage system. These issues were not mentioned in the DSEIS, but should have been, and would now require additional plans and calculations for review.[21]

While not explicitly opposing the project, the comments of the involved agencies thus strengthened the hands of community groups who needed as much expert concurrence as possible. With such responses, ACT and CLEAR could now invoke the spectre of impartiality in contending that their experts' findings had been independently corroborated and could not be disregarded. Regardless of the "light planning" perspective of the majority, the judicial standard requiring the planning board to take a "hard look" at adverse environmental impacts could now be invoked to require Magellan to prepare a responsive SEIS addressing the agencies' commenting concerns. And the adequacy of Magellan's response would be something the community groups could contest.

IDA Concerns

While the SEQRA public comment period was coming to a close, the issue of IDA tax abatements and their role in the financing of the project continued to remain a focus of concern for the coalition of community groups opposing Moselle Plaza. The DMG on January 5th had formally asked the Town Board to oppose any tax abatement for the project and had later submitted a petition with 400 signatures of customers and owners of local businesses. Toward the end of the month, the DMG assembled and distributed another information sheet on the relevant issues, citing strong critiques of IDA policy in a 1992 New York State Senate report and an analysis published by the Fiscal Policy Institute of Albany in the same year.[22]

On February 14th, DMG officers again asked the Town Board to take a formal position against an IDA tax abatement. Specifically, it recommended a non-binding resolution in which the Town Board would publicly state that if the Reading County IDA submitted Medford's application to the Town, as required by state law, the Board would disapprove it, "absent any new information, additional information or supporting documents." The proposed resolution also encouraged Medford to comply with its original representations in the IDA application by simply expanding at its present location rather than abandoning its current store and moving to Moselle Plaza.[23]

The DMG request to the Town Board was strengthened by investigative reporting for the *Tribune* at the end of January. In an article entitled "Bondage: Investigation Reveals Discrepancy in Moselle Plaza Application for Big Tax Breaks," the reporter reviewed overall abatements available through IDA status and then explored the misrepresentations in Medford's application.[24] The *Tribune*'s investigative report could not have been better timed for the DMG's request to the Town Board. CLEAR's January 26th letter to the Town Board reviewed in detail the statements in the article, the application misstatements and the relevant state statute which Medford had violated.[25] All such information made a favorable Board decision on the DMG's proposed resolution politically more palatable. In adopting such a statement, the Town Board could demonstrate support for local business and against welfare for large corporations, while still retaining the free-market "light planning" perspective held by a majority of planning board members. In any event, the resolution would not be risky because of its "non-binding" nature. With ACT and CLEAR support, however, the DMG believed that this symbolic action, along with a lengthy SEQRA process and growing public outcry, would help to discourage Medford from further participating in the joint venture with Magellan and might even encourage it to reconsider expansion on site.

At the Town Board meeting of February 16th, activists had no sense of how the resolution would be received. Once again, it seemed, Devilla's would be the swing vote, given the "light planning" perspective of Schmidt and Kraft and the "regulator" perspective of Lyon and Pelletier. The outcome was a surprise: 4-1 in favor, with only Devilla opposed. Apparently Kraft and Schmidt felt that the action was so moderate and non-committing that they could afford to appease the small business community, without risking their base among "light planning" supporters generally.

In the course of the Board's discussion, however, Schmidt opined that his vote was neither binding nor an accurate predictor of his ultimate disposition on the issue. He stated that if and when Magellan Construction was finally at the point of needing Town Board approval to obtain IDA financing, he would probably vote favorably if they were willing to throw a new fire engine or other infrastructure upgrades into the deal.[26] His statement, commodifying the issue of approval, reminded activists of the offer a few weeks earlier by Reynolds to Turbell, in effect, to buy off the opposition. It gave community groups reason to pause.

PART THREE PROJECT REVIEW

INTRODUCTION

The premise of participatory environmental impact reviews, such as SEQRA, is that grassroots democracy combined with serious science will produce wise land-use policy concerning specific development proposals. The wide variety of perspectives, lay and expert forms of knowledge, attentive listening, lay engagement with and critiques of expertise, and non-personal "community" perspectives, all, in addition to defense of self-interests, could produce a rich context for intelligent land-use judgments. As described in Part II, however, even laying out an appropriate research agenda, the first stage for serious inquiry, was a highly politicized endeavor aimed at restraining participatory involvement. Between community groups which sought more powerful analytical lenses and a developer and its "light planning" board allies and their consultants who sought more superficial review, there was a constant battle to determine the official approach to be adopted. While eventually the worst polarization was reduced through activists' extra-SEQRA political challenge to the authoritarian board chair, the underlying tension, based on basic land-use ideological differences, remained.

After several stages of agenda-setting input from the developer, the planning board, outside agencies, outside experts and the public, culminating in the official public hearing and public comment period, research and analysis responses to this input were now the SEQRA order of the day. If the developer and board would accept the legitimacy of the research agenda proposed in response to the DSEIS, identified issues could be explored with appropriate methodology and likely environmental and economic impacts seriously assessed.

Chapter Nine makes clear that the developer and "light planners" of the board remained committed to only facial compliance with SEQRA's expectation, while evading serious research into issues raised by the public. With the board and its consultant planner censoring significant research suggestions ("substantive comments"), with the developer's marginalization of issues in its Draft Final SEIS, and with the chair's and consultants' blockage and deferral of efforts to explore substantive topics on the table and their sometimes explicit disdain for "scientific" endeavor itself, procedural tactics most often minimalized board engagement with the substantive issues themselves. In effect, the procedural battle over appropriate agenda continued into the substantive phase supposedly dedicated to intensified research and analytical review.

To confront this procedural evasion from and marginalization of substantive analysis, community groups were forced constantly to intrude themselves, through their own and their experts' critiques, into at least the written record dialogue being established. Such self-asserted participatory intervention, however much resisted by the "light planners'" attorney, was required to educate, promote engagement and develop a formal record of attempted, but unsuccessful, "administrative remedy" for later judicial review. At the same time, community groups lobbied to assure that newly vacant planning board seats would be filled by individuals committed to and capable of understanding the participatory spirit of SEQRA, thereby employing its full potential for serious impact assessment.

Chapter Ten moves from the struggle over the SEQRA inquiry's internal operating rules to eventual planning board debates over substantive issues in the realms of stormwater and water quality, traffic and economics. Such debates remained in part epistemological, since there was little agreement among board members as to the proper approach to inquiry itself. The dichotomizing and rivalry of "scientism" versus "common sense" were a constant dynamic, not entirely explained by the land-use ideological orientation of board members.

SEQRA's "hard look" standard demanded at least the pretense of competent scientific engagement, but also permitted wide discretionary latitude for evaluative rigor on the part of the lead agency. When more refined lenses of inquiry were tried, in analytical discourse concerning stormwater, water quality, traffic and economics, untranslated as they were by the board's consultant planner, they threatened the capabilities of the board, and threatened the underlying domination of the SEQRA process by politics. While community groups were confident of their position at "scientific" and "intuitive" levels both, "light planners," for the most part avoided pursuing methodical inquiry too far. In turn, understanding the politicized nature of the arena and for other reasons, outside state agencies were reluctant to contribute their own expertise or even a statement of "professional standards" to facilitate intelligent consideration of the issues at hand. Whatever dialogue occurred, therefore, was primarily between experts of the developer and those of the community groups, far from a participatory model. The board's professional planner had little to say on substantive concerns and seemed mainly concerned with moving the process beyond the participatory SEQRA realm where his technical interventions would be less obviously political in connotation.

As before, at this stage of SEQRA deliberations as well, community groups were forced to attend to extra-SEQRA dimensions of the struggle. In effect, they had to create unofficial participation when the official participatory realm was so constrained. Chapter Eleven thus describes efforts to deepen a community sense of the economic threat of the megamall by focusing on tax abatement welfare sought by the developer and soon to be granted by an out-of-county "shadow government" public corporation. While broadening the grassroots coalition, this strategy also aimed to gain favorable judicial intervention and thereby discourage the developer from proceeding. At the same time, activists sought to engage FoodFeast in a reconsideration of its intent to move, knowing that the chain's refusal to do so would further weaken the image and credibility of the Moselle Plaza proposal generally. A series of picket-line demonstrations outside of FoodFeast accomplished the same goal and brought awareness of the megamall issue to a wider segment of the local population. Finally, community activists decided to acknowledge the underlying adversarial politics of the megamall issue and to appeal to the moral economy of the citizenry by fielding a slate of anti-mall candidates for the Town Board. All of these efforts, it was believed, might also have salutary effects as well on dynamics within the planning board itself which was not isolated in daily life from the community.

NINE   THE PLANNING BOARD'S REVIEW: PROCEDURAL ISSUES

Seeking A Fair Playing Field

While the January efforts by ACT and CLEAR to remove planning board members Ryker and Davis, attorney Rattle and the firm of Harvey & Plonsker clearly raised public awareness of Ashbury's old-boy political network and conflicts of interest within it, they failed to achieve their principal goal of removing these people from positions of power. Rattle remained as the planning board's special attorney, while Davis and Ryker remained on the board, intent on continuing in Moselle Plaza deliberations. The firm of Harvey & Plonsker also stayed on as regular planning board attorneys. Ryker was replaced as chair, but only by his friend Maglie who had publicly always accommodated Ryker's tactics in the past. On the other hand, it was hoped that the level of public exposure achieved in January would now at least moderate "light planners'" procedural manipulations and place their behavior before the public eye as an issue of controversy itself. This would happen, however, only if ACT and CLEAR maintained constant vigilance, ready immediately to intervene to rectify procedural failures.

Vigilance meant that community groups had to attend every planning board meeting, from beginning to end, month after month, whether or not Moselle Plaza was officially on the agenda, since discussion of the issue and decisions could occur at any moment regardless of notice. Vigilance meant carefully recording every discussion of the project or process with handwritten notes and audio cassette for later review (and potential use in court).[1] It also meant reviewing the project file in the planning board office every several days to gain access to the latest written communications among Magellan, outside agencies, Rattle, the board's expert consultants and the board itself.[2]

Continued public participation in the SEQRA process was essential if board members were to have needed information to critique Magellan's response to substantive comments about the DSEIS on the record. The statutory design empowers the developer to respond, but does not require the planning board to allow further participation from the public.[3] The logic is that the planning board, with help from its own consultants, would be able to take a "hard look" at Magellan's responses to determine whether Magellan had adequately mitigated any contested environmental harm and to suggest reasonable alternatives to the original design. However, the gap between theory and practice, at least in Ashbury, was significant. Paid by the planning board at the hourly rate of $125, Busch was hardly independent from the "light planners" who had retained him originally. Rarely would Busch even speak out at a meeting in which Moselle Plaza issues were debated. When he did participate, it was almost always to suggest that the developer's plans for mitigation were reasonable and that the subsequent permitting process by involved agencies would assure adequate environmental protection. The planning board's engineer never attended meetings and would respond by letter only to specific requests without any overall contextual analysis. His work for private developers in the area, in any event, lent credence to the notion that he couldn't be counted upon to critically analyze Magellan's responses to substantive issues of stormwater, water quality and traffic.[4]

Dreyfus was particularly interested in having Wright and Case respond in writing to any analysis or mitigation proposed by Magellan and in having Smith do the same for further data presented by Marvell or anyone else acting on the board's behalf who sought to place Moselle Plaza in a favorable economic light. His concern was not only to create a record which showed the inadequacy of developer and Marvell responses and how they could not be reasonably relied upon by a board committed to SEQRA's "hard look" review standard.[5] His view was also that if Magellan skirted issues and attempted to whitewash critiques with misleading or inaccurate data or generalized pleas for board trust, a "hard look" failure by the board, plus the bias and conflict-of-interest issues, could be used to persuade a reviewing court to reverse board approval and to require a fair and impartial SEQRA review.

Laying the Groundwork

On February 6th, Dreyfus wrote a letter to Maglie with new evidence to justify Ryker's recusal from further discussions on Moselle Plaza and his removal from the planning board. He cited Ryker's statements in the *Tribune* attacking CLEAR and ACT as Nazis and not to be taken seriously "until we know who they represent and where their money comes from," denouncing their leaders as "personally obnoxious," and announcing his intention to make them "feel the hurt, the pain, they tried to inflict on me." Dreyfus stated that "the evidence is overwhelming that he lacks the basic competence to consider these data [from ACT and CLEAR and their experts] objectively as distinguished from their source." Without recusal, Ryker's "continued participation in the Moselle Plaza application process will render that process a sham and any decision made by the Planning Board regarding that application null and void."

On February 13th, the day of the planning board's first meeting following the public hearing, Dreyfus listed by hand-delivered letter a series of procedural requests. At the top was a request for public comment at planning board meetings.

> There is an ongoing need for public dialogue with the Planning Board regarding the SEQRA process related to the Moselle Plaza application. The organizations I represent have submitted substantive comments in writing from experts and lay people. They are concerned that they have an opportunity to respond to the applicant's comments prior to final acceptability of the DSEIS.

Dreyfus pointed out that the DEC's *SEQR Handbook* "specifically provides for consultation with experts and outside consultants by the lead agency prior to preparation of the final SEIS."[6]

On March 3rd, Maglie indicated by letter to Dreyfus (with copies to all board members) that all public hearing and written comments on the DSEIS would be forwarded to Magellan Construction and Marvell and that Busch would prepare an outline of issues raised verbally or in writing. Once responses from Magellan and Marvell were received, they would be forwarded to involved agencies for comment. After that input, a final SEIS would be prepared by the board. All responses would be available to the public. However, with a strikingly different tone from Ryker, Maglie also promised that:

> the Planning Board still encourages public input during the remainder of this process. . . . The Planning Board will evaluate all the information it receives from the developers, involved agencies and the public before it makes its SEQRA determination regarding this project.

Maglie's actions were entirely justifiable under SEQRA since community groups' outside experts would be the principal source of data for critiquing Magellan's responses to comments on the DSEIS. But his exercise of discretion not narrowly mandated by statute was a significant break with the past, demonstrating that Maglie himself was committed to "pragmatic capitalist" concern with at least the appearance that the process wasn't rigged.[7] Hence Ryker's removal as chair had begun to pay a major dividend--the community groups' ability to create a record--regardless of whether it indicated a change in Maglie's substantive thinking. Both the public's right to continue informing the board and the board's promise to consider such input were finally now legitimated. In the past, the public had to assert the right to be heard, unilaterally, with no guarantee of recognition. This was an important first step, however cautious, toward the concept of SEQRA as research and decision-making through community dialogue. At the same moment, however, Maglie also refused to go beyond the Town Board's "resolution" of the issues of bias and conflict of interest and refused to open issues of recusal for discussion among the board.

Filling Planning Board Vacancies

At the time of the January public hearing, there were two vacancies on the planning board, with Pelletier recently elected to the Town Board and Dalrymple having resigned. Filling these vacancies became an issue of ever-greater importance. Given the change in the town's overall political atmosphere, with even traditionally "light planning" residents joining ACT and CLEAR to oppose one aspect or another of Moselle Plaza, community groups thought that the time was ripe to seek applicants with "regulator" views. One of ACT's members suggested Suzi Green, an Ashbury resident for 27 years and administrative assistant to DEC's Region D director. Green chaired the Ashbury Environmental Conservation Commission, was president of the Ashbury-based Van Wyck Valley Rail-Trail Association and had volunteered her candidacy for the one-year vacant Town Board seat in December 1993. According to Fran Killington and others in ACT, she was strongly concerned with protecting the environment and would be a good counterbalance on the board.

Turbell suggested Bob Manley, a young lawyer who had arrived in the community with his family only the previous May. As an attorney in a nearby city and past member of an environmental conservation commission in northern Westchester County, he had immediately applied to fill a vacancy in the Ashbury EnCC. Those who came to know Manley during this first year were impressed with his environmental concerns. Turbell argued that Manley was familiar with SEQRA regulations and would feel free to confront a Rattle-Ryker interpretation which narrowed unnecessarily the board's concerns.

Because of these reputations, activists lobbied Lyon, Pelletier and Devilla for each to be appointed. Manley made an appointment to speak with Devilla individually to reassure her that he could be trusted to follow the law and that she would feel comfortable in appointing him. Devilla seemed particularly pleased by Manley's willingness to accede to her position and personal scrutiny. Both candidates competed with two others endorsed by Ryker. Neither of the latter apparently had credentials in the planning field, although one was a member of the Ashbury Garden Club. Both, however, were outspoken in favor of the free market and the need to increase the economic base of the town through further development. The differing perspectives of the candidates underscored the sub-text that the Town Board's apparent decisions would be viewed by many as a vote up or down on Moselle Plaza.

However, Manley and Green also offered Town Board members predisposed to building a megamall the timely chance to restore public credibility in the decision-making process when the Fall elections were not far away. It had now become risky for Schmidt and other potential candidates to openly ally with Ryker and those who favored a megamall when the DMG and others in the local business community had allied with many residents to visibly oppose the project.

Nevertheless, activists were pleasantly surprised when both Green and Manley were appointed at a February 1995 Town Board meeting. Each gained three out of five votes, with Schmidt joining Kraft in opposing Manley and Devilla joining Kraft against Green. Though "regulators" Manley, Green and Hillman would be still short of a majority, activists now counted on having three board members prepared to give a fair hearing to the community's anti-mall critiques. Four were needed for a majority, but Dreyfus and others believed that Ryker had by now so discredited himself on the record that there was reasonable hope for his vote to be tossed out in a court review of the SEQRA decision.[8] A resulting de facto tie vote would bring a prior SEQRA approval decision back to the planning board.

While Ryker and Davis were seen as committed to approving Moselle Plaza and Maglie almost certainly so, Myers' vote was slightly more in question. Owing his seat to Ryker's manipulation and vocally supportive of Ryker in public, it seemed unlikely that Myers would be capable of crossing his patron. Indeed, rumors circulated during the Spring and Summer that Myers was being primed for nomination as a Republican candidate for the Town Board. Likewise, activists also heard the rumor in early Spring that Magellan Construction and Medford considered the SEQRA vote already locked-up in their favor--which meant Myers was already committed.[9]

Nevertheless, Myers was still untested in any showdown project decision to date. His December "completeness" approval of the DSEIS was not necessarily a decisive test since "regulator" Dalrymple also had felt that the document was ready for public review. Moreover, there was some reason to think that Myers might want to distance himself from Ryker. In a chance Spring 1995 encounter at the local bakery, a member of one of the community groups asked Myers' wife, whom he already knew, whether Myers was capable of voting independently from the person who secured his seat. Her response indicated that while she opposed the megamall, she couldn't speak for her husband; but she believed that he would not automatically follow Ryker's position. In mid-July, local Springtown Road neighbors of Myers even circulated a petition against Moselle Plaza and organized a small meeting with him to share their concerns. From their past experience in the local neighborhood association, Myers had a reputation as a wild card and the July meeting left them with a sense of non-committal and unpredictability both.

Rattle's Legality
At the February 13th planning board meeting, Rattle resumed his attempt to define a narrow path of legitimate SEQRA activity. Rattle was restrictive

rather than inclusive, by implication, when he informed the board at this meeting that its Final SEIS (FSEIS) response to any comments received after February would be discretionary and should only be done if the comments were deemed "substantive" in nature. While a literal reading of SEQRA regulations, Rattle's manner of presenting the issue of legal obligation suggested that he would discourage rather than encourage additional information, in contrast with Maglie's later letter of March 3rd. This was clarified explicitly when the board directly discussed, at this meeting, the issue of the public's right to more input. For Rattle, the only appropriate time for further public comment was in SEQRA's automatic 10-day period following the board's eventual acceptance of the FSEIS.[10] By his view, community groups and their experts would be excluded from critiquing Magellan Construction's responses to the public hearing until the board had accepted them, however modified, as appropriate.

Rattle's restrictive intent at the same meeting was shown further when he referred to allegations by ACT, CLEAR, Hillman and Pelletier that the DSEIS accepted as "complete" in mid-December did not adequately address the outline of the scoping document.[11] Without addressing the merits of this contention, Rattle cited a state court decision holding that it was not necessary for a scoping outline to be "slavishly followed in preparing an EIS,"[12] while he omitted to say that assiduous compliance with detail had never been held by courts to be an abuse of a planning board's discretion under SEQRA.

As for preparing the FSEIS itself, Rattle suggested that Magellan and Marvell prepare proposed responses to the public comments. "[The] board and its consultants can then analyze and evaluate both the comments and the applicant's proposed responses and prepare final responses." The board could also consult, if needed, with involved agencies and "independent professionals" to deal with some of the complex issues. Rattle's advice here was unexceptional. But couched as it was, it conveyed how facial compliance with SEQRA would bias the process in favor of an applicant's framing and agenda, supplemented by the planning board's and involved agencies' own expertise, without regard for the expertise of those retained by the community groups.

Rattle then attempted once again to isolate the relevance of economic analysis from other scoping realms so as to de-legitimate its consideration. This tactic left lay board members with the impression that economics had nothing to do with environmental issues and could not properly be considered under SEQRA. As if this narrowing of legitimate SEQRA issues was not enough, Rattle also told the board that even traffic studies "are 1/3 art, 1/3 science and 1/3 B.S." In other words, leave it to the experts but even then don't take "scientific expertise" too seriously when contrasted with your own "common sense."

By Rattle's implied scenario, professional experts of Magellan, the planning board and outside agencies would handle technical review issues, the public would be excluded and only stormwater issues deserved or could obtain a "hard look" based on science. Appropriate to this logic, Rattle devoted 5 pages of his 7-page letter to the planning board to discuss the process of post-SEQRA site plan review, thereby implying to board members that its remaining SEQRA review would be relatively brief. Indeed, Maglie himself predicted a final SEIS decision in May.[13]

With Maglie's March 3rd assurance that continued written public comments would be welcome, Dreyfus responded to Rattle in a letter to him and the planning board on March 8th. As before, he contended that Rattle's remarks about economic impact analysis, if unchallenged, would significantly cramp board ability to examine the "community character" issue under SEQRA. Maynard Smith and CLEAR had both presented community character and growth-inducement as major areas of evidence and critique in the official public comment period. Furthermore, Rattle had omitted entirely the relevance of economics to the SEQRA cost-benefit balancing analysis which the board would have to undertake once it identified adverse environmental impacts. The relevance of this balancing test was that likely job loss and vacancies in existing plazas and the downtown would drag the local economy, and thus would not overcome, through positive socio-economic effects, otherwise negative environmental impacts on traffic conditions, wetland pollution, and community character.

Busch's Consultation and Advice

The March 13th meeting saw the board's first attempt to develop a list of "substantive" issues which had been raised in the public comment period and which the board therefore needed to seriously address in the FSEIS.[14] It was thus a critical meeting for assessing the degree to which the planning board would take a "hard look" at the issues and thereby assure the integrity of the SEQRA process.

Busch's March 10th "draft/preliminary listing of substantive written comments" offered by the community was the basis for the planning board's discussion. This document, which Busch created without initial input from board members themselves, was an important delegation of planning board responsibility to the board's consultant. After all, board members were present at the public hearing and were assumed to have read those comments which were submitted in writing by experts and others. Thus, if lay common sense meant anything, it would suggest that this was a task within the capacity of the board.

Busch's document first listed 8 substantive topics under "stormwater and water quality management and erosion," 9 under "traffic" and 4 under "economic impact," the same 21 topics that the planning board had listed in its August 8th scope. Busch then quoted distinct comments under each topic which asserted how Magellan had inadequately addressed or neglected the issue in the DSEIS.

Immediately conspicuous to activists in the audience was Busch's omission of any comments made by professional expert Maynard Smith on economics, by McBride/CLEAR on all three scoping topics, by the Forest County Planning Board on stormwater and traffic and by board member Ben Hillman on all three areas. Most of these comments provided an empirical basis upon which to confirm the accuracy of other critiques noted by Busch on the same topic and in many cases raised new significant substantive topics of their own. As the discussion of this list proceeded for several hours, it appeared that no board member was sufficiently familiar with missing substantive comments to enable them to question Busch regarding their omission. When the discussion drew to a close, McBride asked from the floor why Smith's and CLEAR's extensive comments had been excluded. Surprised at the question, Busch himself appeared unfamiliar with these comments and provided no explanation. Maglie attempted to save face:

> I certainly am not prepared now to say that Gene's comments were the final comments and those are the ones we are going to address. But I also intend to focus on, and it's not going to be that much more extensive. There may be other issues that come up. But it will be quick and rapid and we will sign off on it by the 27th. Davis jumped in to claim that CLEAR comments didn't really add significant new issues beyond those already recorded anyway, so it didn't matter that Busch didn't record them in his list. Said Davis, "I think Gene did a wonderful job." Hillman was not present and Manley and Green, who were not on the board at the time of the public hearing, appeared too new to the fray to understand the significance of omitted data. For others of the "light planning" majority, there was apparently no problem.

Only after the meeting did the reasons for Busch's omissions become more clear. Busch stated that he had never even seen the written comments of CLEAR or Smith in the documents he had reviewed for preparing his outline. He stated, "nothing not on the log-in list [prepared by the board's secretary] was looked at." However, board members, Busch and Rattle were all present at the public hearing where Smith and McBride had spoken and where each had announced that he was turning in written remarks as well. In addition, the FCPB was an involved agency and anything it submitted should have been easily flagged.

Apparently, Busch had not reviewed a transcript of the public hearing to determine who had spoken and what they had said.[15] Nor did he appear to have reviewed the planning board file to see what reports had been submitted. Either the package sent to Busch omitted the documents at issue or Busch chose not to review them. Incompetence or intentionality were the only explanations for this major error and for Busch's failure to use the hearing transcript as a further referrant. Beyond this was the complicity of the "light planning" majority and Rattle in not even calling these omissions to Busch's attention once his memo was read.

McBride's was the longest written submission received by the board and provided considerable detail in the areas of traffic and economics. Smith's was the only professional economist's detailed critique of the Marvell report, and his verbal remarks, based on his submission, were a central highlight of the public hearing. It was as if Busch and the "light planning" majority hadn't even heard or listened to Smith's testimony. Caught in flagrant transgression of SEQRA responsibilities[16] which would significantly compromise board adherence to the "hard look" standard, Maglie agreed to correct the record by asking Busch to include those items in a final draft prior to the next board meeting. As much as any single event in the entire SEQRA process, this occurrence demonstrated to activists the need for the community's close scrutiny and critique at each and every step taken by the board and its consultants in order to assure that members addressed the substantive issues.

Beyond these omissions, very conspicuous as well was the fact that the professional engineer acting on behalf of the community groups, Joshua Wright, was recognized by Busch as a source of substantive comments only once. While many of Wright's points had also been covered in Turbell's statement for ACT, the potential impact of such critiques on the board and on the official record was necessarily diminished by citing a lay person only-- however well-informed--instead of a recognized professional expert.[17]

Concerning economic impact issues, Busch stated (without having reviewed Smith's and McBride's submissions) that many of the comments were very speculative and very subjective in nature. Maglie added that the board was getting only rhetoric about fiscal impacts--to which Ryker heartily agreed. Schwab saw his opening and claimed that this was why Magellan Construction had objected to examining economics in the first place. Maglie then echoed Rattle's position from a month earlier, stating that all economic analysis was very subjective, a basically irrational guess about the future. "We could stack up [economic development] reports for and against until we're blue in the face. But it all depends on the future."

> My problem with economic impact statements, doing a number of
> them, is that tell me what assumptions are or tell me what answers

you want and we'll justify the assumptions. And the assumptions change from year to year and day to day. . . . I mean I can do the calculations, there's nothing earth-shattering about it. But I'm not sure I know how to do the calculations correctly.

For his part, Ryker proposed simply deferring the whole subject to the Reading County IDA since that was the "permitting agency" for this realm. Under this logic, if RCIDA thought that Medford was a good risk to re-pay government-backed IDA bonds, then that would end the inquiry--regardless of the economic harm that a Wal-Mart-led megamall would afflict on the tax base of the town and on local businesses. For Myers, Ryker's remark went beyond the pale and it was the first time that he had objected to an approach suggested by a fellow "light planner." He stated that deference to permitting agencies is "exactly the opposite of . . . what we said before. Regardless of what the permitting agency . . . allow[s] or disallow[s], it's still something that we have to do."

Maglie's only concession was that the project's fiscal impact should be calculated by Marvell, including the effect of potential tax abatements. Myers, in turn, thought that potential assessment effects on the older upper Main Street malls should also be examined. However, this was too much for Magellan. Complained David Jankoff, the project manager, "This is getting expensive. Wanting new things like this--things you never wanted before--is just making the whole thing messy."

Nevertheless, with new members Manley and Green virtually silent and Hillman absent from the meeting, the "light planning" majority, fully encouraged by Rattle, Busch and Magellan, steam-rolled over the board's August 1994 scoping intent. Busch's large-scale arbitrary filtering, the board's narrow view of its response to substantive comments on adverse environmental impacts, and Rattle's legal assurance that judicial review was concerned with form over substance, all apparently guaranteed for Magellan a relatively quick and easy approval process.

Maglie's announced schedule confirmed the rush to judgment. On March 27th, he said, the board would finalize its list of substantive comments to be addressed by Magellan in its draft FSEIS.[18] Responses from the developer and Marvell would be returned by April 17th and immediately sent out to involved agencies. By May 8th, all agency comments would be in hand and, by late May or early June, the board would formally accept the draft as final.[19]

On March 15th, Maglie wrote to Marvell requesting responses to public comments on the economic impact portion of the DSEIS.[20] However, Maglie filtered further Busch's already-restricted list and highlighted only six specific comments despite also sending CLEAR's letter. This, in turn, provoked Marvell on March 22nd to send only a brief response. None of CLEAR's letter was addressed. None of Marvell's six specific responses was more than a few sentences in length and only reasserted his original findings without responding to the critiques.

At the March 27th planning board meeting, Busch presented a two-page supplementary list of "substantive comments," based on the written submissions from the Forest County Planning Board, Maynard Smith and McBride/CLEAR, as well as statements made by the public at the public hearing and recorded in the official stenographic transcript. Busch acknowledged that all of these documents provided extensive comments and "many of these are substantive." However, because he elaborated no further, the board could not know which specific comments Busch believed were substantive and deserving of a response.

Perhaps responding to McBride's comments at the previous meeting regarding his omissions in his initial list and the effect of this on his professional reputation, Busch also added the most assertive planning advice, consistent with SEQRA spirit, he had delivered to date:

> Finally, it is my opinion that there have been many substantive comments made on most every scope issue that need to be addressed in the FINAL SEIS. I also believe that the responses cannot be simply "yes/no" or "it's a permit issue" type of responses. Many of the comments will require involved analysis and, perhaps, changes to the proposed project. In any case, I think the Board should be as engaged as practicable in the process of response preparation.

For the first time, Busch also now directly faced the critical issue of whether Marvell's economic analysis had to consider the effect of Wal-Marts on Main Streets throughout the United States. Though the transcript record included a local retailer's testimony that Magellan identified Wal-Mart to him as the principal anchor tenant, Magellan continued to maintain that it had not, as yet, signed a lease with any company and that it could not say, with certainty, what store would be the principal anchor. Busch acknowledged that Smith's and McBride/CLEAR's reports presumed Wal-Mart to be the tenant and that both reports had presented considerable data about Wal-Mart's specific negative impacts on local business communities. He pointed out that the planning board's scope "included a request for mega store ' . . . data, studies or other such information . . .' which thus far has not been provided [by Magellan] or its existence refuted."

He contended that if Wal-Mart indeed had a unique type of impact and if it was planned as the Moselle Plaza anchor, "then comments made with respect to Wal-Mart may be valid and important." Busch also pointed out that various comments had addressed issues of impact on "community character." Though not specifically an item in the board's August scope, he acknowledged, as

McBride had suggested, that the term "community character" had been used in the board's notices of positive declaration and determination of "completeness" of the DSEIS and public hearing. He raised the procedural question, therefore, of whether "community character' ought not to be a valid issue for substantive comments.

Despite omissions and elements of caution in Busch's statement, this March 24th memorandum was a significant procedural breakthrough. Not only did it partially rectify Busch's omissions of two weeks earlier, it also challenged the "light planning" majority to acknowledge that serious issues had been posed on the official record concerning economic impact which were both relevant to community character and a later commodifying cost-benefit "balancing" analysis. Implicit in these cautions was the concern that if the board failed to acknowledge these critiques, it would be vulnerable to a serious court challenge arguing that it had not taken a "hard look" at relevant issues as required by SEQRA case law. The board could not easily ignore such procedural advice from its own planning consultant, now itself on the record.

However, at the same board meeting, "light planners" made only a superficial effort to comply. Rattle's advice was that considering Wal-Mart as a "worst-case" scenario was problematic:

> [P]resumably when you do something like a shopping center, you can't use a catastrophic analysis situation that you would use with, say, with petroleum or something like this. . . . I have a little bit of a problem with saying this is a Wal-Mart because that's purely speculation. . . . [T]he assumption . . . that if this is a Wal-Mart, it'll have the greatest impact of any shopping center or shopping deal or whatever it is--that assumption I don't think is one that could be used here, and maybe shouldn't properly be used here. . . . I think you have to look at what a shopping center is and not any particular shopping center. Well again, the whole premise being made at the public hearing was a Wal-Mart is the worst-case analysis. But I don't know that you can use a worst-case analysis.
> . . . I'm not trying to guess the identity of the ultimate tenant. I don't think it's important.

To re-assure "light planners" that they should avoid the Wal-Mart issue altogether, under Rattle's rubric of speculation, project manager Jankoff reiterated that Magellan did not know the identity of its major anchor. Davis and Ryker assured him that they found his statement credible, without reference to the impeaching contrary testimony from the local merchant at the public hearing. For his part, Myers suggested that perhaps Wal-Mart might even be a "best-case" scenario.

Avoiding implications altogether of a big-box retailer, whether a Wal-Mart or Kmart or other such store, placed "light planners," however, in an untenable position. While Maglie insisted that Wal-Mart impact was probably just the same as Kmart and Rattle asserted that the board couldn't legally focus on just a single chain, both had to admit that potential discount department store impact could and should be examined generically. Indeed, such an economic analysis was specifically called for in the "regulator" majority's July and August scoping documents, however distasteful it was to "light planners" at the time. Nonetheless, Marvell had provided only a brief disclaimer that Wal-Mart would not have a substantial adverse effect.

Conceding the legitimacy of analyzing generic big-box store impacts, however, was not something that Magellan would accept as a rationale for paying further beyond the $12,000 it had already escrowed for Marvell. Magellan made its defense on procedural grounds. Jankoff complained that the process would be too delayed, especially because of these new economic concerns. Hillman and Maglie suggested following Busch's advice to set up a meeting with Marvell to develop a list of substantive issues. Myers remarked that "based on what Mr. Smith said, I'm not sure we should pay [Marvell] in the first place." Smith, he stated, had ripped Marvell's report "to smithereens." Ryker stated that he didn't think Marvell would return for a new meeting. Maglie then suggested simply using Busch's March 13th list of economic impact items, plus the comments by Smith and CLEAR, as the substantive issues to be addressed in the FSEIS. Hillman raised the danger that Marvell would not say enough in response to the list to be meaningful. As he saw it, the biggest problem with Marvell's original December report was that it was simply "a string of one-liners," with little traditional analysis and documentation. From his own position, Ryker began to see the need to disassociate himself from Marvell, whose report he had originally proclaimed to be eminently fair. He pointed out that Marvell was Julia Bellows' choice, not his, thus further reducing Marvell's authority.

Rattle then reverted to his original position, marginalizing the legitimate place of economic impact in SEQRA reviews. "If the impact of this project will cause a major change in the community, then it is ripe for and should be addressed. If it doesn't, it doesn't even need to be included in the EIS." This comment contributed nothing analytically to the board's assessment of whether critiques of Wal-Mart, or any big-box retailer, were substantive and required a response. But it served to caution the board that, in Rattle's view, the whole issue of economics could be dismissed as irrelevant and that in continuing to discuss big-box retailers, the planning board might be treading in legally-dangerous water. The way out of the Wal-Mart morass seemed clear. Avoid it altogether and the board's attorney would use legality as the basis for its defense.

In closing the meeting, Hillman pointed out that his own December 12th lengthy list of critiques of the DSEIS should also have been sent to the developer for response in the FSEIS.[21] However, not even "regulator" members offered remarks about those public and outside expert comments omitted from Busch's March 10th list of stormwater and traffic issues but admitted by him at this meeting as "substantive." The board thus gave tacit approval to Busch's earlier narrowing of the FSEIS agenda, without discussion as to whether any of these newly-admitted "substantive comments" required Magellan's response.[22]

The Draft FSEIS

At the April 17th meeting, Jankoff and Schwab presented Magellan Construction's several inches-thick draft of the FSEIS. Addressing only issues of stormwater and traffic, this new document began with a project description barely revised from that in the DSEIS. Specifically, it now included a new eastbound Rte. 354 turn lane into the Thruway and an enlarged stormwater detention pond in response to the Thruway Authority and the FCDPW. Following this section were copies of all written submissions to the board during the public comment period and specific point-by-point responses to each question raised by Busch's March 10th list of "substantive comments" by involved agencies and the public. For the most part, Magellan's responses were brief and condescending, if not openly dismissive of the questions as irrelevant or answered elsewhere in the document.[23] Responses to economic questions were deferred to the planning board and its consultant.

Maglie had written to Marvell on March 29th and called him a week later, specifically asking that he provide responses by April 17th to the issues raised by Smith and McBride. By fax on April 10th, Marvell sent a summary response defending his earlier brevity, but offering additional services only if an additional $7350, plus expenses, were paid.

The issue of Marvell's availability and even relevance now again became the focus of the board. At the April 17th meeting, Maglie reported on Marvell's reply and questioned whether further work on his part would show anything different or be of any use. Disavowing the value of any further expense and the attendant delay of another Marvell report, he stated, "I don't have much faith in [economic consultants]." Maglie felt that analyses in this realm were an unending chain of events and said that he was more than comfortable working with what was already available, regardless of having no responses to Smith's and McBride's comments about Wal-Mart and big-box retailer impacts. Green added that spending another seven or eight thousand dollars would be unjustified.[24]

Members of the community groups present were frustrated by the "light planning" majority's continued superficial discussion or its decisions to avoid issues entirely. They were also frustrated by "regulator" members' inability to counteract this pattern and thereby obtain compliance with SEQRA's "hard look" requirement. In actuality, the process had degenerated into little more than smoke and mirrors. As Dreyfus said afterwards to the *Tribune* reporter, "[board members] are in no position to engage in an [economic] analysis."[25] Instead of the board's March 27th apparent commitment to a serious agenda, this entire realm of economic impact issues was now in serious danger of being marginalized into a minor footnote of the FSEIS. Magellan Construction, Rattle, Ryker and Davis no doubt favored this procedural outcome, while Busch had again lost his independent voice. On the other hand, because of Magellan's refusal to do an SEIS economic impact study of its own and now the perceived incompetence of Marvell, the board and Magellan were left with no professional expert opinion of their own with which to respond in the FSEIS to serious economic questions raised by Smith, McBride/CLEAR, and other members of the public. This meant that the issue would be glossed over entirely and, if Moselle Plaza were approved, community groups would have to untangle the web and demonstrate to a judge how the planning board had abdicated its SEQRA responsibility.

At the May 15th meeting of the board, following discussion of stormwater and traffic issues, Myers expressed continuing discontent with the lack of a credible economics response section in the FSEIS. He suggested that Marvell's report and the comments it provoked be sent on to another consultant. In his view, Marvell's responses were "very superficial." The board had to demonstrate that at least it had made an effort to meet minimal expectations to satisfy the "hard look" standard.

Maglie resumed his skeptical response: "I have personal feelings about economic consultants. They'll work with statistics and give you any answers you want. . . . I don't think there's anything earth-shattering in any of those documents I've received from any of the consultants that persuade me to say that this is really a science." Hillman agreed with Myers that the economics public comments "have not been adequately addressed." Myers added flatly, "I don't think we're competent, capable or have the time to do [the review] and I don't think it's in the best interest of the applicant." Ryker asserted that the board had hired an economic consultant, in the first place, "against the advice of counsel." As if on cue, Rattle revived his theme about the illegitimacy of economics in the SEQRA equation. However, this time he added, "If they [economics] be taken into consideration by you on making a finding statement, it should be taken, but it's not part of an EIS." This final, confusing, one-sentence caveat, apparently conceded Dreyfus's earlier point that economic impact was indeed relevant in making the cost-benefit balancing test in the final SEQRA determination. Rattle's overall tone and the method by which his remarks were framed left the board with the clear impression that it was now unnecessary to address the issue further until appropriate adverse environmental impacts had first been identified. Ryker asserted that, in any event, economics was only a matter of common sense which members of the board were as capable as anyone of assessing:

> With or without Marvell, with or without the developer, I can take a look at the worst-case scenario of the shopping center in relationship to the presently existing Ashbury area and even in the surrounding area and make an intelligent determination as to whether or not it will have an economic impact. I feel extremely confident that I'm able to make that determination.

Ryker's "lay common sense" approach provoked a response from Busch. Repeating Marvell's claim, he suggested that many of Smith's and CLEAR's comments were "what-if" remarks. However, he questioned if the board was capable of deciding which comments were of this speculative type and which were based on uncontroverted facts. He also suggested that another firm might be reluctant to render a second opinion. Hillman pointed out that many areas of the scope were unaddressed by Marvell, but addressed intelligently by the public. However, both he and Manley supported Myers' assertion that the board was not expert enough to fill the gaps and provide credible responses. Maglie, sensing what appeared to be a coalition majority in favor of further study, then declared that he would take on the analytical burden himself and would report back in a month,[26] a decision he later contended was made by "consensus."

Agency and Community Experts

On April 18th, Rattle sent a letter to "involved agencies," inviting responses to Magellan Construction's draft FSEIS. The key involved agencies who might respond would be the DOT, FCDPW, the Thruway Authority and the DEC, each with seemingly substantial concerns of its own. By Rattle's criteria, agency experts, applicant experts and board consultants Busch and Napoleon were the only legitimate players at this stage of the SEQRA process. Each of the first three agencies responded in May[27] while the DEC waited until July. As well, the USDA Soil Conservation Service (now the Natural Resources Conservation Service) responded on May 11th to Maglie's earlier request for data on stormwater management practices.

Rattle's failure to invite community groups to respond to Magellan's draft FSEIS would seemingly preclude their experts from participating in the review of its adequacy.[28] However, for ACT and CLEAR, the only legitimate SEQRA procedure was one which fully involved the public and its experts as well. Leverage through this alternative set of experts was significant since the planning board would otherwise rely mainly on Magellan/Marvell responses.[29] Armed with Maglie's letter of March 3rd authorizing an open file and the FOIL requirement to which Ryker himself had ultimately acceded, community groups were able to maintain ongoing access to the planning board file. This contained all correspondence and documents submitted to the board and was invaluable in continuing the activist and community groups' experts' ongoing critiques.

The tension between Rattle's narrow approach, requiring notification only to involved agencies, and Maglie's March 3rd exercise of discretion, permitting community groups and their experts to participate, would continue for many months as the latter sought to compete for planning board attention. While the usual "reliable" experts, i.e., those hired by Magellan and those employed by involved agencies, were called upon by Maglie and Rattle, the community groups repeatedly responded with data and analyses provided by their own experts, whether explicitly invited or not. Given the perspective of Magellan's experts and the bureaucratic mentality of agencies primarily concerned with their own permitting process, it was only through this engaged process of critical "peer review" that the community groups hoped to obtain a balanced and in-depth substantive discussion which would demonstrate the inadequacy of Magellan's responses. In each case, responses by experts on behalf of ACT and CLEAR, or supporting their perspective, directly confronted the adequacy of Magellan/Marvell positions. Importantly, at the very least, they created identifiable doubt as to their credibility.

The leading procedural issue now was whether and how Magellan would begin responding to the community's experts.[30] Potentially, a legally sufficient and scientifically credible discourse could be imposed on Magellan by the outside critiques. To an objective reader, this would prevent the planning board from relying solely on Magellan's responses in making its findings. This would mean pitting expert against expert, an unusual occurrence in planning board practice, where normally experts deferred to one another. However, such a dialectic on record would allow "regulator" members to choose sides and to contend that there was an adequate, albeit contradictory, scientific basis for their conclusions.

Moreover, if outsiders could frustrate Rattle's attempt to narrow the discourse, Maglie, Ryker, and Davis would be required to provide non-ideological reasons for supporting a project which provoked serious substantive critiques with which involved agencies and the board's own engineer might come to agree. Forcing the board, in effect, to produce reasons rather than conclusions, community groups gained an important advantage over "light planners" who had rarely before been required to satisfy the "hard look" standard in any way other than to receive documents and to acknowledge that they had been considered and reviewed. Now they would have to read these documents and grapple with the contradictions themselves.

Defensive Maneuvers

The first "light planner" approach to the onslaught of analytical correspondence was to attempt simply to curtail further input. In a May 5th letter, Rattle warned Maglie that as far as he was concerned, enough "new and/or updated data has now been obtained." Planning board discussion must not be allowed to go beyond potentially significant environmental effects of the project that were omitted or inadequately addressed in the earlier Amsterdam Square EIS.

The second approach was to limit the ambit of the board's final SEQRA determination. Rattle stated that the present process should not be "a de facto review and analysis of every environmental impact that was previously reviewed and analyzed in the [earlier] EIS." It was therefore time for the board to decide whether or not the new data and information demonstrated new or different significant adverse effects from those analyzed already for Amsterdam Square in 1990. Such an up-or-down vote would curtail the making of any further record and could potentially foreclose an argument later crafted by community groups that the planning board had not adequately addressed significant issues.

Rattle's strategy of damage control provided "light planners" with a way out of the debate, without ever resolving competing and contradictory assertions of the experts through reasoned analysis. In effect, should a "light planning" majority conclude that there were no new significant adverse environmental effects from those considered by the board in 1990, it could simply re-affirm its earlier approval finding without addressing the currently-competing assertions. This, of course, depended on whether Rattle's client, the planning board, sought a legally justifiable means of approval under SEQRA without further analysis of the issues. Should a majority wish, through the discretion granted by the statute, to pursue the matter further and comply not only with the letter but the spirit of SEQRA, then Rattle's advice would be viewed as an effort to control the decision in a manner favorable to his own predisposition.

Rattle's unwavering support for facial compliance over actual compliance with SEQRA intent emboldened the other "light planners." When confronted with Hillman's objection at the May 15th meeting that no one had considered the Soil Conservation Service's substantive objections to the stormwater management plan, Ryker simply evaded the concern by contending that the USDA SCS had suspect credibility and, in any event, its opinion was non-binding.

It's obvious by their [the Soil Conservation Service's] own admission that they no longer have staff to provide the detailed analysis that some people thought they would be able to do. . . . This [report] is advisory. This is some people who have obviously very good intentions but don't have the staff or the expertise in these areas . . . to do the kind of work that some people are leaning on them . . . . And all I'm saying is let's not hold this up to be the holy bible, the end-all and be-all of this discussion. That's all I'm saying. And you can obviously and will disagree.

In any event, Ryker opined, permitting agencies reviewing the project after SEQRA approval would be much tougher than the planning board. Hence, having received responses from Magellan to public comments, the planning board could leave well enough alone and simply "backload" any further environmental consideration to the permitting agencies.[31]

Undaunted by "light planners'" strategy of discount and evasion, Hillman pointed out that Moselle Plaza's incursion into the on-site southerly lot implied that the board should ask Magellan to provide office-use traffic generation figures for that second lot as well. Amsterdam Square's EIS and Magellan's DSEIS had used light-industrial-use traffic figures for the same area and the town was about to allow office use in light-industrial zones. Ryker and Davis, who had never shown familiarity with even elementary-level traffic analysis, then suggested that the planning board could simply make those calculations on their own. Moreover, Rattle again attempted to foreclose serious consideration of the effects of Moselle Plaza on the light industrially-zoned southerly lot. He contended, "You really have to stay away from the light-industrial area" since Moselle Plaza was a site-specific project which, except for parking and infrastructure, was situated entirely on the northerly lot. Under his view, measuring cumulative impact by considering any potential development on the southerly lot, not directly related to or dependent upon Moselle Plaza itself, was inappropriate.

Here as elsewhere, Rattle defined what was inappropriate in terms only of what was minimally required by SEQRA case law rather than what was within the board's discretionary authority and encouraged under the statute. While courts responding to environmental groups challenging the actions of planning boards under SEQRA have not mandated the doing of a discretionary act, as long as the agency could proffer a reasonable explanation for its refusal, courts have also never held that, out of reasonable caution, a planning board exceeded its discretionary authority, for example, by requiring a cumulative impact analysis.[32] Indeed, courts have cautioned continuously that the SEQRA review process should not be "segmented" to artificially narrow the purview of the board's concerns and thereby allow the board to lose sight of the forest for the trees.[33]

Led by Rattle and Ryker, and with Busch's support, "light planning" members were now prepared to accept Magellan's responses as adequate. Without further deliberation and analysis, they were ready to approve the project and, consistent with the "backloading" approach, defer all further environmental impacts to permitting agencies with greater expertise in areas of specific concern. According to its advocates, not only was such a damage control strategy within the planning board's discretion, it would appear that the planning board had no other reasonable choice. Thus, while "regulator" members Manley and Hillman and seemingly ambivalent "light planner" Myers sought initiatives for the board to develop its own method of analyzing substantive issues and the adequacy of Magellan's responses, the other "light planners," with Rattle's encouragement and support, were invited to eliminate further inquiry. What Busch had accomplished with his narrow filtering of comments from the public comment period was now carried a stage further.[34]

Social Discipline

Maglie set the tone at the next planning board meeting, on June 19th, by indicating that he hoped for an FSEIS "completeness" vote by the end of July. After initially discussing at length Maglie's economic impact report, responding to Smith and McBride, the board returned to issues of stormwater management. When Hillman again raised a concern brought by Wright for an alternative stormwater management design, a need substantiated by planning board engineer Napoleon, Maglie angrily retorted, "Bull crap!" All the board needed was to know conceptually that a change of design was possible. They could get around to changing it in detail in the site plan. Hillman persisted. He wanted to learn about the potential environmental impact of an alternative design first, before the site plan stage, as required by SEQRA.[35] In addition, he demanded an adequate site plan map equivalent to that provided at the SEQRA stage by the developer of Amsterdam Square. Hillman pointed out that the alternative detention basin size and location could well affect other issues as well. Maglie responded by marginalizing Hillman's concerns. He simply overruled the request without a vote by stating, "Let's move on to the next point."

Hillman, however, was persistent, thereby forcing the question of members' normative behavior. Maglie and the "light planners" operated under the guise of consensus. While this meant little more than the board's accession to the will of the "light planning" majority, the etiquette of the situation meant that no member would directly challenge the power of the chair to define the consensus of the board.[36] In this instance, after several more exchanges between Hillman and Maglie about the need for an alternative stormwater design, Maglie exploded, asserting that having only one stormwater plan at this stage "will be legally defensible." He shouted, "What you want is a full-blown site development [plan] down to the last tree planted! . . . You kept asking additional and additional and additional and further and further details!" Busch backed him up. "It may be a little semantical at this point" to have such detail, he said, since the site plan will demand an elaborate review and potential changes anyway. Hillman refused to back down. There was a need to know what impacts would be now rather than later, he asserted. "I feel completely uncomfortable without a level of detail that produces information equivalent to what was presented to the planning board in terms of Amsterdam Square."

Maglie stated that the way to meet such concerns was for board members to place as many conditions as they wanted in the approval findings statement. This response omitted the fact that the board had the authority to disapprove a project under SEQRA because of a failure to present alternatives and that the board was not required to re-design the project through imposing mitigatory conditions. In any event, a "light planning" majority, hostile to requiring Magellan to do anything other than what the company accepted in its responses, realistically would seek to prevent such conditions from inclusion in the board's findings statement. Busch agreed with Maglie, reiterating the "light planning" refrain that "there are regulations beyond planning board design or SEQRA findings that all of these have to go through."

Rattle again invoked the imprimateur of legality by bluntly characterizing SEQRA as a procedural formality with few, if any, teeth. For Rattle, the setting of environmental standards was apparently anathema:

> This whole SEQRA process is not supposed to give you necessarily any answers. It's supposed to call attention to what the problems are, a few alternatives and mitigation measures to consider when you go further on in your site plan approval process, if it goes to the approval process. I mean it isn't supposed to get to the point where you say, "ah, here's what the best thing is." It's to discuss the issues.

In other words, lip service to a collegial process of scientific inquiry would be accepted only as far as Rattle, Maglie and the "light planning" majority considered it appropriate. One danger of controlling "regulator" member voices was that it exposed the board to a subsequent court claim that substantive issues were not pursued by a minimal "hard look" standard and were not adequately supported by sufficient data.[37] But this seemed of little concern to Maglie, let alone Rattle. More relevant to them, it appeared, was to prevent the board from findings that the developer failed to offer adequate mitigation for the potential adverse environmental impacts of Moselle Plaza, thus justifying a SEQRA findings vote of disapproval.[38] If, by some unanticipated circumstance, a planning board majority vote did ultimately disapprove the project, lack of clarity and resolution of contradictory responses at the present stage could leave a negative decision vulnerable to attack by Magellan in the courts, contending that adequate mitigation had been offered and that such a decision was "arbitrary and capricious," without adequate factual basis.

With Rattle's renewed instructions to pursue form over substance, supporting Maglie's efforts to control the behavior of dissident members, Myers, the only conceivable swing vote on procedural issues, again backed down. He agreed that the details Hillman sought could await the site plan review stage. Rattle added that the board could do all the detailed review later and if certain conditions weren't met it could always deny site plan approval. Now, in an effort to resolve the acrimony, Green, a "regulator" member who to date had said very little, went along, "as long as there's that room in the process."

Having restored procedural authority through shouting, through the backing of his legal and planning experts and now through a clear majority, Maglie regained his usual more mellow demeanor. He assured board members that he would try to develop a consensus in wording for the final FSEIS document, taking into account all the material received since the public hearing. However, he cautioned that any subsequent material provided by experts of the community groups "can be looked at or not" by the board. This statement of the board's discretionary authority suggested that the open dialogue invitation that Maglie had extended to the community groups on March 3rd was now something he, at least, felt free to re-define.

But the procedural discussion wasn't over. Manley now asked if the planning board was comfortable having to choose between strongly contrasting traffic reports of Magellan's expert and Case. Perhaps, he said, a third expert should be brought in. As he had expressed concerning the realm of economics, Maglie now stated with traffic. Rather than accepting the rational challenge of comparing methodologies and logic in two competing analyses, Maglie simply devalued the authority of "science." For Maglie now, as Rattle had told the board in mid-February, traffic analyses are not scientific. "There's one traffic study. . . . What Case cites and what the developer cites are both true statements depending on how you read the numbers." Again Busch agreed. "That reconciliation is only done by DOT." They will decide on the adequacy of methodology. And he thought they had no problem with the methodology used in Magellan's report.

Hillman then inquired whether the DOT had even seen Case's critique--in other words, could an expert comparison be made if there was nothing to compare Magellan's report with? His suspicion was correct, since Maglie had not mailed all of Case's responses to the DOT when he asked for the latter's new input on Magellan's FSEIS analysis. Manley added, "And if 300 people get up at the public hearing and scream about traffic, that's no good? . . . Then why have a public hearing?" In his usual blunt (but surely revealing) manner, Ryker responded simply, "To keep people happy." But Rattle felt uncomfortable with such an explicit revelation of the "light planners'" mere facial compliance with SEQRA:

> If somebody's not happy, they have to give some reason. I mean there's a lot of reasons [that] were given. . . . You have to ferret them out and see if those reasons have rational basis and are not just, I mean, on every project that's contested you'll find the courts saying that it doesn't have to be scientific . . . . Then obviously it's not going to be. It's going to be one here and one there and somewhere in the middle is the answer. And it's not easy to get. And you keep on hiring somebody else to take a look at it.

> There's a zone somewhere in here, with this out here, that you can make a decision that's going to be supported. Your decision is presumed to be correct, but you better be able to point to it. . . . These things, traffic usually, I mean Gene knows traffic. I mean, you know, you can get a handle on these things. Stormwater you can get a handle on.

> It's what I said in the very beginning, when you get into things like visual impacts and economic impacts, you know, it's a very subjective situation and you have to be very careful. Read what I gave you about what is an economic impact. For an FEIS, not for a findings statement, but for an FEIS, it's pretty limited what you can do. When you get to findings, then you can have a little more leeway.

Rattle's efforts here apparently were to sanitize a record now containing Ryker's explicit bias in the conduct of the process itself.

At the same meeting, Rattle earlier summarized the concluding FSEIS task for July. If the board felt that there was insufficient information from Magellan, he said, it could request more. However, the May and June meetings had already demonstrated how unwelcome to the "light planners," Rattle and Busch such a request would be. He suggested that the FSEIS group together responses to public and involved agencies' comments, perhaps for a total of ten topics. The August scope had included 21 issue areas and even Busch's admittedly-incomplete early March list of public comment substantive issues had numbered 49. Rattle's suggested number was entirely arbitrary, in that Rattle acknowledged no specific familiarity with the substance of the issues raised. Thus, his suggestion to consolidate the issues into the workable number of 10, while seemingly pragmatic, was little more than reassurance to "light planners" that form could prevail over substance in SEQRA reviews.

But procedural resistance from "regulator" members, sometimes joined by

Myers, delayed the planning board further. At the board's next meeting on July 17th, Rattle explained that he was above all critical of the opportunity being provided for extensive dialogue on substantive issues--though he did not directly name the community groups or their experts:

> . . . what appears to be happening is every time, at least that I'm here, you sit down for a meeting, there are five or six letters from various engineers or other people which then have to be reviewed and we go another month and it looks as if we're <u>never</u> going to get through the process. And I think, from a legal standpoint, that we're getting pretty close to where . . . this FSEIS has to be completed and filed.

Board members were again forced pragmatically to confront the procedural issue of whether certain topics should be discussed as part of the FSEIS or whether they could simply await SEQRA approval and site plan review. Rattle asserted that an up-or-down vote on whether the FSEIS was complete was now appropriate, regardless of unanswered issues about project design and its impact on the environment. If board members felt that the applicant "has not done everything feasible, practical to mitigate identified environmental concerns, you give a negative finding. . . . You won't approve, you won't go on and look at the site plan." By contrast, a vote to accept an FSEIS as "complete" would not necessarily imply SEQRA acceptance of the project. Thus, if the board wished to advance the process further, a "completeness" decision on the FSEIS was the best way to proceed. While acceptance of an uncritical FSEIS as "complete" might appear to "regulators" to be benign, it could also reasonably suggest that, with so many contradictory opinions, the board had no adequate official record to justify a negative findings vote and thus strengthen Magellan's hand. Rattle gave no guidance on this issue. In this sense, to state, as Rattle did, that the findings vote is "really where it comes down" was quite misleading and seemed designed to manipulate the board into a shallower and more arbitrary final decision.

Subsequent comments by "regulator" members disputed Rattle's interpretation of board responsibility at this stage. If a hard decision was not made about the adequacy of applicant responses at this FSEIS "completeness" stage, a majority was likely to vote at the findings stage, without critical analysis, to simply defer further judgment to the board's site plan review process and involved agencies' permit decisions, thus abdicating, through a "backloading" approach, board responsibility under SEQRA.

Board members who believed that Magellan Construction had provided qualitatively or quantitatively inadequate responses or inadequate mitigation plans would have to assert themselves for a decisive board stance at this present "completeness" review stage or risk having only conflicting data as a basis for the final SEQRA determination. After SEQRA approval and when project plans and investments were much further advanced, there would be much less legal leverage for "regulator" critiques.

Following the July 17th meeting, Maglie declared, "I would like to wrap it up. I'm sure there's more to our lives for the next two years than Moselle Plaza." Added Ryker, "I'm sick of this project." Thirty concerned citizens who had sat silently frustrated through tedious and procedurally-bound discussion, never addressing the merits of any public or outside expert critiques, agreed with "light planners" for the first time as they filed out of Town Hall. The question remained whether "regulator" members could continue to be empowered by public participation in what was fast becoming a moribund process.[39]

Magellan's Revenge

While Rattle, Busch and "light planning" members of the board did their best at meetings to hasten the process without meaningful substantive reviews, Magellan Construction attempted to neutralize ACT/CLEAR efforts to the contrary. On July 17th, Magellan's attorney, Morris Schwab, sent a letter to the dean of Dreyfus' law school attempting to silence Dreyfus' voice in the process.[40] His letter criticized Dreyfus' use of the school's letterheads in his many communications to the board. He suggested that this raised a serious question as to whether the law school itself was taking a position about Moselle Plaza--which he assumed was not the case. Since Dreyfus prefaced each letter by indicating that he represented the community groups as an individual, the contention that the law school was somehow implicated in the anti-mall movement seemed meritless. Yet Magellan's efforts to retaliate against an activist leader in the community struggle was consistent with Reynolds' earlier threat to Turbell in January, when he indicated that Magellan would stop at nothing to deter McBride, Turbell and Dreyfus from continuing their oppositional role, including attempting to eliminate their employment. Having apparently succeeded in forcing Turbell to lose her job shortly after that threat, it seemed that Magellan was now moving on to Dreyfus. When Schwab's letter failed to reduce Dreyfus' role in the process, Reynolds escalated the attack in a letter of his own to the dean on August 21st.[41] Claiming legitimacy by introducing himself as representing Magellan Construction Group, "a well-respected commercial real estate developer, that develops commercial properties in five states and has a portfolio worth an excess of $500,000,000.00," Reynolds took aim at Dreyfus directly:

> In all of my years in the real estate business I have never seen an individual use more outlandish statements and hide behind the fine name of an institution, such as yours. This is, in fact, the case of one Mr. Manny Dreyfuss [sic]. He comes to public meetings, writes letters to the editor, town officials at the planning board, town board, the

county and state levels using his status at [your law school].

I do not believe, now or have I believed in the past, that this was done with the knowledge of you or the Board of Trustees of your law school. I reach out to you to take some disciplinary action against Mr. Dreyfuss [sic] so that we do not have any confusion in the future. In pretty short order we are going to be forced to take defensive action against the slanderous allegations that he has made. We do not want the good name of [your law school] to get in the middle of this situation.

This attack on Dreyfus' First Amendment rights was obviously a calculated threat to his job and misrepresented the role of the law school in the process. While Dreyfus was known in the community and to the press as a community activist and law professor, he had never invoked the law school's name as supporting or endorsing his position or that of the community groups. While the letter had no effect on his tenure as a professor, the particularly vicious nature of the attack was intimidating, and it seemed to him a warning to other activists as well. The process of attacking Magellan and its allies on the planning board had high stakes for everyone involved. Magellan was clearly willing to make it a test of strength, using whatever resources it could. Nonetheless, the rather desperate nature of Reynolds' polemically written letter confirmed for activists that Magellan itself felt threatened by the effectiveness of community interventions, and this was a source of new confidence.

At the board's July 24th meeting, Rattle advised on the process of finishing up the FSEIS.

I would recommend you write out what you want and give it back to the applicant and say you do it, then we'll re-review it and here [are] the changes we want, here's our economic analysis and you guys put it together and give it back to us and we'll sit down and look at it for whether we feel it's complete and addresses our changes.[42]

Essentially, after months of sporadic attempts by "regulator" members (occasionally joined by Myers) to engage in more independent analysis of their own, Rattle now moved to place the analytical process back in Magellan's hands. Whatever list of requests the board might convey to Magellan for a final draft, the fact that the developer would frame and edit the discussion would significantly reduce whatever autonomous voice the board might have achieved.

TEN

THE PLANNING BOARD'S REVIEW: SUBSTANTIVE ISSUES

Busch's Filter

Busch's March 10th document was essentially a filter by which certain comments were defined as "substantive" and others unimportant and not meriting further planning board concern. His list was correlated with topics from the board's August 8th scope in each of three major realms. Under each scope topic, Busch listed those written comments which he believed were important enough (and not duplicated by others) for planning board designation to Magellan as requiring responses in the draft FSEIS.

A. Stormwater and Water Quality

The first scope item in this realm asked for a written narrative and detailed graphic description of the stormwater-water quality management and erosion control plans and how they fundamentally differed from those for Amsterdam Square. The 11 comments chosen by Busch raised substantial problems with the DSEIS. In terms of design, the comments indicated that the stormwater system did not meet minimum local and regulatory requirements. The plan did not clarify intended use of federally-designated wetlands. The plan failed to treat the first flush of stormwater runoff for pollutants prior to discharge into federal and state natural wetlands as required by DEC regulations. Comments also contended that the plan failed to analyze (or rule out) the existence of a Creighton Road-Rte. 354 aquifer recharge area and that strict measures were necessary to avoid its contamination. The plan proposed two culvert pipes under South Creighton Road despite the fact that only one culvert was allowed by the FCDPW. This meant that an on-site drainage solution would be required. The plan omitted any consideration of the additional runoff which would be created by the second access road, so a solution to the drainage at that site would be needed. Finally, any fair analysis would show project discharge of unacceptably high levels of salts and organic pollutants into the wetlands.

As for methodological critiques, comments on Busch's list indicated that the drainage area near the Thruway, on the western edge of the site, was not analyzed in a manner acceptable to the Thruway Authority. The technical appendix needed a narrative description of how design storms and runoffs were calculated. Magellan's basis for calculating post-development stormwater flows differed from the basis used with the Amsterdam Square EIS, but such a change, comments showed, was not made for calculations of <u>pre</u>-development flow. This helped create an illusion that post-development flows would be less than or equal to pre-development flows.

While substantial, Busch's list failed to mention many other significant issues raised during the public comment period, among which were several from the DEC, the FCPB and engineer Joshua Wright. For this one scoping topic alone, Busch had therefore filtered from planning board attention a large number of "substantive" comments. None of these was frivolous. Each had the potential of contributing substantially to a reasoned assessment of the severity of adverse environmental impact of the project. Under SEQRA, while the board had the right to create its own list, actual practice in the past, also permissable under SEQRA, suggested that the board would rely heavily on its consultants for guidance. Given a large project of this sort, the nature of the existing majority at the time and the freshness of two new members, such dependence was all the more likely.

In many instances, Busch had diminished the potential significance of particular issues by providing only very brief excerpts from comments quoted though more elaboration would have explained their importance to those unfamiliar with the logic and contents of technical substantive critiques. Finally, Busch frequently cited comments from the lay public rather than similar comments from professional community experts (as Wright) or involved agencies (as the DEC or FCDPW). He thus potentially biased members' attitudes against the credibility of such critiques in advance. Given the predisposition of courts to rely more on opinions from "scientific experts" than on the public, Busch's editing was indeed problematic.

Busch engaged in a similar severe and apparently arbitrary "filtering" process for each of the remaining scope topics concerning stormwater and water quality issues. Most of the excluded important comments were identified by Turbell in a lengthy letter to Busch on March 23rd.

At the March 13th meeting,[1] Magellan Construction began resisting the relevance of certain critiques and guidelines in Busch's original list. Magellan assumed that the planning board would accept it without further analysis despite Maglie's assurance that Busch's list "was only a first run-through, not cast in concrete." Specifically, Magellan argued that aquifer engineering, sewage effluent and pesticide-laden soil analyses were not appropriate matters for the FSEIS to address. Attorney Schwab asserted that it should not be the developer's burden to prove the existence and contours of a hypothetical underlying aquifer. Sewage effluent, Schwab argued, was not an issue in the initial scoping document. (Magellan refused to concede the validity of the August 8th scope which included this issue.) No reference was made to the "changed circumstances" which the board had found necessitated an SEIS in the first place and which related to existing adverse effluent effect on the current state of the watershed.

Several speakers at the public hearing requested the planning board to obtain free expert services from the nearby federal Soil Conservation Service office in reviewing the DSEIS. On March 20th, Maglie wrote to the SCS, asking specifically for its advice on two issues.

One concerned the DSEIS use of the "TR-55 method" for calculating stormwater runoff. Using this method for the pre-development site, engineers for both Amsterdam Square and Moselle Plaza calculated that 25-year storms with the existing culvert would cause flooding of South Creighton Road. However, there seemed to be no historical record of actual flooding in that area. Adding acres of paved surface and buildings to the site obviously would increase stormwater flow significantly and implied the need for more detention ponds on site. The issue here was whether the TR-55 method should continue to be used to provide the data basis for that important policy decision or, given the historical record, whether another method of analysis was more appropriate. Second, Maglie asked the SCS if more detention ponds were needed, whether their location would cause stormwater retention problems in areas with soil types indicating seasonal high water tables.

Magellan Construction's Response

Magellan Construction presented the board with its draft FSEIS at the meeting of April 17th. Despite Maglie's earlier assertions that Busch's March 10th list was only a preliminary draft, Magellan leaped at the opportunity to address Busch's issues alone rather than await further planning board finalization on which issues to prioritize for FSEIS attention. It called Busch's initial list "the Planning Board's identification of substantive comments" and responded to each item therein as if these were the official instructions.

Magellan also reproduced and remarked upon every comment made verbally or in writing during the public comment period, as well as to the two memos from board members Hillman and Pelletier, written before the planning board's DSEIS "completeness" vote of mid-December. However, Magellan unilaterally decided which of these other comments needed detailed responses and chose how detailed those replies should be.[2] By the very nature of these decisions and Magellan's desire to discuss each item as briefly as possible, Magellan was able to assert control of the content of the FSEIS. This, in turn, weakened the quality of the draft FSEIS while preserving the appearance of meeting SEQRA's expectations of responding to all substantive comments in a thoughtful and reasoned manner. Magellan's unwillingness to seriously engage with critics at this stage was also demonstrated in the minimal nature of its design changes in response to the great volume of public and expert critique.

The only significant change proposed was a new stormwater basin in the light industrial zone to the south of the project's wastewater plant. This responded to the County Public Works Department unwillingness to permit either a larger culvert pipe or two culverts under South Creighton Road to accommodate greater volumes of post-development stormwater. The new basin would receive stormwater from the main parking lot as well as the flow previously planned into the Thruway Authority's property on the west. However, Magellan omitted any discussion of the environmental impact of such a design change and whether it could be accommodated without an amendment or variance in the zoning law.

Additionally, Magellan's engineers now altered its pre-development stormwater flow estimate methodology by replacing the TR-55 method with the antiquated "Rational Method" in order to demonstrate that the project would cause no increase in stormwater. The engineer contended that reliance on the Rational Method was approved in a conversation with Marcia Everitt, a representative of the Soil Conservation Service, on April 7th.

Busch's March 10th list of important comments on stormwater, water quality and erosion contained 24 items. Magellan Construction's response to the comments on this list occupied about 12 pages of the draft FSEIS or an average of about 1/2 page per response. Of the 24 items, 8 or 1/3 were answered with no more than one sentence or three lines. Only 4 of the remaining 16 items, according to Magellan, merited a response of at least one page.

The longest response, nearly two pages, was devoted to DEC's request that all feasible wastewater alternatives be examined which might avoid project effluent intrusion into the wetlands. If intrusion was necessary, said the DEC, the FSEIS discussion should show how negative impacts would be minimized. In this instance, Magellan's lengthier response was due solely to the fact that four alternatives had to be described--using the Village treatment plant, increasing the capacity of the North Creighton plant, constructing septic fields and constructing an on-site wastewater treatment plant. Once the three first options were eliminated, because either the village had voted it down or existing facilities were grossly inadequate or because septic fields would be inappropriate, the on-site treatment facility, said Magellan, became the "alternative of choice." Minimization of impact would be guaranteed, it said, by "producing an effluent meeting the SPDES permit requirement." Though DEC had requested that the FSEIS discuss a plan which would meet SPDES standards, Magellan's response, without further elaboration, was that its package treatment plant would satisfy such standards,.

As to Turbell's critique of the DSEIS failure to address surface water regulations protecting receiving waters from excess nutrients associated with stormwater runoff and sewage effluent, Magellan claimed that the main recipient of contaminated stormwater would be the less-than-one-acre wetland in the northeast part of the site. This, they later contended, was little more than a puddle and of no great concern to either federal or state authorities. No potential pollution to large easterly off-site wetlands from stormwater flows through the culvert further south was mentioned. Sewage effluent was also unmentioned as a source of further contamination. Using a table from a metropolitan Washington publication, Magellan claimed that the project's phosphorus and nitrogen pollutant removal from on-site stormwater would be at a higher percent than that required in the DEC stormwater regulation tables and hence acceptable. It also stated that shopping center acreage produces only slightly more phosphorus and nitrogen material than minimally-tilled agricultural land and that applying Magellan's planned higher removal rates would show that managed stormwater would allow less nutrient discharge from the project than would occur from the undeveloped silt-loam soils presently on site. Thus, Magellan's method of stormwater treatment and removal would satisfy DEC's standard that <u>post</u>-development stormwater pollution rates be no higher than <u>pre</u>-development figures for the same site. Stormwater pollutant discharge, Magellan contended, would also be significantly less than the maximum allowed by DEC for wastewater treatment plants, thereby implying that contamination from the former source was comparable with the latter.

Turbell had also commented that the DSEIS failed to describe changes in wetland conditions since 1990 and to calculate cumulative impact of North Creighton sewage plant substandard effluent along with Moselle Plaza effluent, topics which had been part of the Board's August 10th scope. As to the effect on the adjacent wetlands of the effluent produced by the malfunctioning North Creighton sewage plant since 1990, without elaboration, Magellan claimed that no changes had occurred in boundaries or quality of state wetlands in the near vicinity of the site. It said that North Creighton sewage effluent was discharged into state wetlands RC-6, whereas Moselle Plaza effluent will go into "a running body of water which has a defined channel through the wetlands." Therefore, it argued, the impact would not be cumulative. This "Gulf Stream" assumption, while imaginative, lacked any basis in fact and none was suggested.

In reply to Wright's detailed discussion of how the project would not comply with minimum local and regulatory stormwater requirements, Magellan made the conclusory assertion, without further elaboration, that it would meet DEC's regulatory standards. Magellan ruled out engineers' preferred infiltration method of stormwater management because of claimed incompatibility of on-site soils. Magellan's assertions on stormwater issues seemed more like fantasy, in part because Magellan would not descend to particulars and engage in a reasoned response to the data submitted by experts on behalf of the community groups.

In the appendix of the draft FSEIS, Magellan responded to written submissions by others of the public and involved agencies. These responses tended mainly to refer to answers already given by Magellan for items in Busch's list. Most responses to Wright's lengthy critique of project impact on wetlands and the aquifer, for example, repeated statements made elsewhere in the draft FSEIS or dismissed Wright's concerns as not applicable. While Wright had asserted that a 1979 study found phosphorus loading from suburban shopping centers to be 8 times the likely level produced by idle land, Magellan Construction claimed that "idle land" in that study applied to "undeveloped forest and old field abandoned farm land," not to "cropland, cow pasture and other maintained farmlands or lawn areas." The latter condition, it implied, correctly described the Heller property, despite the fact that the land had remained fallow for many years and that the only farming involved haying the field.

At this stage, for the stormwater-water quality realm, regardless of Busch's filtered list and Magellan's responses avoiding substantive issues, the lines were drawn in some substantive areas for a potential refined analytical debate. Continued critical questions and comments by several board members and experts on behalf of the community groups over the next few months forced a much more engaged substantive confrontation than Magellan Construction, through its conclusory assertions, ever expected. Contrary to Magellan's intent, community groups were able to utilize SEQRA to maintain an open process and to force Magellan to participate in a planning dialogue with the community.

Seeking An Official Outside Expert

On May 11th, Marcia Everitt of the Soil Conservation Service replied to Maglie's March 20th request for assistance with several important comments on the DSEIS and Magellan's responses in the draft FSEIS. Specifically, concerning methodology for stormwater runoff calculations, Everitt stated that using the TR-55 method is preferred. She also criticized Magellan's reference to the on-site land as "tilled." In fact, she said, "[t]hese fields were orchard with grassed rows, there is no tillage on these lands and the cover factors for runoff for the BEFORE condition should reflect the grassed condition. . . . The land has been idle for some time and is mainly grass, brush and woods." This comment was important since it supported Wright's lower pre-development "idle land" nutrient flow calculations and thus reduced the threshold beyond which Moselle Plaza's post-development stormwater nutrient flow would be unacceptable. The disparity between pre- and post-development conditions became all the more clear.

Everitt also validated FCPB and public concerns that high water tables on site would limit the volume of stormwater that could be stored in project basins. Finally, she urged that the proposed use of the adjacent southerly parcel should be taken into account before stormwater management plans for Moselle Plaza were considered as final, since "[c]hanges in landuse, drainage patterns and permeability can affect the ability of the stormwater management practices to operate as designed." This validated a "cumulative impact" argument presented earlier by CLEAR but ignored by Magellan and Rattle.

Everitt's critique was substantial. Coming from an independent government expert source, its potential impact was all the more significant and added important credibility to the scientific arguments and critiques of the community groups and their expert.

Community Experts Respond

On May 12th, Dreyfus transmitted to the board two more commentaries about the DFSEIS, solicited by ACT, to respond to Magellan's assertions. The first, from Joshua Wright, substantially overlapped with the letter from Everitt and challenged in detail the reliability and completeness of Magellan's responses, focusing on issues of hydrologic modeling, contaminant loadings and removal and effects on wetlands. The second letter transmitted to the board was from SUNY/Ashbury geology professor Trent Locker and a second expert, a professional hydrogeologist. These two experts critiqued Magellan's dismissal of aquifer concerns in the DFSEIS, stating to the contrary that the project site directly threatened a significant aquifer.[3]

Planning Board Enters the Debate

This new set of evidence and arguments from Everitt, Wright and the two geologists posed a direct challenge to the credibility of the methodology and design assumptions, standards and analysis of Magellan's engineering firm. For Magellan Construction, the new critiques posed the alternatives of downsizing the project, engaging significant more time and money in re-analyzing and redesigning the stormwater and wastewater systems or denigrating the reliability of the critique presented by experts on behalf of the community groups. Not surprisingly, Magellan chose the latter.

Magellan began to attack and marginalize the critiques in whatever way possible. Beyond engaging in procedural arguments as a tactic to limit debate, Magellan directly confronted the accuracy of the community's experts' substantive positions.

The May 15th meeting was the first occasion for such an attack. At this meeting, Magellan contended, contrary to Wright and the SCS, that the

Rational Method and not TR-55 was the appropriate means to determine the extent of stormwater runoff. In the board's lengthy discussion which followed, while Maglie, Ryker, Davis and Busch defended the Rational Method, Hillman underscored the Soil Conservation Service's unwillingness to do so and Myers questioned whether methodologies could be changed in mid-stream, from pre- to post-development.

Ryker distanced himself entirely from the SCS since much of what Everitt's letter stated supported Wright's critique: "This [SCS] report was [not] meant to be held up, quoted from, every time that there's a question on something here." In any event, Everitt's SCS letter, he said, was only advisory. Davis, in turn, wished to resolve these on-site issues on the basis of practical experience above all, a posture which would legitimize his own common sense as the sole basis of an "expert" finding. After all, he was the only one to have grown up on the farm site under question.

> In a worst-case situation, when that whole farm out there is frozen, in the wintertime, and you get a hard rain, it still doesn't flood the road.
> It can't go into the ground, it's frozen. I've seen it. You all have too.

Davis' contention was that wetlands and untilled soils, in the winter, were tantamount to a paved impervious surface. If flooding didn't occur, either would be perfectly acceptable.

Hillman reiterated Everitt's argument that the site's "current land-use" definitional distinction between "tilled" and "not tilled" had important implications. He also raised Wright's point that the on-site federal wetland was likely to be impacted more than Magellan admitted in the DFSEIS. The discussion ended with Maglie agreeing to have analyzed the detention pond's ability to handle first flush runoff for at least 24 hours, but without resolving the methodological dispute regarding the amount of project-generated stormwater. In addition, Maglie accepted the need to test the adequacy of on-site soils for the infiltration method as well as how high water tables would affect detention pond capacity.

The Board's Expert Engineer

For resolution of these technical issues, the board agreed to send the draft FSEIS to its own engineer Tony Napoleon for review. It was obvious, at the least, that Magellan Construction's DFSEIS responses had satisfied neither "regulator" members nor Myers, especially in the face of the subsequent professional expert critiques. On May 22nd, Maglie wrote to Napoleon, requesting his analysis of the points raised especially by Everitt's letter. On the 24th, Dreyfus sent Napoleon copies of the critiques by Wright and by Locker and his associate as well, items Maglie had neglected to include in his own presentation of the debate.

After communication from both Magellan's engineer and Wright, Napoleon sent his own report to the planning board on June 12th. On the issue of Rational vs. TR-55 Methods, Napoleon found that the latter was the appropriate method. "Everyone seems to acknowledge the limitations of the 'Rational Method.' Why use it to quantify peak runoff from a large impervious area [the plaza] for which run-off coefficients and times of concentration are well known?" He suggested that stormwater basins would probably need to be enlarged, though excess volume could be used for the next phase of site development (in the southerly lot) if they proved over time to be unneeded.

Napoleon pointed out that it was impossible to know from existing data whether the first flush basins were in areas of high water table. However, if lined with clay, as Magellan promised, there would be no problem, as Wright had anticipated, with "non-source" pollutants left in basin soil from runoff in dry seasons bleeding back into a basin when the water table rises. Nevertheless, Napoleon was unwilling to dismiss the "preferred" infiltration method and this would eliminate any concerns about the viability of protection from clay linings. He urged that Magellan's engineer analyze actual existing soil boring data rather than using the generalizing county soil survey map to explore the infiltration alternative. Napoleon also agreed with Wright that "the federal wetland at the detention basin will change in shape and will likely change in nature."

The Board Exposed

By now, the lines had been clearly drawn between Magellan's environmental mitigation and that demanded by the community groups. The latter groups had used the opportunity Maglie provided to continue to submit expert critiques of Magellan's responses to the original "substantive comments." The board was thereby better empowered to make the assessment required by SEQRA as to whether Magellan's proposed mitigation minimized adverse environmental impact to the greatest extent possible. The board now had additional expert data and analyses from the developer's own engineer. While several of the remarks by Everitt and Wright had been at least partially addressed by Magellan, several others in their letters, as well as those in the letter from Locker and his associate, had not. More than ever, as the debate among experts evolved, lay planning board members were exposed to increasingly technical language and analyses. While this followed SEQRA's design to enhance the scientific objectivity of the board's determination, it also made the board potentially vulnerable to manipulation by analytical interpretations, and, in defense, more inclined to pursue basic "common-sense" approaches to the project. While two "regulator" members, Hillman and Manley, seemed able to follow the debate with ever more sophisticated questions of their own, the others appeared unable to comprehend the discourse sufficiently and often remained silent, uncertain or defensive. No doubt most of the board hoped that Napoleon, their own engineer, would get them off the hook concerning this whole realm of issues.

At the June 19th meeting, Maglie first urged the board to use Napoleon's June 12th recommendations as the basis for conditionally approving. Under this scenario, the board would approve Magellan's stormwater management plan, but subject to Napoleon's design standards which contradicted it. No further SEQRA deliberation in this realm would be needed. Maglie simply moved on to Napoleon's next point when it became clear that Hillman and Manley were unwilling to acquiesce in his proposal.

For his part, Ryker moved to table the whole discussion by first denigrating Napoleon, ("[he] wouldn't have a clue about the site compared to Red") and later accepting his findings as the final word without further board deliberation: "If you read some of the stuff we got today, and you go along with it, the analysis is there, the findings are there, and the documentation is there." At this point Rattle intervened to urge that all open questions simply be accepted as conditions to be resolved, as Maglie suggested, with detailed study at the site plan stage, after acceptance of the FSEIS and a "conditioned approval" findings statement. Busch agreed and further claimed that design problems could be worked out by the permit agencies themselves without further input from the board.

For them, a "backloading" SEQRA approval could be conditioned upon specific mitigations determined at the site plan stage, without ever confronting whether Moselle Plaza created too great an environmental risk to be worthy of approval. This question could be finessed as had been done with Amsterdam Square. But there was no reason to believe that the board would be more capable at the site plan stage of engaging with the issues or finding acceptable mitigations. Furthermore, as Hillman and Manley kept repeating, the very nature of some of the proposed mitigations might have important new adverse environmental impacts of their own. At that late stage, they would never be considered anew.[4] For Hillman and Manley, Napoleon's document implied intense analysis of project impacts now, as part of the SEQRA process; for Maglie and other "light planners," it meant avoidance of basic environmental risk assessment through delay until after the SEQRA determination.

Ultimately, the fundamental difference between "light planners" and "regulators" as to the purpose of this stage of the SEQRA process prevented that body from any further engagement with Napoleon's or others' issues in this realm. While the experts continued their exchange, substantive debate within the board stopped almost as soon as it had started. Maglie, Ryker, and Davis opposed it. Rattle and Busch and Magellan reenforced this position.

Myers appeared to want to avoid further confrontation and to delay any debate on substantive issues in the stormwater realm until the site plan stage. From the sidelines, a frustrated Green agreed to accept Myers' position.

In a letter of July 12th by William Tholen, the DEC further responded to the DFSEIS, in effect agreeing with Busch that any further substantive engagement with the stormwater issue be deferred to its own later permit reviews. Basically, the DEC opted out of further engagement with issues during the board's SEQRA process. At the same time, Tholen still asked Magellan for precise map locations of the effluent pipeline and pointed out that the status of permission from private land owners and DOT was still "vague and unaddressed" for installing sewer pipes and effluent discharge. Coming from the main permitting agency in the stormwater realm, this brief communication appeared to sound the death knell of SEQRA stormwater issues for the community groups and foreshadowed a similar deferral of traffic issues which the "light planning" majority was more than willing to postpone to the DOT's permitting stage.

Given Tholen's extensive February critique of the DSEIS, his response now to the DFSEIS seemed to completely reverse the DEC's position. To activists, it also reflected the newly altered political context of the DEC generally in the pro-developer regime of Governor George Pataki since the previous January. While Tholen's two remaining issues were potential problems for Magellan, DEC's retreat on stormwater issues offered little encouragement that effluent discharge concerns would be treated any differently.

Wright's Final Word

A final board FSEIS "completeness" discussion of stormwater issues was scheduled for July 17th and activists wanted the last word. Whether or not the board became involved in serious discussion, ACT and CLEAR wanted to highlight the current state of the scientific exchange for the official record to demonstrate that the board had not satisfied its SEQRA responsibility to demand the greatest mitigation possible. Again they prevailed upon Joshua Wright to send along one final letter, defining the primary issues as the choice of stormwater treatment method, stormwater basin sizing and its effect on quantity and quality, and the project impact on federal wetlands. Point-by-point, Wright offered a reasoned scientific perspective about the quality of the inquiry in which Magellan and the board were supposedly engaged.

Based on standard scientific criteria, these were fundamental challenges to the credibility of Magellan's responses. What Wright had dramatically exposed was the unwillingness of Magellan's engineer to confront long-standing issues first placed on the record at the January public hearing. Magellan's rationalizations of existing plans either completely avoided the critiques of

Wright, Everitt and Napoleon or only obliquely faced them with rhetoric, irrelevant diversions or false data. The scientific integrity of Wright's position had been backed by the SCS, the government agency most removed from state and local political pressures. In his own guarded and incomplete manner, even the planning board's engineer could not professionally ignore the validity of Wright's critique.

The Board in Disarray

The data submitted by Wright, the SCS and Napoleon, demystified the issues of stormwater management and their effect on the underlying aquifer and on-site and off-site wetlands. The board was now empowered to determine whether Magellan's engineer's responses mitigated the adverse environmental effects to the greatest extent possible. The data seemed clear that Wright's challenge, corroborated as it was by the board's own engineer and an independent governmental agency, would justify disapproval if the board were to assiduously follow SEQRA's "hard look" standard. The overriding political question, however, was whether the board majority would be willing to accept its SEQRA responsibility. As before, of course, the implication of these challenges for Magellan was either significant downsizing of Moselle Plaza or the further expense of redesign and larger infrastructure facilities in the light-industrial zone. Greater encroachment upon the latter zone, in turn, represented greater non-conformity with the zoning code and thus a further risk of failure when seeking Town Board or ZBA approval for such use.

Magellan was unwilling to consider any significant modifications, choosing to take its chances at bullying its way through the SEQRA process. Once the momentum for SEQRA approval was achieved, through the imprimatur of the local planning board, Magellan was confident that it would succeed in subsequent stages of site-plan, permitting agency and zoning reviews. To serve Magellan in this strategy, "light planning" board members and consultants Rattle and Busch sought, issue by issue, to prevent the challenges presented by the scientific data and re-stated by Manley and Hillman from being considered. While Rattle constantly prodded the board into narrowing its definition of legitimate SEQRA concerns and speeding up the process generally, Busch attempted to minimize the impact of Napoleon's critique by saying that his recommendations were qualified, not definitive statements. Maglie, in turn, backed by Ryker and Davis, consistently diverted discussion to the procedural definition of "completeness" of such topics in the FSEIS, promising further discussion at the later "findings" and site-plan approval stages. Repeatedly, the beginnings of a deliberative process were thus terminated. Said Maglie, "What we have in documentation is what we have. Vote yes or no on this basis."

Discussion of the "completeness" of substantive stormwater issues under

SEQRA, involved the same avoidance and prevarication which characterized the board's procedural posture. While a veneer of consideration was provided by including Magellan's responses to the board's scoping agenda and to the public critique, little more than lip service was given to the "hard look" doctrine. Instead, the same ideological gaps which divided "light planners" from "regulators" at the outset continued to dominate and determine the FSEIS "completeness" debate.

The clearest example of how law's substantive requirement was subordinated was the board's unwillingness to acknowledge Wright's contribution to the stormwater completeness debate--how his critique had informed board members and empowered them to decide, using legal rationality, whether Magellan's responses were sufficient. During the entire four-month review of stormwater and water-quality issues, not one person at any board meeting dared to mention the name of the community groups' expert. Manley and Hillman, whose comments at meetings were informed by data Wright provided in his critiques of Magellan's responses, no doubt were inhibited to cite him for fear their remarks would be discounted as biased out of hand. For the "light-planning" bloc supported by Rattle and Busch, when contrasted with Magellan's engineer, Wright was a pariah, a renegade professional expert to be treated as a non-entity, since he dared to lend his credentials to community critics and challenge the credibility of a developer's positions.

B. Traffic

Essentially, the four-month review of traffic impacts saw the same dynamic as for the stormwater realm. The main differences were apparently simpler issues, a new set of involved agencies and a different expert, Stanley Case, responding on behalf of the community groups. In certain ways, these differences, however, only underlined the fact of a common planning board pattern.

For the traffic impact realm, the most important written critiques of Magellan Construction's DSEIS came from Case himself; McBride, on behalf of CLEAR; and planning board member Ben Hillman, an employee of the DOT. Busch's March 10th filtered list of "substantive comments" relied entirely on the Thruway Authority and Case, as well as one comment from Turbell for ACT. Busch had omitted reading the comments of McBride, Hillman and Henry Fowler of the FCPB.

Case had stated that lane widths at the Rte. 354-Green Corners Road intersection were improperly described as wider than they actually were, thereby implying a faster, more acceptable traffic flow. Busch also included Case's concerns regarding Magellan's data interpretation. Case objected to the DSEIS combining separate right-turn lane and through lane traffic flow ratings into overall intersection directional level-of-service averages, thereby implying unacceptably a reduced significance of major right-turn lane delays. The reason for a standard of lane-by-lane analysis was easy to understand. At a given intersection, if several lanes of traffic have smooth traffic flows but one or two others have large backups and unacceptably long waiting time, the latter genuine problem would not be identified through intersection lane level-of-service averaging. A lane-by-lane analysis, however, would highlight the problem and allow it to be properly addressed. Case contended that Magellan's traffic analysis narrative thus claimed an easier flow of traffic than actually existed.

McBride's omitted comments echoed, to a good extent, those of Case. However, he also had requested peak PM traffic flow analyses for summertime and for Fall foliage, county fair and craft fair weekends (periods with which, as a local resident, he had special familiarity), since traffic during these periods was always significantly higher. For his part, Hillman had requested, among other things, that in Magellan's cumulative traffic impact analysis incorporating light industrial use of the southerly Heller lot, the developer's flow figures should reflect the Town's recent zone use change which permitted office use as well as warehouse potentials.

The DOT's response to the DSEIS, included by Magellan, apparently gave a green light to Magellan's traffic plans, stating:

> The methodology used for analysis seems to be reasonable. The existing 1993 traffic volumes, projected 1995 traffic volumes, traffic distribution, no-build traffic volumes and build traffic volumes all appear to be reasonable.[5]

The DOT simply asked that Magellan's application for a highway work permit be sent on to the DOT so it could initiate its own permit review process. The DOT thereby indicated no further interest in contributing to analytical discourse during the SEQRA stage.

The scope agenda sought to identify highway improvements necessary to mitigate adverse impacts caused by this project's and others' cumulative traffic. Busch mentioned the scope item without incorporating any comments, though Case had estimated "E" or "F" levels of service for certain lanes of Rte. 354 intersections with Green Corners and Creighton Roads--even when Magellan's "improvements" were factored in. Since levels of service below "D" were unacceptable, clearly further mitigation would be needed, a point which McBride included in his comments as well.

Magellan Construction Responds on Traffic

The board barely mentioned traffic issues until its meeting of April 17th when Magellan representatives presented their draft FSEIS. Based on the

DOT's reactions to public critiques, Jankoff assured the board that everything was under control.

> We met with DOT pretty informally. We didn't go over specifics. Again, they reiterated, we pushed it. We said, "Hey, listen. Questions come up about the traffic study and the numbers that we use and the calculations and figures and methods that we use" and they said that they accept those figures and they are not going to go back and make us revise them.

Magellan's formal responses in the DFSEIS reflected this self-confidence and, except for a Thruway turn lane, showed its unwillingness to alter the project design. Busch's March 10th list of substantive issues contained only 9 comments in the traffic realm compared to 24 for stormwater and water quality. Compared to Magellan's 12 pages of response for the latter issues, the traffic realm elicited just 2 pages in its draft FSEIS. The barely 1/4 page response to each comment indicated Magellan's sense that this realm was relatively beyond challenge, especially given DOT's benign response, and that such matters were too technical for SEQRA deliberation. Nevertheless, Case was a professional with technical expertise and impeccable credentials. His critique directly undermined Magellan's assertions and seemingly had to be answered in order to contend that the board complied with SEQRA's "hard look" standard.

Concerning the issue of improper Green Corners intersection lane widths, Magellan claimed that its stated widths were "based on the anticipated restriping of the intersection by NYS DOT," though Magellan now corrected several new intersection analyses in its DFSEIS to reflect some, but not all, current conditions. As to the misleading averaging of overall traffic service for each intersection, Magellan replied simply that lane-by-lane analyses were also provided in the DSEIS. While Magellan's statement was accurate, it was also misleading since lane-by-lane analyses appeared only in the appendix of detailed technical charts, not in its prose narrative interpretation which was the most that lay planning board members could at best be expected to read. It was on the basis of the prose section that Magellan made the claim that all traffic flows would be at an "acceptable" level.

Magellan also briefly responded in the DFSEIS to traffic comments not on Busch's filtered list, including the critique from Ben Hillman. Concerning his request for analysis of an additional intersection, Magellan responded simply, "Comment noted. The Traffic Impact Analysis conservatively takes into account reasonable traffic projections and finds that acceptable Levels of Service will be achieved with the proposed improvements." Despite its calm, assured tone, this response was in fact quite patronizing. It acknowledged the remark and told the planning board member who made it that Magellan proved its case so well, it didn't need to consider anything further. As for evaluating cumulative traffic impact from the southerly Heller lot, including, as Hillman requested, new potential office space in that zone, Magellan stated that the evaluation they offered was based on a "hypothetical maximum development scenario under current zoning." If the Town Board amends the zoning, Magellan said, any new development of that lot will have to undergo a SEQRA review and numbers could be updated at that time. Given the Town Board's definite intent to revise the zone use definition, as Hillman informed Magellan in his December memo (the new definition was passed in April 1995), responding to the request would have anticipated the expanded use numbers and changed the analysis.[6]

As with the stormwater-water quality realm, Magellan had consciously decided to change virtually nothing in its traffic analysis and design in response to critical input--unless it came directly from an official permitting agency it would later have to satisfy. Since its analysis and project design apparently met at least the conditional approval of DOT and seemed to satisfy concerns of the Thruway Authority, Magellan was unwilling to expend money on further analysis and mitigation.

On May 4th, in response to the planning board's request, the DOT sent on a half-page letter supposedly commenting on the April DFSEIS. It stated: "We have completed our review of the above referenced proposal with respect to the project's impacts on the State highway system." It added that the proposed change in access to the Thruway ramp and other mitigations will be reviewed as part of the highway work permit process.[7] In short, the DOT offered no advice to the board after review of the various critiques and developer responses and seemed unconcerned with lending its analysis to the SEQRA stage.

Case Responds to the DFSEIS

At the request of ACT and CLEAR, on May 5th Stanley Case sent to the planning board a critique of Magellan's DFSEIS responses to his original letter. Among other items, Case emphasized that the DFSEIS ignored the combinations of through and right-turn lanes and continued to use improper averaging of lane levels-of-service at each intersection. He also restated his previous finding that Creighton and Green Corners intersections with Rte. 354 would show many "E" ratings and one "F" level of service, even after planned road improvements.

Whereas the DOT spoke in only broad conclusory terms of approval, Case had moved inductively from concrete analytical problems to the conclusion that the project design was unacceptable, under SEQRA, because of adverse environmental impact created by deterioration of traffic conditions. While a debate between DOT and Case was implied by the differing views of traffic impact, the former carefully never stated enough for a clear engagement to occur.

The planning board was thus again placed in a no man's land between competing experts without its own sense of how to monitor and participate in the debate. At the least, the presence of Case, as a critical professional expert, forced the board to acknowledge, as it seemed unlikely to do with lay public comments alone, that a legitimate "scientific" debate existed. Moreover, the growth in traffic experienced by Ashbury over the last decade, often resulting in bumper-to-bumper conditions at peak hours, would seem to provide ample common sense substantiation for Case's contentions. Given SEQRA's purpose of using the tools of reason and scientific analysis to produce thoughtful, informed decisions, at least "regulator" board members would have to directly confront the issues of this realm.

The Board Begins on Traffic

As with the stormwater realm, the May 15th meeting became the board's first attempt to define the areas of difference. Maglie introduced the topic by reading the newest letters from DOT and the FCDPW, but not the response from Case. Maglie reported that DOT and the FCDPW were in general agreement with the conceptual plan.[8] For him, this was sufficient to complete the discussion and approve Magellan's plan.

Once again, however, Hillman took the lead, insisting that traffic flow analysis of cumulative volumes from the southerly "light-industrial" lot should take account of its most intensive potential use. This would mean using the higher number of vehicle trips generated for office use as opposed to figures Magellan employed based on warehouse use only. Maglie denied the relevance of looking at the cumulative impact at all, since the southern lot was no longer attached to the northern one as it had been with Amsterdam Square, given Heller's earlier subdivision of the property. Anyway, said Ryker, "we have an approximation that's close enough." Myers, on the other hand, thought cumulative impact was a legitimate issue since combined traffic generated from both Heller lots might in fact limit development further south on South Creighton Road. After Rattle's warning that the board should stay away from considering the back lot, Hillman responded that use of that lot was already legitimately in consideration since Magellan itself had included it, with warehouse use, in the DSEIS.

A slight diversion in the discussion appeared when Myers questioned whether an "E" level of service (just short of gridlock) was necessarily precluded by existing DOT standards. To head off an implication that the board might establish its own standard of acceptable service, given what was desirable environmentally in Ashbury, Busch in turn asserted that the goal is to have a level of service <u>no less</u> than at present. Busch concluded, without elaboration or analysis of Case's critique, that he thought the Moselle Plaza plan had met that goal.

Myers' comments, however, were most encouraging, coming as they were from a "light planner" whose appointment to the board had been personally secured by Ryker. Myers raised methodological questions originally posed by Case in his response to the DSEIS. How do we deal with Case's comments, he asked, and his estimates of service levels? Maglie responded (incorrectly) that the data wasn't in question, it simply depended on how it was interpreted. In effect, he said, Case simply looked at it differently from the developer. Hillman stopped him in his tracks by pointing out that Case disagreed with the multiple purpose trip generation factor.[9] Maglie acknowledged this, but shifted his defense to the fact that apparently the DOT didn't see it as an issue. Added Ryker, referring to Case's critique, "It's not relevant." This was too much for Myers. Dramatically tossing Case's reports over his shoulder, he said, "If I don't agree with it, I throw it out, it has no relevance. But if it says what I want it to say, then it has relevance. C'mon, Rocky!" Never had a board member so clearly defined Ryker's bias and predisposition. Ryker was speechless.

Rattle backpedaled quickly by conceding that an "F" level of traffic service would be unacceptable. More generously, Maglie stated that he thought everyone would agree on level "E" as being unacceptable. After all, Magellan had stated that the average for each intersection was above the "E" level. Maglie had no problem with this averaging method of analysis despite Case's explanation of how it inadequately labelled actual traffic in any specific lane.

Magellan Responds to Case

Case's critique and the seriousness with which Hillman and Myers received it clearly upset Magellan's strategy. Apparently, it suggested emergence of a new majority (with Myers joining the three "regulator" members) potentially opposed to the approval of Magellan's plans. Quickly, Magellan enlisted its traffic engineer to draw a cleaner line of defense, sanitizing the traffic impact. On May 24th, Jankoff submitted to the planning board the engineer's new report. In contrast to the brevity and sometimes condescending tone of the draft FSEIS responses, the engineer now replied with 9 pages of narrative and a 6-page appendix, specifically addressing comments from several board members and Case. It appeared that Magellan knew the difference between conclusory statements and factual analyses.

Concerning the issue of cumulative impact estimates for the southerly Heller lot, Magellan's engineer continued to assert that a full buildout there with light-industrial use would produce, after Magellan's planned road improvements, levels of service at "D" or better at all the Rte. 354 intersections and at "C" or better at the specific intersection of Rte. 354 and Creighton Road. Once again, Magellan's engineer relied on <u>overall averages</u> of lane service ratings instead of the various <u>lane-by-lane</u> levels. Averaging made the situation look better than it was.

Nevertheless, Magellan's engineer then took the plunge into discussing potential <u>office</u> use of the southerly lot as well. While acknowledging that maximum office-use buildout would produce double the number of vehicles as for light industrial use, he claimed that because of limited lot size and higher parking requirements, in fact an office facility would have to be no more than half the size of any other light industrial facility. Thus, the number of vehicle trips generated would be the same. He likewise dismissed as unproblematic his averaging of right-turn lane and through-lane levels of service at the Creighton Rd.-354 intersection, since "the representation of the delays in the capacity analysis results are in a standard format and have been accepted by NYSDOT."

Case Responds to Magellan - II

Urged by the community groups to respond, Case sent a new letter to the board on June 15th reiterating that:

> levels of service E and F would occur as a result of the development of Moselle Plaza. These are unacceptable conditions and below the levels of service currently provided at these intersections and they would not be mitigated by the NYSDOT [Thruway bridge] improvements.

Magellan's engineer's foray into discussing potential office use of the southerly Heller lot was accepted by Case, but shown to imply something totally different. All it would take, Case pointed out, to have full office space buildout, despite limited acreage, would be multi-level parking. Therefore, the full traffic volume of southerly lot buildout would be nearly twice the amount shown in Magellan's analysis of that particular cumulative impact.

Again, with regard to Magellan's engineer's averaging of different lanes' levels of service, Case stated flatly:

> averaging delays for through traffic and right-turning traffic to develop an overall level of service is like telling a man with one foot in an ice bucket and the other foot in boiling water that, on the average, he should be comfortable. . . . Such practice falsely suggests that the level of service at that intersection is better than it is.

The June 19th planning board meeting was far more preoccupied with economic and stormwater impacts than with traffic. At the least, however, everyone recognized that an impasse existed between experts. Manley asked whether the board felt comfortable choosing on its own between the respective expert claims. Maglie replied that there was only one traffic study and he was satisfied with finding truth in however one read the numbers from either report.

Busch, in turn, assured Hillman that the DOT would reconcile the different methodologies. Under this logic, there was no further role for the planning board at the SEQRA stage once it had obtained the competing views of the experts. No resolution was needed to satisfy SEQRA's "hard look" standard when a permitting agency had final authority over an aspect of the project. Busch contended that DOT had shown no question toward Magellan's approach. Hillman doubted, however, that the DOT had even been shown Case's critiques and insisted that they receive it and offer their response. The board moved on to another realm--though not before Rattle himself was provoked to admit that an "E" level would not be acceptable.

Appealing to the DOT

Determined to put this set of traffic issues to rest, Maglie wrote to the DOT, despite its demonstrated disinterest in the local SEQRA process, requesting its assistance in addressing the issues raised by Case. Again because of the community groups' regular review of planning board files, Dreyfus became aware of Maglie's letter and quickly wrote to DOT on his own. Dreyfus explained the context of the most recent exchange of letters between the experts and enclosed copies of Case's January 30th and May 4th statements as well. Dreyfus' was a necessary intervention because Maglie had already shown his unwillingness to forward community experts' analysis to involved agencies. In Dreyfus' view, confronting DOT directly with specific issues raised in Case's expert critique--especially the critical one about acceptable standards and Magellan's failure to meet them--might challenge DOT's professionalism to the point that it would finally have to engage with the methodological and substantive disputes.

Though by the July 24th meeting, DOT had still failed to respond, Maglie had at least spoken with someone in the regional office. He said that he asked DOT directly about its standard of "acceptable level of service" as well as Magellan's use of overall averages for intersection performance ratings. Answers to these questions were critical to deciding whether Magellan had engaged in sufficient mitigation or the extent to which Case's critique continued to have validity. Maglie reported that DOT said that it didn't approve of any "E" or "F" levels of service. It also agreed that an overall intersection level of service rating was based on its various lane-by-lane component parts. With the DOT adding considerable validity to Case's critique, Maglie decided to wait for DOT's letter before going further with this realm.

DOT's two-page July 27th letter was received by the planning board on the last day of the month. However brief, it was the most extensive set of comments DOT had contributed to the SEQRA process in 18 months of review to date. The letter demonstrated that when forced to respond, the DOT too knew the difference between barebones conclusions and factual analysis. While couched again in language difficult to penetrate (Rattle called it "a study in ambiguity"), the letter finally began to provide the board with an independent third opinion about several of the critical issues at dispute.

Concerning the correct worst-case cumulative scenario for the southerly Heller lot, the DOT said: "If the town has a specific proposal to rezone this property to other uses, such as an office building, then an alternate impact analysis can be prepared as part of the SEQRA process." On the issue of lane level-of-service averaging to determine overall intersection ratings, the DOT said that it would be appropriate to combine a through and a shared through-right-turn lane for level of service analysis, "unless a separate exclusive right-turn lane is provided," as was the case here. The DOT would "review and determine the final design details," including lane widths, "prior to the issuance of highway work permit."

The letter also explained DOT's internal decision-making process. Its Planning and Program Management Group typically reviewed all SEQRA documents to determine the "reasonableness and completeness of the traffic information included." For the DOT, despite its status as an involved agency, all that was needed to satisfy SEQRA was a reasonably complete work plan, not a determination whether that plan adequately mitigated the adverse environmental impacts of a proposed project. If a state highway work permit was required, a separate division within DOT would later determine the amount of "mitigation work necessary to address the impact of the generated traffic," without community involvement. Presumably, DOT letters to the planning board to date were produced by only the first phase of review, thereby explaining the lack of detailed commentary. DOT's abdication of a substantive role under SEQRA, while undermining the purposes of the statute, was consistent with its historical position toward environmental legislation which could impede highway growth.

Importantly, the letter also specified that:

> the Department's basic policy is that the traffic impact of a new development must be mitigated so that the level(s) of service, safety or other measures of traffic can be maintained at the same level as the affected facility would have operated without the new development. A comparison of the no-build and combined scenarios in the [EIS] is done to determine what, if any, changes to the highway system would be required.

With its bureaucratic language, generalizations, deferred judgments and omissions, DOT's letter was hardly a definitive statement on one side or the other. Nevertheless, certain key principles were articulated which were consistent with Case's critique and community groups moved quickly to underline to the board these areas of agreement. Once more, they sought a letter from Case.

Based on the DOT statement, Case now elaborated to the board on each of the major disputed points. He especially underlined that, despite the data base flaws in Magellan's traffic flow analyses, even its own charts demonstrated that after road improvements were made, traffic levels of service would still deteriorate and that unacceptable "E" and "F" levels would occur. Following DOT endorsement of the value of measuring office use of the southerly lot, Case specifically calculated the impact of such additional vehicles on the Creighton Rd.-Rte. 354 intersection. From this, he proved that, even with Magellan's planned road mitigation, northbound traffic on South Creighton Rd. would remain at an "F" level during the afternoon peak traffic flow.

A Final Board Review

For the first time, therefore, at its August 14th meeting, the planning board finally had a foundational irrefutable expert opinion on traffic impact. Almost immediately, however, a major dispute ensued concerning the relevance or not of including cumulative traffic volume data from potential buildout of the southerly Heller lot. The DOT's endorsement of measuring this potential for office use only intensified this previously-debated issue. On this point, Myers and Manley were persistent in pursuing the logic of the recent DOT and Case letters. But Rattle, Busch, Ryker and Maglie all strongly discouraged hypothetical speculation as inappropriate to the task at hand, thereby discounting the growth inducement nature of the project and compartmentalizing the SEQRA decision by limiting it to the northerly lot. Ultimately, Maglie ignored the opposition and proceeded to the next traffic issue.

Maglie acknowledged the lane width issue merely as something the DOT promised to review later on. Next item. Concerning averaging ratings for different lanes at the same intersection, Maglie first read the DOT letter to imply that Magellan's method was acceptable. After Myers contended that Maglie's reading misconstrued DOT's meaning, Maglie admitted that Case's statement of certain unacceptable lane flows was correct, but added that "DOT has already stated that that is unacceptable and [in] the design stage, [it will require] design that prevents 'E' level of service." Next item. The rest of the letter, he said, simply explained the DOT review process. Maglie mentioned nothing about DOT's standard, stated explicitly in that section, that traffic service should not deteriorate beyond present levels.[10] Descending to particulars had flushed out further the degree to which "light planners" were willing to delegate SEQRA decisions to permitting agencies, thereby disengaging themselves from any further substantive environmental decision-making of their own.

Maglie's strategy of denial and avoidance sought to portray analysis of the southerly Heller lot as unreasonable, to defer lane-width and other issues to later DOT review and to generally hurry the board past potentially important issues. Thus, Maglie--with assistance from Rattle, Busch and Ryker--hoped to maneuver the DOT response back to a place of apparently benign objective neutrality, implying nothing critical for the planning board's concern at the SEQRA stage. Maglie was clearly ready to vote for approval.

C. Economic Impact

Busch's March 10th filtering list of "substantive issues" raised in the DSEIS public comment period was even more misleading in the economic realm than for stormwater and traffic. In actuality, Busch totally evaded the most important substantive critiques on Moselle Plaza's economic and fiscal impact by omitting the comments of professional planner Maynard Smith, McBride for CLEAR and Hillman of the planning board. While Busch cited some public comments for each of the four scope items in this realm, in most cases these comments were more general in nature than those of Smith and CLEAR and thus were susceptible to being dismissed as mere hyperbole.

Smith and McBride had pointed out, in considerable detail, that Marvell's report provided no information on costs to Town government, on revenues or costs for the school district, on effects on local taxes through tax abatements and reduced assessments for adversely-affected commercial properties, on the nature of jobs created and on the number of jobs lost. They disputed the methodological assumption that a 7-mile radius retail zone would capture most consumer spending of residents living toward the edge of that zone since they were as close if not closer to other major stores than they would be to Ashbury. They criticized the lack of rationale for projecting only a small inevitable leakage of retail spending outside of the area, apparently not accounting for catalog shoppers, attractiveness of regional malls and other factors. They requested details on the cumulative impacts of other existing and planned regional Hudson Valley Wal-Marts and Kmarts on the regional consumer market. Additionally, they pointed out that Wal-Mart had a much higher sales-per-square foot amount than shown in the report, thereby implying capture of a higher proportion of local spending than estimated by Marvell.

McBride had also questioned important disparities between Marvell's and Magellan's estimates of Ashbury median household income and existing area retail spending. As well, he had stated that Moselle Plaza would cause reduced sales and income taxes from existing stores, the likely imposition of Main Street blight and deteriorated small-town rural community character, and contradictions of the project with the Town's draft comprehensive plan. Contradicting Marvell's optimistic assumptions, both Smith and McBride had cited expert predictions of continued sluggish economic growth in the Northeast over the next few years, while McBride had provided many details on current unemployment and underemployment in the local area. McBride had also pointed out that Marvell's retail spending projections were based on figures no later than 1992, though the effect of IBM layoffs came after that time. Smith and McBride had both predicted a Moselle Plaza-caused demise of major anchors in existing Ashbury shopping centers and a devastating ripple effect on smaller stores dependent on anchor shoppers at the same plaza locations.

Because Maglie discounted from the beginning either favorable or unfavorable economic studies as "all based upon futures we have no way of seeing," he offered no pretense, in contrast to stormwater and traffic realms, that the SEQRA process would follow a model of scientific rationality. His only exception was in the area of fiscal impact, where Maglie believed that tax abatement effects were "a calculation that can be done and I, for one, want to see what it looks like."

Myers suggested that the fiscal impact analysis should go further, such as examining the local tax base effect if existing shopping centers were hurt and sought assessment reductions as a result.

> That's the one thing in all of these economic development discussions that is going to have a real and direct impact on every property owner in this town--as well as on the school district. And yet it might not be a negative impact. We don't really know any of that yet. It could be that a little new competition would lower business rents in the town and actually help local business people.

Despite the public comments on Busch's list, the testimony heard at the public hearing and extensive critiques from Smith and CLEAR already in their possession, other "light planning" members at the March 13th meeting sought to eliminate economics from discussion.

In his March 22nd response to Busch's list of DSEIS public comments, Marvell repeated his assertion that estimates of spending at existing area stores compared with potential area buying power demonstrated:

> that there is a sufficient demand for retailing in the Ashbury area to support both the existing retail establishments and the Moselle Plaza. . . . [I]n the short run there will be no negative impact on existing retailers. However, in the intermediate and long-run time period, the

existing retailers will <u>gain</u> from increased retail activity from the Moselle Plaza.

This optimistic forecast could not have contrasted more with the negative images of Smith, McBride and other project critics who demonstrated the harmful effect that Moselle Plaza would have on the economic viability of the three existing shopping plazas in town and the ripple effect that this would have on the overall economy. Whether the planning board would have to address this large disparity without rose-colored glasses was yet to be determined.

The Paid Expert Departs

The $12,000 already paid for a 22-page report, based on generalities and standard texts, had failed to acknowledge virtually every material issue related to the Ashbury local economy. Now Marvell wanted additional money before he would address what he called the "what if" Ashbury-specific critiques raised by Smith and McBride. Since the model of scientific rationality invites debate about background assumptions, raw data, methodology, and conclusions, the board appeared to be without a method to satisfy its responsibility under SEQRA. The board had to decide how to proceed with economics. Maglie refused to believe that further consultation with an expert in that realm would be useful. All regarded further payment to Marvell as a waste. In the view of the "light planners," there was no potential source of free advice from the outside, since they would refuse (with the possible exception of Myers) to accept as valid anything further from Smith. Therefore, the economic impact review would proceed at the competence level of the board itself. The wagons would be drawn, limiting the basis for decision-making to "common sense."

Smith Responds

The board's plight was magnified when it received Maynard Smith's May 9th two-page additional commentary requested by the community groups. He explicitly endorsed McBride's written comments of February 10th: "I agree with the critiques presented and incorporate them with my own." He referred to Busch's opinion that his and McBride's responses were "substantive" and required answers. Smith stated that "these are not issues which can be responded to solely through lay 'common sense.'" He criticized Marvell's continued optimistic forecasts of Moselle Plaza's effects on local retailers, reminding the board that these forecasts were based on faulty assumptions and methodology, including Marvell's neglect of readily-available data on the adverse effects of Wal-Mart on small-town economies and his failure to address impact on existing shopping centers.

Maglie Attempts A Rescue

The May 15th meeting was an opportunity for the board to begin examining these issues itself since members had chosen to seek no other opinions from the outside. However, after extensive discussion on stormwater issues and additional time on traffic, board members once again discussed no more than their own quandary about economics. Myers and Hillman were again upset at the lack of expertise to draw upon for independent perspective and suggested hiring another consultant to review the present debate. Maglie and Ryker insisted that the board had enough data, that economics was not a science and that members could make the necessary judgments themselves. Busch admitted that while there were many things the board could do for itself in this analysis, there were some that it could not. Eventually, Maglie offered to take on the burden himself of assembling a spectrum of economic scenarios for the next meeting. After all, he said, he had access at his EnergyMax office to various future forecasts for the region.

Maglie contended that someone practiced in number-crunching, such as he, could objectively analyze and explain economic indicators. As in the traffic realm, he thought, there was only one set of data. Thereafter, everything was subject to interpretation and lay people were just as capable of engaging in this process as experts, whose conclusions were subjective and represented only their own predispositions and biases. Such conclusions, he suggested, were of little consequence to lay members of the board, who, as community residents, had an ample basis to form their own opinions.

Maglie issued his 14-page economic forecast to the board on June 12th. His report was more than a mere presentation of data. It contained his own conclusions and predictions, based on data derived, he contended, from a review of Magellan Construction's Spring 1994 economic impact report, Marvell's DSEIS report, the Smith and CLEAR written critiques from the public comment period, and subsequent letters from Marvell, McBride and Smith. To his credit, Maglie's forecast was the first effort to pull all the essential documentation together as the basis for the board's economic decision.

In essence, while conceding higher anchor store projected sales suggested by Smith and McBride, he accepted, without further elaboration, Marvell's and Magellan's very optimistic estimate of consumer market growth in the area, thus concluding that there would be minimal effect on existing retailers. Concerning fiscal impacts, Maglie accepted Marvell's figure for local tax revenue generated by the plaza without verification and then cut the figure in half to find the income produced after tax abatements. While granting that there would be costs to the Town government, he didn't bother to calculate the amount since "commercial property generally pays more in taxes than it receives in benefits." Maglie then factored in potential reduced assessments for existing Ashbury shopping centers, estimated by McBride, and came up with an overall revenue benefit from Moselle Plaza of about $76,000.

Maglie treated specific concerns of Smith and McBride about Wal-Mart practices as "what if" questions, following the lead of Marvell. He agreed that Moselle Plaza would have a major impact on the Ashbury retail market, but believed that the consumer market was large enough to absorb it. In summation, he stated: "In all the cases tested and in all the variations suggested in the public comments, the retail market potential appears to be sufficient to allow the development to occur." The market would correct itself without the need for any outside intervention.

In the end, after his April disclaimer of not knowing how to do economic analysis, Maglie claimed to have brought rationality and objectivity to the planning board process:

> I have tried to take the major issues that have been raised regarding the economic consequences and impact on the community character of the Town that would be created by the Moselle Mall from the rhetoric level to the number level using inputs from the comments made regarding the economic studies included in the DSEIS.[11]

His conclusion was that the project would absorb some of the present spending leakage outside of the area, have a positive impact on the tax base, create new jobs, have at worst a minor impact on tourism and have minimal likelihood of creating long-term economic blight. "Light planning" was all that was needed.

The Community Responds

By June 18th, McBride, on behalf of CLEAR, assembled and transmitted to the board a detailed 13-page critique of Maglie's report.[12] While following step-by-step the same format as Maglie, McBride filled in the gaps of Maglie's analysis and corrected his data, using much of the substantive information previously provided by Smith and McBride, but neglected by Maglie. In contrast to Maglie's optimistic conclusions, but using the same method of analysis and crunching the same numbers,[13] McBride's figures showed a $28.8 million or 21% loss of retail sales to existing business during the first year of Moselle Plaza operation--primarily because of estimating nearly 10% less local consumer spending potential and a 15% irretrievable spending leakage outside of the area. He foresaw ever-greater erosion and decline of local businesses in the years thereafter. He also highlighted the important secondary adverse ripple effect caused by the decline of major existing anchor stores. On the fiscal side, McBride predicted tax revenue losses approaching $2 million at the same time that governmental expenses would increase by millions. There would also be a net loss rather than gain of jobs in the community and a spread of "Main Street" blight which would significantly alter town character.[14]

On the issue of fiscal impacts, McBride underscored evidence already submitted by the DMG about expected overall county and state tax losses of at least $1.5 million due to IDA tax abatements. Beyond additional fire and police costs for serving the new mall, the town government would face greater need for such services with decaying malls. To eventually rehabilitate decayed areas would add further costs for community development and planning. Additionally, off-site highway improvements required by major unmitigated traffic impacts would cost more millions of dollars which Magellan asserted would have to come from public funds. Finally, the new Wal-Mart would even cost the school district about $50,000 annually because of a likely addition of about 6 schoolchildren to the community from families of imported store managers. Beyond these various omissions, McBride indicated that Maglie had not accounted for additional likely reduction of assessments to other commercial and residential town properties adversely affected by Moselle Plaza, beyond the major shopping centers themselves,.

The Board's Substantive Debate

At the June 19th meeting, Maglie explained that his approach was to see if the numbers offered were reasonable, without a claim to precision, and if Moselle Plaza would cause economic blight. He said that economists could give you any answer you want as to how long blight might last. Myers, who appeared to be inching toward an alliance with "regulator" dissenters, pointed out that nearby downtown Poughkeepsie never recovered from the blight imposed by major shopping malls outside of town. Various members then offered specific questions on data availability and analytical approaches, indicating by doing so that they were not content with Maglie's report as the final word. Though never citing McBride's critique, it seemed that at least Myers and others had used some of his points to re-enforce their own original skepticism in this realm.

On the other hand, in Ryker's view, the situation was much too complex and subjective to be understood by rational predictors. From a different starting place, Green seemed to agree. She said that it was important to think about the huge scale of Moselle Plaza and the potential for empty stores in 5-10 years. Ashbury was not healthier than Poughkeepsie before the coming of the latter's megamalls. She thought the board still had "trouble coming up with any kind of objective data that will support or not support some of our gut feelings," but said that she didn't need a lot of figures to tell her what she saw when she drove around. She said that she therefore saw blight in the future of Ashbury.

In response, Rattle then boxed in the issue from the other side by asserting uncharacteristically that the board's findings statement must be based on science, not speculation. "You have to have . . . facts in mind. This worst-case analysis that you were bringing up really is not supposed to be used for shopping centers. You've got to use hard data and then you can extrapolate it." The upshot of Rattle's view was that hard data was unavailable, the matter was purely subjective, and the board shouldn't concern itself further with the problem, having satisfied SEQRA's standard by taking a "hard look" at the contradictions.

Maglie then suggested that SEQRA was not the proper vehicle for the economic concerns voiced by "regulators." Instead, they should petition the town to rezone the area east of the Thruway if they wanted to prevent further commercial expansion in the wake of Moselle Plaza. But to this suggestion, Ryker objected in the name of "progress" and in opposition to forecasting:

> So many people [are] calling for some kind of [job and tax] relief in this community that to call for some kind of a stoppage to commercial growth or industrial growth or business growth is going counter to any kind of life for this community.
>
> . . . You say [people] would be afraid of the monster store, but there are other people who would see that there is a niche in the market, that it's created by the fact that there's, to excuse the expression, a monster store there and another kind of store here . . . . If [currently-discussed large developments are approved in Regent Park and at Midway Park Airport], there may be an upswing in the whole area. How are you going to predict that? You're not going to predict that. You talk about the negative side of it, there's also a positive side of it that you don't seem to want to deal with.

After Maglie took note of topics that members wanted researched, Myers raised the issue of community character. Again Ryker completely dismissed the topic: "You can talk about community character. 'Community character' is in the eyes of the beholder, the resident and the traveler." For Ryker, the whole topic of community character was not an appropriate SEQRA consideration, despite the statutory requirement to the contrary. Since these judgments were inevitably subjective, they should be omitted from board consideration. With Ryker's final suggestion that site screening by planting evergreens and shrubs would mitigate the big-box effect, the discussion of Maglie's report came to a very indecisive end.

Smith's Critique

Though Smith was out of the country when Maglie's report was issued, upon his return he also wrote a critique. Smith's 4-page letter was mailed to the board on July 1st. While giving Maglie "great credit for attempting to clarify the issues and to create a meaningful understanding of the facts and opinions provided by the participants in the process," Smith stated that his response "ignored or underplayed several key factors that must be addressed before a reasonable decision can be made." For Smith, that decision meant something more than simply identifying differing opinions resulting from economic indicators. It meant deciding whether the scale of the proposed project had to be substantially downsized before it could satisfy SEQRA's standard as minimizing to the greatest extent possible the adverse environmental impact on community character. For Smith, it also meant concluding whether the proposed project would have a positive or negative economic impact on the town, in the balancing test, given identified environmental impacts related to stormwater and traffic.

While repeating many of the same points that McBride had argued, Smith also stressed several important themes of his own. He criticized Maglie's description of mall development, in this case, as merely evolutionary.

> It is not simply the latest form of retail evolution. In my twenty years of planning experience, I have never observed as much commercial disruption as occurs when Wal-Mart comes to town. It is a revolutionary form of retail activity.

Beyond the initial Moselle Plaza, Smith foresaw significant additional commercial development attracted to east of the Thruway, becoming a shopping hub of its own "with no connectedness to the community. I find no evidence in any Ashbury planning documents or conversations with citizens that such a shift or such a center was intended." Ashbury would be "willingly giving up its traditional character in exchange for a shopping center that could be placed in 'Anywhere USA'."

Concerning the disputes among various people, consultants and groups about income levels and growth rates in the area, he thought that "it appears most reasonable, in order to protect the community, to take the most conservative and worst case numbers." Smith stated finally that he reviewed the McBride/CLEAR critique of June 18th and agreed with its findings. Given the information available, he recommended that Moselle Plaza be disapproved by the criteria of SEQRA.

In turn, on July 10th, McBride followed up Smith's letter with a detailed evaluation of municipal costs and revenues attributable to Moselle Plaza, using the *Fiscal Impact Handbook* recommended by Smith.[15] McBride's conclusion was that "at best, only part way through the next decade would Moselle Plaza begin to pay more in town revenue than it costs in town government expenses and reduced assessments." Evaluation of school district fiscal impact produced similar results. When county and state revenues and expenses were added as well, the conclusion was inescapable that "taxpayers will shoulder additional tax burdens because of the Moselle Plaza development."

Such was the state of the official record when the board held its final review meeting on economic impact issues on July 24th. Without comments from Magellan Construction and with Marvell dropped from the scene since April, only Maglie's effort to revitalize Marvell's report and the detailed critiques and analyses of Smith and McBride were on the table. While Maglie had been given a list of items to research, it was clear that he had not done so. He offered nothing and no one renewed a request. In fact, this meeting was totally void of dialogue since everyone present now indicated that they had enough information to make a judgment.

<u>Prospects Ahead</u>

The board now moved on to the next stage of finalizing the FSEIS on the basis of all the information it had received. In the absence of any substantive discussion among board members of the economic issues raised and with little more than that for disputed contentions in traffic and stormwater realms, community activists were hardly optimistic regarding the final determination. Only the occasional questions posed, though unanswered, and the procedural debates themselves provided clues as to how substantive issues would be resolved. In the end, differences about substance, like procedure, seemed irreconcilable and presumably would be subject to the politics of competing ideologies represented by "light planners" and "regulators" on the board. Each would vote their original predispositions and now had chapter and verse to cite from various submitted reports to support their conclusions. The decision would be resolved, it seemed, through determining which voting bloc could attract the one board member, Myers, who, at the end of the meetings, had positioned himself as a centrist. Hand-picked by Ryker to replace Bellows and to provide "light planners" with a solid majority for approval, Myers seemed to balk at pleading Ryker's party line.

Myers' potential vote was a thin reed upon which community groups could rest their hopes and it demonstrated activists' frustration with the administration of the SEQRA statute itself. Those who favored disapproval clearly had the better of the argument, it seemed, applying the "hard look" standard to each environmental realm and using the economic and social balancing test also mandated by the statute. While SEQRA was designed to enhance the promise of scientific objectivity, those who opposed the statute and its implications continued to dominate the final SEQRA decision-making process. With Ryker and Davis legally-challengeable because of publicly-disclosed predisposition and conflicts of interest, the only solace the activists had was that should Myers vote for approval, a narrow 4-3 decision might be reversed by the courts because dissenters could demonstrate that the outcome would have been different had each board member satisfied legality's standard for fair and impartial decision-making. Of course, this would mean raising funds to retain an attorney who would represent the groups in court when Dreyfus returned to full-time teaching in the Fall. Having spent all their resources in creating a record of reasoned dissent, activists were by no means sanguine about the possibility of achieving further success in the courts.

ELEVEN
DIMENSIONS BEYOND THE OFFICIAL PROCESS

Symbolic achievements were important for sustaining the spirits of ACT and CLEAR and for reaching out to the broader community, but ultimately there was no real victory unless the project was defeated. While the Town Board's February 1995 IDA resolution no doubt discouraged Medford, it was non-binding. Potential additional costs of developing Moselle Plaza, without IDA status, were one factor among several which would influence the developer's cost-benefit calculation. But the community groups could not know the specific weight of this factor for Magellan compared to the cost of environmental mitigation and the likely profit to be gained for having a Wal-Mart-type mega-store as the principal anchor.[1]

Strategizing

Beyond maintaining their proactive interventionist approach with the planning board, ACT and CLEAR had to address two other major realms of priority activity as well. First would be a continued effort to discourage Moselle Plaza through extra-SEQRA means. This meant activists again having to identify all possible government decision points, including involved agency permits, authorizations and zoning changes, and to intervene in each of these processes as well. This also meant continuing to speak directly to Medford, to encourage corporate officials to understand and consider the alternative of expanding the FoodFeast store on site. A second major priority would be to continue to broaden the coalition and to deepen the politicization process so as to add further pressure on the planning board. As well, the community groups needed to gain more financial resources to cover costs of professional experts and publicity, and to increase the ranks of volunteers.

Should the planning board approve the project under SEQRA, Magellan would still have to obtain Reading County IDA approval in order to gain low-cost financing and tax abatements, zoning approval from the Town Board or ZBA to allow Moselle Plaza's planned extension into the southerly light industrial zone, a series of five DEC permits concerning wetlands, stream protection and removal of hazardous substances, and approval from the Army Corps of Engineers concerning potential threats to on- and off-site federally-designated wetlands.

Pending Magellan's response to substantive comments by the public and involved agencies, ACT and CLEAR met in the third week of February to design a strategy to inhibit Magellan from proceeding further, assuming their FSEIS responses were found by the board's "light planning" majority to adequately address critiques through mitigation. Each of the subsequent flashpoints was analyzed and discussed, beginning with the need to obtain Army Corps approval.

Because of the agency's inadequate resources and more pressing priorities, Army Corps review was typically very slow and indecisive for a project of this size.[2] Despite Ina Turbell's persistent attempts for months to gain immediate Corps review, no more than a standard response was forthcoming, indicating that the Corps awaited more information from the developer.

As for continued involvement with the DEC whose permitting authority over stormwater, sewage and hazardous materials awaited SEQRA approval from the planning board, the plan was to continue to engage the DEC's commentator, William Tholen, upon receipt of Magellan's draft FSEIS. Furthermore, there might be an opportunity for ACT and CLEAR to participate in DEC public hearings should the planning board approve the project and it reached the permitting stage.[3]

At their strategy meeting, ACT and CLEAR decided to explore the legal dimensions of opposing Magellan's needed expansion of the commercial zone through a ZBA variance or a Town Board zoning change. But apparently the developer was content to wait for SEQRA approval before pursuing either of these alternatives, so community activists deferred action here as well.

This left ACT and CLEAR with the IDA issue as the single major point of immediate intervention outside of the planning board's SEQRA process. While the Town Board's non-binding resolution of February 16th provided a warning to Magellan, it failed to stop that approval process at its source--acceptance of the application by the Reading County IDA. Should the Reading County IDA be persuaded that Medford's application misrepresented material facts, it could vitiate the application and declare the process a nullity. Such a decision would eliminate Magellan's opportunity to persuade Schmidt, Devilla, and Kraft, the three "light planner" members of the Town Board, through donation of a fire engine or some other community amenity, to approve the project and overrule the non-binding resolution. Since the community groups knew from Turbell's experience with Reynolds that Magellan was willing to grease the wheel by spending large sums in such a manner, reversal of the Town Board's February 16th resolution seemed a distinct possibility.[4]

Suing the IDA

At about the same time, a worker at a local copy shop which had donated free and cut-rate services to the community groups informed a member of ACT that Wal-Mart was in a legal battle in her mother's home town of Hornell, New

York, near Rochester. She soon obtained news accounts specifically describing the legal points at dispute. Dreyfus immediately contacted the Rochester attorney who filed the challenge and obtained the relevant briefs and court records. A citizens' group in Hornell had successfully challenged an IDA approval which preceded SEQRA review. In Dreyfus' opinion, the argument used might apply to RCIDA's actions as well. Legal action had several advantages. Utmost was the hope that IDA preliminary approval of Medford's application would be voided by the court. In this case, Medford might be unable to re-apply since the IDA statute reform enacted in late 1993 prohibited retail developments from receiving IDA funds.[5] Moreover, legal action, whatever its outcome, would also demonstrate to Magellan and the planning board's "light majority" that the community groups were resolved to utilize the judicial system, if necessary, to overturn an adverse decision failing to comply with the letter and spirit of SEQRA law. As well, the suit might focus media attention on Medford's efforts to use its home-county IDA as a form of corporate welfare to give it a distinct advantage over any Ashbury competitor. Such publicity, it was hoped, would broaden and deepen the community alliance against the mall more generally.

Closer scrutiny of Medford's 1993 application to RCIDA and the Inducement Resolutions revealed another material misstatement. Medford had answered negatively to application questions about whether the project would be for less than 100% supermarket use and would involve leasing to third parties, leaving the impression that IDA funds would be used only to subsidize Medford's on-site expansion.[6] Though the application showed only a 60,000 sq. ft. grocery store for Ashbury, the option agreement with Heller, attached as an application exhibit, clearly showed intent to build a major mall. Regardless of the discrepancy, RCIDA's Inducement Resolution referred to IDA financing for construction in Ashbury of a 160,000 sq.ft. shopping plaza including 100,000 sq. ft. to be leased to other retail tenants.[7] Medford's application also erroneously stated that the Ashbury project would conform to existing zoning. Because of Moselle Plaza's need to intrude into at least several acres of the Light Industrial Zone (explicitly mentioned in the Heller option agreement), the Ashbury project would be non-conforming.

Though IDA Administrator Sanford promised McBride that he would inform him, as requested, about any upcoming IDA meeting related to the Ashbury project, he did so only by accident. On his second visit to Sanford's small office on March 3rd, McBride by chance overheard Sanford informing someone by phone about an IDA meeting six days hence. Knowing that any IDA notice about this meeting was unlikely to appear in the *Post* or any other local media distributed in Ashbury, McBride called the Reading County Office Building directly and found that the Ashbury project was indeed on the agenda.

An Ashbury contingent of six activists, including Turbell, McBride, Dreyfus, Gail and Les Garvey and Peg Turner (of the DMG), was organized to pay RCIDA a surprise visit and to present the case for annulling Medford's Ashbury application. The timing was most fortuitous since March 9th was the very day that the groups' attorney Brad McKenna planned to file suit against RCIDA. Appearing on scene, Ashbury activists would be able to learn directly if their request for a rescinded approval was to be granted or whether a lawsuit would have to be filed.

Sitting in comfortable chairs around a long table in their wood-panelled meeting room, officials seemed a bit irritated and definitely anxious at this unexpected intrusion. As Dreyfus remarked afterwards, the whole atmosphere reeked of the paternalism and nepotism of a 1950s Southern courtroom. While Sanford cautioned his board about engaging in a discussion about the issues, "because we know where that might lead," he informed the Ashbury group that Medford had clarified to his satisfaction the application statements in contention. Tom Lincoln, Medford's Vice President-Comptroller, had in fact thanked Sanford "for keeping us informed as to the various actions the anti-growth forces in the Town of Ashbury are taking. They seem to want to take any avenue they can to slow us down including the mounting of an attack on our I.D.A. status."[8] Said Sanford, the Ashbury group should just go solve its differences with Medford on its own--perhaps ultimately in court. As activists left the room, little did Sanford know that their suit against RCIDA and Medford was to be filed that very day.[9]

In the midst of the legal suit's preparation, without much persuasion, the DMG and Village Board of Ashbury also chose to join ACT and CLEAR as plaintiffs. Politically, this coalition of determined opposition to the mall was impressive. At a press conference at Village Hall the next day, McBride for CLEAR, Turbell for ACT, Jan Winfield for the DMG and Mayor Patton for the Village each explained their reasons for bringing this action. Dreyfus, in turn, explained the legal issues involved and, hopefully, their favorable resolution.

At the same time, the community groups participating now as plaintiffs in the law suit issued a joint press release denouncing the hidden manipulations of Medford and RCIDA to damage Ashbury's future:

> Such backdoor techniques in which Medford, a dominant corporation in Reading County . . . , uses its influence with members of the RCIDA unbeknownst to the community which will be impacted adversely by its act [are] foreign to our own American democratic way. The Reading County IDA and FoodFeast should have immediately notified the town of Ashbury and provided an environmental impact study which dealt with the effect of this mega-

store mall on the area's sensitive wetlands, traffic problems and community character. Instead, the RCIDA and FoodFeast sought unilaterally to engage in a growth-inducing project which would enrich Medford's coffers at the expense of the town and its residents.

It also pointed out the significance of the statutory restriction against IDA funding for mere marketplace advantage:

The purpose of the statute is to encourage new business, not to permit existing businesses to hopscotch from one location to another at taxpayer expense whenever the business thinks it would like a new facility to enhance its competitive standing in the marketplace.

The highly politicized rhetoric of the press release portrayed Medford and its RCIDA ally as willing to exploit the tax base through a coalition of local interest and greed. The community groups hoped that by framing the funding for Moselle Plaza in this wider political context, residents of Ashbury already opposed to inequities in high property taxes would be willing to join the coalition of groups opposed to the mall. Just two weeks later, the Ashbury Chamber of Commerce, a consistently "light planning" organization,[10] itself went on public record opposing these types of tax abatements.

After having reviewed the tax concessions proposed for an IDA-sponsored firm and having read a [critical] paper [on IDA misuse], we believe that an IDA-sponsored retail store would not provide additional benefits to the community and in fact could have a detrimental effect. An IDA-sponsored retail firm would create a zero-sum game in which some of our local businesses would fail and the IDA-sponsored firm would succeed.

The tax concessions provided to an IDA-sponsored business do not provide a level playing field for all business. . . . [N]on-IDA firms are likely to experience an increase in costs in the form of higher taxes to compensate for the concessions in tax given to IDA firms. . . .

. . . IDA subsidies may help relatively inefficient firms to lower their price, thereby underpricing the existing competitors. This will reduce revenues of the existing retail stores and may eventually bankrupt them.

Retail firms tend to serve existing markets without expanding the size of these markets. . . . There is no evidence that IDA-sponsored firms create new jobs.

For these reasons, the Chamber Board agrees with the New York State Legislature's position in not supporting further requests for IDA funding of retail projects. . . . The Moselle Plaza is the last proposed site to fall into the exhausted retail IDA sponsorship.[11]

The wording of the Chamber's statement presented a serious challenge to the

Ryker-led majority on the planning board. The Chamber was the traditional source of Republican support for development and apparently had never opposed any application pending before the planning board. While the wording of this statement omitted reference to the ongoing SEQRA process, the message was clear. The Chamber did not consider Magellan to be a good corporate citizen and disapproved of its ability to thwart local businesses through tax advantage. This was one of the most significant political victories yet achieved by the community groups and, along with the resolution of the Town Board, isolated further the "light planning" majority by severing it from its natural ally. Those who favored building Moselle Plaza were now conclusively unmasked as ideologically favoring welfare for large corporations to the detriment of mom-and-pop businesses. Once again, activists' appeal to saving the community from outside predators had struck a responsive chord.

Magellan's Legal Response

Morris Schwab, the Glens Falls attorney representing Magellan Construction before the Ashbury planning board, answered for Medford and RCIDA two months later. Schwab's response was a procedural argument, omitting discussion of the substantive issues involved. He contended that the challenge to the 1993 preliminary inducement resolution was "untimely" and that the coalition of plaintiffs lacked "standing" to sue a governmental entity. At the same time, he failed to engage with contentions raised by the community groups regarding either Medford's misstatements or RCIDA's failure to engage in timely SEQRA review before agreeing to the preliminary inducement resolution. Despite the credibility and merits of their own position, community plaintiffs were not surprised at the motion to dismiss since it was a typical reply to a broad-based challenge of legality. Courts have traditionally opted out of deciding substantive issues when narrower technical grounds are available because of non-majoritarian concerns that judges not indulge themselves in a quasi-legislative process. Local courts in Forest County were notoriously constrained from any level of activism, in part because they tended to be elected officials thoroughly vetted by local Republican leaders and rewarded for judicial conservatism.

Community groups responded to the "standing" issue easily enough because they had included individuals as plaintiffs whose property was immediately proximate to the Heller site and who could show that they would be harmed beyond the level of general harm to the community. Hence they could be considered sufficiently "aggrieved" as to have the right to sue. There was also substantial case law to back the "standing" of ACT and CLEAR because they represented a wide spectrum of individuals from the entire community, some of whom resided proximately to the site.[12] The more difficult and complex response was to the "timeliness" of the proceeding.[13] The law suit was assigned to a judge from the Albany area who was assisting local Forest County judges in reducing case backlog. By the end of the summer, there was still no decision although the political momentum generated by the action continued to grow in favor of the community groups. Ultimately, if an adverse opinion was received, community plaintiffs would have to decide whether to risk additional funds on an appeal. That decision, in turn, would depend on the larger context of the struggle over Moselle Plaza and its effect on the planning board's decision.

Speaking to FoodFeast

While the lawsuit was pending against Medford and RCIDA, community groups also attempted friendly persuasion with FoodFeast's corporate executives about the alternative of expanding on site. The community would support FoodFeast, it was said, if it chose to be a good neighbor, disassociate itself from Magellan's Moselle Plaza and simply expand on site. Moreover, activists wanted to demonstrate to the community and to business interests that they were not just nay-sayers, but had a positive goal of "appropriate development" consistent with the nature and character of the community. Activists also believed that despite Medford's chilly reception to on-site expansion in recent years, such a "carrot" would gradually seem more appealing to FoodFeast the longer Moselle Plaza was contested and the more its financing was brought into question.[14]

For the record, Turbell also made certain that on-site expansion was presented at the SEQRA public hearing as a reasonable alternative in keeping with the character of the town and without the same adverse environmental effects which Moselle Plaza would bring. By late March, Turbell assembled a working committee of two local architects, a builder and a local artist to draw up conceptual on-site expansion plans for presentation to the Ashbury Development Corporation[15] and eventually to FoodFeast. But the proposal never developed momentum. ACT remained hopeful, however, and the chant of "FoodFeast - Stay on Site!" was to become a consistent presence at outdoor demonstrations led by ACT from August on.

ACT and the Community

If immediate decision-makers on the planning board and elected members of the Town Board were to be influenced by community moral pressure--in addition to the technical discourse of SEQRA--ACT and CLEAR believed that the community voice needed more numbers and volume than ever. Furthermore, to afford the cost of competing in the specialized professional arenas of the planning board and courtroom, ACT needed to raise substantial funds to defer the fees and disbursements it had to expend on its own experts. Hence public appeals became increasingly important.

One immediate priority of the late February strategy meeting was to assess realistic potentials of a sustained fundraising campaign. It was obvious that existing plaza owners and village retail businesspeople had much to gain from the anti-mall efforts and should therefore be approached for contributions. Such appeals had not been made before, though some retailers--such as the two local copy shops--had already contributed much through free or discounted services.

However, the question of receiving contributions from existing retailers and commercial property owners was debated among the activists. The community groups believed that Ryker and his "light planning" allies sought to discredit the anti-mall movement by contending that it was funded by the self-interest of the few but unresponsive to the needs of the community. Ryker kept demanding that since contributors to the Republican party were scrutinized, community groups ought to reveal their sources of funds as well. Secondly, some activists were uncomfortable with being associated with plaza owners and retailers whose involvement in strip-malling the Main Street corridor had ultimately paved the way for the Moselle Plaza proposal east of the Thruway. After all, FoodFeast Plaza, Ashbury Plaza, and Almond Plaza were all aesthetically displeasing, fronted by large blacktop parking areas which replaced the beautiful maple trees and farmland that had once dominated the landscape. Moreover, these plaza owners were not known to be environmentally conscious and the stormwater and traffic problems they caused were considerable.

Realistically, however, ACT knew that funds would have to be raised by commercial contributions, in addition to rummage sales, community events, and individual donations. As with public broadcasting stations, in the absence of state funds, public interest groups without an affluent base would have to appeal to the self-interest of the private market. For local environmental groups opposed to further degradation of the resources and natural ecology of the community, it meant soliciting funds from despoilers themselves who, at the end of the day, hoped to benefit by reduced competition. Nevertheless, ACT decided to speak directly with real estate corporations that managed the large plazas in town.

But support from the commercial sector would not be enough. The IDA suit, it was assumed, would cost at least $8000 in attorney's fees and possibly substantially more if, as seemed likely, the case would have to be appealed to a higher level. Furthermore, ACT and CLEAR would soon need to locate an attorney specializing in environmental law in order to prepare its court petition in time for the expected legal battle over SEQRA approval. Additionally, activists needed legal advice on the technicalities of rezoning and potential legal services for a court contest about that issue as well. Fortunately, experts Smith and Case, hired for the public hearing and subsequent SEQRA process, were available at minimal cost and Dreyfus was willing to continue <u>pro bono</u> representation before the planning board. In addition, sustaining and enlarging visible community activity about the mall issue would require further newspaper ads and leaflets.

ACT planned a series of successive fundraiser events over the next several months. Special committees were set up and many hours spent in planning, publicity and solicitation of contributions-in-kind. The first event, an evening of food and music at a local watering spot adjoining FoodFeast, took place on March 15th and raised a disappointingly small $500. It was a difficult lesson in the disproportionality of resources available to the protagonists in a SEQRA struggle. Magellan liked to contend that it was a company with assets of over $500 million. It proudly displayed its wealth at planning board meetings in the presence of well-heeled managers, lawyers, and engineers. Nevertheless, the March event was a start. Moreover, ACT learned lessons about publicity and potentially-attractive events, acquired a solid core of energetic volunteers and received contributions from at least 17 local merchants in the form of food, publicity materials, and party supplies, as well as selling tickets. The event was thus successful from a coalition-building perspective.

A second ACT fundraiser toward the end of May 1995, at the historic home of two longtime Ashbury residents, gained a net sum of about $1100. Seeking to appeal partially to a more traditional element of Ashbury society, this event took place at an impressive brick structure begun by one of the early Dutch families in the 18th century and completed a few decades later. A third such event raised $3500 at another historic home on the banks of the Van Wyck River. Again, the event attempted to broaden the coalition of opponents to Moselle Plaza by inviting members of the community with some means who were normally unaccustomed to political activism and to identify ACT and CLEAR with the historical and cultural traditions of the community. Speeches as well as folk and classical music were featured, with Town Board member Mark Lyon leading a bluegrass group in songs reminiscent of 60s protest movements. A number attended from the old-boys' network which dominated Ashbury politics over the years and whom activists assumed held "light planning" views. This was particularly impressive in that it signaled growing perception of a major community crisis and growing isolation of Ryker and other "light planners" whose inflexible ideological views, in this context at least, were beginning to be perceived by mainline residents as extreme and destabilizing.

A particular effort was made to depict the struggle with Magellan and Wal-Mart in visual terms which could be easily identified in everyday traffic and in casual encounters in town. The many "Stop Malling Ashbury" and "Stop Wal-

Mart" bumperstickers on cars throughout the town provided frequent reminders of community opposition. Likewise, a specially-designed, often seen, orange tee shirt by a graphic artist member of ACT represented Moselle Plaza and Wal-Mart as a giant shark about to devour the stores of downtown Main Street.

An ACT public information meeting at Village Hall on May 25th showed a video of a recent "60 Minutes" TV expose of Wal-Mart practices and presented a full update of the latest and upcoming stages of the planning board's SEQRA review. This effort meant to empower local residents with arguments about Wal-Mart and megamalls and their effects on small communities throughout the United States. Activists wanted to enlarge the base of articulate supporters such that a greater diversity of people would begin to write letters to the paper and speak at planning board meetings in opposition to Moselle Plaza.

The most controversial action was a series of three large picket-line demonstrations along Main Street directly in front of the FoodFeast Plaza. The decision "to strike FoodFeast" appealed to a wide range in the coalition who viewed demonstrations of this sort as a healthy way of expressing free speech and of further publicizing FoodFeast's recalcitrance. Picket lines also dramatically publicized the growing number of individuals willing to stand up and be counted as opponents of the megamall. With hundreds of participants, many picket signs and printed flyers for all drivers entering and exiting FoodFeast plaza, the three "community actions" on August 12th, September 15th and November 4th turned out to be family events with people of all ages and their children. If activists needed further encouragement, it came from the steady stream of car honks and handwaves of support from hundreds of peak hour drivers up and down the main corridor of Ashbury. By contrast, demonstrators saw and heard little from those that might support the project although Ryker himself circled picketers in his car, glaring at individuals and conferring with FoodFeast authorities and the police. Picket line-demonstrations were important means of outreach in themselves. Despite substantial continuing coverage of the Moselle Plaza struggle in both local weekly newspapers, such media had reached only a limited number in the community.[16]

A final major ACT recruitment strategy dovetailed with continuing concern about the formal political context for local decisions. Local elections in November 1995 would choose the Town Supervisor and two Town Board members, as well as several other officials. It was a natural opportunity to focus community attention on the issues of Moselle Plaza. While some activists also had searched for a way to hold a town referendum on the megamall, there was no authority for this in New York statutes. Local elections focusing on the central issue of Moselle Plaza, however, could become an appropriate substitute.

With a majority of the Town Board at stake and important issues in the struggle still to be resolved by that body, most activists felt that the opportunity must not be neglected. Future Board decisions would include potential boundary changes of the commercial zone to accommodate Moselle Plaza, IDA status approval, reappointing or not Ryker to the planning board at the December 31st expiration of his term, and potentially replacing "light planning" advocates on the ZBA, including the chair, Ernie Davis, who sold the plaza site to Heller and continued to own adjacent property. Activists also hoped to persuade the new Town Board to strengthen the Town Ethics Code to become effective in confronting bias and conflict-of-interest issues made visible in the anti-mall struggle. The community groups recognized as well that even if Moselle Plaza were defeated, a new developer could easily then apply with a modestly-downsized but still inappropriate project. This would require an entirely new SEQRA process and potential struggle which the heavily-strained groups could ill afford. With an anti-mall majority on the Town Board, however, the latter could enact a potential moratorium and rezoning to ban future strip-mall development if and when the Moselle Plaza project was defeated. Seeing the relationship between underlying zoning and short-range planning board SEQRA decisions gave added impetus to those who had previously viewed environmental threats as something to be attacked only on a case-specific basis.

For these reasons, ACT activists began early to develop a solid coalition of anti-mall candidates. The first step was to assure that "regulator" members of the Town Board were re-elected. The old Citizens Party which had served as Mark Lyon's base for two previous elections was once again revived under a new label, the Community Reform Party, more identifiable with the anti-mall movement and with Lyon and Jane Pelletier as candidates.

Of even greater significance was the effort needed to defeat Supervisor Schmidt, a longtime political ally of Ryker, already elected to two terms and now seeking another. Despite describing himself as an "environmentalist," Schmidt, who was proud of his Dutch roots, increasingly symbolized the "light planning" perspective of the dominant majority of elected officials who had willingly presided over years of unchecked growth. Moreover, Schmidt's "bean-counter" image enabled him to curry favor with homeowners and business people who opposed increased town taxes. Schmidt would maintain that taxes had not increased under his tenure because he had prudently administered Town fiscal resources while favoring development to expand the tax base. As a retired IBM manager, he presented himself as businesslike and above the emotional fray of the anti-mall movement. Replacing Schmidt with an anti-mall activist would not only result in a new "regulator" majority on the Town Board, but would create further pressure on existing "light planning" planning board members who contended that they were simply administering majoritarian views.

After much persuasion, a business person and fourteen-year resident of the area, Rachel Wilton, agreed to run. Wilton had worked closely with other ACT activists since early Spring and was fully committed against the mall. Additionally, Wilton's articulate public presence and her experience as a businessperson with responsibility for large accounts in a New York City advertising firm gave her credentials to counter Schmidt's claims of experience as a competent manager. She became a credible candidate for Supervisor under the Community Reform Party banner.

By mid-Summer, the CRP slate was assembled behind a campaign focus of opposition to Moselle Plaza. To successfully defeat Schmidt, however, and possibly the two Republican candidates for the Board, this slate also needed endorsement by local Democrats. Here the stumbling block was Edna Devilla and her tightly-knit longtime clique of supporters within the local Democratic Party club. It was plain that Devilla disliked the community activists whom she considered outsiders in the political process. She was also seen as at best ambivalent about the threat of Moselle Plaza itself, although she generally favored commercial development. Though initially threatening Pelletier with losing Democratic endorsement should Pelletier continue to associate with the activists and Lyon, Devilla backed down when Pelletier, a forceful "regulator" advocate, committed herself to the CRP slate and stated that she would compete, along with Lyon and Wilton, for the Democratic nomination at the September caucus.

The grip that Devilla and her loyalists maintained over the Democratic Party was beginning to erode. Ultimately, with ACT's public endorsement of the CRP slate and ACT's mobilization of party members for the September 14th Democratic caucus, Devilla's committee no longer could select the party candidates. The party caucus endorsed Wilton and the two other CRP candidates for the Town Board. Anti-mall activists had thus expanded their coalition and publicity effort to a much broader mainstream front.

PART FOUR   PROJECT DECISION

INTRODUCTION

The SEQRA stage of project review from February through August 1995 demonstrated the conceptual futility of a de-politicized environmental impact assessment process. From beginning to end, procedural maneuvers and shallow substantive debates by board consultants and most board members were mere shadows of the larger project approval or disapproval outcome already in mind.

Compared to a model of collegial open-ended rational inquiry, board dynamics were a complete failure. By standards of participatory planning, the process also strongly discouraged community involvement. As a context in which respective experts from developer, outside agency and community group perspectives could exchange and critique each others' research and analyses, this SEQRA stage was somewhat more successful, if considered as an abstract refinement and greater sophistication of understandings about a few crucial issues of environmental and economic impact. Having roots largely in an adversarial proceeding to begin with, however, whatever few abstract gains were achieved in perceiving project impacts were immediately enframed by the inevitable political overlay. To the public, the extent that substantive inquiry actually affected the views of any board members was largely unknown.

Nevertheless, the legally-mandated review process had to move toward finality when a definite policy decision would be made. The board had now decided, at the least through mutual exhaustion, that it had all the information it needed to assess, through a "hard look," the relative nature and degree of environmental and economic impact which the project would cause and the extent of mitigation planned by the developer. The first phase of decision-making at this new stage, as described in Chapter Twelve, was now to set forth, for themselves and for a final public and outside agency review, first, a definitive list of "substantive" issues articulated in response to the DSEIS concerning realms of stormwater-water quality, traffic and economics and second, appropriate reasoned responses to the research questions raised. While not meant to draw conclusions about the acceptability or not of the project as a whole, this "comments-responses" section was meant to be the board's own description of its research analysis of the various impact issues. Given the politicized nature of the just-concluded research phase, however, this chapter makes clear how the editing of this board document mainly continued the shallowness and procedural manipulations of the earlier stage. Once again, community activists were compelled to intervene with new substantive critiques and legal interpretations of their own simply to assure a relatively level field of combat for board members of alternative perspectives. Even more, activists increasingly found it necessary to substitute themselves in the dynamics, as a kind of alternative planning board, to provide on the record alternative "comments-responses" drafts which the board's planner would not provide and which, without adequate resources, the critical members of the board were unable to create. As the chapter portrays, a critical political aspect of this phase was to determine even what constituted the official SEQRA record upon which the board's decisions could be based.

With finalization of the "comments-responses" section, the board declared the draft FSEIS as "complete" and thereby available for a final brief period of review by outside agencies and the public. In this next phase, as described in Chapter Thirteen, the board's task was to compile the research results summarized in the FSEIS "comments-responses" section into an extensive narrative "findings" document setting forth the nature and extent of significant adverse environmental impacts and their potential mitigation as well as the balance of economic and social impacts against adverse environmental effects. As expected, the "light planning" board attorney and planner produced draft "findings" which marginalized the community groups' critiques, thus providing a rationale for board SEQRA approval of the project. The earlier series of community groups' expert submissions, in turn, provided a template for an alternative "findings" document justifying SEQRA disapproval. Assuring this clear and more formal basis for contestation to the end diminished the power of procedural maneuvers and forced substantive issues to a head.

Chapter Fourteen describes how the local campaign and election for a new town board provided another dimension of the overall political context for the planning board's SEQRA decision. It then portrays the nature and dynamics of a prolonged series of procedural maneuvers and dramatic decisions made by a board majority to conclude the SEQRA process.

TWELVE

COMPLETENESS: SECOND ASSESSMENT OF THE DEVELOPER'S RESPONSES

Assessing the Planning Board

As the DFSEIS review phase came to a close, ACT and CLEAR activists felt very conflicted. Through continued assertive interventions following the close of the official public comment period, the critical community had remained an active participant at the planning board level in whatever procedural and substantive discussion occurred. Unquestionably, Dreyfus' letters and legal memoranda had helped to inform the potentially receptive members of the board who were now alerted to the skewing of substantive and procedural legality by Rattle and other "light planning" members. Likewise, the continuous, increasingly-refined expert critiques of Wright, Case and Smith (the latter augmented by McBride's comments) had provided "regulator" members with an alternative analysis that had forced more detailed examination of certain issues to be placed in the board's official record. To play by official SEQRA rules, ACT and CLEAR had accepted the terms of "legitimate" bureaucratic discourse--the vocabulary of law, science and commerce--and at the least had objectively neutralized the one-sided presentations of Magellan, Rattle, Busch and the "light planners" on the board.

However, for the most part, planning board substantive discourse concerning the three impact realms from February through mid-August was quixotic, mediocre in content and shockingly brief. Constantly under siege by the procedural attacks of Rattle, Busch and Maglie (assisted more crudely by Ryker and Davis), board discussions typically saw issues raised, then quickly evaded by lengthy procedural discussions and little consistent effort to develop common understandings of the data, methodology and conclusions involved. Perhaps most shocking was the inability of planning board members to come to any resolution about the degree to which adverse environmental impacts were avoidable through either mitigation, downsizing or abandonment.

The three veterans of the "light planning" majority--Ryker, Davis and Maglie--appeared to believe that SEQRA was a pro forma gate which required planning board approval but which had little, if any, significance in deciding the viability of the project. For them, the focus on SEQRA by community activists, independent experts and "regulator" members obstructed and delayed the board's real work of site plan review. It was at this "backloaded" stage, without significant public influence, that the project would be measured, fitted and shaped to satisfy local regulatory standards. What remained would be the responsibility of the involved agencies in the permitting process.

On the positive side, the work of the community groups and their experts took root in the growing sophistication of "regulator" members Hillman and Manley and "light planner" Myers, as shown through the critical questions asked and comments made at successive meetings. Nevertheless, the review process was so dominated by Maglie and his "light planning" allies that any attempt to engage board members in a "quest for knowledge" was stopped almost from the beginning. On numerous occasions, when Manley and Hillman attempted to lead discussion toward an understanding of water quality and traffic issues to enable the board to confront Magellan's assertions directly, their efforts were forcibly cut off by the chair or ambushed by procedural tactics. Manley and Hillman would sooner or later become silent, from either frustration or disgust, knowing of course that they didn't have the votes to force a resolution of any raised substantive issue over the will of the chair.

Manley and Green, more than Hillman, also appeared restrained by a personal desire to maintain calm, civil and even friendly small-group peer relations in public meetings, despite the manipulations of "light planners" Busch and Rattle. Personal discomfort with confrontation--especially in the context of the small numbers on the board, the frequency of meetings and a public audience--often seemed to encourage a surprisingly passive response to "light planners'" aggressive and manipulative power moves attacking "regulator" positions. Given the usual harshly argumentative, power-playing atmosphere of most meetings, Green may have been discouraged from participating for that reason alone.[1] In any case, her verbal contribution was so minimal that whatever perspectives she shared with Manley and Hillman were essentially absent in affecting the dynamics of the group. For the public, it was humiliating to see sympathetic board members treated so badly and the community's own critiques usually so ineffectively articulated and defended by "regulator" board members.

Myers, on the other hand, seemed to have broken his original alliance with his patron Ryker and the other "light planners." He did not like to be viewed as in anyone's pocket and instead cultivated the image of a conscientious, if unpredictable, board member. Whatever his sympathies for developers and the free market generally--explicitly stated on occasion, and whatever his hostility to public tactics of community activists, Myers raised relevant questions, often rejected simplistic responses and sometimes resisted various procedural maneuvers to limit substantive discussion. Whether from genuine concern, argumentative personality, knowledge that his was the crucial vote or intent to make sure the board covered its SEQRA approval tracks for a potential court case, Myers' role was definitely not that of a passive follower of the "light planning" juggernaut. If a majority of the board had possessed the will to proceed with rational inquiry, Myers' further interventions could have been a healthy complementary catalyst in that direction. While he seemed unable or unwilling to do so on his own, Myers' questions sometimes provided the opportunity for Manley and Hillman to pursue further a substantive line of inquiry.

By mid-August, the planning board was at the end of its informational inquiry, but the paucity of engagement and analysis suggested that, by ideal SEQRA standards, in fact the board was only where it should have been months ago when reviewing the Draft SEIS. It was now at a place where sophisticated answers could be demanded of the developer or provided by more careful analysis from other sources. By the standards of a serious research project, the board was now ready to begin, not to abandon its substantive inquiry.[2]

At the August 14th meeting, however, Maglie declared to board members: "We've gotten it all . . . it's time to write the answers"[3]--the board's responses to the substantive exchange between Magellan, the public and the experts acting on behalf of the community groups. True to form, even this statement was not meant to be an open invitation to the board. Already, Maglie had asked Busch to prepare draft definitions of appropriate questions raised by substantive comments and respective answers for the board's official "comments and responses" section within the FSEIS.[4] Under SEQRA, the FSEIS was the planning board's own document. The board could prepare it however it wished. Using its own words, the board had the potential to underscore substantive public critiques that had to be answered and then construct its own responses.[5] Maglie, however, chose the narrowest approach possible by giving responsibility for the first draft of the "responses" section to Busch, whose track record as planner demonstrated his willingness to follow the lead of the "light planners" and to curtail serious, autonomous board inquiry.

Busch's Draft Responses

Community activists were dismayed and outraged when they read Busch's "substantive comments-responses" draft for the stormwater and water quality realm after the August 14th meeting and his similar draft for traffic concerns distributed on the 28th. Busch had been publicly embarrassed earlier by his deeply-flawed March draft of the list of substantive comments that Magellan needed to address. Nevertheless, he now revived the very same list as the basis for organizing the board's "relevant" questions and responses for the final version of the FSEIS. As he explained in introducing his draft on the 28th, Busch simply reproduced Magellan's April draft FSEIS list of priority questions requiring responses. But Magellan had simply reproduced Busch's original faulty list of substantive comments of March 10th. Busch now also used Magellan's April responses to the same list, amending them, in some cases, for the stormwater realm, to account for comments from Napoleon. Direct critical comments from Wright and even from Everitt of the SCS were omitted from Busch's draft.

Obtaining a copy of this draft from the planning board file, Dreyfus directly intervened on August 25th with a letter to the board pointing out "material omissions," among others, concerning the conceptual design and methodology for the stormwater management system, the presence of contaminants in stormwater runoff, and existence or not of an aquifer. At the planning board meeting of the 28th, no one challenged Busch's basic format and no one mentioned Dreyfus' letter. However, "regulator" members criticized Busch's omissions and distortions as already suggested by Dreyfus.

Moving on to his draft on traffic issues, Busch introduced it as only an initial attempt, not an effort to respond to all comments. In actuality, board dynamics were such that first drafts (such as Busch's own March 10th list of substantive issues) were usually determinative. Here, as with the stormwater draft, Busch had simply replicated, with minor amendments, Magellan Construction's own responses in its April draft FSEIS, based on Busch's original faulty list of substantive comments.

Busch's lock-step repetition of Magellan's responses to the traffic issues omitted any reference to Case's critique demonstrating, at the least, that levels of service would be below any acceptable standard. Green asked, as she had the month before, what had happened to the FCDPW's plan for a separate traffic impact analysis. Maglie replied that the FCDPW had just written a letter to the board indicating that, since meeting with DOT, it was now satisfied with the existing study and would need nothing more. With no further explanation, a potential source of independent agency critique had thus disappeared.

In fact, the explanation of FCDPW's change of position seemed comparable to the sudden earlier retreat by DEC. The August 25th letter from FCPDW was signed by the politically-appointed Commissioner of Public Works, as opposed to the civil service staff member who had months before responded to the planning board demanding a separate analysis. Furthermore, copies of the letter were sent to two top Republican leaders of the county legislature (the first a representative from the Ashbury district) and both close political allies of Republican county boss Joe Enrico. By appearances, political pressure had caused the FCDPW to withdraw since nothing had changed from the time of its original request. At that time, the DOT had already indicated acceptance of the methodology, projections and analysis in Magellan's traffic report.

Concerning economic impacts, Maglie then announced that since Busch had no developer document to work from in this area comparable to Magellan's "responses" of April for stormwater and traffic realms, he had asked Green and Manley to work with him in drawing up a draft of relevant questions and responses. Indeed, he asked the two of them to lead the board's discussion on this area at the next meeting. Green reminded the board that she had only joined up after the formal public comment period was over. To help her in preparing a draft, she said, she needed clarification of the board's rationale for requiring an economic study as part of the SEIS in the first place. This was an open invitation for Ryker who asserted:

> There was a lot of internal discussion . . . as to the direction of it,. . . the magnitude of it, the need for it. . . . Specifically, since the original document [the EAF] had an analysis in it, . . . whether we should go out and contract with another analyst was the subject of some discussion. Julia Bellows took it upon herself to contact 3 or 4 people and get bids without really checking with the rest of the board and then it took on a life of its own. . . . A lot of the intent has been lost because of the fury that was generated by the study and the discussion thereafter.

Importantly, for the first time from any board member, Green then stated the relevance of economics in the ultimate decision-making process, refuting Rattle's earlier assertions, which Dreyfus had also countered, that economics was not a matter for SEQRA concern. Green pointed out that SEQRA requires the lead agency to balance economic impact with a project's impacts environmentally. Correctly, she added that if the board is not allowed to consider certain issues from an environmental perspective, the information is out there and we must consider it anyway in terms of balancing against environmental effects. However, Green then undermined her own position-- according to standards of "rational discourse"--by repeating the "light planner" refrain that "we've now passed from science into the realm of religion-- whether you believe that there will be certain results." Again, this was a lead Ryker could appreciate:

> We have visited and revisited this discussion many times. My feeling is still we have the information in front of us. . . . [L]et's make our informed decision. You can take the negative side of it, you can take the positive side of it. But like Suzi says, "it's gone past science, it's gone into," I use "conjecture" instead of "religion."

Even more disappointing was Green's draft economic impact "comments-responses" outline which she distributed to the board. It was the same filtered list which Busch himself had assembled in early March and which two weeks later he had admitted was very inadequate. Busch's own responsibility for reducing the ambit of issues confronting the board was now, in effect, legitimated by one of its "regulator" members. For his part, Manley distributed a draft statement on the relationship of economics to community character and "urban blight." Unfortunately, it was not focused on issues raised by the proposed Moselle Plaza and its generality rendered it essentially ineffective.

As for concluding the FSEIS process generally, Ryker now insisted that there was no need for further information and no need for further meetings. Some of the comments made, he said, were irrelevant to the scope. Supporting Magellan's approach and that of Busch, Ryker said that there was no need to address every particular comment.[6] The board could just note that they were accounted for. Myers added that different approaches to answering the same issue could be mentioned, from different sources, without attempting to resolve competing views.[7] Though a more inclusive approach, community activists saw Myers' suggestion as deferring any reasoned answer to questions posed by substantive comments until the SEQRA "findings" stage, which would be like taking the cart before the horse. After all, the basis of the findings for approval or disapproval should appropriately be derived from answers the board reached in response to questions posed by the substantive comments. By Myers' logic, once a SEQRA determination was made, the findings used to legitimate that determination would simply be the unspoken conclusions of the majority, thereby precluding any further debate.[8]

Members of the community groups present at this meeting were confronted with the reality that through manipulation and shallow rhetoric the planning board might be able to contend that it had satisfied the "hard look" standard without ever lifting a finger to resolve environmental and economic issues. Whatever progress had been achieved in the dialogue by professional experts was now again being funneled through a very restrictive process. The result would be consistent with "light planners'" original "backloading" intent, i.e., to defer environmental issues to other agencies and the site plan process and to absolve themselves of any responsibility for developing standards capable, as SEQRA required, of minimizing to the greatest extent possible adverse environmental impacts posed by the project.[9]

One ACT activist expressed the frustrations of the community groups in her August 30th letter to local papers.

> Mr. Busch . . . said himself that his ["comments-responses"] paper was collated from the developer's materials. . . . [he] submits the developer's material as [the] basis for discussion and omits opposing argumentation. This is really astounding. . . . Public comments are quoted, but answered in generalities. The reasoning and argumentation by opponents to the mall . . . [are] totally omitted.
>
> The result is a sanitized paper, without details, without strong issues, without pros and cons. Any outsider knowing nothing and reading this

would think, "fine; no problems; no engagement necessary." This tenor in the paper is so pervasive that the Board members' reaction seemed to be highly similar to our uninformed outsider. The discussion had no details, no nitty-gritty around the issues. . . . the Board members behaved as though this was some exercise in editing a paper of little or no consequence. Mr. Maglie said several times that the Board has to "get through this thing," instead of steering the Board members to a clearer understanding, and leading in analyzing issues. This is leadership in weakening the issues, and it is appalling.

Newly Assessing the State of the Board

Maglie's aim in inviting Manley and Green to help write the FSEIS "comments-responses" statement on economic impact appeared to be to coopt these members into the "consensus" he frequently spoke of as his goal.[10] Maglie knew that his own previous extensive effort on economic impact would not be easily discarded by members of the board--at the least, because of deference to the chair personally. Moreover, he selected the two "regulator" board members most averse to confrontation who, it appeared, would be least publicly offended by benign generalities uncommitted to a disapproval finding.

Anxiety over the cooptation scenario conformed also to a larger apprehension developing among community activists. At the ACT meeting of August 31st, members discussed the apparent lack of assertiveness generally among "regulator" members on the board. Individuals in ACT and CLEAR and their three professional experts had made enormous efforts in researching, analyzing, and writing about critical issues on the EIS agenda. Both groups felt that the community had done the planning board's own work. They had repeatedly placed abundant and timely questions, data and analyses and articulate conclusions at the table of the board throughout the long months of the SEQRA process to date.

But intimidation by Maglie and the other "light planners" was real. They had seniority on the board in years of service, while their more assertive manner often enabled them to utilize planning discourse to their advantage. In addition, ideological opposition to destructive development, even to a project of this size, appeared to place "regulator" members on the defensive, since they did not wish to be labeled as "anti-capitalist" or, as Ryker described, mere NIMBYs.[11] The three "regulator" members rarely even acknowledged the specific critiques community activists submitted, failed to effectively resist "light planner" power maneuvers at the meetings and appeared frightened to take the initiative of speaking outside planning board meetings with activists who provided the board with critical material. On one occasion, when Dreyfus and McBride attempted to speak with Ben Hillman after a planning board meeting about traffic impacts, Ryker pulled alongside in his car and made a show of listening. This concerned Hillman who said he didn't want to speak further for fear that Ryker would use the conversation against him as evidence of anti-developer bias.[12]

Throughout the process, the chair offered members no guidance regarding the evidentiary basis upon which each of the planning board members could act and whether that basis would be enhanced by speaking with those who had offered critiques and responses concerning the adverse environmental issues in dispute. This left "regulator" members in a quandary regarding the propriety of outside discussion. Were they a jury who could consider only what was said at planning board meetings or could they educate themselves as to the meaning and relevance of data already on the record? If the latter, could this occur only through new discussions at planning board meetings or could they educate themselves on their own through discussion with authors of submitted material? While the question of self-education propriety seemed of less concern to Ryker, an outspoken "light planner" who always appeared to have inside information regarding Magellan's activities and strategy, "regulator" members were anxious about their status and feared recrimination.

At the ACT meeting, members tried to understand possible psychological and political motives for why the three "regulator" board members acted as unassertively and defensively as they did. It was decided that one or two ACT members would converse individually with each of the three "regulators" to share the group's frustrations and to better comprehend their behavior. ACT members understood that however friendly as individuals and however sympathetic to community critiques, "regulator" members on the board might actually feel overwhelmed by the intensity of community feelings and their own responsibility on the megamall, as well as somewhat paralyzed specifically by technical details and complexity for which none was prepared. Subsequent friendly conversations with each "regulator" member confirmed these dynamics. For ACT and CLEAR, the dual problem was thus how to assure "regulator" board members that the knowledge they needed was at hand and then, given these dynamics, how to encourage them to present it articulately so as to affect the deliberative record.

Whatever the gain in better understanding "regulator" personal feelings, nevertheless, again and again, community activist critiques seemed to drift off to a void, without effect on the board. Indeed, given the format of Green's economic impact draft which followed Busch's abbreviated issues list of March 8th, Dreyfus now thought that her SEQRA vote for disapproval was lost. If that were true, the Moselle Plaza FSEIS would potentially be approved by a 5-2 vote, implying that even if a court later determined that votes by Ryker and Davis should have been excluded because of bias and conflict of interest, Magellan could still argue that there were enough votes for approval and that the court should affirm the planning board's decision.

Despite these feelings of frustration, objectively it was also clear that certain inroads had been made on certain issues. A relatively small number of important issues presented by community critics and outside experts had been accepted by the board as relevant to the FSEIS. The TR-55 Method of measuring stormwater, infiltration as an alternative to stormwater basins, lane-by-lane rather than averaged intersection level-of-service traffic ratings, and cumulative traffic impact from the southerly light-industrial lot--all of these items now were at least included as legitimate substantive issues in the present FSEIS draft. This meant that the board would have to address them in making its findings determination.

At the same time, it seemed that even this small number of issues to emerge to date through the planning board's filter was about to be cast to the wind by "light planners." Their "backloading" tact from beginning to end was to defer any controversial decisions regarding mitigation until the site plan stage when SEQRA approval would have been granted and "regulator" members would effectually have very limited leverage. The question remained whether "regulator" members would resist the circumvention and insist upon a merit-based determination of substantive issues as part of SEQRA's final decision.[13]

Community Models for Traffic, Stormwater and Economics

Concerning the traffic realm, while the August 28th meeting produced for the first time board agreement with Case's principle that lane-by-lane levels of service were more important than overall averaged intersection ratings, nobody on the board seemed ready, willing or able to take the next step. This would be to examine the detailed traffic tables in Magellan's document to discover what individual lane ratings actually were and whether such levels of performance would match up with DOT standards of not worsening present conditions and not producing "E" or "F" levels of service. Busch was apparently the only person at board meetings familiar enough with traffic studies to be able to read the data accurately. But he would not take this initiative.

At this point, Case had bowed out from further commentary, fearing that his credibility for objective analysis would be damaged by appearing too much as an advocate on behalf of community activists. Case felt that the board ought to acknowledge the significance of his contribution and ask him, directly, to elaborate on any issue where there might be misunderstanding or difference of opinion. Given the unlikelihood of this scenario, McBride decided to take on the task himself and force the lane-by-lane analysis issue to be advanced. Though by no means a traffic expert, through his years of reviewing similar developers' materials for CLEAR, McBride had learned how to read the basic information in traffic charts, thereby enabling him to disaggregate much of Magellan's raw data.

McBride thus examined every one of the dozens of intersection analysis pages from the DSEIS and DFSEIS to register the level of service for each of the over 30 lanes studied. McBride then calculated from the raw data and charts obvious instances where level-of-service ratings would be altered by corrections for proper lane widths and by accurate Friday peak hours instead of the 22% smaller volumes used by Magellan for less-congested Thursday peak hour counts.

All of this McBride laid out in an easily-accessible narrative form so that the methodology and conclusions could not be avoided. From the existing public record of Magellan's own submissions, in a September 6th 8-page letter to the board, McBride demonstrated that there were many instances, even with planned mitigations, where individual lane service would deteriorate from present conditions and where service would be at unacceptable "E" or "F" levels.[14] On September 8th, McBride complemented this detailed traffic analysis of levels of service with an 8-page alternative traffic realm "comments-responses" draft for the board to consider, in place of Busch's version, in the FSEIS.

In a similar manner, Turbell worked with other ACT activists to prepare a new critique of Busch's draft "comments-responses" statement on stormwater issues. ACT's 3-page document with appendices, submitted to the board on September 7th, suggested major changes in the proposed FSEIS concerning stormwater pond capacity, the underground aquifer, adverse impacts of impervious surfaces and runoffs, proper designation of pre-project on-site soil conditions, and a new location for sewage discharge since the planned site was unavailable. Arguments and documentation were presented by ACT for each of these issues, based mainly on the already-existing official record.

On September 10th, McBride sent on a detailed 14-page alternative FSEIS "comments-and-responses" document for the realm of economic and fiscal impacts. While in late March, Busch had acknowledged that his earlier list of substantive comments in this realm was fundamentally flawed, Busch had never created a new list of those significant comments from CLEAR and Smith which he admitted needed to be addressed. Instead of Busch's flawed list of 16 mainly abstract comments, McBride's list nearly doubled the number of items-- based largely on Busch's omitted submissions by Smith, CLEAR, the FCPB and Hillman. Responses were based on the three letters from Smith and four letters from CLEAR and referred also to claims in the Marvell report.

Once again, the board's work had been accomplished from the outside. The process of preparing an alternative critical FSEIS was demystified and simplified for all three major realms of adverse impacts. "Regulator" members had data and arguments with which to respond to "light planners'" argument that all issues could now be simply put off to site plan review, after deferral to the appropriate permitting agencies. Negative implications of Magellan's traffic study, for example, could no longer be deferred to DOT for lack of knowledge. The obscurity of technical issues was demystified through use of DOT's own standards and methodology.

Between McBride's alternative documents for the traffic realm and economics and ACT's and Dreyfus' critiques of Busch's "comments-responses" draft for stormwater and water issues, the planning board now had clear articulate drafts, based on expert documentation already in the official record, which provided ample justification for "regulator" members to argue for disapproval under SEQRA. In Dreyfus' view, such a vote which adopted the alternative "comments and responses" drafts could now be fully assured of withstanding a court challenge by Magellan because of the well-documented "hard look" process which these materials provided.[15]

On September 8th, however, operating on the familiar "light planning" track, Magellan Construction submitted its own suggested revisions of Busch's document. Apparently, after the August 28th meeting, Maglie had told Busch to give Magellan his August drafts for stormwater and traffic realms, along with board comments. Since Busch's drafts were only a minor revision of Magellan's April document, it was not surprising that Magellan responded within ten days and with little change from Busch's draft.

Alternative Legal Advice

To clarify legal issues muddied again by Rattle in previous weeks as he sought to deter the board from further inquiry, on September 13th Dreyfus wrote another letter to the planning board. While defining existing legal standards for cumulative impact analysis and the economics balancing test, probably most important was his insistence that the planning board's SEQRA decision on the adequacy of proposed mitigations to adverse effects should be ultimately a policy decision, governed by the rule of reasonableness. He contended that the board, as lead agency, must make this determination "without delegation to the involved agencies."[16] The Court of Appeals was very clear about ultimate responsibility:

> To be sure, the lead agency under SEQRA is likely to be non-expert in environmental matters, and will often need to draw on others. The statute and regulations not only provide for this, but strongly encourage it (citations omitted) . . . . Nevertheless, the final determination . . . must remain with the lead agency principally responsible for approving the project.[17]

Under this view of the statute, while the planning board properly and reasonably might rely for advice and information upon involved permitting agencies such as DOT or DEC, the lead agency must not abdicate to these agencies its "hard look" responsibility under the statute.[18] "SEQRA does not alter the jurisdiction between or among state agencies," added Dreyfus. Permitting agencies determine whether proposed mitigations (such as road widening and stormwater basins) meet the regulatory standards of the agencies themselves. Contrary to the advice of Rattle and Busch, he said that it was the planning board's decision, in the first place, to decide whether the mitigations proposed by the applicant adequately protect the environment, when balanced against social and economic considerations.[19]

The Electoral Factor

The lengthy duration of the process to date was now beginning to become an important political factor in itself. Town Board elections were scheduled for the first week of November and new terms would begin on January 1st. Community Reform Party candidates officially opposed the mall, were supported by activists from the ACT-CLEAR coalition, and appeared at the anti-mall rallies. They were endorsed by the Democrats on September 14th and, if elected, would bring to office a clear Town Board majority against the mall which could have an immediate impact on planning board composition. Ryker's 7-year term was coming to an end on December 31st. While no doubt Ryker wished re-appointment, it was inconceivable that an anti-mall Town Board majority would go along. If, unexpectedly, the SEQRA "findings" statement and final SEQRA vote became delayed until after January 1st, a new planning board appointee would replace Ryker and would most likely abstain, having not participated in any project deliberations.[20] This would leave the board with a potential 3-3 split, thus denying Magellan's approval.

Such a scenario depended on a delay of the planning board's SEQRA vote until January, election of the full anti-mall slate, solidarity against SEQRA approval among "regulators" Hillman, Manley and Green, and an FSEIS document providing an ample official record by which to justify turning down the project. None of these factors was assured. If the FSEIS "completeness" vote was taken on September 18th as planned, there still seemed ample time for Maglie to ask the board to pass a findings statement and SEQRA approval before the end of the year. While re-election prospects for Lyon and Pelletier seemed favorable, unknown newcomer Rachel Wilton had a much harder struggle against incumbent supervisor Grant Schmidt--despite the central issue of the mall. As to a solid official record, while Manley and Hillman had critiqued the plaza project in every realm, Green had remained largely silent except for her statement against Moselle Plaza causing "Main Street" blight. On several occasions, she had succumbed to Maglie's argument that certain issues could be resolved at the site plan stage instead of before the SEQRA decision, and her most recent comments on economics seemed to ally her with Maglie's and Ryker's "common-sense" distrust of expert analysis and opinion. Finally, given the "light planning" majority's momentum toward accepting more or less Busch's "comments-responses" section of the FSEIS draft, the wording of that section would provide little basis in traffic and stormwater realms for disapproval of the project.

Empowerment

Community activists remained anxious and concerned about what "regulator" board members really thought of their critiques since discussion was so minimal at public meetings. But they were also uncertain as to the propriety of members speaking with activists privately about substantive issues. To assure that a logical and defensible findings statement incorporating community critiques could be prepared by "regulator" members, activists finally decided that direct communication was required. Knowing that "regulator" members would obtain little assistance from either Rattle or Busch, activists sought to make them conversant enough in the scientific and legal data and analysis which the community groups had submitted and made part of the record so that "regulator" members themselves could produce their own critical board draft. They decided that trial rules precluding juries from discussing evidence outside of their joint deliberations had little relevance to planning board proceedings. Neither Maglie nor Ryker had restricted planning board members from private inquiry to learn as much as possible about substantive issues. Indeed, planning board meetings which should have discussed public critiques were marked by the absence of discussion and discourse and by the presence of what appeared to be settled opinions on the part of "light planners." The nature of planning board deliberations was such that board members considered adverse impact data on their own and arrived at their own individual conclusions. What occurred at planning board meetings was little more than statements of some members regarding positions they had arrived at after independent review and study. What members knew they learned from written and verbal submissions to the board and independently from living in the town and speaking with residents about the project in question. This "evidence" was obtained without witness examination either by attorneys or through inquiry by board members jointly. Self-knowledge of this sort, articulated under the guise of "common sense," was constantly touted by Calimino and Ryker as the best guide to the decision-making process. Davis' statements exemplified this attitude. He contended that his experience in engineering and from living on Heller's land enabled him to arrive at his own conclusions, regardless of what experts and other had said.

Thus, activists believed, it seemed fair to level the playing field by empowering "regulator" members to use their own common sense, informed, as it were, by expert and activist analysis of data submitted to the board. If submitted data had independently persuaded "regulator" members to disapprove the project, now empowering them to articulate their disapproval in logical and knowledgeable discourse seemed appropriate. Beyond the value of critical statements amidst planning board deliberations along the way, "regulator" views now had to be clearly articulated as a counterweight to whatever findings statement the "light planners" might produce. In the event of a majority approval vote, a reviewing court would need to see a dissenting disapproval findings statement when determining whether predisposition and conflict of interest rendered the approval statement reversible.

During the first two weeks of September, ACT and CLEAR leaders thus initiated direct conversations with "serious planner" board members individually and in private to determine whether they wanted assistance in articulating data already on the record which could be used in a draft findings statement. Because Manley and Green now had an announced role in drawing up a draft of FSEIS responses for the economics realm, the need for assistance took on a sense of urgency. All three "regulator" members explained that they welcomed whatever such assistance activists could offer. Green reviewed with McBride the overall logic of the economics predictive model used by Marvell, Smith and CLEAR and how she might, if she chose, critique the various assertions made by each submission according to that model. McBride then spoke with Manley about the traffic issue, since Manley's interest seemed piqued by the detailed levels-of-service analysis McBride had recently submitted to the board. McBride methodically compared his own analysis with Magellan's traffic report documentation to demonstrate how his calculations had been made. Though grasping the meaning of the traffic narrative was difficult at first, Manley was a quick learner and soon gained confidence in his ability to cultivate traffic analyses and autonomous judgments.

The Decisive "Completenesss" Meeting

September 18th was the decisive meeting scheduled to finalize the FSEIS "responses to public comments" section and to vote on the "completeness" of the overall document. Everyone knew that whichever way the board decided, the case could eventually end up in litigation because neither Magellan nor the community activists appeared willing to accept an adverse determination. At least two dozen project opponents were in the audience, intensely aware of the significance of this event.[21]

Maglie opened the meeting, still on the defensive from harsh public comments the week before[22] but determined to turn that experience to his advantage.

While rejecting the claim that publicly-raised issues had not been considered, he assured everyone that public input was welcome, appreciated and taken "under advisement."

Immediately, Myers asked Rattle to clearly define board responsibility and options at this present stage. Specifically, he wanted to know if tonight's "completeness" vote on the FSEIS would preclude the board from using material not in that document as a rationale for subsequent SEQRA findings.[23] This was a critical inquiry because Busch's filter, adopted by Magellan, had omitted much of what community critics and outside experts had submitted. Rattle's response was predictable, given SEQRA's mandate, although his language obscured the issue for non-lawyers:

> The findings statement must be supported by substantial evidence in the record. The record is the EIS [from Amsterdam Square] and the SEIS [for Moselle Plaza]. If it's not there, it won't be supported, be conclusive. You have to be able to point to something in the SEIS that's substantial, that would support your conclusion, your findings of fact. That's what you're making findings of, fact [emphasis follows voice intonation].

Though such a definition was expected, for ACT and CLEAR activists, it was also a dreaded nightmare. It implied that none of the critiques from the public or other agencies excluded from Magellan's April document or from the "substantive comments and responses" section now being finalized (based on Busch's truncated March list) could be referred to when the board prepared its findings. While critical written and verbal remarks from the official public comment period of January and February were legally part of the official record, and thus were at least partially included in Magellan's April document, in that same April draft Magellan, as author, had had the last word. Under Rattle's implied scenario, none of the post-February exchange between experts or other submissions from the public apparently would be included.

Wanting certainty on this point, Myers asked, "Would that [the FSEIS] include every item that's on the record here, like all this [pointing to his huge pile of letters from the public and experts]? Or does that include only those things that have been detailed in our, this final supplemental impact statement?" Rattle clarified that it would also include submissions from the official comment period of early 1995, leaving doubtful the status of continued correspondence and debate beyond that date regarding the adequacy of Magellan's mitigatory responses:

> No, no. The final supplemental is a draft supplemental with the comments and the responses to the comments. All that is the final, or the SEIS. So anything in there can be used to support your findings. It's not just the last little document that's a reply to the comments, a

response to the comments. It's the comments themselves and the document that was originally, you know, the draft supplemental and all of the appendices which include the traffic analyses and the different engineers' analysis. It's the whole ball of wax, but it has to be within the confines of those documents. It can't be something that hasn't been included.

Unsatisfied with this response, Manley then picked up on Myers' line of inquiry with a crucial question of his own: "Would the input that we've had from the community, this ongoing input since the public hearing, would that be included as part of the body of this report?" Rattle's response appeared to deflect the thrust of the question: "If you include it. You've had engineering work done, I mean, your engineer, is a response." While thus conceding the relevance of some post-hearing material, he apparently meant only those opinions solicited by the board itself and which they chose to include in their own final "substantive comments and responses" statement--such as the several Napoleon points made in Busch's August draft on stormwater.

Persistent demands from the board for clear definitions were not Rattle's past experience. One reason for his success in narrowing board inquiry was precisely Rattle's capacity to obfuscate his responses and thereby procedurally outmaneuver any inquiry whose thrust he may have disagreed with. As with professional experts in the employ of Magellan Construction and the various state agencies, Rattle's typical responses were minimal, stating only one part of reality and relying heavily on the aura of expertise and authority. Only when directly challenged by other equally-credentialed experts and under threat of losing their own credibility would Rattle or Magellan's engineers begin to concede a larger field of interpretation and the partial inadequacy of their earlier response. In Rattle's case, while sometimes conceding the board authority to act on a matter which he opposed, he would immediately urge the board not to exercise its discretion.

In the present instance, Myers' inquiry and Manley's persistence backed Rattle into a corner. In response to the pointed question whether the board could rely on post-hearing outside comments, including those from the public and their experts, in making its determination, he answered: "Well, it's not normally done." Myers re-phrased the question: "Is that part of the scope of the document?" Rattle hedged while trying to seem definitive: "I'll have to check that. I don't really. I mean, I would say, if you've made it as such, you've made it as such." Myers again re-stated his concern: "I just need to know, before we go any further, whether or not that information is expected to be part of the record of this project or not." Green suggested that Rattle was implying that ACT, CLEAR and Wright reports could be incorporated as appendices. Myers now amplified:

> Before we go any further, it's important for me to know exactly what is going to be included in this record. . . . I just want to know whether or not that's it. Because based on that information, you know, that's going to affect how I view our work today and our work here on in.

Myers' demand went to the core of legal rationality. What constitutes the record of the proceeding is the first relevant inquiry made by any legal decision-making body. As the board's legal advisor, Rattle would be expected to provide clarity on this issue without expressing a view on the merits of any of the contentions raised by those whose responses constituted the record. Instead, Rattle seemed more than willing to choose the responses he considered acceptable without informing the board of the ambit of the record. It was as if Rattle was saying, "Don't consider what supports that with which I disagree; consider only that with which I agree and you will be proceeding in a legally proper manner." By usurping the substantive decision-making role and not confining himself to matters of procedure and assuring that an adequate record was produced, Rattle disempowered those with whom he disagreed by depriving them of a "professional basis" upon which to disagree and to present their views.

Maglie then responded to Myers and Manley by stating that he'd have no problem attaching an appendix with all items received since April and making a clear chronological record. "That would get into the report and also establish the record of the workings that we've done since the arrival of this report." In other words, for him, including such documents in the report would allow the board to better prove that indeed it had given all comments and issues the "hard look" required. But inclusion in an appendix did not necessarily clarify the underlying question of whether such material could then be cited as justifying reasons for a SEQRA determination. In further prolonged back-and-forth discussion, Myers and Manley persisted, but both Busch and Rattle continued to evade a clear response.

Maglie eventually attempted to sum up what would appear to satisfy legal rationality and to move on, leaving behind the essential concern of Myers, Manley and Green as to whether ongoing public comments, which Maglie had earlier invited, would have equal status as evidence to justify particular findings:

> Hopefully, we have responded either specifically or generically to the documents. I think if we found specific things in there that you had worried that we didn't do or something's raised up and you wanted a particular comment in there and we haven't addressed it, now's the time to do it. But I think we have been on an ongoing effort to respond to the issues as they have presented themselves to it. Now whether some feel that the response that we've made is adequate or not

adequate, that's judgmental on everybody's part. But I think we're consistently trying to respond to the comments when evolved, so I have no problem throwing a correspondence section in there.

What was to be considered a "material," "substantive" part of the record, requiring the board's response, therefore, would be a determination made by the majority and this, in turn, would depend on whether a decision was reached to approve or disapprove the project. Maglie had agreed that all correspondence could be included as an appendix and thus potentially referred to in the findings. But it seemed that he, Rattle and Busch definitely distinguished between unsolicited post-hearing comments from the public and those from the board's engineer or involved agencies as to which ones could legitimately be used to justify particular findings. All Rattle would concede was that the post-hearing unsolicited comments, if accepted by the board, needed responses, but even then those responses could simply be pro forma references to earlier responses already on the record. In other words, from Rattle's perspective, after all the semantic games, nothing had changed and the debate created by the comments made by the public's experts and the developer's responses could be all but disregarded. For Rattle, Busch and Maglie, the situation could continue to be ambiguous and thereby justify an approval statement based upon a selective reading of the received correspondence. For Myers, Manley and Green, their silence after this final exchange seemed to imply a belief that unsolicited comments could be used as findings rationales. Given the rapidity and subtlety of this opening flurry, some among the activists in the audience also felt that this point had been won.

But it was dangerous to rely simply on one's hope that the legality of a procedural principle had been conceded. Rattle had successfully evaded legal clarification of what was to be included, an understanding needed by board members aiming toward disapproval in order for them to proceed logically with the "completeness" vote. To be safe, the "complete" FSEIS should include in its "substantive comments" list remarks such as McBride had compiled (but Busch had omitted) in his drafts on traffic and economics. It also needed to then incorporate in the "responses" section whatever evidence the board wished to include from the critical correspondence received during the summer. This would assure a solid official FSEIS record which could justify a disapproval findings statement--if votes were there to choose that alternative--or at least a dissenting statement which would show the fallacy of the basis for the majority's approval.

Nevertheless, without further clarification of what constituted "the record," board members now proceeded into an item-by-item review of the Busch-Magellan "comments-responses" draft without any additions to the list of issues to be covered. Along the way, in stormwater and traffic sections, there were skirmishes, as several weeks before, with the "responses" wordings as they stood. But now, understanding that board momentum was clearly for a "completeness" finding with no further substantive comments or responses, Maglie agreed to certain definitional changes suggested by Manley. On the other hand, Manley joined Myers in agreeing that certain other critical issues could simply be resolved by DEC or DOT at a later stage.

While superficially conciliatory to the "regulator" perspective of Hillman and Manley, Maglie was simply "word-smithing"--adding or changing words which could ultimately be bargained away at the site plan stage when "regulator" members no longer had significant leverage for project disapproval. Again and again, this same dynamic occurred as the board proceeded through the remainder of the stormwater draft. Certain of Magellan's boldest assertions about present or post-development conditions were eliminated or toned down, but the thrust of the document was still to grant SEQRA approval by accepting, in principle, Magellan's proposed mitigation.

At one point, Rattle's intervention in this discussion revealed explicitly the line he had implied at the beginning of the evening. Reacting against Myers' insistence on including office-use instead of warehouse-use buildout traffic figures, as Case had suggested, Rattle said, "You can't take something out of the comment." By Rattle's interpretation, the evidential status of unsolicited comments by experts for the public was nil.

While the stormwater and traffic "comments-responses" drafts had been consistently compromised by Busch's filtered March list of "substantive comments," discussion of economic impacts was under no such constraint. Though Busch's filter applied in this realm as well, he had also conceded that his list had omitted many substantive comments made by Smith and CLEAR and that they also should be answered in the FSEIS. Busch's failure to construct a revised list gave the board the potential to create its own much larger agenda of substantive-comments-requiring-responses than any list Busch would have produced. Furthermore, since Marvell had backed out of the process so early, the board was not psychologically constrained to merely edit his pre-established set of responses extolling the virtues of Moselle Plaza as it had been with the Busch/Magellan responses for stormwater and traffic realms. Added to this greater potential flexibility was the fact that Maglie had designated Manley and Green to draft the board's September economic "substantive comments and responses" and Green had assembled all of the critical materials on economics to personally review. For various reasons, then, activists felt hopeful that at least issues of economic and fiscal impact would gain a decent wide-ranging and genuinely responsive written discussion.

In fact, Green's draft list of "substantive comments and responses" was almost as inadequate as her initial late-August list of relevant questions.

Though she had a green light to expand beyond Busch's self-admitted flawed list of early March and McBride had explicitly attacked the continued use of that list in verbal remarks to the board one week earlier, Green repeated Busch's list of substantive comments without amendment. It was further depressing evidence that Manley's and Green's desire to be non-confrontational and consensus-oriented could be co-opted by "light planners" into an approval findings statement.

While Green said that she had based tentative responses to Busch's list of substantive comments largely on evidence from ACT and CLEAR, alongside that from Marvell and Maglie, she "tended not to make any really strong statements or conclusions because [she] wanted this to be the board's document." All she had done, in fact, was to collate and juxtapose various remarks from all sides that seemed relevant for the select list of issues on Busch's agenda. Green insisted that the hard decisions regarding the wording and adequacy of the responses would have to be done by the board. Since this occasion was the board's first exposure to her draft, she suggested that members go into it in depth at another meeting. Maglie refused, stating that a month would be lost in doing so. Ryker immediately seconded that plan. The board then proceeded to review Green's document, point by point, with a view toward a "completeness" vote.

Concerning effects of the project on Ashbury area businesses, Myers insisted that Marvell's conclusions should be included in the document, even if they were very generalized. Green agreed on a need for "balance." Citing Maglie's June 12th report and CLEAR's critique of June 18th, Myers said both should be included. "Somewhere in the middle, as Rocky stated, we'll find something." At another point, he insisted that to make "value statements at this particular point I don't think is necessary," suggesting that a response which satisfied the board was premature, despite the fact that the FSEIS was to be the board's document containing its own responses to the substantive comments raised. In passing, Green mentioned that the recent 14-page CLEAR "comment-response" draft on economics had been quite useful. Myers said that he never saw it, despite the fact that it had been distributed to all members. Busch claimed that he never saw any pertinent studies on mega-stores despite McBride's repeated submissions and Dreyfus' earlier attachment of the Muller-Humstone report on the East Aurora Wal-Mart project. We received nothing, Busch said, omitting to add that he also had done no research of his own. Maglie acknowledged having received information on these studies which he characterized as "summaries." This was enough information for him since, as he stated, "I have real problems with all kinds of economic consultants." Nevertheless, he thought Marvell had covered that topic as well, since the latter explicitly referred in several sentences of his December final report to beneficial effects of a Wal-Mart and to adverse effects only of a Home Depot.

Because of his haste to hold the "completeness" vote that night, Maglie urged that the various corrections suggested be made after the fact and included in the finalized FSEIS sent out to involved agencies by October 2nd at the latest. In the meantime, he personally would take responsibility for editing Green's draft to include more balance and annotations as suggested, and would add Bob Manley's draft definition of "economic blight" as well.

Agency comments to the FSEIS would be invited until October 30th. Maglie foresaw October 23rd as the first opportunity to look at a draft "findings" statement. October 30th could be a second review meeting, with nothing finalized until the official FSEIS comment period had come to a close.[24]

Despite the fact that the board had no final document before it, Rattle declared that the "completeness" vote would not be conditional, since all suggested changes would be incorporated by Maglie in the final document. Not surprisingly, Ryker then read a lengthy "completeness" resolution which Rattle had prepared in advance of the meeting, including a phrase stating that "the lead agency is satisfied that the Final SEIS is now accurate, adequate and complete." With that, nearly five hours after the meeting had begun, Maglie polled the board. All but one voted in favor. Only Ben Hillman held out to the end. Hillman then explained his reasons for doing so, emphasizing all the various items which he said the board should have considered in the present stage instead of deferring to the time of site-plan review. Ryker, in turn, read a statement praising the board for its "considerable look" at the project and members' "thoroughness and sacrifice." For the "light planners," the "completeness" vote was a meaningful test of their ability to assure project approval under SEQRA.

In the end, all from the original packed audience who remained past midnight as public witnesses were McBride and a single reporter. For the others, the entire process had been too painful to endure. Despite challenges to Rattle at the beginning about the status of post-February critical comments and responses, the meeting had failed to resolve that issue, continued to defer matters to the site-plan stage, merely tinkered with the Busch-Magellan draft and offered only a contorted, neutral and half-finished draft on economics to be finalized later by Maglie.

All of this produced in McBride, and in those activists who heard about the meeting later, a sense of profound futility. It was true that Myers and "regulator" members had spoken up and even won concessions on various wordings of the document[25] and Green had apparently won some legitimate record standing for the Smith/McBride economic critique. But the overall tone of the FSEIS implied what the "light planners" had sought all along--SEQRA approval, with hard issues left unanswered or to be resolved mainly by involved agencies at the permitting stage.[26] Only one "regulator" member had decided to stick to his principled opposition at the final vote and to insist that the board arrive at its own responses through analysis and study <u>before</u> the SEQRA determination.[27]

THIRTEEN

THE CONSTITUTIVE STRUGGLE FOR A RECORD

The board's process and "completeness" vote on September 18th left community activists extremely discouraged. Despite moments of significant critique and procedural independence, overall the board drifted toward SEQRA approval, just as those officially at the rudder had always intended. With the acquiescence of two of the three "regulator" members, the board had now declared the FSEIS as "complete." It provided, as the planning board's part of that document, a limited number of "substantive comments" deemed worthy of extended reply and a series of official responses, largely based on Magellan Construction's original position. Moreover, the "record" status of correspondence received by the board subsequent to the public hearing remained ambiguous. While the views of community group experts critiquing the adequacy of Magellan's proposed environmental mitigation could serve as a basis for disapproval, "regulator" members could rely on these data only if the correspondence was part of the official record.[1] Furthermore, even if a disapproval majority could be found, it seemed improbable that such members could extract themselves from this morass, based on past performance. Procedurally, it seemed unlikely, given Maglie's, Busch's and Rattle's virtual endorsement of Magellan's perspective.

Continuing Battle on Substantive Issues

Nevertheless, neither Magellan nor community activists were willing to admit that the process was essentially finished. Each sought to have the final word on substantive issues. Despite the fact that the board had already declared the FSEIS as "complete" on September 18th, nine days later Magellan's engineer provided a rebuttal on stormwater issues to Wright's mid-September critique. The new report was simply attached by Magellan as Exhibit B in the FSEIS document it now assembled for the planning board. Magellan had exploited its position months before as the board-authorized originator of the DFSEIS. As the party assigned responsibility of assembling the final version, it now decided itself to determine the contents of the "complete" FSEIS. By virtue of the board's delegation of authority to Magellan to print the final document for distribution, Magellan was able to include its newly-proposed mitigation, even though it had failed to do so before the board's "completeness" decision and the board had never considered the adequacy of the response.[2]

Wright responded to Magellan's rebuttal on October 15th with a detailed analysis of the discrepancies and fallacies in this newest report. In a letter to the planning board on the same date, CLEAR's McBride also responded to the FSEIS. He placed new traffic data on the record as well as economic and social data relevant to the required "balancing test" following board identification of any adverse environmental impacts. Specifically, McBride added more current documentation confirming stagnant retail demand in the local market area, thus further substantiating earlier claims that the local retail spending market was smaller and the likely cannibalizing effect of Moselle Plaza greater than Magellan or Marvell would admit.

McBride also added for the first time a "social impact" to be used by the board in the final SEQRA balancing test once environmental assessments were completed.[3] In practice, this final post-environmental SEQRA evaluation traditionally focused on economic impacts. For many months, Dreyfus and the community groups had consistently called this aspect of SEQRA responsibility to the board's attention, despite Rattle's obfuscation of the issue. However, "social impacts" were also mentioned alongside "economic impacts" in the "balancing test" section of the SEQRA regulations.[4] Thus, McBride contended that the likely radically disruptive effect of Moselle Plaza on existing Ashbury businesses and jobs might well produce, as did massive IBM layoffs and plant closings in a neighboring county, unusual levels of violence, depression, substance abuse and other forms of at-risk behavior. He attached a recent article which described these effects in that county to prove the point.[5]

Continuing Battle on Procedural Issues

The board's September resolution accepting the FSEIS as "complete" was filed by Rattle with the DEC and other involved agencies on October 6th. The resolution set a deadline of November 1st for any outside comments to the planning board. Since the board planned to draft its "findings" statement at meetings of October 23rd and 30th, the November 1st deadline implied that the board might have a decisive final vote on November 6th--one day before the town election. However, on October 20th, the Thruway Authority unexpectedly notified the board that it wished to comment on the FSEIS, but would not be able to do so by the deadline. It thus requested an extension to November 17th. Given the awkwardness of turning down a reasonable request from an involved state agency, at its meeting of October 23rd, the board thus agreed to the extension. The election date factor would no longer potentially rush the judgment of the board.

On October 11th, Rattle transmitted to the board his draft of a proposed findings statement, with conclusory wording as expected, rationalizing SEQRA approval for Moselle Plaza. The remaining twelve pages provided extensive text from the previous Amsterdam Square findings statement, all of which had led to SEQRA approval for that earlier project. For Rattle, these passages were meant to enframe the Moselle Plaza findings as essentially an extension of Amsterdam Square's original design and approval, leaving blank spaces to be filled in with specific Moselle Plaza data.

Additionally, on the same date, Rattle submitted a three-page set of guidelines for the board to follow in its findings preparation process. Virtually the entire letter was based on the assumption that SEQRA approval would be granted. In only two brief phrases, in the final page, did Rattle even mention the "disapproval" alternative. Mainly, Rattle set out the "backloading" scenario he had promoted since July 1994--ways in which the board could condition its approval on certain mitigating site plan specifications and on permitting steps to be taken by other agencies.

Rattle also finally responded to the board's September 18th discussion regarding the legal propriety of using data presented after the public hearing stage as acceptable evidence for supporting a findings statement and SEQRA decision. Said Rattle, quoting from a leading state court decision:

> Findings, as well as any conditions imposed in and by such findings, must be reasonable and supported by substantial evidence. In approving or denying an action the lead agency must state the facts and conclusions in the FSEIS and comments relied upon and the social, economic and other factors and standards which form the basis of its decision.[6]
>
> As to what is "substantial evidence," the New York State Court of Appeals has held that it is "such relevant proof as a reasonable mind may accept as adequate to support a conclusion or ultimate fact" or "the kind of evidence on which responsible persons are accustomed to rely in serious affairs."[7]

Once again, Rattle had evaded directly replying to board member questions. He had promised to research the issue, but in this statement failed even to acknowledge it as a concern to be clarified. In effect, the board was left to its own devices to determine whether post-comment period data not included in the "substantive comments/responses" section fell within the definition of "substantial evidence."

Dreyfus filled the gaps and responded to the assumptions and omissions demonstrated in Rattle's letter and draft findings statement with his own letter to the board on October 20th. Because Rattle's proposed draft contained language assuming SEQRA approval, Dreyfus provided a lengthy model of alternative paragraphs in case a disapproval decision was reached, emphasizing that the board had sufficient data and hundreds of hours of review whereby it could make an informed judgment and pick and choose the data it found most persuasive.

Dreyfus then addressed the issue of the meaning of "substantial evidence," the term which Rattle specifically cited but without adequate definition. He pointed out that the definition for this term came from the Court of Appeals and was therefore binding on the planning board.[8] In actuality, said Dreyfus, "there is ample factual data to satisfy the 'substantial evidence' test for disapproval of the Moselle Plaza application" and a lack of any substantial evidence from the applicant, applying the balancing test, that the town would benefit from the project. Specifically, Dreyfus reiterated the types of pre- and post-public hearing data which supported SEQRA disapproval concerning traffic, stormwater management and community character--whether or not in the "comments/responses" section of the "complete" FSEIS approved by the board in September.

Extra-SEQRA Efforts

Eight days after the FSEIS "completeness" meeting, state Supreme Court Judge Lorenzo D'Elia issued a nine-page decision on the IDA case, dismissing the suit on the procedural ground that it was filed too late.[9] Although his finding was not surprising to Dreyfus and the plaintiffs' attorney who had responded to this argument in answering papers,[10] activists were still disappointed to receive such a narrow technical decision which skirted the merits of their contentions. The only consolation was the fact that Judge D'Elia had obviously considered the issues and arguments as serious enough to warrant an unusually extensive opinion and even to state explicitly that "the Court is mindful that the concerns raised by petitioners are not frivolous."[11] Thus, they were hopeful that if a case soon would have to be brought against the planning board for SEQRA approval of Moselle Plaza, it might be assigned to Judge D'Elia since he had now already become involved in a connected matter and was familiar with the overall dispute. At the county level of the judicial structure, dominated as it was by a one-party electoral system, it was unusual to find a judge apparently as empathetic as D'Elia to concerns of environmental and community activists.

At the planning board level, activists renewed efforts to further politicize the Moselle Plaza application by obtaining a bipartisan statement against SEQRA approval from eleven former planning board members.[12] By showing present members that those with a "light planning" perspective on this project were clearly a minority in the community, even when measured against former board members themselves, activists hoped to persuade anyone on the fence to join the opposition.

A more important potential influence on the planning board was the ongoing electoral campaign for Supervisor and two other Town Board seats. October was traditionally the month of greatest campaign activity and this year's drama was more intense than usual, with primary focus on Moselle Plaza. Following the local Democrat September caucus which overwhelmingly endorsed the anti-mall CRP slate of Wilton, Pelletier and Lyon, veteran Democrat Town Board member Devilla criticized the new Democrat majority and its roots in environmental activism. Devilla's hostility to the activism of the CRP-Democrat candidates was quickly exploited by Ryker and highlighted as a main feature in a four-page vitriolic Republican flyer distributed in mid-October.

Nevertheless, vocal community sentiment ran clearly against Moselle Plaza and obviously favored activist anti-mall candidates over Republican Supervisor Schmidt and his two running mates, close allies of Ryker. By mid-October, correctly reading the community pulse, even Schmidt's running mates announced their opposition to the megamall, although they had never before publicly opposed it or worked with community groups in the anti-mall struggle. As for Schmidt himself, he asserted that Republican Town Attorney Lou Tapani had advised him that Town Board members should not take a stand on the issue since they might be called upon later to make decisions affecting its fate. Schmidt's efforts to cloak himself in the neutrality of a judicial fact-finder, rather than as a legislator with defined policies and goals, was doomed from the start.[13] Schmidt had already said and done enough in past months to indicate his favorable sentiments about Moselle Plaza and development in general.

Furthermore, his opponent Wilton's articulate stand on a variety of local issues and her business background were persuasive for those who liked her anti-mall position, but who feared a one-issue administration consumed entirely in stopping the mega-mall. Additionally, Republicans had succeeded in alienating a significant new group of voters--students at the local SUNY campus--when party leaders Enrico and Ryker, several months earlier, had openly opposed a separate poll location on campus for student voters whom they assumed would vote predominantly Democrat.[14]

While elections to the Town Board would have no direct effect on the imminent planning board SEQRA decision on Moselle Plaza, the campaign and subsequent election became an ongoing survey of community sentiment on the issue. Symbolically for some as well, the campaign and approaching election became a referendum on Ryker and his policies since, as chair of the party, he was visibly identified with the campaign and had led support for Magellan Construction throughout the entire planning board process.

Longer-Range Planning

Two other planning events impacted on the board before its initial "findings" meeting of October 23rd. On October 4th, County Planner Henry Fowler sent to the Town Board the FCPB's strong endorsement of the proposed Town

Comprehensive Plan. Fowler described the plan as providing "the underlying principles upon which to base the Community's future" and "a major step forward from the existing document which is now dated." Such an endorsement further supported the activists' position that the size, scale and location of the proposed megamall would violate the character of the community.

On environmental matters particularly relevant for the megamall decision, the FCPB recommended that east of the Thruway, where Moselle Plaza was to be located, the lack of water and sewer availability, combined with delicate wetlands, poor soils, crowded highways and existing moderate land use patterns, implied the need for more restrained light industrial and commercial development. The FCPB specifically urged that the Comprehensive Plan articulate a goal of fostering those traffic patterns "which reduce trip generation and are capable of being serviced by a multi-modal system." Furthermore, it recommended that major land use decisions "should reflect overall community impact rather than the more narrow significant environmental impact contained in SEQRA. In short should it be done versus can it be done." Finally, the FCPB suggested that a section on economics was sorely missing. Among other things, such a section could "illuminate concerns over retail trade area . . . discuss areas of future growth potential," explore tax revenue and expenditures by land use type and analyze tax incentives.

> The overall intent should be an integration of the values in the Plan with the economics and finances of the community. In addition, the section should serve as guidance in the discussion of tax rateables versus community/environmental preservation.

While never discussing the specific Moselle Plaza proposal, these remarks nevertheless endorsed the types of planning values and methodology promoted throughout the review process by CLEAR and ACT both. Nothing could have satisfied activists more and it came at a critical juncture of the megamall review process, just prior to the up-or-down vote.

With support from a majority of the Town Board and after McBride provided him with model legislation from an upstate town, Mark Lyon now appeared at the planning board meeting of October 16th to propose a revision of town zoning to prohibit shopping centers with retail space outside of a 15,000-45,000 square feet range and site size outside of 5-15 acres. However, the timing of this effort was procedurally problematic. First, it was not at all clear whether those from the "regulator" perspective would achieve a majority to disapprove Moselle Plaza. Second, a favorable rezoning recommendation from the planning board would seem to preempt a finding of approval for the megamall since the retail space caps substantially contradicted Magellan's plans for a 180,000 square foot shopping plaza. Some activists, concerned with obtaining a majority to disapprove the megamall, feared that Lyon's proposal would be associated with "anti-development environmentalism" and could therefore further polarize the planning board, leading to a clear approval majority for the megamall and disapproval of Lyon's proposal. Others, hopeful of a disapproval vote against the megamall, feared that the subsequent absence of revised zoning regulations would enable Magellan or any other developer immediately to submit new plans for a mall, with substantially the same retail space as Moselle Plaza but with other more attractive mitigation.

Though Lyon's proposal was consistent with the Comprehensive Plan's new guidelines, local law required that before passing a zoning change, the Town Board had to submit such a proposal for planning board review of up to 45 days. Lyon explained that the Town Board wished to have new zoning in place, consistent with the new Plan and in case the board rejected Magellan's SEQRA approval. This would avoid a new and similar application from being presented.

> I think the Town Board is interested in having some kind of mechanism ready to go in the event that this one, for one reason or another, withdrew or was rejected, so that we wouldn't have to go through this process a third time.

Lyon suggested alternatively that a temporary moratorium could be enacted, if necessary, to fill a potential time gap before new restrictions were put into place.

> The thing that concerns me is not to get burned for a third time, let's say, where that last superstore pulled out. There was a period of about two years where we might have had a moratorium. We might have had a revision of the zone. Then it came back again.

Very quickly the ire of Myers came to the fore. Over the months since his appointment to the planning board, Myers had attempted to foster the image of an independent decision-maker, influenced only by the data submitted and not by the politics of other board members, the public or the Town Board. Earlier, he had even chastized Ryker for refusing to read Case's traffic submissions on ideological grounds.

> Let me ask you one question. You used the phrase "burned." . . . "The first project came and went and we don't want to get burned [by] a second." . . . Well, I want to know what you mean by that. . . . There's an assumption you're making there. When you say "burned," that means that there's something bad.

Replied Lyon:

> Right. That's my feeling and that's the feeling of a lot of people in town. That [Moselle Plaza's] out of scale with, the zoning is not compatible with the community, the scale of the community or the community's interest. So, I think that's the sentiment of the majority

of the members of the Town Board, anyway.[15]

Myers was outraged that the Town Board was attempting to pre-empt the independent judgment of the planning board by altering zoning <u>before</u> the planning board had judged on the propriety of Moselle Plaza. His sentiments were immediately adopted by the other "light planning" members who sought to discredit the anti-mall sentiment by contending that it was composed of little more than a clique of political operatives opposed to any development. Davis attacked the Town Board's proposal as spot zoning directed solely at the Heller property. He claimed that the Town Board had 27 years to change the zoning if it had wanted to. Lyon replied, in turn, that the planning board had failed to make any such recommendations. Now Ryker joined the attack on Lyon by claiming that the planning board had other zoning revisions on its agenda already--signage and expanded uses in the industrial zone--and that in any case the Ashbury Development Corporation had already shown a desire to study revisions for the commercial zone on its own. "Let's finish one thing before we take on two or three things." Not only did such comments suggest potential problems and delays for the zoning change itself, it also raised the spectre of an untimely provocation now solidifying a pro-Magellan majority including Myers, as some activists had feared.

Beyond the problem of the timing of the proposed zoning change, there was also a question about the degree to which Lyon was able to adapt his remarks to the politics and personalities of planning board members. When Lyon re-emphasized the need for quick action by the boards on this proposal, he reminded planning board members that the Moselle Plaza review had already generated more comprehensive information than the town had ever produced on its own concerning traffic and environmental constraints in this prime commercially-zoned area. Furthermore, "I'm very leery of deferring action on this particular zone change because of my past experience in delays that I've seen on planning documents that are needed for the Town Board to take action on."

These remarks further inflamed Myers who seemed to be grabbing the chance to demonstrate his strong anti-regulatory "light planning" bias. He objected to relying on the megamall data since it involved such a limited area and since most of it, he claimed, had been generated by Magellan itself--which in traffic and other areas he conceded to be unreliable. Concerning minimum and maximum sizes:

> what we'd be doing is perhaps creating something that could harm potential development down the road. In effect, what might be happening is that we'd be taking the flexibility that we do have now away from ourselves by creating the constraint, as I would see it. I think each particular project should stand on its own merits or fall on

its own merits and I'm not sure that 45,000 square feet is the number
. . . .

Davis again backed Myers, insisting that every project should be judged on
its own merit. In any case, he said, in order to survive these days, stores have
to go bigger.

> And if that 50-55,000 or 60,000 square feet is required for them to
> even consider standing or building a building or developing a site in
> this town, if the property is large enough to have some incidental
> secondary stores, that is what the public demands, quite frankly. From
> a marketing point of view, that's what everybody wants. They want
> the one-stop shop. That's exactly what they want.

Davis also warned that a cap of 45,000 sq. feet on retail space might provoke
a developer lawsuit, challenging the zoning as unconstitutional, because in his
view limiting the size of the build-out might be an unlawful "taking."

Consultant Busch said he had never seen such a zoning model and that size
was not necessarily a determining factor for the quality of a development.
Beyond urging that the market rather than regulations determine the
appropriate size of commercial development, Myers then insisted that formal
restrictions would create:

> a negative impact upon the town that could then hold the town people
> hostage to existing retailers who knew that the likelihood that any
> future development would be such that those future sites could not
> compete because of what already exists. So therefore you create a
> reverse situation where you might have, rather than a stranglehold of
> a superstore that comes in and creates a negative economic impact,
> you have no competition from any future development and create the
> reverse happening. There's a great possibility of that.

Furthermore, Myers again expressed his resentment at the procedural posture
of the proposal, coming, as it were, during the present sensitive final stage of
SEQRA decision-making.

> . . . [T]o me [it] seems to be too much of a knee-jerk reaction in terms
> of what's going on with Moselle Plaza, OK? Any discussion of this
> nature should be totally separate and removed from that as not to
> prejudice this Board in any way whatsoever to consider current
> applicant or any future development. And I think that while you may
> have some good intentions, . . . [it] is not really a propos at this
> particular time because I think it's a sensitive issue. And asking us to
> go ahead and suggest some limitations on future development when
> we're considering a project that's so significantly larger, I mean
> somewhere in the neighborhood of four times the size, I think really
> puts us in a difficult position and sort of passes the buck. . . . And

comments on how this whole thing relates to Moselle Plaza really should not be brought to the table.

At this point, Maglie summarized the board's sentiments as wanting to wait for the ADC's Main Street Corridor study to be done by planners from Cooperville Associates.[16] As for an intervening moratorium, even Hillman and Manley failed to endorse it, claiming the need to study such a proposal at more length. Myers was opposed, again asserting that proposals should stand or fall on what the market for land and development would bear. Added Ryker, "Free enterprise. An alien concept, I'm sure." To demonstrate how contentious and inappropriate they viewed Lyon's proposal and how little regard they had for his integrity, in closing the discussion, both Myers and Ryker insisted that the minutes of the planning board discussion be provided to the Town Board directly, rather than relying on Lyon's personal report.[17]

For community activists, the event was a fiasco. Lyon's seemingly-obvious logic of preventing the unwanted opportunity for a new, post-Moselle Plaza, megamall proposal apparently was lost on everyone on the board but Green. The perception that Lyon was trying to stampede the Moselle Plaza decision had resulted in Hillman and Manley failing to endorse even a building moratorium, with Myers seemingly re-aligning himself with Ryker and the "light planners" by articulating a classic laissez-faire perspective. Myers' emotional outrage at the substance and timing of Lyon's proposal seemed to push him into the welcoming arms of Magellan's proponents. If there was consolation from this meeting, it was only from Myers' off-hand denigration of Magellan's data as "unreliable." But this seemed dwarfed by the vehemence of his response generally.

The Findings Meeting of October 23rd

The meeting of October 23rd was the first occasion for the planning board to deliberate upon the nature and intent of its Moselle Plaza SEQRA findings. In the absence of Rattle, Maglie began with a quick introduction of the former's draft framework for an approval findings statement. Busch then handed out a proposed draft findings statement for "Surface Water" to be examined in more detail later in the meeting.

After complaints by Manley and Myers about continued lack of clarity of what was being included in the official FSEIS record and perceiving that he again faced a contrary majority on procedural issues, Maglie then went considerably beyond anything admitted by Rattle at the late September meeting. He re-asserted that anything could be used to justify particular findings, whether in the FSEIS officially or in regular correspondence received after September 18th.[18] Anything was "fair game" for citation in the findings statement. He stated that nothing would be thrown out as illegitimate. "So nothing is thrown out, everything is allowed," even including relevant comments received from now on. Everything <u>can</u> be used if it's useful. All that the findings needed, he said, was a factual basis, from whatever the source, "whether it's in this [FSEIS] document, whether it's in the DEIS, whether it's back in Amsterdam Square, whether it's in the correspondence file or gone back to the findings in fact [the comments-responses section], no problem."

At this point, Busch also volunteered an opinion he had apparently been reluctant to set forth on September 18th:

> I think you're always going to, not always, but the majority of projects that I've ever been involved with, there's always been an overlap. Things come in afterward and things don't always cut on the dotted line, so to speak, on time. And I think, for the basis of your decision-making, your record of what you have, which is all-inclusive, is yours to use as you please.

The board then quickly acquainted itself, section by section, with Busch's draft findings statement on stormwater issues. Busch's draft was unsurprising. In its description of context, development plans, problems and mitigations, it followed the intent and logic and often the exact wording of relevant passages from the "comments-responses" section of the FSEIS. With its "backloading" purpose, it relied on eventual DEC permit and planning board site-plan approvals as mitigating conditions for ultimate SEQRA acceptance, as Rattle had urged all along.

All of the most contentious issues would be ultimately resolved by other agencies or the Town Engineer or the board itself at the site plan approval stage, where the role of the public would be minimal. There was no suggestion from Busch of any adverse environmental impacts unmitigable through one or another of these approaches. For Busch, everything was a matter of details which professionals were better able to resolve in the privacy of their offices. It was sufficient that substantive comments were made in response to the DSEIS, and that an FSEIS had been prepared which contained comments and responses.[19] Under this logic, the "completeness" vote was indistinguishable from a finding of approval, and the planning board was little more than a cipher for information submitted by the developer and its critics.

Following review of Busch's draft, Manley immediately distributed his own unannounced 12-page draft "disapproval" findings statement concerning community character and economic/fiscal/social impacts. He explained that his purpose was simply to hand out and briefly summarize the document for board consideration. Members were invited to look it over on their own for review together at a later meeting. For community activists, to see this document distributed, whatever its reception, was an exciting and gratifying moment. In almost every respect, Manley's draft adopted the analysis and conclusions of earlier Smith and CLEAR reports--this, the result of activists' actions to assure that "regulators" had an on-record document of their own to justify their decision.

Referring repeatedly to the evidence and analyses of Smith, CLEAR's McBride and the similar Humstone-Muller report for East Aurora, New York, Manley identified the key disagreements between these sources and Marvell/Maglie and explicit reasons why the arguments of the former three sources were most compelling. It concluded that Moselle Plaza would cause a wide variety of negative economic and social effects which:

> would fundamentally change the community's character and the cumulative effects of Moselle Plaza with its increased traffic and secondary impacts would irreparably disrupt and tear the fabric of the local economy and the elements of the community which give the Town its identity, vibrancy, attractiveness and stability.[20]

The Findings Meeting of October 30th

To the consternation of the large audience on October 30th, much of the next board meeting was taken up by long periods of silent reading. Board members had a full plate for their attention: Busch's approval findings drafts on traffic and wastewater, Manley's disapproval drafts on stormwater-water and traffic issues and, surprisingly, a draft from Ryker on stormwater as well as the latter's critique of Manley's earlier economics draft.

Busch now stated that his own findings draft would be integrated into Rattle's. In effect, he tried to assure the board that all it needed was to fill in the right colors and his document showed them how. Between Rattle's and Busch's drafts, the board had little to concern itself with. Nevertheless, forced by the weight of evidence on the record and having read Manley's draft on traffic impacts ahead of time, Busch had to acknowledge some apparently significant negative project effects, including some impacts "in conflict with the basic policy of the NYS DOT."

However, Busch's traffic draft then gave conditional approval based on the presumed ability of a revised site plan to show project size modifications that would reduce impacts and bring intersections into conformity with DOT policy. Furthermore, Busch left determination of the adequacy of such measures in the hands of the DOT and FCPWD since they were "the primary jurisdictional agencies for these improvements."

As for wastewater issues, Busch's draft again acknowledged problems but stated ultimately that "the project's impacts . . . will be minimized to the maximum extent practicable" as long as the jurisdictional agencies for this matter approved.

By contrast, Manley's draft findings documents for stormwater and traffic realms clearly set forth numerous expected problems and identified Magellan's failure to provide adequate mitigations. Concerning traffic, Manley introduced his draft by citing DOT standards against reducing present levels of service and requiring lane-by-lane impact analysis.[21] He also specified the board's own decision to not permit traffic service levels to deteriorate to "E" or "F" ratings.

Manley then proceeded with an intersection-by-intersection analysis specifying which lanes, in which peak conditions and buildout scenarios, would cause deteriorations of traffic service to "E" and "F" levels. The draft also insisted that projections should be based on accurate lane widths and a potential office-space buildout of the southerly Heller lot.

In turn, Manley's draft findings statement for stormwater and water quality issues proceeded one-by-one through identifying the quality and significance of wetland and related aquatic resources, likely short- and long-term project adverse impacts and the unmitigable nature of such impacts for the on-site and off-site wetlands and nearby aquifer.

As with his earlier economics findings draft distributed the week before, Manley's analyses in these two new documents were no surprise to ACT/CLEAR activists since they relied heavily on those groups' and Case's and Wright's earlier submissions. Again, however, it was elating to those in the audience to see finally on the table such strong written critiques emanating from within the board itself. If Magellan had an ally in Rattle, Busch and Maglie, the community activists now had a voice through Manley. Whatever the outcome, at least board members would have to choose between two clear findings alternatives. Should a court later be asked to reverse the findings, because Ryker and Davis should have been recused, a clear basis existed now to show how those from the "regulator" perspective had made a reasonable and well-documented judgment.

Ryker's two draft findings documents were a curious contrast. His proposed findings on stormwater management, water quality and erosion control were lifted almost entirely from Magellan's own EIS documents with no indication of issues discussed and refined by the board or outside sources. On the other hand, his findings document on economics was vintage Ryker--the same phrases and abrupt conclusions typical of his reactions to Moselle Plaza issues throughout the whole review process. However, here again, he failed to engage with critical perspectives and relied totally on the Marvell report. Indeed, Ryker claimed that Marvell was:

> the only independent economic consultant who has nothing to gain or lose if the project is built. Since the Board hired them to prepare this study, I feel we should strongly consider their findings as well as [Maglie's].

By contrast, he said, Manley's analysis and conclusion were "non-factual and based upon opinions not supported by the Planning Board's research. Each member must decide on their own using <u>facts</u>."

After reading through the contrasting new documents from Manley and Ryker on stormwater issues, Maglie was the first to speak and expressed accurately the plight of the board.

> I am in somewhat of a quandary with the board since we are now working on two completely opposite points of view in just about every document that we touch in this field. I sometimes wonder if there's any purpose in carrying on a debate.   .   . . reading the literature that we've exchanged and read back and forth, it doesn't appear to be even in the furthest reaches of my imagination any potential of building a consensus on the board. But I wish to have some dialogue on this . . . .

Maglie was obviously aware, from the earliest discussion of the project two years before, that the board contained significantly differing perspectives. Nevertheless, Maglie had worked continuously to achieve an ostensible board "consensus"--through persuasion or manipulation or by simply ignoring the differences.[1] This strategy culminated in the FSEIS "completeness" vote of September 18th. In turn, community activists had been constantly frustrated by how this strategy muted or ignored voices from the "regulator" perspective. But now the board was down to its final SEQRA stage. If a critical perspective was ever to be heard in the SEQRA process, it had to become very articulate and stubborn. So far, this had been achieved through Manley's alternative drafts. Maglie now had to consider that perhaps no meeting ground could be found.

Ryker attempted the classic "mitigations" approach:

> As a veteran of the first war of findings statements [with Amsterdam Square], I think what the board should keep in mind almost above all else is that when you come to mitigations on impacts, some of the key verbiage is "maximum extent practicable." There's no way you will ever get a document that . . . will . . . neutralize every impact. And I think that reasonable people have got to look at all the information and come to some kind of common ground within the law. We did it with the Master Plan, the Comprehensive Plan. We've done it with other projects. . . . We did it last time, that's what we should do this time.

Manley, in turn, stated that the board didn't have a lot of information to draw from in the original documents, so he tried to take it from whatever sources he could. Forthrightly, he admitted that "obviously we're not going to be able to reach a consensus on some things and I guess that's to be expected whenever there's such a different range in ideas about a project such as this." Green's statement was conciliatory but also stubborn.

I appreciate the work that both folks did and Gene Busch to get us going well. In reading Gene's, I felt that some of the points he came up with were well chosen. But the issue of putting them back to site plan and getting alternatives again is not attractive to me at this point. I think we're at a point in which we have what we have and we should try to reach a determination on it.

When Manley tried to get Busch to interpret one of his key findings phrases, "to the maximum extent practicable," when referring to mitigations the board might wish to impose on Magellan, Busch evaded. "I think it's a good legal statement. I'm not sure I could even tell you how to put your finger on it as to exactly what it is as opposed to what it isn't." Manley bounced the evasion back to Busch in paraphrased terms: "So it's all-inclusive and therefore non-inclusive. It means everything. It means nothing." Busch weakly agreed: "I suppose, in a way," but then tried a more sophisticated, though still confusing evasion:

> I think the measure of SEQRA process, SEQRA regulations, asks you to take a hard look at things and to evaluate whether or not practical measures for what's been proposed can be accomplished or can't be accomplished, whether all the alternatives have been viewed or re-viewed that appear to be practical. So that there's a lot of things in there that, sort of weighed together, it then becomes the opinion that to the maximum extent a determination is made.

Myers then jumped in with a new angle on the issue. How, he asked, can this SEQRA process with its "maximum-extent-practicable mitigations" guarantee environmental protection after the fact, after the project is built? These were Myers' strongest statements ever on whether to accept Magellan's mitigations conditioned on later involved agency permitting authority. It was clear, at least on the issue of board deference to other agencies, that Myers wished to decide proposed mitigations on the merits now, thus breaking with Busch, Maglie and Rattle and allying himself with Green, Manley and Hillman. If his earlier remark about the unreliability of Magellan's data, during the moratorium discussion fiasco, was an accurate predictor of his findings stance, activists would have something to celebrate since Myers plus the "regulator" members constituted a majority.

This challenge to the credibility of one of the key phrases in the "light planners'" SEQRA strategy greatly disturbed attorney Rattle, who now himself entered the fray. Rattle appeared concerned because the lack of a site plan and the resulting vagueness of eventual mitigations might tempt Myers not to give SEQRA approval. Rattle's messages throughout the review process had encouraged this "deferral-to-the-end" "backloading" approach since environmental problems had appeared which seemed insurmountable and could have stopped the project with a clear immediate decision.

To save the approval process, Rattle now reversed his earlier tact and sided with Myers against deferring to the permitting and site approval stage. Anticipating that this procedural posture would satisfy Myers' concerns about the delegation of authority, Rattle said that if there were certain things which the board did not want to see happen in the future, as seemed to be the case:

> You must make that decision <u>now</u>. And . . . if the consensus of this board turns out that this project <u>is</u> approvable, with conditions obviously, then I think you must specify those conditions and specify them in detail--not, say, you know, come back or something and we'll look at it. . . . you must set a standard in your findings.

But Rattle's demand for clear, specific and enforceable conditions forced the board to make definite decisions now. As Rattle himself said:

> You impose a condition that is so vague or so unenforceable, you're hurting yourselves because later on, when the thing is built, if it's built, and then the water quality doesn't meet what you specify that it should, doesn't degradate it below the current conditions, I mean no judge in this world is going to shut this project down because there's a minor [contradiction with vague conditional findings]. . . . the town's going to try to enforce it and the judge is going to say, "I'm not shutting down a $25 million project because this has happened."

Myers followed Rattle's unintended lead in criticizing Busch's and Ryker's drafts. "They seem a little bit clinical, a little bit benign, where no clear determination is made as to specifically what needs to be done or is done. Obviously, what Jim has written is clear and specific."

It appeared that Rattle then realized that the logic of his own remarks was becoming too dangerous, but it was also becoming confusing just which procedural message to deliver to the board. To co-opt Myers, Rattle had to support clear and detailed decision-making now. However, the only draft available which provided that level of clarity was Manley's disapproval findings.

As an afterthought, Rattle thus added another defensive obstacle to the slippery slope he had just encouraged. "But don't forget, you're starting from positive findings made in 1990. You have to then show why those findings are no longer valid." Rattle's bromide was to repeat his earlier opposition to the need for any SEQRA investigation at all, given his conclusion that Amsterdam Square's original findings were fine. His approach appeared once again to circumscribe legality to limit board exercise of discretionary authority to undertake an SEIS in the first instance. In other words, a special burden of proof was on the planning board if it wished to contradict its earlier verdict.

At this point, Myers now challenged Rattle's adoption of Myers' own position as imposing an inappropriate task of mitigation design on the board itself.

> To what degree do we wind up having to design the applicant's project for them is really what it comes down to. . . . how far do we go in order to create a framework for the applicant to have a positive finding, so we wind up being the one to create the development? I don't understand that. . . . why suddenly are we the ones who have to be the ones to determine what that will be in some kind of findings statement? If they didn't do their homework in determining that mitigation, then there's a chance for a negative impact. . . . Are we going to design the traffic so that it works right or let the DOT make that decision somewhere down the road? That wasn't our job. Our job was to review what they proposed to do and if we find that it isn't appropriate, then say so. . . . I'm not going to re-write their whole proposal for them to fit our needs.

Myers supported Rattle's admonition to make clear choices now, without acquiescing in Rattle's procedural posture to cast wide legitimacy on the Amsterdam Square findings regardless of changed circumstances. If Magellan had failed to offer mitigation alternatives to choose from, given changed circumstances and substantive comments, it was not up to the board to do that detailed work for them.[23] Green quickly agreed. Rattle's control over the process was clearly waning. While his practice in the past was to take any criticism and turn its meaning on its head, he had now met his match in Myers who was clearly able to do the same, but from a disapproval perspective.

Maglie then tried to move the discussion to a different path by alleging the unbalanced nature of proposed drafts.

> I feel the information we're getting from the board members [has] been one-sided, to say the least, and I'm not getting a judgment view on an equal balance of the material there, but I'm getting a re-hash of the same material that I've gotten for the last six months. And if you've adopted that side, that's fine. But I would be hoping more for a more judgmental viewpoint that balanced both sides of the equation. I haven't gotten that from anybody here.

He then proposed that two overall findings drafts be presented to the board on November 20th--one for approval and the other for disapproval.

Once again, Myers jumped to the challenge. In his view, Maglie's attempt to find a "balanced judgmental statement" was a contradiction in terms. In fact, Busch and Manley had each, in their own ways, balanced a variety of data and had come up with different conclusions. For Myers, what was needed was a vote, not further compromise or watering down of either draft. A judgment one way or another would have to be made.

Rattle then resumed his attempt to take charge by donning again the cloak of legalism. In this case, he attacked the assertiveness of Manley's drafts as unsubstantiated by sufficient evidence.

> I see a lot of language in here--"will" and "shall"--and you're going to have to point to the documents that support that. Because the findings are being made for a judge and when the judge reads them, he'd better be able to go to somewhere in the FSEIS and find support for that. Otherwise, whatever the findings are, positive or negative, they may get reversed. . . . You have to point to some proof. You just can't say [something will happen] or the judge is going to say, "Well, where is it going to do that?"

Myers pointed out that this was an issue for Busch's traffic document as well. Rattle agreed, but then added a substantive claim of his own: "And there's a question whether, you know, some degradation in traffic is probably acceptable. . . . It should be an <u>unacceptable amount of reduction</u> in service. Every project is going to cause some impact" (authors' emphasis). While Myers agreed with this statement, both appeared to forget the DOT standard which both Busch and Manley had cited earlier--that is, that a reduction of service was unacceptable, period.

At this point, Rattle also attempted to turn a substantive issue into a procedural one and again to appeal to legality to restrict the planning board in the exercise of its discretion. Despite his earlier acknowledgment that the board had the discretion to consider the potential build-out of the southerly Heller lot, he objected to reference to this issue in Manley's findings. "I mean getting into things like this is where you get into thin ice."

For the first time, Manley then challenged Rattle directly on a legal issue. Given the interrelationship of the two lots with potential mutual use of the same stormwater and wastewater treatment facilities, Manley said, it would not be an abstract issue to measure potential traffic from the build-out of the other lot in question. "From case law, all the cases, I know the cases on cumulative impact, a reasonable determination of possible impacts from the building of this site [would not be declared] beyond the ken of a planning board."

Rattle refused to concede.

> If you read the regulations about cumulative impacts. . . directly related to this project or other projects already in the works. Nobody is proposing anything for the property next door. The answer is, when they come in, they get reviewed. If you want me to send you a memo on this, I'll do so. But I do not think you should be plugging a speculative project--in fact, a non-existent project--into these figures.

Myers in turn refused to let go, pointing out that the board had merely followed the applicant's DSEIS itself in including projections for buildout of the southerly lot. After a further exchange on the issue, the meeting itself came to an end. A conclusive showdown could potentially come at the scheduled meeting of November 20th.[24]

Reactions varied in the immediate aftermath. Already the next day, Maglie was considering a new tactic. Apparently still trying to find a papered-over semblance of board consensus for approval, Maglie told the *Tribune* that he would put together what effectively would be a "line-item" draft finding statement. Each proposed mitigation measure would be placed up for a vote. A vote against any one item would mean a vote against the whole document. Presumably, "regulator" members might be unable to articulate the inadequacy of any specific mitigation effort and this might render them more susceptible to withdrawing their objection. Moreover, through pragmatic negotiation, perhaps a majority--meaning especially Myers, the critical swing vote--could be convinced to let a SEQRA approval go through with Magellan's proposed mitigations or with alternatives suggested by the board.

Magellan representative David Jankoff, in turn, sounded much like Ryker in his direct critique of Manley's economics draft.

> A lot of information used was mixed and matched from various reports. He took the worst case scenario from each. He didn't use any information from the independent consultant Marvell, but he used reports handed in from the public. He totally ignored the report that I paid $12,000 to have done.[25]

Community activists were by no means convinced of Myers' decisive shift, which would solidify a disapproval majority. All that had occurred was placement of a critical findings draft on the table. While important symbolically in slowing momentum toward approval, it represented no change in the power alignment to date. The "regulator" critique presented was the same critique already on the record from community groups and outside experts for months.

Over the same period, Myers had played the role of board skeptic and had never put himself decisively on the line. Even at this latest meeting, he seemed inclined to be critical or supportive of either side at his own whim. Myers' emotional criticism of the moratorium proposal only two weeks earlier was also fresh in mind. Appointed to the board through Ryker's manipulations, for community activists, Myers' origins left him forever suspect. Ultimately, some thought, he was simply playing a power role to the end--for whatever stakes he could command. Victory continued to be more difficult to foresee than defeat.

FOURTEEN THE PLANNING BOARD'S DECISION: THE PROCESS OF FINALITY

After the meeting of October 30th, neither Magellan nor the community groups felt confident of victory. Magellan placed its hopes on the capacity of Maglie, Rattle and Busch to formulate an approval statement attracting a majority of planning board votes, while the community groups depended upon the persuasiveness of Manley's draft disapproval. Each side continued for the next three weeks to pursue their goals through strategies in substantive, procedural and extra-SEQRA arenas.

Substantive and Procedural Battles

Again, Magellan sought to gain the final word in the debate on stormwater management issues. An October 26th letter from Magellan's engineer was received by the board on November 2nd. The letter responded directly to the five points in Wright's critique of October 15th and tried to minimize potential board concern over each issue. But Wright then submitted his own detailed reply to Magellan on November 20th, the day of the next findings meeting. Meanwhile, a week earlier, local attorney Eric Cretcher, at the urging of the community groups, submitted a letter adding another critique of the Board's process. Attempting to head off the last-minute revised strategy of the planning board chair, Cretcher referred to Maglie's stated desire to still achieve a consensus position on Moselle Plaza through somehow merging opposing findings statements. Cretcher's observations and advice were quite direct.

> There is no requirement under SEQRA that a finding statement reflect the consensus of the Board. In fact, as with most adjudicatory bodies the determination process does not easily lend itself to unanimous resolution. The merger of two diametrically opposed documents will create confusion and would result in a finding statement replete with inconsistencies.

Instead, Cretcher urged the board to set forth its separate positions in two different documents and to simply adopt whichever one gained the majority, with the remaining statement becoming the dissenting opinion.

The Town Election

The first week of November brought to a head the bitter exchange between competing electoral slates for Town Supervisor and the two other contested seats on the Town Board. Concerning the megamall issue, Republicans attempted to play both sides. While ads for the slate endorsed Schmidt's previous opposition to IDA funding ("without special concessions"), one Town Board candidate claimed that he was opposed to the megamall but also against the proposed law concerning shopping centers more generally. He said that the proposed maximum cap of 45,000 square feet was "way too low" since "they say" that a modern supermarket requires almost 100,000 square feet.

> It seems to me that [the law] was only introduced to serve the political interests of the liberals proposing it. However cleverly the liberals disguise it, I believe the entire Moselle Plaza issue has been used as an effective distraction from the Democrats' past records and many other more important issues. . . . There's more to Ashbury than the Moselle mall!

On the side of the Democrat/CRP slate, large ads for Rachel Wilton in the same issue of the *Tribune* proclaimed that her vision of the future was especially "An Ashbury without a megamall" and that "Ashbury is at a crossroads. Because of this it has never been more important to vote."

Letters to the editor from an ACT coordinator and activist directly criticized Schmidt's record specifically on the Moselle Plaza issue. Despite Schmidt's claim at a candidate's night forum that he had no bias one way or the other about the project, one of the letters informed readers of a conversation with Schmidt at the January public hearing where the latter openly acknowledged support of the megamall and spoke favorably of the "benign" effect of a Wal-Mart megamall he had recently visited in Massachusetts.

Ashbury polls on November 7th were unusually crowded for a local election. Ultimately, 3366 voters took part, about 25% more than in the previous local election two years earlier. The total included 376 voters at the booths on the SUNY/Ashbury campus.[1] When the polls closed that evening, it became quickly apparent that the anti-mall slate had swept the election. Political newcomer Wilton had defeated Schmidt for Supervisor by a vote of 1865 to 1501. This was powerful testimony indeed of the significance of the Moselle Plaza issue, since two-term incumbent Schmidt had been relatively popular and had beaten his previous Democrat rival by a 2-1 ratio. Similarly, in the race for two seats on the Town Board, Pelletier gained 1910 votes and Lyon 1890, compared to rival Republican candidates with 1361 and 1172 respectively.[2]

The winning candidates and anti-mall activists were elated at the apparent de facto referendum in favor of their position[3] and obviously hoped that it would have an immediate positive effect on the upcoming planning board decision. An op-ed by a regular *Tribune* writer stated the significance in no uncertain terms:

I don't think the debate on Moselle Plaza, in or outside the confines of politics or rhetoric, ventured on getting elected to anything. This unneeded piece of capitalism is the reason the Community Reform Party came into being. To fight the mall. . . . It was the main issue in [the CRP] platform, understanding as they did and do, that this plaza would be the death of Ashbury as a small college town. And more importantly, they <u>won</u>. And they won <u>big</u>.

. . . [The Republican candidates] would have done nothing to block the plaza. People knew that. And they <u>lost</u>. And <u>big</u>.[4]

Even if the planning board now approved the project, activists believed that their opportunity to stop it through Town Board actions opposing IDA funding, opposing a zoning variance or zoning law change in Heller's southerly lot, and appointing environmentally-friendly people to the planning board and ZBA would be greatly enhanced. Between election results, numbers of signatures on past petitions, participants in demonstrations and contributors to ACT, it was now clear that the anti-Moselle Plaza struggle had the backing of well over half of the community's adult residents. In addition, activists heard that Medford, presumably reacting to the local election, had now indicated willingness to re-examine the scenario of on-site expansion at its existing FoodFeast store location.

The November 20th Meeting

Maglie assumed the chair's prerogative to lead off the November 20th meeting by presenting his own new findings draft--a summary of what he viewed as the resolution of remaining environmental issues. Not implying that he intended a decisive vote at this meeting, Maglie said he just "wanted to give a kind of focus to the discussion tonight in a couple of different areas." Essentially, given the now uncertain voting majority within the board, Maglie now sought with his "summary" document to act the part of a pragmatic, "non-policymaking bureaucrat," simply looking at the "facts" before the board without assuming any final judgments in advance. Intuitively, it seemed, Maglie knew that he had to de-politicize and bureaucratize, as much as possible, the rhetoric and discussion of the issues at hand.

Consistent with "light planner" strategy all along, Maglie now sought to achieve a friendly "consensual" resolution of various disputed areas, while those more problematic in nature would be "backloaded" to a later date--either in the site-plan stage or at the time of project review by permitting agencies. By Maglie's apparent scenario, no "real" conclusions would have to be drawn, since the answers to certain sticky questions would not be gained until later. Thus, SEQRA "approval" would not be real project approval, so no one's principles would be compromised and everyone, including Magellan, would be satisfied. For Maglie, the planning board's role under SEQRA was to be little more than a cipher of information and to thereafter report the comments and responses which had been completed.

Maglie's was the same approach attempted by Busch with his own drafts, but without some of Busch's objectionable "conditional approval" language. In the stormwater-water quality realm, Maglie identified four areas of needed review. Concerning the on-site wetland, he conceded, as had Busch, that a large proportion would be destroyed. In his view, less than 50% would remain as a wetland. Demonstrating new "sensitivity" to environmental issues, Maglie even granted that what remained would not act effectively as a wetland and that it would have to be replaced. In his view, the board would simply have to decide whether such an impact could be mitigated through some form of creative engineering. He had little doubt that it could but did not specify how.

Maglie also granted that the issue of pre-development runoff quality had never been properly determined. At this point, disconcerting to watching activists, Manley implied, through detailed comments on Maglie's approach, that he had now accepted Maglie's document, rather than his own, as the basis for the board's substantive discussion.

Maglie briefly mentioned sewage treatment facility impacts and effects on the wetlands as also requiring mitigations, but failed to identify what those might be in either case. He told the board that this omission was because he wanted the board to make that decision--whether there could be mitigations and what their nature would be. He said:

> in terms of mitigation, move into the design of the project. You propose a mitigation and, in effect, you're making up a design--you will do this, you will do this, you will do this. And you effectively have designed a new project. And I think that responsibility is a planning board responsibility.

Moving on to the traffic realm, again Maglie followed Busch's lead and conceded several examples where traffic levels of service would deteriorate from "no-build" to "build" scenarios. He also noted that Magellan had not included seasonal variations of traffic conditions in its calculations. As for the southerly Heller lot, knowing that the issue could not be avoided, Maglie granted that its development might be limited by the extent of Magellan's planned intersection improvements, but still insisted on employing warehouse-use, instead of larger office-use traffic projections for that zone.

Economics issues posed a major obstacle to Maglie's strategy since it was hard to conceive of designing relevant mitigations in that realm during the later site-plan stage. Thus, Maglie's only hope was to obtain board agreement that economic projections were too unreliable to come to any objective conclusions. In effect, this realm would be permanently set aside as beyond the board's capacity to make any definitive statement.

Maglie thus amiably told the board that he felt better on the issue of economic projections once he reminded himself that even the federal government was divided in its estimates of future growth. In an appeal for "reasonable centrism," he asserted that "the board received economic projections for the retail market area from one extreme to the other. The real truth probably lies somewhere in between." Revealing his underlying bias for approval, he benignly added, "The conclusions raised in the initial [Amsterdam Square] findings statement, which I attached, probably still hold true." (That document had definitively concluded that "the Board finds that there will not be significant adverse environmental impacts to the local economy as a result of the proposed shopping center.") In practical terms, however, Maglie then sought to dismiss the entire realm from effective consideration--as either an environmental impact, in terms of community character, or for the final cost-benefit balancing test with negative environmental impacts generally.

> I feel the planning board should not make decisions that restrict retail competition. Nor should the board make decisions that significantly alter the existing shopping patterns of the town. If the board used either of these in the planning function, it would be detrimental in the long run for the well-being of the community. The information that's been received regarding economic impact of this project should not be used for a definitive decision in regard to the merits of the project. What I mean right there was, if that's the only thing that we've come up with, one way or another, that should not stand because I'm not comfortable with all the information.

Concerning fiscal impacts, again Maglie claimed, "I don't think there's any clear cut black and white answer on this area." To prove his good intentions, beyond his newly conceded acknowledgements of legitimate substantive issues, Maglie pointed out that Manley's own document had provided him with some of the background data he now used in his own.

Impatient with further discussion from Maglie, Myers then agreed that in many cases Maglie's review was "quite congruent to what Bob has to say in his proposal here." However, the conclusion Myers drew from this differed from Maglie's. Myers immediately moved, with Hillman seconding, that Manley's findings statement be accepted "as the policy of the board and that we go from there in critiquing it in principle."

This sudden bombshell, with Ryker-appointee Myers accepting a "regulator" draft disapproval statement, seemed to the audience to leave Maglie in a dazed and defensive position. "I'm not sure where I'm coming out on this. There are parts in there that I definitely agree with Bob on and there are parts in there that I don't think are valid, fair, objective."

In turn, Myers tried now to soften the blow, attempting to present his motion in part as simply a device to get the board moving toward a more definitive statement.

> Well, we have to come from a perspective and I think we have one at least in that we can go from there on out. Whatever changes or modifications the board wants to make, we should make based on this finding statement that Bob presented. So, in effect, I'm saying that we should accept in principle and then work from there.

Appearing incredulous, yet hopeful that perhaps it was Myers' logic, not his intent, that was at fault, Davis immediately sought to alter Myers' resolution: "If you accept it in principle, then you accept it with the conclusions." He urged that the board complete the findings statement first and then come up with conclusions. For this, no motion would be needed. And perhaps Myers would thereafter come to his senses and vote to accept a findings statement which could only serve as a basis for approval. Ryker agreed: "If you agree with its [Manley's] conclusions, then there's not a whole hell of a lot to complete."

What this debate showed clearly once again was that, for the core group of "light planners," the process the board had taken on for two years in reviewing the Moselle Plaza application was nothing more than a means of justifying a pre-determined political outcome. Had "light planning" members wanted to proceed using greater scientific rationality and objectivity, they would have attempted to craft a findings statement which would carefully analyze each of the developer's positions and those of the critics and arrive at a conclusion regarding whether any proposed mitigation was satisfactory. Instead, what had been painfully clear to activists earlier on now became blatant and overt. For "light planners," SEQRA was nothing more than a vehicle through which ideological differences regarding land-use and the environment could be "rationalized." Whatever decisions were reached had only to do with the balance of power on the board and the degree to which one ideological group or another held sway. For "light planners," the strategy of rationalizing pre-determined outcomes had heretofore been employed in a relatively bulletproof fashion, insulating the planning board from any reversal of fortune arising out of court review. Now, led by a renegade "light planner," the tables were turned and "regulator" members, heretofore accepting legal liberalism's principle of fair process=fair result, had adopted the outcome-determinative strategy used against them earlier.

Myers, recognizing the inversion of power through structural realignment of the board and the obvious effect that this had on the outcome, then attempted to appease his shocked "light planning" peers while at the same time clarifying his substantive position. Tipping his hat to the legitimacy of the "fair process" model, he agreed that the board should go through the document, polish it up and change whatever needed to be changed. But he thought the board would act more efficiently if it had a single document to work from, "as opposed to constantly handing out different variations on different themes. . . . I think that this is what you wanted to do a month ago." However, as to outcome, he was decided: "Generally speaking, one of the reasons why I made the motion is that I believe in the conclusions that it does state."

Having caught his breath, Ryker could barely restrain his feelings about this unexpected structural turn. All he could do was to attempt to discredit the draft document, its author and its conclusions.

> Well, I find it [Manley's document] to be more imbalanced than anything else. While he cites different pieces of information that were submitted to us, probably the only information that he's taking as gospel, and most of the conclusions, are directly from one or two pieces of information. He said that . . . the Smith study is the only study that should be relied upon. . . . [H]e makes his own conclusions as to what research he's going to accept as factual and I disagree with that. There's other pieces of information that were submitted that were equally factual, I think, if not more so. But that's his opinion versus mine. And if you're going to take his basic studies and [draw from them] his conclusions, I find to be imbalanced at best and biased at the most.

Ryker's critique of Manley's right to choose among experts flew in the face of SEQRA "hard look" case law (though such choices usually favored developers).

Green then joined in defense of Myers' procedural logic, in effect, agreeing to take the cart before the horse because she agreed with the result. How could the board proceed to draft findings, she asked, if the basic intent of the majority had not been previously determined? For her, the board should get straight onto its work:

> Knowing that we probably will be going to court, regardless of the outcome, it seems to me that this is prudent to try to make a determination now, on a somewhat informal basis, whether or not this is an approval or a disapproval, and then make sure that the writing is as thorough and well-documented as we could possibly make it.

Now Hillman joined in as well, defending Manley's document as "like a lawyer's case," an "excellent job identifying the number of problems at such a site that are not mitigated, whether it's in stormwater or water quality, traffic, etc." Hillman agreed that it was not the board's job to design the project. "There was ample opportunity provided for alternatives and variations of alternatives we could have been looking at, we could have been considering and it's not there." In sum, Manley's statement "definitely reflects my feeling."

Manley, in turn, concerned with the appearance of fair process and more prone to a consensus model of decision-making himself rather than one involving imposition of power, now tried to soften the impact of his document by assuring Maglie that a lot of his own draft "tracks what you summarized," with "a couple little exceptions here and there with stormwater and I did a little bit more detail with traffic. But basically, I think, our conclusions are pretty close to the same." Given that Manley and Maglie were on opposite sides of almost every issue raised by the megamall, and that Manley had adopted an assertive strategy, at the very least, his remarks may have been viewed as disingenuous. However, Manley was conflicted with having disregarded what he viewed as tenets of legal liberalism and having participated in a process which could no longer accommodate "light planners" if disapproval were to be assured. Manley even had praise for Marvell as having done "a good job in providing us with the framework for economic analysis." Nonetheless, perhaps sensing the newfound power of the "regulator" perspective, Manley moved assertively into discrediting Marvell's conclusions by emphasizing the significance of one of the "regulators'" strongest forms of rebuttal evidence, the decline in county tax revenue figures (proof of lower local consumer spending) which Manley himself had researched during the past few days.[5]

Myers now took Manley's lead to summarize the rationale for his conclusions on the substantive environmental issues. Distancing himself from Maglie and echoing the view expressed earlier by "regulator" members, he stated: "I don't think that we have the responsibility to rebuild this plan or re-design it for the applicant." Concerning stormwater quantity: "Sure, there may be some engineering feats of marvel that we might be able to develop to overcome whatever negative impact . . . that there is." He doubted that the board or himself could determine the significance of the project's impact on stormwater quality. As for traffic, he didn't believe the board could legislate needed improvements to keep quality from deteriorating. This was therefore an additional factor to be balanced, in the end, against potential economic benefit. Another would be the potential loss of future aquifer use. Echoing Smith's "big bang" theory, Myers addressed the likely economic impact of the project.

> I don't think, based on the analysis that I've seen, how this town can
> mitigate $30 million loss in its retail sales . . . unless the project's not
> there. The growth potential of this town is not where it was 20 or 30
> years ago. The [inability] to overcome that loss in a short term and a
> long term is so great that I don't think it can be overcome by whatever
> we decide the applicant should do or not do.

Myers' final remark then shifted the direction of the discussion and moved it to what activists perceived as a more precarious ground: namely, that the developer might, on its own, re-submit a re-designed megamall that might meet Myers' standards and achieve an approval majority.

> [The developer] may make a decision to . . . change the scope of the project. But it's his business. But we might be able to suggest mitigations for a few areas; I think there are enough of those that are so significant that we would have to, in effect, re-design the project for the applicant. I don't think it's our responsibility to do that.

Davis, identifying with some of what Myers said, attempted to return to Maglie's original position of withholding judgment until the findings statement was completed and adhering to SEQRA's decision-making requirements:

> I agree that we can't be project designers. . . . The emphasis here though is for us to define what is required, not how to accomplish it. . . . I personally will not vote that we accept [Manley's document] or adopt it because I still feel, and maybe this is semantics, but I think it puts the cart before the horse. I would rather use it as a guide and then adopt it when we feel it is acceptable to at least a majority of the board. The emphasis here should be on the definition of what the problem areas are and it's up to the developer the decision as to how he accomplishes that.

When challenged by Green, he elaborated further and revealed, in doing so, that his suggestion led logically back to the "light planners'" original "backloading" intent to grant SEQRA approval and defer substantive issues to the site-plan review stage.

> [What] we can say is what you've proposed doesn't do it. We're into this gray area where . . . we've all raised the questions at one time or another, about how much and to what detail, do we have to look at this proposal, this plan, this application during the SEQRA process, as opposed to what we look at during the site review process. . . . You're looking at something that isn't finally designed and yet we're trying to make decisions on it.

He then appealed to Busch to interpret the board's responsibility in this context.

Busch welcomed the opportunity to define the planning board's role again in "light planning" terms. The earlier Amsterdam Square findings statement, he said, essentially concluded that some planned mitigations were all right, but others still needed to be agreed to by the developer before the project would be accepted. By contrast, Manley's document specified areas Magellan fell short on and because of these, "the project is denied, period. It doesn't say here are all the parameters that you have to meet to come back with a new plan and then we'll consider it." While not stating specifically that disapproval was not a legal alternative under SEQRA, he urged the board to decide if Manley's was really the kind of approach the board wanted to choose. Ultimately, Busch's argument cautioned the board against employing an environmental statute to preclude future development.

As earlier, Green asked whether Magellan's coming back with a new plan wouldn't simply start the SEQRA process all over again. Busch asserted that, as with the Amsterdam Square findings, SEQRA approval could be given, but conditioned upon specific mitigations being met during the site-plan review. Green saw this as "taking a big step toward project design." Busch admitted that the present Moselle Plaza proposal, as now designed, was unacceptable by the board's criteria on traffic and stormwater management (economics or community character remained unmentioned). But for him, this should not close the door on the project if the developer was willing to satisfy whatever conditions the board set forth.

Davis then argued that at this stage to deny SEQRA approval would be "back-handed design" itself, "in a sense that you're making a judgment that it can't be mitigated." Busch agreed and said what the board would be asserting was that it didn't see any practical way of overcoming certain adverse effects. Davis carried this further: "Well, that's a judgmental thing, too, that we don't see the practicality. That doesn't mean that there aren't engineering designs out there that will in fact do it, with water quality or whatever else."

Busch now offered a final fall-back scenario by contending that even a vote of "disapproval" (which now appeared to be a foregone conclusion) could be conditional, without prejudice to the developer, to allow re-submission of an acceptable design thereafter. Even if the board rejected the project for the moment,

> then the applicant can certainly regroup, say "well, we do have a design that can meet it, we can change this plan, we can re-design this project" and go back and, obviously subject to SEQRA again, but give the board a new project that's been re-designed, that has all the parameters, and more perhaps, that the board has discussed in the past year.

Under this logic, Magellan might contend that, even with the disapproval, it had a vested right to construct a megamall because of the previous Amsterdam Square SEQRA approval and Magellan's own significant expenses to date, regardless of any potential new restrictive rezoning by the new Town Board majority.[6] And this was precisely the scenario activists and Town Board member Lyon wished to foreclose by enacting a shopping center size cap or a building moratorium before potential SEQRA rejection of Moselle Plaza. However, Green reduced Busch's scenario to an absurdity:

> I guess my concern is that we've been talking about it and the

developer's representatives have been here and [heard] all of the concerns of the community which have been well-documented and there has not been much flexibility on the design at all. So I think we ought to take a hint and this is the project that we have to make a value judgment on. Make it and, if it goes negative, then the developer can come back. We can do this forever [outburst of laughter and groans from the board].

Sensing the ideological polarity and uncomfortable with his motion being characterized as anti-mitigation and arguably contrary to SEQRA, Myers now, at least nominally, watered it down. He suggested that after Manley's document was accepted in principle, the board could go through and modify it and even change the conclusions if it could find acceptable mitigations. To expedite the process, he said, the board needed a clear agenda. On the other hand, Myers clarified that the conclusions were not likely to be changed since he believed that they were accurate. Nevertheless, he left the door slightly ajar for the developer.

[The proposal] may have some spots that need to be addressed or tightened up, for whatever legal purposes, or for whatever direction to the applicant to take in the future if need be, then fine, but I think we ought to start right here to complete this thing [emphasis added].

Ryker was not ready to accept Busch's final face-saving scenario or the vague second chance offered by Myers. He again argued that the board should accept the path it followed with Amsterdam Square, granting approval under SEQRA and requiring the re-design of certain items or a stamp of approval from permitting agencies. Allying himself with legality, Ryker sought to interpret the board's mandate under SEQRA as to require approval. In his view, the board didn't even have discretionary power to turn the project down on SEQRA grounds.

It depends on how you look at mitigations. If you look at mitigations as a way of turning down a project or if you look at mitigations as a way of overcoming the obstacles the project presents, that's two different points of view. This is a project that was submitted in good faith. It was submitted under law and it was the planning board's responsibility, is the planning board's responsibility to deal with this project under the existing law.

... I disagree with [Manley's] conclusions, specifically because in the past a lot of projects seemed insurmountable and, like Red says (who has the engineering background), there are many ways to skin the same cat. And if we go forward and accept this document and accept these conclusions, then I think we're starting off right away by saying this project is rejected, this project can't be mitigated. And we're not following the letter of the law or the responsibility that this board has. . . . Because the letter of the law says you're supposed to review this project under the guidelines set forth. And I think that if you use mitigations specifically to reject something, then I think you're betraying your responsibility.

Ryker's interpretation of SEQRA, however, was not supported by Rattle who sat throughout these proceedings, his face reddened, in what appeared to be angry silence. While heretofore Ryker was able to deftly point to the planning board's lawyer as the final arbiter of a legality principle he favored, Ryker was now without Rattle's support on a crucial determinative issue. At this stage, even Rattle could not articulate a rule of law in accord with Ryker's assertions. Although it could be argued that Magellan had presented its application in good faith, that had little or no bearing on the board's capacity to disapprove the project should it conclude that the developer had the opportunity to respond and that the proposed mitigation remained unsatisfactory. While Rattle had argued against the planning board's going "the whole nine yards" by requiring an SEIS, once it had (with Magellan's specific acquiescence), the board could reasonably arrive at whatever findings and conclusions it felt were justified by the data submitted throughout the process. Moreover, while it appeared that Rattle's efforts attempted to constrain the process so as to preclude any refutation of Magellan's responses following the public hearing, Maglie had invited these responses in what he contended, at the time, was the board's desire to consider all relevant information. Ultimately, Rattle's influence was further minimalized by the assertion of power by "regulator" members (joined by Myers) who were supported, in their own view of legality, by community lawyers publicly contradicting Rattle's assertions and showing the fallacy of his arguments.

Maglie now again tried to find a middle ground, again acknowledging that "I think I agree with the membership here that I don't want to design this project." Realizing that there was no majority base for approval under SEQRA, however, he conceded that "I'd be comfortable to use this [Manley's document] as a guideline" with which to devise a final finding statement. However, "when you say 'I accept in principle,' I'm not sure what I'm accepting. That's my problem." Ryker then asked if Myers would compromise by tabling his motion and simply using Manley's document as a draft, as Maglie suggested, without voting in principle on its conclusions.

Myers saw no need to table his motion since it reflected his beliefs and he had a majority. Again he reiterated that if the board came to different conclusions after the review of Manley's document, that would be its prerogative. "So I think we agree on the ends [the need to, as Maglie contended, "word-smith" the findings statement]. The means [Manley's draft and disapproval conclusion] are different and I don't see any reason to change." Davis and Maglie tried to change his mind. Myers refused.

Almost one hour into the meeting, Maglie then polled the board members around the table on Myers' motion. Green, aye. Hillman, aye. Manley, aye. Ryker, nay. Myers, aye. Davis, nay. Maglie, nay. The deed was done. A majority of the planning board had voted, in principle, to disapprove Moselle Plaza on SEQRA grounds.

While Dreyfus immediately cheered from the back of the room, other activists at the front beamed inside but remained silent, in fear that the slightest provocation might switch Myers to the other side. To them, Myers was so volatile, they dared not provide him with the slightest excuse, in this delicate context, to recant. Nevertheless, those in the audience felt finally able to relax their vigilance as the dynamics of the board gradually transformed. For Dreyfus, Myers' decision was final and, like the decision-making of the planning board in general, based upon entrenched differences which none of the members (except perhaps Ryker) were willing to articulate publicly. In switching allegiance, even temporarily, from "light planner" to "regulator" perspective, Myers was irretrievably committed to rejecting Moselle Plaza. Perhaps motivating him was his disdain with having been thought of only as Ryker's nominee, without an independent voice. Or perhaps it was his desire to maintain harmony within his own family and with his neighbors. After all, his wife had stated her opposition to the project privately. His neighbors had visited with him and presented him with their petition showing the number of neighborhood residents who opposed the project as harmful to the character of the community. Or it may have been that the spectre of a Wal-Mart-anchored megamall was just more than Myers was willing to swallow, given his own perceptions of the town's environmental and economic limitations. For whatever the reason, Dreyfus believed that Myers' decision was thought out, calculated, and unbending.

Once the vote was taken, for nearly two hours, the board proceeded step by step through Manley's draft, occasionally altering words and phrases, enduring bitter periodic sniping from Ryker and Davis and listening to Maglie's repeated appeals to make conditional mitigations and to draw no definite conclusions which would bind developers or the board for the future. For the most part, Maglie publicly accepted the problem areas defined by Manley for both stormwater and traffic sections. At the same time, Rattle, whose anger was beginning to protrude, said to Manley that he completely disagreed with how he had prepared the analysis of traffic.

Once again, it was in the realm of economics and community character where the "light planners'" greatest opposition was voiced. If they still hoped for potential developer mitigation in other realms at the site-plan stage, here it was impossible to conceive of acceptable changes short of significantly downsizing the whole project, which Magellan consistently refused to do. To discredit Smith's and McBride's analysis and the data they had relied upon was their only option. Thus, despite acknowledging the significance of Manley's research on the decline in tax revenue, Maglie still insisted that "neither extreme has shown valid economic statistics that project out five years, next year, next week" and the board shouldn't say there is no market for such a development since the board lacked enough information and it wasn't "a board's purview to do economic projections." The board, he said, should take a neutral stand.

To this, Myers responded authoritatively with his voice from the business world: "I absolutely disagree with you 180 degrees. . . . [I]f that were the case, then no developer would ever consider developing anywhere because the models that he might be using for future sales potential for that zone have no validity." For the first time in the whole review, Ryker now assumed Medford's line that FoodFeast had to expand; it was too small for the community. Myers said this was irrelevant. The question at hand was the entire project. Astonishingly, Davis then asked, "What if this happened to be a Home Depot . . . ? We don't know." (That chain was the one store even Marvell had acknowledged as unfit for Ashbury.) For the first time ever, Myers invoked the definite image of Wal-Mart by contending, "Nobody spends this kind of money . . . without knowing exactly what they're doing and exactly who they're dealing with and to have commitments."

Maglie even acknowledged that the project offered <u>no</u> positive economic benefits, though <u>possibly</u> some economic hardships, to balance against adverse environmental impacts. Nevertheless, responding to Myers' earlier statements regarding the capacity of the Ashbury market to absorb a megamall, he objected to the concept that the planning board had the responsibility "to dictate the level of retail competition" in the community. It was a stark admission of the ideological roots for his "light planning" bias and demonstrated, as had Myers' earlier statements, what little respect anyone had for the socio-economic balancing test mandated by SEQRA. Ryker joined in, claiming that the new majority's position was a return to "18th century protectionism."

At the end, after all his "conciliatory" gestures, Maglie attempted to re-assert the "light planning" position by proposing that a new shorter document be written, based on the discussion and suggestions of the past two hours and referring to Manley's draft as a background document. While Manley agreed that some re-phrasing could be done, Myers called the maneuver for what it was, pointing out that such a process would contradict his motion. Davis tried another tack, indicating that he wanted to see a final draft and then have it reviewed by Rattle before the board took a vote, since "we're sued no matter what."

While everyone agreed that a revision was needed, the two ideological positions on the board had very different outcomes in mind. Thus, the process of preparing a final draft would be crucial. Though Manley pointed out that a smaller editing group would simply replicate the disagreements of the larger board, here Myers deserted him--to the dismay of those in the audience—and shifted to a procedural posture now consonant with legal liberalism's notions of inclusion. For Myers, the appropriate committee was Maglie, Manley and the consultants--Busch and Rattle. Armed only with the "straw vote" on principles and Manley's document, but stacked with three opponents to that document and those principles, this seemed a wholly inappropriate and potentially disastrous scenario if disapproval was what Myers hoped to achieve. Nevertheless, after the apparent major accomplishment of the evening, no one from the "regulator" perspective objected. The revision committee was scheduled to report back to the full board on December 18th with a probable formal vote at that time.[7]

For the first time, activists allowed themselves the luxury of fantasizing about a celebration, an existence without endless crises and desperate meetings, and a long-range life in Ashbury without a megamall. Nevertheless, the final action of the board was worrisome and raised the spectre of a potentially pyrrhic victory. Even if ultimately the project was rejected, despite "light planners" as a majority of the re-drafting committee and Manley's predisposition for consensus, another scenario had re-surfaced in the board's discussion. It now seemed possible that Magellan would simply redesign the project after disapproval and re-submit it to the board before a new moratorium or shopping center cap law was in place.

Magellan Construction and Medford were quick to express disappointment. Huge amounts of money had been spent on a project they had been led to believe was a sure thing with the planning board. Despite the possibility of new maneuvers to gain a conditioned approval or the potential to re-submit a new plan, for the moment they were defeated. On the night of the decisive planning board vote, stunned Magellan partner Deke Reynolds called it "absolutely crazy" and "very discouraging" and told a reporter that Magellan was already exploring options to the east. He said that the company would "evaluate its court options," but also added that "the people from CLEAR did a hell of a job."[8]

According to Magellan's project manager Jankoff, "That finding statement is so negative to this project that if they adopt anything along those lines they are going to pretty much deny the project." He said he was frustrated by the board's position. "There's basically nothing we can do." He was also surprised, he said, because he thought ACT and CLEAR represented only a vocal minority. "I never really had a handle on how much of the community they represented. I have to commend CLEAR. They did an outstanding job of being persistent. . . . Obviously, I felt the election had a lot to do with [the planning board vote]." As for alternatives, "We're evaluating all the potential sites in the area. I really don't see another site in the Town of Ashbury or the Village. I can tell you we were approached several times by property owners outside the Town of Ashbury."

In turn, Nelson Silveira, Medford senior vice-president and general counsel, stated that Medford would back Magellan Construction in the search for alternative sites. "Medford has expended many hundreds of thousands of dollars already." As for the alternative of on-site expansion, "It just doesn't work. For a whole host of reasons: traffic flow, parking, loading docks, drainage, fill." Furthermore, "other [plaza] tenants . . . may not want to move."

The day after the planning board vote, a Magellan representative visited the town hall of Ashbury's neighbor, the town of Acton, to discuss with the town building inspector potential alternative sites in that community. The Acton Town Supervisor, a pro-development ideologue himself, welcomed the possibility, claiming that "it would be a wonderful improvement to help offset tax costs. No strain on our school system. No strain on our water or sewer." The Supervisor and building inspector specifically recommended a largely undeveloped site on Rte. 354, a mile to the east of the proposed Moselle Plaza.

As for potential court action by the developer, Maglie predicted, "I don't think Magellan is going to waste the time to go to court." Rattle, however, disagreed, stating, "I think litigation will ensue." It would seem that he hoped for vindication of his two years of advice in court. Claiming that he would not meddle with the board's will in the findings revision committee, Rattle apparently welcomed a Magellan suit challenging a document drafted by Manley and the new board majority. "They have made their finding statement. Let them defend it in court. I don't want to change it."[9]

Ryker's response to the press was predictably angry, but also revealed his sense of betrayal by his own board appointee.

> I was blindsided by [Myers'] motion. I thought Sam still had an open mind about this project. . . . What it looks like to me is you might as well dissolve the planning board and let Manny Dreyfus and Alex McBride review all future applications. . . . It's utterly ludicrous to believe Bob Manley prepared that document himself. He's a capable guy, but he was guided and led by the nose by the opponents.[10]

As for longer-range implications, "No matter what you say in the comprehensive plan or in your [Development Corporation] brochures, you are really telling businesses to go elsewhere."[11]

In a letter to the *Tribune*, Davis claimed to vindicate his name. He stated that "[c]ompliments are due to the [mall] opponents for their very thorough research and the organizational efforts that have been expended." Nevertheless, he also blamed them for "the use of any means to accomplish a purpose." He then sought to provide "a few historical truths" to contradict accusations, "that borders on slander," that he had any conflict of interest in continuing to participate in decision-making about the plaza. He also strongly resented that the planning board had been blamed for what in fact was the town's responsibility generally--not to have re-zoned the area years ago--if that was the community's intent. He assured that "[e]very member of the planning board has nothing but the best interests of the town at heart, despite what some adversaries may say." He claimed that "[t]here are also differing ways to accomplish goals. As an example, my technical background can result in what may be perceived as closer scrutiny during site plan review than SEQR deliberations." Finally, he dared opponents to prove now that they weren't simply against any business-oriented project presented to the community.[12]

Myers explained his action to the press as he did at the board meeting itself. His motion "was designed to have people step over the line and declare themselves--I felt it was time to start counting noses." He said that for him, the negative implications of the project in traffic, environmental and economic realms "each revealed themselves in time," amounting overall to a "disastrous" effect on the community. Though gradually coming to these conclusions, he sought to vindicate the process as consonant with fair fact-finding and said that he and others on the board were scrupulous about not revealing their true feelings in public or even privately. "I didn't even say anything to my wife until maybe two months ago. I wouldn't tell her where I stood, even though she told me where she hoped I stood."[13]

Beyond his public statement, Myers also personally called McBride and Ina Turbell the day after the vote to thank them for the excellent analyses and information they had provided to the board. To McBride, he said that when his own economic calculations roughly matched CLEAR's mid-June analysis, his feelings against the project became decisive. McBride, in turn, thanked him for his crucial swing vote and for his consistently critical questions throughout board review of the project.[14]

The publisher of the *Tribune* summarized the event with the dramatic words it called for:

> The rejection of Moselle Plaza may be one of those watershed events that mark a significant shift in the life of a small community. In turning down this huge mall, Ashbury has, I believe, changed long-held ideas about its own identity and affirmed more recent ones. The

planning board turned down the opportunity to make a large addition to the town's retail space and thereby to reinforce its role as a significant sub-regional retail center.

It was an unprecedented decision in Ashbury, whose planning board had historically been sympathetic to growth. We at the *Tribune* think the decision was both courageous and correct. But we recognize the argument about it won't stop soon. It will reverberate in this community for a long time to come.[15]

One week earlier, a *Tribune* editor specifically addressed the role of the activist community groups themselves:

The saddest part of this story is that if it were not for the Herculean efforts of Ashbury Community Together and CLEAR, our local grassroots watchdog groups, this monster-mall would probably already be built. In the early stages of this project, the *Tribune* was also guilty of not doing its job. Of listening to but a few select voices on the planning board. Call it cronyism, or lack of insight by our then-reporter, but we did the community no service in treating the efforts of ACT and CLEAR as if they were a splinter group, outside of our community.

As we all later found out, particularly Magellan Construction, it simply wasn't the case. There is a great lesson in this for all of us. It's called awareness, and together, as a community of diverse individuals, we must keep seeking it.[16]

First Intermission

In the wake of electoral and planning board victories, however, the anti-mall coalition began to fray at the edges. On December 12th, Magellan's attorney Morris Schwab called Supervisor-elect Rachel Wilton to set up for himself and Deke Reynolds a direct face-to-face meeting to discuss various alternatives they were considering for the Ashbury project. He invited her to bring along planning board members or anyone else she wanted. Encouraged by others to meet with Magellan, Wilton informed McBride and Dreyfus a day later, just several hours before the meeting was to occur.

Dreyfus pointed out that it was inappropriate for elected town officials (with selected planning board members) to meet with Magellan to discuss redesigning the project while the planning board was in the process of drafting a final findings statement. Resentment against this outside interference (similar to that which arose when Lyon had earlier proposed a moratorium) might even cause votes to be lost for Manley's findings statement. Dreyfus also thought it was foolish politically for Wilton to be perceived, after the platform ran with and elected on, as interested in a deal with a company which had demonstrated little interest in the community's environmental and economic concerns. Moreover, he cautioned that, in legal terms, such a meeting might provide a basis for Magellan to demand a "conditioned approval" from the planning board and/or a claim of "grandfathered vested rights" on grounds of ongoing mitigating alternatives being discussed with the town. The latter claim would be especially dangerous since it might allow Magellan to argue that it was exempt from any eventual moratorium or shopping center cap.

McBride and Dreyfus also both predicted that Wilton would be unable personally to sit through a presentation without participating in dialogue. They insisted that she cancel the meeting for all of the reasons Dreyfus offered. After hearing Dreyfus' concerns and not wishing to be viewed as meddling in the planning board process, Wilton reached Reynolds, already in his car heading south on the Thruway, informing him that she could not meet. Reynolds was furious that his plan was subverted and threatened Wilton that the town would be sued if she refused. In turn, this direct threat angered Wilton who told him emphatically that she would not back down to such tactics.[17]

Nevertheless, at this point, everyone recognized that there were imperative common goals to be accomplished. At the top of the list was the need to give the town ample time and space to devise more restrictive zoning concerning shopping centers, thus to prevent a recurrence of the years of community struggle over Amsterdam Square and Moselle Plaza. In transition policy planning meetings of ACT activists before the new regime took office, a specific moratorium ban on shopping center size was seen as the only realistic way in the existing context to fill this gap. Much to the frustration of Dreyfus, McBride and Turbell, however, Wilton still foresaw allowing a large FoodFeast (without a big-box anchor) to be built on the Heller land. Nevertheless, in her inauguration speech on January 1st, Wilton publicly proclaimed that the moratorium was her immediate top priority.

Activists who had spent years bringing the struggle to its present stage now scrambled desperately to assist Wilton and the Town Board in researching and drawing up a draft "interim zoning" law (and the public notice for public hearings) and in transmitting this immediately to the FCPB for its required input.[18] Such haste was needed to get the moratorium in place before the planning board completed and voted upon Moselle Plaza findings. Fortunately, the latter process was delayed as the findings revision committee required more time than expected to come up with a final draft. However, the planning board anticipated reviewing and voting upon a potential final version at its January 22nd meeting.

At the planning board's January 15th meeting, discussion about the moratorium brought worrisome divisions and temporizing in the new disapproval majority. Ryker, of course, spoke strongly against the proposal, as he had for the past nine years. He claimed that zoning restrictions and moratoria illegally infringed on property owners' rights and that it was improper to rush the law through when no one had proposed such a measure during the past years of developing the Comprehensive Plan.[19] Ryker said that it sent a bad message to potential commercial developers and, in any case, the public hearing had been improperly advertised. On the other side, Green and Hillman were clearly in favor of the measure. Manley, whose taste for confrontation had run its course, equivocated, questioning whether it was too arbitrary in the specific capping figure or in applying mainly to the Heller lot alone.

Myers joined Ryker in absolute opposition, again apparently attempting to resurrect his standing in the "light planning" community. He thought the cap was nonsensical, sent the wrong message to the community and might even cause prejudice to the planning board's findings vote. The law would hold the community hostage to existing businesses and implied that people don't trust the planning board to go through another shopping center review process. If Moselle Plaza had been a smaller project, similar to the existing Ashbury Plaza, he said, it could have been accepted. While Myers' vote on Moselle Plaza seemed decided, he wanted to assure his original supporters that he was not opposed to nor would he obstruct reasonable development. And this might include a mall of 150,000 sq. ft. of commercial space, the size of Ashbury Plaza, 35,000 sq. ft. less than Moselle Plaza. For him, rejection of Moselle Plaza was not meant to set precedents. To activists, it seemed that the "light planning" majority had re-constituted itself and some feared its potentially dangerous implications for the ultimate findings vote on Moselle Plaza. Ironically, it was the planning board's regular attorney Don Torelli, whose firm represented FoodFeast elsewhere, who brought this momentum to a halt by explaining the legal legitimacy of moratoria and by suggesting certain reasonable and minor modifications to the Town Board's proposal to assure its viability in court.[20]

At the same meeting, Maglie recommended to the board that it request the Town Board to reappoint Ryker to another seven-year term based, said Maglie, on Ryker's good service over the years, his solid experience with planning issues, and his knowledge both of the community and the network of involved agencies. "Regulator" members asked for an executive session to discuss the issue privately and the meeting re-convened in the small planning board office. Meanwhile, Ryker sat in the larger meeting room conversing with several members of the audience and threatening personally to harass the planning and town boards in the future if they didn't reappoint him. However, the planning board's discussion in the back room was equally intense. Without

Ryker's participation, but with a proxy vote (illegal by case law) from the absent Davis, the board deadlocked at 3-3 (Maglie and Myers joining Davis in favor). While the board was unable to pass a recommendation to the Town Board, the old ideological alliances had again come together.[21]

At the same time that activists were deeply involved in trying to expedite passage of a moratorium,[22] they also wanted to assure that Ryker would be immediately replaced. Without a Town Board appointment for the new 7-year term of his seat, by law Ryker would remain temporarily as a full voting member of the planning board.[23] Beyond this top priority, CLEAR and ACT also sent a joint letter to Wilton requesting that the new Town Board majority replace Maglie as chair, Harvey & Plonsker as the planning board's regular legal counsel and Busch as planning consultant. A lengthy rationale accompanied each request, with detailed accounts of the negative influences of each on Town land-use planning over the past few years.

At the Town Board meeting of January 18th, Ryker promoted himself for the planning board reappointment on the basis of having served over the years "at great sacrifice of my private life and finances." He claimed that he had assisted large numbers in the community through his terms on the board and had done so "willingly and joyfully." Ryker said that his politics were not a mystery but that "they had never influenced my actions on the planning board." While Devilla and Kraft then voted to reappoint Ryker, on this issue the new Town Board majority held firm and Ryker's position was properly opened for other applications. Interviews for the post and a new appointment, however, would not occur until the Town Board meeting of February 23rd,[24] so Ryker would remain on the board for at least another month.

The Second Findings Decision

Advance word of the drafting committee's new proposed findings statement brought out anti-mall activists in great number at the planning board's January 22nd meeting. When released the weekend before, the document quickly was perceived as a desperate new effort by "light planners" to de-rail the disapproval decision. Not surprisingly, given the politics of the drafting committee majority, what Manley's original draft had taken away, essentially the new version gave back. The old list of unresolved project problems was maintained, though with some weakening alterations. But now, more subtly than in Rattle's and Busch's drafts, instead of absolute SEQRA disapproval, the findings again implied the potential to defer mitigation issues to the site-plan stage of planning board review, with some to be resolved simply on the basis of later permitting agencies' approval. It was the old "conditioned approval," shifting-of-responsibility "backloading" scenario all over again, in a disguised, more superficially critical form. Importantly, this draft also included a crucial mitigation escape clause for Magellan, promising that if Moselle Plaza were downsized, the board would entirely reconsider. Maglie, in consultation with Busch and Rattle, once again sought to impose "light planners'" will on the board regardless of the views of the majority. The struggle for domination continued.

Specifically, Maglie's draft stated that appropriate mitigations could be achieved in the following ways:

> . . . the adverse impacts of the project can be eliminated or at least mitigated satisfactorily by obtaining commitments from the various state, county and town agencies involved in this project (i.e. - DOT, DEC, FCDPW, ATB, etc.) for the design and construction of needed infrastructure improvements and the amendment of the land use policies pertaining to this site.

In turn, the new draft contained a downsizing solution never analyzed nor agreed to by the board.

> If such improvements cannot be obtained, or if they do not adequately mitigate the impacts of the project, the project may be downsized so as to reduce the adverse impacts to an acceptable level.

Finally, the draft provided an open-ended general escape clause for resubmitting the project, apparently drafted by Rattle, thus allowing Magellan to claim continuing vested rights in its proposal even if a moratorium was put into effect:

> As the action as currently submitted is not feasible or practicable under existing conditions, such denial is without prejudice to the Applicant submitting a new application which provides the required mitigation of adverse environmental impacts as identified in the FSEIS and in these Findings, including but not limited to alternative sizes of the proposed development infrastructure improvements servicing the proposed development.

Green opened the board discussion by asking who wrote the draft. Maglie replied that it was a combination of Manley, Busch and Rattle. Though Myers' background and loyalty to Ryker made activists fear his susceptibility to at least the new escape clauses, here he was quick to the attack, stating that he was suspicious about Maglie's claim. Inclusion of the old stormwater analysis from the Amsterdam Square approval findings statement, for example, had nothing to do with the planning board's November motion which was to create a findings statement consistent with a disapproval vote. The revision committee's mandate, he said, was not respected. The new document was 180 degrees different from Manley's original version which the board had approved in principle. "It's an absolute travesty and a good portion I consider to be trash." Furthermore, it undermined the board's legal position. The board should not have to devote time now to wordsmithing a bad document.

Now with reddened face, Maglie claimed that the new version merely tried to put Manley's draft in final form. He asserted that there were no conclusions or findings changed. Myers, who had discussed the process with Manley before the meeting, immediately challenged Maglie. He again stated that the document was changed significantly and that the change was not done by the committee, but by the initiative of Maglie himself and/or Rattle. Manley, he said, was not involved.

Finally, Manley joined in, though in a moderate, understated fashion. He thought Myers' suggestion of returning the document to the committee would be a good idea. He didn't agree with substantial portions of the new draft, especially concerning the weakened sections on stormwater and economics.

Maglie and Ryker defended inclusion of Amsterdam Square findings as simply providing a "user-friendly" document for comparative purposes. Myers, however, got Maglie apparently to admit that Amsterdam Square findings had been summarized and edited for this current draft and denounced such "editorializing for whatever the agenda might be." Myers asserted that the committee had met only twice and that only one person wrote the present draft. Maglie claimed that Rattle received the same copy now shown to the board and gave minimal comments on three realms. Busch added that he thought the board simply wanted a laundry list of findings to choose from, not a final draft. Maglie contended, "We just mis-communicated about this." Myers pointed out that the "laundry-list" approach and comparison with the Amsterdam Square statement were appropriate in the early Fall, when the board was deliberating over whether to approve the project, but undercut the purpose of the document now that the board had voted in principle for disapproval. He cited, for example, inclusion of the 1990 Amsterdam Square finding that there were "no black and white conclusions" in the economics realm as contrary to the views of the majority expressed in the board's November straw vote.

Manley, who by nature disliked this sort of confrontation, now asserted that 95% of the traffic section was okay and 90% for economics, hoping to reduce antagonism between the two ideological poles. He thought that one committee meeting could fix it up. Maglie suggested that Manley, Myers and Green form the new committee. Manley then suggested that Maglie himself be on it and assured everyone that he didn't think there was any intent on the part of Maglie, Rattle or Busch to circumvent the committee. Later in the same evening, recognizing just how far he had diverted from the consensus model of local government, Myers himself praised Gene Busch as an excellent planner who could assist the board better than any outside firm in considering future changes to the commercial zone.[25]

Second Intermission

On February 9th, Magellan's potential resubmission scenario was essentially eliminated when the Town Board held a second public hearing on the moratorium, then quickly approved the measure. Only an attorney for Joe Heller, owner of the contested site, spoke in opposition. The potential window of opportunity for a fresh, downsized resubmission, before a ban on such projects was in place, had now closed. To the great relief of community activists, this nightmare possibility kept alive by planning board opposition to a cap or moratorium had fortunately now dissolved because of the slow pace of revising planning board findings.

On February 23rd, Ryker lost his seat on the planning board. The Town Board interviewed several candidates. A caricature of the old-style political boss he apparently fancied himself to be, Ryker presented his case as before. "I deserve the job," he said. "It should be mine because of all the years of service I've given, at great sacrifice to my own personal life. I know everyone in the county. I can make things happen. From the time I first came to the board, my home phone's never stopped ringing." Despite the approval once again of longtime supporters Kraft and Devilla, the newly-elected Town Board majority replaced Ryker with Mark Tischler, a longtime environmentalist, member of the Town Environmental Conservation Commission and a good friend of Manley's.[26]

Third Findings Decision

The final findings version was brought to the planning board for discussion and a vote on March 11, 1996.[27] In this new version, all of the critical conclusions in Manley's November draft were restored and all of the specific Amsterdam Square findings were removed. Contrary to the January version, this document offered no "without prejudice" escape clauses for a Magellan claim of grandfathered vested rights by which to evade the new interim law's ban on large shopping centers. After only short discussion, the new document came to a vote and passed by a 4-2 margin with Tischler abstaining because he had not been part of the deliberative process. In the end, "light planners" Davis and Maglie were all who remained to dissent. Maglie contended that his refusal to join a consensus for disapproval was because of definitive analyses and conclusions in the section on economics. Exhausted and immensely relieved, activists in the audience spontaneously arose with a loud round of applause. Official findings were filed on March 15th. Moselle Plaza was dead.[28]

PART FIVE

CONCLUSION

FIFTEEN

EPILOGUE: THE POST-DECISION CONTEXT

Ashbury Community Together held its long-anticipated celebration party on May 5, 1996, but not before Magellan filed a suit in the state Supreme Court in Regent Park against the Ashbury Town Planning Board three weeks earlier claiming various violations of the SEQRA statute and regulations. The stated grounds for the suit appeared frivolous since the official record of planning board deliberations was a lengthy and rationally-based, factual analysis which satisfied the "hard look" standard. Yet the new Town Board majority did not look forward to a prolonged judicial battle and significant attorney's fees as a preoccupation of its first year in office.[1] At the same time, Magellan still owed $17,400 to the escrow account established to cover the fees of Rattle, Busch, Napoleon and Marvell and litigation by the Town appeared to be necessary to force Magellan's adherence to its contractual obligation. In the end, a deal was struck in early June whereby the Town made no further claims against Magellan and the latter withdrew its suit.[2] Town taxpayers were forced to cover the fees of professional experts, most of whom had so opposed the efforts of grassroots community groups to gain a fair SEQRA hearing.

Meanwhile, Magellan tried a new strategy. In April 1996, the developer submitted an application to the adjacent town of Acton for a second version of Moselle Plaza (including a large FoodFeast and a still publicly-unacknowledged Wal-Mart[3]), now proposed for the site on Rte. 354, one mile east of the Heller property, just across the border from Ashbury.[4]

By this time, local neighbors of the new project site and other interested Acton residents had begun monitoring the first exploratory paperwork submitted by Magellan to the planning board office and several months earlier had formed a new activist organization of their own. While meeting with Ashbury activists and learning lessons from the Ashbury experience, the Acton group (ACCORD) organized its own publicity campaigns, fundraising and large turnouts at Acton Town Board and planning board public meetings when Magellan's project was on the agenda.

By the time of the public scoping hearing on November 14, 1996, the Acton group had organized a sophisticated presentation of important issues to be investigated by an EIS--nearly identical with those in the Ashbury case, but concerning a site whose stormwater, wetland and aquifer problems were even greater than those of the original Heller plot and where the substantial traffic increase generated by a megamall would totally disrupt local residents. After statements by Joshua Wright, Maynard Smith, an expert hydrogeology engineer, other experts, activists and other citizens, and with the encouragement of the planning board's planner and hydrogeological consultant, the Acton planning board voted to accept most of the recommended scoping agenda presented by activists and their experts alike. Magellan's representatives were stunned and activists delighted by an EIS agenda much more stringent than that imposed in Ashbury and, because of the site's proximity to the Heller lots, covering much of the same environmental and economic conditions.

Though Jankoff assured the public and the Acton planning board that Magellan would return with the required draft EIS within six weeks, succeeding months without action made Magellan's failed promise increasingly conspicuous. Despite regular assurances that studies would be forthcoming, by early summer 1997 even Acton town officials favoring Magellan's project admitted that it was dead. Activists and their experts were fully convinced that the required EIS agenda and the activated community presence which promised to hold Magellan and the planning board to its letter were too rigorous for Magellan to proceed. Finally, on January 22, 1998, Magellan's Acton proposal was formally withdrawn.[5]

In Ashbury, the new Town Board majority, supported and encouraged by anti-megamall activists, proceeded in early 1996 toward re-zoning the commercial zone to prevent yet further megamall proposals which the community had clearly disapproved. Following passage of a moratorium prohibiting new free-standing stores of more than 45,000 sq. ft. in February 1996, a special "B-2 [commercial zone] Rezoning Committee" was appointed to research and recommend appropriate changes in that district. The committee, chaired by Mark Lyon, had a strong mandate to ban large-scale commercial development from the east side of the Thruway based on the victorious struggle against Moselle Plaza, the electoral victory and a March 1996 public forum where over 100 participants from various perspectives apparently shared this consensual goal. But committee deliberations dragged on for months and did not encourage public participation since meetings were largely unannounced. More surprisingly, under Lyon's influence, rezoning plans even seemed directed toward intense commercial development, albeit with individual buildings smaller in scale, for that "gateway" area of town.[6]

Through the long anti-Magellan struggle, having effectively claimed "community trusteeship" and even "naming" of the town landscape east of the Thruway (as the "gateway to Ashbury"),[7] activists from CLEAR and ACT strongly appealed for scenarios consistent with the March community meeting and the adverse environmental and economic constraints demonstrated in the Moselle Plaza findings statement. In February 1997, for example, McBride submitted lengthy economic impact analyses, similar to and based upon those developed against the Moselle Plaza project, which once again showed that the local retail market was insufficient for sizeable new retail facilities to be built without creating urban blight.[8] Meanwhile, the ADC adamantly opposed any retail store cap of less than 65,000 sq. ft.[9] The Town Board ultimately endorsed a draft plan with the bulk of B-2 Committee recommendations-- including those for the gateway area.

Despite a GEIS scoping session in September 1997 for the new rezoning scheme, however, by mid-2002, the Draft GEIS itself was still not completed. After a series of temporary moratoria without progress on long-range rezoning, the Board feared that such ad hoc interim measures might be vulnerable to court challenge and the prior zoning status restored. A makeshift rezoning law in early 1999 thus banned any separate retail stores over 35,000 sq. ft. in the gateway district.[10] As a long-range legacy of the community struggle against Moselle Plaza, the GEIS scope and proposed rezoning signified greater community caution, but only the continuing longer-range political struggle would decide whether or not the revised commercial zone east of the Thruway would reflect a partial retreat back to a "light planning" orientation.

Among major actors in the Moselle Plaza struggle, McBride and Dreyfus continued to monitor the Town Board's and planning board's reviews of other development projects[11] and assisted the Acton group in its efforts. Turbell, who had joined local Congressman Francis Grano as an aide in his Regent Park office, also continued to assist efforts in Ashbury, Acton and elsewhere in the region to protect the local environment. Jan Winfield maintained leadership of ACT while that organization offered fundraising and other help to the Acton group and began shifting concern to other land-use issues in Ashbury. Wright became Town Engineer after the new Town Board majority took office and eventually sat regularly as a consultant in town planning board meetings as well, though Busch and the firm of Harvey & Plonsker remained as regular planning board consultants.

On the planning board, Manley became the new chair and Green the vice-chair in 1996. With the resignation of new member Tischler in mid-1997, the "regulator" majority board was clearly still in a tenuous position. Manley and Myers both posed their candidacies for the Town Board in September 1997, each publicly taking responsibility for authoring the Moselle Plaza findings statement. In the Republican caucus of mid-September, Myers, whose Town Board candidate nomination was supported by Ryker and Enrico, barely lost to the anti-Ryker incumbent Town Clerk. Kraft also won re-nomination. For Supervisor, Republicans nominated a local realtor who was the only non-FoodFeast employee publicly supportive of Moselle Plaza at the January 1995 public hearing. Within days of the party caucus at which his domineering style was openly challenged, Ryker resigned from the party chair position[12], claiming that it was time to move on because of bad health and his job as rock band road manager.[13] Manley won the Democratic nomination for one of the Town Board positions without opposition. Devilla decided to retire from the board, but urged her own candidate in her place.[14]

Supervisor Wilton announced her decision to run for a second term in August. Following her own success and victories by Kraft and the anti-Ryker Republican in November 1997, another "regulator" was appointed to the planning board, thereby temporarily prolonging a majority of those with that orientation. At the end of 1998, two new planning board appointments were required. Manley's term had expired and Maglie resigned in late 1998 because of a job transfer to Albany.[15] While Manley was eventually given a new term, the Town Board delayed filling Maglie's remaining one-year post with Ina Turbell until late April 1999 because of Red Davis' threat to resign if this were done.[16] For other reasons, by January 2000, Manley and Myers had resigned as well.

By mid-Summer 1999, Edna Devilla announced her own run for Supervisor despite Wilton's intention to run for a third term, thus verifying Devilla's long-rumored ambition for the job. While defeated in the Democratic caucus, Devilla gladly accepted the Republican nomination in late August, thus confirming her continued identification with the "old boy/girl" "light planning" urban regime. Indeed, Devilla joined Republican nominees for Town Board in calling for Ashbury to return "to the way it was years ago."[17] In November 1999, she barely defeated Wilton's try for a third term. (Two years later, Devilla was soundly defeated by a previous anti-megamall activist, a founding member of CLEAR and ACT, while two more opponents of Moselle Plaza, including Bob Manley, also joined him, Jane Pelletier and another Democrat on the five-person Town Board.)

From 1995 on, Wilton had received strong support from ACT activists, but only after considerable pressure did she back off from her initial encouragement of an expanded FoodFeast (65,000 sq. ft.) standing alone at the Heller site. Thereafter, Wilton's persistent efforts as Supervisor to convince FoodFeast to remain at its existing location, combined with the successful effort of Acton residents to block Magellan's new project in that town, apparently bore fruit. By mid-1997, contrary to its many past assertions during the megamall controversy, FoodFeast announced that it now found that it was feasible to expand on site if arrangements could be made with the plaza owner and existing tenants. In September 1998, FoodFeast presented these formal expansion plans to the Town planning board and within a few months these plans were approved. Nevertheless, by mid-2000, Magellan Construction reappeared in Acton to seek approval for a mammoth FoodFeast store (81,000 sq. ft.) at the same site where its 1996 Wal-Mart/FoodFeast megamall had been defeated.[18] In early 2002, despite significant community opposition and the same underlying environmental issues as in 1996, the Acton ZBA approved a SEQRA negative declaration for the project, a decision quickly challenged in court.

For many months, during the early period of Wilton's administration, Ina Turbell had coordinated efforts to devise an alternative development plan for the Heller site consistent with the "gateway" goals of the March 1996 community meeting. Meeting with a number of interested local citizens and with Heller himself, she was encouraged to believe that Heller would finally understand and accept community values and thus endorse a proposal of appropriate scale and purpose. However, Heller was increasingly impatient with the Town's inability to finalize rezoning for the area and with the lack of Town support in helping to find potential development investors. By June 1998, apparently with Wilton's encouragement, Heller made tentative arrangements to sell a development option to Arnold Forte, a son of LeRoy Forte, one of the founders of Magellan Construction's parent company, Crotty & Forte. Arnold Forte himself had been a partner in Magellan Construction and at least 30 other limited liability corporations over the past decade with Deke Reynolds and others. Though suspicious of Arnold Forte initially because of his involvement with Magellan, Wilton negotiated in detail with him regarding a payment-in-lieu-of-taxes arrangement for a local medical center he was also building in town. Gradually, she came to trust his intentions and to believe his account that he had no knowledge of the Moselle Plaza proposal or community struggle and that in fact he and the other partners of Magellan Construction had completely broken with Reynolds in the Fall of 1997. She was pleased with the appearance of his new medical center and the terms of the IDA payments-in-lieu-of-taxes arrangement she had negotiated.[19] Despite his disclaimers, activists found extensive evidence in the Albany press and Albany County courthouse records to prove that Arnold Forte had misled Wilton and others and that he and Deke Reynolds were still involved together in current projects. They were quite critical of Wilton's collaboration after the long Moselle Plaza struggle.

The continued intervention of well-funded Albany developers in Ashbury, at least partially welcomed by town officials, as well as the insider politics and mixed outcome of commercial rezoning, consistently demonstrated to activists the great power of outside economic forces and their ideological compatibility with influential local collaborators to continually shape the political economy and ecology of this small town. The Moselle Plaza battle was simply one skirmish in an inevitably prolonged political evolution.

Meanwhile, the march of Wal-Mart through New York continued, despite community victories against it in Ashbury, Acton, East Aurora, Ithaca, Lake Placid, and elsewhere. While Sprawl-Buster Al Norman reported some 85 communities across the country by April 1999 as having won victories against mega-store projects,[20] in Reading County the newest and 34th Wal-Mart in New York state was built (including a large supermarket) directly across from a FoodFeast in the Spring of 1999 after town officials succeeded in defeating a Medford suit, on SEQRA grounds, to prevent it. In August 2002, the regional chain providing Ashbury for years with a smaller discount department store folded under market pressure and Ashbury activists braced against a likely new local siege by Wal-Mart.

SIXTEEN THEORIES OF URBAN REGIMES AND PARTICIPATORY DEMOCRACY

A. Grassroots Influence in Local Environmental Planning and Development Politics

Whatever past sociological distinctions between ideal types of rural small-town and urban communities, the persistence of traditional affective bonds and invention of new "communitarian" identities and values in urban areas, the decline of farming populations, the reciprocal population flow between urban and rural locales, and the hegemony of urban-based national mass media can by now be acknowledged as significantly reducing the relevance of past dichotomies.[1] In the present case study, focus on a specific small community much composed of and heavily influenced by second- and third-generation immigrant families, ex-students and faculty of a state university and refugees from the New York City metropolitan area from the 1960s onward adds great weight to arguing against the analytical significance of difference, aside from mere scale, between urban and small-town contexts. Thus, this section of the theoretical discussion presents important themes from the rich literature on urban political economy and urban planning to help contextualize our small town Ashbury case study from upstate New York. Specifically, we focus on the centrality of land-use policy in determining whatever autonomy exists in local regimes, on the major forces contending for power and possible change in local arenas, and on major obstacles to grassroots participation in the exercise of power.

Centrality of Land-Use Policy

As Paul Peterson, Clarence Stone and many others have convincingly argued, because of their minute scale within national and international economies and their constitutional confinement within larger political frameworks of state and national governments, local governments--even at the level of major cities--are inevitably severely limited in jurisdiction.[2] To make their locales satisfactory to existing residents and business and enticing to outsiders, local regimes must strive, above all, to maintain adequate economic opportunities and desirable living conditions. Whether large metropolitan centers, commuter suburbs or rural small towns, these imperatives critically affect, in a land of great geographical mobility, whether people come or stay.

In the present capitalist order, to maintain or expand the economy requires adequate incentives for local and outside capital to invest and remain within the community. Whether concerning individual homeowners' chief investment (the real estate value of their own homes) or business investors' sense of opportunity for financial gain, a climate of economic stability and potential economic improvement is typically the crucial criterion. Thus, assuring adequate employment, opportunities for investment initiative, adequate housing and prevention of eroding quality through higher taxes or deteriorating race relations, environmental and other contexts become typical measures for objectively assessing the performance of any local regime. At the same time, to carry out its functions, however defined, a local government requires adequate revenue, typically about 50% from <u>local</u> sources,[3] the most important of which is typically the local property tax. For all of these reasons, agreed upon in the literature of local political economy and urban planning, "urban politics is above all the politics of land use, and it is easy to see why. Land is the factor of production over which cities [and small towns] exercise the greatest control."[4]

Major Participants in Local Politics and the Spectrum of Policy Priorities

Upon examining specific local case studies, most American community power and urban planning theorists assert that, despite structural boundaries imposed generically by the broader economy and by state and federal governments, significant differences in local political regimes can and do exist and that policy outcomes in the land-use realm will reflect such differences. While "caretaker" ("status quo") vs. "activist" ("entrepreneurial") emphases are one form of regime distinction, more significant in analyzing the potential for participatory planning is the dichotomy (as at the national level) between policymakers prioritizing economic growth or development vs. those prioritizing economic, political and social redistribution, a range from autocratic to progressive populist in nature. Most current American theorists emphasize political arrangements <u>within</u> the local political context which establish a specific balance of power and a corresponding balance of policy definition. Rejecting the old "elite" vs. "pluralist" dichotomy in theories of urban politics, Clarence Stone uses a "regime paradigm" to focus on the informal supra-government prevailing coalition in local governance which must interpret the nature and extent of outside economic and political forces, balance these against locally-articulated interests and accomplish successful implementation of the policy choices made.[5]

Stone argues that while "land-use development" is the central concern of local regimes, "development" must be understood by an expansive definition. As Stone states, "'[D]evelopment policy' might more strictly be termed 'redevelopment policy,'" since "policy makers generally do not start with a clean slate on land use" and their efforts are more a matter of "reshaping the local community than simply . . . shaping it."[6] As Meredith Ramsay suggests, "Economic development acts like a giant asphalt paving machine that tears up the old road in the process of building the new."[7] Furthermore, land has a qualitative use value beyond its "highest and best use" as commercially defined for investment purposes. Thus, residents' identity with friendly, familiar and secure community character, a sense of neighborhood solidarity, a feeling of connectedness with nature or pride in legacies of historical significance may well conflict with a commercial developer's fixation on the proximity of a plot to major transport and utilities infrastructure or sizeable retail markets. In the broader sense of "development," policies which enhance the latter uses ("exchange value") may deplete or "undevelop" the "quality of life" use values of the former sort.

Focusing on this broader potential urban "development" agenda forces greater attention on and thus a better assessment of the culture and dynamics within each community which produce the particular governing coalition, its policies and the possibility of change. It is this focus which has motivated a great variety of local political economy case studies in the past several decades.

As Stone suggests, from the mid-80s on, the urban regime paradigm, especially, has pointed to "value choices that are implicit in efforts to shape policy by one set of arrangements rather than another. Struggle is therefore very much a part of the development picture they paint."[8] And, normatively, the claim that "politics matters is not the final point in [our] argument. Rather, it is the first step in recognizing a responsibility--a responsibility to identify and work for good political practice."[9]

Given the centrality of land-use policy for local government, it is not surprising that Molotch and Logan would conclude that:

> The people who use their time and money to participate in local affairs are the ones who--in vast disproportion to their representation in the population--have the most to gain or lose in land-use decisions. Local business people are the major participants in urban politics, particularly business people in property investing, development, and real estate financing.[10]

Such social forces are recognized everywhere as major direct actors in urban regimes, often enough in the dominant position suggested by Molotch and Logan.[11] As Berry et al. suggest, "Any developer or businessman with a credible and significant proposal can gain immediate attention from local government."[12] Adds Babcock with more specificity, "[f]or the non-residential builder, the discussion with the municipality usually starts from the premise that he is wanted."[13] Nevertheless, as abundant studies especially over the past decade have demonstrated, significant variations in governing coalitions do exist and these variations are rooted in both divisions within the business community and in the presence of various other local social forces demanding attention and particular redistributive or social equity policies.

In Dallas, Stephen Elkin discovered an urban regime at all levels in which a "pure" "entrepreneurial" political economy evolved to a "complex" model from the late 1930s to the present, while both strongly linked city politics around the concerns of business for growth.[14] Under the original arrangement, a Citizens Charter Administration, created and supported by Dallas business leaders, recruited as political candidates individuals from the business community itself or sympathetic to it who would in turn make appropriate growth-friendly official appointments to the city manager post and other significant positions. The Dallas business elite thus conversed about policy with "officials who had no independent political base from which to dissent,"[15] thereby achieving the desired fiscal restraint, aggressive annexation and infrastructure expansion for its growth agenda. "Developers had little need to attempt to corrupt officials" since they in fact "found that public officials were receptive to whatever pace of development they could sustain."[16] Eventually, because of barriers to new boundary expansion, zoning changes, gentrification and new infrastructure costs, pro-growth activity increasingly resulted in "direct, tangible and significant costs to substantial portions of the local citizenry."[17] Because of a more diversified, complex and thus fragmented business community since the mid-70s, the pro-business agenda has become more conflicted and complex, resulting in a new mediator role, though still business-friendly, for public officials, thus a relationship "more like a coalition than like [an] alliance."[18] In short, primarily because of changes within the business community itself and the literal bounds of the polity, the urban regime of Dallas shifted--in terms of the land-use planning spectrum--from a place explicitly dominated by business interests to a somewhat more regulatory orientation, though again with business interests first.

Examining development policy in Kansas City, Dayton, Atlanta, Los Angeles and elsewhere, Susan Clarke discovered variations from submission to business pressures to resisting regimes which forced restrictive terms of private investment on those in the business community.[19] Along with structural constraints of outside economic and political frameworks, Clarke emphasized the need of regimes to sustain their own multi-class political legitimacy, their own institutional long-range resource capacity, and their own long-range power, through imposing non-market redistributive conditions or "linkage policies" on developers. Ultimately, she concluded that it is these institutional concerns, in specific local contexts of sufficiently-organized and articulate clienteles, which caused local officials to diverge sometimes from business-dominated development policy.

John Mollenkopf and Richard DeLeon described the transition from the pro-growth regime of San Francisco Mayor Alioto to the mixed, partially redistributive regimes of George Mascone and his successors from 1975 onward.[20] Similarly, Barbara Ferman provided ample evidence of successful redistributive challenges to growth machines in Chicago and Pittsburgh in the late 70s and 1980s.[21] Along the same line, in 1991, H.V. Savitch and J.C. Thomas collected a series of studies of 13 large American cities which seemed to demonstrate, in all but one case, a splintering of governing coalitions into "hyperpluralist" systems.[22]

In rural Maryland, Meredith Ramsay even discovered at this late date "transitional" community regimes which still evaded, at least temporarily, the apparent imperatives of economic development because of "subsistence economies" and a strong, more traditionalist, cultural context which valued established social and economic relations more than potential materialist gains.[23]

A different research perspective was employed by Elizabeth Howe. Her extensive 1982 survey of ethics in city planning was based on personal interviews with 19 urban planners each in Maryland, New York, Tennessee and Texas and 20 in California. Of the total, two-thirds worked in local agencies. While denying that the sample was representative of all planners, in part because "each state seems to have had a particular 'culture of planning,'"[24] the diversity which Howe described in this spectrum of local planning cultures itself complemented the findings in studies on urban regimes. "Planning," she said:

> was most accepted and, apparently, most powerful in northern California. . . . California also seemed to be characterized by a fairly pluralistic, open, participatory style of politics. . . .
>
> At the other extreme were Texas and Tennessee. . . . The day-to-day politics of planning in most places was characterized by a development-oriented, old-boy network style of politics . . . .

In New York City, because of large agency size, planning was "extremely bureaucratic" and "[t]here was a general sense that the politics was not only hardball but sometimes corrupt. Upstate, in smaller communities and cities, acceptance of planning seemed mixed."[25] It was this variety of political contexts, as with the studies of internal dynamics of urban regimes, which allowed Howe to find various degrees of business dominance in planning and the significantly different versions of land-use development policy which followed. Detailed accounts by "equity planners" themselves, with experience over the past three decades from Jersey City and Hartford to Denver, Portland and San Diego among others, also testified to the potential for urban governing coalitions to differ from the more common growth machine.[26]

Urban politics analysts, planning theorists and equity planners therefore suggest a spectrum of urban development policy and policymaking considerably more complex and variegated than that proposed by emphasizing external economic and political structural constraints.

Participatory Urban Reforms

For proponents of regimes with less dominant business orientation and stronger social equity values (including environmental sensitivity in land use), the obvious alternative to merely enlightening the governing elite was to expand or take over the governing regime itself. Such efforts typically involved broadening electoral participation, using local referenda, forming activist party organizations and organizing communities along neighborhood or single-issue lines, direct action, radical advocacy planning from within the regime, and opening formal space for public participation through mandatory hearings and litigation--all of which received substantial impetus through the larger forces encouraging and forcing more democratic political culture generally in the United States in the 60s, 70s and 80s.

One of the best detailed local case-study analyses of such efforts, by Richard DeLeon, concerns progressive politics in San Francisco from 1975 on, the defeat of a pro-growth regime and the subsequent evolution of what he defines as an "antiregime." The latter, at the time of his 1991 account,[27] had opened the political door to new social forces, was proficient in preventing unwanted development and in accomplishing certain redistributive goals, though had not yet succeeded in creating a solid social coalition and coherent integrated redistributive program to move on with from its primarily negative agenda. Thus, it had not yet assured its own longevity. Nevertheless, DeLeon suggests that San Francisco was the most progressive large American city in recent years. Its agenda "emphasizes human development rather than physical development, the use value of the city's built environment rather than its exchange value, the needs of local residents and communities rather than those of developers and outside investors."[28] It is a city that "imposes as many limits on capital as capital imposes on it,"[29] with a regime that "rejects money and materialism as the taproot of urban meaning."[30] The antiregime's primary instrument of power is "local government control over land use and development,"[31] though this instrument was used only because of citizen intervention, not because of city hall.[32] Yet it was still in a transitional phase, what Manuel Castells called a "wild city,"[33] where the antiregime coalition (of which the "slow growth movement" was a key component) remained in a hyperpluralist, parochial, defensive mode--attacking "the localized symptoms of social decay," such as sprawl, high rises, traffic congestion and displacement, but in terms of local enclave resistance rather than a more effective coordinated trans-enclave transformative program.

Another of the best recent works exploring such issues, Barbara Ferman's study of the established and reform urban regimes of Pittsburgh and Chicago,[34] presented alternative explanations for movement of each toward greater popular inclusiveness, with progress toward non-economic social equity goals of urban revitalization as a result. In brief, neighborhood-based organizations in Pittsburgh were recognized as legitimate by and worked with business and politician regime leaders, while in Chicago such non-business groups were excluded from meaningful roles until the death of Mayor Daley, the breakdown of his successor machine governments, and the rise of an alternative coalition led by Harold Washington in 1983. Essentially, according to Ferman, there are various arenas which comprise local political systems. Which particular social forces dominate the urban regime profoundly affects which arena will be most active. In Pittsburgh, a "civic" arena ("private, nonprofit institutions that distribute resources on a collective basis and foster a cooperative culture") was predominant once financier Richard King Mellon stepped in to actively pressure the government of Mayor Lawrence. In Chicago, until the election of Washington, the predominant "electoral" arena, with resource-distributing partisan institutions, created a highly fragmented and competitive context.[35] With access by non-elite interests, such as working-class neighborhoods and racial minorities, to the decisive political arena in Pittsburgh, but not in Chicago, redistributative housing, for example, prospered in the former but not in the latter. Pittsburgh's priority "civic" arena, said Ferman, encouraged a more participatory political culture. To the extent that neighborhood-based challenges to the growth machine can transcend narrow "reactive" preoccupations (sometimes shielding disguised racism), a potential emerges for more progressive local policy generally.

Pierre Clavel's *The Progressive City*,[36] in turn, found that the failures of market mechanisms to provide basic subsistence for large numbers and to meet grassroots participatory expectations caused new urban progressive regimes in Hartford, Cleveland, Berkeley, Santa Monica and Burlington (Vermont) to take a more cautious view of property rights by direct or shared control of utilities and public developments, by progressive redistributive fees and tax structures, or by rent control and land-development control regulations. They encouraged community-based collectives, as in the realms of housing, social services and food production and distribution. They also encouraged and helped to organize mechanisms for active citizen participation in local policy-making. In the course of mobilizing large numbers to gain and maintain power, progressives depended upon an alternative "structure of thought" demanding new priorities and critiquing the public biases and agendas of the elite- and growth-oriented prior regime. In this evolution, progressive planners, professional and otherwise, were a crucial component.

DeLeon, Ferman, Clavel and many others concerned with the democratizing of urban regimes have described the new urban social movements from the 60s to the present as major contributing factors. Even those, such as Castells, predisposed to emphasizing strong structuralist definitions of urban politics, were impressed enough by the strength and persistence of such movements to grant that urban terrain can be a significant location for currentday transformative politics not based on class.[37] As Fainstein and Hirst state, specific urban-based social movements in the late 60s especially erupted over issues around race and ethnicity, social services client status and neighborhood intrusions by developers and public bureaucracies.[38] While such movements eventually shifted from militant direct action to service delivery, experience with community solidarity and leadership "left an enduring legacy of community activism that would develop into a national neighborhood movement."[39]

From the 70s to the present, typical new urban social movements included community-wide progressive coalitions (as in Santa Monica and Burlington, Vermont), life-style community groups (as in San Francisco), ethnic-based community organizations (as the San Antonio group, Communities Organized for Public Service) and neighborhood homeowner groups, usually middle-class and often defensively exclusivist and conservative in orientation.[40] Despite excessive focus on single issues, sometimes narrow enclave orientations and problems in sustaining mobilization, such movements everywhere pressured for greater participation in local decision-making, won many important battles over land redevelopment policy and often helped to expand or change the nature of specific urban regimes.

Concerning neighborhood-based activist movements specifically, one of their ardent proponents in the late 60s, Milton Kotler, proclaimed: "[T]erritoriality is not only an efficient political tactic: it is a natural impulse of threatened people. Thus, reason and nature move the poor toward territorial control as a lever of political change for greater justice."[41] In more positive terms, from personal experience in the Adams-Morgan district of Washington, D.C. and familiarity with numerous examples across the country, David Morris and Karl Hess wrote in 1975 that:

> the neighborhood, at root, then, can be said to represent the way people naturally live together. It does not represent a political theory. It represents a human reality. . . . [I]n a new birth and building of neighborhood life, all human activity could be brought back together so that work, play, love, life, politics, science, and art could be shared experience by people sharing a space, sharing agreements as to how

to live together, and mutually aiding one another to enjoy the fullest, ripest existence as human beings in a humane setting.[42]

By now, examples of such community activity abound, most dramatically in accounts such as that of Peter Medoff and Holly Sklar in their 1994 book on the community-based and community-controlled redevelopment of the Dudley Street neighborhood in Boston.[43]

John Forester's *Planning in the Face of Power* was specifically written "about planning for people in a precariously democratic but strongly capitalistic society,"[44] focusing on "just what public-serving practitioners can do . . . in practice, in an organizationally messy world of political inequality and economic exploitation . . . ."[45] Inevitably, he says, because of their knowledge and position in land-use policy-making, professional planners above all organize attention. Their choices of what information to emphasize, how to state it and to whom are the core of planners' power. For Forester, planning analysts' responsibility is "to work toward a political democratization of daily communications,"[46] "to anticipate and counteract alterable, misleading, and disabling claims and learn to nurture well-informed, genuinely democratic politics and discourse instead."[47] "Critical" or "progressive" planners can actively inform and encourage citizens groups, ordinarily disadvantaged in the process and thereby assure more equitable, genuinely democratic project reviews and policy decisions.

Such an orientation and practice, advocated by Forester and numerous other theorists,[48] have been demonstrated as important contributions to and products of progressive urban regimes. Krumholz and Clavel report that the "equity planners" they interviewed were "not simply attached to their work, but hooked, driven, possessed by an unusually high level of excitement . . ." and "seemed to be convinced that the struggle for a more open, egalitarian society offered them . . . the hope of a better life for others."[49] They "worked often and intimately with grassroots organizations and public bureaucracies and dealt with the media as an important portion of the planners' attempt to educate and build political support."[50] All were involved in extensive coalition-building efforts. Though politicians rarely articulated equity planning objectives, say the authors, urban planners have sufficient administrative discretion and freedom to define activist roles needed for such efforts. Persistence was an essential quality. Not simply advocating for the disadvantaged, their interviewed planners attempted to translate community concerns and to convert business executives themselves behind their equity objectives. Though such planners were still a minority in the field, Krumholz and Clavel were convinced that equity planning could realistically be placed "more squarely at the center of professional and city policy work."[51]

B. Participatory Politics As A Social Ideal

While "democracy" ordinarily connotes "rule by the people," thus suggesting a "participatory" form of governance, since the American revolutionary era, the political elite in this country has sought to emphasize participation mainly for itself, with only a representative system, at best, for all others. Indeed, for conservative and liberal elites both, the term "democratic" had a fearful radical connotation in the 1780s and 1790s, as large numbers at the grassroots intensified demands for participatory self-rule in the wake of revolutionary ideals and sacrifices from the struggle against Britain. The waves of localist "anarchic" participatory political contexts, forces and demands throughout the new states, most dramatically in the Shays' and Whiskey Rebellions, seemed to elites to embody that "mob rule" which writers of the Constitution and even many Anti-Federalist leaders identified pejoratively with "democracy."[52] The term became more "acceptable" to most elites as it became more constrained in practical content, as more stable national and state regimes gradually evolved, while enfranchising previously-excluded white male workers, women, racial minorities and youth.

While grassroots movements, such as the Dorr War in Rhode Island and the Callico Rebellion in New York in the 1840s, Populists in the 1890s and the IWW and radical farmers in the early 20th century took up the late 18th century grassroots claim that participatory politics, not voting rights alone, were the essence of democracy, establishment political theorists increasingly focused on and glorified the more restricted sense of stable "democracy" in modern, industrialized mass political society. Joseph Schumpeter, Robert Dahl and a host of political scientists described empirical evidence of voter "ignorance" and "apathy," proclaiming a basic (and appropriate) division between relatively passive masses and active, only partially-accountable but also non-conspiratorial "professional citizen" elites.[53] From this perspective, when significant numbers of people of color, women and youth became highly vocal and politically active in the 1960s and 70s, Harvard political scientist Samuel Huntington proclaimed that American democracy could not hold together in the face of such energized grassroots elements.[54]

Political scientists and sociologists have focused in recent years on the demise of political parties and the nature and power of various "linkage" replacements--from interest groups and public opinion polling to internet groups and traditional social movements--as means by which the vast majority of the population indirectly can bring its concerns and perspectives to the policy-making process. Such studies, like the "pluralist" analyses of Dahl and others earlier, also sought to identify new specialized "behavioral" elites (or "counter-elites"), based on entrepreneurial or participatory activism rather than ascriptive criteria of class and status.[55] Yet such "linkage" mechanisms, like more passive periodic voting opportunities, are not the same as active grassroots participation. Whatever their instrumental political value (including sometimes accurately reflecting actual grassroots sentiment[56]) at particular moments of political evolution, at the least they fail to meet the normative concerns of "participatory democratic" theorists.

Participatory Democracy Theorists

Strongly activist social movements of the 1960s and 70s for civil rights, for black power, for empowerment of the poor, for the defense and vitalization of neighborhood communities, for cooperative workplaces, for women's and gay liberation, for student power, against the war and to protect the environment most dramatically revived demands for the "participatory" dimension of democracy.[57] Alongside grassroots activists' demands for "participatory democracy" gradually emerged to the present a body of theoretical works, often seeking insight from historical theoretical and practical traditions of anarchism, socialism, alternative forms of liberal democracy (as far back as Greek and Roman times) and non-Western indigenous cultures, but also gaining sophistication from contemporary empirical analysis[58] and, in many cases, from feminist, ecologist and post-modernist theory. While all sharing a critique of recent elitist democratic perspectives of Schumpeter and others, participatory theorists are found on a wide spectrum of their own. While some wish simply a more energized and diversified grassroots input--beyond mere voting--into existing representative structures, others envision a radically transformed society based on decentralized though interrelated local units of participatory democracy within every realm--economic, social, cultural, as well as the traditionally political.

Discussion in the following section concerns only theorists in this "participatory democrat" spectrum, since democracy theorists of representative government from the elitist "realist" camp have already conceptually marginalized the positive significance of participatory phenomena.[59] Specifically, at this point, we discuss only "moderate" theorists from the participatory democrat spectrum, since participatory aspects of environmental impact assessment are the type of reform commonly addressed by such writers. However, the perspectives of participatory democracy theorists of "radical reformist" (Barber, Mouffe) and "strong radical" (Pateman, Plumwood) tendencies will be discussed in the concluding chapter, as we bring the insight of the Ashbury case-study analysis to assess strengths and weaknesses of "moderate" participatory democracy theory generally.

The latter perspective offers specific reforms designed to foster greater grassroots political involvement and influence, while tempering expectations of a drastic qualitative change in American political society as a result. We chose the ideas of four of these "moderate" theorists-- Michael Walzer, James Fishkin, David Mathews and Harry Boyte--to extract crucial criteria for the meaning of participatory democracy as it has emerged from such writing in these past several decades.[60] A brief summary of major themes from each of these four is followed by short descriptions of several actual participatory democratic experiments in the contemporary United States, again to help clarify important elements in the model of moderate participatory democracy.

Moderate Participatory Democracy Theorists

With his "critical associationalism," Michael Walzer has become a spokesman for "communitarian civil society" from a less traditionalist perspective.[61] While long a staple of democratic theory, the notion of "civil society" was perhaps best known as described and analyzed in de Tocqueville's account from the 1830s.[62] The significance of "civil society" as the protector and nurturer of participatory values in the face of more distant and authoritarian national regimes was revived most recently with the surge of dissident movements in east and central Europe in the 1970s and 80s, contributing to the collapse of Communist governments throughout the region. In Walzer's words, "civil society" refers to "the space of uncoerced human association and also the set of relational networks--formed for the sake of family, faith, interest and ideology--that fill this space."[63] While "civil society" has long been a feature of Western politics, more recent cultural trends of greater work hours, time devoted to television and the internet, and greater attention to private consumerism have led to an atrophy of grassroots associational networks and thus a decline in the production and reproduction of civility in itself.

Walzer advocates more frequent community involvement to counteract the prevalent atomization and privatization which leave citizens unaware of or insensitive to needs and values beyond their own, and ineffective and vulnerable even in defending their self-interests. To enhance the vitality of mutual networks and thus the social capital of a nation, according to Walzer, requires decentralization of the state to allow for more citizen participation, along with more communal or cooperative economic units alongside private entities in the market to allow for similar opportunities in that realm. However, rather than focusing exclusively on greater grassroots political engagement or on producer control of the economy, Walzer proposes enhanced civil society (and thus social capital) overall, but with:

> no singularity of its own. The phrase "social being" describes men and women who are citizens, producers, consumers, members of the nation and much else besides--and none of these by nature or because it is the best thing to be. The associational life of civil society is the actual

> ground where all versions of the good are worked out and tested . . .
> and proven to be [each on its own] partial, incomplete, ultimately
> unsatisfying.[64]

It is associational life where the "civility" learned is "independent and active" rather than the deferential entrapment most men and women have experienced in subordinate relationships.[65] Thus, the crucial test of civil society is "its capacity to produce citizens whose interests, at least sometimes, reach further than themselves and their comrades, who look after the political community that fosters and protects associational networks."[66]

James Fishkin offers a different, but equally modest and consciously non-"utopian," participatory approach. Fishkin rejects the elitist assumption that by nature ordinary citizens, if given a chance, are uninterested in and incapable of deliberating upon important substantive issues. Citizens in a civic community, with high levels of associational social capital, he says, "internalize norms that motivate them to participate and to join with others-- norms that give them satisfaction regardless of any calculation about the effects of their individual actions."[67] He also rejects the empirically-obvious inegalitarianism of representative institutions and the inadequately deliberative nature of "democratic reforms" such as proliferating direct primaries and deference to opinion polls. In his view, political equality is essential for fully-realized democracy and this implies "institutionalization of a system which grants equal consideration to everyone's preferences and which grants everyone appropriately equal opportunities to formulate preferences on the issues under consideration."[68] To avoid tyranny, says Fishkin, is one of the essential conditions for democracy. By this he means "the choice of a policy that imposes severe deprivations when an alternative policy could have been chosen that would have imposed no severe deprivations on anyone." Such deprivations could be defined as "destruction of essential human interests" or "denials of basic human rights" or of "fundamental human dignities."[69]

Fishkin proposes "deliberative opinion polls," not as a panacea but as one of a general range of reforms to "bring 'power to the people' under conditions where the people could exercise their power more thoughtfully,"[70] despite the immense size of the contemporary polity. He seeks to bring the favorable traits of "face-to-face democracy of the Athenian Assembly or the New England town meeting to the large-scale nation state."[71] In effect, Fishkin proposes the old model (as with juries) of representation-by-lot. This constant rotation of office would avoid ossification of leadership and de facto arbitrary exclusion of any category of citizens, activist or not. "Deliberative opinion polls" would assemble a scientifically-based random selection of individuals for two weeks to consider significant political issues. With a full range of competing arguments, such panels would render judgments credibly viewed as reflecting what the vast majority of the population would decide if it also had a similar opportunity.[72]

Fishkin is convinced that "the public can best speak for itself when it can gather together in some way to hear the arguments on the various sides of an issue and then, after face-to-face discussion, come to a collective decision."[73] Citing, as do many theorists in this area, the "ideal speech" model of Jurgen Habermas,[74] Fishkin projects a context where "every argument thought to be relevant by anyone would be given as extensive a hearing as anyone wanted. . . . [P]articipants must be willing to consider the arguments offered on their merits. They listen and participate with an openness to the reasons given on one side or another."[75] In his citizen panel scheme, keeping the deliberative group together for a number of days consciously aims to facilitate identification with the larger social body. Fishkin insists that the deliberative ideal would encourage as open-ended a process as necessary to assure that all participants could express themselves, fully understand each other, and reply to others as needed.[76] ". . . [T]he longer the duration of the event, the more likely would be the effect on the knowledge and sophistication of the participants."[77]

Actual experiments with his deliberative panel model lead Fishkin to believe that participants emerge with "a new appreciation for the complexity of the views, the conflicts of values the issues posed, and the limitations of any one solution."[78] All of this he sees as complementing the structure and basic process of American national politics as it now exists. Fishkin's model of deliberative citizen polling has been tested, to his satisfaction, in various contexts (electoral campaigns and otherwise) at various levels of government concern.[79]

David Mathews, a cabinet member in the Ford administration, has written extensively on the theme of "citizen politics" as distinct from the political activities of government. Relying heavily on obvious expressions of contemporary voter alienation, extensive focus group research by The Harwood Group in the late 1980s and early 90s and his own experience as an organizer of the National Issues Forums,[80] Mathews believes that grassroots citizens justifiably feel manipulated by and angry with politicians, lobbyists, the media and the current operation of government, and also deeply regret a sensed loss of community. Says Mathews:

> There appears to be a public agenda that consists of issues that people identify with as citizens and another agenda, a politics-as-usual agenda, that is different from the public's agenda. . . . For the public to relate to an issue, it has to be framed in terms of what is valuable to people in their everyday lives, not just in terms of technical considerations. . . . People are dismayed when they cannot find

connections between issues as they are presented and their own concerns.[81]

As he points out, "the most essential part of deliberation is deciding on the nature of the issues and all of the possible alternatives for addressing them."[82] Ordinary citizens are consistently interested in voluntary participation in associational public life, in community problem-solving efforts. "The challenge is to connect politics as usual to the politics that people already practice."[83]

Having witnessed enthusiastic and reasonable deliberations of large numbers in issues forums and community associations throughout the country, Mathews is confident in the capacity and motivation of ordinary citizens, if given the opportunity, to exchange perspectives with others and thoughtfully collaborate in finding reasonable solutions to matters of public policy. As Mathews points out, "[A]ctive citizens don't necessarily begin with confidence in their ability to be successful. Part of their decision to become active may be to acquire skills and knowledge they don't have--to become efficacious."[84] Says Mathews,

> [C]itizens want to understand the experts, but they have more than technical concerns. . . . [T]hey don't just want to be lectured or "addressed." . . . [T]hey don't care for all the jargon, statistics, and other forms of "professional speak." This "foreign" language makes it difficult for citizens to talk to citizens.[85]

With adequate information, average citizens without scientific or technical expertise can understand complex technical issues as easily as formal legislators with similar background.[86] While there are experts in fact, "there is no such thing as experts on policy questions, which are really questions of 'what should we do?'"[87]

Furthermore, "[a]cting in cooperation with others energizes people" and "[e]ngaging in politics expands people's sense of themselves . . . aware of and active in the exercise of their inherent capacities as they go about the business of creating better communities and better countries."[88] Harking back to the models of the Athenian polis, settler covenants, early New England town meetings, and Anti-Federalism of the late 18th century, Mathews advocates community-wide discussion, on the basis of full equality, as a way to revitalize American politics. As he states, genuine town meetings "are conducted among equals for the purpose of making decisions."[89] "The idea is to construct relationships conducive to problem solving, even when people aren't happy with, or don't necessarily like, one another."[90] In contrast to the usual politics of "conflict, confrontation and contest" where "[c]itizens playing the game of adversarial politics adopt a language that connotes war," says Mathews, meaningful public dialogue means settings where "people put a high premium on hearing from those who are different and have different perspectives. . . .

People want to find connections with one another and not just further define their differences."[91] As we expect of juries, he says, "To deliberate means to weigh carefully both the consequences of various options for action and the views of others."[92]

In Mathews' view, grassroots citizens should be regarded as "the primary officeholders in a democracy."[93] While not envisioning a system of direct democracy, he asserts that "there are certain things that a democratic public must do in order for a representative government to work."[94] "We can elect our representatives but not our purposes. Political work is done in stages, with each stage doing the preliminary work that makes the next possible. Public choices about purposes are the necessary precondition for the governmental solutions we demand."[95] Furthermore, self-interest does not necessarily contradict community interest. "Common sense tells us that when a public good is threatened, we are all at risk--a hole in one end of the boat is going to bring water to the other."[96] "People have a self-interest in advancing the broader public interest" and the latter "grow[s] out of the varied relationships we have with other people," as when fostered by community associations dedicated to genuine dialogue.[97] While public deliberation is not apt to produce quick results, its long-range effect on official policy-making is likely to be significant.[98] By reviving grassroots assumption of and experience with civic responsibility and by finding meaningful policy solutions, representative government will become genuinely representative, the servant rather than ruler of the public.

For many years Harry Boyte has been one of the leading advocates of grassroots citizen participation. In *The Backyard Revolution*, he portrayed the post-60s extensive nationwide phenomena of local citizen advocacy based on "an old American practice of cooperative group action by ordinary citizens motivated both by civic idealism and by specific grievances. They seek some kind of democratization of power relations--the greater involvement of ordinary people in decisions affecting their lives."[99] With Sara Evans in 1992, he wrote of the need for "free spaces" in everyday life where grassroots movements and the free spaces at their heart "call attention to that vast middle ground of communal activity, between private life and large-scale institutions, as the arenas in which notions of civic virtue and a sense of responsibility for the common good are nourished, and democracy is given living meaning."[100] He agrees with the need to re-orient American politics from its overwhelming emphasis on individual rights, interest group competition and redistributive justice to democracy as aimed toward shared understandings or values. Yet he sees the "deliberative citizenship" model of Jurgen Habermas and others as a limited and misleading vision since "[i]n real life, judgments are dependent on context and perspective, and always suffused with power dynamics."[101]

Furthermore, it emphasizes too much the formal governmental structures of society and a static theory of power, failing to acknowledge the myriad "ways in which citizens act directly to define and solve the problems of society."[102] "Power is not simply one-directional" and "no one is simply a victim nor an innocent."[103]

Boyte cites America's long tradition of a political culture "that was practical, down-to-earth, work-centered and energetic"[104] which infused the proliferation of voluntary associations serving as mediating political institutions. These latter "had local, community dimensions. They also connected people's everyday lives to larger arenas of public life and policy."[105] The activism of the 1950s and 60s, in turn, revived from the privatism of the postwar period a "freedom language" including "a new sense of 'citizenship,' through which people came to experience themselves as participators in governance."[106] However, because significant pre-existing power dynamics, cultural differences and specific histories often generate very different perspectives on issues, Boyte suggests common involvement in practical community-oriented work relationships as a much richer means for understanding civic agency and commonality. Says Boyte, "only through the on-going multi-dimensional work of people with different interests and perspectives who address common problems can we rebuild a sense of 'commonwealth' practice and vision that has a broad and deep appeal and resonance. . . . In the process, citizens also develop the skills and knowledge seriously to address public issues, to become 'co-creators of history.'" "The ideal of a public life of deliberation has emerged . . . as the alternative to the incivility, rancor, and meanness that characterize public talk today." But public values cannot emerge from invoking supposed widely shared normative ideals which, realistically, may not exist. "Rather, meaning and value are constantly reworked and recreated, or created new, in the process of the work itself."[107] Boyte sees practical "public work" relationships as at least temporarily casting aside the hierarchies of power and status which ordinarily divide people and their sense of self-interest. In turn, such experiences then need to be translated into "a language of citizenship that draws attention to the larger significance of local and community efforts."[108] Experience together in pragmatic project contexts can encourage a common language and understanding of citizenship and thus restore the public, rather than government, to the center arena of politics.

Experiments in Participatory Democracy

As Berry et al. state, "Making the case for participatory democracy on theoretical grounds is much easier than demonstrating that it will work." What is more, they say, "[G]enuine participatory democracy has yet to be tried" in the contemporary United States.[109] Nevertheless, attempts in that direction have been made. Illustrating the relevance of criteria emerging from participatory democracy theorists are several contemporary experiments in actual participatory practice: Community Action Programs of the War on Poverty in the 1960s, "citizen juries" of the Minneapolis-based Jefferson Center for New Democratic Processes, select environmental activist groups in California and the common practice of initiatives and referenda.

Among the best-known elements of the federal War on Poverty reform package in the mid-1960s were local community action programs (CAPs), to be "developed, conducted, and administered with maximum feasible participation of residents of the areas and members of the groups served." The phrase "maximum feasible participation" came to mean election by grassroots communities of representatives to a local anti-poverty community action board which in turn would make fundamental policy decisions concerning which specific anti-poverty programs (health care, job-training, legal services, etc.) or community organizing activities would be approved. Beyond the gains from substantive programs themselves, one of the positive outcomes from the Community Action Programs was that board membership and the ensuing development of skills proved to be essentially a step of upward career mobility for inner city leaders (like earlier generations of leaders in urban political party patronage machines).[110]

One of the longest and best-known experiments is the "citizens jury" process developed by the Jefferson Center for New Democratic Processes since 1974. According to the Center's website, 28 projects using this model were undertaken at local, state and national levels through 1999, and similar projects were conducted by other organizations in other countries.[111] The basic assumption is that all citizens realistically cannot be involved in careful, extensive deliberation upon the many various policy alternatives of modern political life. Given their number and variety, such reviews would be impossible even for legislators with best intentions, and the vast majority of people cannot devote as much time and resources to the effort as these elected officials. A next best alternative, it is argued, similar to Fishkin's model, is to randomly select a "citizens jury" from a scientifically-determined representative pool of citizens to meet for intensive mutual research and discussion over several days concerning a focused issue of public policy. Such panels have been solicited from the Center by government officials and private sources alike.[112] Issues have ranged from national health care reform and environmental matters to school district facility needs, low income housing and organ transplants. The process is intended to provide non-interest-group-based, informed, demographically-representative <u>advice</u> to government officials, but also to encourage higher voting rates among the public generally by giving it self-confidence on issues through its own publicized "representative" voice.[113]

According to the Center, the central questions ("the charge") that the jury must address are pre-determined by an advisory committee "composed of individuals knowledgeable on the topic who represent a range of perspectives." The range of expert witness testimonies to the jury is "carefully balanced to ensure fair treatment to all sides of the issue." Adequate time and a variety of formats, facilitated by a trained moderator, are used to assure full dialogue with witnesses and discussion of juror opinions before findings and recommendations are presented in a public forum. An evaluation is completed by jurors at the conclusion of the process to assure the public and potential official decision makers of an unbiased process. There are many process issues inherent in attempting to assure an unbiased, openly communicative and deliberative arrangement. According to Crosby of the Jefferson Center, "It has taken us years to feel comfortable with our solutions to some of the difficult problems of democratic facilitation, agenda setting, witness selection, and juror selection."[114] Fair and open process in each area is critical and is recognized as essential for the credibility of the outcome.

Instead of awaiting others' transformation of official political structures and processes, many in America have asserted participatory democracy on their own. Among such efforts have been creation of and involvement with social change organizations dedicated in part to bringing about a participatory democratic society. A recent empirical study by Paul Lichterman on "personalized politics"[115] helps to elucidate the strengths of such activity. Having closely observed and surveyed several active grassroots environmental groups in California and the regional and national Green movement, Lichterman argues that a "self-fulfillment ethos" does not have to detract from a politics seeking the common good if the social activism engaged in conscientiously seeks to address on-going issues of equality, psychological growth and political skill development within the organization itself. Likewise, commitment to activism for communal goals (such as clean air) does not have to be through a sense of obligation, at the expense of individual growth and fulfillment.

In Lichterman's words, "The personalized commitments [he studied in California environmental groups] . . . both create and are sustained by a form of political community that emphasizes individual voice without sacrificing the common good for private needs."[116] Lichterman's observed "personalist" activists respect and manifest through words and actions an inherently valuable and unique individuality, apart from material and social accomplishment. In his terms, their activist perspective seeks fulfillment of individual potential primarily in a social context, while at the same time continually critiquing traditional or their own obligationist concepts of the public good. Such "a personalized form of political commitment underlies significant portions of numerous recent grassroots movements in the U.S."[117] By his observation, the sense of commitment was a long-range way-of-life focused on an overall sense of multi-issue ecological concerns and their deeper social roots and dedicated as well to non-hierarchical activist contexts respectful and encouraging of individuals' unique contributions.[118] "Ideological talking and writing have been central forms of Green 'doing,' along with specific, local projects and protests . . . ."[119]

Lichterman found a "personalized politics" culture effective and relevant as well among suburban "Airdale" resident activists, not just among Green activists with fewer local roots and greater national movement identity. "Airdale" activists were concerned with participatory values within the group and community both, but tended to be less concerned with theoretical formulations and with linkage to broader social issues--such as the promotion of participatory democracy generally within the society. Members "were neither passive volunteers nor unconcerned spectators. They became involved not as individual agents of social change but as concerned local residents contributing their time and gladly accepting direction from a more experienced activist."[120] In the prevailing "privatist" suburban culture of "Airdale," the shared mutually-encouraging empowerment of personalized politics provided by an environmental activist group proved necessary and sustaining for a context lacking shared "traditionalist" communitarian motivations for participatory civic life.

At the same time, Lichterman's observations of "personalized politics" environmental activism led him to emphasize the need to translate between political cultures, between those already participating more actively and those more privatistic and deferential in orientation. "Airdale" group members successfully "translated" between political cultures, he states, because they inhabited both "communities." As well, he asserts, effective dialogue between different activist political cultures would encourage "personalists" to better grasp the strength of movements based on locale and specific issues,[121] while those more oriented toward these latter would benefit from the "broader moral and political horizon" of the "personalists."

Referenda have been integral to American democratizing reforms and practice since the grassroots participatory political culture of the late 18th century revolutionary era,[122] although referenda are still unavailable at the national level. Popular self-government also gained from state-level voter initiative reforms by the beginning of the 20th century. Such reforms spread quickly during the Progressive period of the next two decades.[123] By now, all states but Delaware submit proposed constitutional amendments to voters, while most states have referenda for statutes and about half permit voter statutory initiatives. Most states also allow for yes/no votes on laws and spending proposals at the local level. As a form of participatory democracy, the model appears simple and direct. Propositions for state constitution amendments or other issues are put forward (if through citizen initiatives, by mass petitions) and the eligible electorate casts a yes or no vote on a set date.[124]

Proponents continue to argue that such a process maximizes the opportunity for equal participation by forcing direct public policy decisions onto ordinary citizens and eliminating usual law-making intermediaries.[125] Its use is spreading and surveys show substantial public support for this tool.[126] Thus, Ronald Libby, writing on three recent prominent initiatives and referenda on environmental and other issues, suggested that voluntary grassroots organizations were able to effectively challenge through such methods the privileged political influence of major corporate interests to a degree inconceivable through normal institutional channels.[127] Supporting his argument, in San Francisco in 1986, voters passed "the most stringent growth-control legislation of any large U.S. city," thereby delivering the death blow to the previous pro-growth machine.[128] Three years later, Seattle voters passed Initiative 31, a major restriction on downtown development. At the local level, one of the first communities to reject a Wal-Mart super store, Greenfield, Massachusetts, did so (by a margin of 9 votes) in 1993 through the means of a local referendum.[129] The potential for widespread citizen involvement is especially shown in sharply-contested local referenda where peer pressure, word-of-mouth discussion and the potential for larger influence by each voter all help to encourage larger turnout proportions.

C. The Integrated Analytical Agenda: Criteria for Participatory Local Land-Use Planning

The relevance and necessity of components discussed above for (1) progressive urban reform and (2) moderate participatory democracy can be tested simultaneously in the integrated context of participatory local land-use planning. As well, we believe that the greatest potential for fulfillment in the latter realm depends on achieving those positive components indicated above in both of these dimensions.[130] The critical question is to what degree, in local land-use planning, the promise of meaningful and influential grassroots participation in decision making is actually fulfilled. This local level of policy experience, where knowledge and intensity of feelings emerge from actually-lived community life, is where citizens potentially can have the greatest responsibility for their own governance. The lived experiment of local participatory land-use planning is thus an excellent test for the premises and promise of current U.S. democracy more generally. Through more broadly expanding our knowledge about the potentials and limits of progressive urban reform and moderate participatory democracy, the present case-study of the potentials and limits of participatory land-use planning helps us to consider the nature and quality of our society's overall continuing political evolution.

Our reading of the literature on progressive urban regimes and moderate participatory democracy theory suggests overlapping but distinct approaches for defining relevant criteria by which to judge the relative degree and effectiveness of any participatory local land-use planning experience. Such criteria involve: (1) macro-level conditions for progressive regimes; (2) micro-level elements of participatory or deliberative democratic process and outcome; and (3) a core condition of local participatory political culture. Participatory culture is encouraged by and infuses progressive urban regimes. It also is strengthened by and stimulates the intrinsic quality of participatory practice. This overlap area between macro and micro dimensions--the local participatory political culture--is the principal focus of the present study, and is uniquely illuminated by our abundance of detailed description from the ongoing official and unofficial record. Yet, again, the core area of participatory political culture depends for success on essential traits from the macro-level of progressive urban regimes as well as from the micro-level of actual participatory democratic process and outcome.

Progressive Regime Traits Contributing to Local Participatory Political Culture

Literature reviewed above on progressive change in urban regimes suggests, at the macro-level, the need for substantial local economic and political autonomy. "Significant local economic autonomy" implies that a local polity has access to state or federal grants, private grants, private investment or local communitarian capital forms (such as credit unions, consumer and producer coops, etc.[131]) essentially subject to local public guidelines. Less dependence on local property tax implies greater freedom from fiscal pressures helping to legitimate the local "growth machine" coalition.[132] It also implies recognizing the wealth of individual talents and resources within the grassroots citizenry itself potentially available for overall community benefit. "Significant local political autonomy" implies broad "home rule" constitutional or statutory powers despite the fact that local municipalities are officially "creatures of the state." In policy realms where "home rule" has not been explicitly defined, it also implies relative freedom from overriding state and federal policy directives, as enforced through the courts or budgetary restraints.

At the same time, progressive urban regimes are characterized by coalition partners sharing a priority of "non-business values"--concern with quality-of-life stability or redistributive/equity goals--as opposed to focus on business growth first and potential trickle-down benefits later. In local politics, this means concern with quality of education, housing, and health services; non-discrimination and equal opportunity in public and private realms; ample recreational facilities; meaningful social networking opportunities; adequate public utilities, community-friendly fire, police and emergency services; protection of valuable socially-created and natural environments; and the intentional fostering of community itself through opportunities for grassroots participation in political decision-making.

Participatory or Deliberative Democratic Process and Outcome Traits Contributing to Local Participatory Political Culture

At the micro-level, exemplary practice within local participatory democracy contexts includes equality of participation, validation of unique individuality, open communication and attentive listening, development of community-mindedness (without presuming a pre-existing "collective will") and personal growth in psychological, social and political skills.

Effective participatory land-use planning demands inclusiveness. Is participation more representational in nature, developing a local (or higher) activist elite, or does it involve a great majority, if not all, of the grassroots population concerned? Does the participatory entity or context become gradually ossified over time, encouraging perpetuation of some in leadership roles and procedural longevity for the mere sake of convenience or are leadership and processes understood to be merely temporary and facilitative for the empowerment of all, continuously subject to critique and alteration? Are those who actively participate concerned with participatory democratic opportunities only for those of similar orientation or do they conscientiously seek to translate between their own participatory democratic ethos and the political culture of others in the community (including non-human life forms) in an attempt to enlarge the number involved and quality of the participatory democratic experience generally? Finally, is the net result of this participatory democratic context likely to discourage or encourage further participation on the part of those who've experienced it?

Quality of deliberative decision-making, in terms of the nature of inquiry and the solution decided upon, involves three major issues. One concerns the scope, depth and open-endedness of the problem definition, agenda, process of inquiry, and the final decision. The second involves the degree to which these stages are open to communication through rationalities alternative to those of a scientistic, technical or legalistic nature and to non-rational expressions as well. The third concerns the degree to which broader community values[133] are balanced with those based on self-interest alone.

Criteria for A Local Participatory Political Culture

A local participatory political culture implies the presence of experienced facilitative community organizers, vital grassroots community organizations active at least partially in the political realm,[134] supportive elected officials committed to ever-greater decentralization of decision-making power, media encouraging of grassroots participation, widespread sharing of participatory democracy values and, at best, a supportive national participatory political culture of the type created in periods of major social crises (as during the 1930s and 1960s in the United States).[135]

Such a culture flourishes best with allies within the bureaucracy from major department heads to street-level administration, committed to what Donald Schon refers to as "creative professional craft."[136] Most important, of course, for the realm of land-use planning are professionals of an "advocate planning," "equity planning" or "deliberative" orientation.

A participatory political culture also implies deliberative structures which exercise power (or have the power to do so) continuously rather than sporadically, thus gaining more respect by other forces in the overall political economy. Similarly, participatory structures fully and directly responsible for decision-making in one or many policy realms will strengthen local participatory culture more than those which must share power with others or which only advise others with decision-making authority. Related to this issue is the degree of finality or independence of decision-making. What may appear to be direct decision-making can be elusive if budget cuts or lack of implementation by some other body prevent participatory decisions from taking effect.

The relative presence or not of the above traits of progressive urban regimes, participatory process, and especially local participatory political culture are the basis for our evaluation of the meaning of the Ashbury case study experience in the next chapter. In our final chapter, we will then critique these original criteria on the basis of structuralist perspectives on urban regimes and more radical participatory democracy theory. This dual-level assessment in the next two chapters, we believe, will best address the bifurcated and often self-contradictory agenda of pragmatic (crisis-oriented) vs. ideal orientations which anyone seriously concerned with participatory land-use planning at the present moment must consider.

SEVENTEEN ENVIRONMENTAL IMPACT REVIEW PROCESS AND THE MODEL OF LOCAL PARTICIPATORY PLANNING

Introduction

While a fascinating and often compelling drama as individuals and one local community experienced it, the evolution of events portrayed in this book, we believe, has far greater value in revealing contemporary political reality at several levels of increasing abstraction, regardless of the particular outcome in Ashbury. We have traced empirically, chapter-by-chapter, the essential stages of development proposal consideration in the New York State SEQRA review process--in terms of formal statutory and regulatory requirements, common interpretation and practice by developers and review agencies at the municipal level, and potential opportunities for public participation. Closely examining actually-experienced dynamics in Ashbury, we believe, provides a valuable pragmatic introduction to typical small-town SEQRA practice throughout New York state as well as grassroots challenges everywhere through environmental impact reviews. However, the Ashbury result of SEQRA disapproval through public participation is not necessarily replicable without a confluence of unpredictable factors similar to those described in this account. In fact, the Ashbury case was a scenario of ad hoc forced adversarial activist participation which happened, in this instance, to overcome the obstructed official participatory promise of SEQRA. The experience fell far short of the positive model of participatory land-use planning.

Our stage-by-stage description has revealed fundamental contradictions, at every step of the process, between the proclaimed environmental protection and participatory democratic intent of the SEQRA statute on the one hand and major opportunities, on the other, inherent in the ambiguities and weaknesses of the law, for developers and their local political allies to escape rigorous environmental critiques and community control and to degrade the environment. Law, after all, is subjective and interpretive. Such contradictions or opportunities for "policy leakage," as demonstrated in the case study of Ashbury, are by now well-known and exploited by large developers, by "light planners" in local planning boards, town boards and ZBA's throughout the state, and by attorneys and professional experts servicing these clients. As Jill Grant benignly states, "regulations that citizens see as protective amulets for neighborhood character are regarded by planners as flexible tools to promote development."[1] They well illustrate the usual workings of the administrative state, where "manipulation regularly masquerades as genuine communication, routinely undermining communicative rationality."[2]

While on the surface SEQRA appears to have a solidly participatory "regulator" orientation, in actuality it depends on elitist and manipulable discourses of legal liberalism, rationalist science, commodity economics and volunteerism, and successful grassroots struggles must battle with each of these as contrary to the ideals of participatory democracy. It is administered most frequently by local "light planner" coalitions which define SEQRA policy operationally by "pragmatic capitalist" rather than "regulator" criteria. The formal "rationality" of SEQRA is betrayed by a politicized non-progressive administration while at the same time falsely promising an easy potential for serious grassroots participatory influence. The result is that in Forest County, where strip malls and megamalls have come to erode local communities, before Ashbury in 1996, no planning board had ever employed SEQRA to disapprove such a project. Indeed, as DEC data have shown, in Forest County and throughout the state, the frequency of EISs has decreased significantly since adoption of the statute.[3] The decline is now at the point where more often than not negative declarations conditionally approve projects on developer compliance with or without guidelines to ostensibly mitigate environmental damage. Expert analysis on behalf of competing ideologies has been replaced with perfunctory stamps of approval reminiscent of pre-NEPA days when SEQRA-type statutes were non-existent. Only with solid organizing, constantly vigilant and sophisticated presence, their own capable and independent-minded attorneys and professional experts, political allies among local decision-makers and considerable good luck can grassroots community groups succeed in plugging the wide gaps between environmental policy and practice to force application of the stringent potential inherent in statutes, such as SEQRA, designed to protect the environment.[4]

Original Evaluative Criteria

At the end of the last chapter, we set forth our intended criteria for evaluating the potential for and actuality of participatory land-use planning in the context of Ashbury's environmental impact review of the megamall. As we discussed, these criteria emerged from substantial theoretical literature on progressive urban regimes and moderate participatory democracy.

Progressive urban regimes provide the overall protective and nourishing framework within which local participatory land-use planning can occur. Eliminating currently great dependence on a local property tax would provide the potential for creative attention to non-business values and quality-of-life stability or redistributive goals in many policy areas--including protection of valuable socially-created and natural environments and the intentional fostering of community itself through opportunities for grassroots participation in political decision-making. To enhance potentials in every policy area, progressive regimes recognize the incomparable value of individual talents and resources within the local grassroots population itself. The need of progressive regimes for significant political autonomy also implies explicit recognition of municipal "home rule" powers by state legislatures; state and federal courts; and any administrative agency or legislative body which might have potential indirect controlling influence through budgetary or other decisions at a higher level of governmental hierarchy.

Participatory democratic process includes above all a concern with full egalitarian inclusion in policy decision-making. This implies equal respect for the dignity and uniqueness of each participant, attentive listening and honest communication. Adhering to such standards inevitably develops community mindedness and personal growth in psychological, social and political skills. It is not enough to satisfy solely those activists who use participatory opportunities with relative ease. Meaningful participation of all must be actively encouraged (though obviously not coerced), and the goal of inclusion is constantly judged by the degree to which those not accustomed to public roles become motivated to participate and the extent to which those who participate are encouraged to continue.

Participatory democratic outcomes are achieved to the extent that problem definition, agenda, process and final decision are the result of open-ended communication and free inquiry by all participants, to the extent that each of these stages is open to contributions from alternative rationalities as well as those of a more common scientistic, technical or legalistic nature, and to the degree that broader community values are balanced with those based on self-interest alone.

The strength of these prerequisites for local participatory political culture is also re-enforced in turn by the continual development of that culture. Components of the latter include experienced facilitative community organizers, vital grassroots community organizations active at least partially in the political realm, supportive elected officials and local administrators (including "serious"/"equity planners") committed to ever-greater decentralization of decision-making power, media encouraging of grassroots participation and widespread sharing of participatory values (in part reflecting national trends in the same direction). Additionally, participatory activity has increasingly more influence in the local political economy through regular structures with continuing and full decision-making and implementation power.

It is impossible to define precise formulas of measurement for any of these criteria. Nevertheless, qualitative judgments can be reasonably attempted, assessing at least whether apparent progress has been made in the participatory direction. Local political contexts, just as wider politics and society generally, are constantly in flux. But the contribution of any community's specific policy resolution (and the stages within it) to that polity's evolution can reasonably be discerned impressionistically and by comparison with similar evidence from similar contexts elsewhere. It is to this evaluative task that we now proceed as we review evidence from our Ashbury case study and broader SEQRA realities generally.

Progressive Urban Regime Prerequisites

Significant Economic Autonomy. The fiscal base of Ashbury government during the period of concern was similar to that of most New York state municipalities--that is, highly dependent on revenues from the local property tax. The impact on town residents of reliance on this source was intensified in Ashbury by the fact that the large local SUNY campus was tax-exempt as state property. The College argues, on the other hand, that it contributes substantially to local residents' prosperity through direct salaries and through local spending by the institution, its employees and students.[5] In balance, there may be a substantial trade-off of this sort. However, because many residents do feel greatly threatened by local tax rates, the local "growth machine" coalition still has significant support in the community and its regular pressures for commercial expansion are important elements in the local political economy.

Specifically, following the collapse of the Amsterdam Square megamall proposal in 1991, Town Board and town planning board reluctance to rezone that "gateway district" east of the Thruway to prevent such projects and their slow efforts to develop a new comprehensive plan generally were no doubt the result of the strength of the local "growth machine" coalition. Indeed, the Ashbury Development Corporation, despite its recognition of the need to emphasize and strengthen the downtown business base, continued to market the rival "gateway" commercial zone and to proclaim a huge unfilled local retail spending demand. It was hardly surprising, therefore, that Wal-Mart and the new Moselle Plaza project were so quick to re-emerge. In turn, the continuous recitation of "minimalist" "growth machine" themes on the part of planning board chair and Republican leader Rocky Ryker, while Moselle Plaza was under review, was obviously a conscious strategy, appealing to what he perceived as a majority constituency in the community.

Following three years of the moratorium, the anti-megamall Town Board majority enacted only a 35,000 sq. ft. cap, a limit which would not preclude a strip mall (albeit on a smaller basis than the previous project). It failed to complete the overall process of rezoning the "gateway" district. While some attributed this failure to leadership or personality issues, no doubt a significant cause was the continued sense of marginal fiscal flexibility for the town,[6] a severe obstacle to the progressive evolution of the local urban regime. Without substantial redistributive tax reform at state and federal levels,[7] only wealthier suburbs will be able to avoid the continued predominant political influence of local "growth machines" and their "light planning" ideologies, and the ensuing forced scenarios of reactive grassroots mobilizations against unwelcome, inappropriate developer initiatives.

Non-Business Values. Ideologically, the Ashbury community was sufficiently liberal to cause most politicians to give at least lip service to public policy goals separate from those of the "growth machine." This was already apparent with the victory of local Democrats in 1975. Nevertheless, the transition to a new urban regime which would manifest such values in practice was slow and quite cautious. With still substantial constituencies of conservative residents and with little fiscal flexibility, articulation of non-business values tended to be followed by practice only when little spending was involved and only in slow increments.[8]

For example, in order to reduce impact on the public budget, efforts by the Wilton administration, to construct a new community center, create a substantial summer recreational program and build new recreational facilities were largely privatized, highly contingent on arrangements with private companies, nonprofit agencies and others for their achievement. Local educational policy, somewhat insulated as it is (with its own taxing authority and single program budget) from the more immediate pressures felt by town government, for a few years until 1999, was probably the most innovative and equity-oriented of all. During this period, intentional fostering of community itself through grassroots participation in policy decisions was more conspicuous by the local school board than by municipal authorities.[9] The latter sought volunteers for consultative committees to advise the Town Board. But, as shown in the case study itself, in areas such as land-use planning with formal deliberative power, the local urban regime has been and remains self-protective. As even one member of the anti-Wal-Mart Town Board majority stated privately, there's a difference between the influence of "insiders" and "outsiders" and, in his view, there should be.

Nevertheless, given the evidence from past elections and the significance of local fiscal limits throughout New York, we suspect that, aside from certain wealthier suburbs and poor and working-class urban neighborhoods, ideologically Ashbury is probably one of the New York communities most likely to share redistributive non-business values.

Significant Political Autonomy. Concerning local land-use planning and environmental impact review specifically, New York state law provides sufficient "home rule" power for a community such as Ashbury to establish and maintain strong zoning and SEQRA standards to protect the environment and encourage grassroots participation. As long as a "hard look" based on adequate reason is the grounds for a SEQRA decision, New York state courts have to date respected local autonomy.

The flexibility of the "hard look" standard and the lack of precisely-defined SEQRA impact criteria also imply significant discretionary power for local decision-makers. As demonstrated in this case study, such discretion is only a necessary condition for participatory planning, not a sufficient guarantee. To the contrary, while community groups continuously encouraged the planning board to follow stringent standards for SEQRA research and evaluation, the board's "light planning" members and consultants demonstrated by their actions that they considered discretion to be a mandate for minimal review. The meaning of SEQRA "discretion," therefore, comes down to the prevailing ideology of the planning board.

As well, municipal governing boards influence planning boards through appointment and budgetary power. In the case study at hand, the Republican-dominated Town Board made a highly-politicized planning board appointment in August 1994 at the request of the pro-developer planning board chair, directly altering the ideological balance of power apparently to favor megamall approval. In January 1995, after major public pressure, the "old guard" majority Town Board replaced Ryker with Maglie as chair, but refused to pursue issues of bias and conflict of interest of pro-developer board members and the "light planning" board attorney. Shortly thereafter, again under the watchful eye of the public, Town Board majorities carefully avoided direct politicized intervention by appointing two new "regulator" board members (Manley and Green) with clearly the best environmental knowledge. The two new appointees merely replaced two others of similar perspective (Pelletier and Dalrymple), leaving "regulators" still in a minority position. Overall, in this instance, the Town Board majority protected the "light planning" majority to the extent that it could without completely discrediting its own legitimacy with the public.

Additionally, through its other legislative responsibilities, the Town Board could have had significant veto power over a favorable SEQRA decision if it chose to deny post-SEQRA applications by Magellan for rezoning the southerly Heller lot and reconfiguring adjacent Davis Lane and if it chose to disapprove IDA financing of the project. It is unclear if any such decisions, however, would ultimately have discouraged the megamall from proceeding. One municipal authority which did intervene decisively was the Village Board when, in June 1994, after public lobbying, it denied access of Moselle Plaza to municipal sewer and water facilities, therefore forcing significant project design changes causing major negative environmental impacts.

Finally, while other involved public agencies at the county, state and federal levels are not empowered to directly contradict local board planning autonomy,[10] the present case study demonstrates their frequent potentially substantial influence on the SEQRA process. On the one hand, by offering initial broadly-worded tacit project approvals, agencies such as the DOT and county IDAs, assist the developer and local "light planners" in creating substantial "frontloading" approval momentum (to the point of discouraging the need for an EIS) by offering the impression that technical "non-partisan" experts, beyond local capabilities, have reviewed project impacts and found them mitigable or acceptable as is.

At the same time, their alleged respect for local autonomy (which hides other motivations as well) causes "involved" agencies usually to refrain from suggesting grounds for an EIS or issues for EIS scoping or from timely assistance to planning board members or the public during substantive EIS review. For developers and "light planning" board members wishing to avoid an EIS through "frontloading" or to "backload" serious project impact review until the legally less participatory post-SEQRA site plan stage, both types of "involved agency" approaches are most welcome.

Quite often, such approaches are explicitly politicized for particular projects, as seemed the case for Moselle Plaza review by the Reading County IDA and the Forest County Public Works Department. More generally, bureaucratic agencies, such as the DEC and the DOT, in turn, are themselves the subject of political pressure by governors and department heads, frequently viewing their responsibility as facilitating construction of a project once a local planning board has given SEQRA approval.[11] Even "regulators" within such agencies are typically inhibited by budget and time constraints, as well as the likelihood of little influence on the lead agency, from issuing more than generalized bland critiques at this stage and are "usually more concerned with the 'stream' of projects improving than with any one project being changed." As well, since outside agency officials expect to be dealing with the various local lead agencies on other issues in the future, "there are strong incentives to be cooperative."[12] Beyond such factors, "the general public's more favorable attitudes toward environmental issues of all sorts is only a vague background fact, potentially decisive if large numbers of people are aroused and persistent, but when not mobilized, as is usually the case, a much diminished influence on agency behavior."[13]

Additionally, as John Cronin and Robert Kennedy, Jr. point out, private industries often "'capture' 'involved' regulatory agencies through frequent exchanges of personnel between industry and regulator" and through many years of close working relationships and professional bonds between agency and industry individuals. Whether slackened regulatory enforcement results from broad business-friendly messages from the state level, staff cutbacks, or other factors is not essential since the effect is the same. As ex-DEC Chief Counsel Nicholas Robinson said about state pollution monitoring programs, a statement applicable to the entire realm of environmental regulation, "Environmental agencies have learned that to make the problem go away, simply ignore it."[14]

Only because of federal agencies' political distance and thus greater autonomy of their own (as with this case study's local SCS office) or because of heavy public expert pressures within the SEQRA process (as with the DOT), are "involved agencies" likely to offer significant substantive input as part of SEQRA's research dialogue with contributions from the public.[15]

In the present case, community groups from the beginning were unwilling to rely on a purely "home rule" local decision-making process, despite the centrality of that factor for genuine local participatory democracy. Having previously witnessed the planning board chair's disdain for participatory values and anti-participatory maneuvers from the commencement of project review, CLEAR and ACT activists made the prudent, "realist" decision to prepare for potential judicial intervention and reversal of a process already flawed by SEQRA legal standards. (The same logic led to the actual suit filed by the anti-megamall coalition against the Reading County IDA.) Moreover, it was likewise prudent and "realistic" to prepare a proper evidential record in case the board unexpectedly decided not to give SEQRA approval and needed a solid record for doing so.[16] Nevertheless, a strategy heavily dependent upon ultimate judicial resolution of adversarial positions was a tacit admission that the participatory model, in the present context, could not succeed. A court process could take years, consume large amounts of money and leave final decision-making almost totally in the hands of both a specialized elite of competing attorneys and, realistically, judges with the same ideology as the "light planners" whose actions the court case would seek to challenge.[17] This is particularly true in Forest County and similar upstate areas where the only review of SEQRA matters is by Republicans whose base of support is mostly individuals identified with the "growth machine" itself.

Prerequisites of Participatory Democratic Process and Outcome

Respect for Individuals, Attentive Listening and Honest Communication. The evidence from our case study is very clear. No doubt the worst violator of this criterion, especially important for those in official authority, was Rocky Ryker, planning board chair for the first fifteen months of project review. In public prejudgments about the worth of the project, denigrating comments and body language with the public and board members alike, his vicious attack on activist leaders as Nazis and with threats to sue, and his attempt to block public access to planning board records, Ryker only re-confirmed what appeared to be his long-standing administrative hostility to respect for individuals with contrary views, to attentive listening and to honest communication. In January 1995, Town Board member Edna Devilla dismissed community concerns about such matters as mere personality differences. In so doing, she marginalized the significance of these dynamics in chilling the atmosphere for democratic discourse. In effect, she legitimized the notion that public (and other board members') input was more a matter of formality than potential substantive contribution.

By comparison, the behavior of the two other long-time "pragmatic capitalist" board members, Davis and Maglie, and the two board consultants, Rattle and Busch, was in tone mostly benign. In actuality, however, their bureaucratic distancing and maneuvers which avoided virtually any engagement with public critiques were equally insulting and dismissive of public and "regulator" members' participation. Rattle's use of legal liberalism to speed the process and undermine the legitimacy of critical research and discourse, Busch's filtered elimination of important substantive issues, Maglie's abrupt conclusions to substantive debate and Davis' easy rejection of the value of important issues presented at the public hearing, all conveyed hostility to critical perspectives and to serious attempts to analyze important impact issues.

While new chair Maglie formally opened the door in February 1995 to the legitimacy of post-public hearing written submissions to the board, his earlier and subsequent actions suggested that he considered these to be of nuisance status at best. Only at the insistence of the "regulator" board majority and mounting pressure from the public in May 1994 did vice-chair Maglie agree to an original informal public hearing, before the critical initial SEQRA determination decision. Only at the later insistence of "regulator" Green did chair Maglie agree in late 1995 to finally permit a brief "public input" period at the beginning of one of the two board meetings each month. And only with his back against the wall, in late 1995, did Maglie apparently attempt seriously, though impossibly at that stage, to pay attention to the public critiques and to bridge with a "consensus document" the huge gap between draft "findings" statements of each side.

Unquestionably, activists' criticism of Ryker, Davis and Rattle on bias and conflict-of-interest grounds encouraged all three to even further distancing and antagonistic behavior toward the public. By January 1995, even some ACT members became critical of continued public reference to these issues. In their view, the very worth and potential of community dialogue was undermined by such an approach. Yet when other activists saw the pro-developer steamroller, led by Ryker and Rattle, refuse to seriously consider reasoned contributions from the public, they were convinced that adversarial politics were needed to at least level the field for an eventual evidential record and judicial review.

Arguably, the entire SEQRA format, with Magellan's "best-case" public relations presentation and "time is money" argument before a "pragmatic capitalist"-dominated board along with "legal liberalist" procedural maneuvers and reliance on chosen experts to distance from public critiques, set up from the beginning an adversarial relationship with the public, contrary to the above fundamental principles of participatory process.[18] As one SEQRA commentator emphasizes, although SEQRA, the Freedom of Information Law and their federal and state counterparts elsewhere are "premised on the idea of full and open disclosure," in fact "[t]he practice, in contrast with the theory of impact review, is suffused with secrecy."[19] Because local "lead agency" boards rely heavily on initial EIS presentations, because these are biased in favor of the developer and because of obstacles to the critical public's timely access to analytical documents for their own intervention, the basic assumptions and data behind technical statements in the EIS are rarely discussed and "project critics are relegated to the periphery on the key substantive issues."[20]

Another issue of individual respect and attentive listening concerns attempts to define "consensus." In the Moselle Plaza review, while the planning board attempted no consensus with the public, chair Maglie appeared to attempt it with the board. Maglie's frequent appeals for at least superficial goal "consensus," if not at the deeper interpretive level, well-illustrated what Torgerson refers to as "uncertainty absorption" in order to reenforce the impression of responsible and rational decisionmaking.[21]

As Taylor points out at the federal level, analysts with a "serious planning" perspective feel compelled to "express their criticism in organizationally acceptable ways. Such self-restraint demands accommodations in both substance and style."[22] While local volunteer planning board members risk no pay or job loss from pressing their critiques in public, lesser potential "sanctions" of being ignored or put down publicly or privately or ostracized for making the board more vulnerable legally are themselves powerful restraints on minority "regulators." "The secret of appearing 'reasonable' to the managers is not 'crying wolf' all the time, or 'too often.' The analysts [or a local planning board's "regulator" minority, as in Ashbury] build up credit, recognizing the unchangeable, smoothing the way for the harmless, doing the little things that grease the procedural wheels in order to appear cooperative and 'discriminating' rather than uniformly 'anti-project'."[23] Meeting after meeting, month after month, members must sit together in a public forum with others of the same small community. Despite ideological differences, there is also, therefore, simply a natural tendency to "get along" at a reasonably affable level. To counterbalance these restraints, outsiders, with social support systems and expertise of their own, must first place essential issues and data publicly on the table while secondly, "regulator" board members must focus on such openings if their own beliefs are to have significant influence. This was especially the case at the level of a local planning board where "regulators" generally lacked technical knowledge of their own to develop sophisticated critiques.[24]

Encouragement For All To Meaningfully Participate. By this criterion, the planning board should at least announce in advance through local media, posted notices around town and/or mailings, every meeting in which it intends to discuss a particular controversial development. Once in attendance, community members should be invited to participate directly in dialogue with the board or, if too numerous, through skillfully-facilitated small-group discussions or other methods to encourage expression from those more inhibited in large gatherings or with apparently unpopular views.[25] Of course, any meaningful direct encounter between the board and the public would have to pursue goals of individual respect and open communication discussed above. As well, the board could solicit further participation through ongoing surveys, informal neighborhood discussions and other similar efforts.

In the actual Moselle Plaza review, the planning board offered only two opportunities for large-scale direct public input--the public "comment" meeting of May 1994 and the official public hearing of January 1995. While hundreds of individuals attended each meeting, demonstrating through their presence and responses overwhelming opposition to the megamall, the fact that so many (including potential supporters) did not feel free to speak their opinion was a failure of the process to meet this participatory criterion. Likewise, when nearly two thousand petition names and hundreds of cards and letters were received by the board in opposition to Moselle Plaza, the fact was barely acknowledged in the official record, let alone as a basis for board discussion of the project's potential social impact on the community. For many, such marginalization no doubt discouraged further involvement.

On two other occasions, the board, on the surface, seemed solicitous of general community input. On December 19, 1994, it voted draft SEIS "completeness" allegedly "so the public could have its turn to officially comment." A month later, at the board meeting of January 23, 1995, Ryker and Davis urged deferral of the community groups' expert testimony to the end of the scheduled public hearing "so that the citizens of the community wouldn't have to wait for outsiders to finish." However, both actions appeared actually to seek diversion from anti-developer critiques. (After all, just nine months earlier, Ryker had publicly stated that 90% of the public's comments at the

May 1994 hearing were irrelevant.[26])

By their nature, hearings allow perspectives to be aired which differ from those of developers and members of the board. Whatever the merits of public comments, jealous defense of their own judgments and prerogatives may thus cause board members automatically to discount or belittle the prospect of public hearings. A "light planning" board majority, as in Ashbury, might therefore easily disregard whatever critical substantive comments are made. More significantly, though recommended by SEQRA, public hearings themselves are not even required.

As Taylor points out, if a NEPA- or SEQRA-type "system of analytical criticism is to work, the burden of proof must be balanced to achieve competing public policy goals. [This implies that] the relative resources of the contending parties must be balanced so that there is a true adversariness, rather than the merely formal adversariness of a *David v. Goliath* situation--in a context in which few plaintiffs can hope to come to as happy an ending as the biblical victor."[27] As federal Judge Carl Bue asserted in *Sierra Club v. Froehlke*, compared to those who spend their working hours promoting and rationalizing projects, the fullest and most independent critique necessarily must come from outside environmentalists, "who must spend the vast majority of the[ir] employment time engaged in occupations other than watching the agencies."[28] To date, NEPA and SEQRA systems have failed to rectify the imbalance through providing community groups with public funds for independent experts.[29] Thus, beyond enormous time demands to monitor and critique the actions of developers and local planning boards, citizen critics must also expend tremendous effort and personal resources to fund serious opposition on their own--hardly an invitation for meaningful participation. In the Ashbury context, ACT and CLEAR gave thousands of hours to making the case against Moselle Plaza persuasive and well-documented, including considerable free time by local professionals in both legal and environmental realms.

For some active participants, the lengthy struggle and its ultimate outcome renewed their dedication to grassroots participatory democracy. But for others, constant battle against a stacked process, dedicated community service met by scorn and cynical political maneuvering, the lack of accessible discourse and genuine dialogue, and/or a bitter taste from lending credibility to an undemocratic and commodifying process simply reenforced a sense of alienation from the political realm generally. As John Forester emphasizes, negative emotional legacies of this sort make effective participatory planning that much more difficult to achieve in the future. In the end, whether Ashbury gained, lost or maintained the same level of "social capital" from the struggle would be difficult to judge and would depend on one's assumption as to whether temporary political alienation might lead in the long run to more radical political activity to change the overall system.[30]

Open-Ended Problem Definition, Agenda-Making, Review Process and Final Decision. Though formal power for final decisions is legally the reserve of the lead agency, proclaimed SEQRA goals appear to welcome public participation in an open-ended process of defining potential impacts, preparing a research agenda and contributing to serious analytical dialogue. If such participation occurred, one might reasonably expect that the final decision itself would reflect much of the public's contribution.

What would emerge from this process is suggested by Taylor in his outline of reasonable intellectual criteria for serious environmental analysis:

> Policy competition would be analytical if the overall system of competition could provide the participants with the following three requisites: (1) motivation to do potentially critical analysis in the first place (exceeding the contrary motivation); (2) sufficient information to make valid criticism effective; and (3) norms of analysis backed up by the power to compel a response to the criticism--either rebutting in an analytically satisfactory manner, or changing the criticized policy.[31]

However, as John Forester suggests and John Dryzek endorses, to assure policy decision making based on "better argument" alone depends also on:

> exposing and counteracting manipulation of agendas, illegitimate exercises of power, skewed distribution of information, and attempts to distract attention. . . . . Analysts cannot avoid taking sides on very basic issues of political structure. . . . [D]efensible policy analysis must side with open communication and unrestricted participation; in other words, with participatory and discursive democracy.[32]

As our case-study record indicates, except for the initial stage of Spring 1994 when a "regulator" majority sufficiently neutralized the quick-paced "frontloading"/"backloading" strategy of Magellan, Ryker, Rattle and Busch, the only "open-endedness" with the public in Ashbury's SEQRA process consisted of procedural requirements themselves for the several legally-mandated stages. In actuality, public dialogue with board members about rational sufficiency at each stage was not invited. In this regard, one of the principal purposes of bureaucratic discourse--such as the SEQRA statute and regulations--may be precisely to disguise the actuality of decision-making as a political instead of scientific-rational process. As seen in our account, its effect is to increase control through resolution of conflict while rendering this use of power invisible.

The 1977 legislative compromise resulting in the final implementation of SEQRA indeed lodged with developers the epistemological power inherent in preparing an EIS.[33] When SEQRA removed lead agency responsibility to prepare an analysis of adverse environmental impacts in the first instance, it rendered lay members of the board captive to the legitimating effect of developer experts.[34] In effect, SEQRA thus invited developers to appropriate environmental discourse for their own purposes, assisted by a new cadre of hired scientific, technical, planning and legal experts ready to meet regulatory planners apparently on their own turf, but even further removed from the level of grassroots discourse and critiques.

In turn, as planning policy expert John Friedmann states, "The key to understanding [these] private analysts is money. Consulting firms must survive in a highly competitive world. . . . [T]hey must . . . learn to work contentedly with their client's basic assumptions: too many challenges of this framework will almost certainly lead to nonrenewal or, worse, cancellation of contract."[35] David Brower, ex-head of the Sierra Club and Friends of the Earth, stated the same point more directly: "After sixty years of working in conservation, I conclude that there are two kinds of science: One is purchased, manipulated, and dispensed at industry's whim. The other cannot be bought."[36] Likewise, as David Schindler wrote:

> Someone is inevitably available to receive these funds, conduct the studies, regardless of how quickly results are demanded, write large reports containing reams of uninterpreted and incomplete description data and, in some cases, construct "predictive" models irrespective of the quality of the data base. . . . [The author's professional title], the mass of the report, the author's salary, and his dress and bearing often carry more weight with the . . . study board, to whom the statement is presented, than either his scientific competence or the validity of his scientific investigation.[37]

As SEQRA commentators point out, the developer's technical consultants who prepare EIS drafts have many discretionary choices to be made in gathering, calculating and channeling raw data into predictive models. "[W]here the developer hires the consultant--as is almost invariably the case under SEQRA--the discretionary choices will tend to be made in one particular direction."[38]

Once the agenda is established, a similar bias of the process against participatory impact appears in substantive issue review. Abundantly described in our case study, the same phenomenon is reflected in Taylor's description of "light planner" project and agency managers' attitudes toward NEPA:

> [They] may only have a strong incentive to analyze an issue after outsiders have demanded it--and the outsiders may demand a very different kind of analysis from what the leaders are prepared to give. . . . Leaders will want analysis that is as little "formalistic" as

possible, that is not inflexible and time-consuming, that can reflect changing priorities and scarce resources, that does not open the agency to political embarrassment.

. . . [T]hese factors all work in the same direction--to make the top leadership less tolerant of scientific norms of analysis, all other things being equal.[39]

Official environmental analysts in federal agencies, local planning board members or public critics with a "regulator" perspective, therefore,

must confront what might be called the managers' "presumption of environmental innocence." . . . [M]anagers will not be persuaded on many important questions unless the specialists can come up with "hard data" to back up their "intuitions" and "hunches." . . . Yet [this] puts the environmental analysts in a Catch-22 situation, for they may have a hard time getting the resources and time that would allow them to "prove" or "disprove" their hunches.[40]

Furthermore, quite frequently a local planning board's young planning consultant, eager for acceptance in the broader professional community, may be intimidated by the developer's planners, well-advanced in the field and with possible useful connections in the future.[41]

In this regard, the "hard look" review standard emerged first in federal courts in an effort to assure that all concerned interests had a chance to make their views known and considered. In effect, however, it was aimed more at process than substance, since courts (at the New York state level as well) became reluctant to second-guess the seriousness with which alternative data and critiques were considered and answered. While this standard improved on earlier court deference to agency expertise, by recognizing agencies' frequent lack of impartiality, the definition of "hard look" itself was wide open to alternative judicial interpretations.[42]

The vacuum of control was thus filled by local political operatives whose attitudes about development only had to be legitimated in language demonstrating compliance with legality.[43] Never was it clearer that politics, the sociology of local government and small-group behavior would determine law's meaning. As Taylor discussed at the federal level with the NEPA process, parallel with the "analyticizing of politics" which dangerously attempted to subsume all value choices to the "objective realm of science" came the "politicizing of analysis" which made a mockery of the scientific pretense.[44]

The fact that in Ashbury the final decision did indeed reflect closely the participatory input of the public was attributable only to the stubborn insistence of activists to continually force their way into the process, to the very merits of the community groups' position and to the willingness of one of the "light planning" majority to fairly consider those merits. It was not SEQRA procedural "guarantees" themselves which led to this outcome. Indeed, in New York state as a whole, by 1982, fewer than 1% of projects reviewed under SEQRA had been rejected on the basis of information provided in that process.[45] At the federal level, even at the early stages of NEPA implementation (before more sophisticated agency formal compliance), NEPA's overview agency, the EPA, in the first part of 1973 applied the "environmentally unacceptable" label to only about 1% of all EISs reviewed. Even its worst rating for EIS information adequacy was applied to only 7% of projects.[46] No doubt reflecting the same pattern across the nation, this same bias of the process toward approval typifies the abundant literature on EIS processes for use generally throughout the country. Even a guide strongly emphasizing the importance of significant public influence, while acknowledging "disapproval" as the most important mitigation, barely mentions this possible EIS outcome anywhere else in the book.[47]

Openness to Alternative Rationalities. At the least, this criterion implies a lead agency's willingness to seriously consider public input in a language other than the rational, techno-scientist, legalistic and commodity discourse usually favored. While the judicial standard of a rationally-based "hard look" implies that a board decision would have to be based ultimately on the latter, SEQRA's invitation for public participation and lead agency discretion means that other sorts of input could legitimately be considered and re-framed by the board in the rationalist language needed.

That scientific or technical issues may be difficult initially for lay understanding is not in dispute. Indeed, developer project managers and engineers appear consciously to use this fact to marginalize public critiques.[48] However, even in as complex a realm as nuclear power, two careful observers of the Atomic Energy Commission licensing process stated directly: "It appears evident to us that utilities and vendors have an obligation to make scientific and technical aspects of nuclear power understandable to the public" and that this can be done "in a manner which makes it possible for the public, and for non-scientist decisionmakers, to evaluate the import of scientific and technical information and to use the information as an input to the decisionmaking process."[49] By now, it is abundantly clear that the lay public can discuss intelligently matters of technology and science if appropriate translations are made.[50]

As Alan Irwin points out, the marginalizing effects of untranslated technical language in fact are often internalized by project critics to the detriment of participatory dialogue: "discourses of expertise can engender a form of self-censorship where objections will not be raised [if the opportunity even existed] since they will be pre-defined as illegitimate." Nevertheless, "[s]ilence in such a context is . . . very different from acquiescence."[51]

Quite arguably, commodifying language of "cost-benefit" analysis, so institutionalized during the Reagan-Bush years, has a similar marginalizing and disempowering impact on the lay public, unused to referring to wetland, aquifer or traffic impacts in monetary terms.[52] In fact, SEQRA (like NEPA and other little NEPAs), with its ultimate "balancing test" to determine potential economic gains for the community which might offset environmental losses, redefines cognizable environmental harm as a function of economic calculations. Months, if not years, of substantial dialogue about the extent of likely environmental harm can all be subsumed, in the end, by a vague formula of economics. The fact that this "balancing test" was turned on its head by community groups in Ashbury, in obtaining a disapproval finding statement for Moselle Plaza, does not diminish the significance of this SEQRA provision in potentially marginalizing an entire environmental discourse--at technical and "citizen science" levels both. In this regard, "Numbers seem to give extra legitimacy to arguments, making points somehow more concrete and less debatable. The impact of numbers can be especially strong on those who are unfamiliar with quantitative analysis and who tend to develop symptoms of mathematical anxiety when confronted with tables, charts, and equations."[53]

Similarly, of relevance to the entire obscuring and disempowering impact of untranslated SEQRA legalistic discourse generally, as Richardson et al. point out, project proponents also frequently employ apparently "objective" euphemisms to neutralize or even make positive the images of negative environmental impacts.[54] Thus, as in the Ashbury case, effluents become "contributions," stormwater pollution becomes "additional mineral loading," traffic jams become "heavier traffic flows," predictable elimination of existing small businesses become "temporary market adjustments," and boarded-up storefronts become "temporary building vacancies."

As demonstrated in our account, the discourses of law, science and economics were equally intimidating to lay members of the planning board itself.[55] This fact could be used as a rationalization for "common-sense" interpretations all the way around, thereby reverting simply to the balance of power of land-use ideologies on the board and exposing the underlying reality of the decision-making process as an arena of political conflict. To the extent that, simultaneously, the illusion of bureaucratic neutrality was maintained through the use of "objective" discourses of legal liberalism, science and commerce, the oppositional lay public experienced a truly Kafkaesque nightmare of apparently constantly shifting targets of authority and accountability. As Woliver states, "The imprimatur of impartiality in political controversies often serves to legitimize the position of those who favor the status quo and to label dissenters as emotional, angry, and subjective."[56]

To empower grassroots citizens who present issues in non-technical terms, a board and consultants who welcomed participatory dialogue could easily translate such contributions into scientific discourse, if needed.[57] At the least, credible counter-testimony in technical language by experts retained by community groups could be seen as neutralizing assertions by developer experts, thereby opening the door to acceptance of additional evidence and analyses from the non-specialist public.[58] In actuality, in the Ashbury case, it was technical discourse presented on the record to the board by lay activists, as much as input from community groups' credentialed experts, which provided the basis for the language of the ultimate SEQRA findings. Their "credibility," of course, was made possible only by the community groups' corroborating professional expert testimony. Without expert testimony to back up lay critiques, even a sympathetic board majority would probably never rely on them alone to justify SEQRA disapproval for fear of later judicial reversal, since courts are likely to give greater deference to experts over non-experts in applying the "hard look" standard.

Lead agency and judicial privileging of "professional science" over "citizen science" (or grassroots-generated knowledge and intuition), combined with the imbalance of resources, means that credentialed experts typically serve, through their specialized discourse, not only to "legitimate" or officialize certain data and conclusions, but also to provide such authority to those already privileged because of their governmental or economic status. However, while no scientific formulation will be wholly objective, some scientific formulations will seem objectively better than others if they produce more reliable predictive explanations. Thus, a truly scientific inquiry in a policymaking process would also examine the relative past predictive success of competing experts. But this level of rationality is rarely attained.

Instead of a neutral arbiter, professional science thus typically gives further advantage to project developers. In this context, "Science is the servant of power--its investigations claim to open up the possibilities for policy-making but instead serve to reenforce the existing social order."[59] SEQRA's denigration of "citizen science" is typical in American regulatory policymaking generally, despite "participatory" devices such as public hearings. Advice to lead agencies from an expert on environmental impact review demonstrates the confusing and understandably suspicious message conveyed to the public about the public hearing process: "a lead agency . . . must convey to the public that . . . the environmental impacts of the proposal are being evaluated, not whether the proposal should be approved or disapproved."[60]

While some of the bias toward technical expert discourse is thus attributable to factors outside of a lead agency itself, the latter still would be free under SEQRA to use lay public critiques as a basis for hiring, at the developer's expense, outside experts of its own. With its temporary early "regulator" majority, the Ashbury board did this in the case of economic impact issues, but failed to challenge the limited budget offered by the developer and subsequently found itself with a minimalistic, discredited economic report. A lead agency could also use the public's lay critiques to justify, as it did in Ashbury to a limited degree, seeking expert analysis by its own already-existing consultants (Busch and Napoleon) or by experts from outside public agencies (the Soil Conservation Service and DOT). But "light planner" board members, in this instance, subsequently attempted to discredit whatever expert analysis was submitted when it was favorable to the community groups' position.[61]

Finally, a participatory-friendly board could potentially translate ethical questions concerning risk assessment models (including concern for future generations), anti-growth perspectives and even the emotional fervor of some members of the public[62] into evidence of significant social impact[63] or a change in community character, each of them legitimate reference points for an ultimate SEQRA decision. At the least, it would suggest to a board that there might be strong reason to further investigate the merits of the issue at hand.

Balance of Community with Self-Interest Values. Adversarial dynamics in place almost from the beginning of the examined SEQRA process left little apparent space for participants to learn from opponents in ongoing dialogue, thereby to potentially transcend whatever self-interest values were in place. As the struggle continued, each side became further and further entrenched, with ultimate resolution seeming likely to emerge only from outside judicial review.

Apart from the obvious defense of self-interests on the part of Magellan Construction, Wal-Mart, and FoodFeast, on the one hand, and local merchants, on the other, probably all remaining major participants--planning board members and community activists alike--saw themselves as acting primarily on behalf of the general community. Additionally, the very experience for activists of developing a prolonged multi-dimensional community struggle brought together numerous individuals with a wide range of perspectives for the first time. Whatever the fate of stripmall development in the Gateway district, this creation of an "oppositional community" was a valuable outcome in itself and also a potential strategic leverage for future grassroots mobilization (obviously not limited to SEQRA battles alone). As well, the very scope of the crisis forced everyone to ponder seriously what was of value to them in the community--beyond their own personal or family well-being. To a good extent, the very concept of an "Ashbury community" was at stake.

It was activists, not the developers, who attempted in mid-course to reach out at least partially to address the stated needed of their opponents--in this case, to FoodFeast management with an alternative on-site expansion plan. That FoodFeast seriously considered and temporarily accepted this alternative only after fully battling and losing two successive megamall wars in Ashbury and Acton speaks volumes to the comparative openness of each side to hear the other's concerns.

FoodFeast and Magellan, of course, also refused to the bitter end to offer any downsized on-site alternative, despite the likelihood that they would have won a planning board majority and possibly considerable community support in doing so. Stubbornly resisting substantial concessions to community concerns, Moselle Plaza developers merely reflected typical developer reliance upon the bias of SEQRA toward approval and the larger "light planning" bias toward property rights above non-materialistic regulatory concerns.[64] While one purpose of the EIS is to require a developer to alter its initial plan after agency consideration of significant adverse environmental impacts, such a process itself is dependent upon the honesty and integrity of the developer and its experts and the will of the agency to consider input from "regulator" members and from outside experts on behalf of the public. The deep flaw in the statute is that it assumes that such an alliance between capital and the state will produce actors who are open-minded and willing to follow proclaimed statutory intent. It is far from credible that profit-maximizing corporations, especially those from outside a local community such as Wal-Mart, Medford and Magellan, would be interested in genuine open-minded dialogue and potential transformation of perspectives which the statutory assumption implies.[65]

Last-minute attempts by Magellan to meet with Supervisor-elect Wilton in December 1995 and by Rattle, Maglie and Busch (most likely in communication with Magellan) to devise a "conditional" SEQRA disapproval in January 1966 apparently were desperate forced efforts to finally acknowledge, at least partially, the strength of community concern. But in this case, so little "learning" so late was not a viable strategy. The fact that Magellan then sued the Town for its disapproval finding, thereby escaping payment of its escrow debts and, next, proposed virtually the same project in neighboring Acton meant that in fact Magellan never recognized legitimate community concerns at all.[66]

Subsequently, some activists and the new Town government attempted to work with Joe Heller, owner of the controversial site, to find scenarios for mutually-acceptable non-megamall development. Such efforts were given despite the ill will created by Heller's encouragement of a succession of potentially-damaging on-site projects and his occasional threats, even after the SEQRA defeat, to battle the community again in court or with new major commercial proposals. But for many of the activists, no matter what the nature of an eventual on-site project, Heller's insistence by 1999 on collaborating again with one of the principals of Magellan Construction, despite activists' personally-stated protests, was a slap in the face of the community, not an example of transcending self-interest.

In a local struggle more divisive among the public than in Ashbury, SEQRA's inadequately guaranteed participatory process can actually leave a legacy of decreased community-mindedness. For example, David Kay, the chair of the Ithaca, N.Y. planning board during that community's similarly long and bitter struggle against Wal-Mart in retrospect had serious misgivings about SEQRA--despite an outcome, which he favored, comparable to that in Ashbury.

> At the heart of my concern was the sense that the planning board was complicit in a significant, systemic misuse of a scarce and valuable resource--the attention and engagement of the energies of a broad cross section of people who cared about their community.[67]

In his view, it was not clear whether elements of reciprocity and mutual trust essential for maintaining and developing community had increased or decreased as a result of the struggle and outcome in Ithaca. Of course, an assessment here would require defining the potential "community" of concern, the relative strength of the four land-use ideology blocs locally, and the rigidity or fluidity of ideological identity.

Traits of Local Participatory Political Culture

Experienced Facilitative Community Organizers. Because of its location, the college and particular community history since the 1960s, the Ashbury area attracted a good number of activist veterans from a variety of political struggles all over the country. This presence, in turn, allowed faster mobilization of community talents once the anti-megamall campaign began. Their experience in prior political struggles also helped to shield them from the initial barbs of "light planners" and their local allies before the strength of anti-megamall sentiment became known.[68]

It is also true, as demonstrated in the evolution of Ashbury's environmental movement, that the SEQRA process itself encourages development of skilled community organizers. The long string of local and regional struggles from the mid-70s to recent battles against the Wal-Mart megamall left a valuable participatory legacy for the community in numerous realms, not just concerning the environment. Again, this is a typical product of any organized community struggle to preserve itself in the midst of crisis, not a byproduct of SEQRA alone.

Nevertheless, the <u>adversarial and crisis nature</u> of the struggle, instead of a process welcoming public participation, tended to develop skills more useful in contexts of confrontation. To the extent that facilitative skills to encourage wider meaningful participation were learned, they were acquired through the process of building the broad anti-megamall coalition itself more than through the opportunity to engage seriously and systematically in open-ended honest communication with megamall proponents. Potential contexts for the latter were not promoted by the planning board and both the adversarial dynamics and the immense time and energy involved simply in building the grassroots coalition and monitoring the board meant that no one was prepared to accept the added burden of attempting to develop even wider community dialogue with ardent megamall supporters.[69]

Vital Grassroots Community Organizations. The case study demonstrates the significance for local participatory political culture of a wide base of volunteer community organizations--some, at least, experienced in political activity. The pre-existence of CLEAR and the DMG, in this instance, were crucial. But the dynamic growth of ACT and its wider supportive network depended greatly as well on an existing rich associational base found in the Ashbury community as elsewhere--from Little League parent friendships and religious affiliations to neighborhood associations, local school contacts, the local arts community and numerous other organized contexts. At whatever level of contribution, dozens of individuals were prepared through past associational experience to offer their talents in the mundane activities of fund-raising, letter-writing, phone trees, distributing petitions and posters, organizing pot-lucks, preparing visual exhibits and walking the picket line.

However much the present account emphasizes the more formal SEQRA context, this wealth of participatory skills, based on pre-existing associational life, was essential to sustain the struggle. And, naturally, the drawn-out anti-megamall campaign itself, in turn, developed further the local reservoir of such talents for future grassroots participatory vitality--whether in political or other realms.

Supportive Elected Officials and Administrators. Without a drastic egalitarian transformation of the wider political system at state and national levels, municipal governments will be formally organized according to hierarchical principles. Nevertheless, even within this official legal context, it is possible to envisage progressive elected officials and appointed administrators (such as "equity" or "deliberative" planners) deciding to share decision-making, in participatory modes, for all but their final legally-required formal votes in the policymaking process.[70] This could logically apply especially to local land-use planning. A local participatory political culture would have to contain elected and appointed officials committed to such sharing. In the Ashbury case, "light planning" Town Board and planning board members and consultants were obviously of the opposite persuasion.

While SEQRA required that some involved agency, such as the planning board, act as the lead reviewing authority, it did not circumscribe how the planning board would interpret its mandate through selection of professionals to advise the board regarding the propriety of any given action.[71] Thus, unless a consultant or planning board member had a financial conflict of interest with the proposed development, with benefit forthcoming as a result of project approval, the board was free to constitute itself and its advisors with individuals whose ideology most mirrored that of the developer itself. Ryker's selection (with Supervisor Schmidt's approval) of "minimalist" attorney Rattle seemed clearly part of a conscious anti-participatory strategy. From Rattle's initial correspondence with the regulatory division of the DEC to his authoritative recitation of whether SEQRA required an SEIS and his usual "minimalist" discourse, his role in the Magellan review demonstrated the interpretive and subjective nature of SEQRA when delegated to individuals with little regard for an inclusive participatory process.

The perspective Rattle presented of legality in the SEQRA process and his role in assuring that the process was legitimate sought to identify himself as a defender of right and reason in a small town. His use of such argumentation admitted no possibility that law and regulations might be subject to a variety of interpretations, and that lawyers are regularly retained to interpret the law in ways favorable to their clients' interests. Nor did it concede that lawyers are often predisposed to representing one side or another in a dispute over legality's capacity to regulate capitalism. More importantly, such a literalist paradigm denied the importance of the interpretive role of a lawyer representing a public body which, with divergent policy views, needs to be informed about the full range of discretionary possibilities in order to arrive at a lawful, socially constructed outcome. It appeared that, under Rattle's view, law was a fixed set of "minimalist" rules, the meaning of which was not subject to debate, which facilitated, without interfering, the orderly workings of the marketplace. In this context, participatory process was viewed at worst as obstruction and at best as unnecessary.

While the public was recognized at official hearings and through the election process, in Ashbury it was an entrenched group of insiders, an established urban regime, who, based on social, political and economic interrelationships, controlled and dominated local government as if it were a family business. It was no coincidence that only lawyers predisposed to development were selected to represent public bodies. Such lawyers depended for their livelihood on local governments' facilitating private interests that were consonant with maintaining the local power structure and development of local and outside capital. Nor is it surprising that those running for elected office and those appointed by elected officials were commonly themselves the very private interests which become the object of local government.[72] This group of insiders is not easily penetrable and resists those aspects of state law which it perceives as contrary to its interests.

It was not until the planning board's lawyer became discredited, as law's messenger, that his voice became silent, along with that of his ally, the planning consultant. This, then, gave rise to a new voice based upon majoritarian principles without regard to the uniformity of consensus. The epistemological basis to discredit law's messenger, therefore, became a prerequisite to substantive decision-making which ultimately satisfied SEQRA's "hard look" standard of legality.

In small town political cultures as in Ashbury, however, raising such questions is often tantamount to questioning the entire legitimacy of the structure of local government which, pragmatically, is littered with similar conflicts and is culturally imbued with the notion that bureaucratic standards of objectivity have no place in a "community of neighbors."[73] Thus, in Ashbury, the local town ethics code permitted only the town official with the conflict to raise the issue before the Town Ethics Board, precluding, thereby, any "outsider" or even other town official from questioning the ulterior motives or objectivity of appointed officials. Additionally, participatory actors are themselves ambivalent about raising these concerns since they are often viewed as "mud-slinging" personal attacks unconnected with the substantive policy issue at stake. In the end, ACT's and CLEAR's efforts to de-legitimize local government structure were met with intimidating demagogic rhetoric, a deterrent to citizen participation. Whistle-blowers who question the propriety of an insider self-interested coalition dominating and controlling local government must be prepared to become vilified themselves in the struggle over legitimacy. Beyond inhibiting barriers of legalism, scientism and professionalism, ACT and CLEAR, like other grassroots groups in similar contexts, had to encounter as well the stigma of "un-American" behavior.

The appointment of Ashbury Town Engineer Joshua Wright by the anti-megamall majority Town Board in 1996 reflected the positive impact of a more participatory attitude, welcoming public input in the planning process.[74] But the prospect for experiencing such planners, especially in local small-town contexts, is not great. According to Howe, Krumholz, Clavel and others, current planners with a participatory-friendly "social equity" orientation are still a minority and in large areas of the country (including upstate New York) very much so.

Meanwhile, the struggle to find or vote in elected officials committed to participatory modes is quite difficult. While a populist electoral campaign can contribute, as in Ashbury, to demonstrating large grassroots opposition to a development project, it can also, like litigation, potentially divert a strong local environmental group from its central objectives. A victory in the electoral arena can in fact lead to subsequent grassroots passivity and thus prove quite ephemeral. An apparent campaign stance is no guarantee of participatory commitment once in office. In Ashbury, for example, even some Town Board members elected on the anti-megamall slate found it difficult to concede, let alone widen, participatory modes (beyond government-appointed committees), as shown in rezoning deliberations concerning the commercial district from mid-1996 on.

Media Encouraging Grassroots Participation. Of all the local and regional media, the Ashbury-based weekly, the *Tribune*, was closest in orientation to the community groups themselves. More positive reporting on local environmental issues and organizing had typified the paper since its origin in 1976. Nevertheless, as the paper itself admitted upon Magellan's defeat, for too long the *Tribune* had neglected encouragement to CLEAR in its many land-use struggles from the mid-80s to the mid-90s. Only with a disillusioned ex-friend of Ryker as editor, as well as his successor, did the *Tribune* take strong positions and engage in investigative reporting generally supportive of "regulatory" values. (This progressive perspective and investigatory journalism has to some degree continued to the present, most likely a political legacy at least partially due to the community's anti-megamall struggle.) In turn, activists spoke frequently with *Tribune* reporters, encouraging their independent investigations and supplying them with copies of all documents sent on to the planning board. As well, a constant stream of letters to both the *Tribune* and the *Ashbury Chronicle* provided an energizing boost to the anti-megamall coalition and continuously informed others in the community of rationales behind the groups' sharp critiques.

While the unexpected support of the more conservative weekly *Ashbury Chronicle* was also quite helpful, it tended to cover impact issues but not the activist community groups which raised them. The regional daily press from Londonville and Riverside ran coverage only on more spectacular events, as the two public hearings and the community groups' efforts to unseat Ryker as planning board chair. The Regent Park *Star* covered most significant meetings, though with no special interest in the perspectives or activist enthusiasm at the grassroots. In turn, radio coverage was minimal. All three dailies did little investigatory journalism of their own and tended to be quite uncritical of potential adverse economic and environmental impacts continually publicized by the community groups.

In general, it would be hard to envisage anywhere a participatory-friendly regional daily press, given their increasing ownership by more distant publishing conglomerates, their priority concern with a strong advertising base of business interests and their attempt to appeal to a broad readership across a wide ideological spectrum. The same is true for radio and TV stations which share similar traits as the regional press. Strongly-"regulator" or even "ecologist" ideological perspectives are unlikely to gain significant coverage except in consciously "alternative" local newspapers, radio or cable television. While local papers of this sort, explicitly committed to participatory democratic values, existed in the late 60s and early 70s in Ashbury, at the time of the Moselle Plaza struggle, such local-based "alternative" media were not present as supportive elements of local participatory political culture.

Widespread Sharing of Participatory Values. Well before the successive anti-megamall struggles, Ashbury, like numerous other communities throughout the state and country, already was home to many residents experienced with and sympathetic to participatory values. Such individuals took the lead and helped to sustain long-range energy and participatory efforts in the megamall SEQRA review process. Those sympathetic to the struggle also were sustained and encouraged by knowing of many similar grassroots struggles in the region and nationally concerning environmental issues generally and anti-sprawl, anti-Wal-Mart concerns in particular. Such networks of information and mutual assistance are important. Shared outrage against outside destructive forces and shared insistence on legitimate grassroots self-determination are intangible, but significant contributions to local participatory political culture.

Additionally, Magellan's easy move across the town line in 1996 and the resulting inter-community collaboration at the grassroots level underscored another important limitation of presentday land-use planning. Legally-located planning in New York and most other states at primarily the local municipal level must be countered by sharing participatory values and political culture across town lines. Though in this case defeated through cross-community collaboration, Magellan's move across town borders illustrated an inherent weakness of isolated "localist" movements: grassroots environmental victory in one locale might simply shift development to an equally inappropriate site in a more vulnerable community. Regionally, nationally and/or internationally, direct and indirect activist mutual assistance (as through the anti-sprawl network) is essential to begin to counter the tremendous power and mobility of large developers.[75]

As in most communities, however, widespread grassroots insistence on meaningful participation tended to emerge in Ashbury only at times of crisis. Typically, long work hours and other competitors for time complemented strong cultural pressures toward "privatized and atomized politics." It is also difficult and painful in our culture for most people to admit that crises represent more basic systemic exploitation, thus requiring a higher level of continuous active political participation. Additionally, political passivity commonly represents a "free rider" assumption that if others watch out for one's community interests, it is unnecessary to be more politically active oneself. Thus, many CLEAR and ACT supporters who actively mobilized in time of greatest need at town meetings, fundraisers and similar occasions were ready to let a small handful of activists carry on the week-by-week and month-by-month monitoring of less spectacular land-use policy-making once the Wal-Mart battle was completed. Again, as in other locales, the same perspective characterized grassroots relations with elections and local government generally. Biennial campaign interest and enthusiasm by a few of the most politically active were followed by moderate grassroots complaints and disillusionment, but little direct participatory involvement, when unmonitored new "insider elites" seemed out of touch with the constituencies which elected them. Of course, as Piven and Cloward argue, elections themselves are a "structuring institution" designed to discourage other forms of more direct participation.[76] While Ashbury political culture possessed more solid participatory elements than in many small communities, therefore, even the megamall crisis failed to move it to a more permanent level of strong demands for regular participation. Because of various generic factors indicated here which transcend the specific Ashbury context, we suspect that this longer-range pattern is typical for most other communities with similar activist episodes.[77]

Regular Participatory Structures with Continuing and Full Decision-Making and Implementation Power. However potentially greater the participatory value base in Ashbury than in most upstate rural communities and however much the anti-megamall struggle temporarily energized the participatory self-confidence of some at the grassroots, therefore, the activist experience described in this case study not surprisingly led to no regularized participatory structures. Ad hoc participatory demands no doubt would continue to arise as various crises emerged, but ideologically, no community majority insisted on on-going participatory structures with power.

Summary. Factors reviewed in this discussion, the authors' experience with many SEQRA reviews in Ashbury and other areas over the years, and available literature on similar environmental impact assessment processes elsewhere suggest to us that the failure of the Ashbury megamall review process to meet the criteria of participatory land-use planning is only typical of the impact review model generally. It is this fundamentally flawed model, not specific Ashbury planning board members or inadequacies in Ashbury's urban regime, participatory process or political culture which must here be especially addressed. Even if, to our delight, the Ashbury community dramatically advanced toward participatory democratic ideals, thereby transforming SEQRA practice into a very different egalitarian and equitable experience from that of the Moselle Plaza process, the overwhelming majority of SEQRA-type battles elsewhere would remain as contorted and obstructed as the anti-megamall struggle in Ashbury. The conclusions from our observations in Ashbury and elsewhere are re-enforced by others' similar impressions in the same realm. The evidence for these broader conclusions is significant and overwhelming.

Despite the great flaws of SEQRA described in our study, New York state is seen as one of the states with the strongest "commitment to environmental goals and the quality of their programs,"[78] thus suggesting an even worse environmental impact review practice in most other parts of the country. Supporting this conclusion, after twenty years in the field, Paul Erickson writes that EISs throughout the US still "tend to serve more as records of decision making than as active tools in decision making"[79] and that "public involvement [in the assessment process] has largely remained an unfulfilled ideal."[80] As he suggests, any public that correctly perceives at best a patronizing attitude on the part of those "inviting" public participation in the assessment process "is fully justified in assuming that the public is being used rather than served."[81] Webler and Renn point out that while environmental impact review processes give citizens an opportunity to influence decisions, the fact that litigation has offered them greater means to shape policy indicates relative failure of the former approach.[82] SEQRA commentators insist that the "relegation of project critics to the periphery" in SEQRA review of key substantive issues because of lack of full disclosure is also typical with other states' environmental impact review processes as well as at the federal level.[83]

Williams and Matheny, in turn, provide extensive evidence about the inability of participatory dimensions in the hazardous waste realm to overcome bureaucratic, legislative and judicial sabotage of regulatory intent.[84] Nicholas Freudenberg states explicitly, "information is rarely the factor that decides who wins or loses an environmental struggle."[85] Similarly, a member of the Forest Service's regional appeals review team in Missoula, Montana described the process by which environmentalist challenges against timber sales were reviewed. The sole task was to assess procedural compliance with NEPA, not the actual environmental impact involved. "NEPA is a law without a conscience that the Forest Service readily exploits. It doesn't tell you what to do; it tells you how to do it. If you have any hope of reforming the Forest Service through NEPA, you're barking up the wrong tree."[86] Finally, while believing federal agencies to be more sensitive to environmental concerns because of NEPA, Taylor's conclusions on the limitations of that process are quite similar to our own,[87] Sirianni and Friedland describe the results of the participatory mandates of the 1970s, such as NEPA, as disappointing,[88] and Gould et al. see "structural barriers" generally as preventing "state-sponsored public empowerment schemes" from effectively constraining government-corporate development alliances.[89]

In an oft-cited 1969 article, federal HUD advisor Sherry Arnstein suggested a spectrum of increasing meaningfulness of citizen participation, depending on the structure, process and intent of those providing such access. Her scale moves from manipulation to therapy, then informing, consultation, placation, partnership, delegated power and, finally, actual citizen control.[90] Our sense is that the vast majority of formal participatory schemes go no further than manipulation or [bad] therapy and, at best, no more than informing, consultation and placation. As Rogers suggests, "The round-table process can create the temporary illusion that those sitting at the table are on a 'level playing-field,' whereas there is a profound difference in the economic and political power of the participants, and, indeed, the table is tipped at a precipitous angle."[91] Given their power in the outside world, developers at this table "do not necessarily act 'in good faith' (to put it mildly) in the creation of environmental policy."[92] In fact, inclusive round-table, multi-stakeholder approaches "merely end up allowing for the domination of economic forces over other perspectives which are temporarily given voice at the negotiating table but are shuffled aside in the decision making process."[93]

Essentially, those who opposed SEQRA's regulatory and participatory intent in the first place, while not able to block the legislation entirely, could not have designed a more ineffective outcome. Given (1) "home rule" devolution to an implementation level preoccupied with expanding the local property tax base, (2) local decision-making boards dominated by anti-participatory "pragmatic capitalists," (3) policy directives and budget limits preventing adequate state agency project critiques, and (4) environmental assessments composed initially by developers themselves, SEQRA's actual implementation became an early template for eventual deregulation and "privatization" schemes throughout many realms--environmental and otherwise--of state and federal public policy. Instead of a democratic research and analysis "marketplace of ideas," SEQRA became essentially a "regulatory marketplace" where the highest bidder prevails. In this particular application of supposed "efficiency"-driven "public choice" and "New Public Management" theory central to conservative privatizers, public grassroots activist groups are defined simply as one of the "private" "interest" competitors whose chances depend wholly on their mobilization of sustained human and money resources against the greater money and political resources of developers.[94]

But not content with remaining "red tape" delays caused by the regulatory shell of SEQRA and continued extra-participatory obstructions by project opponents it still permits, SEQRA's anti-regulatory opponents have continuously attempted to make it "customer"-friendly and "streamline" its process for its developer-"clients." DEC's regulatory revisions of 1996 further limited public participation in reviews and expanded the list of projects exempt from SEQRA. Apparently responding to environmentalist litigation about the changes, Pataki's DEC Commissioner stated that SEQRA "focuses on environmental protection, not process,"[95] despite the fact that the public has served as chief enforcer of SEQRA protection standards from the outset. Most recently, some SEQRA opponents promoted "reforms" of "conditional negative declarations" and Generic Environmental Impact Statements (GEISs) designed to further minimize the likelihood of developers having to prepare an EIS and thus also minimizing the remaining level of public participation.[96] Likewise, the New York State Conservative Party proposes further devolution of SEQRA into the hands of "light planners" and reduction of allowed time for preparing EIS critiques.[97]

The 1997 *Merson* decision may have provided the final blow to regular, if reduced, use of EISs.[98] Given the judiciary's reluctance to substitute its own substantive evaluations of impact issues for those of lead agencies, it is difficult to imagine courts defining more precisely the *Merson* thresholds permitting de facto CNDs. The Court of Appeals sees a developer's Type I project mitigation modifications as merely "legitimate maturation of a development project," not SEQRA-prohibited "conditions of approval," if they are produced "as part of the 'give and take' of the application process" preceding the final submission of the EAF and resulting from an "open process" of examination of large project impacts "with input from all parties involved" and "they clearly negate the continued potentiality of the adverse effects of the proposed action." Without more precise definitions of "clearly negate," "open process," and "input from all parties involved," this ruling is an open invitation for conscious "light planner" erosion of the public's role. Already a Federal court has cited *Merson* to assert that structured public hearings are not required by SEQRA's requirement of public participation[99]

Without even the guarantee of an EIS process of structured public input (whatever its weaknesses) through participation in forming the research agenda (scoping), focused comment on the developer's detailed plans and impact analyses (DEIS public hearing/public comment period), required developer responses to substantive public critiques (draft FEIS) and opportunity for public analysis of developer responses (at the least in the FEIS public comment period), lead agencies are invited to offer only token, makeshift windows for public participation in the research and deliberation process, a far cry from the purpose and spirit of SEQRA. Without an EIS findings statement, there is also no "balancing test" opportunity justified for the public to submit relevant and potentially crucial evidence concerning negative economic and social impacts. With *Merson*, the public will have to scramble for unguaranteed access to relevant documents, meaningful forums where lead agencies and developers must listen, and depend on the "good will" of both to consider its comments in the midst of the obviously more decisive lead agency-developer negotiations. With nothing left to guarantee its own participatory role but the *Merson* threshold of "open examination and input," the public now is also effectively deprived of judicial protection as well. As John Caffry states, because of *Merson*, "[t]he future will no doubt see a significant decline in de facto CND cases."[100]

The New York State Builders Association currently suggests that SEQRA's demise would be most welcome since allegedly it "has done little to change or improve the design of development projects" and "it is one of the reasons why we have a declining population and other areas are receiving some of the growth we should be receiving."[101] In any case, as SEQRA's original author and greatest legislative proponent recently observed, "[i]t is unfortunate that recent interpretations of SEQRA have emphasized how to 'get around' its spirit by devising ways to comply only with 'the letter' of the statute. This has confused and blurred the original intent of SEQRA. Mitigation of negative environmental factors has been downplayed."[102]

EIGHTEEN   SOCIO-POLITICAL CONCLUSIONS

Fundamental Critiques of the Evaluative Model

While proponents of progressive urban regimes and moderate participatory democracy may not have wished to imply that their models were realistically attainable throughout the society, some of their writing easily lends itself to that interpretation. They suggest that if only the right reforms and grassroots strategies are pursued, most Americans could experience a qualitative change in access to political self-responsibility from the ground up. Our detailed analysis to this point suggests that such expectations are unrealistic. Furthermore, our analysis suggests that government and big business have an important stake in maintaining this very illusion, encouraging through "participatory" rituals among an alienated public the continued "legitimacy" of elitist politics, environmental insensitivity and the domination of capital.[1]

We agree that it would be surely valuable for any local community to achieve a local participatory democratic political culture and participatory land-use planning of the sort suggested in Chapters Two, Sixteen and Seventeen above. But if these are presently unachievable in all but, at best, a small number of communities, a new explanatory and predictive model is needed for those who aspire to participatory democratic goals. While evaluative criteria used to this point have demonstrated major flaws of SEQRA and similar processes elsewhere, the same evaluative model also has lent itself, through its own inherent limitations, to the co-optive politics of those who wish to keep opaque the underlying dynamics of American politics.

An improved evaluative model must make such dynamics transparent to better assess the short- and long-range meaning of grassroots participatory activism of the sort described in this book. For this purpose, we wish to look more closely at pragmatic weaknesses in and "structuralist" critiques of urban regime theory. We also wish to examine weaknesses in actually-experienced participatory democracy experiments as well as critiques by radical democracy theorists concerning models like those of the "moderate" proponents examined in Chapter Sixteen.

Pragmatic Weaknesses in Progressive Urban Regimes. While urban regime theorists have presented their case convincingly as to the potential for changed coalitions of preeminent local power, the conditions for change to progressive urban regimes seem much more rare. However impressive the progressive regime examples cited by Clavel, Berry et al., Krumholz and Clavel, DeLeon,

Ferman and others, such regimes were continually the exception and usually only temporary. As Clavel stated, his five major examples "represent[ed] a notable exception to the normal patterns of local government"[2] and ultimately produced business-based backlashes in each case.[3] In turn, Berry et al. found "few other cities that even came close to the five cities [of their study] in the scope of neighborhood-based citizen participation."[4] Krumholz and Clavel discovered "a majority mode of operation that, like the society generally, tended to deny the efficacy of equity work, participated in futile giveaways to growth-oriented projects that failed to produce jobs and seemed not to emphasize the populations equity planners served."[5] Even the equity planners themselves typically felt that they were alone or their innovations vanished from local memory once they moved on.[6] As well, however remarkable the achievement of community-controlled redevelopment in Boston's Dudley Street Neighborhood Initiative, an unusually participatory model, its proponents acknowledged that it was very exceptional in that city and across the country, depending on nearly irreplaceable features of eminent domain power given by the city, massive foundation funding and community participatory control.[7]

Summing up her comparative analysis of regime evolution in Chicago and Pittsburgh, in turn, Ferman sees generally "disappointing experiences of urban progressive movements." Measured against the objectives of "improving the workings of a democratic polity[,] . . . "

> the political implications of the Chicago and Pittsburgh study are quite sobering. Perhaps most disheartening is the fact that many of this study's findings reflect the implications of the direction in which American politics appears to be heading . . . openly hostile to the needs of poor people and minorities, the residents of many of these inner-city neighborhoods.[8]

In her view, "the difficulties of building and maintaining progressive coalitions will be magnified as the existing 'small opportunities' continue to evaporate."[9] Finally, DeLeon's account underscored the precariousness of probably the most progressive large city regime, in San Francisco. There, it was obvious that a multi-racial and multi-class coalition as well as a coherent progressive ideology were essential, especially when the regime faced serious state and federal threats to cut back the economic and political space needed to maneuver.[10]

Structuralist Critiques of Urban Regime Theory. Having made their point that earlier deterministic-appearing structuralist paradigms of urban politics ignored or undervalued a wealth of evolving and fluctuating alternative local power coalitions, urban regime theorists, in turn, would seem now wise to return more to the issue of ultimate regime boundaries. Specifically, despite the rich diversity of alternative urban regime coalitions, to what extent do generic external restraints on local autonomy prevent progressive beginnings from proceeding further or from multiplying across the American landscape?

Though not impressed with or oriented toward the potentials of equity-oriented, redistributive progressive urban regimes, Peterson's *City Limits* argued compellingly concerning the ultimate economic binds faced by local governments in the face of regional and national capital mobility. Positive resolution of equity issues, he said, would have to be addressed by the federal government--the only level in the American political system with adequate resources to do so. Yet in the nearly two decades since Peterson's book, capital mobility has only intensified, now most strikingly at the international as well as national level.

The increase in transnational capital mobility is substantial. A commonly-cited example is the over one trillion dollars of foreign exchange traded privately each day, over 90% of which is pure financial speculation.[11] The threat posed by such volatile mobility, of course, is a strong disciplinary force inhibiting social redistributive spending on the part of urban and national regimes alike. As a writer for the right-wing libertarian Cato Institute wrote, "Equity investors have developed a global perspective, and they prefer markets where government is downsizing and the prospects for economic growth are good."[12] Likewise, while certain privileged centers such as New York City can benefit from "world city" administrative specializations in the new neo-liberal globalizing economy, in general, multinationals have long since learned that "cities can be played off, one against the other. Like restless apartment dwellers who keep moving to the newest complex, multinational corporations move from one city node to another in order to take advantage of the incentives offered" (including regulatory streamlining, tax breaks and cheap labor).[13] To the point, Perry reports that almost 90% of all business start-ups or expansion in western New York manufacturing or production facilities costing at least $750,000 in the mid-80s received some sort of government subsidy or support.[14] Using the recent example of western New York, Perry argues that unfavored regions in the United States can now in fact legitimately be described with the same "dependency theory" terminology as Third World countries.[15]

This transnational identity and potential flight of capital in turn leaves even the federal government, Peterson's salvation, no longer capable--within the bounds of its own prevailing militaristic and capitalistic ideology[16]--of coming to the rescue of urban regimes. From federal to local levels, the resulting priority of luring capital has pushed politicians increasingly to accept or rationalize a revival and more sophisticated version of neo-liberal ideology. This belief system focuses on market freedom and individual wealth accumulation instead of any notion of social solidarity and brings a "New Public Management" orientation to guide government at every level.[17] Shields and Evans define the "New Public Management" as a simultaneous tendency to centralize and more explicitly politicize political authority over bureaucracy, to assure neo-liberal policy agendas, while decentralizing and privatizing public administration. In doing so, it "obscures the fundamentally political nature of these changes through the discourse of efficiency, effectiveness and a refoundation of representative democracy."[18]

Such trends obviously thus cause ever-further erosion of the necessary bases of progressive regimes. (In some cases, as with the new World Trade Organization's power to ban "trade-inhibiting" legislation in any of its members, even local environmental protection measures, such as the serious exercise of SEQRA, could be "vetoed" by the neo-liberal political forces of globalization.[19]) Except for wealthier suburbs, this is surely as much an intense pressure on smaller municipalities as on major cities. Increasingly, whatever movement toward grassroots participatory democracy had been achieved in earlier years becomes all the more threatened in the face of the new intensification of elite politics, business value preeminence and privatization.

Pragmatic Weaknesses in "Moderate" Participatory Democratic Experiments. SEQRA and similar environmental impact review processes provide one model among a number of experiments in "moderate" participatory democracy. While our detailed case study has focused on this single model, SEQRA's basic identified weaknesses in fact typify the wider range of experience in this "moderate" realm.

Among experiments described in Chapter Sixteen, for example, referendums fail, through their simplistic yes/no votes, to acknowledge the individuality or intensity of voters' perspectives and fail to bring participants out of their atomized passive voter roles into open dialogue. Referendum campaigns are typically fraught with emotional appeals often heavily influenced by corporate spending, frequently are loaded with technical discourse to the point of incomprehensibility, and actually invite participation in only very narrow areas of policy choice at infrequent intervals. Even after votes, referendums are susceptible to politically-motivated judicial or budgetary vetoes, thus encouraging that much more disincentive for future voter participation.

The Community Action Program of the 1960s, in turn, while quite decentralized, still elicited voting participation at best by only 5% of those eligible.[20] It also relied on a representative rather than participatory mode on a board where elected community representatives were still usually in a minority.[21] Ultimately local decision-making itself was subject to the heavy hand of budgetary cutbacks from Washington. Such a limited participatory experience no doubt gave little sense of personal growth to most community residents and most likely left little legacy of positive enthusiasm for future participatory models generally.

Concerning citizen juries or deliberative panels, while conscientiously attentive to good process generally, such experiments are easily limited to problems or "responsible" policy alternatives carefully framed by the commissioning body, involve only small numbers of the population, and focus on limited issues at infrequent intervals. Additionally, they are only consultative in nature and are vulnerable to massive corporate spending and propaganda to counter whatever influence they may have on legislative bodies.[22]

Other thoughtful experiments along the "democratic discourse" lines of the "moderate" participatory democratic model have been proposed and experimented with, sometimes in direct response to the weaknesses of SEQRA-type experience.[23] But these new experiments themselves are vulnerable to similar critiques. Thus, "citizens advisory committees," "planning cells," "regulatory negotiation," and "coordinated resource management" have been criticized, among other issues, for their limited number of participants, mere consultative power, limited frames of discussion and restricted opportunities for their use overall, dependent as they are on the interest of exceptional agency or company officials.[24]

"Radical Reformist" and "Strong Radical" Participatory Democratic Theory. While "moderate" participatory democratic theory served to demonstrate many of the weaknesses of SEQRA-type environmental impact assessment processes, even deeper problems are identified when the "moderate" model itself is critiqued by "radical reformist" and "strong radical" participatory democratic theorists. "Radical reformist" theorists recognize a need for more drastic participatory reform, yet apparently still believe in the potential, however difficult, for the present liberal capitalist system to evolve in that direction from within.[25] Important themes of Benjamin Barber and Chantal Mouffe will be examined here to represent this group. "Strong radical" participatory democracy theorists, in turn, advocate a participatory system of greater depth and breadth, one clearly incompatible with liberal capitalism.[26] Of these, important themes of Carole Pateman and Val Plumwood will be discussed here. While authors with radical perspectives distance themselves from most aspects of the present political system, with or without explicit statements on how a transformation might be achieved, their alternative models serve also as a critique of existing practice, and thus, for some readers, a potential guide as well for relevant steps with which to begin.

According to Benjamin Barber, "There is little wrong with liberal institutions that a strong dose of political participation and reactivated citizenship cannot cure."[27] Nevertheless, he says, Western liberalism, in its representative form--

that is, "thin democracy"--"serves democracy badly if at all."[28] At the same time, liberalism generally and the "civil society" orientation, such as represented by Walzer, excessively focus on individualist instead of communitarian rewards. While conceding that local associational activity can help train for democracy, Barber sees the latter as undermined to the extent that the focus is privatistic, parochial or particularistic.[29] Politics in a "strong democracy" is where "the going is as important as the getting there,"[30] where a civic community is created with citizens "endowed with an enlarging empathy."[31] Says Barber, with "strong democratic" talk, "no voice is privileged, no position advantaged, no authority other than the process itself acknowledged."[32] "Strong democracy" encourages the art of careful empathetic listening, seeking a common language for a common good rather than the usual liberal democratic practice of adversarial proceedings where speech becomes another potential form of domination. Barber even goes so far as to assert that majority victories over minorities are a sign that mutualism has failed. To avoid ossification of leadership and thus de facto exclusion, Barber proposes that lower level officials be chosen by lot and that rotation of offices be required. Barber also warns that "[a]dopted piecemeal or partially, such innovations will at best only be assimilated into the representative adversary system and used to further privatize, alienate, and disenfranchise citizens."[33]

Additionally, Barber stresses the importance of affective communication since it is capable of measuring conviction and commitment as well. Implying also the need to break out from confined acceptable discourse, Barber states that it is capitalist logic and epistemology, not capitalist institutions or capitalist values, which offend democracy. On the other hand, Barber states that it is the modern corporation, gigantic, unaccountable, often monopolistic, and far from the free market image of the family enterprise, which "is an enemy of democracy in all its forms" and which strong democracy will have to overcome. Agreeing with Jefferson, Barber believes that America is blessed with such a strong constitution and individualist tradition that it can afford stringent critiques and even, from time to time, outright rebellion.[34] Finally, Barber states that only after thin democracy has been succeeded by strong democracy can it "pursue the economic leveling up and social justice that are the condition of its further growth."[35] "Democracy is the only road to socialism, and patience and humility remain the chief democratic virtues, especially for social democrats."[36]

While Barber speaks of a gradualist participatory approach to social democracy, based on liberal institutions, Chantal Mouffe speaks of a post-Marxist socialist project to push liberal democracy in the logical non-capitalist radical democratizing direction implied by its chief values of liberty and equality. This "radical liberal plural democracy," as she defines it, is a significantly transformative variety of participatory politics. From her post-structuralist perspective, Mouffe rejects the "essentialism" of liberals and leftists alike who define the term "liberalism" as equivalent to capitalism and/or individualism. It is incorrect and a fundamental weakness of "really existing" liberal democratic capitalism to imply that policy issues (as well as economic dynamics) can be explained and based upon mere private agreements--themselves based on private pursuit of instrumental objectives, with only consumerist procedural rules to regulate the plurality of individual interests. Such a perspective ignores the fact that multiple social identities, some dominant and some subordinate, are held by every individual. It also evades the reality that certain of those with common social identities have organized themselves to develop and maintain superior power positions over others.

Active citizenship should become the pre-eminent political identity among each individual's "ensemble of subject positions" (or unique variety and precariousness of identities),[37] while at the same time political agency should not be centered on one's relation to the state, but on one's ensemble of social relations. Mouffe speaks of radical democracy as a vigorous, ongoing, but non-messianic and never fully-resolved struggle to deepen the democratic revolution and the logic of "the egalitarian imaginary" by eliminating those institutions or institutional practice (such as large corporations and centralized big governments) in which subordinate social relations are embedded. She is emphatic on the need to respect individuality. Along with this emphasis, she states that the democratic demands of each oppressed identity group for liberty and equality should lead not only to allied efforts, but also to a new common political identity as "radical democrats."[38] This new citizenship identity is essential, says Mouffe, since some existing "citizenship rights" are "based on the very exclusion or subordination of the rights of other categories."[39] For Mouffe, also, "radical democracy" demands that deep questions be asked, though such a project means neither aiming at total transformation of the society nor at eliminating individuals who resist the radical democratic struggle. At the least, Mouffe says, there must be a common ethical subscription to certain norms of public conduct while pursuing self-chosen actions and satisfactions, rather than the communitarians' substantive definition of the common good or liberals' instrumental promotion of self-interest alone. Out of the experience of public-minded conduct will emerge more likely consensus on many, though not all, public policy means and goals.

Further on in the spectrum is Carole Pateman, one of the most influential "participatory democracy" theorists in recent years. Three decades ago, she sharply critiqued mainstream democratic theorists' reading of "classical" democratic theory and their claim that grassroots political participation was dangerous and unrealistic in modern industrialized society.[40] For Pateman, "'participation' refers to (equal) participation in the making of decisions, and 'political equality' refers to equality of power in determining the outcome of decisions, a very different definition from that in the contemporary theory."[41]

Crucial to her position was the "political" nature of all realms of social authority, especially in the workplace, but also in educational, cultural and other realms,[42] and thus the importance of complementary democratization through participatory decision-making in each of these realms if participatory democracy would succeed. Said Pateman, "for a democratic polity to exist it is necessary for a participatory society to exist, i.e., a society where all political systems have been democratised and socialisation through participation can take place in all areas."[43] At the same time, Pateman saw such changes occurring first at lower levels of everyday decision-making. Higher levels of government, industry and other realms, involving large numbers, would be governed by representative structures, but with a high level of voter interest and responsibility--fostered by lower-level "participatory" experience. Pateman's eventual agenda, in turn, sees individuals involved in decision-making in every social realm of their daily lives, not just the explicitly political.

Australian writer Val Plumwood argues that a non-dualistic mutualist ethic toward and relationship with non-human nature is the pre-eminent grounding for radical participatory democracy in every realm of social life. Plumwood specifically agrees with important aspects of Mouffe and Pateman, but her emphasis on master-subordinate dualism throughout the dominant philosophical traditions of Western culture since ancient times brings her to a unique, deeper vantage point than the others.[44]

> Reason in the western tradition has been constructed as the privileged domain of the master, who has conceived nature as a wife or subordinate other encompassing and representing the sphere of materiality, subsistence and the feminine which the master has split off and constructed as beneath him. The continual and cumulative overcoming of the domain of nature by reason engenders the western concept of progress and development.[45]

This paradigm continues to rationalize the exclusion, subordination and control of women, non-whites, workers, and colonized non-westerners as well since such human categories are cast by the "master identity" as lacking full rationality and closer to animal or nature realms.[46] The master's only valuation of such humans and of non-human nature is in instrumental terms: how much they contribute to the self-defined well-being of the elite.

The spread of genuinely democratic structures and experiences throughout daily life--characterized by a "relational conception of self" and a "rationality of mutuality," will re-enforce and converge with a non-instrumental ecological citizenship as well,[47] whereby animals and all of nature are recognized "as part of the political and moral community."[48]

Of the various theorists, perhaps Plumwood gives most attention to the implicit need to translate between political cultures of those oppressed by the present political system. Through her advocated "relational conception of self" and "rationality of mutuality," individuals will come to recognize that, for each category of "difference," philosophical and institutional dynamics of repression, alienation and domination as well as a potential anti-dualist liberatory strategy are similar and will return to the most basic human-nature split and its defeat. Plumwood argues that resolution of this hierarchical dualism is neither by uncritically merging all categories (as do some deep ecologists), by reversing hierarchy positions, nor by subordinate groups seeking gradual institutional inclusion in the master's framework without dissolution of the master's dualist logic. Non-scientistic "rationality" must also be accepted as legitimate discourse in the public arena, Plumwood states, since "even the challenges to the ruling elites [to date] have been appropriated by the master forms of consciousness or remade in their terms. . . . [T]he master identity is more than a conspiracy: it is a legacy, a form of culture, a form of rationality . . . [which] has come to shape us all."[49]

<u>Summary: Implications for Local Participatory Democratic Culture</u>. Great political and economic external pressures on local regimes and local participatory experiments have been major causes of the very compromised nature of participatory democratic models in the United States to date. As the more radical participatory democratic theorists have suggested, the lack of substantial experience with successful on-going participatory democratic contexts throughout the various realms of daily life, including but also beyond the explicitly political, has severely limited the emergence of a critical mass of individual grassroots organizations, media and facilitative organizers who might, because of the intrinsic and instrumental values of such experience, exude participatory democratic consciousness and lead to its exponential spread throughout a local political culture. Such a spread, in turn, would naturally produce a <u>de facto</u> transformation of local government from its hierarchical mode to a fully inclusive, continuing realm of egalitarian decision-making for every aspect of community policy. Concerning land-use planning specifically, this would imply a majority of local residents with "ecologist" ideology, increasingly sensitized to the self-defeating limits of anthropocentric orientation and the particular definitions of "reason" characterizing dominant forms of Western thought and culture since the Greeks.

Implications for Future of American Democracy and Environmental Protection

Returning to our original theme that any society's land-use form is inherently a statement of basic social relations, we must recognize that "real property" in our society is a particular artificial social construct within larger networks of power relations. The contemporary nexus of capitalism, industrialism, materialism and anthropocentrism, among various immense cultural forces, produces a strong and, to many, unquestionable logic of "light planning" or at best a "regulator" planning approach. Christopher Bosse suggests that "Americans generally are 'Lite Greens,' wary of making major life-style changes in the name of environmental protection."[50] Add to these heavy cultural forces the particularly strong limiting influence of militarism within the American system to maintain and expand capitalist expansion abroad and there seems less room for questioning basic assumptions than ever.[51] With the present historical moment of transnational capital mobility and neo-liberal privatization of decision-making in realms of public policy concern, space for the nourishing and evolution of "ecologist" participatory democratic ideology among large numbers seems even more cramped. At the same time, we suspect that, if better publicized, its emphasis on inclusive local community decision-making rather than governmental intervention would make it far more popular than it is.

Despite the fact that, as Raymond Rogers suggests, "any pretense that the role of government was to promote the 'public good' in the name of equity and rule of law has all but evaporated,"[52] the reaction of most in our society is increasing alienation and further retreat to "private" pursuits, rather than mobilization toward confronting these underlying broad historical forces. Our case study has demonstrated the typical roots of this alienation and why a supposed realm of "participatory democracy," designed in part to counter such alienation, has only led to its intensification. As we stated in Chapter One, if current democracy were to succeed at all it ought to be able to do so in a setting such as the one we described--a local context of immediate major threat and with a legally-mandated process inviting significant public participation. However, as we have shown, while the substantive outcome was positive, the process was not.

Adequate local environmental protection through this procedural template of privatization and illusion is anything but assured. Well-financed struggles by national environmental organizations against the largest development projects-- such as the New York City Westway proposal and the opening of national forests and parks to massive operations by lumber and mineral-extraction corporations--continue to attract the headlines. But thousands of local volunteer low-budget grassroots efforts every year against locally-significant, environmentally-destructive development proposals are of equal import for this country's quality of human lives and ecological well-being. The state of local interpretation and implementation of supposed participatory environmental regulations, where they even exist, therefore, is profoundly significant for our society's ability to survive within nature, just in terms of environmental degradation specific to this country alone. In turn, not even approachable in accountability to grassroots populations and with far more dangerous and complex issues than those faced in Ashbury, regulation at the federal level (let alone internationally[53]) in this most critical of realms appears doomed all the more.[54]

The local case-study described in this book is also symptomatic of the nature of regulatory policy-making in our society more generally. As illustrated throughout our account, between loosely-constructed regulations, a dependence on legal liberalism and "rational" criteria for enforcement, a consensus of decision-makers toward free market dynamics and minimal state intervention (especially at the local level), a preponderance of legal, scientific and technical "experts" committed to market ethics and power, and governmental technicians concerned to preserve their own publicly-unaccountable enclaves of bureaucratic power, regulatory law's proclaimed intent is constantly subverted at ideological and practical levels both.[55] In the context of the hegemony of development, environmental decision-making (even when "participatory") serves to legitimate megamalls by defining them as a benefit to and in harmony with their surroundings.

As social scientist Maarten A. Hajer explained concerning the acid rain controversy in Britain, even when the discursive practices of a capitalist-dominated "technocratic coalition" were supplanted by an "ecological modernization coalition" because of overwhelming public concern, actual routinized institutional policies of government have not changed. "The practical solutions, some of the labels, and many of the ecomodernist formulations were taken over while the traditional pragmatist practice continued," legitimized in fact "as a permanent, natural state of affairs."[56]

Given the consistency of this subversion throughout environmental and other realms of regulatory policy over many generations and the "realist" awareness of politicians, policy-makers, corporate interests and dependent intellectuals of this fact,[57] it is reasonable to conclude that entrenched power within capitalism will pursue whatever strategies of bias and manipulation are deemed necessary to preserve the opportunity for further development and growth. When the popular demand for community responsibility and restraint in any realm of social or economic activity becomes too vocal to be ignored, a legitimizing strategy of establishing new laws such as SEQRA and regulatory bodies such as the DEC is adopted as "evidence" of the corporate state's willingness to assume wider responsibility and accountability. If the popular outcry is so large or if popular suspicions against the legitimacy of new regulatory agency decision-makers develop too quickly, a space for "public participation" is enacted to release existing political tension, while re-enforcing the legitimacy of the decisions reached. Such innovations, however couched in the language of "participatory" consensus, represent a concerted effort at social construction to secure against challenges to capitalist control.[58] As Matthew Cahn suggests, "[t]he manipulation of public opinion through symbolic policy . . . allows [l]iberal society to . . . eliminat[e] the substance of [d]emocratic accountability."[59]

The literature on legal liberalism has, over the years, emphasized the notion that consumers of the law will accept law's outcome, provided it occurred in a manner which, through the auspices of a "fair hearing," was participatory and even-handed. Coerced results, albeit reliable, are less likely to be internalized as acceptable than those which occurred through "due process." The emphasis, therefore, is on proceduralism rather than substantive justice. It is contended that compliance with accepted procedural norms will assure that outcomes, at the least, are palatable, if not reliable. Whether or not one accepts the empirical validity of society's acquiescence to fair process as the guarantor of just outcomes, practice under SEQRA demonstrates that it is through this political process that powerful interests secure outcomes favorable to only a few. Indeed, under the auspices of legal liberalism, brokered and pre-ordained results are socially constructed in the garb of popular mandates, through the guise of compromise and consensus. The history of the environmental impact statement, at both national and state levels, has demonstrated that making decision-making more accessible and subject to poly-vocal discourses has done little to impede the steady progress of state-sponsored capitalism to continuously degrade the quality of life through ever-increasing sprawl.

What is "lawful" becomes a function of the political will of decision-makers and not a superstructure of freely-contracted agreements of mutual objectives and responsibilities. In this process, law itself is manipulative since it is within the realm of the powerful to subvert the very instrument which ostensibly seeks to constrain. Thus, megamalls can be described as not only harmonious with their physical surroundings, but as having been decided upon "lawfully," with full regard to the mitigation of adverse environmental impacts and the health, safety and welfare of the community. Everyone can then breathe a sigh of relief. As Jill Grant states directly, "As used by planners, politicians, and developers, 'democracy' supports the status quo."[60]

In the social ecology of the planning board, law is subservient to and can only be understood in the context of local politics. Should a planning board in a progressive urban regime be comprised of environmental advocates who endorsed SEQRA principles and objectives and retained consultants to ensure literal compliance with the spirit of the statute, an EIS would be required with full public participation and, given judicial discretion accorded to administrative agencies, a court challenge by a developer to such a decision would be unavailable. By contrast, in the more common political context, a decision to not require an EIS by a planning board predisposed to development and based upon data provided by consultants who reviewed potential impacts and characterized them as minimal would be equally impervious to judicial review and would be construed as a proper exercise of discretion. Law in this context is subjective and dependent on the will and interpretation of the dominant political entity.

Law's inaccessibility and reliance on elitist interpretations also help to circumscribe whatever beneficial effects are guaranteed through procedural fairness. After all, regulatory statutes written by lawyers can only be understood through reliance on interpretations by lawyers, whether as advocates or judicial officers. Epistemological empowerment, i.e., the understanding of rights and obligations, is therefore limited to a few and not conducive to the viability of participatory enclaves. Moreover, under capitalist democracy, law is private in that the principal purveyors of the law, the lawyers, must be retained in order to get them to act, while the fees they charge are normally beyond the means of community groups. Law's knowledge is not disbursed based on notions of merit, i.e., the intention to act consistently with law's potential laudatory objectives and purposes, but on profit--which re-enforces the corporate paradigm and, at the outset, biases the result.

In this context, however sincere the intent of some reformers, the legalized existence of participatory enclaves within statist policy-making--such as the opportunities for community input in the SEQRA process---can only be understood as having been incorporated by lawyers and key political actors not decisively to change existing basic power relations, but to assuage the public and thereby further legitimize the dynamics of market capitalism and actually-existing liberal democracy more generally. Nevertheless, well-organized grassroots political initiatives still have the potential, in policy realms such as SEQRA's, to overwhelm elitist constraints imposed upon "participatory democracy" with their own political sophistication and thereby outflank momentarily their law-empowered adversaries, as in the struggle depicted in this book.[61] Through their detailed understanding of procedural and substantive issues and through successful framing of the struggle with the imagery of "community defense against outside predators," local activists achieved what official practitioners of SEQRA would deny them--immediate preservation of the local character of Ashbury, situated as it was in the environmentally-sensitive Hudson Valley.

Such accomplishments must not be belittled. They provide endless evidence of peoples' capacity and will to resist destructive intrusions into their daily lives and communities by development and their capacity to alter law's elitist paradigm. Such accomplishments also offer invaluable experience with the nature and quality of temporary grassroots empowerment.[62] Over a period of months or several years, alternative "insurgent" participatory community decision-making emerges, overlapping with but independent of existing political and regulatory structures and with even greater popular "legitimacy" than the latter. However, as we have argued, the persisting potential for such victories should not lead to the conclusion that an evolution toward participatory democracy can be modeled upon existing participatory enclaves.[63] We believe that though sometimes effective in stopping brushfires on the outskirts of a community and in encouraging local accumulation of participatory wisdom and strength, these temporary volunteer mobilizations are not by themselves sufficient to signal or model true participatory democracy or to establish viable lasting local participatory political cultures. As Rogers suggests, "First and foremost, environmental conflicts are about conflicts of world views, and it is naive to the extreme to think that the world view of capital and technology will be negotiated away in an 'enlightened' manner through collaborative policy making."[64]

Grassroots participatory democrats face not only a well-financed and politically-entrenched corporate state, but also popular opinion heavily-engineered every day in a thousand ways by government pronouncements, corporate propaganda, the media generally, consumerist culture, the cult of bureaucratic and scientific "rationality," and sheer exhaustion to believe in free-market ideology and the legitimacy of those who dominate their existence.[65] It thus seems impossible to envisage within the foreseeable future the emergence of a vital "participatory democratic" polity through a strategy of occupying, expanding and multiplying participatory enclaves within the existing political system. We agree with Grant's conclusion that ultimately, in the face of such pressures, "democratic government does not give people the power to decide the fate of their communities; neither does planning."[66] To attempt serious environmental protection within the present system is akin to seeking to improve conditions of slaves within the institution of slavery.

On the other hand, community struggles such as the "insurgent planning" example described in this book provide a glimpse of an alternative decentralist model of politics and economics, a model increasingly envisioned and acted upon by large numbers in our society as faith in the authority and potential benefits of the old system has declined. This "direct democratic" alternative would begin from the grassroots level and gradually proceed through horizontal networking and upwards, continually focusing on "making community" or democratic "civil society" as it proceeded, through direct non-hierarchical relationships of ordinary people in every realm. At the same time, it would reclaim the political nature of economic relations by rejecting the industrialist/capitalist imperative of constant development through consumption of "resources" in favor of a community-determined, community-centered, and confederated economics in balance with rather than destructive of nature.[67]

We do not pretend to offer here a political strategy to enhance these positive tendencies, but hope that our analysis of the Ashbury experience helps to clarify the nature of the issues and struggle involved. We agree with Rogers that "current relations have a history, and there exists the opportunity to resist their totalization, thereby leading to a recognition that humans can still 'make' history, rather than just laying down and surrendering to the 'logic' of economic and technological expansion."[68] If the Ashbury struggle and other similar grassroots efforts succeed in returning to us an understanding that we have an opportunity to contribute to the broader turning of history toward reconciliation with the "natural history" from which we emerged, they will have succeeded--whatever the immediate political outcome. However, for those consciously aspiring to protect the environment and to live in a participatory democratic political culture, what these enormous obstacles mean specifically--concerning local land-use planning, local community life more generally and in broader regional, national and international contexts--will have to be answered by the actions of each of us in a manner most consistent with our own evolving mutual learnings and vision.

APPENDIX A: TABLES

GLOSSARY

ACT   Ashbury Citizens Together

CLEAR   Citizens Linked for Environmental Action and Responsibility

DEC   New York State Department of Environmental Conservation

DOT   New York State Department of Transportation

DFSEIS   Draft Final Supplemental Environmental Impact Statement

DSEIS   Draft Supplemental Environmental Impact Statement

EIS   Environmental Impact Statement

FCPB   Forest County Planning Board

FCDPW   Forest County Department of Public Works

FOIL   Freedom of Information Law

FSEIS   Final Supplemental Environmental Impact Statement

GEIS   Generic Environmental Impact Statement

NEPA   National Environmental Protection Act

RCIDA   Reading County Industrial Development Agency

SCS   Soil Conservation Service (now Natural Resources Conservation Service), U.S. Department of Agriculture

SEIS   Supplemental Environmental Impact Statement

SEQRA   New York State Environmental Quality Review Act

MAJOR ACTORS (through 12/95)

Magellan Construction
Deke Reynolds (head of shopping center division), David Jankoff (project manager), Morris Schwab (attorney)

Planning Board Consultants
Frank Rattle (attorney), Gene Busch (planner), Tony Napoleon (professional engineer)

Planning Board Members
Rocky Ryker (M), Red Davis (M), Rich Maglie (PC), Julia Bellows (R), Jane Pelletier (R), Ray Dalrymple (R), Ben Hillman (R), Sam Myers (PC), Bob Manley (R), Suzi Green (R)

Town Board Members
Grant Schmidt (Repub., PC), Edna Devilla (Dem., PC), Mark Lyon (C, R), Gertrude Kraft (Repub., PC), Jane Pelletier (Dem., R)

Community Groups' Experts
Manny Dreyfus (attorney), Joshua Wright (professional engineer), Stanley Case (traffic engineer), Maynard Smith (planner and economist)

Community Group Leaders
Ina Turbell (president, Ashbury Citizens Together), Alex McBride (co-chair, CLEAR)

Community Reform Party Candidates
Rachel Wilton (Dem., R), Mark Lyon (C, R), Jane Pelletier (Dem., R)

Alphabetically Listed

Julia Bellows (Planning Board, R)
Gene Busch (planner for Planning Board)
Stanley Case (traffic engineer for community groups)
Ray Dalrymple (Planning Board, R)
Red Davis (Planning Board, M)
Edna Devilla (Town Board, Dem., PC)
Manny Dreyfus (attorney for community groups)
Suzi Green (Planning Board, R)
Ben Hillman (Planning Board, R)
David Jankoff (Magellan Construction project manager)
Gertrude Kraft (Town Board, Repub., PC)
Mark Lyon (Town Board, C, R) (Community Reform Party candidate for
 Town Board)
Rich Maglie (Planning Board, PC)
Bob Manley (Planning Board, R)
Alex McBride (CLEAR co-chair)
Sam Myers (Planning Board, PC)
Tony Napoleon (professional engineer for Planning Board)
Jane Pelletier (Planning Board, R) (Town Board, Dem., R) (Community
 Reform Party candidate for Town Board)
Frank Rattle (attorney for Planning Board)
Deke Reynolds (head of Magellan Construction shopping center division)
Rocky Ryker (Planning Board, M) (Town Repub. Party chair)
Grant Schmidt (Town Supervisor, Repub., PC)
Morris Schwab (Magellan Construction attorney)
Maynard Smith (planner and economist for community groups)
Ina Turbell (Ashbury Citizens Together president)
Rachel Wilton (Community Reform Party candidate for Town Supervisor,
 R)
Joshua Wright (professional engineer for community groups)

Abbreviations: M="minimalist" planning perspective, PC="pragmatic
capitalist", R="regulator", Repub.=Republican, Dem.=Democrat, C=Citizens
Party

CHRONOLOGY OF MAJOR EVENTS

1992

1/8   -   Medford Corporation signs option with Joe Heller, property owner

4/27   -   Medford gains planning board approval for Heller lot subdivision

1993

6/9   -   Reading County IDA gives preliminary approval for Medford shopping center in Ashbury

12/20   -   Magellan Construction first publicly presents Moselle Plaza project to Ashbury planning board

1994

5/5   -   Formation of Ashbury Citizens Together (ACT)

5/23   -   First "public hearing" on Moselle Plaza

6/27   -   Planning Board votes for environmental impact statement

8/8   -   Planning Board adopts final draft for EIS scope

12/19   -   Planning Board accepts DSEIS as "complete"

1995

1/19   -   Planning Board chair replaced by Town Board

1/30   -   Official public hearing on DSEIS

4/17   -   Magellan gives draft Final SEIS to planning board

6/12   -   Maglie gives economics report to planning board

9/18   -   Planning Board accepts draft FSEIS as "complete"

11/7   -   Town Board election

11/20   -   Planning Board's first "findings" vote

1996

3/11   -   Planning Board's final "findings" vote

APPENDIX B: MAPS

Map I - Features of Area Near Moselle Plaza Site

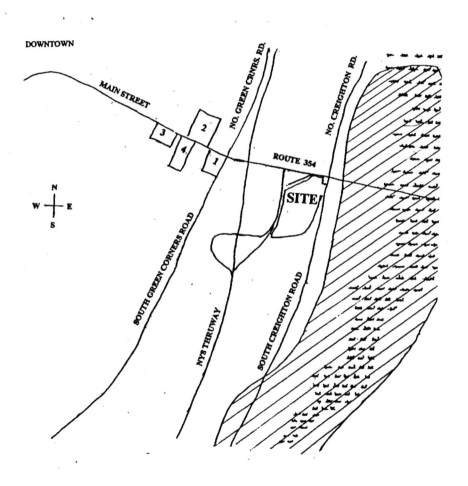

DOWNTOWN

MAIN STREET

NO. GREEN CRNRS. RD.

NO. CREIGHTON RD.

ROUTE 354

SITE

N
W — E
S

SOUTH GREEN CORNERS ROAD

NYS THRUWAY

SOUTH CREIGHTON ROAD

1 = EXISTING FOODFEAST PLAZA

2 = ASHBURY PLAZA

3 = ALMOND PLAZA

4 = MAPLE HILL PLAZA

 ROODEKILL-
CREIGHTON
WETLAND

 UNCONSOLIDATED
AQUIFER

386

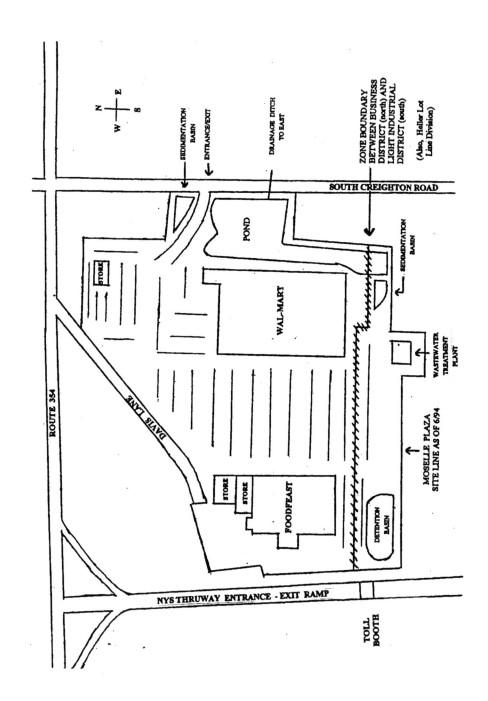

Map II - Tentative Site Plan for Moselle Plaza, June 1994

APPENDIX C: CHARTS

SEQRA FLOW CHART
(With relevant book chapters in roman numerals)

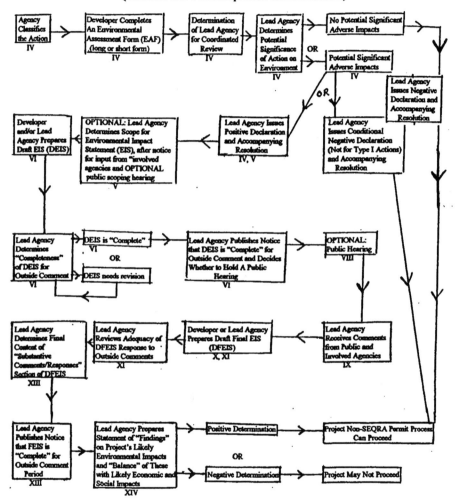

MODEL OUTLINE FOR TRAFFIC ANALYSIS

1. Identify key intersections, in vicinity of project, where traffic flow to be measured (local knowledge, accident records, etc.)

2. Measure present traffic flow at these intersections
   a. "worst-case analysis": peak AM and PM hours, weekdays (usually Friday) and Saturday; busiest season (tourism, peak shopping period, etc.)
   b. actual number of vehicles in every direction, lane-by-lane
   c. determine number of lanes, width of each lane, stop sign or traffic light (and timing of latter)
   d. using standard traffic engineering formulas, determine level of service (how much delay) (A is best, F is worst) for each lane (not just average for whole intersection)

3. Calculate traffic flow figures for year of project completion (or beyond) by adding amounts for annual traffic growth rate in area (such as 4%) to item #2

4. Calculate estimated additional cumulative traffic for year of completion derived from new projects in area already approved or likely to be built

5. Add items 3 and 4 to determine total "no-build" background traffic volumes (and levels-of-service) for each lane

6. Estimate specific traffic volumes (and lane-by-lane distribution) to be generated by the new project (using standard ITE formulas), using peak hours and peak seasons

7. Combine 5 and 6 to determine projected traffic flow and levels-of-service resulting from project (use the four elements identified in item #2)

8. Calculate improved traffic flow and levels-of service resulting from planned mitigation (road widening, additional lanes, traffic lights, etc.) agreed to by developer

MODEL OUTLINE FOR ECONOMIC IMPACT ANALYSIS

A. Overall Comments:

1. Purpose: A detailed economic impact analysis is essential for understanding the project's likely overall effect on community character, the fiscal context and local jobs (in SEQRA analysis, this is especially relevant for potential environmental impacts on "community character" and "visual or aesthetic resources" and also for the "balancing test" which weighs a project's environmental impacts against economic and social impacts)

2. Methodology: All formulas and factual assertions should be justified through detailed explanations and/or citation of reliable sources

B. Impact of Project on Existing Retail Market

1. What is the existing and projected local retail demand? (definition of primary retail zone geographically and taking into account other similar Wal-Mart and Kmart malls in the region; population size and income of this zone; average % of income spent on retail goods--generally and by category)

2. What is the existing (and approved) retail capacity (by sq. ft.) in the retail zone (generally and by category)?

3. What is the likely irretrievable retail spending leakage outside of this zone? (as through mail, phone or internet orders; commuter spending; continued shopping at regional malls, etc.)

4. What are the expected sales from the new mall (overall and by category)? (include current and projected sales per sq. ft. for Wal-Marts)

5. What will be the extent of the new mall's resulting takeover of retail sales from existing retail stores (overall and by category)?

6. What will be the specific impact on major shopping centers in the area?

7. What will be the secondary ripple impact of the new mall on non-directly competing stores in the same major shopping centers with seriously-impacted anchors?

8. What will be the secondary ripple impact of the new mall on non-directly competing stores in the shopping centers and downtowns caused by the discouragement of existing and future tourism through the appearance of urban blight through deteriorated or abandoned centers and boarded-up store fronts?

C. Impact on Jobs

1. Number (overall and by store); full-time or part-time (and definition of each by hours and weeks); average pay scale for each category; long-range vs. first few weeks; new jobs vs. those already existing (as in current local stores of same nature); locally-recruited vs. out-of-town recruited

2. Average rate of Wal-Mart job expansion vs. general retailer job expansion proportional to sales increases

3. Number of jobs to be lost in the retail zone because of the new mall's impact on the existing retail market

D. Fiscal Impact

1. Revenue Impact

   a. Expected property taxes to be paid by the new mall to town (and/or village), school district and county (calculate both with and without potential tax abatements, such as IDA or other business incentive programs, such as 485-B in New York)
   b. Expected loss of property taxes to be paid to town (and/or village), school district and county because of lowered assessments of deteriorated or abandoned malls, other strip shopping centers and existing downtown commercial properties, as well as reduced assessment of residential properties near the new mall and near newly-ghettoized shopping centers and downtown
   c. Expected loss of property taxes to adjacent towns (and/or

villages), school districts and county because of lowered assessments of shopping centers and downtown commercial properties in adjacent towns (and/or villages), as well as reduced assessment of residential properties nearby

d. Decline of state equalization funds to school district because of potential higher local assessment base

e. Expected county sales tax revenues from the new mall

f. Expected loss of county sales tax revenues because of deterioration or abandonment of existing retail stores and tourist spending in the area

g. Expected state and federal income tax revenue from new jobs created by the new mall

h. Expected loss of state and federal income tax revenue because of losses of existing jobs in the area caused by the new mall

2. Government Expenses

a. Costs for additional fire, police and other municipal services at the new mall

b. Costs for additional fire, police and other municipal services at the ghettoized shopping centers and downtown(s) (similar calculation for potentially affected adjacent towns or villages)

c. Costs for community planning, assessment and community development resulting from urban blight caused by new mall in existing downtown (similar calculation for potentially affected adjacent towns and villages)

d. Costs for town, county and/or state road improvements

e. Costs to school district for new schoolchildren from families of new employees

E. Impact on Community Character

1. Growth-inducement effect of shifting commercial center away from existing locations

2. Consistencies or contradictions with town Master Plan

3. Effect on pedestrian access to existing stores

4. Effect on rural, small-town atmosphere

5. Comparison of existing merchants' support level of local volunteer organizations and community activities with typical record of Wal-Mart

6. Similar assessments of these factors for potentially affected adjacent towns and villages

ENDNOTES

CHAPTER ONE

1. A recent anthology which examines various case-studies of "insurgent planning" is Leonie Sandercock, ed., *Making the Invisible Visible: A Multicultural Planning History* (Berkeley: University of California Press, 1998).

2. Formal environmental impact assessment is currently required by statutes in 27 states, the District of Columbia and Puerto Rico. It is also required by federal law for actions by agencies of the United States government and by national law in a large number of countries throughout the world (Diori L. Kreske, *Environmental Impact Statements: A Practical Guide for Agencies, Citizens and Consultants* [New York: John Wiley & Sons, Inc., 1996], Chapter Five). While struggles based on environmental impact analysis can be found throughout the world, we also recognize that "[c]ompared to most other industrial societies, the United States organizes land use in a unique manner, both in the extent of authority given to private developers and in the extreme independence of local government agencies" (John R. Logan and Harvey L. Molotch, *Urban Fortunes: The Political Economy of Place* [Berkeley: University of California Press, 1987], p. 147).

394

3. Opposed to the usual modernist portraits of state-driven planning as a "progressive" and "rational" practice and similar to the intent of the Sandercock volume, our analysis studies local resistance to official planning practices and alternative community-driven and community-building planning from below. As Sandercock states, "planning by and through the state is only one story among many, rather than <u>the</u> story. . . . [An alternative approach addresses] people's need and right to participate in decisions affecting their daily lives in cities and communities" (Sandercock, "Framing Insurgent Historiographies for Planning," in Sandercock, ed., pp. 28-29).

4. Planning expert Jill Grant states: "Seldom have writers fully articulated the values, beliefs, and meanings transacted by the players in the 'planning drama.' Most of the studies of practice have focused on the planner: few have looked at relationships between planners, politicians and citizens" (Jill Grant, *The Drama of Democracy: Contention and Dispute in Community Planning* [Toronto: University of Toronto Press, 1994], p. 18). In the present work's attention to detail, we follow the advice of Grant: "To understand the 'script' of planning dramas, we must listen to the language of participants in planning activities. In the choice of words, in the turns of phrase, in the style of argumentation that actors use, we uncover evidence about relations between actors and the meanings and values they transact" (Ibid., p. 38). Additionally, as John Forester emphasizes, such "stories enrich our critical understanding if they allow us to talk about the 'political passions of planning'--the academic undiscussables of fear and courage, outrage and resolve, hope and cynicism too, as planners and other professionals [and activists, we would add] must live with them, face them, work with them" (Forester, *The Deliberative Practitioner: Encouraging Participatory Planning Processes* [Cambridge: M.I.T.Press, 1999], p. 35). From a phenomenological perspective, we believe that it is important to allow the various subjectivities of actors to emerge, in order to facilitate and strengthen the power of an overall analysis of the entire arena of contestation, the deeply encoded "text" of the environmental impact assessment process.

5. Constance Perin, *Everything in Its Place: Social Order and Land Use in America* (Princeton: Princeton University Press, 1977), p. ix.

6. Nicholas Blomley, "Landscapes of Property," *Law and Society Review*, vol. 32 (1998), no. 3, p. 569.

7. A useful short summary of the centuries-long process in Europe leading to this stage is Daniel W. Bromley, "Rousseau's Revenge: The Demise of the Freehold Estate," in Harvey M. Jacobs, ed., *Who Owns America? Social Conflict over Property Rights* (Madison: University of Wisconsin Press, 1998), pp. 19-28. The most obvious initial stage of government intervention in North America was in forceful takeover or purchase of land from the original Indian inhabitants.

8. Richard F. Babcock, *The Zoning Game: Municipal Practices and Policies* (Madison: University of Wisconsin Press, 1966), pp. 3, 6, 17, 31, 115-119. Says Perin, "Zoning regulations are probably the most significant incentive on behalf of development. . . . Zoning regulations are a major 'insurer' to which some of the risk is passed along, and . . . it is that function that accounts for the decisions of bankers

and investors to accept zoning, and, through their influence, Chambers of Commerce and city councils" (p. 152). Concerning exclusionary motives, in the 1926 *Euclid* case which eventually gained Supreme Court legitimization for zoning, the original trial judge stated that "in the last analysis, the result to be accomplished is to classify the population and segregate them according to their income or situation in life" (as quoted in Babcock, p. 107). Likewise, Robert Wood stated, for example, "Though exceptions exist among its municipalities, Westchester [County in New York] remains, as someone has quipped, dedicated to 'zoning against "Bronxification!"'" (Wood, with V. Almendinger, *1400 Governments: The Political Economy of the New York Metropolitan Region* [Cambridge: Harvard University Press, 1961], pp. 93-94).

9. Blomley, p. 575.

10. Babcock, pp. 6-8, 60, 89.

11. Harvey Molotch, "The City As A Growth Machine: Toward A Political Economy of Place," *American Journal of Sociology*, vol. 82, no. 2 (September 1976), pp. 309-332.

12. See Richard Harris and Sidney Milkis, *The Politics of Regulatory Change: A Tale of Two Agencies* (New York: Oxford University Press, 1989); Elliot Krause, "Functions of A Bureaucratic Ideology: 'Citizen Participation,'" in Terrence E. Cook and Patrick M. Morgan, eds., *Participatory Democracy* (San Francisco: Canfield Press, 1971), pp. 420-427; David Mathews,. *Politics for People: Finding A Responsible Public Voice* (Chicago: University of Illinois Press, 1994); Harold Wolman, "Local Government Institutions and Democratic Governance," in David Judge, Gerry Stoker and Harold Wolman, eds., *Theories of Urban Politics* (London: Sage Publications, 1995), p. 137; Susan S. Fainstein and Clifford Hirst, "Urban Social Movements," in Judge, et al., eds., p. 195; Harry Boyte,"Beyond Deliberation: Citizenship As Public Work," paper presented at the PEGS Conference, February 11-12,1995,Available[Online]:<http://www.journalism.wisc.edu/cpn/sections/new_citizenship/ theory/boyte.html> [8/3/99]; Jeffrey M. Berry, Kent E. Portney and Ken Thomson, *The Rebirth of Urban Democracy* (Washington, D.C.: The Brookings Institution, 1993), pp. 35-36; and Carmen Sirianni and Lewis Friedland, *Civic Innovation in America: Community Empowerment, Public Policy, and the Movement for Civic Renewal* (Berkeley: University of California Press, 2001).

13. Thomas Webler and Ortwin Renn, "A Brief Primer on Participation: Philosophy and Practice," in Ortwin Renn, Thomas Webler and Peter Wiedemann, eds., *Fairness and Competence in Citizen Participation: Evaluating Models for Environmental Discourse* (Dordrecht, The Netherlands: Kluwer Academic Publishers, 1995), p. 19.

14. An interesting and useful "social constructionist" theoretical approach to understanding the tasks and overall methods of effective environmental organizing, in such a context, is John A. Hannigan, *Environmental Sociology: A Social Constructionist Perspective* (London and New York: Routledge, 1995). Our analysis in this book agrees in important respects with Hannigan's described dynamics and we have taken to heart his suggestion that "future research on the environment from

a social constructionist perspective would significantly prosper by incorporating a more explicit emphasis on power relations" (p. 190). Our specific concern with competing constructions of reality and their related discourses is comparable to the postmodern analytical approach of a variety of more recent writers on environmental politics, such as Bruce A. Williams and Albert R. Matheny, *Democracy, Dialogue and Environmental Disputes: The Contested Languages of Social Regulation* (New Haven: Yale University Press, 1995). The competition of discourses matters. As Frank Fischer and John Forester state, "[D]iscursive struggles involve far more than manipulatory rhetoric. The institutionally disciplined rhetorics of policy and planning influence problem selection as well as problem analysis, organizational identity as well as administrative strategy, and public access as well as public understanding" (Fischer and Forester, "Editors' Introduction," in Fischer and Forester, eds., *The Argumentative Turn in Policy Analysis and Planning* [Durham: Duke University Press, 1993], p. 2).

15. Manuel Castells, *The Urban Question: A Marxist Approach* (London: Edward Arnold, 1977), p. 466.

CHAPTER TWO

1. See, for example, those "ideal types" presented in Seymour J. Mandelbaum, Luigi Mazza and Robert W. Burchell, eds., *Explorations in Planning Theory* (New Brunswick, N.J.: Center for Urban Policy Research at Rutgers, State University of New Jersey, 1996); Sue Hendler, ed., *Planning Ethics: A Reader in Planning Theory, Practice and Education* (New Brunswick, N.J.: Center for Urban Policy Research at Rutgers, State University of New Jersey, 1995); Elizabeth Howe, *Acting on Ethics in City Planning* (New Brunswick, N.J.: Center for Urban Policy Research at Rutgers, State University of New Jersey, 1994); and John Friedmann, *Planning in the Public Domain: From Knowledge to Action* (Princeton: Princeton University Press, 1987). The first and last of these sources also provide especially useful discussions of the historical theoretical roots of each major perspective.

In analyzing public policy more broadly, Charles O. Jones describes three generic patterns of policy agenda-setting quite similar to the first three policy orientations outlined here (*An Introduction to the Study of Public Policy* [Monterey: Brooks/Cole, 1984; 3rd ed.], pp. 62-64). In general terms, land-use policy "minimalists" align with an overall "individualist libertarian" or "minimal statist" political perspective, "pragmatic capitalists" with "conservative statism," "regulators" with "liberal" or "socialist" statism, and "ecologists" with "direct democracy" or "communitarian libertarianism."

Competing land-use planning or overall public policy perspectives, in turn, are a sub-set of the competition in "mental structures, appreciations, worldmaking, and framing"--terms "that capture different features of the processes by which people construct interpretations of problematic solutions, making them coherent from various perspectives and providing users with evaluative frameworks within which to judge how to act" (Martin Rein and Donald Schon, "Reframing Policy Discourse," in Fischer and Forester, eds., p. 147). Such framing has philosophical, ethical and political dimensions, among others, with important implications for appropriate behavior in every aspect of community life.

2. Bruce Yandle, "Environmental Regulation: Lessons from the Past and Future Prospects," in Terry L. Anderson, *Breaking the Environmental Policy Gridlock* (Stanford: Hoover Institution Press, 1997), pp. 144-145.

3. Thomas L. Harper and Stanley M. Stein, "A Classical Liberal (Libertarian) Approach to Planning Theory," in Hendler, p. 19.

4. James Howard Kunstler, *The Geography of Nowhere: The Rise and Decline of America's Man-Made Landscape* (New York: Simon and Schuster, 1993), p. 26.

5. Logan and Molotch, p. 27.

6. Ibid., p. 47. As Douglas Torgerson points out, "Perfecting the market would require the abolition of both public <u>and</u> private power in the market, and this would mean a radical transformation of power relationships on a scale that free market advocates do not fully contemplate. . . . What is left of the market, indeed, if it is considered detached from the ensemble of vast public and private power that has historically promoted, shaped, and defended actually existing capitalism and its spectacular wealth?" (Torgerson, *The Promise of Green Politics: Environmentalism and the Public Sphere* [Durham: Duke University Press, 1999], pp. 152-153).

7. As Harvey Jacobs points out, to accomodate newly emerging airplane travel in the early 20th century, U.S. courts repossessed from private landowners air rights above a certain elevation, thus creating a new "public commons" (Jacobs, ed., p. xi). Said no less a "Founding Father" than Benjamin Franklin, "Private property . . . is a creature of society, and is subject to the calls of that society whenever its necessities shall require it, even to its last farthing" (Franklin, "Queries and Remarks Respecting Alterations in the Constitution of Pennsylvania," in Vol. 10 of *The Writings of Benjamin Franklin*, edited by Albert H. Smith [London: Macmillan, 1967 (1789)], p. 59, as cited in Jacobs, ed., p. 37).

8. This "minimalist" perspective is articulated, for example, by individualist libertarian Richard Epstein in *Takings: Private Property and the Power of Eminent Domain* (Cambridge: Harvard University Press, 1985) and by "classical liberal" Robin Paul Malloy in *Planning for Serfdom: Legal Economic Discourse and Downtown Development* (Philadelphia: University of Pennsylvania Press, 1991). Despite differences between the two orientations, they have more in common with each other than with the other three positions. In political movement terms, this "minimalist" position is represented by various elements of the "Wise Use Movement," such as the Alliance for America. Such organizations are critically examined in John Cronin and Robert F. Kennedy, Jr., *The Riverkeepers* (New York: Scribner, 1997), pp. 236-251; Chip Berlet, ed., *Eyes Right! Challenging the Right Wing Backlash* (Boston: South End Press, 1995), pp. 135-154; Harvey M. Jacobs, "The 'Wisdom,' But Uncertain Future, of the Wise Use Movement," in Jacobs, ed.; Philip D. Brick and R. McGreggor Cawley, eds., *A Wolf in the Garden: Land Rights Movement and the New Environmental Debate* (Lantham, Md.: Rowman and Littlefield, 1996); Carl Deal, *The Greenpeace Guide to Anti-Environmental*

Organizations (Berkeley: Odonian Press, 1993); John Echeverria and Raymond Booth Eby, eds., *Let the People Judge: A Reader on the Wise Use Movement* (Washington: Island Press, 1995); and David Helvarg, *The War against the Greens: The "Wise Use" Movement, The New Right and Anti-Environmentalist Violence* (San Francisco: Sierra Club Books, 1994).

An Ashbury highway superintendent explicitly offered a "natural law" rationale for this position when replying to the authors' critique of his failure to abide by New York state environmental impact regulations. "When I place my hand on the Bible, I took the oath of office to God, who is my judge, as He is the judge of the two of you. There are no experts in the field of conservation and/or the environment; we all destroy the Earth in our own way." (Glenn Martin letter to the editor, *Tribune* [Ashbury, N.Y.], 4/20/00 [while we have changed the names of specific local and regional newspapers in order to preserve identity fictionalization, we have retained specific citations to assure readers that sources for our information are quite real]).

9. Perin, p. 145.

10. Howe, p. 58; John R. Logan, Rachel Bridges Whaley and Kyle Crowder, "The Character and Consequences of Growth Machines: An Assessment of Twenty Years of Research," in Andrew E.G. Jonas and David Wilson, eds., *The Urban Growth Machine: Critical Perspectives, Two Decades Later* (Albany: SUNY Press, 1999), pp. 82, 88-89.

11. Charles Hoch, "What Do Planners Do in the United States?," in Mandelbaum, et al., eds., p. 227.

12. Bishwapriya Sanyal underscores the hostility of this perspective to government planners generally as a dangerous interest. They see "the state [as] neither an autonomous nor a benign actor but [one] . . . captured by a 'special-interest' group, internal to the state, whose members are part of a new class that, by controlling the state apparatus, controls some of the means of production and all of the means of distribution" (Sanyal, "Meaning, Not Interest: Motivation for Progressive Planning," in Mandelbaum, et al., eds., p. 138). This provides the motivation behind conservative political forces, as in the Reagan administration, which seek to take over and maintain government agencies, while effectively dismantling from within their capacity to function as originally intended.

13. Howe, pp. 113-124. Her further description of this orientation appears on pp. 6-7, 28, 30, 34, 40-41, 58, 80.

14. John Friedmann, "Two Centuries of Planning History: An Overview," in Mandelbaum, et al., eds., p. 23. See also Howell S. Baum, "Practicing Planning Theory in A Political World," in Mandelbaum, et al., eds., p. 373.

15. Taylor, *Making Bureaucracies Think: The Environmental Impact Statement Strategy of Administrative Reform* (Stanford: Stanford University Press, 1984), pp. 19, 28.

16. Despite the erosion of traditional localist community identities by long-range forces of modernization, this prolonged and continuing disruption itself has now led to a resurgent appeal of new communitarian identities, an important leverage for "growth machine" ideologists to use to their own advantage (Kevin R. Cox,

"Ideology and the Growth Coalition," in Jonas and Wilson, eds., pp. 31-32, 34, and Mark Boyle, "Growth Machines and Propaganda Projects: A Review of Readings of the Role of Civic Boosterism in the Politics of Local Economic Development," in Jonas and Wilson, eds., pp. 60-62). However, as suggested by David Kay, the Ithaca, N.Y. planning board chair during a Wal-Mart battle there in the mid-1990s, while "community" disruption may well be significant, "community-building" may also occur through such struggles, especially among activists and their supporters (all the more in progressive local political cultures) and especially in resistance to major outside developers whose projects pose major disruptive potentials themselves (David Kay, "Community and the Politics of Open Space" [Ithaca: Cornell Local Government Program Paper, 1996], pp. 11-12, 15-16; Available [Online]: <http://clgp.arme.cornell.edu/docs/14-DKOS.pdf> [2/15/01] .)

17. Williams and Matheny, p. 17.

18. Serge Taylor's account of NEPA administration is a highly useful analysis of phenomena at the national level similar to those discussed in this volume at the levels of local and state government. Taylor's description of the perspective and behavior of "environmental analysts" within federal agencies is strikingly similar to our own analysis of "regulator" planning board members locally.

19. Anthologies of leading current planning theorists, such as Mandelbaum, et al., eds. and Hendler, ed., as well as Howe's work on ethics in city planning, address as a central theme the dilemma of the traditionally apolitical planning profession which by now explicitly confronts the extent to which its potential has been politically compromised. John Forester, *Planning in the Face of Power* (Berkeley: University of California Press, 1989) and Norman Krumholz and Pierre Clavel, eds., *Reinventing Cities: Equity Planners Tell Their Stories* (Philadelphia: Temple University Press, 1994) are especially eloquent presentations of current professional planners' acknowledgement of this reality while still strategizing to be effective.

20. James A. Throgmorton, "Ethics, Passion, Reason, and Power: The Rhetorics of Electric Power Planning in Chicago," in Hendler, ed., p. 200.

21. Howe, pp. 129, 132.

22. Throgmorton, p. 201.

23. Howe, p. 126.

24. Throgmorton, p. 201.

25. Howe, p. 137.

26. On the development bias of social science generally, see Jonathan Crush, ed., *Power of Development* (London and New York: Routledge, 1995); Hannigan, p. 9; and Wolfgang Sachs, *The Development Dictionary* (London: Zed Books, 1992).

27. Gary Snyder, *The Practice of the Wild: Essays* (San Francisco: North Point Press, 1990), p. 154.

28. Though significantly different, these several orientations have much more in common with each other than with "minimalist," "pragmatic capitalist," or "regulator" perspectives. For a reasonable discussion of the theoretical differences and commonalities among those with the "ecologist" perspective, see Michael E. Zimmerman, *Contesting Earth's Future: Radical Ecology and Postmodernism*

(Berkeley: University of California Press, 1994). As Friedmann emphasizes, much of the recent impetus behind the social ecologist perspective came from New Left, social anarchist and critical Marxist (not to be confused with the state socialism of contemporary governments) currents of the 60s and later. Other good sources for current ecocentric thinking are Carolyn Merchant, *Radical Ecology: The Search for A Livable World* (New York: Routledge, 1992); David Pepper, *Modern Environmentalism: An Introduction* (London and New York: Routledge, 1996); Robyn Eckersley, *Environmentalism and Political Theory: Toward an Ecocentric Approach* (Albany: State University of New York Press, 1992); the special issue of *Environmental Politics* (London), vol. 4, no. 4 (Winter 1995), "Ecology and Democracy"; and Alan Carter, *A Radical Green Political Theory* (London and New York: Routledge, 1999).

29. Aldo Leopold, *A Sand County Almanac* (New York: Oxford University Press, 1949), p. viii.

30. Kunstler, p. 10.

31. Raymond A. Rogers, *Solving History: The Challenge of Environmental Activism* (Montreal: Black Rose Books, 1998), pp. 1, 9.

32. By Eckersley's definition, the "anthropocentric" orientation conceives assumptions and values in terms of their instrumental worth to human actors. "Anthropocentric" environmentalists, by this interpretation, propose "new opportunities for human emancipation and fulfillment in an ecologically sustainable society. . . . [T]he nonhuman world is reduced to a storehouse of resources and is considered to have instrumental value only . . . ." Those of an "ecocentric" perspective also pursue ecologically sustainable society, but within a broader context of recognizing the moral standing of the nonhuman world "and seek[ing] to ensure that it, too, may unfold in its many diverse ways" (Eckersley, p. 26). "In terms of fundamental priorities, an ecocentric approach regards the question of our proper place in the rest of nature as logically prior to the question of what are the most appropriate social and political arrangements for human communities" (Ibid., p. 28).

33. According to this perspective, as stated by Elizabeth Ann R. Bird, "Every aspect of [natural] scientific theory and practice expresses socio-political interests, cultural themes and metaphors, personal interactions, and professional negotiations for the power to name the world" (Bird, "The Social Construction of Nature: Theoretical Approaches to the History of Environmental Problems," *Environmental Review*, Winter 1987, p. 286). This understanding is one aspect of "post-positivism" generally (Frank Fisher, *Citizens, Experts, and the Environment: The Politics of Local Knowledge* [Durham: Duke University Press, 2000], pp. 68-85, 282, 284).

34. John A. Livingston, "One Man's Celebration," *Ontario Naturalist*, vol. 19 (1979), p. 13, as quoted in Rogers, p. 149.

35. Says Torgerson: "If ecology indicates the interconnection, complexity, and significant unpredictability of nature, we can also hold up the mirror of ecology to reveal the corresponding character of human affairs. . . . We must act with conviction, but with the understanding that we might be (somehow must be) wrong" (p. 103).

36. Also, as Alan Carter points out, whatever an enlightened "regulator" regime may accomplish in the short run, it remains dangerous from its own paternalistic assumption of knowing "the best real interests" of everyone and its tendency to hide the fact that other alternatives might be possible. Both patterns erode democratic political culture and potentially easily cause misguided or malevolent policies later on (pp. 98-103).

37. Torgerson, p. 24. Local, national and international crises naturally compel their attention and force many "ecologists" to concede that stop-gap political action might bring short-range benefit. But they have no illusion that such measures will prevent long-range social and ecological degradation and ultimate collapse. It is also true that many, if not most local land-use struggles across the United States concern potential degradation of primarily the human environment--water supply, traffic, urban blight, etc., though, as Robyn Eckersley suggests, "At best wildlife might emerge [as with wetlands preservation] as an indirect beneficiary of human welfare ecology reforms" (Eckersley, p. 38).

38. Michael Brooks, "Planning and Political Power: Toward A Strategy for Coping," in Mandelbaum, et al., eds., p. 118. As Torgerson states, "Although dissenting professionalism remains primarily attuned to functional politics--and thus a framework of reform--the discursive accent of the approach [emphasizing meaningful participatory politics and non-expert opinions] points to a constitutive prospect, more precisely a discursive redesign of policy processes and the administrative sphere" (Torgerson, p. 137).

39. Philosopher Robert Young presents a thoughtful argument that "monkeywrenching" forms of direct action "should be seen as contributing to the health and vigour of democratic processes." He suggests that "monkeywrenching is far less likely to be coercive than many other activities that are already thought of by objectors as being part of the democratic process," such as those perpetrated by powerful media proprietors, large corporations with their huge campaign donations and bureaucracies which thwart democratically supported outcomes (Young, "'Monkeywrenching' and the Processes of Democracy," *Environmental Politics* [London], vol. 4, no. 4 [Winter 1995], pp. 213, 212).

40. Friedmann, *Planning in the Public Domain*, p. 405.

41. Howe, p. 12.

42. Friedmann, *Planning in the Public Domain*, p. 407.

43. As Mark Warren points out about political ideologies generally, the latter may or may not become fundamental personal identity frameworks, thereby affecting the level of consciousness or zeal in articulating their implications for concrete policy issues (Mark E. Warren, "Can Participatory Democracy Produce Better Selves? Psychological Dimensions of Habermas's Discursive Model of Democracy," *Political Psychology*, vol. 14, no. 2, 1993, p. 222).

44. In actual local land-use struggles, for example, "ecologists" may sound and act much like "regulator" "in-house lobbyists," "forceful researchers," or "participatory advocates," as described above. Conversely, a "pragmatic capitalist" may sometimes temporarily verbalize typical "minimalist" positions (and "regulators" articulate

"ecologist" positions) if there are immediate political advantages to doing so. Thus, appropriate land-use perspective labels are based more reliably on long-range observation of words and actions both.

45. As Rein and Schon state, because those involved in policy disputes usually try to make their objectives realizable, they "often do so by 'hitching on' to a dominant frame and its conventional metaphors, hoping to purchase legitimacy for a course of action actually inspired by different intentions. . . . When participants in a policy discourse begin 'gaming,' they obscure their underlying frames" (p. 151). The particular plight of transformative "ecologists" mobilized by a sense of impending crisis while rejecting incremental instrumentalism, yet desperately wishing to respond effectively to immediate environmental threats, is a central theme of Douglas Torgerson's *The Promise of Green Politics: Environmentalism and the Public Sphere*. One result of this dilemma is the need to use rationalist counter-experts to neutralize or offer more convincing testimony than pro-development experts while simultaneously forcing decisionmaking back into the hands of lay decisionmakers more susceptible to influence of non-expert community peers.

46. As Ronald Beiner states, in the present context of "liberal democracy," it is the state which officially guarantees, but also seeks to render impotent, the free space within which non-statists can have a public judgmental voice. He thus sees it as natural that eventually confined and marginalized non-statists will seek to acquire at least a portion of state control when there is a chance to do so (Beiner, ed., *Theorizing Citizenship*, (Albany: State University of New York Press, 1995), p. 5). The extensive degree of broad shared liberal values of this "governing consensus" is argued in some detail in Thomas L. Harper and Stanley M. Stein, "Contemporary Procedural Ethical Theory and Planning Theory," in Hendler, chapter 3.

CHAPTER THREE

1. There are many useful publications on Ashbury local history relied upon by the authors to understand the background context for this case study. However, these cannot be cited here or in the bibliography without undermining the purpose of fictionalization.

2. *Ashbury Beacon* (hereafter referred to as *AB*), 1/17/30.

3. The Town of Ashbury, with 32.4 sq. miles, contains at its center the incorporated Village of the same name (3.6 sq. miles of the downtown retail and surrounding residential area).

4. "Ashbury Study Club" vertical file and minutes books, Ashbury Library, Ashbury; *AB*, 3/3/38, 3/17/38. In 1937, the Club's Village Improvement Committee, led by the wife of a local doctor, commenced serious zoning research and drafting of a potential ordinance, enlisting the assistance of the American Planning and Civic Association. The APCA, product of a 1935 merger of the American Civic

Association and the National Conference on City Planning, like its predecessors, was in the mainstream of Progressive movement efforts since the turn of the century for "municipal improvement" through healthier environments, beautification, corrupt-free and efficient government and, more specifically, conscientious urban planning.

5. Hoover's support in Ashbury was stronger than in the rest of Forest County. Ashbury had a Democratic Town Supervisor, James Fallin, throughout the 1920s, despite a 3-1 Republican advantage in local voter affiliation, but local elections usually depended far less on party loyalty than did national elections. The 1930 state gubernatorial election saw Ashbury give incumbent Roosevelt a 26-vote majority over his Republican challenger (*AB*, 11/7/30). In general, Herbert Hoover's planning perspective was comparable to "pragmatic capitalists" at the local level while elements within Roosevelt's first-term administration, such as Rexford Tugwell, were more akin to local "regulators." Both approaches aimed to save industrial capitalism from its own self-destruction.

6. As with the laying of earlier railroad lines, the particular routes of the toll road and federal interstate systems were a development bonanza for some towns and a disaster for others. Likewise, the specific route of the Thruway through towns such as Ashbury obviously benefitted some land owners and speculators considerably more than others. The politics behind such decisions would be useful to study.

7. A number of surveys around the country by the late 60s and early 70s indicated that a high percentage of people preferred to live in small towns or rural America (Logan and Molotch, p. 97).

8. A recent tourist guide to interesting, but offbeat, U.S. towns included Ashbury on its list because of the "multifaceted contrarian experience" of mixing small town, campus and historical legacy elements with an overall mellow, but colorful, local atmosphere.

9. 1990 figures (*Forest County 1995 Data Book* [Regent Park: Forest County Planning Board], p. 9).

10. Hippie life-styles and communes thrived in the town and surrounding countryside for at least a decade and a half after the late 60s while student radicalism at the SUNY campus reached a peak in the early 1970s.

11. Blomley, p. 576.

12. Doreen Massey, *Space, Place, and Gender* (Minneapolis: University of Minnesota Press, 1994), pp. 154 and 156, as quoted in Blomley, pp. 581-582.

13. "Basic Studies,"Ashbury Master Plan Committee; *Forest County 1968*, p. 13; *Forest County Data Book*, 1984, p. 51; *Forest County Planning News* (Forest County Planning Board, Regent Park), October 1972. By 1971, John Richards, the Forest County Planning Board director, foresaw an Ashbury population of 30-50,000 people in the next 30 to 50 years (Regent Park *Star* [hereafter referred to as *RPS*], 10/18/71).

14. *Forest County News*, I, 2 (May-June 1988); *Riverside Dispatch* (hereafter referred to as *RD*), 9/15/00.

15. Sources for this brief summary of post-World War II evolution in this and the preceding paragraph include *The Village of Ashbury . . .*; the "Basic Studies"

document for the *Ashbury Community Comprehensive (Master) Plan Report* (Ashbury: Ashbury Master Plan Committee, 1989), chs. 6, 12-14; the *Ashbury Comprehensive Plan* (Manuel S. Emanuel Associates, Inc., 1990); *AB*, March 30, 1966; the Londonville *Post* (hereafter referred to as *LP*), November 14, 1988; and several local Ashbury history publications.

16. Amsterdam Square Draft EIS (1989), section 4, p. 38, in Ashbury Town Planning Board files.

17. "Ashbury Open for Business," flyer of the Ashbury Development Corporation, 1992. Apparently, the ADC saw no contradiction with its precursor, the Ashbury Economic Development Task Force, which advocated two years earlier for "the preservation and continued development of the Village's downtown as the major concentration of retail and commercial businesses . . . ." The AEDTF saw encouragement of a thriving downtown as much "better than trying to develop a large shopping mall" and "far easier and cheaper than putting in new . . . shopping centers outside of town where there are no water and sewer lines and where, more importantly, they would serve no social purpose." ("The Bottom Line: Final Report of the Ashbury Economic Development Task Force," April 1990, pp. 8, 23.)

18. New York State Town Law, Section 271.

19. In this slow reaction, Ashbury reflected prevailing sentiments among the governing bodies of the region at the time. Forest County itself established a planning board only in 1963 and never conveyed to it significantly more than an advisory role for county and local governments.

20. *AB*, 5/20/48, 5/27/48, 12/16/48 and minutes of the Ashbury Village Board.

21. At the public hearing before passage, two spoke against it, including attorney, long-time Republican activist and ex-Village Mayor Kenyon Foster who, through his "minimalist" perspective, insisted that zoning was wholly unnecessary. At the time of the Village's earlier zoning consideration, in 1948-49, Foster had argued that "Ashbury has not experienced any rapid growth or expansion and probably never will," stated that zoning was "worse than communism" since it planned to take value from some properties and give it to others, and quoted Jefferson's admonition, "The people least governed are the best governed" (Letters to editor, *AB*, 12/2/48, 12/23/48, 5/12/49).

22. "Survey of the Town of Ashbury," League of Women Voters, 1954-55 ("League of Women Voters" vertical file, Ashbury Library, Ashbury). Results were also reported in the *AB*, 5/31/55. This was a surprisingly thorough demographic and attitude survey, with responses from the vast majority of households in Ashbury.

23. *AB*, 4/18/57. Attorney Kenyon Foster, who had strongly opposed zoning in the Village, was newly converted to the cause because of "tremendous change and growth due to the Thruway" and his social exclusionist fear of ensuing large, unhealthy and immoral trailer camps and "the menacing tide of Porto Ricans [sic] pounding on our door to the south." In turn, an Ashbury Taxpayers Association activist saw zoning as a "protection racket similar to that given by Hitler and Stalin to the Polish people when they invaded that country." In her view, there was no alternative to relying on "more good will among more people" and loving "THY

NEIGHBOR AS THYSELF" (*AB*, 3/5/58).

24. *AB*, 3/5/58, 3/12/58, 3/26/58. Despite the 1958 vote approving the principle of Town zoning, the Democratic candidate for Supervisor in 1959 argued that the code prepared by the Republican-dominated planning board needed more flexibility since "Ashbury remains primarily a rural community," not a Westchester town or other metropolitan suburb. The Republican platform, presented by candidate Joe Enrico, contained no mention of zoning. (*AB*, 10/21/59). By mid-December 1959, the town planning board, still without a zoning ordinance, had approved 21 subdivisions (*AB*, 12/16/59).

25. Recently converted "minimalist" Kenyon Foster remained as Town Attorney to interpret the new code. His son Happy Foster succeeded him by 1968. (*Ashbury Chronicle* [hereafter referred to as *AC*], 1/6/60, 12/21/67). Among other provisions, the 1960 ordinance permitted trailer camps and tourist homes on the dramatic eastern slopes of the nearby mountain range, large industrial zones (also permitting business) in the plains west of the river and east of the Thruway (south of Rte. 354) and a narrow business strip zone on Main Street-Rte. 354 from the Village line east to the Town of Acton.

26. The accommodating nature of the new land-use regime was demonstrated in Town Supervisor Joe Enrico's willingness to convert a major Main Street residential zone to a commercial zone just months after the 1960 zoning ordinance was passed, thus facilitating the strip-malling of Ashbury east of the village. This amendment directly benefitted a local orchard farmer-turned businessman and a future planning board attorney, both with property on the south side of Main Street. (*AB*, 3/15/61, 5/17/61).

At its 1/7/63 meeting, the board acknowledged to the building inspector that stricter enforcement of the code was needed since contractors were seeking so many variances (Ashbury Town Planning Board minutes). According to Bill Kramer who joined the Planning Board in 1960, official board business until then "had been relegated to the backroom," with meetings "at irregular intervals." His own moves to regularize and open meetings to public scrutiny "startled some and disturbed others" (*AC*, 3/24/66). Official board records indicate that some of Kramer's first meetings were in the law office of Town Attorney Kenyon Foster. Not until late 1962 did the Board decide even to open its meetings to the public when developers made their presentations, though executive sessions were still used for Board discussions and votes. Meanwhile, a significant number of board members (and the Board's attorney Richard Schmidt) in the 1960s had occasion to move from one side of the table to the other as they presented their own developments to their peers on the board.

27. *RPS*, 11/15/68.

28. The new "planning rhetoric" was soon learned by developers and their government allies in the "local growth coalition," with the assistance of paid experts for both sets of players.

29. Perin, p. 154.

406

30. Seven-person planning boards had staggered terms, with only one appointment term expiring each year. The effect was to prevent newly elected municipal boards from significantly changing, if they wished, the ideological orientation of existing planning boards.

31. *AB*, 2/9/66; Ashbury Town Planning Board minutes. Electric utility companies commonly have been ardent growth advocates everywhere since more growth means new customers.

32. Insurance and real estate broker James Fallin, in the 1920s, was the first non-Dutch descendant to attain the office of Town Supervisor. A new resident of Ashbury in the mid-1910s reported over 70 years later that when she first arrived she realized that people in the community worshipped their Dutch ancestors. This same sense of pro-Dutch bias was reported all the way to the 1950s. (Interviews in the Oral History Collection, Ashbury Library, Ashbury.)

33. A sizeable Italian population had emerged in the Ashbury area by the first two decades of the 20th century, originally seeking escape from the ills of urban life and because of jobs on local farms and significant local public works projects such as a major bridge, the Ashbury-Acton trolley line, the Ashbury water works, and Normal School construction. As elsewhere, while Italians in Ashbury experienced distrust and bias from already-established residents, industrious efforts to provide for their families as well as patriotism and military service in World War II significantly diminished such prejudice.

The late 1950s were the critical transition period for the legitimization and ascension of the new Republican leaders. By the 1950s, Italian-Americans represented a sizeable minority of the local population, probably supplanting Irish and Germans as the leading ethnic element behind Dutch descendants.

34. Established in 1937 (succeeding the 1909-organized Dutch Arms Club and the 1930s-organized local Exchange Club) and 1907 respectively, the "good old boys" Ashbury Club, as well as its female Ashbury Study Club counterpart, were almost exclusively northern European in membership until after World War II, but broadened their ranks by the mid- and late-1950s.

35. Enrico ran in 1955 as a Democrat, in 1957 on both slates (gaining nearly 500 more votes from Republicans than from Democrats), and by 1959 solely as a Republican. He was accepted as a member of the Ashbury Club by early 1967. After an unsuccessful Republican primary bid for state assembly in 1968, Enrico remained chair of the county legislature through 1976 and in the legislature itself through 1977.

He left his government leadership post after some decline in local electoral support and an embarrassing fiscal fiasco while also, some alleged, under pressure from fellow Republican legislators who resented his attempts to control decisions through undemocratic means. (*RPS*, 3/11/76, 3/21/76, 3/24/76, 12/16/76, 12/17/76).

However, Enrico then moved on to become chair and power broker of the Forest County Republican party in 1977, a position retained to the present. Again, however, "bossist" lack of accountability and refusal to share information and decision-making caused various Republican leaders in the county finally (though unsuccessfully) to seek his replacement in 1993. The Republican County Legislature Chair's legal suit against Enrico alleged that the latter had "turned his public office into a private office to further his own political objective." (*RPS*, 9/8/81, 10/11/81, 9/29/85, 2/15/93, 8/15/93, 8/29/93, 9/27/93, 10/5/93.)

36. *RPS*, 5/3/68.

37. This town comprehensive plan (the first in Forest County) was prepared by the professional firm of Brown & Anthony City Planners, Inc. and delivered in April 1966. It was funded primarily through a Federal Housing and Home Finance Agency "701" grant and encouraged, as elsewhere in the state, by the New York State Department of Commerce Bureau of Planning. (*AB*, 11/18/64, 11/24/64; *AC*, 10/3/68.) Ashbury was not alone in neglecting a prepared plan. By 1979, Siemon and Larsen declared that "adopted comprehensive plans continue to be few and far between, and comprehensive relationship to implementing land use controls are even less common" (Charles L. Siemon and Wendy Larsen, "Comprehensive Planning Revisited," *Planning, Zoning and Eminent Domain* [Dallas: Institute of Planning, Zoning and Eminent Domain, 1979], p. 106, as quoted in Richard F. Babcock and Charles L. Siemon, *The Zoning Game Revisited* [Cambridge, Mass.: Lincoln Institute of Land Policy, 1985], p. 261).

38. Ashbury was no aberration in Forest County at the time. Only in 1974 did the final town in the county appoint a planning board (*Forest County Planning News*, no. 9 [Spring 1974] and no. 11 [Winter 1974]).

Voices from the public frequently were unabashedly pro-growth through this period. At a Town planning board public hearing on potential future density changes in the zoning ordinance, a local builder stated: "I have heard complaints about urban sprawl, well I want to strike a blow for urban sprawl" and referred to Levittown, Long Island, with its quarter-acre lots, as an attractive model. Another developer, future planning board member Red Davis, commented that if the minimum lot size was increased to two acres, "I fail to see what type of planning that is." He asserted that the present ordinance "puts us 15 years ahead of the next community. I can't see why we can't live with what we have" (*AC*, 6/27/73).

39. One 1975 letter to the *AB*, for example, complained: "Within our recent past certain real estate and legal persons came to agree that the town was ripe for 'development,' that any sort of 'development' which enriched a few could be pushed past a passive majority. . . . Our planning boards have compromised Ashbury to the breaking point. . . . Do our priorities go to advancing the interests of real estate builders and their attorneys? Or do we change tax bases to help local farmers survive, protect our open spaces and natural resources and maintain Ashbury in what remains of its uniquely beautiful setting? We are constantly told that 'growth is good,' and only yokels think otherwise. CANCER IS A GROWTH AND Ashbury IS BEING EATEN AWAY. IT IS WITHIN OUR RIGHTS TO CALL A HALT." (*AB*, 1/2/75.)

40. Objectives included appropriate land-use to conserve and enhance property value, eliminating the spread of strip development, creating a suitable system of open spaces and enhancing the aesthetic quality of the community.

41. RPS, 1/29/71.

42. Letter from Pat Simmons to the Town Supervisor and Village Mayor, in "Chamber of Commerce Newsletter" spiral bound collection, Ashbury Library, Ashbury.

43. As zoning and land-use lawyer Richard Babcock observed about the process two decades earlier, "The indictment of zoning to which all critics subscribe is that its administration is arbitrary and capricious. Procedural due process is continually flaunted in our medieval hearings, our casual record keeping and our occult decision-making" (Babcock, *The Zoning Game*, p. 135).

44. *Tribune*, 3/14/85.

45. *AC*, 8/15/73.

46. *AC*, 9/19/73.

47. A good chronological summary of this campaign is in the *RPS*, 11/24/86.

48. Jim Stapleton, review of Erik Kiviat, *The Northern Shawangunks: An Ecological Survey*, in *The Hudson Valley Regional Review*, vol. 7, no. 1 (3/90), pp. 63-64.

49. The short-lived Community United for Proper Development and the Ashbury Homeowners Association, as CLEAR a decade later, closely monitored land-use planning issues in the village and town while articulating detailed critiques at local board meetings and to the press. The biggest victory of the AHA was in defeating a 260-acre $50-60 million residential project which (with at least 5000 residents) would have nearly doubled the village population (*AB*, 4/12/72; *AC*, 4/26/72; *RPS*, 5/28/72).

50. CLEAR is discussed throughout the book as one of the two principal community groups struggling against the megamall.

51. CLEAR's detailed critique of the proposal was contained in a letter to the editor, *Tribune*, 1/31/85. The PUD project was the first of a long string of local development projects which CLEAR monitored, critiqued and sometimes went to court about over the next few years, most frequently within the framework of the SEQRA process. One of the CLEAR officers, Alex McBride, personally attended the vast majority of Ashbury town planning board meetings over the next decade. Other members attended meetings of the Village planning board or the planning board of the neighboring town to the south. From its beginnings in 1985 through the early 90s, CLEAR activists felt like they were on a non-stop treadmill of endless new developments, but were determined to maintain a strong voice for grassroots citizen involvement in planning.

52. The delay forced on the developer through use of the SEQRA process contributed to the eventual decision of Wal-Mart to pull out in the context of a newly-emerging recession. From such efforts, it is easy for some to conclude, as do Logan and Molotch, that "the main virtue of the [EIS] for those trying to preserve use values is perhaps its capacity to delay projects, helping to buy time, to discourage investors, to mount political opposition" (p. 165).

53. At the same time, articulating a participatory democratic perspective, CLEAR recommended that the Master Plan Committee organize a series of local neighborhood meetings throughout the town to dialogue with citizens about appropriate re-zoning and other measures to protect the environment. Such meetings "would permit a maximum amount of face-to-face grassroots expression of visions, critiques and concrete alternatives. Important process decisions as well as well as drafts of each section of the master plan should be submitted to neighborhood gatherings and the process should not continue until reports from this local level are heard and seriously discussed" (written presentation by CLEAR to the Ashbury Master Plan Committee, 8/7/86).

54. While vice-chair of the Town Planning Board in December 1965, Bob Tapani presented an earlier subdivision for this property involving 74 lots (Ashbury Town Planning Board minutes, 12/6/65). Overall, the Tapanis owned 400 acres of orchard and farmland (*RPS*, 7/23/86).

55. Said the president of the Forest County Builders Association, a 59-year old Ashbury native and "considered the dean of local builders," "they don't want another person coming into Ashbury. The problem is that these people came here the last 10 years and claim Ashbury. They make a lot of noise, but I'm not sure they represent the whole community" (*LP*, 5/17/87).

56. This point was well made in early 1997 when planning board member Red Davis stated in a letter to the local *Tribune* that he was "getting fed up with late-comers to this community who criticize me and the other REAL natives who have dedicated and donated their social and economic lives and livelihood in every way possible to make Ashbury what it is so we can all enjoy it." The editor replied: "I don't think an Ashbury community member's voice should be silenced based on their tenure in town. We are all relative newcomers here in the historical context, even the Dutch." (*Tribune*, 2/13/97.)

57. Parsons was one of the prime targets of Town Board candidate Hurley's strong critique in 1973 (see p. 29 above). Even before her promotion of the two megamalls east of the Thruway, she, her husband and others in 1969 proposed to tear down half a block of old downtown buildings on the south side of Main Street and construct "Dutch Circle," a disproportionately gigantic monolithic commercial center.

58. *AB*, 9/13/73. Revealingly, she said in the early 1970s, "I like to change things and I believe that economics is the only really successful way to get things changed. Money makes things happen. I eat, sleep, and breathe this business" (*Dutch Arms Press* [special issue on Ashbury women], early 1970s). Interviewed by another local paper in the same period, she said, "I don't believe in altruism. People have to be useful. . . . There are a lot of parasites in this world. . . . Anyone who wants to run for something as big as Ashbury should have some business sense. . . . A town is a business." At the same time, she thought Ashbury could have reasonable growth to a population level of 48,000 (*AB*, 9/13/73). In 1980, she complained about the "lunatic fringe" and its opposition to the mountain ridge hotel-condominium proposal and advocated that only taxpayers should have the right to vote on fiscal-related issues of this sort (*Tribune*, 2/6/80, 9/10/80).

Town and county Republican boss Joe Enrico even appeared at several public meetings, threatening on one occasion an immediate lawsuit against the Town Board if it dared to pass a "Critical Environmental Area" designation assuring more careful planning board reviews, for a district including his property (unofficial transcript of audio recording of Ashbury Town Environmental Conservation Commission hearing on CEAs, 12/22/88).

59. A SLAPP (Strategic Litigation Against Public Participation) suit against CLEAR leader Ellen Scott in 1989 was specifically cited by local Assemblyman Francis Grano as a factor motivating him in early 1990 to introduce state legislation to protect activist citizens against frivolous retaliatory litigation by those they criticized (*LP*, 3/13/90). The proposal was enacted in 1992 (see Marnie Stetson, "Reforming SLAPP Reform: New York's Anti-SLAPP Statute," *New York University Law Review*, vol. 70, December 1995, pp. 1324-1361). For more on SLAPP suits generally and how to fight them, see George W. Pring and Penelope Canan, *SLAPPs: Getting Sued for Speaking Out* (Philadelphia: Temple University Press, 1996) and Dwight H. Merriam and Jeffrey A. Benson, "Identifying and Beating A Strategic Lawsuit against Public Participation," *Duke Environmental Law and Policy Forum*, vol. III (1993), pp. 17-36.

60. Far from being the concern of only well-to-do elitists, as ideologists of the "growth machine" would allege, environmental degradation caused by helter-skelter local development affected everyone. As Logan and Molotch point out, "[a] high-quality physical environment constitutes a free public good for those who have access to it. Those who are unable to buy amenities in the market lose most from the unavailability of such resources" (pp. 95-96). Though members and activists of local environmentalist community organizations might sometimes be skewed by class, this is more a reflection of the time, organizational and financial resources required for such activity than others' lack of interest (Ibid., pp. 135-136, 221-222). The "elitist" myth is also belied generally by consistent survey results showing overwhelming public concern about deteriorating environmental conditions as well as by the rapid spread of environmental justice movements in recent years.

CLEAR became formally affiliated with Open Space Institute in 1985 as one of its grassroots Citizen Action Projects.

61. Richard Lingeman, *Small Town America: A Narrative History, 1620-The Present* (New York: G.P. Putnam's Sons, 1980), p. 448, and Edward J. Blakely and Ted K. Bradshaw, "The Impact of Recent Migrants on Economic Development in Small Towns," in Michael W. Fazio and Peggy Whitman Prenshaw, eds., *Order and Image in the American Small Town* (Jackson: University Press of Mississippi, 1981), pp. 34-35.

62 . Overall, platforms of local Ashbury Republicans and Democrats during the 1950s and most of the 60s differed little in content or tone. Essentially, they were all part of the same urban regime. Enrico's successor as Town Supervisor, Bob Tapani, even gained cross-endorsement by the Democrats in the November 1969 election (his second), despite the fact that he was, as the 1967 Democratic candidate for Supervisor stated, one of Enrico's "closest 'cohorts'," as sure a hand-picked "'Enrico

Republican' if there ever was one in the community," having "owe[d] his political start almost altogether to Mr. Enrico" (*AB*, 10/22/69).

By contrast, a SUNY professor in 1969 wrote of the mixed welcome and shock caused by the dramatic expansion of the College and thus new constituents in the community: "The people of the College spend more than five million dollars in this community but they are also loud and boisterous and argumentative. <u>They speak in a language strange to small town America.</u> They speak of ghettos and social inequality, of community power and radical cures. They dream their own dreams of the future. . . . In short, the Ashburyians are shocked to find an urban college in their rural setting" (our underlines) (*AB*, 10/29/69).

63. Official voter registration records, Forest County Board of Election.

64. No doubt the Watergate backlash had an effect on the outcome as well, despite common voter distinctions between the same party at the national and local levels. Republicans ran local developers for three of the four Town Board seats (including Supervisor) up for election in 1975. The fourth Republican candidate complained that the planning board gave "too much emphasis on ecology" and favored the nuclear power plant in neighboring Acton. All three developers, including future planning board member Red Davis, were defeated. In contests for the county legislature, local Democrat Gary Patton won and gained more Ashbury votes than long-time incumbent Joe Enrico, who also kept his seat (*AC*, 10/8/75, 10/15/75, 11/5/75, 11/12/75).

65. Kessler's land-use policy orientation and repeated electoral success exemplified Logan's and Molotch's claim that "[t]he growth machine will sustain only certain persons as politicians"--those, of whatever general ideological learning, who willingly opt to participate in the "growth consensus" (p. 66).

66. *Tribune*, 11/10/83; *LP*, 11/9/89; *RPS*, 11/28/89; *AB*, 1/7/59.

67. Newspaper quotations suggest that Schmidt's 1991 Democratic opponent was even more favorable than Schmidt to a megamall development on the east side of the town (*Tribune*, 10/24/91).

68. *AC*, 9/8/71.

69. This control had been challenged in recent years within the party caucus and in local elections by progressive Democrats and independents forming a Citizens Party behind the election of Lyon and others.

70. At the same time, she was the Ashbury representative to the Forest County Planning Board.

71. In a 1996 interview, Ryker still portrayed himself as "a child of the 1960s" (*Tribune*, 2/8/96).

72. In contrast to Lyon, Supervisor Kessler and Town Board member Devilla supported Ryker's reappointment to the planning board in December 1988 (*RPS*, 12/25/88).

73. A local publisher in 1993 referred to "Enrico's brusque and sometimes menacing style" (*Tribune*, 10/7/93).

74. Quoted in *CLEAR Newsletter*, July 1993.

75. Ryker self-description in interview, *Tribune*, 2/8/96.

76. See endnotes 38 and 56 above in this chapter. *AC*, 10/22/75. In 1999, Davis mentioned that he himself had excavated and graded the site for the FoodFeast grocery store in the early 1970s (Porter personal notes from planning board meeting of 3/8/99).

77. *Tribune*, 2/13/97.

78. Kinsella's predecessor as chair, Ken Halsted, complained in late 1985 that the planning board was so preoccupied with "administering" that it had no time for planning and that other board members were not interested in adding a third meeting per month to create such space (*Tribune*, 11/21/85).

79. See generally, Nicholas A. Robinson, "SEQRA's Siblings: Precedents from Little NEPA's in the Sister States," *Albany Law Review*, vol. 46 (1982), p. 1154.

80. See Sandra M. Stevenson, "Early Legislative Attempts at Requiring Environmental Assessment and SEQRA's Legislative History," *Albany Law Review*, vol. 46 (1982), pp. 1114-1119.

81. See Ibid., pp. 1115-1117. (In 1971, three environmental assessment bills that specified DEC oversight were introduced into the legislature. None of the three passed either house. A fourth bill introduced in 1972 was vetoed by Governor Rockefeller.) The DEC itself was created in 1970.

82. See Ibid., pp. 1115-1119.

83. *1975 New York Legislature Ann.*, pp. 384, 398 (Gov. Carey's 1975 State of the State Message).

84. Report to the Governor, 1975, of the New York State Task Force on the Environment, Section Report of the Subcommittee on Land Use Planning-Critical Areas Bill, "Proposed Critical Resources Management Act" (hereinafter Proposed Critical Management Resources Act) Section 26-0103, pars. 2-3, "Statement of Findings" ("Government Documents" file, New York State Library, Albany). The introduction enumerated the concerns of the task force regarding New York State's "invaluable but limited" resource base.

85. See Ibid. at Section 26-103, par 5.

86. See Ibid. at Section 26-103, par 6.

87. Moreover, the Task Force sought to harmonize the actions of the state Department of Environmental Conservation with the adoption of protective regulations by local government, thus seeking to reduce the tension over the issue of home rule by delegating, in the first instance, regulatory power to local government. See Ibid., par. 5. The proposed act provided that critical environmental resources "would be protected from uncontrolled or incompatible development by local regulation pursuant to state standards" (emphasis added). The proposed act went on to state that if local government failed to "effectively enforce the development regulations, the Commissioner temporarily assumes enforcement powers" (Summary and Section 26-0113). The Commissioner was also given authority to bring civil actions to secure a developer's compliance with the law.

In addition, the proposal authorized citizen suits by any individual against any person or entity undertaking development either without the approval of local government or in violation of its regulatory scheme. Citizen suits were also authorized against the Commissioner or any officer or employee of the DEC or of any local government upon an allegation of failure to perform an act or duty mandated by the environmental regulatory scheme. Citizens were empowered to bring civil suits because courts would be specifically authorized to award costs of litigation to the citizen (including reasonable attorney and witness fees). See Ibid., Summary and Section 26-0115. A citizen's suit provision encourages any individual to monitor and press for enforcement of the law.

88. N.Y.S. 3540-A, N.Y.A. 4533-A, 198th Session (1975). The already-existing California model was crucial according to Paul Bray, Assembly bill drafter at the time (Bray verbal presentation at the SEQRA 25th Anniversary conference, Albany Law School, Albany, NY, March 15, 2001).

89. Says Philip Weinberg, "This statute has bolted the door forever on the notorious era when state and local governments could make land-use decisions in the proverbial smoke-filled room, injuring communities with impunity, exemplified by the oft-quoted line of that consummate builder, Robert Moses, that 'once we put a shovel in the ground, there's no court in the world that will make us remove it'" (Philip Weinberg, "SEQRA: Effective Weapon--If Used As Directed," *Empire State Report*, October 2000, p. 38).

90. Paul Bray, then a bill drafter for the Assembly, asserts emphatically that the SEQRA statute was a product of legislative leaders Herbert Posner (Assembly Democrat) especially and Bernard Smith (Senate Republican) rather than Governor Carey. Indeed, he says, it was only because of the relative disorganization of the new Governor's office at the time that this legislative initiative was able to become law. According to Bray, 1975 was a unique window of opportunity as the Assembly and Governorship went Democratic, a strong Governor (Nelson Rockefeller) had just departed, Posner's Assembly Environmental Conservation Committee leadership was experienced and committed and the Governor's office was still not in control. Even now, Bray doubts that SEQRA could have been enacted in any other context. (Paul M. Bray, "Twenty-Fifth Anniversary of SEQRA," *Empire State Report*, April 2000, pp. 38-39, and Bray public and private comments at the SEQRA 25th Anniversary conference, Albany Law School, Albany, N.Y., March 15-16, 2001.)

91. "Dear Senator" letter in re: Senate Bill 3540 from Sandra Stanley, Research Assistant, New York Conference of Mayors (6/9/75)("SEQRA Bill Jacket" file, New York State Library, Albany).

92. Letter from Edward J. Connelly, President, New York Conference of Mayors, to the Honorable Judah Gribetz, Counsel to the Governor (7/28/75)("SEQRA Bill Jacket" file, New York State Library, Albany).

93. Letter in re: Assembly Bill 4533-A from Robert T. Waldbauer, Mayor of the Village of Patchogue to the Honorable Judah Gribetz, Counsel to the Governor (6/30/75)("SEQRA Bill Jacket" file, New York State Library, Albany). The Forest County Planning Board argued in late 1975 that while SEQRA objectives were

worthwhile, implementation would be "costly," "time-consuming," and "unworkable." As applied by lay boards without technical resources at the local level and without practical enforceability or sanctions, the process was likely to become merely "a pass through operation." It argued that only an enlarged DEC support staff and real agency teeth to discourage environmentally-damaging projects would save SEQRA objectives. Furthermore, it proposed that all environmental impact and other state and county permit reviews be consolidated into one overall review agency process for each development (*Forest County Planning News*, Fall 1975; John Richards, FCPB Director, 11/6/75 letter to Stephen Gordon, Deputy Commissioner of DEC).

94. Memorandum in re: Senate Bill 3540 and Assembly Bill 4533-A, from William C. Finneran Jr., General Manager and Director of Labor Relations, General Contractors Association (6/10/75) and William C. Finneran, Jr. 6/28/75 letter to Gov. Carey ("SEQRA Bill Jacket" file, New York State Library, Albany).

95. N.Y.A. 12175-B, 199th Session (1976). See 1976 N.Y. Legis. Ann. 199 (Governor's Memoranda); 1976 N.Y. Session Laws at 2300 (Tompkins) (Memorandum of State Executive Department); Ibid., p. 2434 (Governor's Memoranda); see Stevenson, p. 1124. In his Special Message on the Economy in 1976, Governor Carey reiterated his support for SEQRA while recognizing the burdens the statute would place on local governments and private industry. Governor Carey proposed phased implementation of SEQRA in order to gauge how to best minimize the onus placed on industry and local government. Carey's deference to anti-SEQRA forces also responded to the simultaneous anti-DEC backlash after the DEC in late 1975 sought potential closure of General Electric manufacturing plants in the upper Hudson River because of their discharge of toxic PCBs (Ross Sandler, "State Environmental Quality Review Act," *New York State Bar Journal*, February 1977, pp. 111-112). (In what persists as a major environmental conflict, GE has strongly resisted responsibility for a full PCB river cleanup all the way to the present.)

96. Stevenson, p. 1125. DEC's original 1976-78 administrative regulations for SEQRA were amended in 1987 and 1996. Both amendment processes saw replays of the mid-70s battles between "serious planner" and "light planner" forces favoring and opposing SEQRA.

97. Act of June 10, 1977 N.Y. Laws ch. 252, Section 1, subd. 9; see Stevenson, p. 1125.

98. Act of August 1, 1975, N.Y. Laws, ch. 612, Section 8-109(1).

99. Act of June 10, 1977 N.Y. Laws ch. 252, Section 3, subd. 8; see Stevenson, p. 1125.

100. While the original bill required that the growth-inducing aspects of any proposed action be included within the assessment, that requirement was modified through the phrase "where applicable and significant" (Ibid., Section 3, subd. 2). An element of circular logic creates a loophole in the mitigation requirements. While there is a rigid requirement that mitigation methods be discussed, they need to be employed only to "the maximum extent practicable." Thus, it is the responsibility of

local planning boards and lead agencies to decide which mitigating measures are reasonable and must be required. See *Jackson v. New York State Urban Development Corp.*, 67 N.Y.2d 400, 422, 494 N.E.2d 429, 439 (1986); see generally, Michael B. Gerrard, Daniel A. Ruzow, and Philip Weinberg, *Environmental Impact Review in New York* (New York: Matthew Bender, 1997), Section 6.02(2).

The result of these amendments meant that many projects with adverse environmental impacts could win approval due to their projected economic benefit. Thus, these amendments had the effect of potentially blunting environmental concerns when contrasted with corporate and developmental projects with alleged financial benefits to the local community. Perhaps, the worst example of this in Ashbury occurred when the DEC approved the hotel-condominium complex proposed for the beautiful and fragile nearby mountain ridge despite the damage that would accrue to the town's viewshed of the ridgeline, the loss and destruction of irreplaceable forest and historic landmarks, the damage to the beautiful on-site mountain lake (the height of which would be depleted for drinking water), and the heavy increase in traffic to the already-congested town and village of Ashbury.

In addition, language was added regarding the scope, content and length of the EIS by stating that it "should deal with the specific significant environmental impacts which can be reasonably anticipated and should not contain more detail than is appropriate considering the nature and magnitude of the proposed action and the significance of its potential impacts." Ibid., Section 3, subd. 2. Use of the term "reasonably anticipated" was specifically alluded to by the Governor as limiting the scope of the EIS.

101. Environmental Conservation Law (hereafter "ECL"), Section 8-0109(2). See *Town of Henrietta v. Department of Environmental Conservation*, 76 A.D.2d 215, 222, 430 N.Y.S.2d 440, 446 (4th Dept. 1980). The court stated that "an [EIS] must be recognized as not a mere disclosure statement but rather as an aid in an agency's decision-making process to evaluate and balance competing factors."

102. ECL, Section 8-0105(2). "Local agencies" include counties and their agencies. See also Gerrard, Ruzow and Weinberg, Section 2.02(3)(1997).

103. ECL, Section 8-0109(2). In determining "significant effect" courts apply the H.O.M.E.S. test described below in note 113. The statute defines environmental effects as including "the physical conditions which will be affected by a proposed action, including land, air, water, minerals, flora, fauna [and] noise . . . ." ECL, Section 8-0105(6). The "environment" also includes "objects of historic or aesthetic significance, existing patterns of population concentration, distribution, or growth, and existing community or neighborhood character." Ibid. In providing this expansive definition of what constitutes "the environment," SEQRA parallels the broad interpretation given to the term in cases involving NEPA. See *Hanly v. Kleindienst*, 471 F.2d 823 (2d Cir. 1972), cert. denied 412 U.S. 908 (1973).

104. ECL, Section 8-0109(4).

105. Ibid. SEQRA Regulations (6 N.Y.C.R.R.) 617.6 and 617.7 provide guidelines for selecting a lead agency and the initial determination as to the necessity of an EIS. (The term "SEQRA Regulations" will be used hereafter instead of the formal 6

N.Y.C.R.R. Also, while the regulatory context for the project review described in this book was the 1987 version of the SEQRA regulations, our citations will refer to the slightly altered 1996 version to facilitate current uses of these references and since no significant changes are involved unless otherwise indicated.)

106. In its significant invitation to "participatory" involvement, this aspect of SEQRA reflected the larger wave of such openings, responding to forceful grassroots activist politicization throughout North America in the 1960s and early 70s-- including "a chorus of voices [which] called for active citizen participation in planning" (Grant, p. 12). Paul Bray insists that the principal architect of SEQRA, Assemblyman Herbert Posner, was strongly committed to significant citizen participation (private comments at SEQRA 25th Anniversary conference, Albany Law School, Albany, N.Y., March 16, 2001).

107. Gerrard, Ruzow and Weinberg, Sect. 3.10(5)(a) (1995). SEQRA regulations urge lead agencies to "make every reasonable effort to involve project sponsors, other agencies and the public in the SEQR process" (emphasis added) (SEQRA Regulations 617.3[d]).

108. To facilitate peer review, SEQRA requires the posting of notices (1) when an initial determination is made that an EIS will be required, (2) of the availability of the draft EIS, (3) of the public hearing at which time oral and written comment is solicited, and (4) upon completion of the Final EIS. To assure that adequate account is given to the responses made by the public and other interested and involved agencies, SEQRA requires that the FEIS include "copies or a summary of the substantive comments received [by the agency to the DEIS] . . . and the lead agency's response to all substantive comments" (SEQRA Regulations 617.9[b][8]). At least 30 days must be allowed for public comment once a draft EIS has been accepted (SEQRA Regulations 617.9[a][3]) and consideration must be given to whether a public hearing should be held (SEQRA Regulations 617.9[a][4]).

The purpose of the EIS "is to provide detailed information . . . and to suggest alternatives to [the action] so as to form the basis for a decision whether or not to undertake or approve [the] action. [The] statement should be clearly written in a concise manner capable of being read and understood by the public . . . ." (ECL Section 8-0109[2]).

109. SEQRA Regulations 617.11(d)(5). Such wording, of course, implicitly acknowledges the "politicization of science" since scientists themselves will disagree on what constitutes effective and practicable avoidance or mitigation of adverse effects (Fischer, *Citizens, Experts, and the Environment*, pp. 96-97).

110. According to Taylor, by 1980, 10% of all NEPA-subject projects with an EIS were brought to court (p. 36). Overall, the number of NEPA cases peaked in 1974 (p. 245). While originally focused especially on demands for an EIS instead of a negative declaration, from 1980 through 1992, as agencies and their lawyers became more acculturated to the statute and its judicial interpretation, litigation has focused almost as much on issues of EIS "adequacy" (p. 356; Kreske, p. 156).

111. Taylor, pp. 82-83, 234-239, 267.

112. See New York Civil Practice Laws and Rules (CPLR), Section 7803(3). Proceedings against New York State officers and agencies are governed under the cited provision ("Article 78"). Four issues may be raised in an Article 78 proceeding: 1) whether the officer or agency failed to perform a mandated duty, 2) whether an officer or agency had jurisdiction, 3) whether a determination was arbitrary and capricious, and 4) whether a determination is supported by substantial evidence. See also, Gerrard, Ruzow and Weinberg, Section 7.03(1) (1997).

113. See *H.O.M.E.S. v. New York State Urban Dev. Corp.*, 69 A.D.2d 222, 232, 418 N.Y.S.2d 827, 832 (4th Dept. 1979). Interpreting the SEQRA regulations, the court required lead agencies to (1) identify the relevant areas of concern,(2) take a "hard look" at each area,and (3) make a "reasoned elaboration" of its determination).

See *Aldrich v. Pattison*, 107 A.D.2d 258, 486 N.Y.S.2d 23 (2d Dept. 1985). The "hard look" standard was extended to review of environmental impact statements as well as determinations of significance (positive or negative declarations) as in *H.O.M.E.S.*. See also Gerrard, Ruzow and Weinberg, Section 7.04(3), 7.04(4)(1997).

114. For example, while the general statute of limitations for judicial review of governmental actions is four months from the time of determination, numerous statutes applicable to local government provide a much shorter period, usually thirty days.

115. *Six Mile Creek Preservation Comm. v. Planning Board of Town of Ithaca*, 82-1397, slip op. at 7 (Sup. Ct. Tompkins Co., Jan. 6, 1983) (explaining that shortened statutes of limitation are permissible in order either to expedite a project or to bring a project to a timely stop before excessive time and money have been invested), cited in Gerrard, Ruzow and Weinberg, Section 7.02(4)(b) (1997). See Village Law, Section 7-740 (imposing a 30-day statute of limitations for challenges to the actions of village planning boards.); Town Law Sections 274-a and 282 (imposing a 30-day statute of limitations for challenges to the actions of town planning boards). For a number of years, the time limitation period in which to bring judicial review has been settled as running from final approval or disapproval of the substantive action, and not from some intermediate step, such as a final SEQRA decision. In the case of a project with a SEQRA positive declaration, the final SEQRA decision is when findings are made after the acceptance of an FEIS. However, for residential subdivisions, preliminary approval is the starting point for the statute of limitations in challenging a SEQRA negative declaration. See also Gerrard, Ruzow and Weinberg, Section 7.02(4)(c) (1997). Two recent Third Department Appellate Division decisions, however, have re-opened the issue of whether the SEQRA final decision or the underlying substantive action decision properly commences the time period involved in which to file a SEQRA challenge. See *McNeill v. Town Bd. of the Town of Ithaca*, 260 A.D.2d 829, 688 N.Y.S.2d 747 (1999); *City of Saratoga Springs v. Zoning Bd. of Appeals*, 279 A.D.2d 756, 719 N.Y.S.2d 178 (2001); and Douglas H. Ward and Michael J. Moore, "SEQRA Challenges and the Statute of Limitations: Sue 'Early and Often,'" *Albany Law Environmental Outlook Journal*, vol. 6, no. 2 (2002), pp. 89-101.

116. See generally, ECL Sections 9, 11, 13, 15-17, 19, 23-25, 27, 29, 33-41, 49, 55, and 71. See also Gerrard, Ruzow, and Weinberg, Section 3.17 (1997), for a complete discussion of the DEC's role.

117. ECL Section 8-0113.

118. See Gerrard, Ruzow, and Weinberg, Section 3.17 (1997).

119. ECL Section 8-0111(6); SEQRA Regulations 617.6(b)(5).

120. ECL Section 8-0109(2); SEQRA Regulations 617.7(a).

121. Figures for SEQRA compliance for the years 1984-1996 were provided to the authors by Charles Lockrow, Environmental Analyst, Division of Compliance Services, Department of Environmental Conservation, in a letter of 1/3/97. Daniel Ruzow attached a chart (based on DEC overall figures) of total SEQRA declarations and followup actions, 1984-2000, to his "Historical Development of SEQRA: The Administrative Process" outline presented at the SEQRA 25th Anniversary conference at Albany Law School in March 2001. DEC's report to us was slightly different for several years from those used by Ruzow, but significantly so only for 1992 "pos decs" (DEC reported 215 to us, but Ruzow states that total as 250). Michael Gerrard published "final EIS completion" figures for 1990-1999 in his article "Ten Years of SEQRA Litigation: A Statistical Analysis," *New York Law Journal*, 3/24/00. Gerrard's and Ruzow's tables indicate a continued decline in Final EISs since 1996.

122. ECL, Section 8-0109(2); 6 N.Y.C.R.R. 617.9(a)(1).

123. The DEC's Region B consists of Forest, Reading and five other counties.

124. Region B is analyzed without its largest county due to the significantly more rural composition of the other counties in the region.

125. The contiguous counties are Reading and three others.

126. Figures for population, employment, retail businesses with payrolls, housing permits and site plans are from the *Forest County Data Book*, 1990 and 1995 editions.

127. As recently as early 1998, a local consulting engineer was unabashedly informed by a planning board member in a town near Ashbury that "we don't do SEQR here." At the national level, according to a survey of NEPA-induced EISs deposited at the official Northwestern University archives through 1996, the number of EISs peaked in 1972 at close to 2000, stayed at from 600 to 1200 per year from 1973 through 1982, then receded dramatically in the Reagan-Bush years to a low of about 250 in 1989 and only modest increases until 1996 (James N. Follin, "Environmental Risks, Decision Making, and Public Perception: A Case Study Involving Environmental Impact Statements," Ph.D. dissertation, Carnegie Mellon University, 1998, p. 68).

128. Torgerson, p. 68.

129. See discussion in Chapter Four, note 37, below, of how courts have found that planning boards have the inherent authority to negotiate with developers prior to the inception of the formal SEQRA process and to thereby avoid having to proceed with an EIS.

130. Vertical file, Ashbury Library, Ashbury.

131. Written statement accompanying his recognition award in retiring as chair of the Town ZBA, on display at Ashbury Town Hall, early 1996.

132. *AB*, 3/20/52. General plans for the Thruway and its likely route were announced in 1938 (*AB*, 12/29/38).

133. Letter to the editor, *Tribune*, 11/30/95; *LP*, 5/10/01.

134. Ashbury Town Planning Board minutes, 12/5/66; *AC*, 12/8/66.

135. The BigBurg chain eventually shifted plans to a central location on Main Street in the village by 1969, thus becoming the second fast-food chain outlet in Ashbury. Despite opposition by local residents and a lawsuit by the Village, BigBurg began construction in 1972 (*AC*, 6/7/72).

136. Village Trustee Patrick Walsh pointed out specifically that the Town planning board's consultant planner and engineer four years earlier had determined that traffic on Rte. 354 was at 250% of its designed capacity while Main Street was at 400%. Ashbury Town Planning Board minutes, 3/5/73, 6/4/73, 7/2/73, 8/6/73, 9/10/73; *AC*, 3/7/73, 5/9/73, 8/8/73, 8/15/73, 9/5/73, 9/19/73; *RPS*, 8/31/73; *AB*, 7/10/73.

137. Red Davis letters to the editor, *Tribune*, 11/3/94, 11/30/95. Davis also blamed "politics" (presumably the Village Board) for the failure of this developer to gain official approval at the time (Letter to the editor, *Tribune*, 2/6/97).

138. Ashbury Town Planning Board minutes, 2/27/84, 4/2/84, 4/30/84; *Tribune*, 3/1/84, 4/5/84, 5/3/84.

139. *Tribune*, 2/7/85, 2/21/85.

140. The absence of local environmental critics in this instance was conspicuous and surprising. In retrospect, the only apparent explanation is that activists were quite distracted by the final stages of the mountain ridge struggle and the concerns west of the river--both described in this chapter above.

141. *Tribune*, 2/6/97.

142. Both had resigned their membership in the grassroots land-use watchdog organization CLEAR before election to the Board.

143. *RPS*, 5/3/88.

144. In the interim, the Town Board had relinquished its legal right as town lead agency for site plan review to the planning board, a power the planning board had sought at least since 1978 and which it had already possessed until 1969 (*AB*, 10/6/69).

145. There were at least two proposals for major shopping centers directly to the east of this site as well: a 168,000 sq. ft. mall with a department store, supermarket, various retail stores and parking for 967 cars proposed in 1986 by a New York City developer and a 150,000 sq. ft. mall (Carmen Plaza) with four large stores, including a supermarket and probable department store, proposed in late 1988 by a developer from Westchester County.

146. As with Moselle Plaza, the developer of Amsterdam Square never announced the identity of its prime tenant during the project review process. However, the local

Tribune newspaper, confirmed that it was Wal-Mart in its article announcing the project withdrawal (10/17/91). After that date, this identity was also confirmed privately to one of the authors by Rodney Kiefer, director of the Ashbury Development Corporation heavily involved in encouraging outside developer investments. Said property owner Heller six years later:

> . . . [NDE] just didn't see a light at the end of the tunnel. Those things do take a lot of time, with the planning board and all, but there wasn't that much opposition except from [the local environmental group] CLEAR; those guys made sure they did everything right--environmentally. (*Tribune*, 2/6/97).

The economic motivation for pulling out was confirmed by Kiefer and in letters to the editor by Red Davis (*Tribune*, 11/3/94, 11/30/95).

147. Cost estimates are based on comments in the *Tribune*, 10/24/91 and 2/17/94 and the option agreement between property owner Joe Heller and NDE.

148. *Tribune*, 1/26/95. By the time Medford transferred the option to Magellan Construction, it had supposedly paid to Heller over $200,000 in option fees, according to Nelson Silveira, Medford's senior vice-president of corporate development. (The terms of the option agreement itself, obtained by a FOIL request to the Reading County IDA, suggest a figure closer to $150,000.)

149. General background details on Crotty & Forte and Magellan Construction come from a 1994 Dunn and Bradstreet report, the Crotty & Forte 1996 web home page and an August 1995 letter from Magellan Construction to the Dean of a Hudson Valley law school.

150. "A Kingdom All Their Own: New York State's Industrial Development Agencies," a report by State Senator Franz S. Leichter, January 1992. A local Albany reporter in 1993 reported on very generous and perhaps illegal campaign contributions from Crotty & Forte, as a company and as individuals, to the local Albany County Democratic Party, raising questions about the propriety of the Albany IDA's frequent bestowal of benefits to the same company. A knowledgeable long-time observer of Albany politics told one of the authors that one of the Magellan partners "wrote the book" on strategic political contributions in the Albany region. In 1997, according to Federal court records, a Crotty & Forte official gave a $10,000 contribution to a Hudson Valley local party boss, apparently in order to assure approvals for a local project.

151. Gary Hoover, Alta Campbell and Patrick Span, eds., *Hoover's Handbook of American Business, 1995* (Austin, Tx.: The Reference Press, Inc., 1994) and *Forbes*, 10/17/94. By 2000, <u>each</u> of the five heirs of Sam Walton, according to *Forbes*, was worth $17-18 billion (*RD*, 9/22/00). Wal-Mart itself had $191.3 billion in sales the same year, $6.3 billion in profits and 1.2 million employees (*New York Times*, 7/8/01). By 2002, Wal-Mart was reported as showing the most revenues of any corporation in the world (*The Times-Picayune*, 4/1/02). The *Forbes* 1985 statement about Sam Walton is mentioned in Bob Ortega, *In Sam We Trust: The Untold Story of Sam Walton and How Wal-Mart is Devouring America* (New York: Times Books, 1998), p. 194.

152. Hoover, Campbell and Span, eds., *op. cit.* Richard Moe and Carter Wilkie, *Changing Places: Rebuilding Community in the Age of Sprawl* (New York: Henry Holt and Company, 1997); Constance E. Beaumont, *How Superstore Sprawl Can Harm Communities* (Washington, D.C.: National Trust for Historic Preservation, 1994); Stacey Mitchell, *The Home Town Advantage: How To Defend Your Main Street against Chain Stores . . . and Why It Matters* (Minneapolis: Institute for Local Self-Reliance, 2000); and James Kunstler, *op. cit.,* provide good overviews on the nature and extent of urban sprawl and the devastation of local communities by big-box corporations such as Wal-Mart. Specific works on the negative impact of Wal-Mart include Bob Ortega, *op. cit.*; Bill Quinn, *How Wal-Mart is Destroying America (and the World): And What You Can Do About It* (Berkeley: Ten Speed Press, 2000; 2nd ed.); Edward B. Shils, *The Shils Report Measuring the Economic and Sociological Impact of the Mega-Retail Discount Chains on Small Enterprise in Urban, Suburban and Retail Communities* (mss.,1997) (Available [Online]: <http://www.shilsreport.org> [10/6/99]); and Al Norman, *Slam-Dunking Wal-Mart! How You Can Stop Superstore Sprawl in Your Hometown* (Atlantic City, N.J.: Raphel Marketing, 1999). A 1996 survey of 30,000 small-business people in New York state found an overwhelming majority opposed to big-box retailers because of their negative impacts on existing local economies (Plattsburgh *Press-Republican,* 2/1/97). A benign account of the rise and predominance of Wal-Mart in the discount retail trade is Sandra Stringer Vance and Roy V. Scott, *Wal-Mart: A History of Sam Walton's Retail Phenomenon* (Twayne Publishers, 1997). A new vivid account of current Wal-Mart working conditions is found in Barbara Ehrenreich, *Nickel and Dimed: On (Not) Getting By in America* (New York: Metropolitan Books, 2001). Quinn (chs. 3 and 5) also has good material on work conditions and recommends especially two websites on the same topic (www.walmartyrs.com and http:// members.aol.com/walmopboy/abuse/index.html). Litigation concerning unpaid overtime work at Wal-Mart stores is described in the *New York Times,* 6/25/02. More on Wal-Mart work conditions and anti-union efforts is in John Dicker, "Union Blues at Wal-Mart," *The Nation,* 7/8/02.

153. *Business Week,* 12/21/92, as quoted in David C. Korten, *When Corporations Rule the World* (West Hartford: Kumarian Press, Inc. and San Francisco: Berrett-Koehler Publishers, Inc., 1995), p. 219. In the more restricted sector of discount store sales alone, the Wal-Mart, Kmart and Target chains together moved from 61% of total sales in 1986 to 85% in 1996. According to Dicker, *op. cit.,* by 2002, the Wal-Mart chain astonishingly took in 60% of all U.S. retail sales. As one commentator thus modestly noted, "Investors, owners and managers of shopping centers anchored by weaker anchor firms will face increasing challenges to their ability to create or maintain asset value" (Dougal M. Casey, "Retail Consolidation," International Council of Shopping Centers white paper, June 1998; Available [Online]: <http://www.icsc.org/ srch/rsrch/wp/ret98.html> [October 20, 1999]).

154. *Wall Street Journal,* 6/10/96, as quoted in Shils, Ch. I, p. 5. Ironically, just days after retiring as Wal-Mart CEO in January 2000, Glass in his role as CEO of the Kansas City Royals baseball team voted for new powers for the major-league

commissioner because "we have to restore competitive balance" (*USA Today Baseball Weekly*, 1/26/00-2/1/00).

155. *New York Times*, 11/28/93.

156. National Market research by that date had defined typical Wal-Mart consumers as less affluent rural dwellers, with less education and 55 or older (David Kay, "Community and the Politics of Open Space" (Ithaca: Cornell Local Government Program Paper, 1996); Available [Online]: <http://clgp.arme.cornell. edu/docs/14-DKOS.pdf> [2/15/01], pp. 6-7). While this profile clearly did not match Ashbury community demographics, another typical Wal-Mart location motivation was to saturate a region with local Wal-Mart stores to eliminate the competition, then withdraw from their less profitable locations once consumer dependency in the region was established (Quinn, pp. 15-18, 124-128; *New York Times*, 3/5/95).

Wal-Mart's "deep pockets" to influence official policymakers were illustrated in the $166,100 given by its political action committee to 147 U.S. Senate and House candidates (98% Republicans) during the 1995-96 federal reporting period (*Sprawl-Busters Alert*, March 1997).

157. Medford Corporation was the largest member of the Evergreen Food Cooperative, the largest retailer-owned wholesale food cooperative in the United States. Evergreen had 1995 sales of $3.6 billion and 3400 employees (*1996 Directory of Corporate Affiliations*, vol. IV - "Private Companies" [New Providence, N.J.: National Register Publishing, 1996]).

158. *Tribune*, 2/2/95. FoodFeast had at least seven major rivals in the region.

159. By November 1995, a Medford vice-president claimed that his company had spent "many hundreds of thousands of dollars already" toward its efforts to build a new store in Ashbury (*Herald*, 11/23/95).

PART TWO - INTRODUCTION

1. "[A]n EIS process is one of discovery" (Kreske, p. 195). "Research is a basic requirement for the analyses in EISs" (Ibid., p. 329).

2. "An EIS that discusses one side of an environmental issue or controversy will present a biased analysis. . . . If the topic is controversial, you should obtain and present the views of experts (written or verbal) on all sides of a controversy" (Ibid., pp. 200-201). "The language of an EIS should reflect its purpose, to present the facts--including both sides of any controversy--to the decisionmaker" (Ibid., p. 317). James Follin states that EPA risk assessment guidelines insist on "proper treatment and communication of uncertainty." He underscores that "a good uncertainty analysis would improve the EIS in many cases" (Follin, pp. 103-104). Similarly, the ultimate federal overseer of proper NEPA practice, the Council on Environmental Quality (CEQ), has declared, as does SEQRA, that reasonable alternatives to the proposed project must also be discussed--and evaluated fairly (Ibid., p. 102).

3. Follin's research on lay citizen reaction to NEPA EISs demonstrated that the more information was provided about potential project impacts, with time to think about the implications, the more negatively the overall project was perceived (Ibid., pp. 139, 148-150).

CHAPTER FOUR

1. Silveira quotation in editorial by Ted Montrose, *Tribune*, 7/6/94.

2. The July 1993 statutory termination of IDA financing for most retail commercial developments was a major outcome of IDA reform efforts in the New York state legislature (*LP*, 5/3/93, 7/22/93). Abundant evidence of IDA conflicts-of-interest, lack of public accountability, taxpayer subsidy of developers without economic benefit and IDA subsidies giving competitive advantage over existing businesses were documented in an Albany newspaper; Robert G. Lynch, *New York State's Industrial Development Agencies: Boon or Boondoggle?* (Fiscal Policy Institute, October 1992); "A Kingdom All Their Own: New York State's Industrial Development Agencies," a report by State Senator Franz S. Leichter, January 1992; and "Time for A Change," final report of public hearings on local Industrial Development Agencies by Francis J. Pordum, Chairman, New York State Assembly Committee on Local Governments (March 1992).

3. While the RCIDA was required, by statute, to give public notice of its meeting and Medford's proposed funding resolution (see New York General Municipal Law, Section 859-a), the notice provision was met merely by publication in the legal notice section of the *Londonville Post* (published in Reading County and circulated also in Forest County) without specific reference to funding the Ashbury project, thus effectively giving no notice to persons concerned with further commercial development of the Heller site or with FoodFeast's plans locally. Only after preliminary approval of the project by the IDA and upon the Ashbury planning board's granting SEQRA and site plan approval would the town board of Ashbury be notified by RCIDA of its intent to fund the project and thereafter be allowed to vote on whether the final approval of the funding arrangement was acceptable to and in the town's best interest. See Chapter Six for a discussion of RCIDA's role in the Moselle Plaza project.

4. This official flyer was discovered only in the course of research for this book. No one from the ADC or other local boosters of Moselle Plaza ever publicly acknowledged that this "invitation" had been made.

5. *Tribune*, 5/19/94, 7/6/94; 9/21/94 letter from Paul Halpern, Medford president and CEO, to community protesters.

6. *LP*, 10/21/93.

7. Specifically, a publicity letter sent to a newspaper in Lake Placid, N.Y. by Sandra Watson of the Wal-Mart Real Estate Division asserted that since Wal-Mart had not announced a store in Ashbury, it was false to suggest that citizens there have fought against it (*Adirondack Daily Enterprise*, 8/30/94). Ashbury activist leaders had earlier contacted leaders of the Lake Placid anti-Wal-Mart struggle and had

informed them of the previous struggle against the Amsterdam Square proposal (including Wal-Mart) in Ashbury and their assumption of Wal-Mart plans to anchor Moselle Plaza. Wal-Mart's policy of stealth entries into communities is discussed in Ortega, p. 186; Norman, pp. 88-91; and Quinn, pp. 30-33.

8. Extensive political contributions to local and state candidates by Magellan Construction principals for many years have been noted by political observers in the Albany area. (See endnote 150 in Chapter Three above.) Deke Reynolds later claimed to an area reporter that developers support incumbents simply because they "like good government and like good candidates" and said that campaign contributions "don't have anything to do with having your bid looked at more attractively . . . ."

9. Magellan's particular timing for presentation to the board may have been designed purposefully to follow local elections. Magellan could secretly support Republican incumbents while also avoiding provoking a major controversy in the middle of the campaign. As one expert on preparing environmental impact statements advised, "Avoid election years to announce your proposed project and start an EIS process unless you are certain of full public support of your project" (Kreske, p. 227).

As is typical, from the beginning and throughout Magellan's many appearances before the board, its own managers, attorney and experts sought to impress the board with their "trustworthiness" through "proper" attire as well as (most of the time) through "rationalist" discourse. Appearance of "the suits" at Town Hall, in turn, always brought deriding comments among activists, attentive to the multi-dimensional communication games played by the developer to influence the board.

10. Rattle began reviewing project material, including the old Amsterdam Square megamall file, on November 30th. By December 20th, at his rate of $150 per hour, Rattle had already amassed fees of $1467.50 (Rattle 2/4/94 invoice to the Town of Ashbury).

11. See notes 65-68 below for a discussion of conflicts of interest and appearances of conflicts in general and those involving specific board members. Rattle's recent representation of a development group (Cairo) in a project involving one of Moselle Plaza's potential unnamed anchor stores (Kmart) also raised the question of a conflict of interest. While Rattle's relationship with Kmart during the specific time period of Moselle Plaza review was unclear, the New York bar is perspicuous in stating that an attorney serving as counsel to public bodies should not represent private clients in real estate matters that might "involve collateral proceedings with the municipality." See New York State Bar Association, Committee on Professional Ethics, Opinion No. 450 (Dec. 13, 1976). Rattle was well-known to CLEAR, having represented the Tapani development in 1987-88 when CLEAR sued the planning board for its approval of the Tapani subdivision carved from the family's extensive apple orchard.

12. Busch's predecessor, the planning board's first planning consultant, was hired in late 1968 or early 1969 (*RPS*, 12/16/68, 4/12/69).

13. Howe, p. 116. Also see pp. 113-120, 153. Most of the "traditional technicians" surveyed by Howe in 1982 worked in "conservative communities" smaller than 500,000 in population.

14. "Supplemental Environmental Assessment for Moselle Plaza Project," 1993.

15. Ironically, given Magellan's early and continuing advocacy of this minimalist EAF review, the developer's original 12/10/93 site plan application referred twice to a forthcoming Supplementary EIS (SEIS).

16. See New York Town Law, Sections 265 and 272-a (zoning ordinances), 266 (variances), and 274-a (site plan approval). For a discussion of variances (which permit a property to be utilized for a type of land use which would otherwise be prohibited by local zoning ordinances), rezoning (a legislative act changing the district classification applicable to the land), and lot line adjustments, see James A. Coon and Sheldon W. Damsky, *All You Ever Wanted to Know About Zoning*, (Albany: New York Planning Federation, 1993; 2nd ed.).

17. Official planning board minutes for 12/20/93 meeting.

18. Jack A. Nasca, Environmental Analyst 2, 12/24/93 letter to Frank Rattle.

19. *Sun-Brite Car Wash, Inc. v. Board of Zoning and Appeals*, 116 A.D.2d 274, 498 N.Y.S.2d 28, (2nd Dept. 1986). Sun-Brite was found to lack standing to oppose a zoning variance granted to a group proposing to build an automatic car wash. The court determined that Sun-Brite was not "aggrieved" merely by the threat of increased competition.

20. *Chinese Staff and Workers Ass'n v. City of New York*, 68 N.Y. 359, 502 N.E.2d 176 (1986). In *Chinese Staff*, the Court of Appeals determined that an urban environment could be affected in a manner that did not include physical alteration of existing structures and that consideration must be given to these effects in determining whether an EIS is required. The court stated, "In sum, population patterns and neighborhood character are physical conditions of the environment under SEQRA and CEQR regardless of whether there is any impact on the physical environment." A later Third Department Appellate Division decision, while relying on *Chinese Staff*, was even more direct on the issue. Referring to a local planning board's SEQRA disapproval of a Wal-Mart store based in part on the expected economic impact on existing stores, the court stated that "it does so in the context of assessing the probability and extent of the change it would work upon the over-all character of the community as a result of an increased vacancy rate among commercial properties in the downtown area--an entirely proper avenue of inquiry, even within SEQRA" (*Wal-Mart Stores, Inc. v. Planning Board of the Town of North Elba*, 238 A.D.2d 93, at 98, 668 N.Y.S.2d 774, at 777 [3d Dept. 1998]).

21. See note 59 below for a discussion of the balancing of economic and social, as well as environmental, factors in determining whether a project should proceed once there has been a finding of potentially adverse environmental impact.

22. *Tribune*, 12/30/93.

23. Ibid. The article also mentioned critical comments from county planner Henry Fowler and benign responses from Town Board member Devilla and the head of the Ashbury Development Corporation.

24. *Tribune*, 12/30/93.

25. Ryker letter to the editor, *AC*, 1/5/94; *Tribune*, 1/13/94.

26. Official planning board minutes of 1/10/94 meeting.

27. *Tribune*, 2/10/94. In the same article, even Supervisor Grant Schmidt backed the concept of an architectural review board.

28. *Tribune*, 3/3/94; *AC*, 3/2/94. On the specific issue of commercial zone definition, essentially both the Master Plan Committee and the planning board offered no change. Specific recommendations on zoning definitions and district boundaries were simply deferred to a later stage of the process.

29. *AC*, 3/2/94. By contrast, Town Board members conservative Gertrude Kraft and libertarian realtor Jay Mosher favored ex-teacher and current real estate manager Sam Myers for the planning board appointment.

30. *Tribune*, 3/13/94.

31. These included the Forest County Health Department, the Forest County Department of Public Works, the Forest County Planning Board, the NYS Department of Transportation, the NYS DEC, the NYS Thruway Authority, the Reading County Industrial Development Agency, the US Army Corps of Engineers, the Ashbury Town Board and the Ashbury Town Zoning Board of Appeals.

32. SEQRA Regulations 617.6(b)(3)(i).

33. Henry Fowler, Forest County Planning Board, 2/10/94 letter to Rocky Ryker.

34. A central program of the Clean Water Act ("CWA"), 33 U.S.C. Section 1251+, was the National Pollutant Elimination Discharge System ("NPDES") by which the pollutants discharged into national waters were to be curtailed. Responsibility for administration of the program was subsequently delegated to the states. See 52 Fed. Reg. 45,823 (1985). In New York, the DEC monitors discharges through the State Pollutant Elimination Discharge System ("SPDES"). See ECL Sections 17-0801-17-0831; see also 6 N.Y.C.R.R. 750-758. Beginning in late 1992, the DEC began monitoring stormwater runoff along with other discharges into the state's waters, taking into consideration the water quality of the discharge where previously only volume was considered. The existence of the SPDES requirements as a separate, post-SEQRA process does not, however, relieve the planning board of its duties and obligations, in the first instance, regarding stormwater discharge under SEQRA.

35. The SPDES requirements relate to SEQRA in that "changes in circumstances" surrounding a proposed development with a prior EIS approval may require an SEIS. The manner in which a project's environmental impact is evaluated can itself be a "change in circumstance" that might trigger an SEIS.

> Supplemental EISs may be needed when: [1] project changes are proposed which may result in one or more significant adverse environmental impacts; [2] newly discovered information arises about significant adverse effects which was not previously addressed; [3] a change in circumstances arises which may result in a significant adverse environmental effect; or [4] site-specific or project-specific analysis of potential significant adverse environmental impact(s) is needed for actions following generic EIS [*SEQR Handbook*, p. 76].

An SEIS may be required even if there are no changes in the actual proposal. "A change in circumstances," such as the manner in which environmental impact is to be evaluated, could necessitate an SEIS. The regulations regarding SEISs specifically distinguish changes in the project, newly discovered information, and changes in circumstances separate from but related to the project as reasons to require an SEIS. See SEQRA Regulations 617.9(a)(7).

36. The tale of wetlands preservation and regulation follows a similar route to that of stormwater runoff regulations. See note 34 above. Also in response to the Clean Water Act, New York passed the Freshwater Wetlands Act ("FWA")(ECL Art. 24). The FWA precludes the alteration of state-designated wetlands by filling, draining, dredging, or other means without a permit issued by the state (ECL Section 24-0701). These regulated alterations explicitly include ". . . running a sewer outfall, discharging sewage treatment effluent or other liquid wastes . . . " (ECL Section 24-0701[2]). The corresponding state regulations (6 N.Y.C.R.R. Sections 662-665) set stringent standards requiring that the "functions and benefits" of wetlands not be severely impaired. See 6 N.Y.C.R.R. Section 663.5. Finally, the 1993 permit requirements specifically address the relationship between stormwater runoff and wetlands preservation and deem it "generally not acceptable" to use wetlands as stormwater retention ponds or otherwise discharge stormwater into wetlands. See SPDES General Permit No. GP-93-06.

A significant difference in federal and state regulation of wetlands came into play in the consideration of Moselle Plaza. New York law requires a permit for alteration of wetlands of 12.4 acres or more (or smaller areas as designated by the DEC commissioner) (ECL Section 24-0301). By contrast, the federal definition of a wetland is a qualitative one without any minimum acreage required. 40 C.F.R. 122.2.

Although it was surrounded by New York state-designated wetlands (in excess of 12.4 acres in area), the Moselle Plaza site also contained a wetlands area of roughly one acre in size, thus raising the question of the applicability of then existing Nationwide Permit No. 26 and the wetlands concerns of the Army Corps of Engineers, concerns which, in the first instance, should also be subject to consideration by the planning board under SEQRA.

37. *Tribune*, 2/17/94. In 1987, the DEC amended its SEQRA regulations, codifying "conditioned negative declarations" ("CND") in 617.6(h) (617.7[d] in the 1996 version). A CND is a finding in which the lead agency does not require the applicant to go through an EIS review as long as the applicant agrees to incorporate measures specified by the lead agency to ameliorate adverse environmental impacts identified during the initial review process (1996 SEQRA Regulations 617.2[h]). However, by terms of the 1987 change, CNDs could only be issued for Unlisted actions (i.e., actions determined to have a significant adverse environmental impact but not explicitly defined in SEQRA Regulations 617.4), and not for Type I actions (SEQRA Regulations 617.7[d]).

Despite the regulatory attempt to limit the application of CNDs to Unlisted actions, the courts have preserved the informal review process for Type I actions by recognizing the inherent authority of lead agencies, such as planning boards, to negotiate plans informally. See *Merson v. McNally*, 90 N.Y.2d 742, 665 N.Y.S.2d 605 (1997) in which the court stated, "We hold that, under certain circumstances, a negative declaration may be issued under the State Environmental Quality Review Act (SEQRA) even where the project--a Type I action--has been modified during the initial review process to accommodate environmental concerns of the lead agency and other interested parties." (See Gerrard, Ruzow and Weinberg, Section 3.06 [2001].) In essence, we regard this as encouraging a "frontloading" developer strategy whereby both the public's potential role and the depth of impact review are considerably diminished. A more detailed critique of the implications of *Merson* appears below toward the conclusion of Chapter 17. (This phenomenon is part of a larger generic trend toward discretionary informal "negotiated" justice discussed generally, for example, in Richard L. Abel, *The Politics of Informal Justice: The American Experience* (New York: Academic Press, 1982).

38. Magellan's attorney Schwab confirmed this DEC pattern at the 2/28/94 board meeting.

39. Taylor, pp. 177, 176. (Taylor discusses this pattern at the federal level NEPA process on pp. 98, 176-181, 262-266, 268-270.) Additionally, while monitoring and enforcement agencies were deliberately not given adequate staffing under Governor Cuomo and agencies themselves were among the worst polluters (*New York Times*, 10/3/92), their politicization and failings were all the more pronounced after the election of Governor George Pataki in 1994. His new State Economic Development Commissioner Charles Gargano promised that "business will no longer be stifled by a bureaucracy too bloated to act" (*RPS*, 6/28/95). Earlier translating this priority in the environmental realm, Pataki's transition team purged DEC's legal staff by 18%, firing substantial numbers of those who could do enforcement against pollution. Meanwhile, his new DEC commissioner made clear that DEC's mission was to facilitate development and progress, not to obstruct it, and that corporations would be treated as customers rather than having a "command and control" "in-your-face" attitude. Likewise, state pollution monitors were drastically cut. In 1995, therefore, DEC collected only 1/4 of the fines it had collected in 1994 (*Albany Times-Union*, 3/15/95, 3/21/95, 1/8/96). The result was that, as one attorney for corporations and developers stated, "The agency is no longer taken seriously in the regulated community" (Cronin and Kennedy, p. 183). As a former DEC chief counsel stated: "Environmental agencies have learned that to make the problem go away, simply ignore it" (Ibid., p. 185).

40. Frank Rattle 2/23/94 letter to Rocky Ryker.

41. Ironically, in an essay he published on SEQRA the year before, Schwab argued that "larger projects with truly significant environmental impacts . . . can (and should) afford both the time and expense of EIS preparation." He stated that "the SEQRA process is open and public and lends itself especially well to the exchange of information and arguments among interested parties. The evolving body of SEQRA case law requires rigid procedural compliance." He even suggested, to facilitate this process, that "applicants' attorneys should consider offering (politely) to lend a helping hand to the agency from which they seek approval."

42. See Chapter Three, note 113, for a discussion of the "hard look" standard applied by courts in reviewing SEQRA decisions rendered by administrative agencies; see Gerrard, Ruzow and Weinberg, Section 7.04. See note 37 above for a discussion of informal methods of SEQRA review that seem in conflict with the "hard look" standard.

43. Official planning board minutes for 2/28/94 meeting.

44. *Tribune*, 3/17/94.

45. Rocky Ryker 3/14/94 memo to David Jankoff. Notions of ecological interconnectedness of environmental impacts are discouraged by the reductionist SEQRA format. Thus, increased traffic jams or aesthetic blight may be considered separately, but their effects on the tourist trade essential for the town's economic well-being will be unlikely to be recognized. This is similar to analyzing toxic contaminants in water supplies, where pollution levels relatively inconsequential when considered one-by-one may have significant toxic effect when considered cumulatively. The 3/14/94 meeting details are based on personal notes and *Tribune*, 3/17/94.

46. Ibid.

47. An initial Magellan Construction 3-page economic impact statement submitted on 3/25/94 asserted that Moselle Plaza would have a positive effect on local existing retailers, including the several local shopping centers. Magellan's economic consultant's report came to the same conclusion.

48. *Tribune*, 3/17/94; 3/24/94.

49. *RPS*, 4/15/94. Remarks by Ryker and the Town Board members were cited in *Tribune*, 3/24/94. Patton specifically recalled how Village businesses were decimated by the earlier development of Ashbury and Almond Plazas uptown.

50. Actually, SEQRA regulations even encourage public involvement prior to a determination of significance. "Early consultations initiated by [lead] agencies can serve to narrow issues of significance . . . , thereby focusing on the impacts and alternatives requiring in-depth analysis in an EIS" (SEQRA Regulations 617.3[d]). See also *SEQR Handbook* 32-33 (1992). The handbook goes even further than DEC regulations, encouraging interested individuals and groups to request information from and establish rapport with involved agencies during that pre-determination period.

51. The account of this 4/25/94 meeting is based on planning board minutes and personal notes.

52. In fact, Village Mayor Patton and the trustees were already being lobbied by several people to stall their decision. Given the dislike already expressed by Village officials for the project, not too much persuasion was needed. The Village Board had offered the potential hook-up only pragmatically to minimize adverse environmental effects on the wetlands and aquifer if the project went through. Village Board members were now informed by a growing anti-mall constituency that town planning board approval might be blocked altogether and that not allowing a hookup would contribute to that outcome.

53. Among the latter were an article by Al Norman, "Up Against Wal-Mart: Eight Ways to Stop the Store," *The Nation*, 3/28/94, and detailed impact studies from Lake Placid, N.Y., Chestertown, Md., and St. A lbans, Vermont where Wal-Marts had been proposed.

54. The generic process of "socially constructed" framing of the struggle, designed intentionally to recruit sympathizers and gain general legitimacy among the broad public, is well-analyzed in Kevin Fox Gotham, "Political Opportunity, Community Opportunity, and the Emergence of A Local Anti-Expressway Movement," *Social Problems*, vol. 46, no. 3 (8/99), pp. 332-354.

55. Such an alliance would be a major breakthrough since "small retailers are often supporters of local growth machines, even when it means bringing in directly competitive operations. In this instance, ideology seems to prevail over concrete interests and the given record" (Logan and Molotch, p. 83).

56. 5/10/94 meeting account based on personal notes.

57. Paramus, N.J. was the most frequently cited negative model in Ashbury discussions. This close suburb of New York City became the site of the largest shopping complex in the U.S. by late 1957. The entire Route 17 corridor of which it is a part seemingly never slowed its strip-mall expansion ever since. By 2001, Paramus contained 30 million sq. ft. of retail space (*New York Times*, 4/15/01). Kenneth Jackson has described the impact of strip malls nationwide over the past five decades: "Small towns across the nation, whether on the open plains of Nebraska or the winding rivers of West Virginia, have see their downtown shopping districts wither and die. Old businesses and buildings are boarded up and abandoned; other structures, poorly maintained, struggle along with marginal firms as tenants. Meanwhile, several miles away, often adjacent to an interstate highway, a Wal-Mart, a K-Mart, or some other discount retailer rests in the midst of a large parking lot" (Jackson, "All the World's A Mall: Reflections on the Social and Economic Consequences of the American Shopping Center,"*American Historical Review*, vol. 101, no. 4 [October 1996], p. 1120).

58. Additional documentation demonstrated the appropriate retail trade zone to use for impact analysis and included pages of the DEC stormwater regulations as well as a copy of relevant pages from an economic impact study of a similar Wal-Mart project in St. Alban's, Vermont.

59. See ECL Section 8-0103(7); see also SEQRA Regulations 617.1(d). Both the statute and the accompanying DEC regulations explicitly state that environmental factors are only one consideration in deciding whether to approve a proposed project. The regulations state, "It is not the intention of SEQR that environmental factors be the sole consideration in decision-making." Once the environmental impact of a project has been evaluated, that impact along with "economic and technical benefits" undergo a "systematic balancing analysis" to determine whether "environmental amenities" outweigh other benefits. See *Town of Henrietta v. Department of Envtl. Conservation*, 76 A.D.2d 215, 223, 430 N.Y.S.2d 440, 447 (4th Dept. 1980).

When a proposal fails to demonstrate economic benefit, the consideration of economic impact accentuates adverse environmental impacts and weighs against approval of the project. The burden is on the applicant to prove that there are positive economic gains which outweigh the adverse environmental impacts or face disapproval of the proposal, and the burden varies dependent upon the degree of adverse environmental impact. See *In re Onondaga Valley Farms* (DEC Comm'r Decision June 16, 1982) and *In re Pyramid Crossgate Co.* (DEC Comm'r Decision Nov. 28, 1980). Moreover, in *Meschi v. New York State Dep't of Envtl. Conservation*, 114 Misc.2d 877, 452 N.Y.S.2d 553 (Sup. Ct. Albany Co. 1982), the court found that the DEC, as lead agency, acted in violation of SEQRA and without a rational basis when it failed to consider the negative economic effect that a solid waste transfer facility would have on nearby property developments and future commercial developments. Thus, were an analysis of the Moselle Plaza project to demonstrate that it would have a negative drag on the economy of the Ashbury community and the surrounding area, once adverse environmental impact were identified, the project could be disapproved despite the developer's efforts at mitigation. See generally Gerrard, Ruzow, and Weinberg, Section 5.12[10][a].

60. The same argument was made in 1973 by then Town Board member Peter Parise concerning the megamall proposal at that time for the same property. Schmidt had already attempted publicly to marginalize project opponents two months earlier (see p. 65 above).

61. Dreyfus, who taught criminal procedure and practice at a law school in the Hudson Valley, was aware of the kickback scheme recently uncovered by U.S. Attorney Rudolph Giuliani's office whereby appointed officials (including the Ashbury highway superintendent, a friend of Ryker) had been indicted for payments made to them by contractors and suppliers. As Logan and Molotch, keen observers of local "growth machine" politics around the country, commented, "Although we shall never have 'good data' on the number of bribes and illicit contributions to politicians, officeholders often seem to face criminal indictment on the basis of conduct related to land use. . . . Such incidents of corruption, it is often said, are like cockroaches: for each one you see, there are a thousand more in the woodwork" (p. 157).

62. *LP*, May 25, 1994. Meeting account also based on official planning board minutes; *Tribune*, 5/26/94; and personal notes.

63. See endnote 20 above.

64. See New York Public Officers Law, Sections 84-90. Section 87 mandates public accessibility to all documents except in designated instances when disclosure might imperil the life or privacy of a person, reveal trade secrets, interfere with a criminal investigation, or violate other statutory restrictions.

65. See *Washington Cease, Inc. v. Persico*, 120 Misc.2d 207, 230, 465 N.Y.S.2d, 965, 979 (Sup. Ct. Washington Co. 1983), aff'd, 99 A.D.2d 321, 329, 473 N.Y.S.2d 610, 615 (3d Dept. 1984), aff'd, 64 N.Y.2d 923, 477 N.E.2d 1084 (1985). In this case, both the trial court and the Appellate Division found an apparent conflict of interest sufficient reason to nullify the permit when the defendant was chairman of the Industrial Hazardous Waste Facility Siting Board and general counsel to the DEC at the time that the department went before the board seeking approval to

locate a toxic waste dump in the town of Fort Edward. The decision was the first to consider the issue under SEQRA. The holding that an apparent conflict of interest could vitiate the decision-making process was in compliance with settled law. See *Beer Garden, Inc. v. State Liquor Authority*, 171 A.D.2d 565, 566, 568 N.Y.S.2d 25, 25 (1st Dept. 1991), aff'd 78 N.Y.2d 1026, 582 N.E.2d 590 (1991), where the court held that a SLA commissioner should have recused herself from a license revocation hearing upon the request of the petitioner because she had been serving as SLA counsel during the time that charges against the petitioner were being formulated. Again, apparent prejudgment was sufficient indication of a conflict of interest.

66. The decisions of the courts in *Persico* were consistent with prevailing law regarding conflict of interest in relation to administrative decision-making. A conflict that raises a question whether a potential decision-maker can decide an issue impartially is grounds to remove that person from the decision-making process or to vacate decisions in which that person has participated. Cases involving conflicts of interest raise either the issue of prejudgment or bias or pecuniary interest of the decision-maker as grounds to vacate a board's decision. See *1616 Second Avenue Restaurant, Inc. v. New York State Liquor Authority*, 75 N.Y.2d 158, 162 N.E.2d 910, 912 (1990), in which the chairman of the State Liquor Authority ("SLA") made reference to and expressed opinion concerning the appellant when testifying before a legislative oversight committee. The Court of Appeals held that the statements were indicative of prejudgment of the facts and that the chairman should have recused himself from the licensing hearing involving the appellant. Similarly, see *Withrow v. Larkin*, 421 U.S. 35, 46 (1975), in which the Supreme Court held that when members of an administrative licensing board evidenced a pecuniary conflict of interest with a licensee, the licensee could challenge the decision based on denial of due process stemming from the conflict of interest.

67. Both Davises' positions as adjacent property owners not only raised a question of pecuniary conflict of interest but appeared to violate state and local ethics laws. See Ashbury Town Ethics Code, Section 15-8; see also New York General Municipal Law, Section 808 (authorizing the establishment of county and municipal boards of ethics). Ashbury Town Ethics Code, Section 15-5(F) reads as follows:

> Investments in Conflict with Official Duties. He shall not invest or hold any investments directly or indirectly, in any financial, business, commercial or other private transactions which creates a conflict with his official duties.

Pursuant to the provisions of General Municipal Law Section 806, ethics codes adopted by local ethics boards, may "regulate or prescribe conduct which is not expressly prohibited" by state law. See also *Zagoreos v. Conklin*, 109 A.D.2d 281, 491 N.Y.S.2d 358 (2d Dept. 1985). Section 15-3(F) of the Ashbury Town Ethics Code, precluding investments in conflict with official duties, is such a law, applying a more stringent standard for public officials' conduct than that mandated by state law.

68. A 1988 Attorney General's opinion issued statewide advised local boards and administrative bodies of specific circumstances by which adjacent property owners may present apparent or actual pecuniary conflicts of interest:

Neighbors often act out of their own self-interests as influenced by concern about property values and the interests and concerns of their families. In our view, they may be incapable of measuring the merit of the application in light of the overall public interest or, stated differently, the overall needs of the municipality. They may be blinded in parts by the overriding parochial concerns of neighbors. [Op. Atty. Gen. (Inf.) 88-59 at 2 (1988)].

The concern voiced by the Attorney General's opinion and articulated in the Ashbury Ethics Code is consistent with the decisions of courts concerned that those who are members of local boards be free from pecuniary conflicts, actual or apparent, in order "to keep the official so far from temptation as to ensure his unselfish devotion to the public interest." *Mills v. Town Planning and Zoning Commission*, 144 Conn 493, 498, 134 A.2d 250, 253 (1957). See also *Zagoreos v. Conklin*, 109 A.D.2d 281, 287, 491 N.Y.S.2d 358, 363 (2d Dept. 1985); *Tuxedo Conservation and Taxpayers Assoc'n*, 69 A.D. 320, 325, 418 N.Y.S.2d 638, 640 (2d Dept. 1979).

69. *RPS*, 6/26/94.

70. *RPS*, 6/19/94.

71. Ibid.

72. With the same disdain for the "appearance" issue," a few months later, Ryker defended his sale of cleaning supplies to the Town, stating that municipalities should do business with their own citizens, even if public officials, since it keeps money in the community (*Tribune*, 8/31/95).

73. *Tribune*, 7/7/94.

74. Meeting account based on transcript of unofficial audio recording.

75. Around this same time, Kennedy Smith, a knowledgeable observer of local planning practice concerning retail sprawl throughout the country, stated, "Very few municipal planning offices have any idea how much commercial space is supportable in their communities." Thus, they "have failed to balance new commercial development with their capacity to support new commercial development" (Moe and Wilkie, p. 147). However, for residents of Ashbury, even "common sense" should have produced concern on this issue, since significant overbuilding of retail facilities in surrounding Hudson Valley cities of Londonville, Regent Park and Riverside had produced large strips of closed stores and shopping centers.

76. *Tribune*, 6/30/94.

77. Magellan had sent on to the Board a one-page internal DOT memo of June 10th which indicated that a review of Magellan's March 1994 traffic impact study used "reasonable" methodology and that existing and projected traffic volumes indicated were also apparently "reasonable." Though quite brief, it was potentially a strong piece of evidence for the developer if the board wished to defer to the DOT.

78. Statement transcribed from author's audio recording of this meeting. Other quotations from this meeting are derived from the same source unless otherwise noted.

79. "The lead agency will make every reasonable effort to involve project sponsors, other agencies, and the public in the SEQR process" (SEQRA Regulations 617.3[d]).

Furthermore, "[e]ach agency involved in a proposed action has the responsibility to provide the lead agency with information it may have that may assist the lead agency in making its determination of significance, to identify potentially adverse impacts in the scoping process, to comment in a timely manner on the EIS if it has concerns which need to be addressed and to participate, as may be needed, in any public hearing" (SEQRA Regulations 617.3[e]).

80. *Tribune*, 6/30/94.

81. See SPDES General Permit No. GP-93-06, Appendix D(II)(4)(C). Detention ponds must meet certain capacity guidelines that require minimum detention times before discharge into water systems and a maximum yearly outflow rate.

82. *Tribune*, 6/30/94.

83. Ibid. and personal notes.

84. *AC*, 6/29/94.

85. *Tribune*, June 30, 1994 and *RPS*, June 30, 1994.

CHAPTER FIVE

1. An individual State Pollutant Discharge Elimination System ("SPDES") permit would have to be obtained through application directly to the DEC for the discharge of wastewater of 10,000 gallons per day or more coming from a sewage treatment facility. See New York State Department of Environmental Conservation, Water Division, *Design Standards for Water Treatment Works* 1 (1988) ("DEC Design Standards").

2. Mayor Patton had come to Ashbury in 1967 as a SUNY political scientist and was neither a member of the property elite nor of the old boys' network identified with the Republican party and the leadership of Enrico, Schmidt and Ryker. In fact, as an activist Democrat, in 1971 Patton accused Enrico's protege, Town Supervisor Bob Tapani, of mismanagement, conflict of interest and nepotism during his campaign against Tapani for that office (*AB*, 9/29/71, 10/6/71). He then attacked the recordkeeping practice and "entrenched and arrogant leadership" of Enrico and his associates at the county level before and during Patton's run for county legislature in 1973 (*AC*, 10/10/73; *RPS*, 10/12/73; *AB*, 6/26/73). He won a seat there in 1975, nearly matching the total vote for Joe Enrico in the district and beating him among Ashbury voters. Patton had served as Village Mayor since 1987. He was to be re-elected, unopposed, for a third term in March 1995.

3. *AC*, 7/6/94.

4. A supplemental EIS is subject to the same procedures, including scoping, as a draft EIS (SEQRA Regulations 617.9[a][7][iii]). Scoping is:

the process by which the lead agency identifies the potentially significant adverse impacts related to the proposed action that are to be addressed in the draft EIS including the content and level of detail of the analysis, the range of alternatives, the mitigation measures needed and the identification of nonrelevant issues (SEQRA Regulations 617.2[af]).

Scoping was added to the SEQRA process in 1987 in order "to focus the EIS on potentially significant environmental impacts and to eliminate consideration of those impacts that are irrelevant or nonsigificant." Scoping is an optional step initiated by either the lead agency or the project applicant (SEQRA Regulations 617.8[a]).

5. Although not the purpose of SEQRA or environmental impact statements generally, the amount of time required for serious review sometimes has the benefit for project opponents of prolonging the process sufficiently to discourage developers financially or otherwise from proceeding toward full project approval.

6. *SEQR Handbook*, pp. 55-56.

7. A commonly employed legal principle, waiver is "the voluntary and intentional relinquishment or abandonment of a known existing legal right, advantage, benefit, claim, or privilege . . . ." (57 New York Jurisprudence Second *Estoppel, Waiver, and Ratification*, Section 74). The problems in asserting waiver in the context of the Moselle Plaza dispute, specifically the skirmishes involving the scoping process, are several. Most importantly, SEQRA regulations specifically provide for the amending of the scoping document if those seeking amendment can show good cause. Whether to accept alterations to the scoping document is at the discretion of the lead agency (see SEQRA Regulations 617.8[g]).

8. DOT Region C Planning and Program Management official 6/10/94 memorandum to DOT Region C Traffic Engineering and Safety official.

9. See ECL Section 8-0109(7)(a) and SEQRA Regulations 617.13(a).

10. See SEQRA Regulations 617.13(c).

11. Both Rattle and Busch as well as planning board engineering consultant Tony Napoleon were already being paid for their reviews of the project from the Magellan Construction escrow fund. By July 21st, at $150 per hour, Rattle had already received $6473.75 for his efforts; between the two of them, Busch and Napoleon had received $1015.50.

12. Rattle 7/11/94 memorandum to the planning board.

13. SEQRA Regulations 617.12(a)(2)(ii).

14. Positive declarations should "thoroughly analyze the identified relevant areas of environmental concern" and contain a "reasoned elaboration" (with supporting documentation) for the positive declaration (SEQRA Regulations 617.7[b][3][4]).

15. The language of the SEQRA regulations and DEC recommendations make clear that local lead agencies are to take an active role in preparation of documents related to the SEQRA process.

16. In New York, the judicial review of administrative decisions (known as an article 78 proceeding, after the process' codification in New York's Civil Practice Laws and Rules) is based upon the administrative record to the exclusion of some evidence that might be allowed in other actions. See Civil Practice Law and Rules ("CPLR") 7804(d), (e); see also Weinstein, Korn, & Miller, *New York Civil Practice*

– *CPLR* paragraph 7804.06-07. Similarly, the rules of evidence are circumscribed for appellate courts reviewing article 78 proceedings, requiring that decisions be based upon the formal record. See CPLR 5526. Courts may refuse to consider affidavits or other evidence that is not in the formal record and, thus, cannot be shown to have been provided prior to the initial administrative decision. See *Jackson v. New York State Urban Development Corp.*, 67 N.Y.2d 400, 424, 503 N.Y.2d 298, 309 (1986)(dismissing petitioner's objections to post-FEIS documents entered into the record as irrelevant because the balance of the record was sufficient to support the findings of the lower court); see also *Carpenter v. City of Ithaca Planning Brd.*, 190 A.D.2d 934, 593 N.Y.S.2d 582 (3d Dept. 1993) (nullifying the permit issued by a planning board because drainage runoff studies had yet to be completed, and refusing to allow the subsequent results of those tests into evidence). Thus, it is of key importance to admit the necessary evidence into the record during an administrative proceeding in order to preserve a reasonable opportunity for objections to prevail upon judicial review.

While it was not difficult to include correspondence in the record, there was little guarantee that planning board members other than the chair would receive or review the correspondence prior to meetings to become familiar with issues raised.

17. Prior to 1996, SEQRA scoping regulations did not guarantee the public a voice in the process. Although the DEC recommended public involvement in some instances, the lead agency possessed full discretion of whether to include the public in the scoping process and to what degree. See *SEQR Handbook*, pp.56-57.

18. Meeting account of this meeting based on personal notes.

19. Morris Schwab 7/11/94 letter to Frank Rattle.

20. 7/14/94 letter from McBride and Turbell.

21. See Chapter 4, note 20 above.

22. Weeks before, Bellows had volunteered to seek bids from outside consultants. Because the results of her research could be critical to the eventual EIS outcome for the project, McBride provided Bellows with names of Wal-Mart impact experts he obtained from the National Trust for Historic Preservation, the Washington, D.C. organization cited by anti-sprawl activist Al Norman as providing assistance to small communities facing similar megamall threats. But Bellows apparently did not vigorously pursue such leads, choosing instead to rely on names passed on by a neighboring county planning board. For McBride, this seemed ominous, since that particular county, across the Hudson River, had experienced enormous megamall growth in the recent past.

23. Meeting account based on official planning board minutes, *Tribune*, 7/21/94, and personal notes.

24. As a business person herself, Bellows was by no means anti-business. In 1996, Bellows became director of the Reading County Partnership, a private agency with government support, which sought to lure potential businesses to Forest County's southern neighbor. Two years later, in that capacity, she articulated a strong pro-business perspective for extensive development of thousands of acres adjacent to Midway Park Airport, a position offensive to environmentalists in the area (*LP,*

10/3/98). At the same time, her Reading County Partnership promoted a "fast-track" municipal approval process for commercial development in the county (*Economic Developments* [publication of R.C.P.], vol. XIII, no. 7 [9/98]) and Bellows herself endorsed broad generic EISs for potential development locations even before specific projects were proposed so as to make "shovel ready" sites readily available to developers (*LP*, 11/22/98, 6/1/99).

25. Sources for the account of this meeting are the unofficial planning board minutes, author's personal notes and an unofficial transcription of an audio recording.

26. Meeting account based on official planning board minutes and personal notes.

27. See note 7 above.

28. *SEQR Handbook*, p. 57. The *Handbook* states that "involved agencies have an obligation to provide input reflecting their agency's concerns, permit jurisdictions, and information needs." However, the failure of an involved or interested agency to participate in the scoping process is insufficient grounds to nullify the results of that process or the ensuing DEIS.

29. Official planning board minutes for the 9/26/94 board meeting and audiotape of the same.

CHAPTER SIX

1. Whatever technical uncertainties may have been voiced internally by Magellan Construction's internal or hired experts were of course filtered out in this document to enhance its authoritative effect.

2. James Wiggins, Engineers, P.C. of Oakdale, N.Y.

3. The legitimacy of this "peak-hour" standard and its implicit value assumption were never challenged by project proponents throughout the extended megamall SEQRA process in Ashbury since the standard is accepted by the DOT and nationwide. But more lenient definitions of respective letter-grade ratings for traffic delays (thus tolerating greater delays without lower ratings) have more recently been adopted in newer editions of the standard Highway Capacity Manual, no doubt in part because of pressures from the development community. In the Ashbury case, community groups and their expert were to challenge the sufficiency of a "peak-hour" analysis alone for "worst-case" analysis, since important seasonal variations were also significant.

4. Wilson & Klein of Reading County, N.Y.

5. SEQRA Regulations 617.9(b)(5)(v). Because of time and money factors, it is obvious that Magellan Construction had little motivation to provide more than what it minimally could get by with in its DSEIS submission.

6. New York law requires the mapping of every wetland area of 12.4 or more acres in area (and smaller areas designated by the DEC commissioner). See ECL Section 24-0301. East of the proposed site of Moselle Plaza were several such wetland areas designated by the DEC as "RC" (for Roodekill-Creighton Watershed wetlands) and numbered (thus, the state recognized these areas, for example, as "RC-4"or "RC-6"). In order to maintain delicate ecological systems such as the Roodekill-Creighton wetlands, both the state and federal government have implemented special measures to prevent alteration of the wetlands in any manner. These measures create a review process separate from SEQRA but also inform the standards of review to be applied by the statute. See Chapter 4, notes 34 and 36 above for a discussion of state and federal wetlands protection provisions and their relation to SEQRA.

7. Prior to February 1997, developers could disturb wetlands of less than one acre without permit. However, before disturbing wetland areas in excess of one acre, developers required a permit from the Army Corps of Engineers, Nationwide Permit No. 26. Thus, the size of the wetland area on the site proposed for Moselle Plaza was significant.

8. "It is generally not acceptable to discharge untreated stormwater directly into naturally existing wetlands" (SPDES General Permit No. GP-93-06, Appendix D[III][4][B][2]). Except for limited situations incorporating wetlands into a larger filtration situations, DEC guidelines do not allow for the use of wetlands as detention or retention ponds.

9. Among such projects were a super-regional outlet mall several exits south of Ashbury on the Thruway; a 500,000 sq. ft. retail "power center" near Londonville; other shopping centers in nearby counties; and a massive planned community of 14,000 dwelling units and 8.5 million sq. ft. of non-residential space in Reading County. Still attempting to control terms of EIS analysis of the one realm they continued to regard as illegitimate, Magellan sent a letter to the board on 9/12/94 requesting that the board hire a third alternative firm, one whose only admitted "related experience" was an economic/fiscal impact analysis for a huge Home Depot store in New Rochelle.

10. Quotations and statements referred to from this meeting are taken from the official Ashbury Town Planning Board minutes and from a transcript of our own audio recording of the meeting.

11. Meeting account based on personal notes.

Wal-Mart's national public relations coordinator, Lee Copeland, claimed in late 1995 that the company had several years earlier decided not to announce prematurely its intention to locate in a specific town because to do so before getting fully approved would be "a disservice to the customer" (*The Peninsula Gateway* [Gig Harbor, Wash.], 11/15/95). But Bob Ortega states that by the late 1980s, Wal-Mart's top officials had consciously adopted a "strategy of being as secretive as possible when trying to build a new store"--not only to avoid local site price inflation, but also to keep potential local "troublemakers" from stalling or blocking approvals (p. 186).

12. Both programs, under state law, were designed to induce new or expanded business through major tax abatement benefits. See later in this chapter and Chapter

11, endnote 4 below, for more details on IDA and 485-B programs respectively.

13. David Jankoff, in a 9/12/94 letter to the Town Board, claimed that a report costing no more than $10,000 "should be able to provide the Board with enough information."

14. *LP*, 9/20/94. FoodFeast had demonstrated similar arrogance toward community values 21 years earlier when proposing its original store in Ashbury. According to the local press, FoodFeast's Board chairman had stated that if his company was forced to meet all the town planning board's standards (however inadequate at the time), FoodFeast would have to increase its prices at the new store (*AC*, 5/9/73; *Dutch Arms Press*, 5/16/73).

15. Ted Montrose reported this comment slightly over a year later. In the same article, he contrasted the remark with the reality of much of the opposition. He mentioned recently seeing a friend of his driving though town, "80 years old, and . . . raised a conservative Italian girl in New York City. Throughout her life she has never been a bomb-thrower, literally or figuratively. But on the back of her car is a sticker that reads: STOP MALLING ASHBURY" (*Tribune*, 11/30/95).

16. Halpern admitted in an October 26, 1994 letter to ACT that FoodFeast had received over 300 postcards.

17. He later stated that even if the existing FoodFeast location was available for expansion at a reasonable price, site grades, existing trees and other issues would pose numerous difficulties.

18. Worthy was apparently a disillusioned old friend of Ryker. In 1992, he had chastised Town Board Democrats in an editorial for their delay in appointing Ryker to succeed Abe Kinsella as planning board chair since "[t]here is no one more qualified" and "[h]e knows the underlying principles of sound land-use planning" (*Tribune*, 2/27/92).

19. *AC*, 12/6/89.

20. Two weeks later Ryker made the same claim of ignorance, adding, "My personal hope is that it will be a Bloomingdale's" (*LP*, 10/17/94).

21. Ryker's remarks complemented nicely those a few months later by a spokesperson for the trade organization, the International Council of Shopping Centers, "It's Darwin's theory, the strong will get stronger and the weak will have to find a way to survive" (*New York Times*, 11/3/95, as quoted in Moe and Wilkie, p. 147).

22. All quotations and references are taken from a certified transcription of a studio recording of this program.

23. Michael B. Gerrard, "The Dynamics of Secrecy in the Environmental Impact Statement Process," *New York University Environmental Law Journal*, vol. 2 (1993), no. 2, p. 283.

24. *LP*, 9/28/99.

25. SEQRA regulations require that the adequacy or "completeness" of a DSEIS is determined by the lead agency. See SEQRA Regulations 617.9(a)(2). Once a DSEIS is determined to be complete the lead agency must file a notice of completion,

allowing for public review. See SEQRA Regulations 617.9(a)(2)(4). This notice must identify the type of EIS (whether draft, supplemental, generic, or final), provide information on how to view or obtain copies of the draft, and provide information as to the duration of the period of public review. See SEQRA Regulations 617.12(a)(2)(iii). See, generally, *SEQR Handbook*, pp 69-72.

26. Though no friend of CLEAR, his predecessor as chair in fact had no such policy.

27. This length of time was estimated on the basis of various time periods allowed by state law for agencies to respond to original FOIL requests or appeals of earlier denials.

28. Before this reversal, Ryker had also refused to provide a copy even to the Town Clerk at her request as official Town records custodian. McBride had asked her for a copy if it came into her hands. Given her strict adherence to FOIL in the past, he anticipated that she would comply.

29. Several months after RCIDA's preliminary final approval, Magellan went to the Ashbury planning board for SEQRA review and a site-plan permit. After the latter, Magellan would ask the Town Board for approval of RCIDA funding. This was the required procedure when IDA funding is used for out-of-county projects and the local community and county have not yet had a chance to comment on the propriety of low interest bonds and abatements for sales and property tax.

30. Use of this loophole was pioneered by the Golub brothers, owners of the Price Chopper supermarket chain. The Golub brothers were based in Schenectady and were able to obtain funding from their local IDA to build mega-stores in adjacent counties. Because of low-interest rate bond funding and tax abatements, these new stores had a competitive advantage over existing supermarkets and the ability to drive them out.

31. The question raised is whether the statute sought not to create empty facilities in local towns but to assist local businesses in expanding on site.

32. A developer of seventeen shopping malls across the country boasted at about this time, "Inducement packages are a significant part of the development of every one of our centers, averaging well into seven figures per project." He stated that his firm had received "a total of fifty million dollars of inducements" between those local, county and state governments involved. This phenomenon led one observer to aptly comment, "Historic downtowns don't automatically dissolve into sprawl-- taxpayers actually <u>pay</u> developers to do the job" (both quotations from Moe and Wilkie, p. 148).

33. Courts have upheld decisions despite minor procedural errors. See *Webster Assoc. v. Town of Webster*, 59 N.Y.2d 220, 464 N.Y.S.2d 431, 451 N.E.2d 189 (1983); see also Gerrard, Ruzow, and Weinberg, section 7.16[7].

34. See Chapter 4, endnote 53 above. McBride also attended a December 1994 conference in Boston, sponsored by the National Trust, which gathered representatives from many local grassroots groups struggling with such issues across the country.

35. A dramatic videotape, "Back Against the Wal," produced in Vermont by similar Wal-Mart opponents, was a powerful feature of the ACT program. (*RPS*, 12/2/94; *Tribune*, 12/8/94.)

36. *SEQR Handbook*, p. 70.

37. In actuality, such limits were never or rarely enforced by courts if the lead agency was still regularly proceeding with focused proposal review, though a developer's threat to seek judicial intervention could be intimidating.

38. Unofficial audiotape recording of 11/28/94 meeting.

39. This final quotation is from *RPS*, 12/6/94.

40. *Tribune*, 12/15/94.

41. *LP*, 12/6/94; *Tribune*, 12/8/94. On November 28th, Ryker told the board that he had recently personally conducted Marvell on a tour of the business areas of Ashbury, no doubt using the opportunity to provide the "light planner" perspective on economic issues involved.

42. Both Ryker and his predecessor Abe Kinsella had already demonstrated antipathy for public hearings in earlier statements to the press.

43. *Tribune*, 12/22/94. Quotations and verbal statements referred to in this account of the December 19th meeting were taken from the official planning board minutes, personal meeting notes and a transcript of an unofficial audio recording.

44. When Turbell later reported her meeting to Dreyfus, the latter saw Magellan's action for what it was. He urged her to set up a new meeting, with an FBI-authorized wiretap to record the offer. Indeed, he contacted the FBI and the U.S. District Attorney's office in Albany to inform them of the issue and to provoke interest in a federal investigation. For those agencies, however, the matter was apparently too minor compared with other issues in the area. They asked only to be kept informed if new developments occurred.

CHAPTER SEVEN

1. In addition, they would call for replacing the Harvey & Plonsker firm as regular attorneys for the board more generally.

2. Town Law, Section 271; Op. Atty. Gen. (Inf.) 84-52.

3. Town Law, Section 271(2); See Chapter 4, notes 11, 65-68 above, for a discussion of bias and conflict of interest.

4. See Town Law, Section 271. Planning boards exist at the discretion of the town boards who fund them even as they may act independently as lead agencies in the SEQRA process.

5. See Chapter 4, notes 65-68 above. Accounts of this meeting generally are in *RPS*, 1/3/95, and *Tribune*, 1/5/95.

6. This information came from private conversations and McBride was reluctant to create awkwardness for board members involved by releasing it. On the other hand, he thought, abuse is often stopped only by revealing it openly to the public. In this case, it was highly relevant and potentially decisive for the request being made.

7. See Town Law, Section 271(1). Planning board members are appointed by the town board. Initial appointments for the board are of staggered lengths of between 1 and 7 years with succeeding appointments of 5 to 7 years (depending upon the size of the board). This causes one seat on the planning board to come up each year for appointment of a new member or reappointment of the old.

8. Turbell furthermore explained that the law firm also represented the estate which sold FoodFeast the Reading County land, implying that they thus represented both sides in a sweet land transaction.

9. *RPS*, 1/3/95.

10. See General Municipal Law, Section 808(3) authorizing the establishment of local boards of ethics.

11. Three months earlier, for example, concerning a totally unrelated matter--the forced resignation of the town police chief because of moonlighting and tax evasion using a false name--Ryker wrote in a letter to the *Tribune*, ". . . worst of all, this community is poorer because of the vigilante way he was driven to retire and poorer because because if we allow this to happen to [him], this small cadre of personal agendas can drive anyone from this allegations [sic]. This above all else is wrong" (10/6/94).

12. *RPS*, 1/3/95.

13. *RPS*, 1/9/95.

14. *Tribune*, 1/5/95.

15. *LP*, 1/3/95.

16. *RPS*, 1/11/95.

17. *Tribune*, 1/5/95.

18. See Chapter 4, note 11 above, concerning this defense.

19. *Tribune*, 1/12/95.

20. Rattle had represented brother Bob and their father when CLEAR sued the town planning board in 1987 because of its approval of the Tapani residential subdivision. Rattle had drafted and filed a SLAPP countersuit against CLEAR on their behalf.

21. *RPS*, 1/9/95; *Tribune*, 1/5/95.

22. In actuality, the Harvey & Plonsker firm was deeply enmeshed in a developer nexus with FoodFeast itself, beyond its later role as FoodFeast's attorneys. Torelli admitted that partners of Harvey & Plonsker were partners in a Reading County development project from 1990 for which he was the attorney. A co-applicant for the project was a national commercial management corporation which happened to manage many Hudson Valley shopping centers with FoodFeast as a tenant. The

former's local office was in the same building in Reading County as Medford's corporate headquarters, a building owned by the same national company which owned the centers managed by Medford's co-applicant. Though FoodFeast was not formally a co-applicant in the specific Reading County development at issue, it was intended from November 1990 on that it would be included there as an anchor store and a lease formalizing this arrangement was signed in September 1991.

23. Interestingly, the *Tribune*'s diligent reporter during this period, Patti Owens, discovered that Harvey & Plonsker provided legal counsel as well to the planning board of a wealthy municipality where Nelson Silveira, a Medford vice president, principal owner, director, counsel and secretary, served as mayor from 1989 on (*Tribune*, 1/19/95).

24. Non-verbal signals to denigrate unwanted public testimony was one of the traits by which Ryker most revealed his lack of commitment to the proper bureaucratic norm of "neutrality." His failure in "image management" here and in other aspects of his behavior clarified his inability to subscribe to a "pragmatic capitalist" use of bureaucratic behavior and discourse even for public relations reasons alone. Non-verbal image contradictions were also pointed out in the behavior of Atomic Energy Commision-appointed licensing board members, in a work by Ebbin and Kasper. The authors observed on many occasions "headholding, eye shading, eye rolling, looks of disgust, grimacing, tight closing of eyes, etc., indicating clear appearance of annoyance if not outright demonstration of bias" (Steven Ebbin and Raphael Kasper, *Citizen Groups and the Nuclear Power Controversy: Uses of Scientific and Technological Information* [Cambridge: The MIT Press, 1974], p. 187).

25. See Town Law, Section 271(1). The Town Board may remove a member of the town board "for cause after a public hearing."

26. See Chapter 4, note 11 above.

27. He accused Turbell of acting until recently on behalf of a mall thirty miles away where she had worked as part of management, he blamed McBride for disliking him ever since he, instead of CLEAR's Kevin Scully, was chosen for the planning board and he stated that Dreyfus had a grudge because of losing the CLEAR case against the board about the Tapani development several years earlier.

28. Ryker's statement was transcribed from an unofficial audio recording of the meeting. Other quotations and descriptions are based on accounts of the *Tribune*, 1/19/95; *AC*, 1/18/95; *LP*, 1/13/95; and *RPS*, 1/13/95; as well as the authors' personal observations.

29. *RPS*, 1/17/95.

30. Devilla's statements were unofficially transcribed from an audio tape of this meeting. Schmidt's resolution is part of the official Town Board minutes. Other statements were reported in the *Tribune*, 1/26/95, 2/2/95; *RPS*, 1/20/95; *RPS*, 1/22/95; *LP*, 1/20/95. Interestingly, one decade earlier, Ryker himself had asked for Village Mayor Gary Patton's resignation in part because of the latter's alleged rudeness to the public and his preference for avoiding public input and accountability (*Tribune*, 10/10/85).

31. *RPS*, 1/20/95, 1/29/95; *LP*, 1/20/95; *Tribune*, 1/26/95, 2/2/95.

32. *AC*, 1/25/95.

33. Similarly, William Chafe writes of the power of the "progressive mystique" during the Greensboro, N.C. civil rights struggle. By emphasizing courtesy and civility, good manners over substantial action, the mystique "served as a masterful weapon of social control. By promoting the appearance of enlightenment and tolerance, the mystique obstructed efforts to mobilize sustained protest. The enemy was elusive and flexible, not immediate and brutal" (Chafe, *Civilities and Civil Rights: Greensboro, North Carolina and the Black Struggle for Freedom* [New York: Oxford University Press, 1980], pp. 238-239). See also footnote 73 in Chapter Seventeen below. In another respect, the tension among anti-megamall activists on this issue illustrates the constant potential for splits between expert advocates and non-expert citizens as to proper tactics and strategy (Fischer, *Citizens, Experts, and the Environment*, pp. 38-39).

34. Unofficial audiotape recording of the 1/23/94 meeting.

35. *Tribune*, 2/2/95. Another account of the meeting was in *LD*, 1/28/95.

CHAPTER EIGHT

1. The minimum period for public comment is 30 days from the filing of a notice of completion of a draft EIS (or draft SEIS) although the lead agency can extend the public comment period at its discretion (SEQRA Regulations 617.9[a][3]). Furthermore, the comment period must remain open for at least 10 days after any public hearing (SEQRA Regulations 617.9[a][4][iii]). However, a lead agency must issue a Final EIS (or FSEIS) within 45 days of the close of any hearings or within 60 days of the filing of a notice of completion, whichever is later, and the period for public comment must be scheduled within this time frame (SEQRA Regulations 617.9[a][5]).

2. See *SEQR Handbook*, p. 73.

3. Environmental policymaking's privileging of specialized "technical expert" language at the expense of the discourse of "local knowledge" is a core theme throughout Fischer's *Citizens, Experts, and the Environment*.

4. The regulations provide for public feedback but not for funding to assist the public in obtaining necessary professional evaluation for a project under review.

5. While a local university campus might be assumed to be shielded enough from such pressures, ACT and CLEAR received no self-initiated offers of voluntary professional expertise from SUNY/Ashbury faculty throughout the struggle against Moselle Plaza. While Turbell had taught part-time within the business department, a SUNY/Ashbury geologist later provided useful data on request and a number of SUNY/Ashbury faculty were supportive in ways similar to others in the community, SUNY/Ashbury as an institution was conspicuously absent during the 2 1/2 years of

struggle. This was not for lack of institutional interest in planning and development issues, since the campus had an official program which provided resources and advice for businesses and regional elites.

6. Since the 1970s, the National Trust has played an important informational and supporting role for local communities nationwide trying to combat sprawl and revitalize existing downtowns. During the Ashbury struggle, Beaumont published her own useful handbook, *How Superstore Sprawl Can Harm Communities*. More recently, Richard Moe, National Trust president, co-authored a well-written, more extensive overview of causes and effects of urban sprawl and positive efforts to reverse the damage and trends involved (*op. cit.*). While critical of political, economic and cultural factors encouraging urban sprawl, the Trust's emphasis on working within the parameters of the present political system and market economy prevents a deeper analysis of the limits of anti-sprawl reform. Among the Trust's greatest achievements was its major role in stopping the Disney proposal for a massive "historic theme park" in the midst of historic northern Virginia in 1993-94, a development which Moe and Wilkie describe as this country's probably "largest and most significant sprawl battle to date" (Ibid., p. x. Also see Ibid., Chapter 1).

7. Details about the DMG's presentation to the Town Board on 1/19/95 are reported in the *Tribune*, 2/2/95. Especially influential among DMG members were the IDA analysis by a SUNY/Cortland economics professor, Robert G. Lynch, *New York State's Industrial Development Agencies: Boon or Boondoggle?* (1992); a transcript of testimony by economist Thomas Muller before the House Small Business Committee on the "Impact of Superstores on Small Business: A Case Study of Wal-Mart;" and a highly critical report on IDA abuses by New York State Senator Franz S. Leichter, "A Kingdom All Their Own: New York State's Industrial Development Agencies" (1992).

8. *RPS*, 1/20/95.

9. *Tribune*, 1/26/95.

10. This particular distortion was initially intuited by Case on the basis of his longtime professional experience. In mid-January, he asked McBride to go out and measure actual lane widths at these usually busy intersections. With two other CLEAR members, McBride did so one evening at midnight. Case's critical guess was validated. Narrower lane widths than those reported in the traffic survey meant slower traffic flow ratings.

11. Within a short time, ACT treasurer Robert Monroe also discovered the same information when a secretary at Magellan Construction headquarters in Albany inadvertently revealed Wal-Mart as the planned anchor (Monroe 1/6/95 letter to Grant Schmidt).

12. All but the quotations in the final paragraph in this section describing the public hearing were taken from the official stenographic transcript. Newspaper accounts were in the *Tribune*, 2/2/95; *AC*, 2/1/95; *RD*, 1/31/95; *RPS*, 1/31/95; and *LD*, 1/31/95. The description of Medford and Magellan Construction officials was included in a 2/2/95 letter from ACT treasurer Robert Monroe to Nelson Silveira, Executive Vice President of Medford.

13. This phase of the SEQRA process, if well-organized by project opponents, inevitably is one of the few peak experiences in the long and difficult struggle, since the public finally can vocalize its feelings while the planning board listens. The chair of the Ithaca, New York planning board during the anti-Wal-Mart battle in that community said that "[t]he hearings themselves eventually achieved an almost festive tone" (Kay, p. 11). The power of this feeling generically is well-captured by Albert O. Hirschman: "The sudden realization (or illusion) that I can act to change society for the better and, moreover, that I can join other like-minded people to this end is . . . pleasurable, in fact intoxicating, in itself" (Hirschman, *Shifting Involvements: Private Interest and Public Action* [Princeton: Princeton University Press, 1982], pp. 89-90, as quoted in Laura R. Woliver, *From Outrage to Action: The Politics of Grass-Roots Dissent* [Urbana: University of Illinois Press, 1993], p. 116).

14. See *SEQR Handbook*, pp. 71-73. Under SEQRA, the term "involved agencies" refers only to a governmental body that has "a discretionary decision to make regarding some aspect of the action" (Ibid., p. 29).

15. See *SEQR Handbook*, pp. 29-30.

16. Most important were letters from Henry Fowler of the Forest County Planning Board, William Tholen of the DEC, Phillip Brown of the Thruway Authority and Carmen Tarinelli of the Forest County Department of Public Works.

17. FCPB 1/17/95 letter to Rocky Ryker.

18. FCDPW 2/10/95 letter to Town of Ashbury Planning Board.

19. NYSDOT 2/10/95 letter to Rocky Ryker. DOT's Commissioner under Governor Carey had been appointed initially by Governor Rockefeller. He later helped found the state's most powerful business lobbying group, the Business Council (*New York Times*, 11/27/00).

20. See Chapter 4, notes 34 and 36 above, for discussion of DEC regulations regarding stormwater and wetlands.

21. New York State Thruway Authority 2/13/95 letter to Rocky Ryker.

22. See endnote 7 above. The Fiscal Policy Institute advocates for fair state taxes and adequate state services and is supported by a variety of community, religious and labor organizations in New York State.

23. On behalf of the Village Board, Mayor Patton also wrote the Town Board on February 10th opposing any tax abatement for Moselle Plaza.

24. *Tribune*, 1/26/95.

25. See General Municipal Law Section 862.

26. *AC*, 2/22/95; *Tribune*, 3/16/95. Devilla rationalized her opposition as a rejection of non-binding resolutions on principle and because she didn't want to be seen as pre-judging an application before it was formally received. Given her earlier lack of interest in the "pre-judgment" issue as applied to Ryker's continuing tenure on the planning board, her sudden concern for this principle, especially in the face of Medford misrepresentations, convinced no one and provided further evidence that she would side with other "light planners" when it came to any vote the Town Board

would have to make on Moselle Plaza.

CHAPTER NINE

1. See Chapter 5, note 16, above for a discussion of how to create the official record upon which administrative decisions are judicially reviewed.

2. This level of scrutiny and documentation made possible the detail and source accountability in the present book.

3. Once a DSEIS has been accepted and the necessary public comment period observed, the lead agency is not required to consider other input from the public. See SEQRA Regulations 617.9(a)(4)(5). However, it is within the lead agency's discretion to consider comment made after the mandatory public comment period. See *SEQR Handbook*, p. 75.

4. Many months later, while representing a Magellan Construction offshoot on a different project in Ashbury, Napoleon informed the board that he always tried to avoid an EIS for his developer clients whenever possible (personal notes of 5/13/96 town planning board meeting).

5. See Chapter 3, note 113, above for a discussion of the "hard look" standard.

6. See *SEQR Handbook*, pp. 74-75.

7. This apparent procedural demonstration of impartiality and Maglie's frequent appeals for board "consensus" on goals, if not interpretations, are typical tactics in bureaucratic management generally.

8. See Chapter 5, note 16, above (discussing the record upon which SEQRA decisions are reviewed in court).

9. The asset manager for the owner of FoodFeast plaza stated in January 1995 that Medford officials had strongly suggested that "Moselle Plaza was a done deal." He was thus later surprised to find that the project had not yet received final approval (*Tribune*, 1/26/95).

10. See SEQRA Regulations 617.11(a).

11. See *SEQR Handbook*, pp. 69-70.

12. *Southern Clarkstown Civic Ass'n v. Holbrook*, No. 4813/89 (Sup. Ct. Westchester Co. Dec. 11, 1989) aff'd mem., 166 A.D.2d 651, 560 N.Y.S.2d 976 (2d Dept. 1990), appeal denied, 77 N.Y.2d 806, 568 N.Y.S.2d 913, 571 N.E.2d 83 (1991).

13. Rattle's remarks in this section came from his 2/13/95 letter to the planning board, presented at the meeting of that date, and his verbal statements on the same occasion as recorded in personal notes. Maglie's prediction was in the *Tribune*, 2/16/95.

14. See SEQRA Regulations 617.9(b)(8).

15. While the board's official stenographic transcript of the hearing apparently was available only shortly before this meeting, informal notes could have been taken by Busch at that time or his memo delayed until that document was available. However, on behalf of ACT and CLEAR, Dreyfus had already transmitted to the board on February 10th a certified stenographic transcript of the most important substantive presentations at that meeting.

16. See SEQRA Regulations 617.9(a)(4)(iii) which requires lead agencies to "receive and consider" comments from the public.

17. Given major flaws of the DSEIS obvious to people in Ashbury, it was also striking to see how relatively few were the substantive comments from experts in outside involved agencies. As already observed, such agencies, for their own reasons, did not participate as substantially as the public in this critical phase of SEQRA review.

18. See SEQRA Regulations 617.9(b)(8).

19. The account of this meeting, including quotations, comes from personal notes, a transcript of an unofficial audio recording, and press reports in the *Tribune*, 3/16/95, and *RPS*, 3/14/95.

20. Marvell had assured the board in December that he would be ready to assume that task once the hearing and comments period were completed.

21. See SEQRA Regulations 617.9(b)(8).

22. Official planning board minutes for this meeting are very abbreviated. The above account, with quotations, is based on personal notes, a transcript of an unofficial audio recording and a press account in the *Tribune*, 3/30/95.

23. Discussion of these issues in detail appears in the next chapter.

24. However, she forgot to mention that, under SEQRA, the developer should have to foot the bill. Official planning board minutes of April 17, 1995; unofficial transcript of audio recording; *Tribune*, 4/20/95.

25. *Tribune*, 4/20/95.

26. Official planning board minutes of May 15, 1995 meeting; personal notes; transcript of unofficial audio recording of meeting; *Tribune*, 5/18/95.

27. May 4th, 12th and 17th, respectively.

28. See SEQRA Regulations 617.9(a)(5) which does not require the lead agency to hear public comment upon an FSEIS.

29. Ibid. See generally, Gerrard, Ruzow, and Weinberg, Section 3.11.

30. See SEQRA Regulations 617.9(b)(8), which calls for the lead agency to respond to substantive questions raised during the public comment period but fails to define the appropriate manner of the response. See generally, Gerrard, Ruzow, and Weinberg, Section 3.11.

31. See ECL Section 8-0109(5) mandating lead agencies to undertake SEQRA considerations regardless of the permitting requirements.

32. See generally, Gerrard, Ruzow, and Weinberg, Section 5.10.

33. See Ibid.

34. 5/15/95 official planning board minutes.

35. See SEQRA Regulations 617.9(b)(5)(v).

36. As Kathy Ferguson points out, "In bureaucracy, . . . goal consensus is merely a shorthand term for the enforcement of the official definition of reality. Individuals recruited into the organization are subjected to a socialization process in which they learn to embrace the goals of the organization, or to give the impression that they have done so, or both" (Kathy Ferguson, *The Feminist Case Against Bureaucracy* [Philadelphia: Temple University Press, 1984], p. 103). According to one veteran of Ashbury official boards, this "acculturation process" generally takes about one year.

37. See Chapter 3, note 113 above.

38. See SEQRA Regulations 617.11(d)(5).

39. Quotations and discussion summary based on personal notes; transcript of unofficial audio recording; *Tribune*, 7/20/95.

40. Morris Schwab 7/17/95 letter.

41. Deke Reynolds 8/21/95 letter.

42. Transcript of unofficial audio recording of this meeting.

CHAPTER TEN

1. Source citations for each meeting discussed in this chapter are found in the previous chapter's endnotes unless otherwise noted.

2. Magellan also decided which comments from one person essentially duplicated comments from another and thus when it could simply indicate that a response to the issue was found elsewhere.

3. They stated that while at a deeper level, folded shale and sandstone bedrock does extend for at least a mile eastward from the site, "the soils and overburden (unconsolidated sediments) overlying the bedrock provide significant pathways for transmission of stormwater runoff from the site."

4. Paul Erickson entirely agrees, recommending that "each proposed mitigation measure should be considered an activity like any other undertaken in the course of project development" and thus "should be assessed for all its potential impacts on . . . the environment, just as every other project-related activity (e.g., land clearing, excavation) should be assessed" (Paul A. Erickson, *A Practical Guide to Environmental Impact Assessment* [San Diego: Academic Press, 1994], p. 250).

5. In actuality, the DOT's brief endorsement basically repeated the wording of DOT's internal memo of the previous June responding to the same set of traffic analyses as in the DSEIS.

6. The adjustment would be simple for Magellan's computerized traffic analysis format.

7. This permit was applied for in October 1993.

8. In actuality, the FCDPW had reserved judgment.

9. This factor concerned how much estimated potential traffic caused by Moselle Plaza could be reduced because of multiple consumer destinations at the same site. Case had questioned Magellan's reduction as excessive, thus implying lower overall traffic impact of the megamall on local roadways.

10. The discussion summary and quotations from this meeting are based on official planning board minutes, personal notes and a transcription of an unofficial audio recording of the proceedings.

11. While having earlier discounted the virtues, let alone possibility, of a cost-benefit analysis or commodification of policy in this realm, because of the credible challenge by that approach from the community groups and Smith, Maglie now felt confident that this traditional method--so popular in the Reagan years at the federal level--could be used to his advantage. As at the federal level, the invitation to cost-benefit analysis implied by SEQRA's "balancing test" was clearly favored generally by developers and light planners throughout the state as a way to counter-balance traditionally non-market values such as reduced traffic congestion or avoidance of wetlands pollution.

A good presentation of "ecologist" perspectives on the cost-benefit analytical approach generally is found in Frank Fischer, *Evaluating Public Policy* (Chicago: Turbell-Hall, Publishers, 1995), ch. 9 - "Environmental Policy and Risk-Benefit Analysis: The Green Critique of Technocratic Ideology." See also, Frank Fischer, "Hazardous Waste Policy, Community Movements and the Politics of NIMBY: Participatory Risk Assessment in the USA and Canada," in Frank Fischer and Michael Black, ed., *Greening Environmental Policy: The Politics of A Sustainable Future* (New York: St. Martin's Press, 1995).

12. In the meantime, Dreyfus had sent to the board a copy of a 17-page report made in February 1995 by economists Elizabeth Humstone and Thomas Muller for a DEIS concerning the Wal-Mart proposal for East Aurora, N.Y. It was the next best arrangement to actually having both economists at hand to rebut Maglie since, covering most of the same issues as he did in Ashbury and using the same methodological model, they came to an opposite conclusion.

13. Once again, as with traffic and stormwater-water quality realms, the choice was made not to contest the dominant mode of planning analysis in the economic realm. The same materialist "dollars and cents" cost-benefit paradigm used by Magellan, Marvell and Maglie was viewed as quite sufficient to undermine the case of Moselle Plaza proponents. No doubt, because of its standing as the dominant form of legitimate discourse in this realm, this model would more easily influence those still undecided and, importantly, would be the only approach recognized as "legitimate" by an eventual court review of the record.

14. See Chapter 4, note 20, above.

15. Robert W. Burchell and David Listokin, *The Fiscal Impact Handbook: Estimating Local Costs and Revenues of Land Development* (Piscataway, N.J.: The Center for Urban Policy Research, 1978).

CHAPTER ELEVEN

1. In fact, activists were not sure if Medford's IDA application even carried over to Magellan Construction (RCIDA administrator Sanford had implied to reporter Owens that it did) or, if FoodFeast pulled out, whether Magellan would carry on with a different grocery store anchor. Another symbolic achievement, the replacement of Ryker, was only one of the issues concerning the biased decision-making context which ACT and CLEAR had tried to have resolved. The particular impact of this single change also was still to be seen.

2. Taylor points out that while nominally part of the Defense Department, the Army Corps in actuality is more an arm of Congress because of its needs for specific congressional authorization and appropriations approval (p. 58). Nevertheless, an issue of this scale was relatively minuscule compared with potential public works projects concerning flood control and in any case was susceptible to intervention by Congressmen representing interests from several different districts.

3. By law, DEC had the discretion to call a trial-like adjudicatory hearing concerning a DEC permit application. At such an occasion, a discovery process can require developer consultants to turn over all the notes and data upon which their analyses were based. But, by 1997, such hearings were "being granted less and less frequently," and in fact "have been denied on major projects, such as landfills and incinerators" (Michael B. Gerrard, "The Dynamics of Secrecy in the Environmental Impact Statement Process," *New York University Environmental Law Journal*, vol. 2 [1993], no. 2, p. 288). While less formal "legislative hearings" for permit applications were still routine, participants have no opportunity for discovery and the public is not allowed to question developer technical experts.

4. Financially, an IDA denial would be important. It was true that if IDA status were denied, the developer could still receive similar property tax abatements through a different business incentive program--N.Y. Real Property Tax Section 485-B--subject to approval at the town and school district level. If the Town was willing to grant abatements, potentially the developer could still lose these for the school district property tax. Though the Ashbury School District also had adopted 485-B incentives, the percentage of tax break was not automatically 50% for the first year, 45% for the next, etc., as with the Town. Thus, activists thought there was reasonable cause to believe that the school board could be convinced to withhold all but the smallest incentive possible under the law. (The same activist tactic had been attempted, though unsuccessfully, in local efforts against the nearby mountain range hotel-condominium development project in the 1970s.) An IDA denial would also eliminate tax abatements for county sales tax on construction items and the mortgage recording tax. All of this might amount to over $1 million or 10% of the stated construction cost of the project. Additionally, the developer would no longer have the special incentive of state income tax-free IDA bonds.

5. This was precisely the logic of the anti-Wal-Mart group which brought and won the suit in Hornell. However, in this latter case, local IDA and city officials now

sought special relief legislation from the State Legislature permitting them to "grandfather" the new shopping center's eligibility for IDA status when it re-applied following the court decision. On behalf of CLEAR, McBride wrote a letter on February 8th to the Committee on Local Government of the State Assembly opposing such legislation and pointing out its dangers as a precedent for other contexts around the state, as in Ashbury.

6. Medford RCIDA funding application of 3/9/93.

7. RCIDA inducement resolutions of 3/11/93 and 6/9/93.

8. Tom Lincoln, Medford Vice-President-Controller, 3/6/95 letter to Abe Sanford.

9. The lawsuit was filed in the New York State Supreme Court in Regent Park with RCIDA and Medford as listed defendants/respondents. It challenged the legality of RCIDA's March and June 1993 Inducement Resolutions as violations of SEQRA. In addition, because RCIDA relied upon various application misstatements of Medford without further investigation, that agency had itself adopted those misstatements as its own and had therefore acted beyond its jurisdiction. The suit thus asked the court to annul the Inducement Resolutions. Accounts of the 3/9/95 meeting are based on personal notes and *RPS*, 3/10/95, 3/13/95.

10. Pat Simmons, president of the Chamber of Commerce, had sent members a misleading and inflammatory letter in September 1986 about the motives and nature of CLEAR's proposed town moratorium. By a decade later, however, some younger members of the community who shared CLEAR's orientation and who had become small business people themselves were beginning to have influence within the Chamber itself.

11. Letter to the editor, signed by Michael Starr, Chairperson, Ashbury Chamber of Commerce, *Tribune*, 3/23/95. The letter was sent to all local newspapers, Mayor Patton, Supervisor Schmidt and planning board chair Maglie. The critical report on IDA impact referred to in this statement was Robert G. Lynch, *New York State's Industrial Development Agencies: Boon or Boondoggle?*.

12. *Douglaston Civic Association, Inc. v. Galvin*, 36 N.Y.2d 1 (1974); *Society of the Plastics Industry Inc. v. County of Suffolk*, 77 N.Y.2d 761 (1991). See Gerrard, Ruzow and Weinberg, Section 7.07, for a detailed discussion of the concept of "standing" to request judicial relief.

13. Generally, Article 78 proceedings, those against public officers and agencies (see Chapter 3, note 112, above), must be brought within four months of the decision being contended. See Civil Practice Law and Rules ("CPLR"), Section 217; see also Weinstein, Korn, & Miller, *New York Civil Practice – CPLR* Section 217. Some statutes shorten this statute of limitations to as little as 30 days. See Gerrard, Ruzow, and Weinberg, Section 7.02[4][b] (limitations as applied to SEQRA challenges). However, most challenges to the IDA statute would seem to adhere to the four month time frame. Literal adherence to the statutory time frame is essential. Violation of this technical issue or others most frequently results in a case being dismissed without judicial consideration of the substantive merits involved.

14. Some involved in the prolonged battle against Medford were not enamored with the idea of assisting that corporation out of its own jam and many thought an

expanded FoodFeast store was unnecessary. A larger store would encourage more needless consumption and more environmental problems, while also threatening the viability of several more preferable small food retailers. However, almost all agreed that expansion on site was better than a megamall on the eastern side of the Thruway. There was therefore no vocal opposition to such a plan.

15. The ADC, with representatives from Town and Village Boards as well as from the Chamber of Commerce, was currently initiating an overview study of Main Street-Rte. 354 Corridor commercial development potentials.

16. After months of substantial visibility and bitter struggle, activists were continually surprised, while handing out handbills, to encounter local residents completely unaware of the issue. When activists responded that it was "about Wal-Mart," most people seemed pleased with the demonstration and in accord.

CHAPTER TWELVE

1. Whether applicable or not in Green's case, Kathy Ferguson's *The Feminist Case Against Bureaucracy* presents solid arguments that because women historically "tend to experience their social worlds differently than do men as a group," they are less dominated by and susceptible to the controlling discourse of bureaucracy (p. 23).

2. At the least, community groups and their experts had raised significant enough questions and critiques to create a "reasonable doubt" about the credibility of Magellan Construction's "scientific" assertions. But activists knew that ultimately the planning board would have to go beyond an acknowledgement of "scientific stand-off" if it was to reject Moselle Plaza on SEQRA grounds. A court would require that there be a reasonable basis for concluding that negative impacts would be too severe to permit the project. At this stage, therefore, the planning board had to move toward resolution of the conflict--through further inquiry or through a choice between rival professional evidence and argumentation. The board's direction here, in turn, would depend on the underlying land-use ideologies of its members, not on disengaged principles of scientific inquiry.

3. Official planning board minutes for August 14, 1995 meeting.

4. See SEQRA Regulations Section 617.9(b)(8) and *SEQR Handbook*, pp. 74-75.

5. See SEQRA Regulations Sections 617.9(b)(8) and 617.11(d), as well as Gerrard, Ruzow, and Weinberg, Section 3.11[5] and *SEQR Handbook*, pp. 74-75.

6. See SEQRA Regulations Section 617.9(b)(8) requiring responses to all substantive comments.

7. Personal notes, transcript of unofficial audio recording and *Tribune*, 8/31/95.

8. See SEQRA Regulations Section 617.11(c)(d) for a discussion of post-FSEIS standards and procedures.

9. See ECL Section 8-0109(1) (requiring agencies to "minimize or avoid adverse environmental impacts") and Section 8-0109(5) (requiring full SEQRA review even

for projects contingent upon other permitting conditions).

10. See Chapter 9, endnote 7 above.

11. With a classic "blaming the victim" strategy, the NIMBY epithet ("Not in My Backyard") is commonly used by developers and their supporters within government and the community to discredit or marginalize critics of particular projects who live nearby. Aside from those with a "social exclusionist" agenda, the image of opposition derived solely from self-interest (supposedly the opposite from community interest) can be turned on its head by demonstrating that those who know the project neighborhood the best are precisely those in the community most aware of important adverse environmental impacts which must be considered in project review. By its ruling on "standing" eligibility for litigation in *Society of Plastics*, New York's Court of Appeals has actually forced those citizens closest to a project to be the best, if not the only, defenders of community environmental concerns if SEQRA legal recourse is needed (*Society of the Plastics Industry Inc. v. County of Suffolk*, 77 N.Y.2d 761 [1991]).

12. However, Ryker had already admitted at the 6/27/94 board meeting that he'd received "an exceptional amount" of personal input about the project from phone calls to his home and street conversations. Likewise, in June 1995, Myers told a reporter that he had initiated much private dialogue with the public about the project and Green stated that she valued the input to date from CLEAR and ACT (*Tribune*, 6/1/95).

13. See SEQRA Regulations Section 617.11(d).

14. A reasonable "worst-case" analysis, McBride argued, would add further traffic volumes, beyond those reported by Magellan, to account for heavier seasonal traffic in the peak shopping period between Thanksgiving and Christmas or in summer weekends with heavier county fairground use. It should also include projection of traffic beyond 1995 and a higher DOT-approved background growth rate than that used by Magellan. Such corrections would show even worse degradation of traffic conditions than already calculated.

15. See Chapter 3, note 113 above.

16. *Matter of Coca-Cola Bottling Co. v. Board of Estimate*, 72 N.Y.2d 674 (1988).

17. Ibid. at 682.

18. *Ames v. Johnston*, 571 N.Y.S.2d 831 (3rd Dep't., 1991).

19. Ibid. at 833.

20. See Chapter 7, note 7 above concerning planning board appointments.

21. As the meeting began, Ryker chose to grab immediate attention and mock community concern with Moselle Plaza by replacing his name card on the table with a target sign of concentric circles. Several weeks earlier, a crudely written note sent to the planning board on an ACT flyer warned: "Approve this mall and you will be dead!! Don't ruin our town and your live [sic]." Ryker at the time acted scandalized, turning the note over to the police to investigate and seeking police presence at the meeting. Many in ACT wondered if Ryker had written the note himself to marginalize the opposition and demonstrate the great "sacrifices" the board endured in the face of a "dangerous mob."

22. After long-standing public complaints and the specific urging of board member Green, the planning board had finally initiated a brief "public comment" opportunity before each monthly workshop meeting.

23. See SEQRA Regulations Section 617.11(c)(d) for a discussion of post-FSEIS standards and procedures.

24. See SEQRA Regulations Section 617.11(a)(c) (providing for post-FEIS comment); see also ECL Section 8-0109(5) (allowing the lead agency to manipulate the review periods in order to assure appropriate SEQRA scrutiny).

25. If the activists' three "regulator" friends on the board stuck together and if Myers swung to their side, suddenly the whole situation could change. But despite Myers' forthright public skepticism, activists were doubtful that he would shift from his "light planning" orientation when the decisive moment came. Myers' base was in Ryker's camp, to which he owed his original appointment. In any case, the board still needed a solid "comments-responses" FSEIS critique of Magellan's proposal if it was to have a legally-credible rationale to turn down the project.

26. Similarly, in his study of federal agencies' responsiveness to the comparable EIS process demanded by NEPA, Taylor concluded that "[m]ost of the [EIS] replies [to comments by the public and outside agencies] are ritualistic defenses of the development agency's original arguments" (p. 183).

27. Personal notes and transcript of unofficial audio recording of September 18, 1995 meeting; *Tribune*, 9/21/95; *AC*, 9/20/95.

CHAPTER THIRTEEN

1. See Chapter 5, note 16 above.

2. See SEQRA Regulations 617.9(b)(8) and 617.11 concerning the FEIS (or FSEIS) and its consideration.

3. Actually, at the January public hearing, McBride and others had mentioned "social impact" factors such as the importance of maintaining a distinctive small-town rural character. While in official SEQRA terms, these references did not necessarily fall within court-accepted definitions of "community character," they clearly were relevant considerations under potential "social impact" for the ultimate balancing test. However, McBride's October 15th letter was the first explicit attempt to place "social impact" factors on the official record.

4. See Chapter 4, note 59 above.

5. In terms of procedure, McBride also urged the board not to defer its environmental assessment responsibilities to state agencies, citing a recent expose ("A Powerful Fund-Raiser Who Also Oversees State Contracts," *New York Times*, September 3, 1995) on significant Pataki administration political pressure threatening to compromise the independence of state agency judgment. Exemplifying this very danger, on November 6, 1995, DEC's acting director of Region B issued

a memorandum suggesting ways in which the DEC could block "frivolous" citizens' lawsuits against polluters (*LP*, 12/9/95).

6. *WEOK v. Planning Board*, 79 N.Y.2d 373, 381 (1992).

7. Ibid. at 383.

8. Ibid.

9. Since technically, though not in reality, RCIDA's inducement resolution of preliminary approval "became a matter of public knowledge immediately after its enactment," D'Elia claimed that the statutory 4-month time period in which to file an Article 78 legal challenge was applicable. Since the suit was filed two years after the IDA decision, albeit within four months of litigants' discovery of the IDA resolution, he ruled that it was untimely and therefore dismissed.

10. The plaintiffs' response to RCIDA contended that the four-month time period in which to file a suit challenging the preliminary approval resolution only began when McBride learned of the action RCIDA had taken regarding Medford's proposal for the Heller property.

11. Judge D'Elia's opinion.

12. This was inspired by the fact that three ex-board members had been actively involved in one of the first picket-line demonstrations. The statement itself was drafted by McBride and circulated by ACT activists Ken Halsted (ex-planning board chair) and Jan Winfield (the successor toTurbell as ACT chair in June 1995 when Turbell began working as a liason aide to the local Congressman).

13. Devilla later claimed the same concern as her rationale for not taking a stand at the time (*Tribune*, 12/16/97).

14. Confirming Republican fears, the local NYPIRG chapter, actively involved in the struggle against Moselle Plaza, now also developed an intense voter registration campaign on campus to provide students a voice they had never previously attained. Further appealing to the student vote, the Community Reform Party and the Democratic caucus majority had nominated a current SUNY student as candidate for Town Clerk.

15. Lyon's proposal, while endorsed by Pelletier, did not necessarily have the backing of Devilla and the two Board Republicans, Schmidt and Kraft. All the Board had done was to authorize Lyon to present the proposal to the planning board since that board was empowered by law to review and comment on any proposed zoning change.

16. This was the outside firm hired by the Village and Town Planning Boards to do the recently-completed Green Corners Corridor study and GEIS.

17. Personal notes; transcript based on unofficial audio recording.

18. See SEQRA Regulations 617.11(a).

19. See SEQRA Regulations 617.9(b)(8).

20. Account of this meeting based on unofficial audiotape recording.

21. These DOT standards were specified in the 7/27/95 letter from the DOT Civil Engineer to Rich Maglie.

22. See Chapter 9, endnote 7 above.

23. See SEQRA Regulations Section 617.9(b)(5)(v).

24. Personal notes; transcript of unofficial audio tape; *Tribune*, 11/2/95.

25. After-meeting comments of Maglie and Jankoff reported in the *Tribune*, 11/2/95.

CHAPTER FOURTEEN

1. Dynamics during poll day typified the growing campaign tension leading up to the election. This was especially true at the campus polling station where Republican poll watchers tried through various methods, ultimately unsuccessfully, to intimidate and otherwise discourage students from voting. In one incident, a voter asked if there was a place on the ballot for a referendum on Moselle Plaza. Dreyfus, a poll watcher all day on the other side, told the voter that while there was no such referendum, he/she could vote for the candidates who opposed the mall. Apparently this intervention so scandalized another Democrat poll watcher and close ally of Devilla that she immediately went off to inform Ryker. This event, as well as Devilla's choice to follow election results at the Republican, rather than Democrat, gathering that evening, well illustrated the essentially one-party system prevailing among the "old guard" party leadership locally.

2. Even without her 313 campus votes (out of 379 total cast there by students), Wilton carried the rest of Ashbury by 51 votes. However, Schmidt immediately blamed his defeat on the student vote, claiming that another 300 or so registered students who lived off campus also voted at the main polling location, no doubt overwhelmingly for the Wilton ticket. Election results and Schmidt's statement came from *LP*, 11/8/95, 11/9/95; *RPS*, 11/9/95; *AC*, 11/8/95, 11/15/95, 11/22/95; and *Tribune*, 11/9/95, 11/16/95. (Figures varied slightly from one newspaper to another.)

3. Pelletier stated that her re-election "says there's a big environmental movement here. I am an environmentalist and I have always run as one. That's what I am. People know what they're getting when they vote for me" (*RPS*, 11/9/95). It is revealing to compare the results of this election with that for the Town Board two decades earlier, in 1973, when issues of uncontrolled growth and a megamall on the same property now chosen by Wal-Mart were prime issues (see Chapter Three, p. 44 above). In that election, the Republican Supervisor candidate defeated his anti-mall Democratic opponent, 1826 to 1038 (*AC*, 11/7/73). Perhaps better organizing, but certainly the continued demographic shifts, worsened traffic congestion and greater environmental consciousness in the local population by 1995 were chief factors in this dramatic reversal from a "pragmatic capitalist" to a "regulator" victory.

4. *Tribune*, 11/16/95.

5. Manley's original research on this issue was open-ended. He could not foresee the outcome, whatever his suspicions beforehand. However, the county assessment

458

office provided him with past yearly sales tax records from 1990 on, dramatically demonstrating a very low growth rate in consumer spending. Contrary to Marvell's and Maglie's optimistic projections, this implied that the Ashbury consumer spending market would not soon significantly expand and that therefore the megamall would be that much more likely to cannibalize existing retail facilities.

6. See endnote 25 below for more on the "vested rights" issue.

7. Personal notes; transcript based on unofficial audio recording; *Tribune*, 11/23/95; *AC*, 11/22/95.

8. *LP*, 11/21/95; *RPS*, 11/22/95. Reynolds told the *RPS* reporter that Magellan had spent hundreds of thousands of dollars on the SEIS.

9. The various post-decision actions described and statements quoted were from the *Tribune*, 11/23/95, and *AC*, 11/29/95.

10. *LP*, 11/25/95. Two and a half years later, Ryker saw the whole review process and outcome as a rationale for even tighter control. He said that he should have "stuck to my guns and been more forceful in following the law. I gave the public more opportunity to be heard than I had to, and, in doing so, ceded control of the process to the opposition. It was a nasty fight and once they got control of the timetable, they were very effective in using it" (*LP*, 3/29/98).

11. *Tribune*, 11/30/95.

12. Ibid.

13. *LP*, 11/25/95.

14. *Tribune*, 11/30/95. Myers later stated that his efforts in preparing the findings statement were one of his finest accomplishments on the planning board (personal notes, Town Board meeting, 1/23/97).

15. *Tribune*, 12/7/95.

16. *Tribune*, 11/30/95.

17. Manley informed Dreyfus on December 13th that he and, he assumed, the other three planning board members favoring the disapproval statement would not want any meeting with Magellan until after the SEQRA disapproval was completed and filed. Myers admitted later that Magellan had also called him at this stage for a private meeting. He stated that he told them only a fully-public meeting would be acceptable. (Personal conversation, 1/16/97.)

The Wilton-Magellan near-meeting was only the first of various issues during this transition period and in the weeks and months after Wilton and the new Town Board took office where serious strategic and tactical political differences caused distancing within the anti-mall alliance, despite continuing friendship at the personal level. Lyon continued to argue that Wilton's initial acceptance of Magellan's invitation was correct and that she should expect that Dreyfus and McBride would have different perspectives since the latter were "outsiders" and Wilton and Lyon were "insiders." A similar dispute arose over Wilton's decision to appoint Devilla as her Deputy Supervisor, even after Devilla informed her that she was unsure how she would vote on Ryker's reappointment to the planning board. While Wilton explained that she was not a "power politician," preferred a friendly, consensual·approach, and had received only a limited electoral mandate, to Dreyfus,

McBride, Turbell and several others who had closely observed local politics for years, Wilton's perspective seemed naive, unrealistic and doomed to failure against individuals and interests who had for long pursued a "light planning" and sometimes vicious personal agenda.

18. This ad hoc scramble to assure rapid passage of the moratorium and the direct involvement of McBride and Dreyfus in doing so led Devilla to complain vociferously against the process and the role of "civilians" in it.

19. This was a patently false claim, since CLEAR, Lyon and others had urged for years that a moratorium should be enacted until the master plan and ensuing zoning revisions were finalized.

20. While New York has no explicit statutory authority for enacting a moratorium on development project local permit review, state case law has established several key elements which make it legally defensible: a short term appropriate for the deliberation to be accomplished; a land-use plan or code revision which, while under consideration, might cause precipitous landowner actions jeopardizing new plan/code effectiveness; advantages to be gained by the municipality which outweigh hardships for landowners generally; strict adherence to the enabling act procedure; and a certain time of expiration (New York State Department of State, *Moratoria* [Albany: Legal Memorandum No. 8, late 1980s]).

21. Personal notes and transcript based on unofficial audiotape of the meeting.

22. At the January 18th Town Board meeting, the hasty moratorium strategy caved in. Devilla became incensed that Wilton's "civilian" advisors had rushed through an improvised process without following "correct procedure." Wilton gave in to Devilla's pressure. While a public hearing did occur, with strong support for the interim law capping new shopping centers or retail stores at 45,000 square feet, Devilla forced the Board to repeat the process, now scheduling a new public hearing for slightly more than two weeks beyond the coming planning board meeting on the findings. (Official Town Board minutes; personal notes.)

23. Public Officers Law, Section 15; 1977 Op. Atty Gen (Inf) 276.

24. Official Town Board minutes; personal notes; and unofficial audiotape of the 1/18/96 meeting.

25. *Tribune*, 1/25/96; personal notes; and transcript based on unofficial audiotape. Following the meeting, Maglie admitted that he, Rattle and Busch had "modified" the draft document after the three meetings of the designated revision committee (which included Manley). Nevertheless, he said he was "pissed" by comments in the board meeting about the process. However, Maglie's intent to save Magellan's project was made clear when he claimed that even if the interim capped-store size zoning law was passed, Magellan's vested rights would be grandfathered unless the project itself was withdrawn (*RPS*, 1/23/96). Presumably, a "vested rights" argument would be based on the claim that, despite the project's compliance with zoning requirements at the time of the application, the planning board improperly and willfully delayed the SEQRA review process, thereby preventing Magellan from proceeding with project construction before the zoning amendment was passed. See *Huntington Ready-Mix Concrete, Inc. v. Town of Southampton*, 112 A.D.2d 161, 491

N.Y.S.2d 383 (1985) and *Pokoik v. Silsdorf*, 40 N.Y.2d 769, 390 N.Y.S.2d 49 (1976).

26. *LP*, 2/24/96; official Town board minutes; personal notes. Ryker's claim to political power based on unique pragmatic ability and knowledge of the community directly echoed the claims of his mentor Joe Enrico three decades earlier (see Chapter 3 above).

27. Account of this meeting based on unofficial audiotape recording.

28. According to County Planner Henry Fowler, this was the first time in Forest County that a project of this sort had been stopped cold by SEQRA, with no mitigation possible (personal conversation with Fowler, 10/21/96). The outcome was all the more remarkable since the whole process piggybacked, as a Supplementary EIS process, on a previously-approved EIS with positive "findings" for a similar project at the same site.

CHAPTER FIFTEEN

1. This was all the more a concern in the face of Magellan's apparent threat to introduce additional suits as well. Just three months earlier, project manager David Jankoff stated that Magellan would not sue the Town if a negative findings statement was filed (*Tribune*, 1/25/96). Now, Ryker more openly than ever identified with the developer and tried to legitimate the suit, stating that if he were Magellan he would probably do the same (*Tribune*, 4/25/96).

2. The Town's stipulation agreement with Magellan to drop litigation was signed on May 13 and filed one month later.

3. Eventually, in early 1997, Heller himself publicly confirmed that Wal-Mart was the planned main anchor of Moselle Plaza (*Tribune*, 2/6/97), while Wal-Mart spokesmen soon thereafter identified the Ashbury area to a local reporter as a planned location for a new store (*LP*, 5/11/97, and personal conversation with the reporter for this article). Reynolds had acknowledged to local Congressman Grano privately a year earlier that Wal-Mart was the planned anchor for the new version of Moselle Plaza in Acton. (See also *Tribune*, 10/31/96.)

4. *Tribune*, 5/2/96. Magellan obtained agreements with site property owners to develop this project in March 1996.

5. David Jankoff 1/22/98 letter to Town of Acton Planning Department.

6. While denying the contradiction between the committee's de facto public mandate and his own recommendation for more commercial development in that area, Lyon most likely feared that without significant compromise on this issue, the Town Board would be unlikely to muster a 4-out-of-5 majority needed to pass the zoning amendment. (A majority-plus-one was required by state law for any zoning change challenged by property holders with a majority of land in the district concerned. Such a challenge was reasonably anticipated.) Manley and Hillman,

whom activists counted on to support "regulator" Pelletier on the committee, attended very irregularly.

At one meeting in the late summer of 1996, McBride was shocked to discover that the committee proposed, with Lyon's strong encouragement, an "urban neighborhood" concept which, despite a potential retail store cap of 35,000 square feet, would allow up to 200,000 square feet of new retail stores--a size exceeding even the total square footage of Moselle Plaza. ACT activists' and McBride's suspicions became full-blown when, at a following meeting, Heller himself brought before the committee a representative of his new chosen mall developer from Connecticut. While Heller praised the ADC director for spending hours with him on the phone and pleaded with the committee to give him a break, the developer assured the group that he would be sensitive to design standards. He stated, however, that he would need a grocery store anchor of at least 60,000 square feet and a minimum of 125,000 square feet overall.

7. For discussion of this concept of collective oppositional "property claims," see Blomley.

8. The "mixed-use neighborhood" concept promoted by Lyon and the committee's consultant, Cooperville Associates, was a typical "New Urbanist" planning approach commonly rationalized as restoring the vitality and sense of community found in traditional urban neighborhoods and which supplied, in easy pedestrian distance, the daily retail needs of their residents. (See James Howard Kunstler, *Home from Nowhere* and Peter Calthorpe, *The Next American Metropolis: Ecology, Community, and the American Dream* [New York: Simon and Schuster, 1993] for elaboration of "New Urbanism" concepts.) However, as tentatively formulated in the rezoning proposal, the potential huge size of retail units and disproportionately large retail sector generally in the Gateway District directly contradicted the scale and community concept which "New Urbanists" promote. Additionally, of course, it raised all the environmental and economic impact concerns about such a build-out considered with Moselle Plaza. As Moe and Wilkie warn and as the new Ashbury proposal suggested, "New Urbanism" will continue to be regarded with suspicion so long as it's used for "simply finding more ways to develop open land" (p. 249).

9. The ADC representative on the B-2 committee, a local realtor, insisted that zoning for the Heller property should accommodate its "highest and best use." As Logan and Molotch point out, this phrase "means whatever the market circumstance dictates--if it means anything at all--. . . [and] serves to align the work of planning officials with the needs of local growth machines" (p. 156).

10. Ultimately, at least part of the reason for the endless delay appeared to be the conflicting personal/political agendas of Lyon and Wilton, and later Edna Devilla, and thus the lack of clear zoning objective signals to Town Board planning consultants on the issue.

11. The most significant among these was a highly controversial solid waste transfer station proposed in Ashbury and ultimately built by the Forest County Rural Recovery Agency. CLEAR actually sued the RRA and Town Board in late December 1995, just before the new Town Board majority took office, so as to give the Town

the opportunity and leverage to renegotiate a contract with the RRA more favorable by environmental and fiscal standards both.

12. He was replaced by close associate Kathy Marino, one of the party's Town Board nominees in 1995 and bookkeeper for the local scandal-ridden firm of Bruce Spinelli. According to a federal bankruptcy judge in a September 1994 decision, the latter hindered, delayed and defrauded creditors by transferring and concealing property knowingly and fraudulently and by making false oaths in an effort to claim that he was without funds and eligible for bankruptcy relief. The judge also suggested that Marino was implicated in the sham transfers of real property and cash. (*Tribune,* 10/26/95; *LP,* 10/25/95.)

13. After losing his post on the planning board in early 1996, Ryker had been considered for, but apparently never offered, positions of a regional economic development post for the Pataki administration and county elections commissioner (to replace his retiring mentor Joe Enrico). However, Governor Pataki eventually rewarded Ryker with a seat on the board of a state performing arts council in Albany. Intermittently thereafter involved in attempting to shape the local Republican party, Ryker appeared as well at an April 2001 planning board meeting and, in opposing a gas station expansion, astonishingly proclaimed himself committed to environmental protection of the gateway district and protective of existing small businesses that might be hurt by the new project.

14. Obviously keeping herself in the political ring for the future, Devilla became president of the Ashbury Development Corporation while also serving as secretary to the Forest County Democratic Party.

15. As planned, after his two years as board chair, Manley was replaced in that office by Suzi Green. Interestingly, during ACT's late 1996 rummage sale effort to raise funds for the activist Acton group's struggle to keep Magellan's revived megamall project out of that neighboring town, Maglie brought a donation of items for the cause.

16. Davis indeed resigned one month after Turbell's appointment.

17. *Tribune,* 9/1/99; *AC,* 9/1/99. Consistent with this perspective, *Ashbury Chronicle_* editor Burt Tompkins saw this as "an election [contest] between people who have lived in Ashbury for between 15 years and their entire lives and those who have lived in the town for less time. I view it as an effort by the townies to take back control of their town" (*AC,* 9/8/99). Devilla was nominated by ex-Supervisor Grant Schmidt and longtime Enrico ally in town and county politics Peter Parise. The same theme was articulated in 1996 by an Ashbury Republican county legislator who urged that Ryker be reappointed to the planning board since "[h]e has been the choice of people who have lived in Ashbury for generations" (letter to editor, *Tribune,* 2/15/96).

18. Medford claimed that the Rite-Aid pharmacy chain still had a lease at the Ashbury FoodFeast plaza and would not let FoodFeast take over its space to expand on site. Yet by that date Magellan Construction had bought the FoodFeast plaza as well. Deke Reynolds, head of this new Magellan Construction offshoot had represented Rite-Aid developments in the Albany area, a fact which made activists

suspect that hidden insider schemes were at work. Despite community acceptance of FoodFeast expansion on site, Medford was ready to abandon Ashbury to the fate of having no major grocery store at all. By mid-2001, it was rumored that if FoodFeast moved to Acton, Rite-Aid would expand into a mega-pharmacy at the old Ashbury FoodFeast site. Later that year, Medford declared bankruptcy and it was unclear whether it would maintain any presence in the Ashbury area.

19. Before and after Wilton's defeat by Devilla in late 1999, there were constant rumors of a new attempt (by Wilton and Devilla successively) to rezone the gateway district to allow for greater commercial development, with the contested Heller lots as the prime beneficiary.

20. Sprawl-Busters home page; Available [Online]: <http://www.sprawl-busters.com> [8/8/01]

CHAPTER SIXTEEN

1. In explaining a theoretical framework for her analysis of economic development policy in a rural Maryland county, Meredith Ramsay argues persuasively against such dichotomies and summarizes similar critiques by others (Ramsay, *Community, Culture and Economic Development: The Social Roots of Local Action* [Albany: State University of New York Press, 1996], pp. 18-22). Castells agrees with this argument (pp. 446-448). While arguing the point, Ramsay's case study even concerns local "subsistence economies," certainly not the condition of Ashbury discussed in the present study. Similarly, Paul Lichterman's study of "personalist politics" focuses greatly on the creation of new "communitarian" identities, separate from but as influential as traditional sources, in providing non-materialist values (Lichterman, *The Search for Political Community: American Activists Reinventing Commitment* [Cambridge: Cambridge University Press, 1996]).

2. Paul E. Peterson, *City Limits* (Chicago: The University of Chicago Press, 1981) and Clarence N. Stone, "The Study of the Politics of Urban Development," in Clarence N. Stone and Heywood T. Sanders, eds., *The Politics of Urban Development* (Lawrence, Ks.: The University of Kansas Press, 1987).

3. Castells, p. 301.

4. Ibid., p. 25.

5. Despite Stone's wish to distinguish regime theory from pluralist theory, there are indeed similarities, as David Judge discusses in his essay on "Pluralism," in Judge, et al.. Judge argues that by now "regime theory" overlaps considerably with later pluralist writings, such as by Dahl and Lindblom, in their mutual recognition of governing alliances of varied interests, with predominant influence by business elites. While admitting these important overlaps, Gerry Stoker emphasizes areas of analysis where regime theory moves beyond neo-pluralism (Stoker, "Regime Theory and Urban Politics," in Judge, et al., pp. 54-71).

6. Stone, in Stone and Sanders, eds., p. 7.

7. Ramsay, p. 7.

8. Stone, in Stone and Sanders, p. 16.

9. Ibid., p. 18.

10. Logan and Molotch, p. 62.

11. "Direct" roles by business come from their command of resources to immediately influence politicians. The indirect "structural" advantage of business interests is derived from what Charles Lindblom refers to as its "privileged position" in our society, since government depends on capital accumulation, most of which comes directly or indirectly from business prosperity (Lindblom, *Politics and Markets* [New York: Basic Books, 1977]). Useful summaries of strengths and weaknesses of the Molotch "growth machine" thesis are Alan Harding, "Elite Theory and Growth Machines," in Judge, et al. and Jonas and Wilson, eds.

12. Berry, et al., eds., p. 118.

13. Babcock, p. 56. By 1999, sociologists Logan, Bridges Whaley and Crowder could declare: "There is remarkable consensus today among urban theorists that growth is at the core of local politics . . ." (p. 75).

14. Stephen Elkin, "State and Market in City Politics: Or the 'Real' Dallas," in Stone and Sanders, pp. 25-51.

15. Ibid., p. 31.

16. Ibid., p. 37.

17. Ibid., p. 40.

18. Ibid., p. 43.

19. Susan Clarke, "More Autonomous Policy Orientations: An Analytic Framework," in Stone and Sanders, pp. 105-124.

20. John H. Mollenkopf, *The Contested City* (Princeton: Princeton University Press, 1983) and Richard E. DeLeon, *Left Coast City: Progressive Politics in San Francisco* (Lawrence, Ks.: University Press of Kansas, 1992).

21. Barbara Ferman, *Challenging the Growth Machine: Neighborhood Politics in Chicago and Pittsburgh* (Lawrence, Ks.: University Press of Kansas, 1996).

22. H. V. Savitch and John C. Thomas, eds., *Big City Politics in Transition* (Newbury Park, Ca.: Sage, 1991).

23. Ramsay, *op. cit.*

24. Howe, p. 11.

25. Ibid., pp. 13-14.

26. Krumholz and Clavel, *op. cit.*

27. DeLeon, *op. cit.*

28. Ibid., p. 3.

29. Ibid., p. 2.

30. Ibid., p. 11.

31. Ibid., p. 98.

32. Ibid., p. 123.

33. Manuel Castells, *The City and the Grassroots* (Berkeley: University of California Press, 1983), p. 326.

34. Ferman, *op. cit.*

35. Ibid., p. 5.

36. Pierre Clavel, *The Progressive City: Planning and Participation, 1969-1984* (New Brunswick: Rutgers University Press, 1986).

37. Castells, *The City and the Grassroots*, pp. 291, 319-320.

38. Fainstein and Hirst, p. 186.

39. Ibid., p. 187.

40. For example, see Mike Davis, *City of Quartz: Excavating the Future* (New York: Vintage Books, 1992), ch. 3, on the conservative enclave exclusionist orientation of southern California homeowner groups. In contrast, DeLeon cites multi-class and multiracial "linkage" concerns of at least large numbers of "slow-growth" activists in San Francisco.

41. Milton Kotler, *Neighborhood Government: The Local Foundations of Political Life* (Indianapolis and New York: The Bobbs-Merrill Company, 1969), p. 98.

42. David Case and Karl Hess, *Neighborhood Power: The New Localism* (Boston: Beacon Press, 1975), pp. 11, 13.

43. Peter Medoff and Holly Sklar, *Streets of Hope: The Fall and Rise of An Urban Neighborhood* (Boston: South End Press, 1994). Such movement accomplishments are also cited throughout the accounts of David Mathews and Harry Boyte, writers discussed below in the next section on participatory democracy.

Extensive empirical comparative analyses of neighborhood politics were carried out by Berry, Portney and Thomson in St. Paul, Portland, Birmingham, Dayton and San Antonio, all characterized by rare city-wide systems of neighborhood organizations which were "the primary agent of political dialogue and citizen influence" (Berry, et al., p. 12). Once established with adequate resources, authority and autonomy, "the balance of power between business and the neighborhoods is altered" (Ibid., p. 287) and such systems have proven to be "positive forces that enrich and improve city politics" (Ibid., p. 284). Furthermore, such systems can be maintained over time. "The systems in these communities have been going strong for more than fifteen years. . . . [T]hey have weathered many a political storm" (Ibid., p. 70).

44. Forester, *Planning in the Face of Power*, p. 3.

45. Ibid., p. 13. Forester has written in this vein consistently to the present, most recently in *The Deliberative Practitioner*.

46. *Planning in the Face of Power*, p. 21.

47. Ibid., p. 22.

48. See, as well, the discussion in Chapter 2 above on "regulatory" and "ecologist" planning.

49. Krumholz and Clavel, p. 228.

50. Ibid., p. 229.

51. Ibid., p. 238.

52. Alfred F. Young, "Introduction," in Young, ed., *Beyond the American Revolution: Explorations in the History of American Radicalism* (DeKalb: Northern Illinois University Press, 1993), p. 10; Jackson Turner Main, *The Anti-Federalists: Critics of the Constitution, 1781-1788* (New York: W.W. Norton and Company, 1974), pp. 104-105, 116-117, 130-131, 171-173; and Gordon Wood, *The Creation of the American Republic, 1776-1787* (University of North Carolina Press, 1998).

53. Joseph A. Schumpeter, *Capitalism, Socialism, and Democracy* (3rd ed.; New York: Harper and Row, 1950) and Robert A. Dahl, *Who Governs? Democracy and Power in American Society* (New Haven: Yale University Press, 1961). (From 1970 on, Dahl began advocating some participatory democracy themes as well.) A more recent theoretical work against participatory democracy and for a "democracy" characterized by a "selective polyarchy . . . of merit" is Giovanni Sartori, *The Theory of Democracy Revisited* (Chatham, N.J.: Chatham House Publishers, Inc., 1987). David Mathews states, "Now the established view is that, at most, a very small percentage of the population, perhaps as little as 5 per cent, takes the responsibility of citizenship seriously" (pp. 54-55).

54. Huntington in Michael Crozier, Samuel P. Huntington and Joji Watanuki, *The Crisis of Democracy: Report on the Governability of Democracies to the Trilateral Commission* (New York: New York University Press, 1975). Carole Pateman points out that it was already known to the empirical democratic theorists that the supposed apathetic voters they had come to accept as natural were disproportionately of lower socio-economic status groups and women (Pateman, *The Disorder of Women: Democracy, Feminism and Political Theory* [Stanford: Stanford University Press, 1989], pp. 7-8). The extremely volatile policy demands of people of color, women and youth to end racism, sexism, militaristic foreign aggression and cultural alienation stated bluntly the great social justice cost of American "elite democratic" regimes in their previous biased exclusionary policies.

55. Examples of this writing include Suzanne Keller, *Beyond the Ruling Class: Strategic Elites in Modern Society* (New York: Random House, 1963); David Lebedoff, *The New Elite: The Death of Democracy* (Franklin Watts, 1981); Althea K. Nagai, Robert Lerner and Stanley Rothman, *Giving for Social Change: Foundations, Public Policy, and the American Political Agenda* (Praeger, 1994); and Robert Lerner, Althea K. Nagai and Stanley Rothman, *American Elites* (New Haven: Yale University Press, 1996).

56. As Mancur Olson (*The Logic of Collective Action* [Cambridge: Harvard University Press, 1965]) claims, many interest-group organizations may indeed have legitimate claims to representing the views of large numbers, despite the fact that their professional staffs are the only activists involved. Simple dues-paying members and those who simply use the existence of such groups as justification for not acting themselves are defined by Olson as "free riders."

57. Students for A Democratic Society (SDS) was apparently the first movement group to use the term explicitly, in its founding Port Huron Statement of 1962. According to Jane Mansbridge, it was Arnold Kaufman, a University of Michigan professor, SDS advisor, and admirer of sociologist C. Wright Mills, who introduced

the phrase in his essay, "Human Nature and Participatory Democracy," in Carl Friedrich, ed., *Nomos III: Responsibility* (New York: Liberal Arts Press, 1960), p. 184 (Mansbridge, "Does Participation Make Better Citizens," *The Good Society*, vol. 5, no. 2 [9/95], Available [Online]: <http://www.civnet.org/journal/issue3/ cmjmans. htm> [7/13/01]).

58. Among the most relevant of more contemporary practical participatory democratic experiences were large-scale workers' self-management in Yugoslavia (before 1989) and Algeria (1962-65), kibbutzim in Israel, and anarchist urban and rural collectives during the Spanish revolution of the 1930s. The most universal, however brief, explosion of participatory democratic political culture in Western Europe in recent years came during the 1968 "May Days" in France.

59. The boundary between "elitist" democracy and the more moderate form of "participatory" democracy has become opaque to the degree that government bodies themselves and others now begin using the latter term to signify what in the past was known simply as "civic education" or "active citizenship." Thus, the National Council for the Social Studies, "the largest association in the country devoted solely to social studies education," defines its clientele's purpose in the following terms: "Social studies educators teach students the content knowledge, intellectual skills, and civic values necessary for fulfilling the duties of citizenship in a participatory democracy" (NCSS home page; Available [Online]: <http://www.ncss.org/ home.html> [10/20/99]). Likewise, in Nevada, an Advisory Committee on Participatory Democracy was created by state law in 1998 with a mission of "identifying and proposing solutions to any problem concerning the level of participatory democracy, increasing or facilitating the interaction of citizens with governing bodies, and improving the operation of government." It also advises the Director of the Department of Museums, Library and Arts on "special projects such as election training and get-out-the-vote programs, awards for citizen participation, and humanities-based outreach projects" (NDED home page; Available [Online]: <http://www.clan.lib.nv.us/docs/ cpd/ cpd.htm> [10/20/99]). A similar mission "to maintain and enhance a vigorous, fully participatory democracy" was given to "Project Democracy" by the Connecticut Secretary of State in the same year (home page; Available [Online]: <http://www.state.ct.us/sots/DemReport/probro.htm> [10/20/99]).

60. Works consulted included: Michael Walzer, *Radical Principles* (New York: Basic Books, 1980); *Spheres of Justice: A Defense of Pluralism and Equality* (New York: Basic Books, 1983); and "The Civil Society Argument," in Chantal Mouffe, ed., *Dimensions of Radical Democracy: Pluralism, Citizenship, Community* (London and New York: Verso, 1992); James Fishkin, *Democracy and Deliberation* (New Haven: Yale University Press, 1993) and *The Voice of the People* (New Haven: Yale University Press, 1996); David Mathews, *op. cit.*; and Harry Boyte, *The Backyard Revolution: Understanding the New Citizen Movement* (Philadelphia: Temple University Press, 1980), Boyte, *Commonwealth: A Return to Citizen Politics* (New York: Free Press, 1990), Sara Evans and Harry Boyte, *Free Spaces: The Sources of Democratic Change* (Chicago: University of Chicago Press, 1992), Harry Boyte and Nancy N. Kari, *Building America: The Democratic Promise of Public Work*

(Philadelphia: Temple University Press, 1996), and Boyte, "Beyond Deliberation, *op. cit.*.

61. "Communitarianism" has both very broad and relatively specific current connotations in the United States. In very broad terms, it signifies a desire for stronger community bonds to replace eroded traditional forms of social identity and solidarity formed by family, neighborhood, religious association and the like. Those with more conservative bent use this agenda as a critique and non-governmental remedy for current "breakdowns of morality" in individual behavior. But the same program is articulated by those who decry capitalism's reliance on individual greed and traditional dynamics of classist, sexist and racist oppression and who wish to eliminate such barriers through new forms of egalitarian community organization (with or without the help of the state). A more specific connotation of "communitarianism" is the intellectual and more popularized writing and movement promoted by sociologist Amitai Etzioni and others in *The Responsive Community* magazine, the Communitarian Network and the Institute for Communitarian Policy Studies--a "centrist" attempt to synthesize traditionalist conservative moral concerns with more liberal political ideals and emphasizing localist voluntary associations of "civil society" rather than government.

62. Alexis de Tocqueville, *Democracy in America*, ed. J.P. Mayer (Garden City, N.Y.: Anchor Books, 1969), pp. 189, 513-24.

63. Walzer, "The Civil Society Argument," p. 89.

64. Ibid., pp. 97-98.

65. Ibid., p. 107.

66. Ibid., p. 105.

67. Fishkin, *The Voice of the People*, p. 148-149.

68. Fishkin, *Democracy and Deliberation*, pp. 30-31.

69. Ibid., p. 34.

70. Ibid., p. 12. Fishkin discusses other related practical proposals in Ibid., pp. 95-101.

71. Ibid., p. 4.

72. On the use of chosen-by-lot representation in ancient Athens, see Ibid., pp. 86-91, and Fishkin, *Voice of the People*, pp. 18-19, 54-55.

73. Ibid., p. 4.

74. This is the model of unbounded critical dialogue advanced by critical theorist Jurgen Habermas in his *Theory of Communicative Action*, vol. II (Boston: Beacon Press, 1987) and elsewhere.

75. Fishkin, *Democracy and Deliberation*, pp. 36-37.

76. Ibid., p. 37.

77. Ibid., p. 83.

78. Fishkin, *The Voice of the People*, p. 168.

79. Beyond his own account of such experiments in his 1996 book, numerous others among the "moderate participatory democracy" advocates--such as David Mathews--have explored the same or similar models. One of the best such accounts,

along with a sketch of the historical evolution of the "moderate participatory democracy" movement in the last several decades is Carmen Sirianni and Lewis Friedland, *Civic Innovation in America: Community Empowerment, Public Policy, and the Movement for Civic Renewal* (Berkeley: University of California Press, 2001). At present, the Loka Institute in Boston, emulating existing European models, is helping to lead the movement in the United States to organize lay citizens consensus panels to deliberate for a week or so on technically complex policy areas (such as telecommunications, biotechnology, and military weaponry) so as to emerge with responsible, informed policy recommendations. Reports on the Institute's activities are found at its current home page (<http://www.loka.org> [2/21/01]). Also, see descriptions of the similar activities of the Civic Practices Network (CPN) and its affiliates at the CPN home page (<http://www.cpn.org> [2/21/01]). (Harry Boyte is the CPN Co-Chair and David Mathews is on its advisory board.) A useful case-study analysis of such a model is Thomas Webler, Hans Kastenholz and Ortwin Renn, "Public Participation in Impact Assessment: A Social Learning Perspective," *Environmental Impact Assessment Review*, 15 (1995), pp. 443-463. Ian Budge, *The New Challenge of Direct Democracy* (Cambridge, Mass.: Blackwell, 1996) is another excellent source.

80. More background on Mathews appears in Sirianni and Friedland, pp. 256-257. Also, see endnote 111 below on the National Issues Forum.

81. Mathews, pp. 43-44.

82. Ibid., p. 182.

83. Ibid., p. 123. Berry et al. cite a 1989 Gallup Poll showing that 41% of citizens are involved in charitable or social service volunteer activity for community benefit (p. 4). Grassroots aversion to consciously connecting associational activities with "politics" is well demonstrated in the extensive research study by Nina Eliasoph, *Avoiding Politics: How Americans Produce Apathy in Everyday Life* (Cambridge: Cambridge University Press, 1998).

84. Mathews, p. 37.

85. Ibid., pp. 44-45.

86. Ibid., p. 187. Mathews cites research studies which have proved this point: Jean Johnson, *Science Policy Priorities and the Public* (New York: Public Agenda Foundation, 1989) and John Doble and Jean Johnson, *Science and the Public: A Report in Three Volumes* (New York: Public Agenda Foundation, 1990).

87. Mathews, p. 188.

88. Ibid., pp. 133, 208-209.

89. Ibid., p. 47.

90. Ibid., p. 144.

91. Ibid., pp. 31, 41.

92. Ibid., p. 111.

93. Ibid., p. 3 (underlining is ours).

94. Ibid., p. 100.

95. Ibid., pp. 110-111.

96. Ibid., p. 62.

97. Ibid., p. 62.

98. Ibid., p. 184.

99. Boyte, *The Backyard Revolution*, p. 8. A brief biographical sketch of Boyte, emphasizing his advocacy activities, appears in Sirianni and Friedland, pp. 245-249.

100. Evans and Boyte, p. 202.

101. Boyte, "Beyond Deliberation."

102. Ibid.

103. Ibid.

104. Ibid.

105. Ibid.

106. Ibid.

107. Ibid.

108. Ibid.

109. Berry, et al., p. 21.

110. Francis Fox Piven and Richard A. Cloward, *Regulating the Poor: The Functions of Public Welfare* (New York: Vintage, 1972), pp. 261, 274; Berry, et al., p. 34; Sirianni and Friedland, pp. 38-39; James A. Morone, *The Democratic Wish: Popular Participation and the Limits of American Government* (New York: Basic Books, 1990), pp. 245-248.

111. Jefferson Center home page; Available [Online]: <http://www.jefferson-center.org> [3/10/01]. For more on the Center's activities and model generally, see also Ned Crosby, Janet M. Kelly and Paul Schaefer, "Citizen Panels: A New Approach to Citizen Participation," *Public Administration Review*, March-April 1986, pp. 170-178; Ned Crosby, "Citizen's Juries: One Solution for Difficult Environmental Questions," in Renn, Webler and Wiedemenn, eds., pp. 157-174; and Audry Armour, "The Citizens' Jury Model of Public Participation: A Critical Evaluation," in Renn, Webler and Wiedemann, eds., pp. 175-188. Crosby states, as of 1995, that his Center and the National Issues Forum (the latter supported by the Kettering Foundation) were among the six U.S. organizations established independent of universities and government "to work to improve democracy without taking policy stands" (pp. 158-159). On the National Issues Forum, see also Sirianni and Friedland, pp. 193, 257-258.

112. Those contracting with the Center have included a Minnesota county board, the Minnesota Pollution Control Agency, a local school board, a Minnesota Congressman and a state department of agriculture, as well as state Leagues of Women Voters and the Twin Cities Area Presbytery of the Presbyterian Church.

113. Says Ned Crosby, co-director of the Jefferson Center, "Once the public sees there is some way to vote intelligently, turnout will increase" (*The Dallas Morning News*, 1/14/96, as reproduced on Teledemocracy Action News and Network website; Available [Online]: <http:// www.auburn.edu/ tann/tann2> [7/1/99]).

114. Ned Crosby, Jen Romslo, Sandra Malisone and Bruce Manning, "Citizen Juries: British Style" (Available [Online]: <http://www.frontpage.auburn.edu/tann/cp/juries.htm> [8/8/01]).

115. Paul Lichterman, *op. cit.*

116. Ibid., p. 4.

117. Ibid., p. 5.

118. Ibid., pp. 34-36.

119. Ibid., p. 40.

120. Ibid., p. 96.

121. "Civic activist" writers of the "moderate participatory democracy" perspective are especially adamant in their critique of ideological radical activists' failure to connect with most people at the grassroots because of their tendency to self-righteously moralize and engage in abstract theoretical diatribes (see, for example, Harry Boyte, "The Critic Criticized," in Len Krimerman, Frank Lindenfield, Carol Kortz and Julian Benello, eds., *From the Ground Up: Essays on Grassroots and Workplace Democracy by C. George Benello* [Boston: South End Press, 1992], pp. 209-213).

122. Laura Tallian, *Direct Democracy: An Historical Analysis of the Initiative, Referendum and Recall Process* (1977) and David Butler and Austin Ranney, eds., *Referendums: A Comparative Study of Practice and Theory* (Washington: American Enterprise Institute for Public Policy Research, 1978).

123. Worldwide, initiatives and referenda are formally possible in many national political systems, including liberal democracies comparable to that in America. The Research and Documentation Center for Direct Democracy at the University of Geneva (Switzerland) maintains a website archive of such provisions and their use throughout the world (Available [Online]: <http://www. c2d.unige. ch/> [2/21/01]).

124. More recent suggested variations would permit votes to be cast by interactive television or internet.

125. Current advocates include Thomas E. Cronin, *Direct Democracy: The Politics of Initiative, Referendum and Recall* (Cambridge: Harvard U. Press, 1989); David D. Schmidt, *Citizen Lawmakers: The Ballot Initiative Revolution* (Philadelphia: Temple University Press, 1989); and Patrick B. McGuigan, *The Politics of Direct Democracy in the 1980s: Case Studies in Popular Decision Making* (Washington: The Institute for Government and Politics of the Free Congress Research and Education Foundation, 1985).

126. Vivien Lowndes, "Citizenship and Urban Politics," in Judge, et al., p. 168.

127. Ronald T. Libby, *Eco-Wars: Political Campaigns and Social Movements* (New York: Columbia University Press, 1998). Libby's three case studies in the late 1980s and early 90s included animal rights issues in Massachusetts, a multi-dimensional "Big Green" ballot in California and secondhand smoke issues in the same state. Elizabeth R. Gerber comes to a similar conclusion after analyzing 168 direct legislation campaigns in eight states (Gerber, *The Populist Paradox: Interest Group Influence and the Promise of Direct Legislation* [Princeton: Princeton

University Press, 1999]).

128. DeLeon, p. 41.

129. The Greenfield experience is discussed by campaign leader Al Norman in his book, *Slam-Dunking Wal-Mart! How You Can Stop Superstore Sprawl in Your Hometown.*

130. For example, however insightful and promising the participatory democratic land-use planning experiments undertaken in isolated local contexts, they seem essentially dependent upon the unique interest of specific agency administrators at the time, rather than an institutionalized commitment to continuous sharing or decentralizing of basic decision-making power (see Margaret A. Moote, Mitchell P. McClaren and Donna K. Chickering, "Theory in Practice: Applying Participatory Democracy Theory to Public Land Planning," *Environmental Management*, vol. 21, no. 6, pp. 877-889 and Webler, Kastenholz and Renn, *op. cit.*

131. See, for example, Michael H. Shuman, *Going Local: Creating Self-Reliant Communities in A Global Age* (Free Press, 1998).

132. However, the growth machine's demands for more speculative investment opportunities and business growth generally no doubt would continue.

133. Such values, according to eco-centric theorists, would include those of non-human life forms.

134. Relevant here is the notion of "social capital," such as described by Robert D. Putnam in his study of contemporary Italy (*Making Democracy Work: Civic Traditions in Modern Italy* [Princeton: Princeton University Press, 1993]) and his essays on American civic life ("The Prosperous Community: Social Capital and Public Affairs," *American Prospect* 13 [Spring 1993], "Bowling Alone: America's Declining Social Capital," *Journal of Democracy* [January 1995], and "The Strange Disappearance of Civic America," *American Prospect* 24 [Winter 1996]). Sirianni and Friedland nicely define "social capital" as "those stocks of social trust, norms, and networks that people can draw upon to solve common problems" (p. 13).

135. Such periods of deep social crisis and mass political questioning are what constitutional law historian Bruce Ackerman refers to as "constitutional moments" (Ackerman, *We the People: Transformations* [vol. II] [Cambridge: Harvard University Press, 1998]). Of course, such periods can produce authoritarian mass movements as well, so the overall strength of and balance between "participatory" and "authoritarian" tendencies is crucial.

136. Donald A. Schon, *The Reflective Practitioner: How Professionals Think in Action* (New York: Basic Books, 1983).

CHAPTER SEVENTEEN

1. Grant, p. 133.

2. Torgerson, p. 141.

3. See Chapter 3, above, discussing the decline of SEQRA-related activity.

4. As Hannigan suggests more generally, "constructing and implementing knowledge claims about the environment is far from a single, straightforward task . . . . [P]otentially successful environmental claims must undergo trials by science, public opinion and politics." (Hannigan, pp. 189-190.)

5. A SUNY/Ashbury study in 1995 estimated over $25 million of such spending contributions to the local economy (*LP*, 8/26/01).

6. Along with her attempt to open local government to a broader constituency and establish new community services, Supervisor Wilton was under great pressure in her first two terms to maintain a tight budget with no tax increase.

7. Redistribution of federal spending from bloated military budgets and corporate welfare, for example, to local school districts and municipalities to assure equitable high quality schools, decent housing and solid local economies would relieve local governments from these immense tax pressures and free up local political cultures to once again focus on a full range of meaningful policy choices, including how best to preserve open space, natural beauty and important natural resources.

8. By contrast, major advantages of and experiences with "asset-based community development," as opposed to the usual deficit model, are discussed in Sirianni and Friedland, pp. 63-66.

9. The last-minute hiring of an unexpectedly conservative and authoritarian superintendent of schools, plus a state-imposed accountability system based on higher school test scores, produced from 1999 on a dramatic reversal of progressive trends in this particular local policy realm.

10. The only exception is the county planning board which can reject site plans it has the power to review (NYS General Municipal Law, Section 239m). Even here, however, local autonomy reasserts itself with the local board's authority to overcome such a veto by a majority-plus-one decision. The county planning board has only advisory power in SEQRA reviews. Other involved agencies at county, state and federal levels have significant potential power at the permitting stage if they choose to use it.

11. Jim Baca, the fired whistleblowing director of the federal Bureau of Land Management under Clinton and later mayor of Albuquerque, is more direct in stating that scientists working for state and federal public land management agencies "have come under mounting pressure to 'fix' their findings for political and economic reasons" (Todd Wilkinson, *Science under Siege: The Politicians' War on Nature and Truth* [Boulder: Johnson Books, 1998], p. xviii). Similarly, employees of the U.S. Army Corps of Engineers reported that budgetary cutbacks and headquarters pro-developer bias have caused wetland regulatory enforcement to become lax and easily manipulated (*Boston Globe*, 8/8/99). Todd Wilkinson introduces his book on governmental repression of honest environmental agency officials by asserting that "[a] campaign of stifling attacks on the essence of scientific truth is present and thriving both within the ranks of the nation's largest employer, the federal government, and among natural resource agencies in most of the fifty states" (p. 4). Likewise, Thomas Devine, legal advisor for many recent whistleblowers, states, "Scientists in the civil service bureaucracy face the type of

job-related repression common in the Soviet Union before glasnost" and provides a revealing list of eight common tactics used against agency scientists and officials who advocate environmental protection (Ibid., p. 6). In New York state, Department of Health scientists sought continuously to narrow the research parameters of the Love Canal disaster and to recommend cheaper remediation, apparently under pressure from their political superiors (Nicholas Freudenberg, *Not in Our Backyards: Community Action for Health and the Environment* [New York: Monthly Review Press, 1984], p. 57).

In a well-publicized action after the fact, Governor Pataki's chief fundraiser Charles Gargano, who became Commissioner of the State Department of Economic Development, intervened on behalf of the Pyramid Corporation, two months after Republicans received a $25,000 check from Pyramid, in order to speed up DOT and DEC approvals for its long-delayed and controversial mammoth shopping mall in Nyack, N.Y. (*New York Times*, 9/3/95).

Cronin and Kennedy have provided reams of evidence about the effective political influences inhibiting the DEC and federal environmental agencies. While restrained under Democratic Governors Carey and Cuomo, the DEC was rendered virtually a non-entity under Republican Governor Pataki--himself beholden to conservative Wall Street millionaires largely responsible for his rapid rise from obscurity to statewide power. (Cronin and Kennedy, pp. 35, 38, 159, 162, 177-199, 221; *New York Times*, 12/29/94; *Albany Times Union*, 12/11/95; Schenectady *Sunday Gazette*, 6/30/96.) Repressive actions toward outspoken DEC wildlife pathologist Ward Stone and the purge of DEC enforcement attorneys were the best known of these actions under Pataki.

In more general terms, "[w]hile in rare instances, . . . bureaucracies interpret legislative intent in favor of the lower classes, by far the more usual situation is to go the other way, to put into practice what legislators hesitate to put into words" (Susan Fainstein and Norman I. Fainstein, "The Political Economy of American Bureaucracy," in Fischer and Sirianni, p. 318).

12. Taylor, pp. 176, 177. (Taylor discusses this pattern at the federal level NEPA process on pp. 98, 176-181, 262-266, 268-270.) Gould <u>et al.</u> even refer to environmental agencies typically functioning as "'containment' vessels for ecologically concerned individuals . . . confined within a bureaucratic structure . . . which largely precludes their active pursuit of [ecological] goals" (Kenneth Gould, Allan Schnaiberg and Adam Weinberg, *Local Environmental Struggles: Citizen Activism in the Treadmill of Production* [Cambridge: Cambridge University Press, 1996], pp. 121-122).

13. Taylor, p. 125.

14. Cronin and Kennedy, p. 185. According to DEC's own figures, "[f]ar fewer polluters [were] being investigated and fined under Gov. George Pataki's administration than during Mario Cuomo's last years in office" (*LP*, 2/2/97).

15. This same dynamic of federal experts helping to legitimate popular challenges to more local government agencies and the developer occurred in the detailed Alberta environmental impact review process described in Mary Richardson, Joan Sherman and Michael Gismondi, *Winning Back the Words: Confronting Experts in*

An Environmental Public Hearing (Toronto: Garamond Press, 1993), p. 15.

16. According to Gerrard, fewer than 10% of SEQRA EISs were challenged in court in the early 1990s, but nearly 18% in the last several years of that decade. The average number of EIS challenges per year during this decade was less than 50% of the number of SEQRA challenges not involving an EIS (Michael B. Gerrard, "Ten Years of SEQRA Litigation: A Statistical Analysis," *New York Law Journal*, 3/24/00). According to Taylor, by 1980, 10% of all NEPA-subject projects with an EIS were brought to court (p. 36). Overall, the number of NEPA cases peaked in 1974 (Ibid., p. 245). While originally focused especially on demands for an EIS instead of a negative declaration, from 1980 through 1992, as agencies and their lawyers became more acculturated to the statute and its judicial interpretation, litigation has focused almost as much on issues of EIS "adequacy" (Ibid., p. 356; Kreske, p. 156).

17. Close observers of SEQRA's litigation record state bluntly: ". . . [T]he outcome of SEQRA litigation in court has something of a lottery quality--the results are influenced not only by the technical soundness of the EIS and the effects of the project, but also by the quality of the advocates and of the judges, and by a host of procedural complexities. These factors, combined with the very constrained standard of review, make the courts a highly unreliable forum of last resort for those dissatisfied with an EIS or other SEQRA determination" (Michael B. Gerrard and Monica Jahan Rose, "Possible Ways to 'Reform' SEQRA," *New York Law Journal*, 1/23/98). As one attorney in 1995 commented to us, "we all know that 90% of the cases are decided on technicalities, not the substantive merits."

Often, of course, judicial interpretations of technical procedural matters can be clearly politicized, just as depicted in the policymaking process described in this book. Roger Beers, an experienced environmental attorney insists that "the most political cases are environmental cases. Often, as important as the law being sued under, or the specific situation at hand, is the political attitude of the judge. If the judge thinks what you want is trivial or will impede economic growth, you may not get very far if the law is ambiguous" (Tom Turner, "The Legal Eagles," *The Amicus Journal*, Winter 1988, p. 36).

However, Gerrard also has demonstrated that plaintiffs are almost three times more likely to prevail in court if they challenge a negative declaration rather than the adequacy of an EIS itself. From 1990 through 1999, the former plaintiffs were victorious in 28% of cases (Gerrard, "Ten Years of SEQRA Litigation: A Statistical Analysis").

18. These biases against the public are starkly revealed when contrasted with a strong alternative scenario: an open-ended time frame and, as Torgerson suggests, a shifting of the burden of proof onto developers to demonstrate compellingly that assumed adverse environmental impacts will not occur (p. 159).

19. Gerrard, "The Dynamics of Secrecy . . . ," p. 279.

20. Ibid., p. 280.

21. Torgerson, p. 82. See also Chapter 9, endnote 7 above.

22. Taylor, p. 29. (The repressive consequences against those who press their positions too ardently are emphasized in endnote 11 above.)

23. Ibid., p. 127.

24. Taylor describes this same relationship between outsiders and "regulator" administrative allies in federal NEPA reviews (Ibid., pp. 131, 306).

25. As Elisabeth Noelle-Neumann has stressed, there is a "spiral of silence" caused by the fear of "separation and isolation" from others in the community and the desire "to be respected and liked" (Noelle-Neumann, *The Spiral of Silence: Public Opinion--Our Social Skin* [Chicago: University of Chicago Press, 1984], p. 41 [as quoted in Laura R. Woliver, *From Outrage to Action: The Politics of Grass-Roots Dissent* (Urbana: University of Illinois Press, 1993), p. 16]).

26. His predecessor as chair, Abe Kinsella, had said much the same after a similar public hearing on the comprehensive plan (*CLEAR Newsletter*, 9/90). Contempt for grassroots research is typical. For example, two New York State Health Department doctors dismissed early systemic Love Canal resident survey data as "totally, absolutely and emphatically incorrect" and as "information collected by housewives that is useless" (Freudenberg, p. 43). By now, the similar early dismissal of grassroots residents' cancer data in Woburn, Massachusetts by state health officials has been well-publicized in the film, *A Civil Action*, and Jonathan Harr's book upon which it is based (New York: Vintage, 1996). A comparable account is Phil Brown and Edwin J. Mikkelsen, *No Safe Place: Toxic Waste, Leukemia, and Community Action* (Berkeley: University of California Press, 1990).

27. Taylor, p. 84.

28. *Sierra Club v. Froehlke*, 359 F.Supp.1334 (S.D. Texas 1973), as quoted in Ibid., p. 85. Gould et al. also point out that their central focused location in the growth machine gives "state participants and developers easy access to financial capital, political ties with elected officials, time and technical expertise; these resources [are] a part of their everyday experiences" (p. 77).

29. Potential funding exists in New York state for community groups critiquing new power plant sites (NYS Public Service Law, Article 10), but this statute is separate from SEQRA.

30. Forester, *The Deliberative Practitioner*, pp. 5, 140, 206, 211, 215-217. Gould et al. suggest that "[w]hen local movements fail, people become apathetic, convinced that they cannot fight city hall. They feel they are powerless to make any difference" (p. 196).

31. Taylor, p. 26.

32. John S. Dryzek, "Policy Analysis and Planning: From Science to Argument," in Fischer and Forester, eds., pp. 228-229. See Forester, *The Deliberative Practitioner*, pp. 236-237.

33. As originally enacted in 1975, SEQRA provided that the applicant would furnish an advisory "environmental impact report" at the request of the lead agency but the agency would always provide the actual DEIS. See Act of August 1, 1975, N.Y. Laws ch. 612, Section 8-0109(3). The 1977 amendments made it permissible for the applicant to provide the DEIS. See Act of June 10, 1977 N.Y. Laws ch. 252,

Section 3.

34. An expert on environmental impact review makes this point directly: "The discussion of environmental consequences of a proposed action and its alternatives is the most important part of the analyses; many reviewers go straight to this section and forego the rest. However, prior discussions in the EIS provide much of the rationale for the analyses. . . .[T]o fully understand how the analyses and conclusions were derived, the foundation and framework of an EIS must be read and understood as well" (underlining ours) (Kreske, p. 285).

35. Friedmann, *Planning in the Public Domain*, p. 162.

36. Wilkinson, p. x. A pool of pro-development expert advocates emerged from the mid-70s on to cope with discursive challenges of SEQRA and its NEPA and "little-NEPA" regulatory cousins around the country. This coincided with the broader strategic recognition by conservative forces generally of the need to develop and subsidize their own policy "think tanks" and networks of conservative academics in order to neutralize, disempower from within and privatize the regulatory and social welfare reform policies of liberal national government administrations. This overall strategy, which William Simon described as creating a "conservative intelligentsia," and its effect on public policy debate generally is discussed in Frank Fischer, "Policy Discourse and the Politics of Washington Think Tanks," in Fischer and Forester, pp. 21-42. In New York state, the Manhattan Institute and CHANGE-NY's Empire Foundation for Policy Research helped to provide similar neo-liberal intellectual underpinning and concrete policy recommendations for the regime of George Pataki. (Tom Carroll, the director of CNY and the EFPR, for example, was past executive director of the state Legislative Commission on Public-Private Cooperation and served as deputy director of Pataki's Office of Regulatory Reform.)

37. Schindler, "Impact Statement Boondoggle," *Science*, 5/7/76 (quoted in Richardson et al., p. 84).

38. Gerrard, "The Dynamics of Secrecy . . .," p. 282. This same widespread pattern of corporate corruption and manipulation of science throughout realms of environmental and health regulation is well-documented in Sheldon Rampton and John Stauber, *Trust Us, We're Experts--How Industry Manipulates Science and Gambles with Your Future* (New York: Tarcher/Putnam, 2001).

39. Taylor, pp. 28-29.

40. Ibid., p. 116.

41. Gerrard, "The Dynamics of Secrecy . . .," p. 283.

42. Of relevance to the issue of "hard look," as Richardson et al. point out, "the process of simplifying issues for lay understanding [is] not always innocent" (Richardson, et al., eds., p. 78). In the company presentation described in that book, toxic dioxins and furans appeared to be eliminated or as harmless as table salt. The issue of how detailed the EIS must be to provide for informed or reasonable decision-making and public participation has been hotly contested in NEPA litigation as well (Ibid., pp. 77-78). As Taylor points out (and as exemplified in detailed defense tactics at the O.J. Simpson murder trial), "'level of detail' questions are ultimately burden-of-proof questions . . . ." (Taylor, p. 118).

43. Gerrard acknowledges this stark conclusion. Given the wide range of lead agency discretion under SEQRA, he says, "Provided that other binding standards are not violated, an agency may approve a project that will be environmentally destructive, if the agency has followed all necessary procedures and made a formal finding as to the reasons for its decision" (Michael B. Gerrard, "Municipal Powers under SEQRA," *New York State Bar Journal*, December 1997, p. 6). Even if an EIS is ultimately required, "[projects] which are represented by experienced legal counsel, and by consultants who will write anything in an EIS regardless of its accuracy, will successfully withstand legal challenge, so long as the procedural i's are dotted and t's are crossed. This will occur even if one or more significant adverse environmental impacts goes virtually unanalyzed in the EIS or unmitigated in the SEQRA findings process" (John W. Caffry, Esq., "Substantive Reach of SEQRA: Aesthetics and Findings," paper presented at SEQRA 25th Anniversary Conference, Albany Law School, March 15-16, 2001, Albany, N.Y.).

44. Taylor, pp. 321, 324.

45. Langdon Marsh, "Introduction--SEQRA's Scope and Objectives," *Albany Law Journal*, vol. 46, no. 4 [Summer 1982], p. 1113. Michael Gerrard estimates that a similar tiny percentage of SEQRA rejections is typical two decades later (private conversation, 3/16/01). Reflecting this minute number of instances, apparently only in 2000 did a New York appellate court expressly rule that a project application could be denied solely on SEQRA grounds, regardless of whether grounds exist for such denial in the underlying statute (such as presumably a zoning law) which require the permit application itself (*Lane Construction Co. v. Cahill*, 270 A.D.2d 609 [3d Dept.], *app. den.*, 95 N.Y.2d 765 [2000]). One authority in the area also denied that by 1982 that there was "any demonstrable evidence of material delays in the implementation of public or private projects as a result of SEQRA" (Philip H. Gitlen, "The Substantive Impact of the SEQRA," *Albany Law Journal*, vol. 46, no. 4 [Summer 1982], p. 1241), while Marsh reported that only 3% of reported actions experienced delays because of SEQRA (Marsh, p. 1113). Opinions on this issue varied considerably at the SEQRA 25th Anniversary Conference, Albany Law School, March 15-16, 2001, Albany, N.Y.

46. Taylor, p. 175.

47. Erickson, *op. cit.*

48. For example, concerning the renowned expert consultants used by the Army Corps of Engineers to review impacts of the Westway project in New York City, Cronin and Kennedy assert that they claimed minimal impact on the striped bass habitat by deliberately massaging the numbers involved, "confident that no one would be able to retrace their steps among the dense thicket of fractions and decimals to find the proof of their deceit" (Cronin and Kennedy, p. 161).

49. Ebbin and Kasper, pp. 228-229.

50. Fisher, *Citizens, Experts, and the Environment*, pp. 233-234.

51. Alan Irwin, *Citizen Science: A Study of People, Expertise and Sustainable Development* (London and New York: Routledge, 1995), p. 98. Especially absurd is the effort "to relate the spiritual aspect of one's beliefs to the marketplace that could

care less what you believe and what you don't believe" (comment by native speaker Bernie Carlson, in an Alberta environmental impact assessment hearing, quoted in Richardson, et al., eds., p. 65).

52. As Frank Fischer points out, the Reagan years were the period when the new cadre of conservative experts largely succeeded in restricting policy discourse generally. New conservative symbols and decision-making models were based on "the ideology of the marketplace and such market-oriented decision techniques as cost-benefit analysis, which became the dominant approach to policy analysis" (Fischer, "Policy Discourse and the Politics of Washington Think Tanks," in Fischer and Forester, eds., p. 35). As in most areas of public policy, this shift to conservative discourse persisted through Bush and Clinton administrations both, and surely has continued in the regime of George W. Bush. Forester correctly states that it is "a recipe for producing resentment . . . when a citizen's deeply felt values are treated as purely financial matters" (*The Deliberative Practitioner*, p. 241). As Fischer puts it, "Ignoring or hiding important social and health impacts [through statistical analysis] . . . functions as a form of moralizing in the name of mathematical objectivity" (Fischer, *Citizens, Experts and the Environment*, p. 56).

53. Mary Grisez Kweit and Robert W. Kweit, "The Politics of Policy Analysis: The Role of Citizen Participation in Analytic Decision Making," in Jack DeSario and Stuart Langton, eds., *Citizen Participation in Public Decision Making* (Westport, Ct.: Greenwood Press, Inc., 1987), p. 21. It could be said that Magellan Construction not only commodified the SEQRA process through constant refrains of "time is money" and alleged economic benefits for Ashbury, but also through attempting to materially influence community opposition leaders through non-site community benefits or threats to their jobs, as well as forcing the town to accept non-payment of its escrow debt.

54. Richardson, et al., eds., p. 17.

55. As Kweit and Kweit observe in the public budgetary process, but of equal applicability here, "The awe of the unfamiliar and the unwillingness to admit ignorance may be adequate for some to attempt to avoid confrontation with bureaucrats bearing a budgetary request supported by policy analysis. One means of avoidance, of course, is accession to the request" (Kweit and Kweit, p. 21).

56. Woliver, p. 155. It is not uncommon for lay environmental critics to be labeled as superstitious, caught up in irrational fantasies, and even "mentally ill" by policymakers, risk assessment experts and social scientists. Studies have even been commissioned to examine such "mental abnormalities" (Kristin Shrader-Frechette, "Scientific Method, Anti-Foundationalism and Public Decisionmaking," *RISK: Health, Safety and Environment*, vol I, Winter, pp. 23+; Available [Online]: <http://www.fplc.edu/RISK/vol1/winter/Shrader. htm> [8/9/01].

57. As Fischer suggests, the ideal is "to understand and reconstruct that which we are already doing when we engage in scientific inquiry. Recognizing reality to be a social construction, the focus shifts to the circumstantial context and discursive processes that shape the construction" (Fischer, *Citizens, Experts, and the Environment*, pp. 74-75). An excellent discussion of generic translation needs and

methods of this sort is Hugo Slim and Paul Thompson, *Listening for A Change: Oral Testimony and Community Development* (Philadelphia: New Society Publishers, 1995).

58. This dynamic was experienced in Alberta environmental impact hearings described in Richardson, et al., eds., p. 174. On the other hand, it might just cause board members, like Maglie on economic impact analysis, to suggest that the board ought to split the difference down the middle.

59. Irwin, p. 29.

60. Kreske, p. 267. As Kweit and Kweit also emphasize, "Although benefit-cost analysis often appears as though the analysis is based on scientific inevitability, it is actually based upon valuations and judgments which are subjective" (p. 29). Indeed, "even when competent researchers review the same set of data, their estimation of the benefits of regulation can differ by a factor of one hundred or one thousand" (Freudenberg, p. 78). As technology historian David Noble stated, cost-benefit analysis actually "is a political strategy designed and fostered, quite deliberately, to undermine, stall and hamstring the regulatory agencies" (Noble, "Cost-Benefit Analysis: The Regulation of Business or Scientific Pornography?" *HealthPAC Bulletin* 11, no. 6 [1980], p. 7, as quoted in Freudenberg, p. 80).

61. What Elizabeth Bird summarizes as Latour's and Woolgar's understandings of "scientific truth" could be also applied to any environmental impact review "findings" statement as well: "scientific consensus is reached not when the 'facts' accumulate to the point where they might be said to 'speak for themselves,' but rather when the political, professional and economic costs of refuting them are such that further negotiation becomes untenable" (Bird, p. 257; her quotation summarizes the perspective of Bruno Latour and Steve Woolgar, *Laboratory Life: The Social Construction of Scientific Facts* [Beverly Hills: Sage Publications, 1979]). However, as Bird asserts, the fact as well that complaints about negative environmental impacts are "grounded in individual, collective, historical, cross-cultural, and visionary experience, are socially constructed . . . and socially interpreted . . . does not diminish their role as a legitimate ground for political claims. On the contrary, their very historicity gives them enormous normative weight" (Bird, p. 260).

62. As Forester states, "emotional sensitivity [by planners] works as a source of knowledge and recognition--and . . . as a mode of moral vision too" (*The Deliberative Practitioner*, p. 41).

63. While acknowledging its relative neglect in the environmental impact analysis process around the country, Paul Erickson presents an excellent introduction to the importance of social impact analysis and elements which might therein be considered (pp. 7, 23-29 and part III). In their analysis of the permit process for nuclear power plants, Ebbin and Kasper view "the emphasis on the physical as opposed to the social and human environment" as one of the basic failures of environmental impact statements as information sources for citizens (p. 238).

An attempt to delineate principles, guidelines and methodology for social impact analysis in NEPA EISs is discussed in Interorganizational Committee on Guidelines and Principles for Social Impact Assessment, "Guidelines and Principles for Social

Impact Assessment," *Environmental Impact Assessment Review*, 15, 1995, pp. 11-43. Among other impacts, this report mentions the importance of assessing the significance of risk perceptions in the community, separate from actually-proven risks.

A new area of "social impact" analysis, though not raised in the Ashbury case, concerns stress-related negative health effects caused at least partly by visual obscenities, such as the visual clutter of sprawl development (see the writings of Roger Ulrich and others in the new field of "green psychology"). If development proposals are in part reviewed with an eye on their potential to encourage economic dis-investment in the area, surely the potential dangers of dis-investment in existing "social capital" elements such as "sense of community," thriving networks of horizontal interdependence, psychological well-being and community self-determination ought to be as seriously considered in meaningful impact assessment. Harvey Molotch, in turn, emphasizes the specific need to measure the social impact of development projects in encouraging or not greater social inequality (Molotch, "Growth Machine Links," in Jonas and Wilson, eds., p. 263).

64. Similarly, as Cronin and Kennedy point out, the non-compliance of polluters with environmental laws results in economic benefits for the polluter, while compliance has a cost. "Unchecked by aggressive enforcement, these pressures will systematically undermine any system of environmental law." Unfortunately, "[e]nforcement is underfunded, abused, and ignored in nearly every environmental bureaucracy" (Cronin and Kennedy, p. 178).

65. As one experienced professional planning consultant stated recently, "when you [the developer] have money and you have experts, you can create a juggernaut and get whatever you want," assuming that opponents cannot match your resources (Frank Fish, verbal remarks at "A Review of Three Projects: An Audit of SEQRA Efficacy" panel at SEQRA 25th Anniversary Conference, Albany Law School, March 16, 2001, Albany, N.Y.).

66. This conclusion well complements the more general observation about mall developers overall: "Suburban retailers are predatory by definition. Most new malls, big-box outlets, and other shopping centers are built not to satisfy unmet demand but to steal demand from existing retailers. . . . [M]alls survive by undermining other malls (and main streets) . . . " (Andres Duany, Elizabeth Plater-Zyberk and Jeff Speck, *Suburban Nation: The Rise of Sprawl and the Decline of the American Dream*, as quoted in Peter Hanson, "Malls Come Tumbling Down," *Metroland*, May 3-9, 2001).

67. As Kay suggests, opportunities for decisionmakers' "[d]eliberate, self-conscious development of social capital" and proactive encouragement of less activist stakeholders do exist as discretionary potentials already within review processes such as SEQRA, if board members have the will and vision to take advantage of them (Kay, pp. 16-17).

68. As Robert Bellah and his co-authors stated, they were members of "communities of memory" and "communities of hope" (Robert N. Bellah, Richard Madsen, William M. Sullivan, Ann Swidler and Steven M. Tipton, *Habits of the*

Heart: Individualism and Commitment in American Life [Berkeley: University of California Press, 1985], p. 153). These are communities "that provide an ideology to name oppression and a group solidarity that provides emotional support" (Woliver, p. 165).

69. ACT advertised open informational meetings on several occasions throughout the town, so project proponents could have attended and dialogued if they wished. (At one meeting, even Rocky Ryker hung out, leering, at the doorway of the meeting room, though by refusing to comment on the issues he seemed only further to cast doubt on his interest in actual community concerns.) To our knowledge, no open meetings were advertised or held by project proponents.

70. See examples from Berry, et al and others cited in Chapter 16.

71. See ECL Section 8-0111(6).

72. To the point, in his Fall 1997 campaign, Ashbury Republican Supervisor candidate Ron Schulz stated: "I have the experience [as a real estate developer/broker] that underlies all the budget and tax issues that our community faces . . . and as Supervisor, the town will be my number-one client" (*Tribune*, 10/30/97).

73. The pressure on activists to restrain their critique of the motives and legitimacy of local officials is comparable to the pressure on critical members of dysfunctional families to be only "co-dependent enablers"--to accept and work only within the bounds of logic (and emotion) imposed unilaterally by those in power in the name of systemic solidarity. As responsible family therapists observe, whatever the discomfort involved, to preclude discussion of those limited defined bounds of critique is almost always to preclude effective change and long-range healing for family members concerned.

74. A good list of behaviors by which planning officials could encourage and help to organize citizen participation appears in Forester, *Planning in the Face of Power*, pp. 155-156.

75. Precisely because local struggles always involve regional, national or transnational corporations or economic forces, Gould et al. advocate local environmental group "embeddedness in larger extralocal networks" (p. 184). Only in this way can important information and experience be shared and developer shifts from one locale to another be combatted.

76. Cloward and Piven, *Poor People's Movements: Why They Succeed, How They Fail* (New York: Vintage Books, 1979), pp. 1-2, 15-18.

77. As Sirianni and Friedland point out, "as a 'moral resource,' social capital . . . tends to accumulate when it is used and be depleted when not . . ." (p. 13).

78. Daniel J. Fiorino, *Making Environmental Policy* (Berkeley: University of California Press, 1995), p. 87. (See also Cronin and Kennedy, p. 184 and Barry G. Rabe, "The Promise and Pitfalls of Decentralization," in Vig and Kraft, eds., p. 47.)

79. Erickson, p. 4.

80. Ibid., p. 164.

81. Ibid., p. 168.

82. Webler and Renn, pp. 20, 24.

83. Gerrard, "The Dynamics of Secrecy . . .," p. 280.

84. Williams and Metheny, chapters 5 and 6.

85. Freudenberg, p. 90. Concerning public hearings specifically, Forester observes that they are "pathological rituals that often minimize responsive interaction and maximize exaggeration and adversarial posturing" (*The Deliberative Practitioner*, p. 147). The formal public hearing is a "magic wand of public polarization . . . where all loud voices might be heard but where no dialogue or collaboration will be possible" (Ibid., p. 235). Another observer of official participatory modes points out that while public hearings are the most common direct form of public involvement, there were nearly universal criticisms of their failure to provide meaningful participation (Thomas C. Beierle, *Public Participation in Environmental Decisions: An Evaluation Framework Using Social Goals* [Washington, D.C.: Resources for the Future Discussion Papers, November 1998], p. 20; Available [Online]: <http://www.rff.org/CFDOCS/disc_papers/ PDF_files/9906.pdf> [8/10/01]).

86. Wilkinson, p. 208. The Forest Service apparently issues more EISs than any other federal agency (Follin, p. 73), thus making this cynical use of that procedure all the more striking. Additional observations on the failure of the Forest Service's (and other federal agencies') "participatory" approach are in Sirianni and Friedland, pp. 111-115, 135-136.

87. Taylor, pp. 131, 150-151, 163, 165, 222, 251-257.

88. Sirianni and Friedland, p. 90. (These authors also describe these failures as a learning experience leading to useful collaboration once the adversarial power of grassroots activists is demonstrated. As indicated below, we do not share that optimistic assessment.) See also the conclusion of Molotch and Logan in Chapter 3, endnote 52 above. While enacted more recently, participatory environmental assessment processes in other countries have demonstrated weaknesses similar to those described here. (For example, see L. Del Furia and J. Wallace-Jones, "The Effectiveness of Provisions and Quality of Practices Concerning Public Participation in the EIA Procedures in Italy and the UK," paper presented at the World Congress of Environmental Resource Economists, Venice, June 25-27, 1998.)

89. Gould et al., p. 40.

90. Arnstein, "A Ladder of Citizen Participation," *Journal of the American Institute of Planners*, vol. XXXV, no. 4 (July 1969), pp. 216-224. At the time, Arnstein was Chief Advisor on Citizen Participation for the federal Department of Housing and Urban Development.

91. Rogers, p. 117.

92. Ibid., p. 15.

93. Ibid., p. 177. Fischer is explicit about these dynamics in most presently-practiced efforts at environmental mediation. "Mediation, as such, is an attempt to substantially depoliticize public environmental disagreements by enabling professional mediators to shape the context of decision making. . . . It didn't take long for the environmental movement to recognize that the subtle ideological foundations of mediation conveyed criticism of the citizen environmental movement.

The movement was quick to point out that the atmosphere around environmental mediations was one of criticism of citizen action rather than of the business community" (Fischer, *Citizens, Experts, and the Environment*, p. 107).

94. This "competition" of resources occurs both at the level of individual project reviews and at the time of electoral campaigns.

95. *Albany Times-Union*, 1/30/96.

96. "Conditioned negative declarations" (CNDs) were proposed in 1994 by the DEC for Type I actions (beyond their use already for Unlisted actions) as a new alternative to "positive declarations" requiring an EIS. The former are negotiated settlements between lead agencies and developers which identify potential significant adverse environment impacts as well as their mitigations--all potentially before the public has any official role whatsoever in discussing the projects concerned. This change was rejected because of public outcry against its short-circuiting of the SEQRA process for major projects. Potential GEISs were part of the SEQRA regulatory scheme from the beginning and could have been used, as CLEAR proposed in the late 1980s in Ashbury, as the basis for regular updates of different aspects of local comprehensive plans. Presently, GEISs are being encouraged by SEQRA opponents as a way to define general environmental parameters within particular districts with which new projects would have to conform. However, they are then seen as green flags for fast-track development with potentially no public participation concerning site-specific environmental impacts.

97. New York Conservative Party home page; Available [Online]: <http://www.cpnys.org199legpro.html#XI> [9/22/99]. Among various other lobbying groups, the International Council of Shopping Centers, meanwhile, works closely with the neo-liberal American Legislative Exchange Council to promote pro-growth policies across the country at the state level, including streamlined "one stop" environmental permitting and "economic impact analysis" as a prerequisite for any new "smart growth" restrictive legislation (ICSC home page; Available [Online]: <http://www.icsc.org/srch/grr/back/9811/2> [10/20/99]).

98. In *Merson v. McNally*, 90 N.Y.2d 742, 665 N.Y.S.2d 605 (1997), the Court of Appeals allowed "conditioned" negative declarations for Type I actions (despite the DEC rejection of this change in 1995) if an "open and deliberative process" is used with ample opportunity for public participation. (See Chapter 4, endnote 37 above). Given common practices, as identified in this case study, which restrict meaningful public participation, this decision must be viewed as a further significant erosion of original SEQRA intent which encourages an evasive "frontloading" strategy. The *Merson* decision fails to define how much or what quality of public participation is needed for this de facto CND in Type I reviews and in most cases would encourage a hastier, more superficial impact research process. By eliminating important structured gates and schedules of public access to documents and potential accountability found in the traditional EIS review process, the de facto CND reduces the public's role while increasing the discretion of lead agencies.

99. *Lucas v. Planning Board of the Town of LaGrange*, 7 F.Supp.2d 310 (S.D.N.Y. 1998).

100. Caffry, *op. cit.*

101. Phil LaRocque and Bruce Boncke, "SEQRA's 25th Anniversary: A Building Industry Perspective," *Empire State Report*, August 2000, pp. 27-28.

102. Herbert A. Posner, book review of William R. Ginsberg and Philip Weinberg, eds., *Environmental Law and Regulation in New York State* (St. Paul: West Publishing Co., 1996), in *New York University Environmental Law Journal*, vol. 6 (1997), no. 1, p. 268. To the point, Forest County planner Henry Fowler, for example, frankly suggested that SEQRA stood for "public participation" without participation and in fact offered less environmental protection than in pre-SEQRA days. (Personal conversation, October 26, 1995.) This observation echoed remarks by an Army Corps of Engineers general in the early 1970s who claimed that at the federal level "NEPA was just the sort of paperwork exercise that the bureaucracy would use to avoid being more environmentally sensitive" (Taylor, p. 67).

CHAPTER EIGHTEEN

1. Following Foucault, Adam Ashforth suggests that public hearings, for example, are "symbolic rituals within modern States, theatres of power" for their own legitimization. Through public testimony at hearings, like confessions before a priest, they establish a controlling "pastoral" relationship to pacify grassroots anxiety while demonstrating a tolerance justifying continuing ultimate power (Ashforth, "Reckoning Schemes of Legitimation: On Commissions of Inquiry as Power/Knowledge Forms," *Journal of Historical Sociology* 3, no. 1 [March 1990], pp. 1-22 [as cited in Richardson et al., p. 13]). We believe that most presentday environmental impact assessment processes, such as SEQRA, could be understood in the same light.

2. Clavel, p. 1.

3. Ibid., p. 219.

4. Berry, et al., p. 294.

5. Krumholz and Clavel, p. 238.

6. Ibid., pp. 237-238.

7. Medoff and Sklar, Chapter Nine.

8. Ferman, pp. 151-152.

9. Ibid., p. 147.

10. DeLeon, pp. 172-175.

11. Alejandro Bendana, *Power Lines: U.S. Domination in the New Global Order* (New York: Olive Branch Press, 1996), pp. 75, 243.

12. Paul Craig Roberts, "How Clinton is Bashing the Buck," *Business Week*, 8/8/94, as quoted in Korten, p. 203.

13. Edward Mozley Roche, "'Cyberopolis': The Cybernetic City Faces the Global Economy," in Margaret E. Crahan and Alberto Vourvoulias-Bush, eds., *The City and the World: New York's Global Future* (New York: The Council on Foreign Relations, 1997), p. 56.

14. David C. Perry, "The Politics of Dependency in Deindustrializing America: The Case of Buffalo, New York," in Michael Peter Smith and Joe R. Feagin, eds., *The Capitalist City: Global Restructuring and Community Politics* (Oxford: Basil Blackwell Ltd., 1987), p. 129.

15. Ibid., pp. 113-137. On the other hand, transnational capital mobility seems less at present than many claim and is still potentially (if not in actuality) subject to significant national controls. In any case, neo-liberals proclaim such mobility as so inevitably uncontrollable that evermore competitive deregulation is essential. See Samir Amin, *Capitalism in the Age of Globalization: The Management of Contemporary Society* (London: Zed Books, 1997); Jerry Mander, ed., *The Case Against the Global Economy: And For A Turn Toward the Local* (San Francisco: Sierra Club Books, 1997); Paul Hirst and Grahame Thompson, *Globalization in Question* (London: Polity Books, 1996); John R. Logan and Todd Swanstrom, eds., *Beyond the City Limits: Urban Policy and Economic Restructuring in Comparative Perspective* (Philadelphia: Temple University Press, 1990); and Korten, *op. cit.*. As Hirst and Thompson argue, "globalization" is a myth "that robs us of hope," "a myth that exaggerates the degree of our helplessness in the face of contemporary economic forces" (p. 6).

16. U.S. capitalism and militarism, of course, are tightly interrelated. As Hirst and Thompson state, U. S. military strength "ensures that no other state can use political power to restructure the international economy. . . . [T]he United States remains the only possible guarantor of the world free-trading system against politically inspired disruption and thus the openness of global markets depends on American policy" (p. 14).

17. Gould et al., pp. 175-176; John Shields and B. Mitchell Evans, *Shrinking the State: Globalization and Public Administration "Reform"* (Halifax: Fernwood Publishing, 1998), pp. 80-81.

18. Ibid., p. 78. Osborne and Gaebler's *Reinventing Government*, popular in the early 90s, presents the basic principles of this perspective (David Osborne and Ted Gaebler, *Reinventing Government* [Reading, Mass.: Addison-Wesley, 1992]). As Shields and Evans point out, not only Reagan and Bush in the United States, but Clinton as well essentially adopted this program, as symbolized in a review of the federal regulatory framework led by Al Gore and published in the final report of the National Performance Review (Shields and Evans, pp. 86-87).

19. Hirst and Thompson, p. 138; Korten, pp. 174-177.

20. Saul Alinsky considered a 5% "participation" rate in any community "a tremendous democratic phenomenon" (Alinsky, *Reveille for Radicals* [Chicago: University of Chicago Press, 1945], p. 201). However, 5% voting in a single election is much less impressive than would be a 5% rate of more-or-less regular activism in community organizing or grassroots program development. Of course, even in the

latter case, the other 95% gain no exposure to, nor the community benefit from, their own intrinsic self-development through the participatory experience itself. In effect, acceptance of the 5% proportion is similar on the local scale to acceptance by "realist" theorists of elitist democracy nationally.

21. The rest would be appointed by state or local authorities from among public officials, the business community, local community agencies and other local interest groups. The 1/3 quota for community representatives was later expanded to as much as 2/3 in some cases. (Lillian B. Rubin, "Maximum Feasible Participation: The Origins and Implications," in Susan S. Fainstein and Norman I. Fainstein, eds., *The View from Below: Urban Politics and Social Policy* [Boston: Little, Brown and Co., 1972], pp. 110-111.) Sirianni and Friedland identify further problems with effective participation in this context (pp. 39-40), as does Morone as well (pp. 223-244).

22. See similar critiques in Armour, *op. cit.*

23. See Sirianni and Friedland, *op. cit.*; Renn et al., *op. cit.*; Thomas Webler, Hans Kastenholz and Ortwinn Renn, "Public Participation in Impact Assessment: A Social Learning Perspective," *Environmental Impact Assessment Review* 1995; 15: 443-463; and Tom R. Burns and Reinhard Ueberhorst, *Creative Democracy: Systemic Conflict Resolution and Policymaking in A World of High Science and Technology* (New York: Praeger, 1988).

24. See Anna Vari, "Citizens' Advisory Committee As A Model for Public Participation: A Multiple-Criteria Evaluation," in Renn et al., pp. 103-116; Hans-Jorg Seiler, "Review of 'Planning Cells': Problems of Legitimation," in Renn et al., pp. 141-156; Susan G. Hadden, "Regulatory Negotiation As Citizen Participation," in Renn et al., pp. 239-252; and Moote, et al., pp. 877-889. As well, a long-time leading advocate of fully-inclusive participatory or deliberative planning, John Forester, while commendably defining qualities needed for public sector dispute resolution, also admits that most planners probably fail to meet these criteria (*The Deliberative Practitioner*, p. 237). Douglas Torgerson, in turn, admits that existing examples of public decisionmaking contexts designed for genuine communication "are no doubt sparse and imperfect" (p. 138).

25. "Radical reformist" participatory democracy theorists include, among others, Benjamin Barber, Frank Bryan, John McClaughry, John Dryzek, Ernest LaClau, Chantal Mouffe, Jane Mansbridge and Sheldon Wolin. Leading works of these writers, illustrative of this perspective, include Benjamin R. Barber, *Strong Democracy* (Berkeley: University of California Press, 1984; 4th printing with new preface, 1990), *The Conquest of Politics: Liberal Philosophy in Democratic Times* (Princeton: Princeton University Press, 1988), *A Passion for Democracy: American Essays* (Princeton: Princeton University Press, 1998) and *A Place for Us: How To Make Society Civil and Democracy Strong* (New York: Hill and Wang, 1998); Frank Bryan and John McClaughry, *The Vermont Papers: Recreating Democracy on A Human Scale* (Post Mills, Vt.: Chelsea Green Publishing Co., 1989); John S. Dryzek, *Discursive Democracy: Politics, Policy and Political Science* (Cambridge: Cambridge University Press, 1990) and "Political and Economic Communication," *Environmental Politics* (London), vol. 4, no. 4, pp. 13-30; Ernest LaClau and

Chantal Mouffe, *Hegemony and Socialist Strategy: Towards A Radical Democratic Politics* (London: Verso, 1985), Chantal Mouffe, "Democratic Politics Today" and "Democratic Citizenship and the Political Community," in Mouffe, ed., *Dimensions of Radical Democracy: Pluralism, Citizenship, Community* (London and New York: Verso, 1992), "Radical Democracy or Liberal Democracy?," in David Trend, ed., *Radical Democracy: Identity, Citizenship, and the State* (New York and London: Routledge, 1996) and *The Return of the Political* (London: Verso, 1996); Jane Mansbridge, *Beyond Adversary Democracy* (New York: Basic Books, 1980); and Sheldon Wolin, *Politics and Vision: Continuity and Innovation in Western Political Thought* (Boston: Little Brown, 1960), *The Presence of the Past: Essays on the State and the Constitution* (Baltimore: Johns Hopkins Press, 1989), and "Norm and Form: The Constitutionalizing of Democracy," in J. Peter Euben, et al., eds., *Athenian Political Thought and the Reconstruction of American Democracy* (Ithaca: Cornell University Press, 1995).

26. "Strong radical" participatory democracy theorists include, among others, Carol Gould, Stanley Aronowitz, Gar Alperovitz, Hannah Arendt, Carole Pateman, Brian Tokar, Kirkpatrick Sale, Val Plumwood, and John Burnheim. Leading works of these writers, illustrative of this perspective, include Carol C. Gould, *Rethinking Democracy: Freedom and Social Cooperation in Politics, Economy, and Society* (Cambridge: Cambridge University Press, 1988); Stanley Aronowitz, "Towards Radicalism: The Death and Rebirth of the American Left," in Trend, *op. cit.*; Gar Alperovitz, "Notes Toward A Pluralist Commonwealth," in Staughton Lynd and Gar Alperovitz, *Strategy and Program: Two Essays Toward A New American Socialism* (Boston: Beacon Press, 1973); Hannah Arendt, *On Revolution* (New York: Viking Press, 1965); Carole Pateman, *Participation and Democratic Theory* (Cambridge: Cambridge University Press, 1970), *The Problem of Political Obligation: A Critical Analysis of Liberal Theory* (Berkeley: University of California Press, 1985), *The Sexual Contract* (Palo Alto: Stanford University Press, 1988) and *The Disorder of Women*; Brian Tokar, *The Green Alternative: Creating An Ecological Future* (San Pedro, Calif.: R. and F. Miles, 1987); Kirkpatrick Sale, *Human Scale* (New York: Perigree Books, 1980) and *Dwellers in the Land: The Bioregional Vision* (San Francisco: Sierra Club Books, 1985); Val Plumwood, *Feminism and the Mastery of Nature* (London and New York: Routledge, 1993), "Noam Chomsky and Liberation Politics" (paper presented to the "Visions of Freedom" conference, January 17-20, 1995, Sydney, Australia; Available [Online]: <http://www.vof.cat.org.au/versions/val.htm> [8/8/01]), "Has Democracy Failed Ecology? An Ecofeminist Perspective," in *Environmental Politics* (London), vol. 4, no. 4 (Winter 1995), pp. 134-168, and *Environmental Culture: The Ecological Crisis of Reason* (London and New York: Routledge, 2002); and John Burnheim, *Is Democracy Possible? The Alternative to Electoral Politics* (Berkeley: University of California Press, 1985).

Traditional and contemporary anarchist political theory falls squarely within this category. Among anarchists more generally, beyond classic theoretical works of Pierre-Joseph Proudhon, Michael Bakunin, Peter Kropotkin, Rudolf Rocker, Errico Malatesta and others are more recent elaborations of relevance to the present discussion in Murray Bookchin, *The Limits of the City* (Montreal: Black Rose Books,

1986), "From Here to There," in Bookchin, *Remaking Society* (Montreal: Black Rose Books, 1989) and "The Meaning of Confederalism," *Society and Nature*, I, 3, pp. 41-54; Janet Biehl, *Finding Our Way: Rethinking Ecofeminist Politics* (Boston: South End Press, 1991); Andrew Light, ed., *Social Ecology after Bookchin* (New York: Guilford Press, 1998); Colin Ward, *Anarchy in Action* (New York: Harper and Row, 1973); April Carter, *The Political Theory of Anarchism* (New York: Harper and Row, 1971); Giovanni Baldelli, *Social Anarchism* (Chicago: Aldine-Atherton, Inc., 1971); Thom Holterman and Heve van Maarseveen, eds., *Law and Anarchism* (Montreal: Black Rose Books, 1984); and Howard J. Ehrlich, ed., *Reinventing Anarchism, Again* (San Francisco: AK Press, 1996).

27. Barber, *Strong Democracy*, p. xix. While Barber in this and many other statements (as well as in his close working relationship with "moderate participatory democrats of the sort discussed in the Chapter 16 and well-represented in Sirianni and Friedland, *op. cit.*) appears little different from the "moderate participatory democrat" position generally, others of his statements (as indicated below) seem far more critical of and pessimistic about the existing U.S. political context. It is this latter dimension of Barber which, we believe, represents the "radical reformist participatory democrat" perspective.

28. Ibid., p. xxii. Contrary to mainstream elite democratic theorists who emphasize ignorance and poor judgment in the vast majority of citizens, Barber believes that to the extent this is true, "it may be the fault of too little rather than too much democracy" (Barber, *The Conquest of Politics*, p. 211).

29. *Strong Democracy*, p. 235. Nina Eliasoph's detailed *Avoiding Politics* provides ample proof for this assertion.

30. Barber, *Strong Democracy*, p. 120.

31. Ibid., p. 133.

32. Ibid., p. 183.

33. Ibid., p. 264.

34. *A Passion for Democracy*, p. ix.

35. Ibid., p. 39.

36. Ibid., p. 40.

37. Mouffe, "Democratic Politics Today," p. 10.

38. Mouffe, *The Return of the Political*, p. 84.

39. "Radical Democracy or Liberal Democracy?," p. 24. This point was well-illustrated by the comment three decades ago of recently-retiring American Political Science Association president Samuel Huntington, as mentioned in Chapter Sixteen above.

40. Pateman, *Participation and Democratic Theory*.

41. Ibid., p. 43.

42. Having integrated feminist theory by 1989 in *The Disorder of Women*, Pateman criticizes her earlier work and other participatory democracy theorists for not having included the home as a workplace and the family and gender relations as equally important realms for participatory democracy (pp. 220, 222).

43. Ibid., p. 43.

44. Plumwood extensively analyzes the origin and evolution of master-subordinate dualisms from Plato, Christianity and Descartes to Locke, humanism, behaviorism and holism in her *Feminism and the Mastery of Nature*. While admiring much in Noam Chomsky's project of seeking a liberatory form of democracy, for example, Plumwood criticizes him for identifying it with classical liberals such as Locke and Adam Smith and with a supposedly apolitical "singular, unquestionable model of disengaged reason" (Plumwood, "Noam Chomsky and Liberation Politics").

45. Plumwood, *Feminism . . .* , p. 3.

46. In her 1988 *The Sexual Contract*, Carole Pateman makes this same point (p. 226).

47. Val Plumwood, "Has Democracy Failed Ecology? An Ecofeminist Perspective," in *Environmental Politics* (London), special issue on "Ecology and Democracy," vol. 4, no. 4 (Winter 1995), p. 158.

48. Ibid., pp. 159-160. Because of this convergence with ecological citizenship and her fundamental attention to a non-dualistic approach, Plumwood explicitly distinguishes herself from what she refers to as Mouffe's "liberal socialist" politics of inclusion in the structures of liberal democracy (Plumwood, "Noam Chomsky . . ."). Endangered species protection policies are currently among the best, though very limited, examples of such recognition, to the extent they are not simply motivated by hopes of future exploitation. By contrast, Plumwood's "deep democratic" political culture, emulating various traditional "wisdom cultures" of the non-West, would recognize and value the "agentic and dialogical potentialities of [non-human] earth others" and would find ways to hear and respect their voices within egalitarian structures of openness, mutuality and negotiation in decision-making (Plumwood, *Environmental Culture*, pp. 33, 87-89, 177, 224-226).

49. Plumwood, *Feminism and the Mastery of Nature*, p. 190.

50. Christopher J. Bosse, "The Challenge to Environmental Activism in the 1990s," in Vig and Kraft, eds., p. 56.

51. The U.S. role as forceful disciplinarian to keep the world safe for capitalism both immensely depletes socio-economic resources and intensely reenforces the meta-logic of hierarchy in every realm.

52. Rogers, p. 125.

53. Transnational degradation, of course, is of vast significance. Crises such as global warming, depletion of the ozone layer, the disappearance of rain forests, the loss of untold species, pollution of the seas, depletion of soil and the spread of monoculture are quite capable on their own of threatening the well-being and even existence of humans and other life-forms throughout the planet. Adequate transnational regulation and reduction of such trends have to date proven impossible.

54. The basic argument of Matthew Cahn's *Environmental Deceptions* is precisely that the dominance in American politics of private-property concerns and self-interest inherited from the Lockean roots of the system has to date prevented environmental regulation from significantly preventing continued degradation. Just as our own account develops this conclusion through its detailed examination of the environmental impact review process, Cahn provides the rationale for his conclusion through examining, one-by-one, America's liberal capitalist regulatory approach toward air and water pollution, waste management and energy consumption (Matthew Alan Cahn, *Environmental Deceptions: The Tension between Liberalism and Environmental Policymaking in the United States* [Albany: State University of New York Press, 1995]). Similarly, Vig and Kraft state that to adequately address the major environmental crises of the future, "much more innovative strategies and tools than have characterized past regulation" are required, yet "[p]olitical opposition is also likely to grow among antienvironmental and property rights organizations" (Norman J. Vig and Michael E. Kraft, "The New Environmental Agenda," in Vig and Kraft, eds., pp. 367, 366).

55. In accord with the evidence and themes of our account, policy analysts Frank Fischer and John Forester state, "planning and policy arguments can be skewed by inequalities of resources, by outstanding and entrenched relations of power and production, and by the deliberate play of power, and in such cases we find not what Robert Reich calls 'civic discovery' but civic manipulation instead" (Fischer and Forester, p. 7). Precisely because of existing "entrenched relations of power and production," we believe that such patterns are the general rule rather than exceptional cases.

56. Hajer, "Discourse Coalitions and the Institutionalization of Practice: The Case of Acid Rain in Britain," in Fischer and Forester, eds., p. 69. Another version of Hajer's analysis appears as "Acid Rain in Great Britain: Environmental Discourse and the Hidden Politics of Institutional Practice," in Frank Fischer and Michael Black, eds., *Greening Environmental Policy: The Politics of A Sustainable Future* (New York: St. Martin's Press, 1995), pp. 145-164.

57. Indeed, it is clear that the conscious combination of democratic rhetoric and removal of genuine power from most citizens characterized the federal constitution of 1787 itself. As Daniel Kemmis states:

> The republican approach to public policy required a high level of interaction among citizens. In particular, it assumed that citizens were presented with many opportunities and much encouragement to rise above a narrow self-centeredness. Only if citizens were, in various contexts, putting themselves in one another's shoes could they be expected to identify with and act upon a personally perceived vision of the common good.
>
> . . . .
>
> Republicanism was an intensive brand of politics; it was, heart and soul, a politics of engagement. . . . The federalist alternative to this republican politics of engagement was a politics of radical disengagement"

(Daniel Kemmis, *Community and the Politics of Place* [Norman, Okla.: University of Oklahoma Press, 1990], pp. 11-12). Kemmis sees the federalist substitution of the large-scale "procedural republic" and the frontier as the means by which to keep citizens apart. With the passing of the frontier, the new phase of American imperialism abroad and the launching of the regulatory bureaucracy in the late 19th century became new barriers to a politics of direct engagement (Ibid., pp. 13, 31-33).

James Morrone similarly describes various stages in U.S. history of cooptation of populist participatory democratic movements from the American Revolution to recent times. In his portrayal, a constant dynamic is that "[r]eformist energy that might have been mobilized on more radical purposes are spent on (newly legitimated) conflicts within a narrow institutional context. . . . Potentially radical forces gain participation and focus on the limited (and limiting) conflicts of organizational life" (pp. 12-13).

The larger historical themes of modern political economic regimes in general relying for control on disciplinary discourse and impersonal bureaucracy (which non-regulating "regulatory systems" exemplify) are the hallmark of theorist Michel Foucault.

58. Our conclusions on the motives and impact of regulation and participatory space are echoed by social scientists specifically covering the environmental realm, such as Alan Schnaiberg, *The Environment: From Surplus to Scarcity* (New York: Oxford University Press, 1980); N. Moldavi, "Environmentalism, State and Economy in the U.S.," *Research in Social Movements, Conflicts and Change* 13: 261-273; and M. Radcliff, "Redefining the Environmental 'Crisis' in the South," in J. Weston, ed., *Red and Green: The New Politics of the Environment* (London: Pluto Press, 1986).

59. Cahn, p. 18.

60. Grant, p. 187.

61. In contexts of environmental crisis, at the local as well as national levels, however, a continuing danger is that the need for immediate action will lead toward "command" hierarchy and over-rationalist mentality within the movement itself, thus subverting major dimensions of "ecologist" values at the same time as temporary victories are achieved (Torgerson, pp. xi, 27, 84-85, 94-95, 106-107, 126, 155).

62. As Cronin and Kennedy emphasize, "environmentalism is a battle to save neighborhoods" as much as anything else. As such, the NIMBY acronym (Not in My Backyard), used as a pejorative label by opponents of community groups since the early 1980s, should not be avoided but worn "as a badge of honor" (pp. 163, 164). In their view, "the Hudson has been saved, sewer plant by sewer plant, wetland by wetland, by the work of citizens at every bend in the river, on every tributary, fighting for every inch of riverfront" (Ibid., p. 171).

63. Cronin and Kennedy, for example, see such enclaves as "a revolutionary disbursement of power to the grassroots" and the best hope for democratizing American society (pp. 174-175).

64. Rogers, p. 20.

65. Timothy W. Luke, *Screens of Power: Ideology, Domination, and Resistance in Informational Society* (Urbana: University of Illinois Press, 1989) and various works by Noam Chomsky are especially revealing about such major inhibiting forces.

66. Grant, p. 206.

67. Elaboration upon this theme could easily take another book. However, interesting and suggestive discussions of such an alternative are found, for example, in Roy Morrison, *Ecological Democracy* (Boston: South End Press, 1995); Bookchin, *The Limits of the City*, "From Here to There," *op. cit.*, and "The Meaning of Confederalism," *op. cit.*; John Clark, "Municipal Dreams: A Social Ecological Critique of Bookchin's Politics," in Light, ed., *op. cit.*, pp. 137-191; Dryzek, "Political and Economic Communication," *op. cit.*; Freya Mathews, "Community and the Ecological Self" (except for the conclusion), in *Environmental Politics* (London), vol. 4, no. 4, pp. 66-100; Tokar, *op. cit.*; Burnheim, *op. cit.*; Ferguson, *op. cit.*; Sale, *Human Scale*, *op. cit.*; Friedmann, *Planning in the Public Domain*, *op. cit.*; and Alan Carter, *op. cit.*, chs. 6-7.

68. Rogers, p. 11.

Bibliography

A. **Official Documents** (fictional local location names used, when needed, consistent with those in the text)

"A Kingdom All Their Own: New York State's Industrial Development Agencies," a report by State Senator Franz S. Leichter, January 1992

Ashbury Comprehensive Plan (Manuel S. Emanuel Associates, Inc., 1990)

Ashbury Ethics Code

"Ashbury Open for Business," flyer of the Ashbury Development Corporation, 1992

Ashbury Town Board minutes

Ashbury Town Law

Ashbury Town Planning Board minutes and official files

"Basic Studies" document for the *Ashbury Community Comprehensive (Master) Plan Report* (Ashbury: Ashbury Master Plan Committee, 1989)

Forest County Data Book (Regent Park: Forest County Planning Board), 1990 and 1995 editions

Forest County Planning News (Forest County Planning Board)

Elizabeth Humstone and Thomas Muller, "Comments on the Draft Environmental Impact Statement for National Project Investment Corporation's Proposed Commerce Green Shopping Plaza for East Aurora Villagers for Responsible Planning, Inc., East Aurora, New York," February 1995

Thomas Muller and Elizabeth Humstone, "Phase One Report: Retail Sales Impact of Proposed Wal-Mart on Franklin County [Vt.]," 10/15/93

New York Code of Rules and Regulations, vol. 6 (6 N.Y.C.R.R. [DEC SEQRA Regulations])

New York State Attorney General's Opinions

New York State Bar Association, Committee on Professional Ethics, Op. No. 450 (Dec. 13, 1976)

New York State Civil Practice Law and Rules

New York State Department of Environmental Conservation, Division of Regulatory Affairs, *SEQR Handbook* (1992)

New York State Department of Environmental Conservation, Water Division, *Design Standards for Water Treatment Works* 1 (1988)

New York State Department of State, *Moratoria* (Albany: Legal Memorandum No. 8, c. late 1980s)

New York State Environmental Conservation Law

New York State General Municipal Law

New York State Public Officers Law

N.Y.S. 3540-A, N.Y.A. 4533-A, 198th Sess. (1975)

New York State Town Law

New York State Village Law

1975 NY Legis. Ann. 384, 398 (Gov. Carey's 1975 State of the State Message)

Population: Forest County, 1970 (Regent Park: Forest County Planning Board, 1972)

Reading County Industrial Development Agency official files

Report to the Governor, 1975, of the New York State Task Force on the Environment, Section Report of the Subcommittee on Land Use Planning-Critical Areas Bill, "Proposed Critical Resources Management Act" ("Government Documents" file, New York State Library, Albany)

"SEQRA Bill Jacket" file, New York State Library, Albany

"The Bottom Line: Final Report of the Ashbury Economic Development Task Force," April 1990

"Time for A Change," final report of public hearings on Local Industrial Development Agencies by Francis J. Pordum, Chairman, New York State Assembly Committee on Local Governments (March 1992)

Town of Ashbury, New York Planning Study (Brown & Anthony City Planners, Inc., 1966)

Vermont Environmental Board, "Findings of Fact, Conclusions of Law, and Order re: St. Albans Group and Wal-Mart Stores, Inc. Application #6F0471-EB," 12/23/94

B. Books and Monographs

Richard L. Abel, *The Politics of Informal Justice* (New York: Academic Press, 1982)

Bruce A. Ackerman, *We the People: Transformations* [vol. II] (Cambridge: Harvard University Press, 1998)

Saul Alinsky, *Reveille for Radicals* (New York: Vintage Books, 1969)

Gar Alperovitz, "Notes Toward A Pluralist Commonwealth," in Staughton Lynd and Gar Alperovitz, *Strategy and Program: Two Essays Toward A New American Socialism* (Boston: Beacon Press, 1973)

Samir Amin, *Capitalism in the Age of Globalization: The Management of Contemporary Society* (London: Zed Books, 1997)

Terry L. Anderson, ed., *Breaking the Environmental Policy Gridlock* (Stanford: Hoover Institution Press, 1997)

Hannah Arendt, *On Revolution* (New York: Viking Press, 1963)

Audrey Armour, "The Citizens' Jury Model of Public Participation: A Critical Evaluation," in Ortwin Renn, Thomas Webler and Peter Wiedemann, eds., *Fairness and Competence in Citizen Participation: Evaluating Models for Environmental Discourse* (Dordrecht, The Netherlands: Kluwer Academic Publishers, 1995), pp. 175-188

Stanley Aronowitz, "Towards Radicalism: The Death and Rebirth of the American Left," in David Trend, ed., *Radical Democracy: Identity, Citizenship, and the State* (New York: Routledge, 1996), pp. 81-101

Richard F. Babcock and Charles L. Siemon, *The Zoning Game Revisited* (Cambridge: Lincoln Institute of Land Policy, 1985)

Richard F. Babcock, *The Zoning Game: Municipal Practices and Policies* (Madison: University of Wisconsin Press, 1966)

Peter Bachrach, ed., *Political Elites in A Democracy* (New York: Atherton Press, 1971)

Giovanni Baldelli, *Social Anarchism* (Chicago: Aldine-Atherton, Inc., 1971)

Benjamin R. Barber, *A Passion for Democracy: American Essays* (Princeton: Princeton University Press, 1998)

Benjamin R. Barber, *A Place for Us: How To Make Society Civil and Democracy Strong* (New York: Hill and Wang, 1998)

Benjamin R. Barber, *Strong Democracy* (Berkeley: University of California Press, 1984; 4th printing with new preface, 1990)

Benjamin R. Barber, *The Conquest of Politics: Liberal Philosophy in Democratic Times* (Princeton: Princeton University Press, 1988)

Howell S. Baum, "Practicing Planning Theory in A Political World," in Seymour J. Mandelbaum, Luigi Mazza and Robert W. Burchell, eds., *Explorations in Planning Theory* (New Brunswick, N.J.: Center for Urban Policy Research at Rutgers, State University of New Jersey, 1996), pp. 365-382

Constance E. Beaumont, *How Superstore Sprawl Can Harm Communities* (Washington, D.C.: National Trust for Historic Preservation, 1994)

Ronald Beiner, ed., *Theorizing Citizenship* (Albany: State University of New York Press, 1995)

Robert N. Bellah, Richard Madsen, William M. Sullivan, Ann Swidler and Steven M. Tipton, *Habits of the Heart: Individualism and Commitment in American Life* (Berkeley: University of California Press, 1985)

Alejandro Bendana, *Power Lines: U.S. Domination in the New Global Order* (New York: Olive Branch Press, 1996)

C. George Benello and Dimitrios Roussopoulos, eds., *The Case for Participatory Democracy* (New York: Viking, 1971)

Chip Berlet, ed., *Eyes Right! Challenging the Right Wing Backlash* (Boston: South End Press, 1995)

Jeffrey M. Berry, Kent E. Portney and Ken Thomson, *The Rebirth of Urban Democracy* (Washington, D.C.: The Brookings Institution, 1993)

Janet Biehl, *Finding Our Way: Rethinking Ecofeminist Politics* (Montreal: Black Rose Books, 1991)

Edward J. Blakely and Ted K. Bradshaw, "The Impact of Recent Migrants on Economic Development in Small Towns," in Michael W. Fazio and Peggy Whitman Prenshaw, eds., *Order and Image in the American Small Town* (Jackson: University Press of Mississippi, 1981)

Carl Boggs, *The End of Politics: Corporate Power and the Decline of the Public Sphere* ((New York: The Guilford Press, 2000)

Murray Bookchin, *Remaking Society* (Montreal: Black Rose Books, 1989)

Murray Bookchin, *The Limits of the City* (New York: Harper and Row, 1974)

496

Christopher J. Bosse, "The Challenge to Environmental Activism in the 1990s," in Norman J. Vig and Michael E. Kraft, eds., *Environmental Policy in the 1990s* (Washington, D.C.: Congressional Quarterly Press, 1997; 3rd ed.)

Mark Boyle, "Growth Machines and Propaganda Projects: A Review of Readings of the Role of Civic Boosterism in the Politics of Local Economic Development," in Andrew E.G. Jonas and David Wilson, eds., *The Urban Growth Machine: Critical Perspectives, Two Decades Later* (Albany: State University of New York Press, 1999), pp. 55-72

Harry C. Boyte and Nancy N. Kari, *Building America: The Democratic Promise of Public Work* (Philadelphia: Temple University Press, 1996)

Harry C. Boyte, *CommonWealth: A Return to Citizen Politics* (New York: Free Press, 1990)

Harry C. Boyte, *The Backyard Revolution: Understanding the New Citizen Movement* (Philadelphia: Temple University Press, 1980)

Harry C. Boyte, "The Critic Criticized," in Len Krimerman, Frank Lindenfield, Carol Kortz and Julian Benello, eds., *From the Ground Up: Essays on Grassroots and Workplace Democracy by C. George Benello* (Boston: South End Press, 1992)

Jacob I. Bregman and Kenneth M. Mackenthun, *Environmental Impact Statements* (Chelsea, MI.: Lewis Publishers, Inc., 1992)

Mark D. Brewer and Jeffrey M. Stonecash, "The Economy, Taxes, and Policy Constraints in New York," in Jeffrey M. Stonecash, ed., *Governing New York State* (Albany: State University of New York Press, 2001; 4th ed.), pp. 205-213

Philip D. Brick and R. McGreggor Cawley, eds., *A Wolf in the Garden: The Land Rights Movement and the New Environmental Debate* (Lanham, Md.: Rowman and Littlefield, 1996)

Daniel W. Bromley, "Rousseau's Revenge: The Demise of the Freehold Estate," in Harvey M. Jacobs, ed., *Who Owns America? Social Conflict over Property Rights* (Madison: University of Wisconsin Press, 1998)

Michael P. Brooks, "Planning and Political Power: Toward A Strategy for Coping," in Seymour J. Mandelbaum, Luigi Mazza and Robert W. Burchell, eds., *Explorations in Planning Theory* (New Brunswick, N.J.: Center for Urban Policy Research at Rutgers, State University of New Jersey, 1996), pp. 116-133

Phil Brown and Edwin J. Mikkelsen, *No Safe Place: Toxic Waste, Leukemia, and Community Action* (Berkeley: University of California Press, 1990)

Frank Bryan and John McClaughry, *The Vermont Papers: Recreating Democracy on A Human Scale* (Post Mills, Vt.: Chelsea Green Publishing Co., 1989)

Susan Buckingham-Hatfield and Susan Percy, eds., *Constructing Local Environmental Agendas: People, Places and Participation* (London: Routledge, 1999)

Ian Budge, *The New Challenge of Direct Democracy* (Cambridge: Polity Press, 1996)

Robert W. Burchell and David Listokin, *The Fiscal Impact Handbook: Estimating Local Costs and Revenues of Land Development* (Piscataway, N.J.: The Center for Urban Policy Research, 1978)

John Burnheim, *Is Democracy Possible? The Alternative to Electoral Politics* (Berkeley: University of California Press, 1985).

Tom R. Burns and Reinhard Ueberhorst, *Creative Democracy: Systematic Conflict Resolution and Policymaking in A World of High Science and Technology* (New York: Praeger, 1988)

David Butler and Austin Ranney, eds., *Referendums: A Comparative Study of Practice and Theory* (Washington: American Enterprise Institute for Public Policy Research, 1978)

Sherry Cable and Charles Cable, *Environmental Problems, Grassroots Solutions: The Politics of Grassroots Environmental Conflict* (New York: St. Martin's Press, 1995)

Matthew Alan Cahn, *Environmental Deceptions: The Tension between Liberalism and Environmental Policymaking in the United States* (Albany: State University of New York Press, 1995)

Peter Calthorpe, *The Next American Metropolis: Ecology, Community, and the American Dream* (New York: Princeton Architectural Press, 1993)

Alan Carter, *A Radical Green Political Theory* (London and New York: Routledge, 1999)

April Carter, *The Political Theory of Anarchism* (New York: Harper and Row, 1971)

Manuel Castells, *The City and the Grassroots: A Cross-Cultural Theory of Urban Social Movements* (Berkeley: University of California Press, 1983)

Manuel Castells, *The Urban Question: A Marxist Approach* (London: Edward Arnold, 1977)

William H. Chafe, *Civilities and Civil Rights: Greensboro, North Carolina and the Black Struggle for Equality* (New York: Oxford University Press, 1980)

John Clark, "Municipal Dreams: A Social Ecological Critique of Bookchin's Politics," in Andrew Light, ed., *Social Ecology after Bookchin* (New York: The Guilford Press, 1998), pp. 137-191

Ray Clark and Larry W. Canter, eds., *Environmental Policy and NEPA: Past, Present, and Future* (Boca Raton, Fla.: St. Lucie Press, 1997)

Paul Barry Clarke, *Citizenship* (London: Pluto Press, 1994)

Paul Berry Clarke, *Deep Citizenship* (London: Pluto Press, 1996)

Susan E. Clarke, "More Autonomous Policy Orientations: An Analytic Framework," in Clarence N. Stone and Heywood T. Sanders, eds., *The Politics of Urban Development* (Lawrence, Ks.: The University of Kansas Press, 1987), pp. 105-124

Pierre Clavel, *The Progressive City: Planning and Participation, 1969-1984* (New Brunswick: Rutgers University Press, 1986)

Richard Cloward and Francis Fox Piven, *Poor People's Movements: Why They Succeed, How They Fail* (New York: Vintage Books, 1979)

Roger D. Congleton, ed., *The Political Economy of Environmental Protection: Analysis and Evidence* (Ann Arbor: University of Michigan Press, 1996)

Brian J. Cook, *Bureaucracy and Self-Government: Reconsidering the Role of Public Administration in American Politics* (Baltimore: Johns Hopkins University Press, 1996)

Terrence E. Cook and Patrick M. Morgan, eds., *Participatory Democracy* (San Francisco: Canfield Press, 1971)

James A. Coon and Sheldon W. Damsky, *All You Ever Wanted to Know About Zoning* (Albany: New York Planning Federation, 1993; 2nd ed.)

Kevin R. Cox, "Ideology and the Growth Coalition," in Andrew E.G. Jonas and David Wilson, eds., *The Urban Growth Machine: Critical Perspectives, Two Decades Later* (Albany: State University of New York Press, 1999), pp. 21-36

Margaret E. Crahan and Alberto Vourvoulias-Bush, eds., *The City and the World: New York's Global Future* (New York: The Council on Foreign Relations, 1997)

John Cronin and Robert F. Kennedy, Jr., *The Riverkeepers: Two Activists Fight to Reclaim Our Environment As A Basic Human Right* (New York: Scribner, 1997)

Thomas E. Cronin, *Direct Democracy: The Politics of Initiative, Referendum and Recall* (Cambridge: Harvard University Press, 1989)

Ned Crosby, "Citizen's Juries: One Solution for Difficult Environmental Questions," in Ortwin Renn, Thomas Webler and Peter Wiedemann, eds., *Fairness and Competence in Citizen Participation: Evaluating Models for Environmental Discourse* (Dordrecht, The Netherlands: Kluwer Academic Publishers, 1995), pp. 157-174

Michael Crozier, Samuel P. Huntington and Joji Watanuki, *The Crisis of Democracy: Report on the Governability of Democracies to the Trilateral Commission* (New York: New York University Press, 1975)

Jonathan Crush, ed., *Power of Development* (London and New York: Routledge, 1995)

Robert A. Dahl, *Who Governs? Democracy and Power in An American City* (New Haven: Yale University Press, 1961)

Mike Davis, *City of Quartz: Excavating the Future in Los Angeles* (New York: Vintage Books, 1992)

Carl Deal, *The Greenpeace Guide to Anti-Environmental Organizations* (Berkeley: Odonian Press, 1993)

Richard E. DeLeon, *Left Coast City: Progressive Politics in San Francisco, 1975-1991* (Lawrence, Ks.: University Press of Kansas, 1992)

Jack DeSario and Stuart Langton, eds., *Citizen Participation in Public Decision Making* (Westport, Ct.: Greenwood Press, Inc., 1987)

Alexis de Tocqueville, *Democracy in America*, ed. J.P. Mayer (Garden City, N.Y.: Anchor Books, 1969)

Mike Douglass and John Friedmann, eds., *Cities for Citizens: Planning and the Rise of Civil Society in A Global Age* (New York.: John Wiley & Sons, 1998)

John S. Dryzek, *Discursive Democracy: Politics, Policy and Political Science* (Cambridge: Cambridge University Press, 1990)

John S. Dryzek, "Policy Analysis and Planning: From Science to Argument," in Frank Fischer and John Forester, eds., *The Argumentative Turn in Policy Analysis and Planning* (Durham: Duke University Press, 1993), pp. 213-232

Andres Duany, Elizabeth Plater-Zyberk and Jeff Speck, *Suburban Nation: The Rise of Sprawl and the Decline of the American Dream* (New York: North Point Press, 2000)

Steven Ebbin and Raphael Kasper, *Citizen Groups and the Nuclear Power Controversy: Uses of Scientific and Technological Information* (Cambridge: The MIT Press, 1974)

John Echeverria and Raymond Booth Eby, eds., *Let the People Judge: A Reader on the Wise Use Movement* (Washington: Island Press, 1995)

Robyn Eckersley, *Environmentalism and Political Theory: Toward an Ecocentric Approach* (Albany: State University of New York Press, 1992)

Barbara Ehrenreich, *Nickel and Dimed: On (Not) Getting By in America* (New York: Metropolitan Books, 2001)

Howard J. Ehrlich, ed., *Reinventing Anarchism, Again* (San Francisco: AK Press, 1996)

Nina Eliasoph, *Avoiding Politics: How Americans Produce Apathy in Everyday Life* (Cambridge: Cambridge University Press, 1998)

Stephen L. Elkin, *Politics and Land Use Planning: The London Experience* (London: Cambridge University Press, 1974)

Stephen L. Elkin, "State and Market in City Politics: Or the 'Real' Dallas," in Clarence N. Stone and Heywood T. Sanders, eds., *The Politics of Urban Development* (Lawrence, Ks.: The University of Kansas Press, 1987), pp. 25-51

Richard A. Epstein, *Takings: Private Property and the Power of Eminent Domain* (Cambridge: Harvard University Press, 1985)

Paul A. Erickson, *A Practical Guide to Environmental Impact Assessment* (San Diego: Academic Press, 1994)

Sara M. Evans and Harry C. Boyte, *Free Spaces: The Sources of Democratic Change* (Chicago: University of Chicago Press, 1992)

Neil Evernden, *The Natural Alien: Humankind and Environment* (Toronto: University of Toronto Press, 1985)

David L. Faigman, *Legal Alchemy: The Use and Misuse of Science in the Law* (New York: W. H. Freeman and Co., 2000)

Susan S. Fainstein and Norman I. Fainstein, "The Political Economy of American Bureaucracy," in Frank Fischer and Carmen Sirianni, *Critical Studies in Organization and Bureaucracy* (Philadelphia: Temple University Press, 1984), pp. 309-320

Susan S. Fainstein and Norman I. Fainstein, eds., *The View from Below: Urban Politics and Social Policy* (Boston: Little, Brown and Co., 1972)

Susan S. Fainstein and Clifford Hirst, "Urban Social Movements," in David Judge, Gerry Stoker and Harold Wolman, eds., *Theories of Urban Politics* (London: Sage Publications, 1995), pp. 181-204

David John Farmer, ed., *Papers on the Art of Anti-Administration* (Burke, Va.: Chatelaine Press, 1998)

Michael W. Fazio and Peggy Whitman Prenshaw, eds., *Order and Image in the American Small Town* (Jackson: University Press of Mississippi, 1981)

Kathy E. Ferguson, *The Feminist Case Against Bureaucracy* (Philadelphia: Temple University Press, 1984)

Barbara Ferman, *Challenging the Growth Machine: Neighborhood Politics in Chicago and Pittsburgh* (Lawrence, Ks.: University Press of Kansas, 1996)

Daniel J. Fiorino, *Making Environmental Policy* (Berkeley: University of California Press, 1995)

Frank Fischer, *Citizens, Experts, and the Environment: The Politics of Local Knowledge* (Durham: Duke University Press, 2000)

Frank Fischer and Carmen Sirianni, *Critical Studies in Organization and Bureaucracy* (Philadelphia: Temple University Press, 1984)

Frank Fischer, *Evaluating Public Policy* (Chicago: Nelson-Hall, Publishers, 1995)

Frank Fischer and Michael Black, ed., *Greening Environmental Policy: The Politics of A Sustainable Future* (New York: St. Martin's Press, 1995)

Frank Fischer, "Hazardous Waste Policy, Community Movements and the Politics of NIMBY: Participatory Risk Assessment in the USA and Canada," in Frank Fischer and Michael Black, ed., *Greening Environmental Policy: The Politics of A Sustainable Future* (New York: St. Martin's Press, 1995), pp. 165-182

Frank Fischer, "Policy Discourse and the Politics of Washington Think Tanks," in Frank Fischer and John Forester, eds., *The Argumentative Turn in Policy Analysis and Planning* (Durham: Duke University Press, 1993), pp. 21-42

Frank Fischer and John Forester, eds., *The Argumentative Turn in Policy Analysis and Planning* (Durham: Duke University Press, 1993)

James S. Fishkin, *Democracy and Deliberation: New Directions for Democratic Reform* (New Haven: Yale University Press, 1991)

James S. Fishkin, *The Voice of the People: Public Opinion and Democracy* (New Haven: Yale University Press, 1995)

Eben Fodor, *Better Not Bigger: How to Take Control of Urban Growth and Improve Your Community* (Gabriola Island, B.C.: New Society Publishers, 1999)

James N. Follin, "Environmental Risks, Decision Making, and Public Perception: A Case Study Involving Environmental Impact Statements," Ph.D. dissertation, Carnegie Mellon University, 1998

John Forester, *Planning in the Face of Power* (Berkeley: University of California Press, 1989)

John Forester, *The Deliberative Practitioner: Encouraging Participatory Planning Processes* (Cambridge: MIT Press, 1999)

Charles J. Fox and Hugh T. Miller, *Postmodern Public Administration: Towards Discourse* (Thousand Oaks, Cal.: Sage, 1995)

Nicholas Freudenberg, *Not in Our Backyards!: Community Action for Health and the Environment* (New York: Monthly Review Press, 1984)

John Friedmann, *Planning in the Public Domain: From Knowledge to Action* (Princeton: Princeton University Press, 1987)

John Friedmann, "Two Centuries of Planning History: An Overview," in Seymour J. Mandelbaum, Luigi Mazza and Robert W. Burchell, eds., *Explorations in Planning Theory* (New Brunswick, N.J.: Center for Urban Policy Research at Rutgers, State University of New Jersey, 1996), pp. 10-29

Gerald Garvey, *Facing the Bureaucracy: Living and Dying in A Public Agency* (San Francisco: Jossey-Bass, 1993)

Elizabeth R. Gerber, *The Populist Paradox: Interest Group Influence and the Promise of Direct Legislation* (Princeton: Princeton University Press, 1999)

Michael B. Gerrard, Daniel A. Ruzow, and Philip Weinberg, *Environmental Impact Review in New York* (New York: Matthew Bender, 1995+)

Carol C. Gould, *Rethinking Democracy: Freedom and Social Cooperation in Politics, Economy, and Society* (Cambridge: Cambridge University Press, 1988)

Kenneth Gould, Allan Schnaiberg and Adam Weinberg, *Local Environmental Struggles: Citizen Activism in the Treadmill of Production* (Cambridge: Cambridge University Press, 1996)

Jill Grant, *The Drama of Democracy: Contention and Dispute in Community Planning* (Toronto: University of Toronto Press, 1994)

Adolf G. Gunderson, *The Environmental Promise of Democratic Deliberation* (Madison: University of Wisconsin Press, 1995)

Jurgen Habermas, *Theory of Communicative Action*, vol. II (Boston: Beacon Press, 1987)

Susan G. Hadden, "Regulatory Negotiation As Citizen Participation: A Critique," in Ortwin Renn, Thomas Webler and Peter Wiedemann, eds., *Fairness and Competence in Citizen Participation: Evaluating Models for Environmental Discourse* (Dordrecht, The Netherlands: Kluwer Academic Publishers, 1995), pp. 239-252

Maarten A. Hajer, "Acid Rain in Great Britain: Environmental Discourse and the Hidden Politics of Institutional Practice," in Frank Fischer and Michael Black, eds., *Greening Environmental Policy: The Politics of A Sustainable Future* (New York: St. Martin's Press, 1995), pp. 145-164.

Maarten A. Hajer, "Discourse Coalitions and the Institutionalization of Practice: The Case of Acid Rain in Britain," in Frank Fischer and John Forester, eds., *The Argumentative Turn in Policy Analysis and Planning* (Durham: Duke University Press, 1993), pp. 43-76

John A. Hannigan, *Environmental Sociology: A Social Constructionist Perspective* (London and New York: Routledge, 1995)

Alan Harding, "Elite Theory and Growth Machines," in David Judge, Gerry Stoker and Harold Wolman, eds., *Theories of Urban Politics* (London: Sage Publications, 1995), pp. 35-53

Thomas L. Harper and Stanley M. Stein, "A Classical Liberal (Libertarian) Approach to Planning Theory," in Sue Hendler, ed., *Planning Ethics: A Reader in Planning Theory, Practice and Education* (New Brunswick, N.J.: Center for Urban Policy Research at Rutgers, State University of New Jersey, 1995), pp. 49-65

Thomas L. Harper and Stanley M. Stein, "Contemporary Procedural Ethical Theory and Planning Theory," in Sue Hendler, ed., *Planning Ethics: A Reader in Planning Theory, Practice and Education* (New Brunswick, N.J.: Center for Urban Policy Research at Rutgers, State University of New Jersey, 1995), pp. 11-29

Jonathan Harr, *A Civil Action* (New York: Vintage, 1996)

Richard A. Harris and Sidney M. Milkis, *The Politics of Regulatory Change: A Tale of Two Agencies* (New

500

York: Oxford University Press, 1989)

Paul Hawken, *The Ecology of Commerce* (New York: HarperCollins Publishers, 1993)

David Helvarg, *The War against the Greens: The "Wise Use" Movement, The New Right and Anti-Environmental Violence* (San Francisco: Sierra Club Books, 1994)

Sue Hendler, ed., *Planning Ethics: A Reader in Planning Theory, Practice and Education* (New Brunswick, N.J.: Center for Urban Policy Research at Rutgers, State University of New Jersey, 1995)

Paul Hirst and Grahame Thompson, *Globalization in Question: The International Economy and the Possibilities of Governance* (London: Polity Books, 1996)

Charles Hoch, "What Do Planners Do in the United States?," in Seymour J. Mandelbaum, Luigi Mazza and Robert W. Burchell, eds., *Explorations in Planning Theory* (New Brunswick, N.J.: Center for Urban Policy Research at Rutgers, State University of New Jersey, 1996), pp. 225-240

Thom Holterman and Henc van Maarseveen, eds., *Law and Anarchism* (Montreal: Black Rose Books, 1984)

Gary Hoover, Alta Campbell and Patrick Span, eds., *Hoover's Handbook of American Business, 1995* (Austin, Tx.: The Reference Press, Inc., 1994)

Elizabeth Howe, *Acting on Ethics in City Planning* (New Brunswick, N.J.: Center for Urban Policy Research at Rutgers, State University of New Jersey, 1994)

Alan Irwin, *Citizen Science: A Study of People, Expertise and Sustainable Development* (London and New York: Routledge, 1995)

Harvey M. Jacobs, "The 'Wisdom,' But Uncertain Future, of the Wise Use Movement," in Harvey M. Jacobs, ed., *Who Owns America? Social Conflict over Property Rights* (Madison: University of Wisconsin Press, 1998), pp. 29-44

Harvey M. Jacobs, ed., *Who Owns America? Social Conflict over Property Rights* (Madison: University of Wisconsin Press, 1998)

R. K. Jain, L. V. Urban and G. S. Stacey, *Environmental Impact Analysis: A New Dimension in Decision Making* (New York: Van Nostrand Reinhold Co., 1981; 2nd ed.)

Andrew E.G. Jonas and David Wilson, eds., *The Urban Growth Machine: Critical Perspectives, Two Decades Later* (Albany: State University of New York Press, 1999)

Charles O. Jones, *An Introduction to the Study of Public Policy* (Monterey: Brooks/Cole, 1984; 3rd ed.)

David Judge, "Pluralism," in David Judge, Gerry Stoker and Harold Wolman, eds., *Theories of Urban Politics* (London: Sage Publications, 1995), pp. 13-34

David Judge, Gerry Stoker and Harold Wolman, eds., *Theories of Urban Politics* (London: Sage Publications, 1995)

Arnold Kaufman, "Human Nature and Participatory Democracy," in Carl Friedrich, ed., *Responsibility* (New York: Liberal Arts Press, 1960)

Suzanne Keller, *Beyond the Ruling Class: Strategic Elites in Modern Society* (New York: Random House, 1963)

Daniel Kemmis, *Community and the Politics of Place* (Norman, Okla.: University of Oklahoma Press, 1990)

Cornelius M. Kerwin, *Rulemaking: How Government Agencies Write Law and Make Policy* (Washington, D.C.: Congressional Quarterly Press, 1994)

Cheryl Simrell King and Camilla Stivers, *Government is Us: Public Administration in An Anti-Government Era* (Thousand Oaks, Cal.: Sage, 1998)

Kim Patrick Kobza, *There Goes the Neighborhood: Protecting Your Home and Community from Poor Development Choices* (Naples, Fla.: Neighborhood America Press, 1998)

David C. Korten, *When Corporations Rule the World* (West Hartford: Kumarian Press, Inc. and San Francisco: Berrett-Koehler Publishers, Inc., 1995)

Milton Kotler, *Neighborhood Government: The Local Foundations of Political Life* (Indianapolis: The Bobbs-Merrill Company, 1969)

William Severini Kowinski, *The Malling of America: An Inside Look at the Great Consumer Paradise* (New York: William Morrow, 1985)

Elliot Krause, "Functions of A Bureaucratic Ideology: 'Citizen Participation,'" in Terrence E. Cook and Patrick M. Morgan, eds., *Participatory Democracy* (San Francisco: Canfield Press, 1971), pp. 420-427

Diori L. Kreske, *Environmental Impact Statements: A Practical Guide for Agencies, Citizens and Consultants* (New York: John Wiley & Sons, Inc., 1996)

Len Krimerman, Frank Lindenfield, Carol Kortz and Julian Benello, eds., *From the Ground Up: Essays on Grassroots and Workplace Democracy by C. George Benello* (Boston: South End Press, 1992)

Norman Krumholz and Pierre Clavel, *Reinventing Cities: Equity Planners Tell Their Stories* (Philadelphia: Temple University Press, 1994)

James Howard Kunstler, *Home from Nowhere: Remaking Our Everyday World for the Twenty-First Century* (New York: Simon and Schuster, 1996)

James Howard Kunstler, *The Geography of Nowhere: The Rise and Decline of America's Man-Made Landscape* (New York: Simon and Schuster, 1993)

Mary Grisez Kweit and Robert W. Kweit, "The Politics of Policy Analysis: The Role of Citizen Participation in Analytic Decision Making," in Jack DeSario and Stuart Langton, eds., *Citizen Participation in Public Decision Making* (Westport, Ct.: Greenwood Press, Inc., 1987), pp. 19-38

Ernest LaClau and Chantal Mouffe, *Hegemony and Socialist Strategy: Towards A Radical Democratic Politics* (London: Verso, 1985)

William M. Lafferty and James Meadowcroft, eds., *Democracy and the Environment: Problems and Prospects* (Cheltanham, U.K.: Edward Elgar, 1996)

David Lebedoff, *The New Elite: The Death of Democracy* (New York: Franklin Watts, 1981)

Aldo Leopold, *A Sand County Almanac, And Sketches Here and There* (New York: Oxford University Press, 1949)

Robert Lerner, Althea K. Nagai and Stanley Rothman, *American Elites* (New Haven: Yale University Press, 1996)

Ronald T. Libby, *Eco-Wars: Political Campaigns and Social Movements* (New York: Columbia University Press, 1998)

Paul Lichterman, *The Search for Political Community: American Activists Reinventing Commitment* (Cambridge: Cambridge University Press, 1996)

David S. Liebschutz and Sarah F. Liebschutz, "Political Conflict and Intergovernmental Relations: Federal-State and State-Local Relations, in Jeffrey M. Stonecash, ed., *Governing New York State* (Albany: State University of New York Press, 2001; 4th ed.), pp. 25-41

Andrew Light, ed., *Social Ecology after Bookchin* (New York: The Guilford Press, 1998)

Charles Lindblom, *Politics and Markets: The World's Political Economic Systems* (New York: Basic Books, 1977)

Richard Lingeman, *Small Town America: A Narrative History, 1620-The Present* (New York: G.P. Putnam's Sons, 1980)

John R. Logan and Todd Swanstrom, eds., *Beyond the City Limits: Urban Policy and Economic Restructuring in Comparative Perspective* (Philadelphia: Temple University Press, 1990)

John R. Logan, Rachel Bridges Whaley and Kyle Crowder, "The Character and Consequences of Growth Regimes: An Assessment of Twenty Years of Research," in Andrew E.G. Jonas and David Wilson, eds., *The Urban Growth Machine: Critical Perspectives, Two Decades Later* (Albany: State University of New York Press, 1999), pp. 73-94

John R. Logan and Harvey L. Molotch, *Urban Fortunes: The Political Economy of Place* (Berkeley: University of California Press, 1987)

Vivien Lowndes, "Citizenship and Urban Politics," in David Judge, Gerry Stoker and Harold Wolman, eds., *Theories of Urban Politics* (London: Sage Publications, 1995), pp. 160-180

Timothy W. Luke, *Screens of Power: Ideology, Domination, and Resistance in Informational Society* (Urbana: University of Illinois Press, 1989)

Robert G. Lynch, *New York State's Industrial Development Agencies: Boon or Boondoggle?* (Albany: Fiscal Policy Institute, October 1992)

Jackson Turner Main, *The Anti-Federalists: Critics of the Constitution, 1781-1788* (New York: W.W. Norton and Company, 1974)

Robin Paul Malloy, *Planning for Serfdom: Legal Economic Discourse and Downtown Development* (Philadelphia: University of Pennsylvania Press, 1991)

Seymour J. Mandelbaum, Luigi Mazza and Robert W. Burchell, eds., *Explorations in Planning Theory* (New Brunswick, N.J.: Center for Urban Policy Research at Rutgers, State University of New Jersey, 1996)

Jerry Mander and Edward Goldsmith, eds., *The Case against the Global Economy: And for A Turn toward the Local* (San Francisco: Sierra Club Books, 1997)

Jane J. Mansbridge, *Beyond Adversary Democracy* (New York: Basic Books, 1980)

Brian Martin, ed., *Confronting the Experts* (Albany: State University of New York Press, 1996)

David Mathews, *Politics for People: Finding A Responsible Public Voice* (Urbana: University of Illinois Press, 1994)

Patrick B. McGuigan, *The Politics of Direct Democracy in the 1980s: Case Studies in Popular Decision Making* (Washington, D.C.: The Institute for Government and Politics of the Free Congress Research and Education Foundation, 1985)

502

Peter Medoff and Holly Sklar, *Streets of Hope: The Fall and Rise of An Urban Neighborhood* (Boston: South End Press, 1994)

Carolyn Merchant, *Radical Ecology: The Search for A Livable World* (New York: Routledge, 1992)

Kay Milton, *Environmentalism and Cultural Theory: Exploring the Role of Anthropology in Environmental Discourse* (New York: Routledge, 1996)

Stacey Mitchell, *The Home Town Advantage: How To Defend Your Main Street against Chain Stores . . . and Why It Matters* (Minneapolis: Institute for Local Self-Reliance, 2000)

Richard Moe and Carter Wilkie, *Changing Places: Rebuilding Community in the Age of Sprawl* (New York: Henry Holt and Company, 1997)

John H. Mollenkopf, *The Contested City* (Princeton: Princeton University Press, 1983)

Harvey Molotch, "Growth Machine Links: Up, Down and Across," in Andrew E.G. Jonas and David Wilson, eds., *The Urban Growth Machine: Critical Perspectives, Two Decades Later* (Albany: State University of New York Press, 1999), pp. 247-265

James A. Morone, *The Democratic Wish: Popular Participation and the Limits of American Government* (New York: Basic Books, 1990)

David Morris and Karl Hess, *Neighborhood Power: The New Localism* (Boston: Beacon Press, 1975)

Roy Morrison, *Ecological Democracy* (Boston: South End Press, 1995)

Chantal Mouffe, "Democratic Citizenship and the Political Community," in Chantal Mouffe, ed., *Dimensions of Radical Democracy: Pluralism, Citizenship, Community* (London and New York: Verso, 1992), pp. 225-239

Chantal Mouffe, ed., *Dimensions of Radical Democracy: Pluralism, Citizenship, Community* (London and New York: Verso, 1992)

Chantal Mouffe, "Radical Democracy or Liberal Democracy?" in David Trend, ed., *Radical Democracy: Identity, Citizenship, and the State* (New York and London: Routledge, 1996), pp. 19-26

Chantal Mouffe, *The Return of the Political* (London: Verso, 1996)

Althea K. Nagai, Robert Lerner and Stanley Rothman, *Giving for Social Change: Foundations, Public Policy, and the American Political Agenda* (Westport, Ct.: Praeger, 1994)

1996 Directory of Corporate Affiliations, vol. IV - "Private Companies" (New Providence, N.J.: National Register Publishing, 1996)

John R. Nolon, *Well Grounded: Shaping the Destiny of the Empire State, Local Land Use Law and Practice* (White Plains: Land Use Law Center, Pace University School of Law, 1998)

Al Norman, *Slam-Dunking Wal-Mart! How You Can Stop Superstore Sprawl in Your Hometown* (Atlantic City, N.J.: Raphel Marketing, 1999)

Mancur Olson, *The Logic of Collective Action: Public Goods and the Theory of Groups* (Cambridge: Harvard University Press, 1965)

Neil Orloff, *The Environmental Impact Statement Process: A Guide to Citizen Action* (Washington, D.C.: Information Resources Press, 1978)

Bob Ortega, *In Sam We Trust: The Untold Story of Sam Walton and How Wal-Mart is Devouring America* (New York: Times Books, 1998)

David Osborne and Ted Gaebler, *Reinventing Government: How the Entrepreneurial Spirit is Transforming the Public Sector* (Reading, Mass.: Addison-Wesley, 1992)

Carole Pateman, *Participation and Democratic Theory* (Cambridge: Cambridge University Press, 1970)

Carole Pateman, *The Disorder of Women: Democracy, Feminism and Political Theory* (Stanford: Stanford University Press, 1989)

Carole Pateman, *The Problem of Political Obligation: A Critical Analysis of Liberal Theory* (Berkeley: University of California Press, 1985)

Carole Pateman, *The Sexual Contract* (Palo Alto: Stanford University Press, 1988)

David Pepper, *Modern Environmentalism: An Introduction* (London and New York: Routledge, 1996)

Constance Perin, *Everything in Its Place: Social Order and Land Use in America* (Princeton: Princeton University Press, 1977)

David C. Perry, "The Politics of Dependency in Deindustrializing America: The Case of Buffalo, New York," in Michael Peter Smith and Joe R. Feagin, eds., *The Capitalist City: Global Restructuring and Community Politics* (Oxford: Basil Blackwell Ltd., 1987), pp. 113-137

Paul E. Peterson, *City Limits* (Chicago: The University of Chicago Press, 1981)

Francis Fox Piven and Richard A. Cloward, *Regulating the Poor: The Functions of Public Welfare* (New York: Vintage, 1972)

Val Plumwood, *Environmental Culture: The Ecological Crisis of Reason* (London and New York:

Routledge, 2002)

Val Plumwood, *Feminism and the Mastery of Nature* (London and New York: Routledge, 1993)

Daniel Press, *Democratic Dilemmas in the Age of Ecology: Trees and Toxics in the American West* (Durham: Duke University Press, 1994)

George W. Pring and Penelope Canan, *SLAPPs: Getting Sued for Speaking Out* (Philadelphia: Temple University Press, 1996)

Robert D. Putnam, *Bowling Alone: The Collapse and Revival of American Community* (New York: Simon and Schuster, 2000)

Robert D. Putnam, *Making Democracy Work: Civic Traditions in Modern Italy* (Princeton: Princeton University Press, 1993)

Bill Quinn, *How Wal-Mart is Destroying America (and the World): And What You Can Do About It* (Berkeley: Ten Speed Press, 2000; 2nd ed.)

Barry G. Rabe, "Power to the States: The Promise and Pitfalls of Decentralization," in Norman J. Vig and Michael E. Kraft, eds., *Environmental Policy in the 1990s* (Washington, D.C.: Congressional Quarterly Press, 1997; 3rd ed.), pp. 31-52

M. Radcliff, "Redefining the Environmental 'Crisis' in the South," in Joe Weston, ed., *Red and Green: A New Politics of the Environment* (London: Pluto Press, 1986)

Sheldon Rampton and John Stauber, *Trust Us, We're Experts--How Industry Manipulates Science and Gambles with Your Future* (New York: Tarcher/Putnam, 2001)

Meredith Ramsay, *Community, Culture and Economic Development: The Social Roots of Local Action* (Albany: State University of New York Press, 1996)

Martin Rein and Donald Schon, "Reframing Policy Discourse," in Frank Fischer and John Forester, eds., *The Argumentative Turn in Policy Analysis and Planning* (Durham: Duke University Press, 1993), pp. 145-166

Ortwin Renn, Thomas Webler and Peter Wiedemann, eds., *Fairness and Competence in Citizen Participation: Evaluating Models for Environmental Discourse* (Dordrecht, The Netherlands: Kluwer Academic Publishers, 1995)

Mary Richardson, Joan Sherman and Michael Gismondi, *Winning Back the Words: Confronting Experts in An Environmental Public Hearing* (Toronto: Garamond Press, 1993)

Dean Ritz, ed., *Defying Corporations, Defining Democracy: A Book of History and Strategy* (New York: The Apex Press, 2001)

Edward Mozley Roche, "'Cyberopolis': The Cybernetic City Faces the Global Economy," in Margaret E. Crahan and Alberto Vourvoulias-Bush, eds., *The City and the World: New York's Global Future* (New York: The Council on Foreign Relations, 1997), pp. 51-69

Raymond A. Rogers, *Solving History: The Challenge of Environmental Activism* (Montreal: Black Rose Books, 1998)

Lillian B. Rubin, "Maximum Feasible Participation: The Origins and Implications," in Susan S. Fainstein and Norman I. Fainstein, eds., *The View from Below: Urban Politics and Social Policy* (Boston: Little, Brown and Co., 1972)

Wolfgang Sachs, ed., *The Development Dictionary: A Guide to Knowledge As Power* (London: Zed Books, 1992)

Kirkpatrick Sale, *Dwellers in the Land: The Bioregional Vision* (San Francisco: Sierra Club Books, 1985)

Kirkpatrick Sale, *Human Scale* (New York: Perigree Books, 1980)

Leonie Sandercock, ed., *Making the Invisible Visible: A Multicultural Planning History* (Berkeley: University of California Press, 1998)

Bishwapriya Sanyal, "Meaning, Not Interest: Motivation for Progressive Planning," in Seymour J. Mandelbaum, Luigi Mazza and Robert W. Burchell, eds., *Explorations in Planning Theory* (New Brunswick, N.J.: Center for Urban Policy Research at Rutgers, State University of New Jersey, 1996), pp. 134-150

Giovanni Sartori, *The Theory of Democracy Revisited* (Chatham, N.J.: Chatham House Publishers, Inc., 1987)

H. V. Savitch and John C. Thomas, eds., *Big City Politics in Transition* (Newbury Park, Ca.: Sage, 1991)

David D. Schmidt, *Citizen Lawmakers: The Ballot Initiative Revolution* (Philadelphia: Temple University Press, 1989)

Alan Schnaiberg, *The Environment: From Surplus to Scarcity* (New York: Oxford University Press, 1980)

Donald A. Schon, *The Reflective Practitioner: How Professionals Think in Action* (New York: Basic Books, 1983)

504

Joseph A. Schumpeter, *Capitalism, Socialism, and Democracy* (New York: Harper and Row, 1950; 3rd. ed.)

Hans-Jorg Seiler, "Review of 'Planning Cells:' Problems of Legitimation," in Ortwin Renn, Thomas Webler and Peter Wiedemann, eds., *Fairness and Competence in Citizen Participation: Evaluating Models for Environmental Discourse* (Dordrecht, The Netherlands: Kluwer Academic Publishers, 1995), pp. 141-156

John Shields and B. Mitchell Evans, *Shrinking the State: Globalization and Public Administration "Reform"* (Halifax: Fernwood Publishing, 1998)

Edward B. Shils, *The Shils Report: Measuring the Economic and Sociological Impact of the Mega-Retail Discount Chains on Small Enterprise in Urban, Suburban and Retail Communities* (mss.,1997); Available [Online]: <http://www.shilsreport.org> [10/6/99]

Michael H. Shuman, *Going Local: Creating Self-Reliant Communities in A Global Age* (New York: Free Press, 1998)

William Shutkin, *The Land That Could Be: Environmentalism and Democracy in the 21st Century* (Cambridge: MIT Press, 2000)

Carmen Sirianni and Lewis Friedland, *Civic Innovation in America: Community Empowerment, Public Policy, and the Movement for Civic Renewal* (Berkeley: University of California Press, 2001)

Hugo Slim and Paul Thompson, *Listening for A Change: Oral Testimony and Community Development* (Philadelphia: New Society Publishers, 1995)

Michael Peter Smith and Joe R. Feagin, eds., *The Capitalist City: Global Restructuring and Community Politics* (Oxford: Basil Blackwell Ltd., 1987)

Gary Snyder, *The Practice of the Wild: Essays* (San Francisco: North Point Press, 1990)

Gerry Stoker, "Regime Theory and Urban Politics," in David Judge, Gerry Stoker and Harold Wolman, eds., *Theories of Urban Politics* (London: Sage Publications, 1995), pp. 54-71

Clarence N. Stone and Heywood T. Sanders, eds., *The Politics of Urban Development* (Lawrence, Ks.: The University of Kansas Press, 1987)

Clarence N. Stone, "The Study of the Politics of Urban Development," in Clarence N. Stone and Heywood T. Sanders, eds., *The Politics of Urban Development* (Lawrence, Ks.: The University of Kansas Press, 1987), pp. 3-22

Jeffrey M. Stonecash, ed., *Governing New York State* (Albany: State University of New York Press, 2001; 4th ed.)

Laura Tallian, *Direct Democracy: An Historical Analysis of the Initiative, Referendum and Recall Process* (Los Angeles: People's Lobby, 1977)

Serge Taylor, *Making Bureaucracies Think: The Environmental Impact Statement Strategy of Administrative Reform* (Stanford: Stanford University Press, 1984)

James A. Throgmorton, "Ethics, Passion, Reason, and Power: The Rhetorics of Electric Power Planning in Chicago," in Sue Hendler, ed., *Planning Ethics: A Reader in Planning Theory, Practice and Education* (New Brunswick, N.J.: Center for Urban Policy Research at Rutgers, State University of New Jersey, 1995), pp. 195-220

Brian Tokar, *The Green Alternative: Creating An Ecological Future* (San Pedro, Cal.: R. and E. Miles, 1987)

Douglas Torgerson, *The Promise of Green Politics: Environmentalism and the Public Sphere* (Durham: Duke University Press, 1999)

David Trend, ed., *Radical Democracy: Identity, Citizenship, and the State* (New York: Routledge, 1996)

Sandra Stringer Vance and Roy V. Scott, *Wal-Mart: A History of Sam Walton's Retail Phenomenon* (New York: Twayne Publishers, 1997)

Anna Vari, "Citizens' Advisory Committee As A Model for Public Participation: A Multiple-Criteria Evaluation," in Ortwin Renn, Thomas Webler and Peter Wiedemann, eds., *Fairness and Competence in Citizen Participation: Evaluating Models for Environmental Discourse* (Dordrecht, The Netherlands: Kluwer Academic Publishers, 1995), pp. 103-116

Norman J. Vig and Michael E. Kraft, eds., *Environmental Policy in the 1990s* (Washington, D.C.: Congressional Quarterly Press, 1997; 3rd ed.)

Norman J. Vig and Michael E. Kraft, "The New Environmental Agenda," in Norman J. Vig and Michael E. Kraft, eds., *Environmental Policy in the 1990s* (Washington, D.C.: Congressional Quarterly Press, 1997; 3rd ed.), pp. 365-389

Michael Walzer, *Radical Principles: Reflections of An Unreconstructed Democrat* (New York: Basic Books, 1980)

Michael Walzer, *Spheres of Justice: A Defense of Pluralism and Equality* (New York: Basic Books, 1983)

Michael Walzer, "The Civil Society Argument," in Chantal Mouffe, ed., *Dimensions of Radical Democracy: Pluralism, Citizenship, Community* (London and New York: Verso, 1992), pp. 89-107

Gary L. Wamsley and James F. Wolf, eds., *Refounding Democratic Public Administration: Modern Paradoxes, Postmodern Challenges* (Thousand Oaks, Cal.: Sage, 1996)

Colin Ward, *Anarchy in Action* (New York: Harper and Row, 1973)

Thomas Webler and Ortwin Renn, "A Brief Primer on Participation: Philosophy and Practice," in Ortwin Renn, Thomas Webler and Peter Wiedemann, eds., *Fairness and Competence in Citizen Participation: Evaluating Models for Environmental Discourse* (Dordrecht, The Netherlands: Kluwer Academic Publishers, 1995), pp. 17-34

Jack B. Weinstein, Harold L. Korn, and Arthur R. Miller, *New York Civil Practice – CPLR* (New York: Matthew Bender, 1963+)

Todd Wilkinson, *Science under Siege: The Politicians' War on Nature and Truth* (Boulder: Johnson Books, 1998)

Bruce A. Williams and Albert R. Matheny, *Democracy, Dialogue and Environmental Disputes: The Contested Languages of Social Regulation* (New Haven: Yale University Press, 1995)

Sheldon S. Wolin, "Norm and Form: The Constitutionalizing of Democracy," in J. Peter Euben, et al., eds., *Athenian Political Thought and the Reconstruction of American Democracy* (Ithaca: Cornell University Press, 1995)

Sheldon S. Wolin, *Politics and Vision: Continuity and Innovation in Western Political Thought* (Boston: Little Brown, 1960)

Sheldon S. Wolin, *The Presence of the Past: Essays on the State and the Constitution* (Baltimore: Johns Hopkins Press, 1989)

Laura R. Woliver, *From Outrage to Action: The Politics of Grass-Roots Dissent* (Urbana: University of Illinois Press, 1993)

Harold Wolman, "Local Government Institutions and Democratic Governance," in David Judge, Gerry Stoker and Harold Wolman, eds., *Theories of Urban Politics* (London: Sage Publications, 1995), pp. 135-159

Gordon S. Wood, *The Creation of the American Republic, 1776-1787* (University of North Carolina Press, 1969)

Robert C. Wood, with V. Almendinger, *1400 Governments: The Political Economy of the New York Metropolitan Region* (Cambridge: Harvard University Press, 1961)

Bruce Yandle, "Environmental Regulation: Lessons from the Past and Future Prospects," in Terry L. Anderson, ed., *Breaking the Environmental Policy Gridlock* (Stanford: Hoover Institution Press, 1997), pp. 140-167

Alfred F. Young, ed., *Beyond the American Revolution: Explorations in the History of American Radicalism* (DeKalb: Northern Illinois University Press, 1993)

Michael E. Zimmerman, *Contesting Earth's Future: Radical Ecology and Postmodernity* (Berkeley: University of California Press, 1994)

C. Articles, Papers and Web Sites

Robert J. Alessi and Yvonne E. Marciano, "Environmental Justice, Public Participation and Standing under the State Environmental Quality Review Act," paper presented at SEQRA 25th Anniversary Conference, Albany Law School, March 15-16, 2001, Albany, N.Y.

Sherry Arnstein, "A Ladder of Citizen Participation," *Journal of the American Institute of Planners*, vol. XXXV, no. 4 (July 1969), pp. 216-224

Thomas C. Beierle, *Public Participation in Environmental Decisions: An Evaluation Framework Using Social Goals* (Washington, D.C.: Resources for the Future Discussion Papers, November 1998); Available [Online]: <http://www.rff.org/CFDOCS/disc_papers/PDF_files/9906.pdf> [8/10/01]

Elizabeth Ann R. Bird, "The Social Construction of Nature: Theoretical Approaches to the History of Environmental Problems," *Environmental Review*, Winter 1987, pp. 255-264

Nicholas Blomley, "Landscapes of Property," *Law and Society Review*, vol. 32 (1998), no. 3, pp. 567-612

Peter Bogason, "Public Administration and the Unspeakable: American Postmodernism As An Academic Trail of the 1990s," Research Paper no. 5/99, Department of Social Sciences, Institut for Samfundsvidenskab og Erhversokonomi, Roskilde University, Denmark; Available [Online]: <http://www.sscnew.ruc.dk/download/5-99.pdf> [9/8/01]

506

Murray Bookchin, "The Meaning of Confederalism," *Society and Nature: The International Journal of Political Ecology*, I, 3, pp. 41-54

Harry Boyte, "Beyond Deliberation: Citizenship As Public Work," paper presented at the PEGS Conference, February 11-12, 1995; Available [Online]: <http://www.journalism.wisc.edu/cpn/sections/new_citizenship/ theory/boyte.html> [8/3/99]

Paul M. Bray, "Twenty-Fifth Anniversary of SEQRA," *Empire State Report*, April 2000, pp. 38-39

John W. Caffry, "Substantive Reach of SEQRA: Aesthetics and Findings," paper presented at SEQRA 25th Anniversary Conference, Albany Law School, March 15-16, 2001, Albany, N.Y.

Dougal M. Casey, "Retail Consolidation," International Council of Shopping Centers white paper, June 1998; Available [Online]: <http://www.icsc.org/ srch/rsrch/wp/ret98.html> [10/20/99]

Civic Practices Network (CPN) home page; Available [Online]: <http://www.cpn.org> [2/21/01]

Lizabeth Cohen, "From Town Center to Shopping Center: The Reconfiguration of Community Marketplaces in Postwar America," *The American Historical Review*, vol. 101, no. 4 (October 1996), pp. 1050-1081

Peter G. Crary, "Procedural Issues under SEQRA," *Albany Law Review*, vol. 46, no. 4 (Summer 1982), pp. 1211-1240

Ned Crosby, Jen Romslo, Sandra Malisone and Bruce Manning, "Citizen Juries: British Style"; Available [Online]: <http://www. frontpage.auburn.edu/tann/cp/juries.htm> [8/8/01]

Ned Crosby, Janet M. Kelly and Paul Schaefer, "Citizen Panels: A New Approach to Citizen Participation," *Public Administration Review*, March-April 1986, pp. 170-178

L. Del Furia and J. Wallace-Jones, "The Effectiveness of Provisions and Quality of Practices Concerning Public Participation in the EIS Procedures in Italy and the UK," paper presented at the World Congress of Environmental Resource Economists, Venice, 25-27 June 1998; Available [Online]: <http://www.feem.it/web/activ/wp/abs98/53-98.html> [11/15/01]

John Dicker, "Union Blues at Wal-Mart," *The Nation*, 7/8/02

John S. Dryzek, "Political and Economic Communication," in *Environmental Politics* (London), vol. 4, no. 4 (Winter 1995), pp. 13-30

Environmental Politics (London), vol. 4, no. 4 (Winter 1995), special issue on "Ecology and Democracy"

Karen Evans, "Imagining Anticipatory Government: A Speculative Essay on Quantum Theory and Visualization," *Administrative Theory and Practice* 19 (3) (1997), pp. 355-367

Michael B. Gerrard, "A SEQRA Retrospective: Whose Predictions Were Correct?" *Environmental Law in New York*, vol. 11, no. 1 (January 2000), p. 19

Michael B. Gerrard, "Municipal Powers under SEQRA," *New York State Bar Journal*, December 1997, pp. 6-8

Michael B. Gerrard and Monica Jahan Rose, "Possible Ways to 'Reform' SEQRA," *New York Law Journal*, 1/23/98

Michael B. Gerrard, "Ten Years of SEQRA Litigation: A Statistical Analysis," *New York Law Journal*, 3/24/00

Michael B. Gerrard, "The Dynamics of Secrecy in the Environmental Impact Statement Process," *New York University Environmental Law Journal*, vol. 2 (1993), no. 2

Philip Gitlen, "The Substantive Impact of SEQRA," *Albany Law Review*, vol. 46, no. 4 (Summer 1982), pp. 1241-1254

Kevin Fox Gotham, "Political Opportunity, Community Opportunity, and the Emergence of A Local Anti-Expressway Movement," *Social Problems*, vol. 46, no. 3 (August 1999), pp. 332-354

Thomas W. Hanchett, "U.S. Tax Policy and the Shopping-Center Boom of the 1950s and 1960s," *The American Historical Review*, vol. 101, no. 4 (October 1996), pp. 1082-1110

Peter Hanson, "Malls Come Tumbling Down," *Metroland* (Albany), May 3-9, 2001

International Council of Shopping Centers home page; Available [Online]: <http://www.icsc.org/> [8/8/01]

Interorganizational Committee on Guidelines and Principles for Social Impact Assessment, "Guidelines and Principles for Social Impact Assessment," *Environmental Impact Assessment Review*, 15, 1995, pp. 11-43

Kenneth Jackson, "All the World's A Mall: Reflections on the Social and Economic Consequences of the American Shopping Center, *The American Historical Review*, vol. 101, no. 4 (October 1996), pp. 1111-1121

Jefferson Center home page; Available [Online]: <http://www.jefferson-center.org> [3/10/01]

David Kay, "Community and the Politics of Open Space" (Ithaca: Cornell Local Government Program Paper, 1996); Available [Online]: <http://clgp.arme.cornell.edu/docs/14-DKOS.pdf> [2/15/01]

Phil LaRocque and Bruce Boncke, "SEQRA's 25th Anniversary: A Building Industry Perspective," *Empire State Report*, August 2000, pp. 27-28

Loka Institute home page; Available [Online]: <http://www.loka.org> [2/21/01]

Jane Mansbridge, "Does Participation Make Better Citizens," *The Good Society*, vol. 5, no. 2 (9/95), Available [Online]: <http://www.civnet.org/journal/ issue3/ cmjmans.htm> [7/13/01]

Langdon Marsh, "Introduction--SEQRA's Scope and Objectives," *Albany Law Review*, vol. 46, no. 4 (Summer 1982), pp. 1097-1113

Freya Mathews, "Community and the Ecological Self," *Environmental Politics* (London), vol. 4, no. 4 (Winter 1995), pp. 66-100

Joan Leary Matthews, "Standing under the State Environmental Quality Review Act--Not An Open Door Policy," paper presented at SEQRA 25th Anniversary Conference, Albany Law School, March 15-16, 2001, Albany, N.Y.

Dwight H. Merriam and Jeffrey A. Benson, "Identifying and Beating A Strategic Lawsuit against Public Participation," *Duke Environmental Law and Policy Forum*, vol. III (1993), pp. 17-36

Sidney M. Milkis, "Remaking Governmental Institutions in the 1970s: Participatory Democracy and the Triumph of Administrative Politics," *Journal of Policy History*, vol. 10, no. 1 (1998), pp. 51-74

Chester L. Mirsky and David Porter, "Ambushing the Public: The Socio-Political and Legal Consequences of SEQRA Decision-Making," *Albany Law Environmental Outlook Journal*, vol. 6, no. 2 (2002), pp. 1-54

N. Moldavi, "Environmentalism, State and Economy in the U.S.," *Research in Social Movements, Conflicts and Change*, vol. 13, pp. 261-273

Harvey Molotch, "The City As A Growth Machine: Toward A Political Economy of Place," *American Journal of Sociology* 82 (1976), pp. 309-330

Margaret A. Moote, Mitchell P. McClaran and Donna K. Chickering, "Theory in Practice: Applying Participatory Democracy Theory to Public Land Planning," *Environmental Management*, vol. 21, no. 6, pp. 877-889

National Council for the Social Studies home page; Available [Online]: <http://www.ncss.org/home.html> [10/20/99]

Nevada Advisory Committee on Participatory Democracy, Department of Museums, Library and Arts home page; Available [Online]: <http://www.clan.lib.nv.us/ docs/cpd/cpd.htm> [10/20/99]

New York Conservative Party home page; Available [Online]: <http://www. cpnys.org199legpro.htm#XI> [9/22/99]

Al Norman, "Up Against Wal-Mart: Eight Ways to Stop the Store," *The Nation*, March 28, 1994

Neil Orloff, "SEQRA: New York's Reformation of NEPA," *Albany Law Review*, vol. 46, no. 4 (Summer 1982), pp. 1128-1154

Peter Park, "Participatory Research, Democracy, and Community," *Practicing Anthropology*, vol. 19, no. 3 (Summer 1997), pp. 8-13

Val Plumwood, "Has Democracy Failed Ecology? An Ecofeminist Perspective," *Environmental Politics* (London), vol. 4, no. 4 (Winter 1995), pp. 134-168

Val Plumwood, "Noam Chomsky and Liberation Politics," paper presented to the "Visions of Freedom" conference, January 17-20, 1995, Sydney, Australia; Available [Online]: <http://www.vof.cat.org.au/ versions/val.htm [8/8/01]

Herbert A. Posner, book review of William R. Ginsberg and Philip Weinberg, eds., *Environmental Law and Regulation in New York State* (St. Paul: West Publishing Co., 1996), in *New York University Environmental Law Journal*, vol. 6 (1997), no. 1

"Project Democracy", Connecticut Secretary of State; Available [Online]: <http://www.state.ct.us/sots/ DemReport/ probro.htm> [10/20/99]

Robert D. Putnam, "Bowling Alone: America's Declining Social Capital," *Journal of Democracy* (January 1995), pp. 65-78; Available [Online]: <http://www.press.jhu.edu/demo/journalofdemocracy/ v006/ putnam. html> [9/8/01]

Robert D. Putnam, "The Prosperous Community: Social Capital and Public Life," *American Prospect*, vol. 4, 13 (Spring 1993); Available [Online]: <http://www.americanprospect.com/print/V4/13/putnam-r.html> [9/8/01]

Robert D. Putnam, "The Strange Disappearance of Civic America," *American Prospect*, vol. 7, 24 (Winter 1996), pp. 34-48; Available [Online]: <http://www.americanprospect.com/print/V7/24/putnam-r.html> [9/8/01]

The Research and Documentation Center for Direct Democracy at the University of Geneva (Switzerland) home page; Available [Online]: <http://www.c2d.unige.ch/> [2/21/01]

Nicholas A. Robinson, "SEQRA's Siblings: Precedents from Little NEPA's in the Sister States," *Albany Law Review*, vol. 46, no. 4 (Summer 1982), pp. 1155-1176

Daniel A. Ruzow, "Historical Development of SEQRA: The Administrative Process," outline paper presented at SEQRA 25th Anniversary Conference, Albany Law School, March 15-16, 2001, Albany, N.Y.

Ross Sandler, "State Environmental Quality Review Act," *New York State Bar Journal*, February 1977, pp. 111-117

"SEQRA 25th Anniversary Conference," oral and written presentations, Government Law Center, Albany Law School special symposium, March 15-16, 2001, Albany, N.Y.

Kristin Shrader-Frechette, "Scientific Method, Anti-Foundationalism and Public Decisionmaking," *RISK: Health, Safety and Environment*, vol I, Winter, pp. 23+; Available [Online]: <http://www.fplc.edu/RISK/vol1/ winter/ Shrader. htm> [8/9/01]

Matthew A. Sokol, "Enacting SEQRA: The Legislative Debates and A 25-Year Look Back," *Environmental Law in New York*, vol. 11, no. 1 (January 2000), pp. 1, 13-18

Eva Sorensen, "Democratic Governance and the Changing Role of Users of Public Services," Research Paper no. 3/99, Department of Social Sciences, Institut for Samfundsvidenskab og Erhversokonomi, Roskilde University, Denmark; Available [Online]: <http://www.sscnew.ruc.dk/dowload/3-99.pdf> [[9/8/01]

Sprawl-Busters Alert

Sprawl-Busters home page; Available [Online]: <http://www.sprawl-busters.com/ [6/20/01]

Jim Stapleton, review of Erik Kiviat, *The Northern Shawangunks: An Ecological Survey*, in *The Hudson Valley Regional Review*, vol. 7, no. 1 (March 1990)

Marnie Stetson, "Reforming SLAPP Reform: New York's Anti-SLAPP Statute," *New York University Law Review*, vol. 70, December 1995, pp. 1324-1361

Sandra M. Stevenson, "Early Legislative Attempts at Requiring Environmental Assessment and SEQRA's Legislative History," *Albany Law Review*, vol. 46, no. 4 (Summer 1982), pp. 1114-1127

"Symposium on the New York State Environmental Quality Review Act," special issue, *Albany Law Review*, vol. 46, no. 4 (Summer 1982)

Teledemocracy Action News and Network home page; Available [Online]: <http://www.auburn.edu/tann/tann2> [2/21/01]

Tom Turner, "The Legal Eagles," *The Amicus Journal*, Winter 1988, pp. 25-37

Thomas A. Ulasewicz, "The Department of Environmental Conservation and SEQRA: Upholding Its Mandates and Charting Parameters for the Elusive Socio-Economic Assessment," *Albany Law Review*, vol. 46, no. 4 (Summer 1982), pp. 1255-1284

Roger Ulrich, et al., "Stress Recovery during Exposure to Natural and Urban Environments," *Journal of Environmental Psychology*, vol. 11 (1991), pp. 201-230

Douglas H. Ward and Michael J. Moore, "SEQRA Challenges and the Statute of Limitations: Sue 'Early and Often,'" *Albany Law Environmental Outlook Journal*, vol. 6, no. 2 (2002), pp. 89-101

Mark E. Warren, "Can Participatory Democracy Produce Better Selves? Psychological Dimensions of Habermas's Discursive Model of Democracy," *Political Psychology*, vol. 14, no. 2 (1993)

Val Washington, "SEQRA: 'Big Bad and Little Bad'," *Empire State Report*, August 2000, pp. 28-29

Thomas Webler, Hans Kastenholz and Ortwin Renn, "Public Participation in Impact Assessment: A Social Learning Perspective," *Environmental Impact Assessment Review*, 1995, 15, pp. 443-463

Philip Weinberg, "SEQRA: Effective Weapon--If Used As Directed," *Empire State Report*, October 2000, p. 38

Robert Young, "'Monkeywrenching' and the Processes of Democracy," *Environmental Politics* (London), vol. 4, no. 4 (Winter 1995), pp. 199-214

D. Newspapers (fictional location and newspaper names used, when needed, consistent with those in the text)

Adirondack Daily Enterprise (Saranac Lake, N.Y.)
Albany Times-Union
Ashbury Beacon
Ashbury Chronicle
Dutch Arms Press (Ashbury, N.Y.)
New York Times
The Peninsula Gateway (Gig Harbor, Wash.)

The Post (Londonville, N.Y.)
The Press-Republican (Plattsburgh, N.Y.)
Riverside Dispatch
The Star (Regent Park, N.Y.)
The Sun (SUNY/Ashbury campus newspaper)
The Tribune (Ashbury, N.Y.)

E. Court and Administrative Decisions

Aldrich v. Pattison, 107 A.D.2d 258, 486 N.Y.S.2d 23 (2d Dept. 1985)
Ames v. Johnston, 169 A.D.2d 84, 571 N.Y.S.2d 831 (3rd Dep't., 1991)
Beer Garden, Inc. v. State Liquor Authority, 171 A.D.2d 565, 568 N.Y.S.2d 25 (1ˢᵗ Dept. 1991), aff'd 78 N.Y.2d 1026, 582 N.E.2d 590 (1991)
Carpenter v. City of Ithaca Planning Brd., 190 A.D.2d 934, 593 N.Y.S.2d 582 (3d Dept. 1993)
Chinese Staff and Workers Ass'n v. City of New York, 68 N.Y. 359, 509 N.Y.S.2d 499, 502 N.E.2d 176 (1986)
City of Saratoga Springs v. Zoning Bd. of Appeals, 279 A.D.2d 756, 719 N.Y.S.2d 178 (2001)
Douglaston Civic Association, Inc. v. Galvin, 36 N.Y.2d 1 (1974), 364 N.Y.S.2d 830
Hanly v. Kleindienst, 471 F.2d 823 (2d Cir. 1972), cert. denied, 412 U.S. 908 (1973)
Hickey v. Planning Bd. of Kent, 173 A.D.2d 1086, 571 N.Y.S.2d 105 (3d Dept. 1991)
H.O.M.E.S. v. New York State Urban Dev. Corp., 69 A.D.2d 222, 418 N.Y.S.2d 827 (4th Dept. 1979)
Huntington Ready-Mix Concrete, Inc. v. Town of Southampton, 112 A.D.2d 161, 491 N.Y.S.2d 383 (1985)
Jackson v. New York State Urban Development Corp., 67 N.Y.2d 400, 503 N.Y.S.2d 298, 494 N.E.2d 429 (1986)
Lane Construction Corp. v. Cahill, 270 A.D. 2d 609, 704 N.Y.S.2d 687 (3d Dept), appeal denied, 95 N.Y.2d 765 (2000)
In re Marriott Corp.(DEC Comm'r Decision, June 2, 1981)
Matter of Coca-Cola Bottling Co. v. Board of Estimate, 72 N.Y.2d 674, 536 N.Y.S.2d 33 (1988)
McNeill v. Town Bd. of the Town of Ithaca, 260 A.D.2d 829, 688 N.Y.S.2d 747 (1999)
Merson v. McNally, 90 N.Y.2d 742, 665 N.Y.S.2d 605 (1997)
Meschi v. New York State Dep't of Envtl. Conservation, 114 Misc.2d 877, 452 N.Y.S.2d 553 (Sup. Ct. Albany Co. 1982)
Mills v. Town Planning and Zoning Commission, 144 Conn 493, 134 A.2d 250 (1957)
In re Onondaga Valley Farms (DEC Comm'r Decision June 16, 1982)
Pokoik v. Silsdorf, 40 N.Y.2d 769, 390 N.Y.S.2d 49 (1976)
In re Pyramid Crossgate Co. (DEC Comm'r Decision Nov. 28, 1980)
Sierra Club v. Froehlke, 359 F.Supp.1334 (S.D. Texas 1973)
Six Mile Creek Preservation Comm. v. Planning Board of Town of Ithaca, 82-1397, slip op. (Sup. Ct. Tompkins Co., Jan. 6, 1983)
1616 Second Avenue Restaurant, Inc. v. New York State Liquor Authority, 75 N.Y.2d 158, 551 N.Y.S.2d 461, 162 N.E.2d 910, 912 (1990)
Society of the Plastics Industry Inc. v. County of Suffolk, 77 N.Y.2d 761, 570 N.Y.S.2d 778, 573 N.E.2d 1034 (1991)
Southern Clarkstown Civic Ass'n v. Holbrook, No. 4813/89 (Sup. Ct. Westchester Co. Dec. 11, 1989) aff'd mem., 166 A.D.2d 651, 560 N.Y.S.2d 976 (2d Dept. 1990), appeal denied, 77 N.Y.2d 806, 568 N.Y.S.2d 913, 571 N.E.2d 83 (1991)
Sun-Brite Car Wash, Inc. v. Board of Zoning and Appeals, 116 A.D.2d 724, 498 N.Y.S.2d 28 (2ⁿᵈ Dept. 1986)
Town of Henrietta v. Department of Environmental Conservation, 76 A.D.2d 215, 430 N.Y.S.2d 440 (4ᵗʰ Dept. 1980)
Tuxedo Conservation and Taxpayers Ass'n, 69 A.D.2d 320, 418 N.Y.S.2d 638 (2d Dept. 1979)
Wal-Mart Stores, Inc. v. Planning Board of the Town of North Elba, 238 A.D.2d 93, 668 N.Y.S.2d 774 (3d Dept. 1998)
Washington Cease, Inc. v. Persico, 120 Misc. 2d 207, 465 N.Y.S.2d, 965 (Sup. Ct. Washington Co. 1983), aff'd, 99 A.D.2d 321, 473 N.Y.S.2d 610 (3d Dept. 1984), aff'd, 64 N.Y.2d 923, 477 N.E.2d 1084

(1985)

Webster Assoc. v. Town of Webster, 59 N.Y.2d 220, 464 N.Y.S.2d 431, 451 N.E.2d 189 (1983)

WEOK Broadcasting Corp. v. Planning Board of the Town of Lloyd, 79 N.Y. 2d 373, 583 N.Y.S.2d 170 (1992)

Withrow v. Larkin, 421 U.S. 35 (1975)

Zagoreos v. Conklin, 109 A.D.2d 281, 491 N.Y.S.2d 358 (2d Dept. 1985)

F. **Miscellaneous** (fictional location, organizational and personal names used, when needed, consistent with those in the text)

Ashbury Library, Ashbury, N.Y. vertical file local history collections and oral history collection

Ashbury Town Board and Planning Board Meeting unofficial transcripts from audio recordings

CLEAR Newsletter

Paul Halpern (Medford Corporation president and CEO) 9/21/94 letter to community protesters in Ashbury

David Porter personal notes of Ashbury Town Board and Planning Board meetings and interviews with Ray Black, Paul Bray, Henry Fowler, Michael Gerrard, Paul Hurley, Sam Myers, Kevin Scully, and Ina Turbell

Deke Reynolds 8/21/95 letter to law school dean

John Richards (Director, Forest County Planning Board) 11/6/75 letter to Stephen Gordon (DEC Deputy Commissioner)

Morris Schwab 7/17/95 letter to law school dean

NAME INDEX (individuals from the case study context not included)

514

SUBJECT INDEX (important themes, issues, organizations, firms, agencies, places) (fictional names included as used in the text)

518

ISBN 155369855-X

9 781553 698555